1 Ashley,J M Address before Ohio Soc. of N.Y ,1890
2 Barrett,J O "Old Abe" the war eagle of Wis.1876
3 Brooks,J Speech in N Y Dec.30,1862
4 Calendar of the Civil War
5 Cook,H J Our national inheritance,1883
6 Curtis,G T True condition of Amer. loyalty,1863
7 Dix,J A Arrest of Hawley D.Clapp,1864
8 Dix,M Death of Pres.Lincoln1865
9 Duffield,G Our soldier-dead,May 30,1884
10 Eliot,T D Address to his constituents,Feb.1861
11 Fleetwood,C A The Negro as a soldier,1895
12 Hamilton,A J Letter to Pres of U.S July 28,1863
13 Walker,F.A. Hancock in War of Rebellion,1891
14 Kelley,W.D. Way to attain peace,1862
15 Laboulaye,E Upon whom rests the guilt of the war?
16 Lowe,C Condition of South,1865
17 McClelland,R. ,,Arrest of C.L Vallandigham,1863
18 McPherson,E Oration at dedication of Adams Co. Soldiers'Monument,Gettysburg,1892
19 Matthews,A F Address at Orange,N.J Decoration Day,1884
20 Meade,G.G Letter on Gettysburg,Mar.16,1870
21 Soc.for Diffusion of Polit.Knowledge.Constitution
22 Morton,E.G. Minotity report of Committee on Federal Relations in House,Wash.1865
23 Philippoteaux,P Battle of Gettysburg cyclorama
24 Rosecrans,W S Resolutions of thanks to 1863
25 Seymour,H Speech before Democratic State Convention,Albany,Sept 10,1862
26 Soule,H From the Gulf to Vicksburg,1894
27 Thomas,B.F Remarks in House,Wash Apr 10,1862
28 Turpie,D Speech in Sen of U.S Feb.7,1863
29 Wade,B.F Report of Joint Committee on conduct of present war,May,1,1862
30 Wood,B. Speech on state of the Union,May 16,1862
31 National entail,a sermon in Brookline,July 3,1864

With Compliments of J. M. Ashley

ADDRESS

—OF—

Hon. J. M. ASHLEY

—BEFORE THE—

"OHIO SOCIETY OF NEW YORK,"

At its Fifth Annual Banquet, Wednesday evening, February 19, 1890.

PUBLISHED BY REQUEST.

Evening Post Job Print.

NEW YORK, February 20, 1890.

MY DEAR GOVERNOR ASHLEY:

At the banquet of the Ohio Society of New York last evening, the President of the Society was, by unanimous vote, directed to ask you to furnish to the Society for publication a copy of your admirable paper on the passage through the House of Representatives of the United States of the Thirteenth Amendment to the Constitution. In performance of this duty, I beg leave to present to you their request.

Let me add, personally, that this formal expression was supplemented individually by every one of those present with whom it was my fortune to converse. I am sure that I speak for all present in expressing my individual appreciation of the greatness and historic value of that action of which you were so largely the inspiration, and in which you were the foremost actor.

Yours, very truly,

WAGER SWAYNE.

HON. J. M. ASHLEY.

NEW YORK, February 21, 1890.

GENL. WAGER SWAYNE,

President Ohio Society of New York,

195 Broadway.

MY DEAR SIR:

Herewith please find copy of my address as delivered before your Society at the fifth annual banquet on the 19th inst.

It gives me pleasure to comply with a request in which is conveyed so complimentary an approval by the Society and yourself of the address.

I only regret that I did not have time to speak more in detail of the personality of the immortal twenty-four who voted with us, and thus made possible the passage of the Thirteenth Amendment.

Truly yours,

J. M. ASHLEY.

Mr. President and Gentlemen of the Ohio Society of New York:

The official acts of the great actors in the conflict of civilization with the barbarism of slavery are faithfully recorded in the nation's archives and open to the inspection and compilation of the coming historian.

You will not expect me to-night to do more than briefly notice some few of these men with whom it was my good fortune to be associated during the time Congress had under consideration the propositions to abolish slavery at the National Capitol and the Thirteenth Amendment.

When the story of our great anti-slavery conflict shall have been written it will make one of the most ideal chapters in our matchless history.

That chapter will tell the coming generations of men the story of the immortal victory achieved by the American people for democratic government and an undivided Union; a victory whose far-reaching consequences no man can even now foresee.

In the fullness of time to every nation and people great leaders are born, and some one or more of these earnest leaders, by the utterance of a simple moral truth in a brief couplet or in a single epigrammatic sentence, have often in the world's history changed the opinions of thousands.

Especially true was this of the written appeals and public addresses of the great anti-slavery leaders in this country for more than a quarter of a century before the rebellion. He was indeed a dull and insensible man who during our anti-slavery crusade did not grow eloquent and become aggressive when writing and speaking of slavery as the great crime of his age and country. To me, as a boy, the men who made up this vanguard of anti-slavery leaders always appeared to be exceptionally great men, men who walked the earth with unfaltering faith and a firm tread, with heads erect, so that their prophetic eyes caught the dawn of Freedom's coming morn. They were brave, strong, self-reliant men, whose words and acts all testified that their great hearts "burned to break the fetters of the world." These men had no thought of witnessing during their lifetime the triumph of the cause which they had so unselfishly espoused; they were tireless and invincible workers. The alluring promise of success nowhere held out to them hope of political reward. To an unpopular cause they gave all they had of time, money and brains, not doubting that those who should come after them would be able to command and so to direct the moral forces of the nation as ultimately to enact justice into law by "proclaiming liberty throughout all the land to all the inhabitants thereof." Under this banner they went forth, conquering and to conquer, and in all their impassioned appeals they "sounded forth the bugle that never called retreat."

To have voluntarily enlisted and fought with this liberating army until our starry banner was planted in triumph on the last citadel of American slavery, is an honor of which the humblest citizen and his children may justly be proud, an honor which will grow brighter in all the coming years of the Republic.

I was so young when I enlisted in this liberating army that I cannot fix the date.

At the home of a neighbor, a Virginian by birth, and until the close of his manly life a resident of Kentucky, I heard, with wondering emotions, the first song in which a slave was represented as appealing to his captors for his freedom. I was but nine years old, but that song with its story touched my heart, and, though I never saw it in print, I never forgot it. The verse of this song that arrested my attention and remained fixed in my memory is as clear to me *to-night* as it was more than half a century ago.

It was the plaintive appeal of an escaped slave, in simple rhyme, such as slaves often sang to tunes with which all are familiar who have heard the old-fashioned plantation melodies.

In that appeal to his captors

> " He showed the stripes his master gave,
> The branded scars—the sightless eye,
> The common badges of a slave,
> And said he would be free or die."

I did not know until then that the slave-master had the right to whip, brand and maim his slave. It was at the home of this venerable anti-slavery man (who made the world better for his having lived in it) that I first learned this fact, and it was at his house that I first heard repeated many of the fiery utterances of Cassius M. Clay, of Kentucky. After showing an appreciation of these anti-slavery sentiments I was frequently lifted on a chair or table by our old anti-slavery neighbor and taught to declaim from the speeches of Cassius M. Clay and others. I was so fascinated by a paragraph from a speech made by Governor McDowell, of Virginia, that it always gave me pleasure to speak it, as I often did, with such earnestness as to secure me as honest applause in that quiet anti-slavery household as any I ever commanded on the platform in after years.

I never forgot that appeal of Governor McDowell, and often used it after I grew to manhood, and quoted it in one of my early speeches in Congress, as I again quote it here:

"You may place the slave where you please, you may dry up to your uttermost the fountain of his feelings, the springs of his thought, you may close upon his mind every avenue to knowledge, and cloud it over with artificial night, you may yoke him to labor as an ox—which liveth only to work, and worketh only to live; you may put him under any process which without destroying his value as a slave, will debase and crush him as a rational being—you may do all this; and yet, the idea that he was born free will survive it all. It is allied to his hope of immortality—it is the eternal part of his nature which oppression cannot reach. It is a torch lit up in his soul by the hand of Deity, and never meant to be extinguished by the hand of man."

I speak of these seemingly unimportant incidents of my boyhood to confirm what I said in opening touching the influence which one brave, truthful man can exercise over thousands, and to illustrate the tremendous power a single thought may often have over the acts and lives of reader and hearer. From my ninth to my thirteenth year my father was preaching on a circuit in the border counties of Kentucky and West Virginia, and afterwards in Southeastern Ohio.

During our residence in Kentucky and West Virginia I did not know a single abolitionist except the family which I have described, and not until I was in my seventeenth year did I meet and become acquainted with Cassius M. Clay and John G. Fee. Sometime afterwards I met James G. Burney, who became the abolition candidate for President in 1844.

The leaders of the church to which my father belonged, and, indeed, the leaders in all Southern churches in those days, publicly affirmed "that slavery *per se* could exist without sin," a doctrine which I regarded then, as I do now, as a perversion of the teachings of Christ. It has always been a source of satisfaction to me that my mother, who was a conservative woman, never gave in her adhesion to this rascally defense of "the sum of all villainies."

At that time, in all the border counties of Kentucky, slavery existed in a milder form than in any other part of the Southwest, and the slave owners whom I knew were much better men than one would in this day believe possible under any slave system.

And yet the system in its practical working was so monstrous that before I had grown to manhood I had publicly pronounced against it, and, as many before me know, I fought it with an energy which never tired, and a faith which never faltered.

While entertaining the anti-slavery opinions of Jefferson and the men of 1776, and everywhere proclaiming them without concealment, I was elected to Congress in 1858, when in my thirty-fourth year, and for the first time took my seat in a deliberative body in the Thirty-sixth Congress during the administration of Mr. Buchanan.

At that time the pro-slavery conspirators were preparing for armed rebellion, and for the desperate attempt, which they soon made, to establish a slave empire on the ruins of the Republic.

There I met many anti-slavery leaders of age and experience, to whose ranks I was eagerly welcomed.

I entered upon the straight and narrow path that led to victory. I faltered but once. That was on the vote on the Crittenden Resolution in July, 1861. The vote was 117 yeas; noes, 2. Mr. Potter of Wisconsin and Mr. Riddle of Ohio voting *No.*

I had been appealed to by almost every public man of my acquaintance in Washington and by my personal and political friends to vote for the resolution, and not assume the responsibility of separating myself at such a time and on so important a matter from my party. When my name was called I shook my head, as was then the custom; my name was called the second time, and I again shook my head, the blush of shame tingling my face, as it has every time I have thought of that act or looked at the record since and read, "Not voting, J. M. Ashley." I never felt the sense of shame so keenly before nor since; and turning to Mr. Corwin, my venerable colleague, as the vote was announced, I said, with emotion, "Governor, that is the most cowardly act of my life, and no power on earth shall again make me repeat it." "Why, General," he exclaimed, with evident warmth, "*I voted for it.*" I saw that I had, in the excitement of the moment, offended him, and I made haste to assure him that I intended nothing of the sort, as all would have done who had offended so lovable, companionable and just a man as Governor Corwin. I promptly extended my hand and said, "Yes, Governor, but you do not see things as I do." I need hardly add that after this I did not again refuse to vote on any question, nor did I, during my entire service, give a single vote that to-night I would change.

Great occasions produce great men. The State of Ohio furnished her full quota for the crisis of 1861:

Joshua R. Giddings, the leader of the "old guard, one blast upon whose bugle horn was worth a thousand men."

Salmon P. Chase, Senator, Governor, Cabinet Minister and Chief Justice, who ranked next to Lincoln in leadership.

Thomas Ewing, profound statesman, great lawyer, and Cabinet Minister under General Harrison in 1841.

Edwin M. Stanton, the great War Secretary, earnest, fearless, tireless.

Judge McLean, the ideal Judge, representing on the bench the coming civilization, the writer of the dissenting opinion in the Dread Scott case.

Judge Swayne, judicial, conscientious, a great worker and the early friend and confidant of Lincoln.

Benjamin F. Wade, bluff, positive, ready to meet the enemy in the field or forum.

John Sherman, keen, politic, far-sighted and successful.

In the House—Thomas Corwin, Bingham, Lawrence, Hutchins, Spaulding, Schellaberger, Schenck, Hayes and Garfield.

Our War Governors, Dennison, Todd and Brough, unequaled as organizers and in administrative power.

On the Democratic side there were Senator Thurman and Representatives Vallandigham, Pendleton, Cox and Morgan, with many able men in private life, who were active in demanding our "authority and precedents" for all we proposed, and much that we did for which we had no "precedent."

In the army Ohio eclipsed the world. That wonderful triumvirate of commanders, Grant, Sherman and Sheridan, were without models and without equals. And then we had McPherson, Garfield, Steadman, Swayne, Cox and Buckland, and hundreds besides, who, on the field and in the forum, made the name of Ohio everywhere synonymous with great deeds and heroic acts.

In such a cause, with such leaders, success was foreordained.

When the official records of Congress during the administration of Mr. Buchanan are examined by the historian of the future, and the so-called compromise proposition of the Union-saving Committee of thirty-three (of which Charles Francis Adams of Massachusetts was Chairman) is compared with the Thirteenth Amendment, which three years later became part of our National Constitution, it will be difficult for him to find reasons for the extraordinary revolution in public opinion which these two proposed amendments to our National Constitution present. And here I wish I could walk backward with averted gaze, and with the broad mantle of charity cover the political nakedness of our own beloved State, which, by the vote of its Legislature, committed the indefensible folly of ratifying the proslavery amendment proposed by the Committee of thirty-three, and thus officially consented to its becoming a part of our National Constitution.

To me the propositions of the so-called "Peace Congress," over which ex-President John Tyler, of

Virginia, presided, were preposterous and offensive, and the "pledge" of the "Crittenden Resolution" a delusion and a snare, cunningly designed to paralyze and manacle us.

Every sane man who to-day reads the numerous proposed constitutional amendments with which Congress at that time was deluged will recognize the fact that they were all studiously and deliberately prepared for the avowed purpose of protecting slavery by new and more exacting guarantees.

This celebrated Compromise Committee of thirty-three reported and recommended an amendment which practically made slavery perpetual.

It was in these words:

"ARTICLE 12th. No amendments shall be made "to the Constitution which shall authorize or give "Congress the power to abolish or interfere within "any State with the domestic institutions thereof, "including that of persons held to labor or service "by the laws of such State."

Imagine, if you can, what the other propositions were, if *this* was the most favorable which the Compromise Committee of thirty-three could obtain for us.

Two days before Mr. Lincoln's inauguration this abasement was made to the slave barons by a two-thirds vote of both Houses of the Congress of the United States, and the act was approved by President Buchanan.

I do not believe a more shameless exhibition on the part of a civilized people can be found in history.

Prior to this proposed surrender to the slave barons, a number of the Southern States had passed ordinances of secession, and defiantly organized a government, with Jefferson Davis as President.

That such humiliating concessions were as defenseless then as they would be now, and as offensive to the civilization of the nineteenth century, will not be questioned.

The nation had not then learned that the strength of a statesman lies in his fidelity to justice—not in his concessions to injustice.

Our official records, for nearly half a century before the Rebellion, presented one unbroken series of fruitless compromises with the slave barons, until in their pride and arrogance they believed themselves able to direct successfully any revolution and ride with safety any storm.

At last we came to know that all our concessions were regarded by them as irrevocable; that nothing but new concessions would be accepted by them, and that they would only consent to remain in the Union on the express condition that we should bind ourselves for all time to record their pro-slavery decrees in every department of the National and State governments.

The rebels witnessed our efforts at an adjustment with shouts of derision and defiance, and said, "Now we have the Yankees on a down grade, and on the run."

They learned afterwards to their sorrow that, however true this might have been under the leadership of Buchanan, it was no longer true under the leadership of Lincoln. Yet, alas! it is true, that immediately after the election of Mr. Lincoln and before his inauguration, many men who had been active anti-slavery men quailed before the approaching storm, which their own brave appeals for liberty had aided in producing.

They comprehended what civil war, with all its attendant horrors, meant to a civilized people, and shrank from its terrible consequences, and as the acts of their representatives proved, they were willing to do everything in their power to avoid it. These timid anti-slavery men were representatives of the wealth, the manufacturing industry, the commerce, the peaceful farm-life of the North and West, and the best civilization of the age. They were for peace; they believed in an appeal to the conscience and heart of the nation, at the ballot box, and in loyally submitting to the verdict when rendered. They never would have appealed from the ballot box to the cartridge box. The great heart of the North was still and for a time held its breath while re-echoing with hope the sentiment of their beloved Quaker Poet, when, just before the Rebellion, he uttered this sublime prayer:

" Perish with him the thought,
That seeks, through evil, good;
Long live the generous purpose
Unstained by human blood."

While I did not adopt, without qualification, the memorable utterances of Daniel O'Connell, the great Irish leader, when he declared "that no revolution was worth the shedding of one drop of human blood," I everywhere proclaimed "that in this country, so long as the press was free and speech was free, and the ballot was free, no revolution was worth the shedding of one drop of human blood."

The speeches, appeals and acts of the leaders of the two sections were entirely characteristic.

The Southern leaders, instead of quailing before the storm which their passionate appeals had raised, defiantly mounted and rode the storm, fit types of the barbarism which they championed.

When the North, with the loyal men of the border States, fully comprehended the fact that there could be no peace nor union unless the Rebellion was suppressed by force, and slavery, which made the Rebellion possible, was abolished, they buckled on their armor and went forth to conquer.

During the first session of Congress, after Mr. Lincoln became President, I introduced a bill for the abolition of slavery in the District of Columbia. It contained but one short section, and simply enacted "that slavery, or involuntary servitude, should cease in the District of Columbia from and after the passage of this act." I sent it to the Committee on the

District of Columbia, of which I was a member, and Roscoe Conkling, of New York, was chairman. When the bill was read in the District Committee, it was by common consent referred to me, as a sub-committee of one. The excitement and indignation which that bill caused in the District Committee, and the undisguised disgust entertained for me personally by the pro-slavery members of the Committee, would be amusing now, but it was a matter of serious moment then.

I felt certain that a majority of that Committee did not intend to let me report that bill or any other of like character to the House for a vote. As soon as it was known that I had the matter in charge, by direction of the District Committee Mr. Chase sent for me, and discussed the proposition which I had introduced, and suggested instead, a bill which should compensate the "loyal slave owners" by paying them a "ransom," which should not exceed three hundred dollars a head for each slave, and enforced his argument by adding that Mr. Lincoln was seriously considering the practicability of compensating the border States if they would take the initiative and emancipate their slaves, and he added, "I want you to see the President, and if possible prepare a bill which will command the necessary votes of both Houses of Congress and the active support of the Administration."

I saw the President next day and went over the ground with him, substantially as I had with Mr. Chase, and finally agreed that I would ask for the appointment of a Senator on the part of the Senate District Committee to unite with me to frame a bill, which the Senate and House Committees would report favorably, and which should have the President's approval, and the support of as many of the Representatives from the border States as we could induce to vote to "initiate emancipation," as Mr. Lincoln expressed it.

Fortunately for the success of the compensation policy, the Senate District Committee designated as that sub-committee-man, Lot M. Morrell, of Maine, to confer with me and prepare such a bill as Mr. Lincoln and Chase had outlined.

After several meetings a bill was finally agreed upon which appropriated one million dollars to pay loyal owners for their slaves at a price not to exceed $300 each.

This bill had the approval of Mr. Lincoln and Chase and other anti-slavery leaders, before it was submitted to the District Committees for their action and recommendation to each House of Congress.

Personally, I did not agree with Mr. Lincoln in his border State policy, but was unwilling to set up my judgment against his, especially when he was supported by such men as Chase, Fessenden, Trumbull, and a large majority of Union men in both Houses of Congress. I therefore yielded my private opinions on a matter of policy, for reasons which I then gave and will presently quote, and because I was determined that that Congress should not adjourn until slavery had been abolished at the National Capital.

I did not want to appropriate a million of dollars from the National Treasury to pay the slave owners of the District of Columbia for their slaves, because I was opposed to officially recognizing property in man, and for the additional reason that I was con fident that before the close of the war slavery would be abolished without compensation. And I believed then, and believe now, that at least two thirds of all the so-called "loyal slave owners" in the District of Columbia who applied for and accepted compensation for their slaves, would at that time have welcomed Jefferson Davis and his government in Washington with every demonstration of joy.

On the 12th of March, 1862, by direction of the Committee for the District of Columbia, I reported the bill to the House as it had been agreed upon by Mr. Morrell and myself, with the approval of Mr. Lincoln, Mr. Chase and others.

On the 11th of April, 1862, the bill, as amended by the Senate, passed the House by a vote of 92 for to 38 against, and at once received the signature of the President.

In the speech which I delivered that day I said: "I do not believe that Congress has any more power to make a slave than to make a king," and added, "If then there is, as I claim, no power in Congress to reduce any man or race to slavery, it certainly will not be claimed that Congress has power to legalize such regulations as exist to-day touching persons held as slaves in this District by re-enacting the slave laws of Maryland, and thus do by indirection what no sane man claims authority to do directly." * * * "If I must tax the loyal people of the nation a million of dollars before the slaves at the National Capital can be ransomed I will do it. I will make a bridge of gold over which they may pass to freedom on the anniversary of the fall of Sumter, if it cannot be more justly accomplished."

As the nation had been guilty of riveting the chains of all the slaves in the District, and Mr. Lincoln and Mr. Chase, and so large a majority of the friends of the Union desired the passage of this act, believing that it would aid them in holding the border slave States, I yielded my own opinions, and voted to pay the loyal owners of the District for their slaves, and thus aided Mr. Lincoln in initiating emancipation by compensation. But events were stronger than men or measures, and this was the first and last of compensation.

On the 14th of December, 1863, I introduced a proposition to amend the Constitution, abolishing slavery in all the States and Territories of the nation, which, on my motion, was referred to the Committee on the Judiciary. In a speech during that session of Congress urging the submission of such an amendment, I said: "I advocated from the first the emancipation of all slaves, because I believed ideas more formidable than armies, justice more powerful than prejudice, and truth a weapon mightier than the sword."

The fall of Vicksburg and the great victory of Gettysburg had solidified the Union men North and South, and assured them of ultimate success.

The crushing defeat of Hood at Nashville by Thomas, the investment of Richmond by Grant, and Sherman's triumphant march from the mountains to the sea, was an announcement to the world that all armed opposition to the Government was approaching its end.

It now only remained, that the statesmen who had provided for and organized our great armies should crown their matchless victories with unfading glory, by engrafting into our National Constitution a provision which should make peace and union inseparable by removing forever the cause of the war, and making slavery everywhere impossible beneath the flag of the Republic.

On the 15th of June, 1864, the House voted on the proposed constitutional amendment, and it was defeated by a vote of 94 for it and 64 against it. I thereupon changed my vote before the announcement was made, as I had the right to do under the rules, and my vote was recorded with the opposition in order that I might enter a motion for reconsideration.

In the *Globe*, as the vote stands recorded, it is 93 for to 65 against. This vote disappointed, but it did not discourage me. Had every member been present and voted, it would have required 122 votes to pass the amendment, whereas we could muster but 94, or 28 less than required.

As I now look back, and review with calmer emotions than I did then the great battle we were fighting, I comprehend more fully the power of that simple and sublime faith which inspired all the living heroes in that historic hour.

In his "Twenty Years of Congress" Mr. Blaine has given me credit, in full measure, for introducing and pressing the first proposition made in the House of Representatives for the abolition of slavery in the United States by an amendment to the National Constitution, and for effective parliamentary work in securing its passage. Personally, I never regarded the work which I then did as entitling me to special recognition. It was to me a duty, and because I so felt, I have never publicly written or spoken about my connection with it, and should not have done so before you to-night but for the pressing invitation of our President, who acts as if he regarded it as part of his duty, while charged with the care of this Society, to bring every modest Ohio man to the front.

There was at that time so many noble and unselfish men in the House of Representatives entitled to recognition for effective work in behalf of the Thirteenth Amendment, that I have always preferred not to single out any one member as entitled to more credit than another. I certainly did not expect any such complimentary recognition as Mr. Blaine has so generously given me.

Educated in the political school of Jefferson, I was absolutely amazed at the solid Democratic vote against the amendment on the 15th of June. To me it looked as if the golden hour had come, when the Democratic party could, without apology, and without regret, emancipate itself from the fatal dogmas of Calhoun, and reaffirm the doctrines of Jefferson. It had always seemed to me that the great men in the Democratic party had shown a broader spirit in favor of human liberty than their political opponents, and until the domination of Mr. Calhoun and his States-rights disciples, this was undoubtedly true. On the death of General Harrison in 1841, and after John Tyler became the acting President, I date the organized conspiracy of the slave barons, which culminated in the Rebellion.

A man of singleness of purpose and disinterestedness, possesses a wonderful power which is soon recognized by his associates in the Congress of the United States. The leading men in both Senate and House, and in nearly all the executive departments, knew that my only ambition was to accomplish the task with which (as Mr. Blaine expresses it) I was "by common consent, specially charged." The only reward I expected, and the only reward I ever had, or shall ever have, is the satisfaction of knowing that I did my whole duty, nothing more, nothing less. I at once gave special care to the study of the characters and antecedents of thirty-six of the members who did not vote for the amendment on the 15th of June, and made up my mind that if we could force the issue of the Thirteenth Amendment into the pending presidential contest, and Mr. Lincoln should be elected in November, that the requisite number of liberal Democrats and border State Union men who had voted against and defeated the amendment in June might be prevailed upon to vote with us after Mr. Lincoln had been re-elected on that issue. In this faith, and with this hope, I at once began a systematic study of the characters of the men whose cooperation and votes must be secured as a condition to success.

During this six months' experience I learned something of the tremendous power of a single man when making earnest appeals to his colleagues. One source of ever-present embarrassment to me was the fact that I had but little experience in legislation, and that nearly every one of my colleagues to whom I was addressing myself was my senior in years. In this great work I had the earnest support of the Administration, the great majority of the Republican party, and many earnest men in public and private life.

On the 28th of June, 1864, Mr. Holman, of Indiana, rose in the House, and said "that he desired to know whether the gentleman from Ohio (Mr. Ashley) who entered the motion to reconsider the vote by which the House rejected the bill proposing an amendment to the Constitution abolishing slavery throughout all the States and Territories of the United States, proposed to call that motion up during the present session." In reply, I said that I did not propose to call the motion up during the present session; "but as the record had been made up, we would go to the country on the issue thus presented." And I added: "When the verdict of the people shall have been rendered next November, I trust this Congress will return determined to engraft that verdict into the National Constitution." I thereupon gave notice that I would call up the proposition at the earliest possible moment after our meeting in December next (See *Globe*, June 28th, 1864).

Immediately after giving this notice, I went to work to secure its passage, and it may not be uninteresting if I outline to you the way I conducted that campaign.

The question thus presented became one of the leading issues of the Presidential Campaign of 1864.

The Administration—the Republican party—and many men who were not partizans, now gave the measure their warm support.

Knowing that Henry Winter Davis, of Maryland, and Frank P. Blair, of Missouri, would vote for the amendment whenever their votes would secure its passage, I went to them to learn who of the border-State members were men of broad and liberal views, and strong and self-reliant enough to follow their convictions, even to political death, provided they could know that their votes would pass the measure.

The following is the list of the names of the border-State men, as made up within two weeks after the defeat of the amendment in June, 1864: James S. Rollins, Henry S. Blow, Benjamin F. Loan, ex-Gov. King, S. H. Boyd, Frank P. Blair and Joseph W. McClurg of Missouri; Green Clay Smith, George H. Yeaman, Brutus J. Clay and Lucius Anderson of Kentucky; John A. J. Cresswell, Gov. Francis Thomas, E. H. Webster and Henry Winter Davis of Maryland; Kellian V. Whaley, Jacob P. Blair, and William G. Brown of West Virginia, and N. B. Smithers of Delaware. Of the 19 thus selected 13 voted for the amendment, and marched to their political death.

After conferring with Reuben E. Fenton and Augustus Frank of New York, I made up the following list of liberal Northern Democrats, whose votes I hoped to secure for the amendment:

Moses F. Odell, Homer A. Nelson, John A. Griswold, Anson Herrick, John B. Steele, Charles F. Winfield, William Radford and John Ganson of New York; S. S. Cox, Warren P. Noble, Wells A. Hutchins, John F. McKenney and Francis C. Le Blond of Ohio; Archibald McAllister and Alex. H. Coffroth of Pennsylvania; James E. English of Connecticut, and Augustus C. Baldwin of Michigan.

Of the 17 Northern Democrats thus selected, eleven voted for the amendment, two were absent, and one who had promised me to vote for it and prepared a speech in its favor, finally voted against. Of the 36 members originally selected as men naturally inclined to favor the amendment, and strong enough to meet and repel the fierce partisan attack which were certain to be made upon them, 24 voted for it, two were absent, and but *ten* voted against it.

Every honorable effort was made by the Administration to secure the passage of this amendment.

At my request Tuesday, January 31st, 1865, was the day fixed for the vote to be taken on the amendment.

A faithful record of the final act of the 38th Congress on this question will be found on pages 523 to 531 of the *Congressional Globe*.

The Speaker stated the question, and announced "That the gentleman from Ohio was entitled to the floor," which under the rules gave me one hour in which to close the debate.

Never before, and certain I am that never again, will I be seized with so strong a desire to give utterance to the thoughts and emotions which throbbed my heart and brain.

I knew that the hour was at hand when the world would witness the complete triumph of a cause, which at the beginning of my political life I had not hoped to live long enough to see, and that on that day, before our session closed, an act, as just as it was merciful to oppressor and oppressed, was to be enacted into law, and soon thereafter became a part of our National Constitution forever.

The hour and the occasion was an immortal one in the Nation's history, and memorable to each actor who voted for the amendment.

Every available foot of space, both in the galleries and on the floor of the House, was crowded at an early hour, and many hundred could not get within hearing. Never before, nor afterwards, did I see so brilliant and distinguished a gathering in that hall, nor one where the feeling was more intense. The Judges of the Supreme Court, the members of the Cabinet, the Vice-President and Senators, most of the foreign Ministers and all the distinguished visitors who could secure seats, with their wives, daughters and friends, were present to witness the sublimest event in our National life.

You will readily understand that this was an occasion to inspire any man of my temperament with a strong desire to speak, and yet it was beyond question my duty to yield all my time to gentlemen of the opposition, who had promised to vote for the amendment, and desired to have recorded in the official organ of the House the reasons for the vote which they were about to give.

The first gentleman to whom I yielded was the Hon. Archibald McAllister of Pennsylvania, an old-fashioned Democrat of the Jackson school. He was not a speaker, and the brief "statement," as he called it, which he sent to the Clerk's desk to be read for him as he stood on the floor, with every eye in that great hall fixed on his tall form, is so characteristic, and withal expresses so tersely the reasons which impelled him and thousands of other loyal and conservative men to demand the immediate abolition of slavery, that I quote what he said entire.

I will read it to you, and repeat what he said, as nearly as I can, with the same intonation of voice and manner as he read it to me in my Committee room that morning, a few minutes before the House convened.

He said "That it was due to his constituents that they should know why he changed his vote, and that he could not make a speech, that he was so nervous that he dare not even trust himself to read what he had written, and asked me if I would yield him the floor long enough to allow him to send to the Clerk's desk, and have read what he desired to say to his constituents." I never was more anxious to yield the floor to any man than I was to him, and answered, "Certainly, I will be glad to yield you all the time you ask." He then read me this short, and now historical, speech, and I said to him then, as I say to you now, that it was, under all the circumstances, the best and most eloquent speech delivered in the House of Representatives in favor of the Thirteenth Amendment. This is the speech, and the way he read it to me:

"When this subject was before this House on a former occasion, I voted against the measure. I have been in favor of exhausting all means of conciliation to restore the Union as our fathers made it. I am for the whole Union and utterly opposed to secession, or dissolution in any shape. The result of all the peace missions, and especially that of Mr. Blair, has satisfied me that nothing short of the recognition of their independence will satisfy the Southern Confederacy. It must therefore be destroyed, and in voting for the present measure, I cast my vote against the corner-stone of the Southern Confederacy, and declare eternal war against the enemies of my country."

As soon as he had finished reading it, I grasped his hand with enthusiasm, and heartily congratulated him, and said, "Mr. McAllister, that is a better and more telling speech by far than any which has been made for the amendment, and I believe that it will be quoted hereafter more than any speech made in Congress in its favor."

When the Clerk of the House finished reading this brief speech of this plain, blunt man, it called forth general applause on the floor and in the galleries, and when I afterwards read it to Mr. Lincoln, Chase and others, they were then as pronounced in its endorsement as I am now.

To the end that there should be no pretext for "filibustering" (as I knew the amendment might be defeated in that way), I determined from the start to so conduct the debate that every gentleman opposed to the amendment who cared to be heard should have ample time and opportunity.

After the previous question had been seconded, and all debate ordered closed, there could be but two roll-calls (if there were no filibustering) before the final vote.

The first roll-call was on a motion made by the opposition, to lay my motion to reconsider on the table. Such a motion is generally regarded as a test vote.

Hundreds of tally sheets had been distributed

on the floor and in the galleries, many being in the hands of ladies. Before the result of the first roll-call was announced, it was known all over the House that the vote was *two* less than the necessary *two-thirds*, and both Mr. Stevens of Pennsylvania and Mr. Washburn of Illinois excitedly exclaimed: "General, we are defeated." "No, gentlemen, we are not," was my prompt answer. The second vote was on my motion to reconsider, which would bring the House, at the next roll-call, to a direct vote on the passage of the amendment.

The excitement was now the most intense I ever witnessed; the oldest members, with the Speaker and the reporters in the galleries, believed that we were defeated. When the result of the second vote was announced, we lacked *one vote* of two-thirds, whereupon many threw down their tally sheets and admitted defeat. I now arose and stood, while the roll was being called on the final vote and said to those around me, that we would have *not less* than four (4), and I believed seven (7) majority over the necessary two-thirds.

As the roll was completed, the Speaker directed that his name be called as a member of the House, and when he voted he announced to an astonished assemblage, "that the yeas were 119, and the nays 56, and that the bill had received the two-thirds majority required by the Constitution." It was a moment or two before the House or the galleries recovered from their surprise and recognized the fact that we had triumphed. When they did, a shout went up from the floor and galleries, and the vast audience rose to their feet, many members jumping on their desks, with shouts and waving of hats and handkerchiefs, and gave vent to their feelings by every demonstration of joy. It was a scene such as I had never before witnessed, and shall never witness again.

Mr. Ingersoll of Illinois said: "Mr. Speaker, in

honor of this sublime and immortal event, I move that this House do now adjourn," which motion was carried.

When this vote was taken, the House had but 183 members, 94 of whom were Republicans, 64 Democrats, and 25 border-State Union men.

If the vote is analyzed, it will be seen that of the 119 votes recorded for the amendment 13 were by men from the border States, and eleven (11) were by Democrats from the free States. If but 3 out of the 24, who voted with us, had voted against the amendment it would have failed. If but four (4) of the 8 members who were absent had appeared and voted against, it would have been lost. Had all the Northern Democrats who supported the amendment voted against, it would have been defeated by 26 votes. Had all the border-State men who voted for it, voted against, it would have failed by 32 votes.

If the border-State men and Northern Democrats who voted for the amendment had voted against, it would have failed by 65 votes.

Mr. Lincoln was especially delighted at the vote which the amendment received from the border slave States, and frequently congratulated me on that result.

Bancroft, the historian, has drawn with a graphic pen the characters of many of the able and illustrious men of the Revolution which achieved our independence. In writing of George Mason, of Virginia, he said: "His sincerity made him wise and bold, modest and unchanging, with a scorn for anything mean and cowardly, as illustrated in his unselfish attachment to human freedom." And these identical qualities of head and heart were pre-eminently conspicuous in all the border statesmen who voted for the Thirteenth Amendment.

It would be difficult in any age or country to find grander or more unselfish and patriotic men than Henry Winter Davis and Governor Francis Thomas of Maryland, or James S. Rollins, Frank P. Blair and Governor King of Missouri, or George H. Yeaman of Kentucky, or N. P. Smithers of Delaware, and not less worthy of mention for their unchanging fidelity to principle are all the Northern Democrats who voted for the amendment, prominent among whom I may name Governor English, of Connecticut; Judge Homer A. Nelson and Moses S. Odell, of New York; Archibald McAllister, of Pennsylvania; Wells A. Hutchins, of Ohio, and A. C. Baldwin, of Michigan.

Of the twenty-four border State and Northern men who made up this majority which enabled us to win this victory, all had defied their party discipline, and had deliberately and with unfaltering faith marched to their political death. These are the men whom our future historians will honor, and to whom this nation owes a debt of eternal gratitude.

But seven of this twenty-four are now living, the others have gone to

> "Join the choir invisible
> Of those immortal dead, who live again
> In minds made better by their presence; live
> In pulses stirred to generosity,
> In deeds of daring rectitude, in scorn
> For miserable aims that end with self."

From Dr. C. L. Ford

Just Issued from the Press of Atwood & Culver, Madison, Wis.

"OLD ABE."

THE LIVE WAR-EAGLE OF WISCONSIN.

BY J. O. BARRETT.

A Book of Fact, Thrilling in Interest, and full of Beautiful Morals.

When an infant bird, this renowned Eagle was captured by a Chippewa Indian, A-GE-WAH-WE-GE-ZHIG, on the Flambeau river, Wisconsin, in the spring of 1861; was sold to Company C, Eighth Wisconsin Regiment, the subsequent summer; went to the front with his braves that fall, leading the van in march and battle, during a campaign of three years in the Great Rebellion. His career is most remarkable in military life. Col. J. W. JEFFERSON, who led the gallant Eighth in many of its battles, says:

"'Old Abe' was with the command in nearly every action. He enjoyed the excitement; and I am convinced, from his peculiar manner, he was well informed in regard to army movements, dress parade and preparations for the march and battle. Upon parade, after he had been a year in the service, he always gave heed to '*attention!*' With his head obliquely to the front, his right eye directly turned upon the parade commander, he would listen and obey orders, noting time accurately. After parade had been dismissed, and the ranks were being closed by the sergeants, he would lay aside his soldierly manner, flap his wings and make himself generally at home. When there was an order to form for battle, he and the colors were first upon the line. His actions upon those occasions were uneasy, turning his head anxiously from right to left, looking to see when the line was completed. Soon as the regiment got ready, faced and put in march, he would assume a steady and quiet demeanor. In battle he was almost constantly flapping his wings, having his mouth wide open, and many a time would scream with wild enthusiasm. This was particularly so at the hard-fought battle of Corinth, when our regiment repulsed and charged, or, you might say, made a counter-charge on Price's famous Missouri brigade."

"Old Abe" was in about twenty-five great battles and as many skirmishes. In the South, he was everywhere an object of marked attention, reminding the populace of their fealty to the Union of States. Given to the State of Wisconsin, in 1864, he has since been frequently on exhibition at Sanitary Fairs and other benevolent entertainments, earning large sums of money for public charities. At military reviews and reunions of the Grand Army of the Republic, he has ever been the central figure of attraction, and popular enthusiasm, being universally hailed as the emblem of the American Union. The Wisconsin legislature of 1876 passed a resolution instructing Gov. LUDINGTON to send the war-bird to the National Centennial, at Philadelphia, under the superintendence of one of his old war bearers. He is there, having his seat of honor at the Wisconsin Headquarters, where he greets his companions in arms again and the millions that are curious to see the world-renowned Eagle of the United States.

"OLD ABE" FUND.

As "Old Abe" is a National bird, the author pledges a liberal percentage of the sales of his history and pictures for the eventual establishment of a National institution, entitled the "Old Abe Ornithological Museum," designed for the benefit of the masses. Gov. LUDINGTON, the State Treasurer, the Wisconsin Centennial Board of Managers, and others, cordially endorse Mr. BARRETT's enterprise:

EXECUTIVE OFFICE, MADISON, *April 12, 1876.*

J. O. BARRETT, Esq.—*Dear Sir*—I seriously object to any one's using "Old Abe" on exhibition for personal speculation, in any shape whatever; but as you propose to devote your history and pictures of this State Bird to the public good, by raising a National fund for Ornithological Science and Fine Art, I heartily approve of your undertaking to sell the same at the Centennial in Philadelphia, and elsewhere, and trust that this promise will be faithfully executed, with a credit to our State and Nation.

H. LUDINGTON,
Governor of Wisconsin.

STATE TREASURER'S OFFICE, MADISON, *April 12, 1876.*

J. O. BARRETT, Esq.—*Dear Sir*—In reply to your inquiry, whether I will take charge of the "Old Abe" fund, which you propose to raise by the sale of your history and pictures of the War-Eagle, "Old Abe," and which you devote to Science and Art, I have to say: You are at liberty to make the State Treasury your bank of deposit, and that said money will be safely kept in the State safe, and receipted by me as fast as you see fit to tender the same. I regard your enterprise as eminently worthy, and trust it can be made a success.

Yours, respectfully,

FERD. KUEHN,
State Treasurer.

Published by ATWOOD & CULVER, Madison, Wis. Price, 50 cts. Postage paid. Illustrated, bound, $1.00. Postage paid.

Beautiful photographs of "Old Abe," identified by Gov. LUDINGTON and others; also, of his Indian captor; sold at 25 cts. each. Liberal discount to the trade on books and pictures.

For sale at the Wisconsin Headquarters, within the Centennial Grounds, at Philadelphia, by J. O. BARRETT; also by ROBERT WOOTTON, General Agent, Madison, Wis.

No. 3.

PAPERS FROM THE SOCIETY

FOR THE

Diffusion of Political Knowledge.

SPEECH OF THE HON. JAMES BROOKS,

AT

932 BROADWAY, TUESDAY EVENING, DECEMBER 30, 1862.

"WHEN A PARTY IN POWER VIOLATES THE CONSTITUTION AND DISREGARDS STATE-RIGHTS, PLAIN MEN WILL READ PAMPHLETS."

READ—DISCUSS—DIFFUSE.

PRESIDENT, PROF. S. F. B. MORSE,
SECRETARY, WM. McMURRAY,
TREASURER, LORING ANDREWS,

OFFICE OF THE SOCIETY,
No. 13 PARK ROW, NEW-YORK.
C. MASON, COR. SEC'Y.,
To whom all communications may be addressed.

Resolved, That it be recommended to all citizens in the various cities, counties, and villages of this and other States, who approve of the objects expressed in this Constitution, that they organize auxiliary societies, and open communication with the New-York Society for the purpose of procuring and circulating our papers.

SPEECH OF THE HON. JAMES BROOKS.

THE President of the Union Democratic Association, after some appropriate remarks upon the services rendered by the Association, said, that a speaker would now address them, by whose ability and eloquence, the large audience present would be well rewarded for their attendance on so stormy an evening. He, therefore, introduced the Hon. JAMES BROOKS. After the repeated and prolonged cheering that welcomed Mr. Brooks, had subsided, he said:

MR. CHAIRMAN AND GENTLEMEN: If any of you expect from me this evening, any exciting, or excited remarks, you will be disappointed. There are times so impressive, crises in public affairs so solemn, that any flourishes of rhetoric, any pompous display of periods, or sesquipedalian words, but detract from the gravity and dignity of the theme. Hence, in the crisis of a civil war like ours, where the blood of kith and kin is poured forth like water, and when the civil war is becoming complicated in fresher, and yet more fearful issues, the simplest language becomes the sublimest expression. (Applause.) The ancient heathen orators in times like these, when they were wont to address their public assemblies invoked their *Dii Immortales*, their Immortal gods. How much more then, should Christians, who assemble now, in the midst of Battle and Blood, invoke *the* immortal God to guide our deliberations. (Applause.)

THE TWO PROCLAMATIONS AND WAR ORDER OF SEPTEMBER, 1862.

When I last had the honor of addressing this Association, late in September last, there were threatening the people two PROCLAMATIONS and one WAR ORDER: One Proclamation threatening the people of the North, that if they discussed the other, the War Order would, through Courts Martial or Provost Martials, suspend Process, Bail, Jury Trial, Habeas Corpus, and arrest and incarcerate all engaged in such discussion. The Civil Courts were to be suspended, and Military Courts were to be substituted in their places. The very first opportunity after the promulgation of these Edicts, I ventured in this Hall to denounce them, as in violation, not only of *Magna Charta*, the Common Law of England and of the United States, and of the rights of man, but of the Constitution of the United States, and of our State of New-York; and you, in your responses, here in this Hall and elsewhere, so ably, so eloquently supported and cheered me, that the Edicts fell powerless before a brave and determined People. The President, indeed, who fulminated these Edicts, under the influence of our, and other elections, the offspring of what we proclaimed, we *would* have, namely, free discussion, recalled, nullified, abrogated his War Order, and that Proclamation Edict which threatened to subvert all Liberty in the North. The Provost-Marshals shrank back before the majesty of an indignant People, and the Judges and the Courts were reïnaugurated, reïnstalled by that People. (Cheers.)

THE PROCLAMATION OF JANUARY, 1863.

But, gentlemen, there is left now another proclamation, not annulled—that, for the South and South-West—in force, or if possible, to be put in force January first, 1863 — which I propose this evening more fully to discuss. (Applause.) The President does not claim, nor do the President's friends claim, that for this Proclamation he has any warrant, in, or under the Constitution of the United States — whereby, thus, he subverts, or attempts to subvert, whole States with all the organizations of their society — their statute, their civil, their municipal, as well as their constitutional laws; nor does he claim, that under the laws of nations, he has any such prerogative or power, save what is indefinitely declared to be the laws of war, the war power, or the military necessity of war. I propose, this evening, gentlemen, to discuss all these weighty matters, and you must put up with, as a necessity of this discussion, the recitation of some of our past history, and with the reading of such documents as proof makes necessary, however heavy such reading may be in a popular assembly. (Cries of "Go on. It is what we want to hear.")

WAR FOR THE CONSTITUTION.

Gentlemen, as I said at the start, we are in the midst of a bloody civil war, the magnitude of which is unlike any thing in the record of human history, except the civil wars of Rome, that drenched the huge Roman Empire in human gore. We, who are not of the Administration, were driven into this war, reluctantly driven in, by the force of unhappy events, and by the then solemn pledge of the Administration, that it was a war, only to maintain the Government and the Constitution of the United States, with the integrity of the Union. (Applause.) We are not now, and we never pretended to be, supporters of the Administration. We drew at first, as we draw now, the constitutional distinction between supporting the Government, and a temporary Administration of that Government. (Applause.) We recognize no loyalty, nor fealty, nor allegiance due to any mere administration of the Government, to no mere man, in no one branch of it—Executive, Legislative, or Judicial—but we do recognize fealty, loyalty, love, devotion, with the whole heart and soul, as due to that great charter of human liberty known as the Constitution of the United States. (Loud and prolonged cheering.) That Constitution in my earlier days, when not as well booked up as I am now I supposed to be some impromptu inpiration of Divine Wisdom, far above all human intelligence, or human instinct—the work of men inspired, as were the Holy Apostles, who handed down to us the Holy Scriptures, and I revered and worshiped that Constitution as the Bible guide on earth to men struggling for Law and Liberty. But upon fuller and maturer reading, I discovered, that our Fathers of the Constitution were not so much inspired men, as condensers or codifiers of centuries of human wisdon, the writers up, and abridgers of human law, the common law of England—of the principles, rights, liberties, our British forefathers, after five or six centuries of struggle, wrested from the Kings and Despots of England, and affixed to great charters of Human Rights, the *Magna Charta* of 1215 won sword in hand by the Barons of England from King John, or the Petition of Rights, 1628, or the *Habeas Corpus*, 1679, or the Bill of Rights, 1689. The Constitution of the United States brought to a *focus* these great Lights of Liberty, Law, Human Progress and Civilization. The eyes of our fathers were then but the lenses of the Past to see their Present, and so to provide for the great Future. (Applause.)

THE IMMEDIATE CAUSE AND THE PLEDGE OF THE WAR.

Hence, when in December, now two years gone by, after the Presidential election, there assembled in South-Carolina, a Convention of the States, enacting an ordinance of secession, separating that State from the United States and from the Constitution of the United States, which had not gratified South-Carolina in that election; hence, when in the subsequent February there assembled in Montgomery, Alabama, a convention of a few other States, subverting and annulling the Constitution of the United States, and not only that, but creating a new Constitution, and changing the old Flag—both the reason and the sentiment of the country felt indignant, and uprose to express that indignation. The magazine so well prepared for explosion during twenty-five years of preparation by extreme men, both North and South, was fired at Fort Sumter, and the explosion took place, involving some thirty millions of people in its destruction. The North uprose in mass almost—not to maintain or uphold Abraham Lincoln, or the Cabinet Administration of Abraham Lincoln—but to uphold the Constitution, the three branches of the Government of the United States, its Judiciary as well as its Executive and Legislative authority. (Applause.) "The Constitution *shall* be maintained:" "The Flag *shall* be respected:" "The Union *must* and *shall* be preserved," were the universal rallying cries of the Northern People. (Applause.) The Rebel Enemy authoritatively, through one of its Cabinet officers, (Mr. Walker,) avowed its intent to march upon, and to seize, Washington;—and hence, when the President called for his 75,000 men, more than a million were earnest to volunteer to protect the Capital, to uphold the Flag, to stand by the Constitution. The war then, was solely and avowedly for the maintenance of the Constitution, and the Flag as the symbol of that Constitution.

THE PLEDGE OF THE INAUGURAL.

The President himself, in his Inaugural, March 4th, 1861, thus pledged himself against the Abolitionists in his own party, and against his Proclamation of Abolitionism:

"I have no purpose, *directly* or *indirectly*, to INTERFERE with the institution of slavery in the States where it exists. I believe *I have no lawful right to do so, and I have no intention to do so.*"

THE PLEDGES OF THE HOUSE.

The House of Representatives, by a nearly unanimous vote, in February, 1861, passed the following resolutions:

Resolved, That neither the Federal Government nor the people or government of the non-slave-holding States *have a purpose or a constitutional right to legislate upon or interfere with slavery in any of the States of the Union.*

Resolved, That those persons in the North who do not subscribe to the foregoing proposition *are too insignificant in numbers and influence* to excite the serious attention or alarm of any portion of the people of the Republic, and that the increase of their numbers and influence does not keep pace with the increase of the aggregate population of the Union.

THE CRITTENDEN PLEDGE.

In July, 1861, was introduced into the House, and passed almost unanimously, (only two dissenting,) the well-known Crittenden Pledge or Resolution, namely:

"That the present deplorable civil war has been forced upon the country by the disunionists of the Southern States, now in arms against the constitutional government, *and in arms around Capitol:* that in this national emergency, Congress, banishing all feeling of mere passion and resentment, will recollect only its duty to the whole country; that this war is not waged on their part in any spirit of oppression, or *for any purpose of conquest or subjugation, or purpose of overthrowing or interfering with the rights or established institutions of those States, but to defend and maintain the supremacy of the Constitution, and to preserve the Union* with all the dignity, *equality* and *rights* of the several States unimpaired; and that, as soon as these objects are accomplished, the war ought to cease."

THE SENATE PLEDGE.

In the Senate, Mr. Sherman, of Ohio, had introduced, and the Senate had passed, a like resolution. Thus, three branches of the Legislative Government—the Executive, the Senate, the House—solemnly pledged itself to the country to carry on a war, only for the SUPREMACY OF THE CONSTITUTION. The armies were created, and the soldiers were enlisted upon that solemn pledge—and, upon many a battle-field, many a life has been freely offered up to carry out, defend, protect, and promulgate that pledge. This was the war, the North entered into—the war of the Conservative men of the North—the war of the great Democratic Party. We never committed ourselves to any other war, (cheers,) and they who are for breaking these pledges, or for creating another war—or who have committed us to, or enlisted us in this war, under what now seems false pretences or false pledges—they are in honor bound to dismiss us from this war, and to carry it on, themselves. (Loud and prolonged cheering, many of the audience rising and waving their hats.)

THE REVERSE PICTURE—THE PROCLAMATION OF SEPTEMBER 22D.

These being the pledges of Mr. Lincoln, the President, and of the Congress assembled in Washington, now look at the reverse picture, and say, who can, that the whole purpose, the whole *programme* of the war have not been changed? Say, who can, that twenty millions of Northern white men are not now called upon to endure Conscription and Taxation, and to sacrifice themselves in Southern latitudes, mainly to free three or four millions of negroes. (Applause.) The President in his September 22d Proclamation says:

"On the first day of January, in the year of our Lord one thousand eight hundred and sixty-three, all persons held as slaves within any State, or any designated part of a State, the people whereof shall then be in rebellion against the United States, *shall be thenceforward, and then, forever free ;* and the *Executive Government* of the United States, including the military and naval AUTHORITY thereof, will recognize and maintain the freedom of such persons, or any of them, in ANY effort, they may make for their actual freedom."

THE PRESIDENT'S EXTRAORDINARY USE OF WORDS.

Let me first call attention here to the extraordinary words of the Proclamation. The President speaks of himself, elected but for four years, two of them now nearly expired, as the EXECUTIVE GOVERNMENT OF THE UNITED STATES? Who created Abraham Lincoln the *Government of the United States?* Who created, who elected him, a man made of no better flesh and blood than the rest of us, to be the GOVERNMENT of thirty millions of people in the United States?

A VOICE — The people. (Cries of "No, no;" "Put him out," "Let him be.")

MR. BROOKS — The people! *Never!* (Exciting cheers.) Never, NEVER did the people give him a majority of their suffrages. (Continued cheers.) He is a minority President, *appointed* by the operations of the Constitution in spite of the people of the United States. (Cheers.) A large majority of the people voted against him, and he was created President in and under that very Constitution he would overthrow by his proclamations. (Great and continued cheers.)

In this Proclamation, the President also speaks of "the Military and Naval AUTHORITY." Authority is a legal power, or a right to command, such as Prince over subject, as Parent over child. The Government has authority: or, the President acting in obedience to Law, and so the Precedents or Decisions of a Court are *authority* or *authorities;* but the AUTHORITY of the Army or Navy is more novel even than this declaration of Mr. Lincoln, that I am the Executive Government of the United States—for there is a precedent for that, in the French *L'etat c'est moi,* (I am the State.) The Army and Navy are the agencies of civil authority—but, under our form of Government, they are no authority of themselves. When the State is the Emperor or the King, the Army or the Navy are only his means of executing his authority—but, under our form of Government, they are no *authority,* only the military Agencies of the Civil Government of the United States. As names often are things, or more than things, I thus dwell in verbal criticisms upon these words. When a President sets himself up as the Executive Government of the United States, and calls the Army and Navy his *authority* for overriding States, and the Laws of States, and the Constitution of the United States, we can not be too watchful of mere words. Naval and military men, then, be it understood, are but Agents, only, of civil authority, to execute Civil and Constitutional Law. (That's so ; cheers.) The Army and the Navy are, certainly, not "authority," under any known or recognized "Executive Government of the United States." (Cheers.)

There is another part of the Proclamation which chalks out, or seems to chalk out, a servile war, which contemplates, or seems to contemplate, the exciting of the slaves to the destruction not only of their masters, but of women and children, and to add the horrors of a servile, thus to the civil war. The words are—

> "The Executive Government . . . will recognize and maintain the freedom of such persons (negro slaves) . . . in any effort they may make for their actual freedom."

I do not know that the President means to excite a servile insurrection. I will not impute to him the horrible intent of converting the Southern country into a Hayti or St. Domingo, with the "Authority" of his army and navy to help, but I say, that the language is susceptible of that meaning, and such meaning has been given to it throughout the civilized world. (Applause.) When the "Executive Government" thus addresses negroes or slaves, words ought to be used that negroes or slaves can not pervert into authority to burn, slay, destroy, without regard to condition, age, or sex. (Applause.)

THE HOUSE BREAKING ITS PLEDGES.

But the President alone is not responsible for this violation of the Pledge and Principle, that enlisted the conservative men of the country in this war. The House of Representatives thus, December, 1862, reversed the Crittenden Resolution of July, 1862, the Hon. Sam. C. Fessenden, of Me., offering the following Resolution, which passed, ayes 78; noes 51.

Resolved, That the Proclamation of the President, of the date of Sept. 22d, 1862, is warranted by the Constitution; that the policy of emancipation as indicated therein is well adapted to hasten the restoration of peace, is well chosen as a war measure, and is an exercise of power with proper regard to the rights of citizens and the perpetuity of a free government.

ISSUE TAKEN ON PROCLAMATION POWER.

And now, my friends, here we take issue on that Resolution, such as we took in September, here, in this Hall, on the Proclamation, pending that reign of terror, when moral courage was needed to speak, not as now, when we can speak, and dare, to speak with freedom, of all the efforts of the administration of the government to subvert the law. When I said to you in the beginning of my remarks, that the Constitution of the United States was the embodiment of the common law of England and of the wisdom of our British ancestors for 500 years, I omitted to say that there was nothing in that Constitution which forbade Executive Proclamations. There are certain things so settled in human life, that it is not necessary to stipulate against them, such as the right to eat, to breathe, to live. When our British forefathers, in their second Revolution, stipulated against almost every form of executive despotic power, they did not deem it necessary expressly to stipulate against Proclamations, or to define the limits of uttering a Proclamation — because the common law of England had long settled, that Kings could not make law by proclamation, or ordain law, or override law. When our Constitution was formed, such a practice had not been set up in England for 200 years. No monarch of England, for that long period of time, had attempted to exercise, by proclamation, such powers and prerogatives as the President of the United States sets up in his Proclamation of September 22, 1862. (Applause.)

Queen Elizabeth as long ago as 1580 began to make Law by Proclamation, then, against the Anabaptists of England, and against Irishmen straying away from home, and against seditious and schismatic books tending to prejudice the then rising Church of England. James the First prohibited by Proclamation country gentlemen from coming to London, and regulated, or attempted to regulate, the habiliments of their women and children. (Laughter.) Charles the First, unfortunately for himself, in prohibiting by Proclamation, emigration to New England, prohibited Cromwell and Hampden from emigrating there. Queen Elizabeth, however, respected her People enough to listen to, and to yield to some of the remonstrances of that People against this power of Proclamation. Charles the First went to the Block, because of the unlawful exercise of this, and similar Prerogatives and Powers. (Applause.) The Tudors and the Stuarts claimed not only the power to proclaim and to ordain Law by Proclamation, but the power to dispense with Law, and to suspend Law. What cost these dynasties their existence is that which calls itself "*the Executive Government*" of the United States, and is now attempting upon us, Americans. (Applause.) Abraham Lincoln *suspends* Law—the *Habeas Corpus*—*dispenses* not only with Law, but even with the Courts of Law, and, by Proclamation, *ordains* Law. (Cheering.) Our Fathers did not stipulate against these Executive or Royal Prerogatives, in the Constitution — because for 200 years in England, the exercise of such Prerogatives had scarcely been thought of. But what no King of England for two centuries dared to do—what broke down the Tudors and the Stuarts, Abraham Lincoln is doing, and his upholders are claiming that he has a right to do. (Applause.)

A PRONUNCIAMENTO, NOT A PROCLAMATION.

Now, no man doubts the right of the President to utter a Proclamation; at times, it is his duty even—but a *Procla-*

mation is one thing, and a PRONUNCIAMENTO is another. The one is English, on English precedent; the other is Spanish, and comes to us from Spain, or, from the Revolutions of Spanish America. The Kings or Queens of England, utter Proclamations now—and there are numerous precedents for them, from the Administration of Washington, on to this era and age—but the Kings of England, now, and the previous Presidents of the United States, utter Proclamations, not to MAKE Law, or to ORDAIN Law, but to proclaim what the Law *is*, and to forewarn ill-disposed people against the violation of existing Common, Constitutional, or Statute Laws. The Queen of England, Queen born, has forewarned her British subjects not to violate British (neutrality) Law—but our four-years old President suspends Law, dispenses with Law, ordains Law, and overthrows both Constitutional and Statute Law. He *pronounces*, (in the Spanish meaning of the word,) not *proclaims* law. He scorns Common Law, Statute Law, Constitutional Law, Latin *Magna Charta*, and *Habeas Corpus*, and English, as well as American written Constitutions, and introduces here, not from England, the PROCLAMATION, but from Spanish America, the *Pronunciamiento*, that is, REVOLUTION. A Proclamation upholds Law; the Pronunciamiento overthrows Law. The President has fulminated a Spanish Pronunciamiento.

NO SUCH MILITARY POLICY NECESSARY.

But, we are told this *Pronunciamiento* against whole States or upon whole States, is, as a matter of mere military policy, or necessity, a wise exercise of the War Power; and it is insinuated that when the negro is thus "pronounced" free on paper, then Sambo, and Scipio and Cæsar will embrace their Rebel masters, and bring them into the ranks of our army, and surrender them as prisoners of war to the utterer of this Paper Proclamation. (Laughter and applause.) We shall see. We shall see. But I deny that there is any wisdom in this Paper as a war measure. I deny that it is a military policy. Its first effect has been to disunite the North, and to raise up a large majority in that North, certainly in the central States of the North, in opposition to this species of Administration. (Applause.) And the next effect has been, while thus disuniting the North, to unite the whole South as one man against a government carrying on a war on such principles. (A voice — "That's so.") We, who were united, have become a *divided* People, and they who were divided, have become a united people;—and if this be military policy, I must say, I don't see it. Do you? (Laughter.) It is a matter of record, too, that since the utterance of this Paper, while Providence before blessed our arms, when fighting for the Constitution and the Laws; now, Providence in a good degree has ceased to smile upon us. Delaware, Maryland, Western Virginia, Kentucky and Missouri came to us under the Inaugural of the President and the Crittenden Resolutions; New-Orleans was taken; Norfolk surrendered; nearly the whole coast of North-Carolina became ours; a Union party more or less existed every where in the South; while now, vast armies are in the field against us, fighting not alone for Independence, but for life, home, family, fireside, wife, children, every thing dear to man. The military policy of the President has made popular, South, what was there but an odious conscription, and what the people were preparing to resist. A war, becoming unpopular, has there been made popular; while a war here, at the start popular, is becoming unpopular, because of the false pretenses under which men were engaged or enlisted in it. (Applause.) Hence, I deny that there is any military necessity for this Paper, or that there is any military policy in it. (Cheers.) It is costing us already seas of blood, and will cost us, if thus persisted in, the entailment of a debt upon generation after generation, so that labor, for centuries, will be subjected to capital. (Cheers.)

NEGRO PROCLAMATIONS IN THE WAR OF THE REVOLUTION.

And now, as a matter of history, gentlemen, there is no one thing upon which the American people, or the United States Government, are more committed than against this use of negro-freeing Proclamations, or the use, in any way, of negroes in war, civil or foreign. The British Generals on our own Continent, pending our own Revolution of 1776, uttered Proclamations like this of Abraham Lincoln. Sir Henry Clinton and Sir William Howe *proclaimed* in New-York, New-Jersey and Pennsylvania the freedom of our negroes; Lord Dunmore did the like in Virginia, and Lord Cornwallis, further South. Our Statesmen and our Generals made good points of appeal to the civilization of the world against this British employment of Indians and negroes in civil war, and they spoke of the Indian savage and negro barbarism in the same breath. The use of such means and men, by Englishmen to subdue Englishmen, was pronounced to be against the law of nations, the law of nature and the law of God. (Applause.) That great man, Edmund Burke, whom Heaven had so gifted with intellect, that he seemed able to concenter the great lights of the Past, and to spread and to reflect them all over the Future — that great man foresaw what England was driving America into, and often held up the lights of that luminous intellect to forewarn his countrymen to beware. What he, what Lord Chatham, and others, said in the British Parliament, ought now to be read and re-read by every North-American. In an address to the King of England, exhorting that King not to drive the war to extreme measures, said Burke:

"To excite, by a Proclamation issued by your Military Governors, an universal insurrection of negro slaves in any of the Colonies, is a *measure full of complicated horrors, absolutely illegal, suitable neither to the practice of war nor to the time of peace.*"

In an address to the then British Colonies, Mr. Burke said:

"We likewise saw with shame the African slaves, who had been sold to you in public faith, and under the sanction of acts of Parliament, to be your servants and guards, employed to cut the throats of their masters."

The effect of these remonstrances from Burke, from Chatham, and other liberal Englishmen, upon Parliament, against these proclamations for the use or sudden liberation of negro slaves by the British generals, did more than any thing to destroy the popularity of the war in England and to tempt the British government and people to end so wicked a war, by the recognition of their colonies as independent States. (Applause.) Great Britain herself, as a government, confessed the Proclamation respecting the negroes to be so wrong that in the treaty of 1783, 7th article, is this solemn stipulation:

That His Britannic Majesty should, "with all convenient speed, and without causing any destruction, or *carrying away of negroes*, or other property of the American inhabitants, withdraw all his armies, garrisons and fleets from the United States, and from every part, and place, and harbor within the same."

When the treaty came to be executed, long controversies arose upon what definition should be given to this "*carrying away of negroes, or other property.*" Whoever will look into the American archives will find long diplomatic papers, and then long diplomatic controversies, — and he will find, too, that not only such Southern men as Jefferson and Edmund Randolph, of Virginia, were committed against the abduction, use, or employment of negroes in war, freed by proclamation or otherwise, but such New-Yorkers as John Jay and Egbert Benson. In the end the British government acquiesced in the justice of these remonstrances, and paid for the deported negroes, thus freed or abducted. (Applause.)

NEGRO PROCLAMATIONS IN THE WAR OF 1812.

A like passage of history was repeated after the war of 1812. Admiral Cochrane, upon the waters of the Chesapeake, issued a Proclamation, which, while it avoided the use of the word slave, in order to seem thus not to violate the understanding, or law of nations, that forbade the use of slaves, or the stirring them up to insurrection, nevertheless invited such persons to enter his Majesty's service, or to emigrate to British possessions in North-America. Admiral Cochrane, in short, was following in the footsteps of Clinton, Howe, Dunmore, and Cornwallis, of the Revolution. When the treaty of Ghent was made, (1815,) in the first article was inserted a stipulation resembling that in the 7th article of the Treaty of 1783, namely:

"That all places captured by either party should be restored without delay, without carrying away any private property captured in such places, or *any slaves or other private property.*"

OPINION OF JOHN QUINCY ADAMS.

John Quincy Adams, to whose name and memory, the Republican party profess to look up with so much respect, it so happens, was Minister at the Court of St. James, charged with the negotiation of this Treaty on the part of the United States. In a letter to the Secretary of State, August 22, 1815, he reports his conversation with Lord Castlereagh upon a subject, in part, as follows:

"Had the British plenipotentiaries asked of us an explanation of our proposal to transpose the words, [of the treaty,] we should certainly have given it; we evidently had an object in making the proposal; and we thought the words themselves fully disclosed it. Our object was the restoration of all property which, by the usages of war among civilized nations, ought not to have been taken. All private property on shore was of that description; it was entitled by the laws of war to exemption from capture—*slaves were private property.*" Further on he continues: "It was true, proclamations inviting slaves to desert from their masters had been issued by British officers; we believe them *deviations from the usages of war;* we believe that the British government itself would, when the hostile passions arising from the state of war should subside, consider them in the same light. . . . . . Lord Liverpool manifested no dissatisfaction at these remarks, nor did he attempt to justify the proclamation to which I partially alluded."

In a letter of instructions (July 5th, 1820) to Mr. Middleton, our Minister to St. Petersburgh, where this article of Treaty of Ghent had been referred, upon difficulties arising as to construction similar to those in the Treaty of 1783, Mr. Adams enters into a sustained argument to prove that the emancipation of an enemy's slaves is not authorized by the laws of war. The following extract is sufficient to clearly exhibit his opinion:

"It has been repeatedly alleged on the part of the British Government that it could not be supposed they would have agreed to an article which would oblige them to deliver up to their masters slaves who, during the war, had taken refuge under their protection. The reply to this observation is, that if that had been an objection to their agreeing to the article, it should have been made before the signing of the article, and the engagement not to carry away slaves, at all. They had in fact numbers of slaves by these different modes of capture—one of such as had been seduced to run away from their masters by proclamations from British officers, a second of voluntary fugitives whom they received; and a third of such as had been taken in predatory excursions. You will find in Niles's Register, vol. vi. p. 242, the proclamation of Admiral Cochrane, instigating the desertion of slaves from their masters. . . . . It is not openly addressed to slaves, nor does it avow its real object. From the use of the phraseology which it adopts, the inference is conclusive that the real object was such as the Admiral did not choose to avow, and the only supposable motive for the disguise is the consciousness that it was not conformable to the established usages of war among civilized nations. The wrong was in the proclamation. Admiral Cochrane had no lawful authority to give freedom to the slaves belonging to the citizens of the United States. The recognition of them by Great Britain in the treaty as property is a complete disclaimer of the right to destroy that property by making them free. An engagement contracted with them to that effect was, in relation to the owners of the property wrongful; and, if, in relation to the slaves themselves, it was an engagement which the British Government assumed upon themselves and sanctioned, it could not divest the owners of the slaves of their property, nor release the British government from the obligation to the United States, and to the owners, to evacuate the place without carrying them away."

Mr. Adams wrote to Mr. Rush, at London, as follows:

"The only equity of the British side is that they signed the article without being aware of its full import, and that the stipulation was incompatible with their previous promises to the negroes. This is the real knot of the question between us, and its solution is, that they had no right to make any such promises to the negroes. The principle is, that the emancipation of an enemy's slaves is not among the acts of legitimate war—as relates to the owners; it is a destruction of private property, nowhere warranted by the usages of war. This principle must, I think, be peculiarly familiar to the Emperor of Russia, and may be pressed upon his attention in the case of reference with effect."

On the 18th of October, Mr. Adams again wrote to Mr. Middleton, and expressed his views in the strongest language. He said:

"In the statement of the British ground of argument upon the claim in the submission, they have broadly asserted the right of emancipating slaves—private property—as a legitimate right of war. This is utterly incomprehensible on the part of a nation whose subjects holds slaves by millions, and who, in this very treaty, recognize them as private property. No such right is acknowledged as a law of war by writers who admit any limitation. The right of putting to death all prisoners in cold blood and without special cause might as well be pretended to be a law of war, or the right to use poisoned weapons, or to assassinate. I think the Emperor will not recognize the right of emancipation a legitimate warfare, and am persuaded you will present the argument against it."

Now, gentlemen, no language can be stronger than this, which Mr. Adams here uses against what Mr. Lincoln has done, or is to do. "The Emancipation of an enemy's slaves (he says) is *not* among the acts of legitimate war," almost the language of Edmund Burke. "No such right is acknowledged as a law by writers, who admit of any limitation." Mr. Adams expresses his horror of such war, by classing it "*with putting to death all prisoners* in cold blood," or "*the use of poisoned weapons*," or "*assassination.*" The Emperor of Russia decided on the words of the Treaty, that the slaves must be paid for, and they were paid for, $1,200,000 under this, the Treaty of Ghent, and the Treaty of 1783.

It is now said, that at a late period of life, Mr. Adams retreated from these positions, and excused himself for so doing, that he wrote under instructions from the then administration, and did not express his own opinions. It is true, that after Mr. Adams had been defeated for the Presidency in 1828 — as he deemed, by the South, exasperated, it may be by that defeat, he did argue, that "the War Power" could abolish slavery, but his "War Power" was not laid down to be in a Proclamation from the President of the United States, but in Congress. CONGRESS, he said, (speech of 1842) has power (thus) to carry on the war, and not the President alone. One of the laws of war, he sets down to be:

"When a country *is invaded* and two hostile armies are set in martial array, the Commanders in both armies have power to emancipate slaves *in the invaded territory.*"

But our President in the White House, with no sword buckled on his belt, even, 1000 miles or more from Texas, etc., which our armies have never *invaded*, fulminates from that White House, in a mere Proclamation, a law of war, liberating the slaves in a Territory he has never even seen. (Applause.)

It matters not, however, what Mr. Adams said, in the heat of debate in 1842 — for then he was but Mr. Adams — whereas as Minister to England, and as Secretary of State, representing and acting for the Government of the United States, he committed this Government, and the People, in 1815 and in 1820, to principles which no honest, consistent successor in that Government can now retract. Mr. Adams in 1815 and 1820 spoke for the United States: in 1842, he spoke for Mr. Adams alone. *There* is our record, a record made up from 1776, on to 1818, in two Treaties of Peace, in diplomatic correspondence, and in the receipt of moneys thereon, and this record can not be got over, or put under — for it stares us in the face, on every side we turn. (Applause.) The emancipation and the use of negro slaves, as President Lincoln is using and emancipating them, is, then, in violation of every principle and every precedent of our intercourse in such matters, with foreign states. (Great cheers.)

Gentlemen, these historical recollections, I am well aware, in a popular assembly, like this, are somewhat dull — but I feel in addressing you, that through this Association I am addressing no inconsiderable portion of our Northern countrymen, and I trust, directly or indirectly, some of the conservative people of the South. (Applause.) Hence it is not declamation that is useful now, but instruction, the right reading of the right records. We must show both the North and the South, that the war waged was a war for the Constitution and the Laws, not a war to break Constitutions and Laws, and a war to be waged according to the laws of nations, as expounded by such eminent men as John Jay and John Quincy Adams, when they were addressing other nations.

THE WAR POWER.

But we are told, gentlemen — no matter what Constitution, no matter what the laws of nations, this is a war power President Lincoln is using to support the very life of the nation. He has the right to exert any, and whatsoever power he may deem best fitted to subdue the common enemy. Or, in other words, the President of the United States has but to involve the people in a war, with any body, ostensibly to maintain the Constitution, and he can then pervert that war, to subvert that Constitution, and to extinguish the life of the nation. (Applause.) What proposition more absurd? What better confutation than the mere simple statement of such an absurd proposition. (Applause.) In an abstract struggle, then, for the Republic, we must die in Despotism! To live, we must commit suicide! To restore the Union, we must make the Union not worth a restoration! Now this is not the sort of Government under which we bargained to live, or to die even. (Cries of "no, no.") We have never agreed to subvert the Constitution in order to restore the Union. We have never agreed to surrender Liberty, Property, Free Speech, Free discussion, or Freedom in the concrete or abstract to any Executive Government, or Executive Power. (Cries of Never, never.) And if ever the time comes, when under any "War Power," it may be necessary to subvert the Constitution, and thus to give up our Rights and Liberties, it is a matter of indifference to me, whether a Union thus achieved, be maintained or not; and I say here, and hesitate not to say, that the quicker we be rid of such a Union, under such a Government, the better for all concerned. (Loud, and prolonged, and reïterated applause, the audience rising and giving three cheers for Mr. Brooks.) This War Power is a new name for a very old thing. It is the new name of Despotism, and of Military Despotism, the very worst sort of despotism on earth. When the Roman Republic was changed into the Roman Empire — when the Romans lost their Consuls, their Tribunes, their Senate, all but in the name, and thus lost all their rights and liberties, their IMPERATOR, the Latin name for their Abraham Lincoln, their Commander-in-Chief, was scarcely changed by the War Power into the modern word, EMPEROR. Augustus, or Tiberius Cæsar, but became *Kaiser*, or *Czar*, that is, Cæsar. Hence, let us put down our foot at the start, and declare, we recognize no Presidential War Power, no *Imperator* to be turned into any *Emperor*, no Cæsar to be made into any *Kaiser*, or *Czar*. He who attempts to govern the People, under any other Power than the Powers of the Constitution; he who leaps over the Laws of Civil Liberty, and the Civil Law, into that boundless field of Despotism, claimed as a War Power, establishes principles and precedents, from Emperors and Cæsars, and merits the execrations of every free man. (Applause.) Hence, I say, when a President ordains Law by Proclamation, under the pretense that he has such right, under any unknown, illimitable War Power, his Proclamation is not to be regarded as Law; it is not Law — (cheers) — and the President of the United States has no more right to declare it Law, than you or I, or any other man. (Tremendous and long-continued cheering.)

Gentlemen, your cheers remind me, that this is strong language— but it is such as the crisis demands. Some body must speak, when the great bulwarks of Law are being broken down, and every thing is thus being put in peril, and I may as well speak as other men. Some humble sentinel must stand on the outposts of the Constitution, and the Law, and standing there, must speak, and cry out against Proclamation Law, against Executives dispensing with, or suspending Law. Two months ago, I know it would not have been safe thus to uphold Law, or to declare against the violation of Law— but it is safe now. Then the casernes of Fort Lafayette or Fort Warren would have been my doom. (Cries, not now, never; we've put a stop to all that.) But when a President is unfaithful to his oath to uphold the Constitution and the Law, and subverts that Constitution and the Law— it is my duty, it is your duty, before God and man, to denounce all his arbitrary uses of power. (Great applause, and three cheers for the speaker.)

SUBJUGATION IMPOSSIBLE.

In the beginning of this war—when

it was a war for the Constitution, and for the whole United States, not only were the people of the North a unit, or nearly so—but we had a great and powerful party in some of the Southern States of the Union; and for that Constitution, and under that Flag, which was the symbol of the Constitution, there was a fair prospect, not of subjugating, not of exterminating, not of crushing out the people of the South —but by prudence and wisdom, and a fair adhesion to the principles of the Constitution, and of the Laws of Civilization as well as of Nations, of bringing back the great body of the Southern people to the embrace of the Union, and to the reverence of that ancient and honorable Flag. It was their Flag, as well as our Flag—and the associations connected with it, were as dear to them as to us. (Applause.) But I hesitate not now to say — what hitherto I have refrained from saying, though often felt, that it is vain, utterly vain, to attempt to subjugate, extinguish, or exterminate six or seven millions of Anglo-Saxon people. (Applause.) Their race is our race. The blood that runs in our veins is their blood. The same pulsations that beat in our hearts, beat in theirs. The same current of life that flows in us, flows in them. Now, who of us, standing here on this Northern soil, believes, Southron or Saxon, Celt or Teuton, or Frank, can invade, or conquer, or subjugate us? All Britain, all France, the whole South combined, could never shake us from our propriety, and make us tremble, and yield, under invasion. (Applause.) Subjugation—*subjugo*—is not a word of Anglo-Saxon derivation, or origin. (Cheers.) Anglo-Saxons never were, never are, never will be, brought under the yoke—*subjugated*, conquered, crushed out, exterminated. (Cheers.) Edmund Burke well comprehended all this, and in that masterly speech of his on "Conciliation with America," cited four cases where, for years and years, the British government had attempted to subjugate a neighboring people—the people of Ireland, of Wales, and of the Counties Palatine of Durham and Chester. Ireland was, five hundred years, he shows, in the process of subjugation, and arms never did conquer her. "It was not English arms, (says Burke,) but the English Constitution that conquered Ireland." The British, at last, threw over her the protecting mantle of British liberty, and Ireland then began to be subjugated. When England piled fifteen acts of penal legislation upon Wales and Welshmen, "no Englishman traveling in that country could go six yards from the high road without being murdered." (Laughter.) "When, after two hundred years of struggle, the day-star of the English Constitution," adds Burke, "had arisen in their hearts, all was harmony, within and without—

> ———Simul alba nautis
> Stella refulsit,
> Defluit saxis agitatus humor, etc. etc.

And the like is said of the Counties Palatine, Durham and Chester. Hence how vain this attempt to subjugate, crush out, or exterminate millions of our own people, of our own flesh and blood —protected as they are by an almost boundless territory stretching from the Potomac to the Rio Grande—a territory almost without high roads, in large plantations, without visible population, in winter, no inconsiderable portion under water; in summer, the heat so oppressive that the man of the North can hardly endure exposure to the rays of the sun. Such a territory, if there were no defenders upon it, would be almost unconquerable, geographically, or climatically, if I may coin the word. The subjugation, therefore, of such a people, or such a territory, in such a climate, may as well be abandoned first as last. If we wish then to bring them back into the Union, we must bring back to them the Constitution and the Protection of the laws. We must do what Burke said, was done for Ireland and Wales, throw over them the protecting folds of the Constitution, in the spirit in which that Constitution was formed. We must re-lift up from the ground where it was trodden under foot, the Constitution, and only the Constitution. (Applause.) We must do Equity and Justice, and then we can exact Equity and Justice. We must hold out Equality for the States, and then we can enforce Equality. We must respect our own rights, and the rights of States, and then we can compel respect for these rights upon others. We must rear up here in the North, a Conservative, Constitutional Party, and when that party is reared up, which accepts the Constitution not as this man or that man expounds it—but as the Supreme Court has expounded it, (cheers,) then, and not till then shall we be a reünited States. Then, and not till then, shall we begin to subjugate the South. Force nor Violence can ever win back a People to love. Conquest would but impose the necessity for re-conquest, until here, as in Europe, we should ever be revolving in the ruinous circle of War and Despotism. We hold in the South, now, only what is under the range of our guns. Our conquest is only of the soil on which we are treading. To hold all this, to possess, to occupy a territory so vast, not alone are one million of men indispensable to hold—but a million more, to conquer, to subjugate, as well as to occupy, or to re-fill the ever-thinning ranks of those who do conquer and subjugate. How much better, then, how much wiser is the law of self-Government, or of that home Government, that State Government, which relieves a nation from obligations so vast, and impresses the duty of Government upon every individual. Rely upon it, then, the only army for subjugation is the Constitution of the United States, and the principles of free self-government, interwoven in every part of it. But what we are doing now — organizing and arming negroes, forming negro Battalions, Regiments, and Brigades—is but outraging public sentiment. All Europe is crying out against it. The whole civilized world shrinks from and abhors any prospect of the repetition of the bloody scenes of Hayti and St. Domingo. That European sympathy and civilization which has hither looked up to us as the model Republic, now turns with horror from white men cooperating with African slaves to shed fraternal blood. We have no hope, then, from the world; we can have no hope in ourselves, until we retreat from this disgraceful exhibition of twenty millions of white men calling on four millions of negroes to fight eight millions, at the most, of white fellow-men. Let us, then, hasten back to the principles of Washington, and of the Fathers of the Republic, as soon as possible, and put the Republic back upon the old track of the Constitution. These were principles of compromise and concession, the North to the South, and the South to the North, and under them, from 1776, on to 1860, we carried on a successful and united government. (Applause.) I do not expect an immediate, nor an early, reëstablishment of confidence between the North and the South; the demagogues have been too long successfully at work in parting us —but I do expect, that when we can successfully reëstablish the principles and spirit of the Constitution in the North, we shall be answered by a corresponding party, South. Or, in other words, when we can effectually subvert Abolitionism, North, a corresponding party in the South will successfully subvert Secessionism there. (Applause.)

THE PURPOSES OF THIS GOVERNMENT.

But, I am asked—what is our *programme?*—what we intend to do? Do we intend to lay down our arms, we are tauntingly asked, and to submit to Rebellion, and let Rebellion ride roughshod over us? Do we intend to let the capital of our country be taken — our armies surrender— and our cities, perhaps, be sacked? No; we have no such intent, no such purpose. (Applause.) We now have no such idea, and we never had. We think, and we feel, first — that if we act upon the purpose and upon the principles, which created this Government, the war will soon, of itself, cease. When the Constitution in 1787 was created, it was not altogether the work of Patriotism, or the love of Liberty that inspired our Fathers. The treaty of 1783, with Great Britain, had secured the Liberty of the People, and the Independence of the States. There was not a right then, we have now, that every body had not then. The great principles of British and of American personal Liberty were as well secured under the old Confederation of States, as under the Constitution of the United States. But there were other things wanting we had not under the Confederation — free trade, free intercourse, a common currency — and, above all, protection and security from European intervention or invasion. Thirteen independent States had thirteen different custom-houses, and thirteen different laws, and regulations of commerce, and of trade. There was one rate of duties in Newport, Rhode Island, and another in New-York, and yet another in Baltimore, or Norfolk. The Fathers of the Republic then felt the great business necessity of creating order out of this chaos — and of adding to a Free People, a system of Free Trade, and of Free intercourse. It was INTEREST, then, SELF-INTEREST, as much as patriotism, that laid the foundations of our Government. There were debts to be discharged, obligations to be met, a navy to be created for the protection of commerce, that could only be achieved by a government of the United States. Under the guidance of these impulses of self-interest, on the 11th of September, 1786, Commissioners from several States assembled in Annapolis, Md., "to consider upon the best means of remedying the defects of the Federal Government." Their very platform was "to take into consideration the TRADE and COMMERCE of the United States, and to consider how far an uniform system, in their commercial intercourse and regulations, might be necessary to their common INTEREST and permanent harmony." The vulgar inspiration of Trade started the Convention held in Philadelphia, afterwards, in 1787. Such men as Washington, Hamilton, Madison, Franklin, Roger Sherman, Rutledge, and Pinckney, did not hesitate to assemble, and to act upon this great inspiration of self-Interest, and of Commerce and Trade. Free-trade, a free intercourse, free rivers, they well reasoned, were indispensably necessary among a free people. The main purpose for which this Government was created, our Constitutional history shows, was to have but one system of customs and of duties, from Georgia to Maine. Or, in other words, more tersely expressed, this is an *exterior*, not an *interior*, Government. The Federal Government was created, not for morals, not for religion, not for slavery or anti-slavery — but to promote the "general welfare," or, in other, more vulgar parlance, to collect duties, to raise revenue thereby, to *coin* money, to have uniform weights and measures, to have one patent-office, and to regulate commerce with foreign nations. I repeat, our great Fathers created a Government of, and founded it upon, self-interest, and only upon these principles of self-interest can it be maintained. When we interfere with morals, or religion, or attempt to govern by Theology, or Philosophy, our Government fails. When we attempt to enforce opinions, or to use Government to enforce opinions, the Government fails — for it never can do what it never was created to do. Hence, when an attempt is made to free negroes, or emancipate negroes in the South, the Government fails, just as if it attempted to emancipate them in Brazil or Cuba, or to emancipate the Sepoys of the East-Indies. Hence, when we prosecute war to free four millions of Southern negroes — though there are twenty millions of us, North concerned it — we must fail, under our form of Government; for the Government was created exactly for reverse purposes, — the purposes of *self-interest* — South as well as North — (applause) — and it is not the *interest* of the South to live among free negroes. (Continued applause.) If, then, we wish to end the war, we must resort to the principles of interest that laid the foundations of the Government, and we must make it the interest of the South to live with us — as our fathers did, when they created the Government. We must, then, go back and remember, this is an exterior, not an interior Government, and that slaves and slavery in Georgia or in Carolina do not concern us, as it is our concern to regulate commerce, to collect duties, to have uniform weights and measures, and common patent laws — not to free negroes. We want one system of trade—one uniform commerce upon the sea-coast, and the free navigation of such great Rivers as the Mississippi, Missouri, Ohio, the Red River, the Arkansas, etc. The true programme, then, is to go back, and go back as fast as possible, to the rëestablishment of our Custom-Houses, our uniform system of duties. What they are doing in the interior of Virginia, whether they are in rebellion or not in Texas, or Georgia, but little concerns us, if we hold on to Galveston, to Fort Pulaski, to New-Orleans, to Norfok, and collect the Revenue, and attend to the weights and measures. (A laugh.) If in Tennessee, even, they choose to rebel, let them rebel till they are tired of it, provided at New Orleans they will pay the duties, and let us alone in Kentucky, and on the navigation of the Rivers. The beauty of our form of Government is, that we have little or nothing to do with what is going on in Tennessee, or Alabama, or Mississippi. If the people there think it their interest to be in rebellion, let them rebel, as long as they will confine their rebellion in their own limits. I do not propose to surrender New-Orleans, no, never. (Applause.) That Post and that Port are indispensable to the great West — where millions and millions more of people are hereafter to live, and who can not even run the risk, that England or France, or some other Power may take it from the South, as we took it from her, under Farragut. What Gibraltar is to the great Mediterranean, New-Orleans is to the Great West — the Key, the gateway of the commerce of thirty or forty thousand miles of interior River Navigation. (Applause.) I do not propose to surrender Key West. The possession of it is indispensable to our navigation of the Gulf of Mexico. It is our self-interest to hold it, and hold it we must. I do not propose to surrender Norfolk or Fortress Monroe. They are the keys of the Chesapeake, and the gates to the Capital in Washington. The duty of this Government is to collect duties in Mobile, in Charleston, as well as in North Carolina, Georgia, and Florida, and Louisiana — and I would remove any thing which stands in the way of the execution of this exterior duty.

UNION A NECESSITY.

The God of Nature, I may say here, to the Southern People,—(Oh! that they may heed it to avert eternal wars!)—the God of Nature has written upon our very geography — "One Country, one Constitution, one Destiny." (Applause.) It is written on the long lines of the Missouri and Mississippi, on the Ohio, and all their numerous tributaries, that empty into the Gulf of Mexico. The Father of his Country is not more eloquent in his Farewell Address upon this necessity of Union and Indivisibility, than is the Father of Waters, for four thousand miles — as he gathers up his reasons in the rising rivulets of the icy Rocky Mountains, and rolls them on, into volumes of irresistible logic toward the Gulf of Mexico. (Applause.) These great waters must — it is the law of inexorable necessity — belong to one people, and be in one country. The holding on to what we have got, on the Mississippi, on the Gulf, on the Chesapeake, on the Capes of Virginia, is as indispensable to our safety as it is for the safety of the South to have them too. We are bound together thus, we are linked together, for weal or woe—and no wise man will fight to put asunder what God has thus joined together. (Applause.) If we part by Treaty, we part but soon to meet again in war. Eternal War, or Eternal Union, seems to be our Destiny. (Applause.) Tell me not that the Ohio can divide us as the Rhine divides France and Germany, or, as the Danube parts Nationalities—tell me not all this, unless you tell me, in the same breath, the numbers of the huge standing armies, that garrison the Rhine and the Danube, and secure Peace only by bristling in arms, eternally. (Applause.) England could not live without Scotland and Wales, and France perished in provinces, and Germany has been drenched with human gore — because *there*, there was one people, speaking one language, cut up, divided into Kingdoms, Dukedoms, Landgraves, etc. It is essential, indispensably essential, for the security of our American Liberty, that we be one People. (Applause.) If but a river part us, or a chain of mountains, huge standing armies must stand as sentinels on every such river, or on every such mountain-pass—and there must be cordons of custom-houses, and passports, and restrictions, all utterly destructive of human liberty. Standing armies are the Death of Freedom. Where the sword reigns, the Genius of Liberty runs off in terror and affright—and the People soon yield up to Despotism. (Applause.) Three hundred thousand men on your side, and three hundred thousand on our side, to act as Policemen, will be indispensably necessary to keep apart a People speaking one tongue, and these inflamed by discordant free, and slave institutions. Your negroes would run off, and we should keep them, and you, in revenge, would burn, pillage, and destroy. Eternal war, or huge standing armies, I repeat then, would be our destiny—and where War is, we see now, both North and South, there is no Liberty. In the name of God, then, if we will throw down our arms, throw down yours, and come back to us, or, if God has abandoned men to passion, and blood, in the name of Liberty, that hereditary Liberty, bequeathed to us all, we invoke you, to unite with us, and rescue our country from a destiny that shocks the patriot even in imagination to contemplate. (Great applause.)

UNION OUR SALVATION.

But, gentlemen, Union is not only essential to Liberty, but essential to our salvation. Republics exist on earth only as exceptional governments. Monarchies and despotisms are the common Law, if not the common destiny of nations. All Europe smiles, or seems to smile, upon our divisions, our battles, and the torrents of blood we shed in order to destroy the only great Republic on earth. Monarchy and Despotism both grin their ghastly smile—while Liberty, the earth over, shrieks over the unnatural, the suicidal war.

Gentlemen, "Divide and Conquer" is the principle of monarchies against republics every where. Divide and conquer is the principle which now inspires the British Government, if not the Emperor of France. Divide the North and South, and then if possible conquer both when both are exhausted. Unity and universality of government are therefore a necessity for us both North and South, and the quicker and deeper, and wider, this principle is comprehended universally, the quicker we shall lay down our arms and stop this horrible effusion of human blood. (Applause.)

PRACTICAL RESOLUTIONS.

Gentlemen, I love to speak for practical purposes, and hence I have prepared two or three resolutions to present for your consideration, for your discussion hereafter, not for action at this time and this place, but for submission to this Democratic Association. I see nothing else that is left to us except the principles that are embodied in these resolutions. Revolution is the last thing to be thought of, under a form of government like ours, where grievances can be redressed at the ballot-box. We have to endure this Congress, we have to endure this President; it is wiser to endure them than to overthrow them by revolution. It is possible, barely possible, that at last they may be awakened and may hear and heed the voice of the people. Hence I have selected a State as a medium through which my resolutions may be presented to the people both of the North and the South. A State of the Revolution; one of the Old Thirteen, of high and holy history, which has never been alien, either to the North or to the South, and which has ever been faithful to the Constitution of our common country, and that is, the State, the glorious State, of New-Jersey. (Loud cheers.) I propose, therefore, the following resolutions, to be submitted to the Democratic Association for discussion, for action, and if you approve of them, for presentation to the Government of New-Jersey. And let me remark here that the Government of New Jersey is a homogeneous government; the three branches are all of one faith and one opinion, and hence I name her in preference to the Government of our own New-York.

Mr. Brooks then submitted certain resolutions, the time for action upon which being over, it is not necessary to publish them here.

From Dr. S. A. Green

CALENDAR

OF THE

CIVIL WAR.

INCLUDING THE IMPORTANT MILITARY AND POLITICAL EVENTS OF THE WAR OF THE

REBELLION,

From Lincoln's nomination in 1860 to the Capture of the Last Confederate Privateer in November, 1865.

PRICE, TEN CENTS.

PRESS OF
ROCKWELL & CHURCHILL,
BOSTON, 1890.

CALENDAR

OF THE

CIVIL WAR

INCLUDING

EVERY MILITARY AND NAVAL ENGAGEMENT (EXCEPT THE SMALLEST SKIRMISHES), THE SECESSION CONVENTIONS, PRESIDENTIAL NOMINATIONS, CALLS FOR TROOPS, PEACE NEGOTIATIONS, IMPORTANT ARMY MOVEMENTS, AND OTHER EVENTS OF INTEREST

PRICE, 10 CENTS

BOSTON
PRESS OF ROCKWELL AND CHURCHILL
1890

JANUARY.

1.—Mason and Slidell sailed for England, '62. Emancipation proclamation took effect; Galveston captured by Magruder, '63. Sloop of war San Jacinto lost off Florida, '65.

2.—Gov. Ellis of North Carolina seized government property, '61. Battle of Stone River or Murfreesboro' ended, '63.

3.—Florida state convention, '61. Slight action at Moorefield, Va., '63. Action at Jonesville, Va., '64.

4.—National fast day by presidential proclamation, not observed in the South, '61. Bragg abandoned Murfreesboro', '63.

5.—Confederate fort captured on Little River, N.C., '63. End at Vicksburg of Grierson's raid, '64.

6.—Kirby Smith put in command of confederate troops west of the Mississippi River, '64.

7.—Alabama and Mississippi conventions, '61. Battle of Blue Gap, Va., '62. 1,600 Indians attacked Julesburg, Col., '65.

8.—Secretary Thompson, of the Interior department, resigned, '61. Action at Springfield, Mo., '63. Loyal mass meeting in New Orleans to form free state government, '64. Gen. B. F. Butler removed from command of the army of the James, '65.

9.—Mississippi seceded, 84 to 15; Star of the West fired upon at Charleston, '61. 20,000 men exchanged, '63. Confederate government conscripted every man in Cleveland, Tenn., '64.

10.—Florida seceded, 62 to 7, '61. Battle of Middle Creek, Ky.; Senators Johnson and Polk expelled from the United States senate, '62. Cavalry fight at Strawberry Plain, '64.

11.—Alabama seceded, 61 to 39; Secretary Thomas, of the Treasury, resigned; the governor of Louisiana seized government property; New York pledged its whole support to the national government, '61. Battle at Fort Hindman, Ark., '63. Longstreet, with 46,000 men, fortified at Bull's Gap, Tenn.; meeting in New York to aid people in Savannah; F. P. Blair, sr., arrived in Richmond on a peace mission, '64.

12.—Confederate raid on Holly Springs, Miss., '63. Gen. Marston raided successfully in Virginia, '64.

13.—Pensacola navy yard surrendered by Com. Armstrong, '61. Simon Cameron resigned as secretary of war, and Edwin M. Stanton was appointed, '62. Second attack on Fort Fisher, '65.

14.—Gunboat Queen of the West captured in the Red River by the confederates; battle of Bayou Teche, La., '63.

15.—Mound City, Ark., burned to clear out guerillas, '63. Fort Fisher captured, '65.

16.—The Crittenden compromise defeated by Clark's substitute that the constitution was good enough, and that secession ought to be put down, '61. Pirate Oreto escaped from Mobile, '63. Magazine exploded at Fort Fisher, '64.

F. P. Blair, sr., returned to Washington; Forts Caswell and Campbell, N.C., evacuated and blown up by the confederates, '65.

17. — Pollockville, N.C., taken, '63. Action near Bainbridge, Tenn., '64. Monitor Patapsco sunk off Charleston by confederate torpedo, '65.

18. — The Massachusetts legislature pledged its whole support to the government; Virginia appropriated $1,000,000 for defence, '61. Two blockade runners captured by Admiral Porter, '65.

19. — Georgia seceded, 208 to 89, A. H. Stephens and Herschel V. Johnson voting no, '61. Battle of Mills Springs, Ky., Zollicoffer, confederate commander, killed, '62.

20. — Gen. Woodbury's expedition (Union) to Ponta Rosa, '64. F. P. Blair, sr., went to Richmond the second time, '65.

21. — Alabama congressmen resigned; Jefferson Davis left the senate, '61. Fitz John Porter dismissed from the service, '63.

22. — Burnside failed to cross the Rappahannock, '63.

23. — Georgia congressmen resigned, '61. Stone fleet sunk in Charleston harbor, '62. Successful Union raids in Virginia and North Carolina, '64.

24. — Augusta arsenal seized by the state, '61. Battle of Woodbury, Tenn., '63. Gen. Rhoddy, confederate, driven across the Tennessee with loss of trains and supplies, '64. Holiday in Louisiana to celebrate the abolition of slavery in Louisiana, Maryland, Tennessee, and Missouri, '65.

25. — Organization of the first colored volunteers at Port Royal, '63. Maj. Burroughs, guerilla, shot while escaping from Fortress Monroe, '64. Savannah meeting to thank New York; Gen. Lee issued a call to arms, '65.

26. — Louisiana seceded, 113 to 17, '61. Hooker succeeded Burnside in command of the Potomac army, '63. Debate in the confederate house on enlisting negroes, '65.

27. — Bombardment of Fort McAllister, Ga., '63. Union cavalry victory at Sevierville, '64. Blair returned from second peace mission; confederates fired Savannah, Ga., '65.

28. — Texas convention, '61. Large meeting at Nashville, Tenn., to restore state government, '64. Confederate house passed bill for employment of negroes, '65.

29. — Gen. Banks promulgated emancipation proclamation at New Orleans, '63. Confederate attack on Cumberland Gap defeated, '64.

30. — Floyd indicted for malfeasance and conspiracy, '61. Union supply train captured near Petersburg, Va., '64. A. H. Stephens, Gen. R. M. T. Hunter, and Judge Campbell came within Grant's lines as peace commissioners, '65.

31. — Three ironclads attacked Charleston blockaders, one sunk; attack on United States troops in Indiana arresting deserters, '63. Lee made general-in-chief of the confederate armies; thirteenth amendment adopted, '65.

FEBRUARY.

1. — New Orleans mint and custom-house seized; secession of Texas submitted to popular vote, 166 to 7, '61. Second attack on Fort McAllister, Ga., '63. Battle of Cumberland Iron Works, Tenn.; Lincoln ordered draft of 500,000 men on March 10, '64. Secretary Seward left Washington to meet confederate peace commissioners at Fortress Monroe, '65.

2. — Queen of the West ran the Vicksburg blockade, '63. Gen. Scammon and staff captured by confederates on the steamship Levi, '64. Lincoln met confederate peace commissioners at Fortress Monroe; gold at 4400 premium at Richmond, '65.

3. — The steamer Nashville ordered out of Southampton (Eng.) harbor; Senator Bright of Indiana expelled from the United States senate, '62. Confederate attack on Donelson defeated, '63. Sherman, with 25,000 men, crossed the Big Black and reached Bolton, '64.

4. — Delegates at Montgomery, Ala., to form a confederate government, '61. Governor-general of Canada signed the bill to prevent confederate raids across the border, '65.

5. — Skirmish on Bear Creek, Mo., '63. Expedition left Port Royal, '64. Battle of Hatcher's Run, Va., '65.

6. — Fort Henry captured by Grant and Foote, '62. Col. Cushman (confederate cotton-burner) captured near Ripley, Tenn., '63. Army of the Potomac reconnoitred in force toward Orange Court-House; Sherman moved south from Vicksburg, '64. Battle of fifth corps and Gregg's cavalry with confederates (Union victory), '65.

7. — Montgomery convention adopted provisional constitution, '61. Battle of Roanoke Island, '62.

8. — United States arsenal at Little Rock surrendered, '61. Confederate meeting at Dalton and Decatur, '64. Electoral votes counted in congress, — 212 for Lincoln and Johnson, and 21 for McClellan and Pendleton, '65.

9. — Jefferson Davis and A. H. Stephens elected provisional president and vice-president of the confederacy, '61. Gen. Rosecrans ordered the summary execution of confederates in Union uniform, '63. Action at Morgan's Mill, Ark., '64.

10. — Fight at Old River, La., '63. Col. Streight and 110 other Union officers escaped from Libby prison by tunnelling, '64. Sherman's right column, in part, landed on James Island, near Charleston, '65.

11. — Gens. Grierson and Smith began raid through Mississippi, '64. Gen. Terry reconnoitred in force toward Wilmington, '65.

12. — The gunboat Indianola ran the Vicksburg batteries, '63.

13. — Lincoln and Hamlin officially declared elected, '61.

14. — Union cavalry surprised at Anandale, Va.; Queen of the West lost. '63. Sherman occupied Meridian, Miss., and destroyed the state arsenal and much property, '64.

15. — Cavalry engagement near Gainesville, Tenn., '63.

16. — Fort Donelson taken with Gens. Buckner and Tilghman, '62.

17. — Confederates captured a forage train near Romney, Va., '63. Sherman occupied Columbia, S.C., and confederates evacuated Charleston, '65.

18. — Jefferson Davis inaugurated at Richmond, '61. Mortar boats opened fire on Vicksburg; copperhead state convention at Frankfort, Ky., dispersed, '63. Charleston occupied by Union troops, '65.

19. — Confederate congress met at Richmond; confederates seized Fort Keane, Kan., '61. Hopefield (opposite Memphis) burned by Gen. Hurlbut's order, '63. Fort Anderson, N.C., captured by Schofield and Porter, '65.

20. — Gunboat reconnoissance up the Rappahannock, '63. Battle of Olustee, Fla.; Gen. Seymour's expedition (Union) badly defeated at Sanderson, Fla., and Smith's expedition repulsed, '64. Gen. Cox defeated the confederates near Wilmington, N.C.; confederate house passed bill to arm negroes, '65.

21. — Jefferson Davis appointed his cabinet, '61. Battle of Valverde, N. Mex., '62. Confederates evacuated Wilmington, N.C., '65.

22. — Michael Hahn elected governor of Louisiana, '64. Union troops occupied Wilmington, N.C., '65.

23. — Confederates evacuated Nashville, '62. Forrest's attack on Smith repulsed, '64. Georgetown and Fort White, S.C., occupied by Union troops, '65.

24. — The Indianola captured near Grand Gulf, Miss., by four confederate steamers, '63. Burning of Columbia, S.C., '65.

25. — Cavalry fight near Hartwood church, Va., '63. (Feb. 25 to 27) battle of Buzzard's Roost, Ga., '64. Johnston took command as Beauregard's successor, '65.

26. — Cherokee national council repealed secession ordinance and abolished slavery, '63. Grierson and Smith returned to Memphis after a successful expedition, '64.

27. — The peace congress submitted a plan to the senate, '61. Sherman returned to Vicksburg after a 22 days' raid, '64.

28. — Confederate ironclad Nashville was captured in Ogeechee River, '63. Col. Richardson, guerilla, was captured near the Cumberland River; Kilpatrick started on a raid in Virginia, '64.

29. — Kilpatrick's raid continued, Stevensburg to Richmond, extended to March 4, '64.

MARCH.

1. — Fight near Bradyville, Tenn.; Duke's guerillas routed, '63. Confederate salt-works at St. Marks, Fla., destroyed, '64.

2. — Gen. F. W. Lander died; action at Pittsburg Landing, Tenn., '62. Sheridan captured nearly all of Early's force near Staunton, Va., '65.

3. — Sheridan defeated Van Dorn at Shelbyville, 63. Fort McAllister, Ga., again bombarded fruitlessly, '63. Grant made commander-in-chief over Halleck, '64. Skirmish between Sherman's and Wade Hampton's cavalry, '65.

4. — Lincoln inaugurated, '61. Battle of Memphis Station, Tenn.; battle of Thompson's Station, Tenn., '63. Col. Dahlgren murdered, '64. Lincoln inaugurated, '65.

5. — Beauregard took command of the army of the Mississippi; battle of Pea Ridge, Ark., from March 5 to 8, '62. Battle in Yazoo City, '64.

6. — Gen. Hunter ordered negroes drafted in the South, '63. Sherman's army crossed the Pearl River at Jackson, '64. Successful Union expedition up the Rappahannock, '65.

7. — Return of successful Union scouting expedition from Belle Plain, Va., '63. Sherman's cavalry occupied Brandon, '64.

8. — The Congress and the Cumberland sunk by the Confederate ram Merrimac, '62. Mosby captured Gen. Stoughton, '63. Confederate senate passed negro enlistment bill, '65.

9. — Engagement of Monitor and Merrimac, '62. Slight action below Port Hudson, '63. Sherman at Hillsboro'; Grant commissioned lieut.-gen., '64.

10. — Jacksonville, Fla., captured by the first South Carolina colored regiment, '63. Red River expedition embarked at Vicksburg, '64. Action at Wilcox's Bridge, N.C.; defeat of confederate Gen. Bragg at Kinston, N.C.; Grant forbade trade at points within confederate lines in Virginia, North Carolina, South Carolina, and Georgia, '65.

11. — McClellan removed, Halleck assigned to the department of the Mississippi, and Fremont to mountain department, '62. Hoke's confederate division defeated at Kinston, N.C., '65.

12. — Successful Union reconnoissance from Franklin, Tenn., '63. Grant appointed commander-in-chief of the armies of the United States, '64. Schofield occupied Kinston, '65.

13. — Battle of New Madrid, Mo., '62. Fort Greenwood on the Tallahatchie, Tenn., silenced by gun-boats, '63. Indianola evacuated by Union troops, '64. Sheridan destroyed the railroad between Richmond and Hanover, '65.

14. — Battle of Newbern, N.C., '62. Admiral Farragut, with seven vessels, passed Port Hudson after a fierce engagement, '63. Fort De Russy captured; call for 200,000 men for three years, '64.

15. — The Jeffersonian office at Richmond, Ind., destroyed by soldiers,'63. The confederate house, 36 to 32, suspended the habeas corpus act, '65.

16. — Union victory at Cumberland Mountain, '62. Union victory near Fort

Pillow, '64. Arkansas voted herself a free state, '64. Union victory at Averysborough, N.C., '65.

17. — Fitzhugh Lee's cavalry defeated at Kelly's Ford, Va., '63. Fort De Russy blown up, '64. Gen. Canby moved against Mobile, '65.

18. — The Nashville escaped from Beaufort, S.C.; battle at Salem, Ark., '62. Confederate congress adjourned, '65.

19. — Steamer Georgiana, with arms for the confederates, destroyed off Charleston, '63. Confederate attack on Port Royal failed, '64. Union victory at Bentonville, N.C., '65.

20. — Battle of Vaught's Hill, near Milton, Tenn., '63.

21. — Fight at Cottage Grove, Tenn., '63. Confederate raid on Magnolia, '64. Junction of armies under Sherman, Terry, and Schofield; Wilson's cavalry defeated Roddy's cavalry at Marion and Plantersville; Goldsboro', N.C., taken by Union troops, '65.

22. — Mount Sterling, Ky., captured by guerillas, '63. Ferguson's guerillas massacred 24 Union cavalrymen at Johnson's Mills, Tenn., '64.

23. — Battle of Winchester, Va., '62. Action at Calf Killer Creek, Tenn., '64.

24. — Pontachoula, La., taken by Union troops, '63. Union City, Mo., attacked by Forrest, '64.

25. — Rams Lancaster and Switzerland lost in running Vicksburg batteries, '63. Owen Lovejoy died, aged 53, '64. Battle of Fort Steadman (before Petersburg), '65.

26. — Action at Apache Cañon, 26th to 28th, '62. Burnside took command of the department of the Ohio, '63. Forrest sacked Paducah, Ky.; Col. Clayton's victory at Longview, Ark., '64.

27. — Fast day in the confederacy, '63. Investment of Spanish Fort, the principal defence of Mobile, '65.

28. — Louisiana popular vote on secession, 20,448 yes, to 17,296 no, '61. Union victory at Cane River, '64. Attack on the defences of Mobile, '65.

29. — Blockade runners captured at Poplar Creek, Md., '63. Confederate ram Stonewall ordered to leave Lisbon; United States war steamer Niagara fired upon by Portuguese authorities; action at Quaker Rood, Va., '65.

30. — Mississippi convention ratified the confederate constitution, 78 to 7, '61. Battle near Somerset, Ky., Union victory, '63. Copperhead riot at Charleston and Mattoon, Ill., '64. Fighting before Richmond, '65.

31. — Gen. Heron appointed to the command of the army of the frontier, '63. Union victory at Crump's Hill, '64. Confederate victory before Richmond, '65.

APRIL.

1. — Farragut passed the Grand Gulf batteries with the Hartford, Switzerland, and Albatross, '63. Confederate ram Tennessee sunk near Grant's Pass, '64. Union victory at Five Forks, '65.

2. — Women's bread riot at Richmond, Va., '63. Action at Spoonville, Ark.; Forrest defeated Grierson near Summerville, '64. Grant advanced on Petersburg; heavy fighting; Richmond and Petersburg evacuated by night; Jefferson Davis left at 8 P.M.; capture of Selma, Ala., '65.

3. — South Carolina convention ratified the confederate constitutien, 114 to 16, '61. Arrest of Knights of the Golden Circle in Reading, Pa., '63. Action at Okalona, Ark.; Petersburg occupied by Union troops at 4 A.M., and Richmond at 7 A.M., '65.

4. — Virginia convention refused, 89 to 45, to submit the secession ordinance to the people, '61. Slavery abolished in the District of Columbia, '62. New York metropolitan sanitary fair opened; Sheridan made cavalry commander of Potomac army, '64. Lincoln in Richmond, '65.

5. — Troops sent from Newbern to rescue Gen. Foster, '63. Action at Roseville, Ark.; confederate Gen. W. P. White assassinated by his own men, '64. Jefferson Davis proclaimed the evacuation of Richmond, and that they would never abandon one state of the confederacy, '65.

6. — Battle of Pittsburg Landing; Gen. A. S. Johnston killed, '62. Confederate Gen. Buford attacked Fort Halleck, Columbus, Ky., '64. Battle of Deatonsville between Grant and Lee, '65.

7. — Communication with Fort Sumter cut off, '61. Island No. 10 surrendered, '62. Dupont's bombardment of Sumter failed, '63. Action at Wilson's Farm, La.; fight with Lee at Farmville, '65.

8. — State department refused to recognize confederate commissioners, '61. Gen. Stoneman defeated at the battle of Pleasant Grove, La.; Gen. Franklin, of Banks's expedition, defeated at Mansfield, La., '64. Lee concentrated his army at Appomattox Court-House, Va.; battle of Appomattox (8th–9th), '65.

9. — Pascagoula, Miss., taken by Union troops and abandoned, '63. Lee surrendered; Spanish Fort, near Mobile, and other forts, captured, '65.

10. — Fort Pulaski surrendered, '62. Battle of Franklin, Tenn., '63. Action at Prairie D'Ann (10th–13th), Ark., '64. Evacuation of Mobile begun, '65.

11. — Surrender of Sumter demanded, '61. Union troops under Gen. Q. A. Gillmore captured Fort Pulaski, Ga., '62. Montgomery, Ala., surrendered to Gen. Wilson, '65.

12. — Beginning of the war — Sumter bombarded; Pennsylvania appropriated $500,000 to arm the state, '61. Action at Pleasant Hill Landing, La., '64. Capture of Fort Pillow and murder of the garrison, '64. Mobile occupied by Union troops; Stoneman defeated 3,000 confederates at Grant's Creek, '65.

13. — Sumter surrendered, '61. Battle of Irish Bend, La., 12th to 14th, '63. Action at Moscow, Ark., '64. Sherman occupied Raleigh, N.C., '65.

14. — Bombardment of Fort Pillow, '62. Battle of Bayou Teche, La., '63. Gunboat expedition from Butler's army captured prisoners and stores at Smithfield, Va., '64. President Lincoln shot by J. Wilkes Booth in Ford's theatre, Washington, '65.

15. — Lincoln's proclamation for 75,000 volunteers issued; extra session of congress called; New York legislature voted 30,000 men and $3,000,000, '61.

Action at Liberty, Ark.; gunboat Chenango exploded, '64. President Lincoln died at 7.22 A.M.; Vice-President Johnson sworn in as president, '65.

16. — Confederate government called for 32,000 troops; Govs. Magoffin of Kentucky, and Letcher of Virginia, refuse to furnish troops to the federal government; action at Lee's Hills, Va., '61. Admiral Porter's fleet ran the Vicksburg batteries, '63. Columbus, Ga., captured, '65.

17. — Virginia seceded, 60 to 53, the result to be submitted to the people; Jefferson Davis issued letters of marque; the Massachusetts Sixth regiment started for Washington, '61. Col. Grierson's cavalry raid (ended May 3 at Baton Rouge, La.) began from Lagrange, Tenn., '63. Mosby surrendered to Hancock, '65.

18. — Pennsylvania volunteers in Washington; Harper's Ferry arsenal burned to save it from the confederates; two men killed by the confederates, '61. Bombardment of Forts Jackson and St. Philip below New Orleans, '62. Action at Poison Springs, Ark.; Baltimore sanitary fair opened, '64. Truce between Sherman and Johnston, '65.

19. — Attack on the Massachusetts Sixth regiment in Baltimore, four men killed and seven wounded; eleven of the mob killed and many wounded; blockade of southern ports, '61. Battle of Camden, N.C., '62. Lincoln's funeral, '65.

20. — Confederates seized U.S. arsenal at Liberty, Mo., '61. Fight at Patterson, Mo., '63. Gen. Wessels surrendered Plymouth, N.C., to confederates, '64. Macon, Ga., occupied; Gen. Howell Cobb and others captured, '65.

21. — Norfolk navy yard destroyed; Union government took the Philadelphia and Baltimore railroad, '61. Salt-works near Wilmington, N.C., destroyed, '64. Gen. E. Kirby Smith proclaimed that he could continue the rebellion; Sherman's truce disapproved by the authorities, '65.

22. — Arsenals at Fayetteville, N.C., and Napoleon, Ark., seized by the confederates; Vermont legislature in extra session, '61.

23. — First South Carolina regiment started for the Potomac, '61. New York metropolitan sanitary fair closed; Grant received the sword by vote of 30,291 to 14,509 for McClellan, '64. Jefferson Davis fled to Georgia, '65.

24. — Fort Smith, Ark., seized by confederates; Virginia proclaimed a member of the confederacy, '61. Union fleet passed Forts Jackson and St. Philip, '62. Tuscumbia, Ala., occupied by Union troops, '63. Battle at Cane River, '64.

25. — New Orleans evacuated by the confederates; Fort Macon surrendered, '62. Confederate batteries at Duck River shoals in the Tennessee River silenced by gunboats, '63. Action at Marks' Mills, Ark., '64.

26. — Cape Girardeau, Mo., attacked unsuccessfully by confederates under Marmaduke, '62. Johnston surrendered 29,900 men to Sherman; Booth was shot, and Harold captured, '65.

27. — Blockade of Virginia and North Carolina ports, '61. Union flag raised at New Orleans, '62. Stoneman's raid in Virginia (ended May 8); Gen. Hooker moved on Fredericksburg; Streight's expedition from Tuscumbia, Ala., to Rome, Ga. (captured by Conf. Forrest, May 3), '63.

28. — Forts Jackson and St. Philip surrendered, '62. Hooker crossed the Rappahannock, '63. War department issued orders to reduce army expenses, '65.

29. — Indiana legislature voted $500,000 to arm the state with; first confederate congress at Montgomery, Ala.; Maryland house by 53 to 13, and the senate unanimously, voted against secession, '61. Battle of Fairmont, W. Va.; Porter's fleet bombarded Grand Gulf, Miss., '63. Proclamation by the president removing restrictions on international trade, '65.

30. — Siege of Corinth, Miss., '62. Grant's army landed near Port Gibson, Miss., '63. Action at Jenkin's Ferry, Ark., '64. Paroling of Johnston's troops at Greensboro', '65.

MAY.

1.—Butler occupied New Orleans, '62. Union victory at Port Gibson; beginning of Grant's campaign against Vicksburg, '63. Commodore W. D. Porter died, '64.

2.—The guerilla Morgan captured Union troops at Pulaski, Tenn., '62. May 2 to 4, battle of Chancellorsville, between Hooker and Lee; confederate victory, '63. Reward of $100,000 offered for capture of Jefferson Davis, '65.

3.—Connecticut voted $2,000,000; Virginia militia called out; President Lincoln called for 42,000 three years' volunteers, '61. Battle of Farmington, Miss., '62. Grant's army crossed the Rapidan toward Chancellorsville and the Wilderness, '64.

4.—Battle of Williamsburg, Va., '62. Siege of Suffolk, Va., raised; end of the battle of Chancellorsville, '63. Reconstruction bill passed, '64. Lincoln buried; Gen. Dick Taylor surrendered, '65.

5.—Battle of Williamsburg, Va., '62. C. L. Vallandigham arrested, '63. Lee attacked Grant at the Wilderness, May 5 to 9; battle of Rocky Face ridge, Ga.; action at Dunn's Bayou, La., '64.

6.—Arkansas seceded, 69 to 1; confederate congress published the war and privateering act, '61. Hooker retreated across the Rappahannock, '63; battle of the Wilderness continued, '64.

7.—Military league formed between Tennessee and the confederacy, '61. Battle of West Point, Va., '62. Kilpatrick's cavalry completed the circuit of Lee's army, '63. Lee attacked Grant; Butler defeated at Bermuda Hundred; battle of Stony Creek station, Va., '64.

8.—Tennessee seceded, '61. Monitor and gunboats attacked Sewall's Point; battle of McDowell, Va., '62. Bombardment of Port Hudson, '63. Action at Todd's Tavern, Va.; Grant pursued Lee to May 18 to Spottsylvania Court-House, '64.

9.—Confederate congress authorized the president to accept all volunteers, '61. Gen. Hunter issued emancipation proclamation; Pensacola evacuated by the confederates, '62. Virginia battles continued — Swift Creek and Cloyd's mountain; Gen. Sedgwick killed; Sheridan's cavalry raid (9th–13th), '64.

10.—Gen. R. E. Lee put at the head of the confederate army in Virginia, '61. Surrender of Norfolk; Gosport navy yard burned; gunboat battle at Fort Pillow, '62. Stonewall Jackson died; Port Hudson batteries silenced, '63. Battle of Spottsylvania, '64.

11.—Confederates destroyed the Merrimac, '62. Battle of Horse-shoe Bend, Ky., '63. Grant "proposes to fight it out on this line, if it takes all summer;" Butler intrenched at Bermuda Hundred, '64. Davis and Reagan captured at Irwinville, Ga., by Lt.-Col. Pritchard; Jeff Thompson surrendered, '65.

12.—Natchez taken by Union troops, '62. Battle of Raymond, Miss., McPherson defeated the confederates under Gregg, '63. Action at Fort Darling, Va. (12th–16th); Sherman carried the confederate position at Dalton; Conf. Gen. J. E. B. Stuart killed in Va., '64. Engagement near Boco Chico, the last engagement of the war, '65.

13.— Queen Victoria's proclamation of neutrality, '61. Yazoo City, Miss., captured by gunboats, '63. Gen. McPherson captured nine trains of military stores, '64. Action at Palmetto Ranche, Tex., '65. Jefferson Davis released on bail, '67.

14.—Jackson, Miss., captured, '63. Battle of Drury's Bluff, '64.

15.—Gov. Hicks of Maryland called for volunteers, '61. Grant defeated Pemberton at Edwards Station, Miss., '63. Union victory at Resaca; Gen. Sigel defeated at Newmarket, Va., 64.

16.—Lincoln nominated for president, '60. Bridges on the Baltimore and Ohio railroad destroyed, '61. Battle at Princeton, W. Va., '62. United States transport Oriental wrecked; Grant defeated Pemberton at Champion Hills, Miss., '63. Fighting (16th–30th) at Bermuda Hundred, Va., '64.

17.—Spies arrested in Washington; confederate congress authorized treasury notes, '61. Confederates driven across the Chickahominy, '62. Battle of Big Black River, Miss., '63. South Carolina union convention at Beaufort; Rome, Ga., captured, '64.

18.—Arkansas admitted to the confederacy; express packages not sent south of Washington, '61. Grant besieged Vicksburg, '63. Action at Calhoun Station, La., '64.

19.—Lincoln revoked Hunter's emancipation proclamation; battle of Searcy Landing, Ark., '62. Blackiston's Island lighthouse destroyed by confederates, '64. Davis arrived at Fortress Monroe, '65.

20.—North Carolina seceded: Gov. Magoffin proclaimed Kentucky neutral, 61. Fighting before Vicksburg, '63. Confederates attacked Ames's division of Butler's army, '64. Confederate ram Stonewall surrendered to Spanish authorities in Cuba, '65.

21.—Confederate Congress adjourned, '61.

22.—Union troops destroyed Ship Island fortifications, '61. Grant's attack on Vicksburg repulsed; battle at Gum Swamp, N.C., '63. Southern ports opened, '65.

23.—Part of McClellan's army crossed the Chickahominy; battles at Front Royal, Lewisburg, and Mechanicsville, Va., '62. Action (23d–27th) at North Anna River, Va., '64.

24.—Col. Ellsworth shot at Alexandria; southern mails stopped, '61. Banks retreated to Winchester; battle of the Chickahominy, '62. Sheridan destroyed the Danville railroad near Richmond, '64.

25.—Banks retreated to the Potomac; battle of Winchester, Va., '62. Union victory near Dallas, Ga., '64.

26.—New Orleans blockaded; strong Union vote in West Virginia, '61. Torpedo explosion at Bachelor's Creek, N.C.; fighting (20th–29th) at Decatur and Moulton, Ala.; Louisiana state convention abolished slavery, '64. Gen. E. Kirby Smith and army surrendered to Gen. Canby, '65.

27.—Gen. McDowell put in command at Washington; Mobile blockaded; Mississippi River blockaded, '61. Battle of Hanover Court-House, Va., '62. Bank's assault on Port Hudson repulsed with heavy loss, '63. Lee retreated toward Richmond, '64.

28.—Savannah blockaded, '61. Confederates retreated from Corinth, Miss., '62. First colored regiment from the North left Boston, '63. Action at Salem church, Va.; Sherman repulsed Longstreet's attack at Dallas, '64.

29.—Jefferson Davis reached Richmond, '61. Action near Thoroughfare Gap, Tenn., '63. Grant crossed the Pamunky, '64. President Johnson issued an amnesty proclamation, '65.

30.—Union troops occupied Front Royal; battle at Booneville, Miss., '62. Grant begun earthworks at Vicksburg, '63. Grant repulsed Lee's attack north of the Chickahominy, '64.

31.—Maj.-Gens. Banks and Freemont commissioned, '61. Battle of Seven Pines and Fair Oaks, Va., '62. Freemont nominated for president and Gen. Cochrane for vice-president, '64. Brazil withdrew belligerent rights from the confederates, '65.

JUNE.

1. — Cavalry action at Fairfax Court-House, '61. Battle at Seven Pines, '62. Confederate attack at Cold Harbor defeated, '64. Day of humiliation and prayer on account of Lincoln's death, '65.

2. — Burnside prohibited the circulation of the New York World and Chicago Times in the department of the Ohio, '63. Action at Bermuda Hnndred, Va., '64. Kirby Smith and Magruder formally surrendered at Galveston, '65.

3. — Action at Phillippi, W. Va.; Border State Convention, '61. Union troops land on James Island, near Charleston; Lee took command of confederate army, '62. New York supreme court decided against legal-tender notes; convention of New York peace democrats, '63. Battles of Cold Harbor and Panther Gap, '64.

4. — Confederates abandoned and burned Fort Pillow, '62. Burnside's order regarding World and Times revoked; Gillmore relieved Hunter of the department of the South; battle of Franklin, Tenn.,'63. Hampton's cavalry defeated at Howe's store, '64.

5. — Raid to Warwick River, Va., '63. Sherman's army fell back toward Atlanta; battle of Piedmont, Va., 64.

6. — Union troops occupied Memphis; fierce gun-boat fight; battle of Harrisonburg, Va., '62. Fight at Milliken's Bend, '63. Action at Lake Chicot, Ark.; night attack on Burnside repulsed, '64.

7. — Confederate battery silenced at Chattanooga; confederate executed for tearing down a Union flag at New Orleans; battle of Cross Keys, Va., '62. Lincoln and Johnson nominated for president and vice-president; Philadelphia sanitary fair opened; Morgan's raid on Kentucky begun, '64.

8. — Two confederate spies shot at Franklin, Tenn., '63. Sherman's advance on Kenesaw range; Gillmore's raid on Richmond fortifications, '64.

9. — Battle of Fort Republic, Va., '62. Part of Hooker's army crossed the Rappahanock; battle of Beverly Ford, '63; Gen. Burbridge defeated the confederates at Mount Sterling. June 9 to 30, battle of Kenesaw Mountain, '64.

10. — Confederate victory at Big Bethel, '61. Battle of James Island, S.C., '62. Confederate congress adjourned; battle of Brice's Cross Roads, Miss., '64.

11. — Wheeling convention, '61. Democratic peace meeting in Brooklyn, '63. Sheridan's victory at Trevillian Station; action at Cynthiana, Ky., '64.

12. — Confederate privateer Clarence captured six vessels off Chesapeake, '63. Grant crossed the Chickahominy, '64.

13. — Confederate fast day, '61. Battle of Winchester, Va., '63. Fugitive slave law repealed in the house of representatives, 63 to 15; battles of White Oak Swamp Bridge, and Charles City Cross Roads, Va., '64. All ports east of the Mississippi proclaimed to be open, July 1, '65.

14. — Confederates evacuated Harper's Ferry, '61. Banks's attack on Port Hudson repulsed, '63. Grant crossed to the South of the James; Gen. Polk killed, '64.

15. — Lee invaded Maryland; Lincoln called for 100,000 men, '63. Battle of Baylor's Farm; action at Samaria church, Va., '64.

16. — Battle at Secessionville, S.C., '62. Confederate attack on Harper's Ferry defeated, '63. Attack on the Union line at Petersburg repulsed, '64.

17. — West Virginia voted itself independent of the other part of the state; Union victory at Booneville, Mo., '61. Battle at St. Charles, Ark., '62. Confederate ram Atlanta captured by the Weehawken; battle at Aldie, Va., '63. Confederates abandoned intrenchments at Bermuda Hundred; action at Lynchburg, Va., '64. A. H. Stephens and R. E. Lee applied for pardon, '65.

18. — Skirmish before Richmond; Union defeat near Hernando, Miss., '62. Grant's attack on confederate works repulsed, '64.

19. — Confederate cavalry raid into Harrison County, Ind., '63. The Alabama sunk off Cherbourg by the Kearsarge, '64.

20. — McClellan took command in West Virginia, '61. Union troops occupied Holly Springs, Miss., '62. West Virginia admitted to Union; Vicksburg bombarded, '63. Fitzhugh Lee and Hampton repulsed at White House, '64.

21. — East Tennessee Union convention, '61. Battle of Battle Creek, Tenn., '62. Battle of La Fourche Crossing, La.; battle of Upperville, Va., '63. Battle of Davis's Farm, confederate victory, '64.

22. — Skirmish at Frederick, Md., '63. House of representatives resolved to abolish slavery; battle on the Weldon road, '64.

23. — Battle of Big Black River, Mo.; battle of Brashear City, La.; confederates occupied Chambersburg; beginning of Rosecrans's Murfreesboro' campaign, '63. Attack on the Weldon railroad, confederate victory, '64. Presidential proclamation rescinding the blockade on all United States ports, '65.

24. — Tennessee voted itself out of the Union, 104,019 to 47,238, '61. Maryland constitutional convention abolished slavery; confederate victory at Staunton Bridge, '64.

25. — Virginia seceded by vote of 128,884 to 32,134; Iowa issued war loan of $600,000, '61. Beginning of the seven days' battle before Richmond; battle of Mechanicsville; confederates destroyed their gunboats on the Mississippi; Gen. Pope in command of the army of Virginia, '62.

26. — Confederates occupied Gettysburg; death of Admiral Foote, '63.

27. — Bombardment of Vicksburg; Fremont relieved, '62. Battles of Gaines's Mill and Golding's Farm, '63. McPherson's and Thomas's attack southwest of Kenesaw Mountain repulsed, '64.

28. — Battle of Chickahominy, '62. Battle of Donaldsonville, La., '63. Meade superseded Hooker, '63. Battle of Stony Creek, '64.

29. — Battle of Savage's Station, '62. Battle of Reams's Station and of Peach Orchard, '64. Close of the conspirators' trial at Washington, '65.

30. — Battle of White Oak Swamp, '62. Johnston evacuated Kenesaw Mountain; Salmon P. Chase resigned as secretary of the treasury, '64.

JULY.

1. — Lincoln called for 300,000 troops; battle of Malvern Hill; Sheridan defeated Chalmers at Booneville, Miss., '62. Battle of Gettysburg begun; Gen. Reynolds killed, '63. W. P. Fessenden accepted the secretaryship of the treasury, '64.

2. — West Virginia legislature organized at Wheeling; action at Falling Waters, Md., '61. Battle of Gettysburg continued, '63. Confederate Gen. Ewell invaded the Shenandoah Valley in three columns, '64.

3. — Arkansas called out 10,000 men, '61. Battle at Elvington Heights, Va., '62. Union victory at Gettysburg, '63. Travel on B. & O. road stopped; fighting (3d–5th) at Smyrna, Ga., '64.

4. — Executive session of congress; New Hampshire voted $1,000,000 loan, 61. Battle of Helena, Ark.; Vicksburg surrendered to Grant, '63. Mosby's cavalry crossed the Potomac at Point of Rocks, '64.

5. — Battle at Carthage, Missouri, '61. Confederate attack on colored brigade near Port Hudson defeated, '64. July 5 and 6, battle of Jackson, Miss., '64.

6. — Battle of Grand Prairie, Ark., '62. John Morgan's confederates invaded Indiana, '63. Hagerstown, Md., evacuated by Union troops; action (6th–10th) on the Chattahoochee River, Ga., '64.

7. — Union victory at Bayou Cache, Ark., '62. Bragg retreated across the Tennessee River, '63. Confederate raiders held Harper's Ferry, '64. Execution of Harold, Payne, Atzerodt, and Mrs. Surratt, '65.

8. — Surrender of Port Hudson; the Mississippi River opened, '63. Gen. Wallace evacuated, and the confederates occupied, Frederick, '64.

9. — Fremont put in command of the Western department, '61. Beginning of actions about Jackson, Miss. (9th–16th), '63. Confederate victory at Monocacy, Md., '64.

10. — Gilmore landed on Morris Island and captured the forts; assault on Fort Wagner, '63. Johnston retreated to the fortifications around Atlanta, '64.

11. — Union victory at Rich Mountain, Va., '61. Halleck appointed commander-in-chief, '62. Destruction of confederate salt-works at Tampa Bay and stores at Dutch Gap, '64.

12. — Morgan invaded Ohio; martial law at Cincinnati, Newport, and Covington, '63. Confederate raid seven miles from Washington, '64.

13. — Battle of Carrickford, W. Va., '61. Confederates captured Murfreesboro', '62. Action at Jackson, Tenn.; draft riot in New York, '63. July 13, 14, and 15, Forrest defeated in five battles, '64.

14. — Battle of Fayetteville, Ark.; Gen. Pope took command of the army of Virginia, '62. Battle of Falling Waters, Md.; battle of Elk River, Tenn.; New York draft riot continued, '63.

15. — Confederate gunboat Arkansas ran the Union fleet and reached Vicksburg, '62. Battle of Halltown, Va.; draft riots in New York, Troy, and Boston, '63.

16. — End of New York draft riot; many rioters killed, '63. Sherman's army crossed the Chattahoochee in pursuit of Johnston, '64.

17. — Battle of Honey Springs, Ind. Ter.; battle of Canton, Miss.; orders issued to enforce the draft at all hazards, '63. Union victory at Grand Gulf, '64.

18. — Confederate victory at Blackburn's Ford, Va., '61. Action at Memphis, Mo., '62. Gillmore's assault on Fort Wagner defeated, '63. Crook defeated Early at Snicker's Gap; Union victory at Peach Tree Creek; call for 500,000 men, '64.

19. — Banks superseded Patterson in command on the Potomac, '61. Battle at Memphis, Tenn., '62. Battle of Buffington Island, O., 63.

20. — Confederate congress met in Richmond, '61. Battle before Atlanta, '64.

21. — Battle of Bull Run — confederate victory, '61.

22. — McClellan put in command of the army of the Potomac, '61. Hood's assault on Sherman at Atlanta defeated; Louisiana state convention adopted constitution abolishing slavery; Gen. McPherson shot in Hood's first sortie from Atlanta, '64.

23. — Battle of Manassas Gap, '63. Gen. Averill defeated at Winchester, Va., '64.

24. — Skirmish with Morgan at Washington, O., '63.

25. — Lincoln's proclamation of the confiscation act, '62.

26. — Halleck superseded McClellan, '62. Morgan and all his men captured near New Lisbon, O., '63. Gen. McCook defeated by confederates on the Macon and Western railroad, '64.

27. — Confederate victory at Richmond, Ky., '63. July 27 and 28, battles at Deep Bottom, New Market, and Malvern Hill, Va., '64.

28. — Union victory at Moore's Mills, Mo., '62. Second sortie from Atlanta, '64.

29. — Guerillas defeated at Mount Sterling, Ky., '62.

30. — Action at Paris, Ky., '62. Lincoln issued an order for retaliation of barbarous treatment, '63. Mine explosion before Petersburg, Va.; Union defeat; Chambersburg burned, '64.

31. — Lee and Meade again on the Rappahannock, '63.

AUGUST.

1. — McClellan reorganized the army, '61. Action at Newark, Mo., '62. Union cavalry victory at Kelly's Ford, '63. Bradley, Johnson, and McCausland defeated at Cumberland, losing part of their plunder from Virginia, '64.

2. — Skirmish at Ozark, Mo., '62. Col. Stout captured by McCausland and Johnson, '64.

3. — Gen. Foster's reconnoissance on the James River, '63.

4. — Confederate ram Arkansas destroyed; Secretary Stanton ordered draft of 300,000 men, '62. McCausland and Johnson defeated at New Creek; Jefferson Davis's sugar-mill at Manitee totally destroyed, '64.

5. — Union victory at Athens, Mo., '61. Gen. McCook murdered while wounded; battle of Baton Rouge; battle of Malvern Hill, '62. Aug. 5 to 23, Farragut's great victory in Mobile Bay, '64.

6. — Hooker abandoned Malvern Hill; battles of Tazewell, Tenn., and Kirksville, Mo., '62. Sherman's unsuccessful assault on Atlanta, '64.

7. — Confederates destroyed Hampton, Va., '61. Confederates advanced across the Rapidan; battle of Trenton, Tenn., '62. Sheridan took command of the middle military division; battle of Moorefield, Va.; McCausland and Johnson defeated by Averill, '64.

8. — Habeas corpus suspended; orders issued to arrest those who discourage enlistments; no passports to be issued, '62. Fort Gaines, in Mobile Bay, surrendered; confederates withdrew from the Maryland side of the Potomac, '64.

9. — Battle of Cedar Mountain, Va., '62. Butler began Dutch Gap Canal, '64.

10. — Battle of Wilson's Creek, Mo.; Gen. Lyon killed, '61. Battle of Nueces River, Tex., '62. Sherman bombarded Atlanta, '64.

11. — Battle of Independence, Mo., '62. Battle of Sulphur Springs Bridge, Va., '64.

12. — Battle of Gallatin, Tenn., Aug. 12 and 13, '62. Toombs exposed the bankruptcy of the confederacy, '63. Northern New York threatened by an invasion from Canada, '64.

13. — Steamboat collision on the Potomac; 80 soldiers killed, '62. Confederate cavalry captured five Union steamers with cattle at Shawneetown, '64.

14. — Fremont declared martial law in Missouri, '61. Union victory at Strawberry Plains, battle from Aug. 14 to 18, '64.

15. — Jefferson Davis ordered Northern men to leave the South within forty days, '61. Gen. Steadman drove the confederates from Dalton, '64.

16. — Lincoln proclaimed non-intercourse with the confederacy; passport system established, '61. Battle of Lone Jack, Mo.; Cols. Corcoran and Wilcox reached Fortress Monroe from Richmond prison, '62. Battle of Deep Run, '64.

17. — Pope's retreat begun, '62. Union bombardment of Sumter begun, '63.

18. — Union raid in North Carolina, '63. Battle of Six Mile Station on Weldon railroad, N.C., '64.

19. — Union raid on Grenada, Miss., '63. Confederate victory at Six Mile Station; Mosby massacred the wounded and prisoners at Snicker's Gap, Va., '64.

20. — Quantrell, the guerilla, sacked and burned Lawrence, Kan., and murdered citizens, '63.

21. — Confederate attempt to cross the Rappahannock, '62. Rosecrans attacked Chattanooga, '63. Confederate attack on the Weldon railroad repulsed; battle of Summit Point, Va.; Forrest took Memphis and was driven out, '64. Trial of Wirz, the Andersonville jailer, '65.

22. — Reception to Col. Corcoran in New York, '62. Gen. Jeff C. Thompson and staff captured, '63. Union victory at Canton, Ky.; Johnson, the confederate commander, killed, '64.

23. — Battle of Big Hill, Ky. Fight between Pope and the confederates, '62. Charleston shelled at nearly six miles distance, '63. Fort Morgan surrendered, '64.

24. — Cavalry skirmishes near Fredericksburg and Fairfax, '63. Gens. Heron and Lee took Clinton, Miss.; actions at Bermuda Hundred, Va. (24 and 25), and (24–27) at Halltown, Va., '64.

25. — Confederate attack on Donelson, '62. Battle of Reams's Station — Hancock lost heavily; battle of Smithfield, Va., '64.

26. — Union expedition sailed for Fort Hatteras, N.C., '61. Confederates took Manassas Junction, '62. Battle of Rocky Gap, Va., '63. Kilpatrick's raid on the Macon railroad, '64.

27. — Battle of Bull Run Bridge, Va.; battle of Kettle Run, Va., '62. John B. Floyd died, '63.

28. — Bombardment and capture of Forts Hatteras and Clark, '61. Second battle of Manassas, '62. Early driven through Smithfield, '64.

29. — Battle at Groveton and Gainsville, Va.; battle at Manchester, Tenn., '62. McClellan nominated for president and Pendleton for vice-president, '64.

30. — Second battle of Bull Run, confederate victory; battles of Bolivar, Tenn., and of Richmond, Ky., '62. Sherman put his whole army between Atlanta and Hood at Jonesboro', '64.

31. — Fort Smith, Ark., captured by Gen. Blunt, '63. Battle of Jonesboro', Ga., Aug. 31 and Sept. 1, '64.

SEPTEMBER.

1. — Battle of Chantilly, Va.; Gens. Kearney and Stevens killed; Burnside evacuated Fredericksburg; battle of Britton's Lane, Tenn., '62. Hood evacuated Atlanta, '64. Removal of all restrictions on Southern ports, '65.

2. — McClellan assigned to command the defences of Washington, '62. Confederates before Petersburg cheered McClellan's nomination; Atlanta captured by Sherman, '64.

3. — Union cavalry victory near Murfreesboro'; Union victories at Darkesville and Perryville, Va., '64.

4. — Oreto ran the blockade into Mobile, '62. Burnside occupied Knoxville, '63. Morgan was routed and killed by Gen. Gillam at Greenville, Tenn., '64.

5. — Confederates invaded Maryland, '62. Women's bread riot in Mobile, '63.

6. — First capture by the Alabama (the whaler Ocmulgee); battle of Washington, N.C., '62. Morris Island evacuated by the confederates, '63. Battle of Matamoros, '64.

7. — Gen. Pope relieved of command of the army of Virginia, '62. Union troops captured Fort Wagner, S.C., '63. Confederate Gen. Dibbles surprised at Readyville, '64.

8. — Gen. Lee's proclamation to Maryland, '62. Confederate Col. Jessie and 100 men captured near Ghent, Ky., '64.

9. — Confederates evacuated Fredericksburg, '62. Cumberland Gap captured by Gen. Shackleford, '63. Sherman concentrated near Atlanta, '64.

10. — Rosecrans defeated Floyd at Carnifex Ferry, Va., '61. Levy *en masse* in Pennsylvania to repel invasion, '62. Grant advanced his permanent line half a mile, '64.

11. — Hagerstown, Md., occupied by confederates, '62. Little Rock, Ark., occupied by Union troops, '63.

12. — Hooker occupied Frederick City, Md., '62. Failure of the Sabine Pass expedition, '63.

13. — Fight at Middleton, Md., '62. Harper's Ferry battle, Sept. 12 to 15, '62.

14. — Battle of South Mountain, Va.; battle of Mumfordsville, Ky., Sept. 14 to 16, '62. Price and 10,000 men crossed the White River for Missouri, '64. Chiefs of the rebel Indians renounced the confederacy, '65.

15. — Harper's Ferry surrendered to the confederates; attempt to blockade the Ohio River, '62. Lincoln suspended the habeas corpus act, '63.

16. — Skirmishes at Chattanooga, '63. Thirteenth Pennsylvania regiment and 2,500 cattle captured at Sycamore church; action (16th–18th) at Fort Gibson, I.T., '64.

17. — Battle of Antietam; Union troops evacuated Cumberland Gap, '62.

18. — Maryland legislature closed by the provost-marshal, and all the confederate sympathizers sent to Fort McHenry, '61. Confederates evacuated Sharpsburg and recrossed the Potomac, '62. Gen. Averill drove the confederates out of Martinsburg, '64.

19.—Battle of Iuka, Miss.; confederates evacuated Harper's Ferry, '62. Beginning of the battle of Chickamauga, '63. Battle of Winchester; Sheridan sent Early "whirling up the valley:" battle at Powder Mill, or Little Rock River, '64.

20.—Confederate Gen. Price captured Col. Mulligan at Lexington, Mo., '61. Battle of Blackburn's Ford, Va., '62. Confederate victory at Chickamauga, '63. Forrest captured Athens, Ala., '64.

21.—John C. Breckenridge joined the confederacy; engagement at Osceola, Mo., '61. Rosecrans retreated from Chickamauga to Chattanooga, '63.

22.—Lincoln's emancipation proclamation issued, '62. Sheridan's victory at Fisher's Hill, '64.

23.—Meade's army reached the Rapidan, '63. Price occupied Bloomfield, Mo., '64.

24.—Count de Paris and the Duc de Chartres became aides to McClellan; great review at Washington, '61. Convention of loyal governors at Altoona, Pa., '62.

25.—Mosby broke the railroad near Fairfax, '63.

26.—Federal fast day, '61. Early retreated to Brown's Gap in the Blue Ridge; battle of Pilot Knob, Mo., '64.

27.—Fremont opened his campaign, '61. Augusta, Ky., destroyed by the confederates, '62. Three Union companies of 39th Missouri regiment at Centralia massacred by Price, '64.

28.—Confederate attack on Burnside near Knoxville repulsed, '63. Battle of New Market Heights; night attack on Hancock's front on Jerusalem plank-road repulsed, '64.

29.—Gen. Davis shot Gen. Nelson at Cincinnati; Union defeat above Port Hudson, '63.

30.—Battle of Newtonia, Mo., '62. Confederate cavalry defeated at Harrison's Landing, Tenn., '63. Renewed fighting at New Market Heights, confederate victory; action at Poplar Springs church, Va., '64.

OCTOBER.

1. — Lincoln visited McClellan's army and urged movement across the Potomac; battle of Shepardstown, Va.; Buell's army left Louisville, '62. Battle of Anderson's Gap, Tenn., '63.

2. — Union victory at Anderson's Cross Roads, Ky., '63. Battle of Saltville, Va., '64.

3. — Union victory at Greenbrier, Va., '61. Battle of Corinth; Gen. Morgan retreated from Cumberland Gap, '62. Sherman crossed the Chattahoochee with 15 days' rations, '64.

4. — Battle of Buffalo Hill, Ky., '61. Confederates defeated at Corinth, '62. Four steamers burned at St. Louis by fire-bugs, '63.

5. — Gen. Robert Anderson in command in Kentucky, '61. Battle of Metamora, Miss., Union troops occupied Galveston, '62. Confederates bombarded Chattanooga from Lookout Mountain, '63. Hood captured the garrisons of Big Shanty and Ackworth; battle of Allatoona, Ga.; Sheridan's victory at Tom's Brook, '64.

6. — McClellan ordered to cross the Potomac and to give battle, '62. Action at Baxter Springs, Ark., '63. Hood's attack on Allatoona repulsed, '64.

7. — Battle of La Vergne, Tenn., '62. Confederate steamers destroyed on the Red River, '63. Battle of Darleytown Road and New Market Heights; pirate Florida captured at Bahia Bay, by U.S. steamer Wachusett, and sunk, '64.

8. — Battle of Perryville, Ky., '62. Union victories near Farmingham, Ky., and Salem, Miss., '63. Union victory at Woodville, '64.

9. — Union forces advanced beyond the Potomac; action at Santa Rosa, Fla., '61. Battle of Lawrenceburg, Ky., '62. Defeat of confederate operations against Rosecrans, '63. Battle of Boonesville, Mo., 9th to 11th; action at Strasburg, Va., '64.

10. — Battle of Harrodsburg, Ky.; Stuart's cavalry raid in Maryland and Pennsylvania, '62. Battle of Blue Springs, Tenn., '63.

11. — Steamer Nashville escaped from Charleston, '61. Confederate Gen. Buford and 1,200 cavalry crossed the Cumberland River at Harpeth Shoals, '64.

12. — Stuart's cavalry recrossed the Potomac, '62. Battle of Ingham's Mills, Miss.; Mead withdrew to the north bank of the Rappahannock; battle of Merrill's Crossing, Mo., '63. Drawn battle of three hours at Strasburg, between Longstreet and Sheridan, '64. Proclamation ending martial law in Kentucky, '65.

13. — Gen. Bragg evacuated Camp Dick Robinson, '62. Battle of Catlett's Station, '63.

14. — Fight at Bristow Station, '63.

15. — Three steamers from New York pursued the Nashville; battle of Lime Creek, Mo., '61. Draft in Boston and Baltimore, '62. Battle at McLean's Ford, Va., '63. Action at Glasgow, Mo., '64.

16. — Confederate raid on Brownsville, Miss., '63.

17. — Battle of Ironton, Mo., 17th to 21st, '61. Lincoln called for 300,000 men, '63. Price occupied Lexington, Mo., '64.

18. — Morgan occupied Lexington, Ky., '62. Maj.-Gen. Birney died at Philadelphia, '64.

19. — Fight near Nashville, '62. Lee recrossed the Rappahannock and marched south, '63. Battle of Cedar Creek; Sheridan's arrival from Winchester (11½ miles away) turned defeat to victory, '64.

20. — Grant succeeded Rosecrans, '63. Battle of Philadelphia, Tenn., '63. Early retreated by night to Mount Jackson, '64.

21. — Battle of Ball's Bluff; Gen. Baker killed; Gen. Zollicoffer defeated at Wild Cat, Ky.; Union victory at Fredericktown, '61. Confederates left West Virginia, '62. Battle of Cherokee Station, Ala., '63. Battle of the Little Blue, Mo., '64.

22. — Confederate salt-works in Florida destroyed, '62. Skirmishes at Columbia and Kingston Spring, Tenn., '63.

23. — Union victory at Maysville, Ark.; battle of Pocotaligo, S.C., '62. Fight at Beverley Ford on the Rappahannock, '63. Battle of Independence, Mo., '64.

24. — Rosecrans succeeded Buell over the army of Kentucky, '62.

25. — Major Zagonyi's charge at Springfield, Mo., '61. Fight near Manassas, '62. Battle of Pine Bluff, Ark., '63. Price defeated with loss of camp equipage at Fort Scott road, '64.

26. — Battle of Romney, W. Va., '61. McClellan's advance begun, '62. Grant moved on Lookout Mountain, '63. Pleasonton defeated Price at Mine Creek; Marmaduke and Cabell captured, '64.

27. — Battle of Labadiesville, La., '62. Battle of Wauhatchie, Tenn., '63. Hooker defeated the confederates at Brown's Ferry, '63. Grant's attack on the South side railroad failed; battle of Hatcher's Run, Va.; battle of Fair Oaks, Va., Oct. 27 and 28, '64.

28, — Capture of Lookout Mountain by Grant; afterward abandoned and occupied by the confederates, '63. Confederate ram Albemarle destroyed by a torpedo boat on the Roanoke River, 64.

29. — Great naval expedition under Dupont from Fortress Monroe, '61. Rhoddy's attack on Col. Morgan's colored troops at Decatur, Ala., repulsed, '64.

30. — Gen. Mitchell died at Port Royal, '62. Heavy bombardment of Charleston, '63.

31. — Skirmish at Maysville, Ky. Bank's expedition landed at Brazos Island, '62.

NOVEMBER.

1. — Gen. Winfield Scott resigned as commander-in-chief, and General McClellan succeeded him, '61.

2. — Gen. Fremont removed; steamer Bermuda ran the Savannah blockade, '61. Gen. Foster's expedition left Newbern, '62. Union victory at Roan Springs, Tenn.; boat attack on Sumter failed, '63. National thanksgiving for peace, '65.

3. — Union rising in East Tennessee, '61; battle at Grand Coteau, La.; actions at Columbia and Colliersville, Tenn., '63. Ram Albemarle destroyed, '64.

4. — Grant's army occupied Lagrange, Miss.; Georgia salt-works destroyed, '62. Banks's expedition occupied Brownsville, '63.

5. — Order issued for the removal of McClellan; battle of Nashville, Tenn., '62. Confederates shelled Chattanooga, '63. Butler took command of troops in New York City, '64.

6. — Lincoln elected, '61. McClellan's advance occupied Warrenton, Va.; battle of Garrettsburg, Ky., '62. Guerillas plundered Blandville, Ky.; battle of Droop Mountain, Va., '63. Confederate ram Shenandoah surrendered in the Mersey to an English man-of-war, '65.

7. — Brig.-Gen. Grant commanded at battle of Belmont, Mo., '61. McClellan removed and Burnside appointed; battle of Marianna, Ark.; negro troops engaged at Port Royal, '62. Meade's army engaged the confederates at Kelly's Ford and Rapidan Station, '63.

8. — Mason and Slidell taken, '61. Battle of Hudsonville, Miss., '62. Lincoln and Johnson elected, '64. McClellan resigned commission; Sheridan made major-general of regular army, '64.

9. — Butler's sequestration order issued, '62. Meade in line of battle, '63. Sherman issued marching order for advance through Georgia, '64.

10. — Senator Chestnut of South Carolina resigned; bill in the South Carolina legislature for 10,000 volunteers, '60. Union demonstration in Memphis, '62. Confederates concentrated on the south bank of the Rapidan, '63. Night fighting before Richmond, '64. Execution of Captain Wirz, '65.

11. — Senator Hammond of South Carolina resigned, '60. Gen. Halleck in command of the Western department, '61. Charleston and Sumter shelled regularly, '63.

12. — Union meeting in Arkansas, '63. About 10,000 prisoners exchanged near Fort Pulaski; Atlanta evacuated by the confederates, '64.

13. — Holly Springs, Miss., occupied by Union troops, '62. Confederates across the Potomac at Edward's Ferry, '63. Gen. Gillam defeated with heavy loss at Bull's Gap, '64.

14. — Gen. Stahel's forces passed Snicker's Gap, '62. Longstreet forced Burnside back at Knoxville; battle of Huff's Ferry, Tenn., '63.

15. — Great public meeting at Mobile declared the causes of secession, '60. Frigate San Jacinto brought Mason and Slidell, taken from the English steamer Trent, to Fortress Monroe, '61. Action at Fayetteville, Va , '62.

16.—Order for Sabbath observance issued, '62. Battle of Campbell's Station, Tenn.; Sherman's corps joined Thomas at Chattanooga, '63. Sherman left Atlanta on his march to the sea, '64.

17.—Artillery fight near Fredericksburg, '62. Siege of Knoxville, Tenn., begun; battle of Mustang Island, Tex., '63. Gen. Slocum burned the railroad station at Locust Circle, '64.

18.—Georgia voted $1,000,000 for arming the State; Maj. Anderson ordered to Fort Moultrie, '60. Burnside advanced opposite Fredericksburg, '62. Slocum cut the Macon railroad; the Georgia legislature fled from Milledgeville, '64.

19.—Executive session of the Louisiana legislature ordered, '60. Confederate congress met, '61. Gettysburg cemetery dedicated, '63. Madison captured and burned by Sherman, '64.

20.—Bank suspensions in Richmond, Baltimore, Washington, Philadelphia, Trenton, and the South, '60. Missouri confederate legislature passed secession ordinance, '61. Gen. Howard captured Milledgeville, '64.

21.—Surrender of Fredericksburg demanded, '62. Union victory at Liberty, '64. Sherman defeated Wheeler's cavalry at Gordon, '64.

22.—Order issued for the release of all State prisoners, '62. Part of Knoxville burned, '63. Action at Griswoldville, Ga., '64.

23.—Action at Fort Pickens, Fla., '61. Reconnoissance in force by Thomas at Chattanooga, '63.

24.—Mason and Slidell put in Fort Warren, '61. Capture of Lookout Mountain; Hooker's fight above the clouds, '63. Potomac, James, and Valley armies celebrated Thanksgiving with delicacies from the North, '64.

25.—Raid on Pooleville, Md.; Confederates attacked Newbern, '62. Capture of Missionary Ridge, '63. Confederate attempt to burn New York, '64.

26.—Lincoln visited Burnside; Sherman left Memphis, '62. Meade crossed the Rapidan, '63. Action at Sylvan Grove (26th–29th), and Browne's Cross Roads, Va. Beauregard's siege of Decatur repulsed, Nov. 26 to 29, '64.

27.—Fighting between Meade and Lee, near Mine Run, Va.; battle of Ringgold and Taylor's Ridge, Ga.; steamer Greyhound burned on the James River, '64.

28.—Burnside visited Washington; battle of Cone Hill, Ark.; confederate cavalry crossed the Rappahannock, '62. Morgan and six officers escaped from the Ohio penitentiary, '63.

29.—Mississippi sent commissioners to the other Southern States, '60. Union victory at Frankfort, W. Va., '62. Longstreet's attack on Knoxville repulsed, '63. Action (29th, 30th) at Spring Hill, Tenn., '64.

30.—Jefferson Davis elected president of the confederacy for six years, '61. Battle of Franklin; Hood repulsed with heavy loss; Attorney-General Bates resigned; Roger A. Pryor captured; battle of Grahamsville, S.C.; battle of Honey Hill, S.C., '64.

DECEMBER.

1. — Great secession meeting at Memphis, '60. Meade recrossed the Rapidan, '63. Banks resumed command of the department of the Gulf, '64.

2. — Confederates in Tennessee and Mississippi retreated before Grant, Dec. 1 to 3, '62. Confederate Gen. Hardee superseded Bragg in Georgia; battle of Walker's Ford, W. Va., '63.

3. — Gen. Geary occupied Winchester, Va., '62. Union foray toward Canton, Miss., '63.

4. — John C. Breckenridge unanimously expelled from the U. S. senate, '61. Longstreet abandoned the siege of Knoxville, '63.

5. — Confederate victory at Coffeeville, Miss., '62. Confederate attack on Murfreesboro' blockhouses repulsed, '64.

6. — Skirmish near Lebanon, Tenn., '62. Ex-secretary Chase appointed justice of the supreme court; capture of Pocotaligo bridge, S.C.; action (6th–9th) at Deveaux's Neck, S.C., '64.

7. — Gen. Butler's expedition at Port Royal, '61. Union victory at Prairie Grove, Ark., '62. Electoral colleges met; Forrest routed by Rousseau near Murfreesboro, '64.

8. — Lincoln issued amnesty proclamation, '63. Confederates established a battery on the Cumberland River; action at Hatcher's Run, Va., '64.

9. — Congress authorized the exchange of prisoners; Confederate congress admitted Kentucky to the confederacy, '61. Direct communication established with Sherman near Savannah, '64.

10. — Howell Cobb, secretary of the treasury, resigned; Senator Clay of Alabama resigned; Louisiana legislature appropriated $500,000, '60. Battle of Union gunboats and confederate batteries at Port Royal, Va., '62. Gunboat Otsego sunk by confederate torpedo on the Roanoke River, '64.

11. — Bombardment of Fredericksburg, '62. Battles of Bean Station and Morristown, Tenn. (10th–14th), '63.

12. — Burnside occupied Fredericksburg, '62. Col. Morgan was captured at Kingston, Tenn., '64.

13. — First military execution; Deserter Johnson shot; engagement at Buffalo Mountain, W. Va., '61. Confederate victory at Fredericksburg, '62. Gen. Hazen captured Fort McAllister, '64.

14. — Lewis Cass, secretary of state, resigned, '60. Union victory near Kingston, N.C., '62. Union victory at Bean Station, Va., '63. Gen. Dix ordered operations against the confederates on the Canadian frontier, '64.

15. — Retreat of Burnside; the advance of Banks's expedition arrived at New Orleans, '62. Victory of Gen. Thomas near Nashville; raid of Stoneman in southwest Virginia; Forrest defeated near Murfreesboro', '64.

16. — Burnside retreated across the Rappahannock; Banks put in command of the department of the Gulf, '62. Hood routed near Nashville, '64.

17. — Union victory at Mumfordville, Ky., '61. Baton Rouge occupied by

Union troops, '62. Resolutions offered in the confederate house to send peace commissioners to Washington, '64.

18. — Battle of Milford, Mo., '61. Confederates seized Lexington, Ky.; Quantrell defeated by Phillips's Indian brigade near Fort Gibson, '62. Secretary Seward required all persons coming to the United States, except immigrants, to have passports, '64.

19. — End, at Oxford, Miss., of successful six days' raid of Col. Dickey's scouting party, '62. Battle of Barren Fork, Ind. Territory; confederates repulsed Standthwaite's attack on Fort Gibson, Ark., '63. Draft and call for 300,000 men, '64.

20. — South Carolina seceded, '60. Battle at Drainesville, Va., '61. Gen. Foster returned to Newbern after a successful expedition; Holly Springs, Miss., sacked by confederates; Sherman's army embarked at Memphis for Vicksburg, '62. Hardee evacuated Savannah; navy yard burned, and salt-works blown up, '64.

21. — Fight on Wolf River, Miss., '61. Sherman occupied Savannah, '64.

22. — Confederate success in Isle of Wight Court-House (Va.); skirmish, '62. Gen. Corcoran killed by fall from his horse, '63.

23. — Union troops occupied Winchester, Va., '62. Union raid on Luray, '63. Fight near Gordonsville, Va., '64.

24. — Ten miles of railroad destroyed west of Vicksburg, '62. Choctaw Indians deserted the confederacy, '63. Porter's fleet attacked Fort Fisher, '64.

25. — Skirmish at Bacon Creek, Ky., '62. British bark Circassian seized in the North River by a U. S. marshal, '63. Porter's attack on Fort Fisher repulsed, '64.

26. — Maj. Anderson and 80 men went to Fort Sumter, '60. Sherman disembarked at Yazoo, '62. The ironclad Dictator launched at New York, '63.

27. — Mason and Slidell were surrendered to the British minister, '61. Sherman marched on Vicksburg; action at Dumfries, Va., '62.

28. — South Carolina seized the U. S. custom-house, post-office, and arsenal, '60. Action at Mt. Zion, Mo., '61. Battle of Chickasaw Bayou, Vicksburg; Gen. Blunt captured Van Buren, Ark.; battle of Elk Fork, Tenn., '62. Action at Charleston, Tenn., '63. Reconstruction meeting at Savannah, '64.

29. — J. B. Floyd, secretary of war, resigned, '60. Sherman repulsed at Vicksburg with heavy loss, '62.

30. — Sherman raised the siege of Vicksburg; battles of Jefferson and of Parker's Cross Roads, Tenn.; Monitor foundered off Hatteras, '62. Great naval expedition left New Orleans, '63.

31. — Battle of Stone River, or Murfreesboro', begun; McClernand succeeded Sherman before Vicksburg, '62. Large quantity of confederate money seized in New York, '63.

1803
STOCK COMPANY.
Imperial
Fire Insurance Co.
OF LONDON, ENGLAND.

COLUMBIA CYCLES
For 1890
SAFETIES
FOR LADIES OR GENTLEMEN
ORDINARIES
TANDEMS
TRICYCLES
HIGHEST GRADE ONLY
CATALOGUE FREE
POPE MFG. CO.
77 FRANKLIN ST.
BOSTON
BRANCH HOUSES
12 WARREN ST. NEW YORK
291 WABASH. AVE. CHICAGO

LOVELL HIGH GRADE "DIAMOND" SAFETY.

$85.

Diamond Frame, Steel Drop Forgings, Steel Tubing, Adjustable Ball Bearings to all Running Parts, including Pedals, Suspension Saddle. Finest material money can buy. Finished in enamel and nickel.

STRICTLY HIGH GRADE IN EVERY PARTICULAR.

NO BETTER MACHINE MADE AT ANY PRICE.

LOVELL LADIES' AND BOYS' SAFETY.

$35.

26 INCH WHEEL.

STEEL DROP FRAME.

Only Steel drop frame 26-inch machine in the Market at $35. Be sure you get a 26-inch wheel. Take no other.

Sent C. O. D. on receipt of $10.00 to guarantee express charges.

SWIFT AUTOMATIC HAMMERLESS REVOLVER.

5 SHOTS, 38 CALIBRE.
(Using 38 S. & W. C. F. Cartridge.)

PRICE,
$11.00.

Latest and best Hammerless Revolver in the market.

SWIFT DOUBLE ACTION REVOLVER.

5 SHOTS, 38 CALIBRE.
(Using 38 S. & W. C. F. Cartridge.)

PRICE,
$10.00.

The most improved Double Action Revolver in the market.

Sent by registered mail, POST-PAID, on receipt of price.

CHAMPION Single B/L SHOT GUN.

Best in the world. It has no equal.

PRICES.	
PLAIN STEEL BARRELS.	
12 Bore,	$11.25.
10 "	12.00.

PRICES.	
IMPORTED TWIST BARRELS.	
12 Bore,	$13.50.
10 "	14.25.

Sent C. O. D. on receipt of $5.00 to guarantee express charges.

The Youths' Companion says of this well known Boston concern:—"THE JOHN P. LOVELL ARMS CO. have been in business for fifty years, and their integrity is beyond question. They are among the largest dealers in Sporting Goods, Fire Arms, etc., in America, and on receipt of 6 cents in stamps, they will send to any one their 100 page illustrated catalogue of Guns, Rifles, Revolvers, Fishing Tackle, Bicycles, Tricycles, Cutlery, Base Ball, Police and Sporting Goods of every description, and you can feel perfectly sure that any goods ordered of this firm will be just as represented.

JOHN P. LOVELL ARMS CO.,

147 WASHINGTON STREET, COR. BRATTLE, BOSTON, MASS.

Capt. WILLIAM L. ROSS,

THE Manager of the American Branch of Messrs. Singer & Co.'s great Cycle House, is one of the best-known men in cycling trade circles in this country. A thorough business man, conservative, while energetic and practical, with an invincible regard for fair play. The manifold interests of the American Branch, with its Agencies throughout the United States, and all the subsidiary issues of the business here are under the direct management of Capt. Ross, who has demonstrated his ability to serve the interests of his House, to the mutual satisfaction of Singer & Co., and their large American following. The works of Singer & Co., at Coventry, England, are the largest in the world, and the wheels they produce are of the highest grade only.

Born in 1842, Wm. L. Ross enlisted in 1864, in the Sixty-fourth Regiment, New York Veteran Volunteer Infantry. Promoted to First Sergeant, Company B; commissioned Second Lieutenant (Company G) from September 24th, 1864; First Lieutenant, December 9th, 1864; Captain, May 18th, 1865. Mustered out with his Regiment, July 14th, 1865. His war record embraces service before Petersburg, Va., in the engagements at Poplar Spring Church, Forts Fisher, Va., Wadsworth, Howard, Hays, Sedgewick, Rice, Morton, Haskell, Stedman, etc., Hatcher's Run, Vaughan Road, Boydton Plank Road, Weldon Railroad, White Oak Road, Dinwiddie Court House, South-Side Railroad, Sutherland Station, Amelia Court House, Jetersville, High Bridge, Deatonville, Farmville. At the last named place he was taken prisoner, while charging a rebel battery, at the head of his Company, April 7th, 1865, and was kept with Lee's Army until released at Appomattox Court House, April 10th, 1865, when he rejoined his Regiment. Capt. Ross is a member of Gettysburg Post 191, Department of Mass. G. A. R., and resides in Boston,— the head-quarters of Messrs. Singer & Co. in the U. S., being in Odd Fellows' Building, cor. Tremont and Berkeley Sts., that city.

Our National Inheritance.

A

MEMORIAL DISCOURSE

DELIVERED

BEFORE SOLDIERS IN THE LATE WAR AND THE CITIZENS OF COLDWATER, ON

SUNDAY, MAY 27, 1883.

UNDER THE AUSPICES OF BUTTERWORTH POST, G. A. R.,

BY

THE REV. HERBERT J. COOK.

COLDWATER, MICH.:
A. J. ALDRICH & CO., PRINTERS.
1883.

OUR NATIONAL INHERITANCE.

A

MEMORIAL DISCOURSE

DELIVERED

BEFORE SOLDIERS IN THE LATE WAR AND THE CITIZENS OF COLDWATER, ON

SUNDAY, MAY 27, 1883.

UNDER THE AUSPICES OF BUTTERWORTH POST, G. A. R.,

BY

THE REV. HERBERT J. COOK,

COLDWATER, MICH.:
A. J. ALDRICH & CO., PRINTERS.
1883.

✠ DISCOURSE. ✠

Will the war never end? Shall we never cease from this fearful expenditure of blood and treasure? Shall we continue forever this breaking of human hearts—this desolation of happy homes?

These are the questions, dear friends, which we were asking so anxiously twenty years ago. Thank God, our prayers for peace were answered, and for more than two decades we have enjoyed the blessings of a happy and a united nation.

Ye shall hear of wars, and rumors of wars.—Matt xxiv, 6.

One generation shall praise thy works to another, and shall show thy mighty acts.—Ps. cxlv, 4, 11.

Decoration Day has won a place in history. Originating in a general order from the Commander of the "Grand Army of the Republic" to strew with flowers the graves of their fallen comrades on the 30th of May, 1868, that day at once took rank among our popular anniversaries The idea simple, pathetic, beautiful, touched the great heart of the nation, and the act has never wanted the co-operation of millions of loving hands. For no public occasion can be more appropriate than one born of the desire and purpose to express a nation's gratitude for costly sacrifices made in her behalf, and to pay a sincere tribute to the heroes who live only in sacred and cherished remembrance.

All these heroes were men, and as such had other and more tender relations in life than grew out of the hard soil of strife and bloodshed. They were husbands, fathers, brothers, sons. They left their homes to answer the urgent call of their country. And in those homes were anxious hearts, sending after them messages of love, daily offering up earnest prayers, but often destined to bleed in the general woe. These personal associations have ever thrown their hallowed influence around the day, and have invested its every act with a tender solemnity. Hands of little children have been taught to weave the garland for a father's monument. Widows' tears have watered the grassy mounds, and circles of bereaved friends have stood with clasped hands around the grave of fallen manhood to say with eloquent silence, broken only by a sigh, a sob, or the sad notes of the funeral dirge, "This is what the nation's life cost *him* and those he loved; this is the price of liberty!" So long, therefore, as the Reaper spares enough of scarred veterans to keep up an organization, and so long as these personal mourners survive their own, and their Country's dead, it is not likely that Memorial Day will cease to be observed. As before, these many years, we shall receive from the open palm of each returning Spring a profusion of God's beautiful and fragrant flowers, and with reverent hands scatter them on every soldier's grave.

Meanwhile, in many a grove that shadows a city of the dead, shall be heard the beating of muffled drums; beneath the blue sky shall float the tattered and war-stained battle-flags, and harmonious choirs shall chant the ode that sweeter grows with the lapse of years:

"How sleep the brave who sink to rest,
By all their country's wishes bless'd!
*   *   *   *   *   *
By fairy hands their knell is rung;
By forms unseen their dirge is sung;
There Honour comes, a pilgrim gray,
To bless the turf that wraps their clay;
And Freedom shall awhile repair.
To dwell a weeping hermit there."*

---

* Collins.

You remind me that I am anticipating another occasion? Let it be so. Thought waits not for lagging hours. Tender associations pay no tribute to time and space. When the sympathies are kindled and the heart is touched we live our truest, noblest life, unfettered by ordinary limitations. Still I do not forget that the present hour has its special claims on him who would voice the religious teachings of the great conflict and our subsequent history. I do not forget the day, the place, the waiting congregation, or the responsibilities of my sacred office. As I understand it, this occasion is in the interest of religion and patriotism. It is a recognition of the God of battles and the God of history. It is to instruct the generation which has grown up since the war, in some of the deep lessons of the mighty struggle for national existence, and to kindle in their minds and ours the holy flame of Christian manhood and womanhood. And if we grasp firmly the deeper thoughts of the hour, it may be that we shall discover in assemblies like this and for this purpose, fulfillment of the poet-prophet's words: "One generation shall praise thy works to another, and shall declare thy mighty acts. They shall speak of the glory of thy kingdom, and talk of thy power; to make known to the sons of men his mighty acts, and the glorious majesty of his kingdom. Thy kingdom is an everlasting kingdom, and thy dominion endureth throughout all generations."†

In this view of history God has his own true place, in all and above all. Men act their parts well or ill; nations rise and fall; wars rage or peace and plenty smile on happy homes; but the Almighty changes not. He is King of all kings, Lord of all lords, and the Supreme Disposer of all events. His plans and his purposes are sure of their just result.

Gathering up the materials for an historic discourse, they are;

1. *The War and its Causes.*
2. *Subsequent Events.*
3. *The Nation of To-day, and*
4. *The Outlook into the Future.*

The purpose is not to make a history or a philosophy of history, for the matter of this discourse is far more than the manner of it can be. A few salient features only will be noted, and the progress of our country, under the guidance, as we devoutly believe, of an all-wise Providence, thoughtfully observed.

Did you see the young man who last Autumn cast his first ballot? He was an infant in the cradle when in 1861 the first gun was fired in Charleston harbor, the rumbling of which shook the whole country to the farthest Pacific shores. It were well for that youth to spread out for earnest study the scroll on which is written the history of the last two decades. It is well for us all to see how Time has been weaving the annals of this fair country, to notice the golden thread of Divine purpose running through the whole, and to know assuredly that the white-haired Weaver has not once thrown the shuttle amiss or of his own direction.

† Psalms cxlv, 4, 11-13.

THE WAR.

Allusion has been made to the opening of hostilities. There was something more than powder which sent that missile hurtling through the air against the walls of Sumter. There was what, if it has not wholly disappeared, has since been greatly modified and reduced in amount and intensity by the logic of events. Sectional hatred, determination to perpetuate human bondage, false ideas of independence and of State sovereignty, had at last reached the desperate point of firing upon the old flag, and thus hurling defiance at the nation. It is painful, now, even to allude to this, and I will do no more. The result of the demonstration you all know. Volunteers were asked for, and volunteers came, for three months, for three years and for nine months. Out of these raw materials was soon constructed the truly grand Army of the Republic, of which, not the majority by any means, lived to return home. Thousands and tens of thousands fell on hard-fought battlefields, in hospitals and in prison; and their sacrifice for native land, I trust, will never be forgotten by a grateful people.

Out of almost nothing, in the course of a few months, a formidable navy was guarding every southern port, and to the end the naval force maintained its right to be called the other arm of our national service.

How fiercely the contest raged four long, weary years, need not be repeated here. The advantage, at first, was not with the defenders of the Union. Men disciplined and ready for duty, ships and munitions of war, alike were wanting and had to be provided. But the plan was laid out early in 1862 to blockade all ports, open the Mississippi River, and to move "On to Richmond." This reduced the matter to a vast siege, varied only by such invasions as those into Pennsylvania and Ohio. The difficulties were stupendous, the fortunes of war variable, but with many disasters, many mistakes on both sides, the conflict at last drew to a close, and the final surrender was made on the 9th of April, 1865. The Proclamation of Emancipation was issued by President Lincoln on the 22d of September, 1862, taking effect the first day of January following, and in the surrender of General Lee the hopes of secession were brought to an end let us hope forever.

Peace once more visited our suffering country, and we hope and pray that she may go no more out forever. Happily we have all gained some wisdom since those troublous times, and now it is rare to hear sectional names and epithets. Both sides in the great struggle are fast coming to rejoice in the grand result, and to regard it not as a victory of North over South, but as a national triumph in the cause of good government and human rights.

The immortal words of Mr. Lincoln's second Inaugural, in 1865, cannot be too often quoted nor their noble sentiments too deeply impressed on the hearts of the whole American people. Speaking of the two sides to the then closing war, he said: "Both read the same Bible, and pray to the same God; and each invokes His aid against the other. * * * The prayers of both could not be answered. That of neither has been answered fully. The Almighty has His own purposes. * * * With malice towards none, with charity for all, with firmness in the right, as God gives us to see the right, let us strive on to finish the work we are in, to bind up the the national wounds, * * to do all which may achieve and cherish a just and lasting peace among ourselves and with all nations."

Sublime utterance of a noble man and a true patriot! Let these weighty sentences. breathing the very essence of the Gospel of Christ, be taught by mothers to their little ones, by teachers to their pupils; and let their spirit, like a benediction, brood over a prosperous and united country, to the end of time! "With malice towards none, with charity for all, with firmness in the right." How would these New Testament principles once thoroughly engrafted and allowed to grow in Church and State, revolutionize society. The fires of contention would die out; jealousy would have nothing on which to feed, and every man would be free to attain at once the highest happiness and the greatest good in character and life, unfettered by those bonds which now shackle the loftiest aspirations, the holiest endeavors.

SUBSEQUENT EVENTS.

And was it not a benediction thus spoken by our moribund President? In five days from that solemn hour the surrender at Richmond flashed over the wires; and in five more—O! sad, sad memory,—the lips that uttered this universal word of blessing for his country and the brotherhood of nations, were sealed in death. The great and bloody sacrifice was ended, thanksgivings had gone up to the God who gave the final victory; but the pure soul of him who had watched and wept, who had toiled and prayed for the glorious result, had entered Paradise. Spirits of light, angelic convoys, who hover around the Christian's dying bed to soothe, and comfort, and sutain, ministered ye ever among the sons of men to one more true and more noble than he? Carried ye ever through the portals of the blessed to the Paradise of God, the divine and immortal spirit of one greater than Abraham Lincoln? Could ye now bend over us in your gentle ministries and audibly whisper the true answer to these queries, we know what it would be. It is the same that we find in our hearts; and even now we seem to hear the echoes of the inspired words solemnly chanted in many a place of worship throughout the land, at the hour of the funeral: "I heard a voice from Heaven saying unto me: Write, Blessed are the dead who die in the Lord, from henceforth. Yea, saith the Spirit, that they may rest from their labours; and their works do follow them."‡

Rest, then, servant of God; rest from the toils and labors of a life that knew no repose; rest, safe in the arms of Him who heard the voice of thy prayers at noon, at midnight and in the mists of the early dawn: rest, as heroes rest, remembered with universal affection and love. And whenever future generations shall write on their entablatures the names of the true, the noble and the great, thy name shall shine in letters of ineffaceable light and glory!

I need not tax your patience with minute recital of public history, from that eventful April, 1865, until the present hour. At the close of the war, the world saw a wonderful sight in the glad return of a million veterans to their homes, families, and ordinary avocations. You, soldiers, do not require a speaker to remind you of those joyous days. The glad welcome greeted you everywhere, on the streets of distant cities, at railway stations, in your native town, and in the sacred privacy of reunited homes. Not a few predicted that you had become so accustomed to camp and field that you would not willingly resume the tranquil pursuits of peace. A great mistake, monstrous blunder! Does the melting snow of our northern hills, as it dissolves flake by flake, quarrel with rivulet, stream, river, ocean? No more did the scarred and tanned soldiers find it difficult or unnatural to doff their uniforms and exchange their hard life for the citizen's clothes and the pursuits of former years. They were ready to go, would be again, in such an emergency, but the love of friends, of peace and of home drew them like a magnet, each man to his place; and to-day the Grand Army of the Republic is an organization of comrades, a confederation of citizens to whom military life is nothing but a satisfying, though terrible, reminiscence.

Reconstruction was something new on the face of the earth. But America was equal to the problem, and, the formal accomplishment of it early effected, the great work has been going on ever since. The recent daily papers tell of an obscure old man down yonder, once called "president," who denies that reconstruction is, or is possible. But the moving civilization of the word seriously smiles at him, as an anachronism—out of time and place and waiting, - waiting for the rolling years to close of an unenviable career.

Our currency was largely inflated by a conflict which had cost $4,000,000,000. Could we ever pay this enormous debt, greater for each year of the war than the entire expenses of "the Government from Washington to Buchanan?" A loan was called for and in five months $530,000,000 was taken — mostly in this country; and to-day the people prefer the bonds to their money; and, because the day of payment was originally so long deferred, the

‡ Rev. xiv, 13.

Treasury is obliged to lock up vast sums of money in the vaults, since it cannot pay the obligations until they mature.

Slavery, of course, exists no longer, and the people who fought for it are generally glad that the knot was cut which no human skill could untie. It was to be expected that a generation of freedmen, with their late masters, would suffer more under the new order of things than the old. They have suffered; they are suffering to-day. But liberty always brings light, education, prosperity. The signs of the times are now in this direction, and I sincerely believe that Congress should inaugurate measures for introducing generally and effectively, free, yes and compulsory, schools for this much-injured race. The same policy might well be tried among the Indians.

Many are the indications of advancement and prosperity in the the last twenty years.

The Atlantic cable was laid in 1866, and it has long since become a factor of our civilization. Few persons then believed that it would be a common occurrence for people of the United States to have, with the thousand other matters printed in our daily papers, sermons preached in London the day before, at their Monday morning breakfast table. We have lived to see this among other wonders of a wonderful period. In the month of May 1869, Maine and California clasped hands by the driving of the last spike of the Union Pacific Railroad. This was but one prominent mark of the great extension of those mighty highways of commerce and travel—our great railway systems. The railroad business has been overdone—at times disastrously—and with some reason there is complaint about their management and mismanagement; but without them our progress would cease and we should relapse into a state of semi-barbarism.

By the side of the railway runs the telegraph, and it has made rapid advances in perfecting machinery and operation. Everything, in fact, pertaining to the electrician's art, including the magnificent light and the telephone, has been moving forward in a manner truly astonishing. Each discovery fills us with wonder and awe, and what may yet be accomplished by further knowledge of this mighty agent is probably beyond our imagination's reach.

The Centennial year was one long series of triumphs. It demonstrated to other nations and to our own people the marvelous products and industrial achievements of America, and the almost unfathomable resources of the country yet undeveloped and unsettled. It proved, too, that the older states were rapidly advancing in all that pertains to individual and national importance. The stimulus of that great public festival will long be felt in the best life of the Nation.

Politically, we may mention as prominent features in the pathway of the Nation, the establishment soon after the war of the "Freedman's Bureau," the passage of the "Civil Rights Bill, the impeachment of a President.

In 1867 Alaska was purchased. Nebraska was admitted and Wyoming organized in 1868.

The important Embassy from China came over the same year, and did much to establish political relations with our Asiatic neighbors on the west.

March 30, 1870, witnessed the return of the last of the Southern members of Congress to their seats, and the proclamation of the adoption and ratification of the Fifteenth Amendment to the Constitution. The "Specie Resumption Act" was passed in 1876, and Colorado, the source of much of our gold and silver, was admitted that year. The bloody fights with the Sioux, when the gallant Custer fell and with him one of our own brave boys, forms a red scar on the fair face of the centennial year.

Railroad riots and communistic outbreaks next attracted public attention. But these fifty millions of people soon forget, often too soon, matters of that degree of importance.

We were destined to another shock from Presidential martyrdom. I will not recount the too familiar story of an exciting campaign; of an administration which had in it so much of personal and public satisfaction; of the assassin's dastardly shots; of the Summer's long sickness, wherein President Garfield "suffered many things of many physicians;" of the final release in death; of the nation in tears. All these things are fresh in your memory, and no poor words of mine are needed to recall the keenness of our sense of loss, and the way in which this city, with the whole nation, strove to honor him who had been our second martyr.

Like Abraham Lincoln, James A. Garfield rose to his exalted position from among the common people. Unlike him, he had the advantages of a liberal education, and so, in a higher degree, represented the advancing culture of the age. Both were men in all that makes exalted manhood. Both were patriots true, and both will be remembered with the highest honors, until the mother forgets her children —Columbia her noblest sons.

THE NATION OF TO-DAY.

In the hush and reverent silence of a sacred memory we leave this hasty sketch of the past. We are brought face to face with current affairs and with the present administration. The latter is now before the people on trial, and there it must be left; for this is not the place nor the hour either to praise or to blame. But in the wider view there is not a little which is hopeful and inspiring as well as monitory and threatening above the horizon of our beloved land. The extent of our territory, the vast resources of the several States, our wealth in commerce, manufactures, minerals, agriculture—these have often been rehearsed. Liberty of speech, of the press and of the individual conscience—these things we have inherited from our fathers. Educational and religious advantages, with the deep love of home and the opportunity for every industrious man to have and to hold one of his own—let us thank God for such inestimable privileges Why then should we not be a contented and prosperous people? I believe we may be—many of us are now. These brave veterans learned, if they needed any such schooling, by the deprivations of military service, how to appreciate and enjoy the public and personal blessings I have named, with many more that I have not. There is no reason why this country should not be approximately the ideal country, the home of the foremost nation of the earth, unless such reason be found in the people themselves. God has given us every natural advantage, and no holiday orator can possibly exaggerate these gifts of Heaven. But

THE OUTLOOK.

Is it all fair and beautiful? Is there no hidden rock in the course of the ship of State? Is there no gale or tempest overhead that sometimes threatens her safety? No thoughtful person can fail to observe many causes for serious consideration as he turns his face towards the future of this great and growing country. He need not be an alarmist—ought not to be; for then he will lose head, if not heart. But if there be one thing that should be studied by every good citizen soberly, wisely and in the fear of God, it is the question, "Whither is this nation tending? Is its great progress all in the right direction?" Then, if he be true to his position, he will use all the influence of his words and example to put down the wrong and to build up and strengthen the right.

Bear with me then, brethen, and fellow-citizens of the fairest land on the globe, while I point out a few subjects for our best and wisest thought.

National greatness is in itself a peril. The rapidly increasing millions and the widening of domain involve always new problems of government and citizenship. Washington was President of the United States—a strip of seacoast commonwealths sparsely settled with a few hundred thousand homogeneous people. Arthur is President of the United States: but the domain is a continent of States inhabited by more than fifty millions of all "people nations, and languages." By the present rate of increase, and at no very distant period, there will be two hundred millions. There is no need for a public speaker to point out the infinite complications which this simple fact of increase puts into all public questions. The danger is, as recently, of sectional differences, and of the introduction, by indiscriminate and endless immigration of ideas which have been perilous elsewhere and which to-day are menacing some of the "strong governments" of the old world. Welcome and honor to the sturdy immigrant who comes to our shores to become an American citizen! But let us beware of dynasties of destruction springing up among us, ungoverned and ungovernable, save as they are controlled by unscrupulous and reckless leaders. We want workmen, laborers, heads of families, good citizens. We do *not* want the penal and pauper classes of Europe in our emigrant ships, nor the plotters of mischief, whose desire is to promote general ruin in order to gather up something for themselves from the wrecks—to put an end to the living in order to plunder the dead.

Ignorance is always a source of danger. The ignorant classes are the dupes of designing knaves. Education, to a limited degree, therefore, should be compulsory. The Negroes, Indians, the foreign population of our cities should be taught, and in *the English language*, the rudiments of knowledge. Great pains also should be used at home and in schools of all grades, in circulating good literature and the endeavor should be made by means of the Press to instruct the young in the first principles of government, in a clear knowledge of our history; and they should be taught in every way through sermons, lectures and public assemblies, that *we have a country*, and that a country which is worth taking life in hand to defend, as these brave men have done, is worth knowing something about, worth living for, and, if need be, worth dying for. In the generations of noble youth so educated and nurtured in the home, in the school, in the church there lies, in my opinion, the hope of the country.

Human Greed and selfishness is a fertile source of danger.

Men there are who seem to believe, judging by their actions, that the Government exists for office-holders alone, and that the State is a fat body, the flesh of which is to feed political cormorants.

It were a difficult matter for wise and earnest statesmen to govern this great nation when they do their best work; how then does the subject become tangled like the inextricable labarynth, when the endeavor seems to be most prominent and constant to promote party feeling, to secure "the spoils" and to advance personal interests at the expense of public advantage.

Unjust, indeed, would it be to say that we have no patriotic and rightminded counsellors and legislators; but, I believe I am not wrong in the assertion that political corruption and huge scheming monopolies, both growing out of the same root of selfishness and both detrimental to the public good are threatening this Republic with danger, and therefore these things should be frowned upon and fought against by all good citizens. The most effectual way to cure political intrigues and the rapacity of monopolies, is to make such matters odious to the people and then to hold up their promoters to public scorn.

And finally, great public peril inheres in the neglect of Divine institutions. Here is material for many sermons, none of which it is purposed to preach here. The evils must be named, however, for the completion of our theme, and for their intrinsic importance. These institutions go back to the beginnings of human society and government. They have never been, and never will be annulled. Fitted to our nature by Him who made us and understood our requirements, no changes of belief or custom on our part, can ever change their perfect adaptation to individuals and society or release either from the sure penalty for disregarding them.

The sacredness of the Lord's day is one of these things to be remembered. God claims one seventh of our time, not indeed for His advantage, but for ours, and He has always most honored the people who have kept Sunday most faithfully. If then we give up our English and American Sunday for the continental holiday, and make it a day for drinking, for races, for theaters and amusements, we may well tremble for the consequences. There is no reason why the place of worship should be neglected, but every reason why each consecrated place should be crowded with worshipers, not only on special occasions like this, but always ; for, thus sought, the blessing of God in a personal and public sense will be given us abundantly for common days and for the great crises and exigencies whenever they arise.

The sacred character of home is another point. In this is involved the sanctity of marriage as the foundation-stone, with permanent divorces granted only for the one cause named in the Pentateuch and reiterated in the New Testament; the sacred responsibility, too often overlooked, of man as the head of the family ; the true position of woman in the home and in the widening sphere of usefulness when she is not called to the holy duties of wife and mother ; *the life* and well-being of children with their proper nurture and education in all the duties of life. Alas! that we should ever forget the sanctity of the place where angels delight to be, where the smiles of Heaven gives unceasing light, and where are rooted the hopes of the whole nation — the happy, well-ordered Christian home. Not only on our wall mottoes ; not only in our public assemblies, dear friends, but in our heart of hearts let us find the words—the prayer, never forgotten in letter or spirit: "God bless our homes."

We shall do well as a people to reverence and to keep all of the ten commandments. Tell me not that these are only arbitrary, or that they were given to one nation. They are not arbitrary, but a covenant of love. There is not one of them that it would not be infinitely better to keep if they had never been written. Consequently they are of universal benefit and obligation. As in the case of the fourth, so of all the decalogue, their observance will bring peace, prosperity, blessing. Such obedience, in the spirit as in the letter, will unite this nation together and to their Maker. The ship of state will not be wrecked, for God will guide her course and send her favoring winds. She will sail triumphantly into the haven of eternal peace, and when she drops her anchor it will be not far from the foot of the great white throne.

Dear friends and fellow-townsmen, soldiers of the Grand Army: It is time to close these extended remarks. They have been spoken in the deep love of our common country, and in full appreciation, as far as that were possible, of the sacrifices that have been made in her behalf. We have spoken with our eyes, as it were, upon past and present, and with our vision stretching on towards the unknown future.

We believe in the Holy Being who presides over the destinies of nations, and to whom we are sure the fate of America is most dear. Believing thus we recognize the finger of Duty pointing us all onward and upward towards better things. "In God we trust," and in Jesus Christ His Son. His kingdom alone is an everlasting kingdom, and His dominion only endureth throughout all generations. Light then, Brethren and Christians, the torch of human liberty. Strive that every man shall be free both in the state and in the full freedom of christian manhood. Let the fathers and mothers, the educators, the statesmen of this country be true to their high responsibilities. Let them do their duty in word and example, in instruction and high endeavor. Then let the children and youth follow their wise leading. Let Statesmanship, Science, Art, Literature, Education, Domestic Peace and the True Religion of the Son of God go hand in hand through all the flying years. Then shall it be heralded by the voice of some shining Arch-angel, as he points to our beloved land; and the choirs who celebrate the welfare and the happiness of the mortals for whom Christ has died, shall take up and prolong the strain: "These are they who love their God and whom God doth love. 'Happy is the people that are in such a case; yea, blessed are the people, whose God is the Lord.' "

No. 5.

PAPERS FROM THE SOCIETY

FOR THE

Diffusion of Political Knowledge.

THE TRUE CONDITIONS OF AMERICAN LOYALTY:

A SPEECH DELIVERED BY

GEORGE TICKNOR CURTIS,

BEFORE THE

DEMOCRATIC UNION ASSOCIATION,

MARCH 28TH, 1863.

OFFICE OF THE SOCIETY,
No. 13 PARK ROW, NEW-YORK.
C. MASON, COR. SEC'Y,
To whom all communications may be addressed.

READ—DISCUSS—DIFFUSE.

Resolved, That it be recommended to all citizens in the various cities, counties, and villages of this and other States, who approve of the objects expressed in this Constitution, that they organize auxiliary societies, and open communication with the New-York Society, for the purpose of procuring and circulating our papers.

SPEECH OF GEORGE TICKNOR CURTIS.

MR. PRESIDENT AND GENTLEMEN OF THE DEMOCRATIC ASSOCIATION:

Nothing but a sense of the duty which every man owes to society, according to the measure of his ability to serve it, would have induced me to address you in a time like this. It is a time of strange excitements and strange acts. No man who does not join in a wild, undiscriminating support of the measures and dogmas of a dominant party, can hope to escape detraction and obloquy. The utmost exertions are made to suppress ordinary freedom of speech; every device is employed to misrepresent, and every effort is made to misunderstand, the purposes of those who are in political opposition to the party in power. The vocabulary of political slang is exhausted to find terms of reproach and infamy, with which to stigmatize men whose motives have in their favor all the ordinary presumptions of purity, and whose arguments and opinions are at least entitled to a respectful hearing. This process, which has been going on for many months, with a violence unexampled even among a people whose political discussions are never marked by too much temperance, has culminated from time to time in outrages upon the rights of persons and property, and may do so again. It is no time when one would choose to utter opinions, without being impelled by a strong sense of duty.

But if we are not prepared to suffer for our convictions, they must be very feeble convictions. If we do not love our country and its institutions well enough to encounter all the hazards that may attend an honest effort to save them, our love must be cold indeed. Such, I am sure, is not your case, or my own. Meaning to utter here nothing but words of truth and soberness—the truth as I hold it, in the soberness that becomes me—I accept all the responsibility to public opinion which may justly fall thereon.

I propose to speak to you to-night upon a subject which seems to me to be strangely misapprehended by many good men, and strangely perverted by many who are not good. I mean the subject of "LOYALTY." The word itself, at least in the sense in which it is used in those countries from which we have lately borrowed it, can scarcely be said to have an appropriate place in our political and social system. But it is a word, at present, in great use among us; and we must take it as we find it, and are bound to inquire what are the moral duties which its just and true signification embraces. This inquiry, and the certain consequences of accepting and following out the doctrines which are now forced upon us, will form the topics of my discourse.

The true conditions of American loyalty are not to be found in the passionate exactions of partisan leaders, or in the frantic declamations of the pulpit, the rostrum or the press. People who do not like my political opinions may hurl at me the epithet "disloyal;" but when they have thrown this missile, they have not taken a single step towards defining, to me or others, what the true conditions of loyalty are. It is important that this step should be taken; for whether we are to go on or to cease, in this course of idle and unmeaning abuse, it concerns us all to know what measure of public duty may rightfully be exacted of us. To know the hight and depth of those great virtues which are comprehended in the term "patriotism"—to feel at once that they are seated in our affections and enthroned in our reason—is to "get wisdom and to get understanding," in the largest of earthly concerns.

The true conditions of American loyalty are to be found in the law of the land; in the institutions under which we live; in the duties flowing from the Constitution of our country; in the political system which we have inherited from our fathers, with all its manifold relations, through which we may trace the clear dividing-line that separates perfect from imperfect obligations.

The text of our fundamental law is the guide, and the sole guide, in all ethical inquiries into the duties of the citizen. To that source all must come, rulers and people alike; to that fountain all must resort. The vague and shifting standards that are drawn from supposed dangers to what is called "the national life," or which spring from the conflicting judgments of men respecting public necessities, can determine nothing. These things can furnish no *rule.* We must have a *rule*, for loyalty is a moral duty; and it must therefore be capable of definition. A people whose "national life" exists only by virtue of a written constitution, and who can have no necessities that lie out of or beyond that written necessity, can find no rule of loyalty in any of the necessities which their constitution of government does not cover. They may find grounds of expediency, in one or another supposed necessity for destroying their constitution; but it would be extremely absurd to say that this expediency could be made the object of their "loyalty." Let us go then to the fountain head — the source of all our national obligations.

The Constitution of the United States itself prescribes the full measure of our loyalty in these words:

"This Constitution and the laws of the United States *which shall be made in pursuance thereof*, and all treaties made or which shall be made, under the authority of the United States, shall be THE SUPREME LAW OF THE LAND."

Observe how precise as well as comprehensive this great rule of our duty is. It expresses without ambiguity the whole of our obligations towards the Federal Government. It makes a *supreme law;* — a law paramount to all other human laws — an obligation transcending all other political obligations. It leaves no room whatever for the intrusion of another or a rival claimant to our civil obedience. That claimant can neither be a person invested or uninvested with office, nor an idea of public necessity, nor an imaginary national life beyond or apart from the life created under the Constitution. The only possible claimant of our obedience is the LAW; for as that law is made supreme, all other demands or demandants upon our submission are of necessity excluded.

What then does this supreme law embrace? The text on which I am commenting itself furnishes the answer. "This Constitution," it says — what this *Constitution* contains, and the laws that *shall be made in conformity with it.*—*these* shall be the supreme law, rising in authority above all other laws. No public necessities, save as they are embodied in the Constitution; no "national life" save as it exists under the Constitution; no legislation that is not in accordance with the Constitution — is the supreme law; but what the Constitution ordains or authorizes, *that* is the public necessity, *that* is the national life, because it is the supreme civil obligation.

Such is the fundamental character of our political system; and so perfect is it in its consistency with itself and with the rights of all who are subject to it, that it contains a machinery by which the conformity of all acts of the Government with the principles of the Constitution may be peacefully tested, without forcible resistance. If the acts of the Government are complained of as unconstitutional, they may be brought to a judicial test, or the people may themselves pass upon them at the ballot-box, through the instrumentality of frequent elections.

Now when we look into the Constitution of our country to discover the full scope of the obligations which are embraced in the supreme law of the land, we find that it grants certain political powers and rights to the central or national government, and reserves all other political powers and rights to the States or the people. Hence it is plain that the reserved rights of the States or the people are just as much a part of the supreme law of the land, just as much comprehended within the duty of our allegiance, just as much the rightful objects of our "loyalty," as the powers and rights vested in the national government. If the political existence created by the Constitution is the national life, called into being by the supreme law of the land — and he would be a bold and reckless sophist who should undertake to find that national life any where else — then the rights which the Constitution reserves to the States or the people are equally comprehended in that life, for they are equally declared to be parts of the supreme law of the land. For this reason, all idea of a supremacy of the national rights or powers or interests, when founded on something not embraced in the Constitution, is purely visionary. No duty of "loyalty" can possibly be predicated of any claim that is not founded in the supreme law of the land. When it is once ascertained what are the rights and powers vested in the national authorities by the Constitution, they are parts of the supreme law, and our "loyalty" is due to them. When we know what are the rights and pówers reserved to the States or the people—and we know that they are the whole residue of all possible political rights and powers — they are equally the objects of our "loyalty," for the self-same reason, namely, they are parts of the supreme law of the land.

Again: the Constitution not only contains some political powers and rights granted to the Federal Government, and a reservation of all other political powers and rights to the States or the people, but it also embraces rights of person and property guaranteed to every citizen in his individual capacity; and these are equally made, not by implication but expressly, parts of the supreme law of the land, and are therefore equally the objects of our "loyalty." All pretence, therefore, of any paramount authority in the central government to override these personal rights of the citizen, or to claim our "loyalty" in disregard of these coordinate parts of the supreme law, is a perversion of the very idea of American loyalty. As well might the citizen claim, because the Constitution has made his personal rights part of the supreme law, that therefore the loyalty of his neighbor is due to him alone, as the Government can claim that loyalty is due solely, or chiefly, or primarily, or ultimately to the functions which *it* is appointed to perform. The rights of the Government, the rights of the States, and the rights of individuals, all and equally, are comprehended in the supreme law of the land, and our loyalty is due to that law, to the whole and to every part of it, and public officers are in the same sense and for the same reason bound to obey every "jot and tittle" of it.

These positions are very plain and familiar truths; too familiar, perhaps, you will say, to require to be stated. But in these days, nothing that is true is too fundamental or too plain to be inculcated. The extravagant language and ideas that are current in the mouths of even sensible people, on this subject of loyalty, would have exceeded all capacity of belief in any other period than this. If one were to undertaké to reduce this language and these ideas to something like a definite moral proposition, it would be found that the doctrine is something like this. In a time of war, when there are great public dangers, the rights of the States and of individuals must give way; and if those who administer the government are satisfied that public necessity requires them to use powers that transcend the limits of the Constitution, he who does not acquiesce in their judgment, or who questions their authority to do particular acts, is a "disloyal" citizen. This statement of the doctrine is the best that I know how to make; for I know not how else to interpret or to apply the denunciations which we find in the proceedings of public meetings, in the columns of party newspapers, and in the common speech and action of very many persons. I need only point to the utter prohibition that is attempted to be placed upon all discussion of any plan for bringing this dreadful civil war to a close, except-

Treasury is obliged to lock up vast sums of money in the vaults, since it cannot pay the obligations until they mature.

Slavery, of course, exists no longer, and the people who fought for it are generally glad that the knot was cut which no human skill could untie. It was to be expected that a generation of freedmen, with their late masters, would suffer more under the new order of things than the old. They have suffered; they are suffering to-day. But liberty always brings light, education, prosperity. The signs of the times are now in this direction, and I sincerely believe that Congress should inaugurate measures for introducing generally and effectively, free, yes and compulsory, schools for this much-injured race. The same policy might well be tried among the Indians.

Many are the indications of advancement and prosperity in the the last twenty years.

The Atlantic cable was laid in 1866, and it has long since become a factor of our civilization. Few persons then believed that it would be a common occurrence for people of the United States to have, with the thousand other matters printed in our daily papers, sermons preached in London the day before, at their Monday morning breakfast table. We have lived to see this among other wonders of a wonderful period. In the month of May 1869, Maine and California clasped hands by the driving of the last spike of the Union Pacific Railroad. This was but one prominent mark of the great extension of those mighty highways of commerce and travel—our great railway systems. The railroad business has been overdone—at times disastrously—and with some reason there is complaint about their management and mismanagement; but without them our progress would cease and we should relapse into a state of semi-barbarism.

By the side of the railway runs the telegraph, and it has made rapid advances in perfecting machinery and operation. Everything, in fact, pertaining to the electrician's art, including the magnificent light and the telephone, has been moving forward in a manner truly astonishing. Each discovery fills us with wonder and awe, and what may yet be accomplished by further knowledge of this mighty agent is probably beyond our imagination's reach.

The Centennial year was one long series of triumphs. It demonstrated to other nations and to our own people the marvelous products and industrial achievements of America, and the almost unfathomable resources of the country yet undeveloped and unsettled. It proved, too, that the older states were rapidly advancing in all that pertains to individual and national importance. The stimulus of that great public festival will long be felt in the best life of the Nation.

Politically, we may mention as prominent features in the pathway of the Nation, the establishment soon after the war of the "Freedman's Bureau," the passage of the "Civil Rights Bill, the impeachment of a President.

In 1867 Alaska was purchased. Nebraska was admitted and Wyoming organized in 1868.

The important Embassy from China came over the same year, and did much to establish political relations with our Asiatic neighbors on the west.

March 30, 1870, witnessed the return of the last of the Southern members of Congress to their seats, and the proclamation of the adoption and ratification of the Fifteenth Amendment to the Constitution. The "Specie Resumption Act" was passed in 1876, and Colorado, the source of much of our gold and silver, was admitted that year. The bloody fights with the Sioux, when the gallant Custer fell and with him one of our own brave boys, forms a red scar on the fair face of the centennial year.

Railroad riots and communistic outbreaks next attracted public attention. But these fifty millions of people soon forget, often too soon, matters of that degree of importance.

We were destined to another shock from Presidential martyrdom. I will not recount the too familiar story of an exciting campaign; of an administration which had in it so much of personal and public satisfaction; of the assassin's dastardly shots; of the Summer's long sickness, wherein President Garfield "suffered many things of many physicians;" of the final release in death; of the nation in tears. All these things are fresh in your memory, and no poor words of mine are needed to recall the keenness of our sense of loss, and the way in which this city, with the whole nation, strove to honor him who had been our second martyr.

Like Abraham Lincoln, James A. Garfield rose to his exalted position from among the common people. Unlike him, he had the advantages of a liberal education, and so, in a higher degree, represented the advancing culture of the age. Both were men in all that makes exalted manhood. Both were patriots true, and both will be remembered with the highest honors, until the mother forgets her children —Columbia her noblest sons.

THE NATION OF TO-DAY.

In the hush and reverent silence of a sacred memory we leave this hasty sketch of the past. We are brought face to face with current affairs and with the present administration. The latter is now before the people on trial, and there it must be left; for this is not the place nor the hour either to praise or to blame. But in the wider view there is not a little which is hopeful and inspiring as well as monitory and threatening above the horizon of our beloved land. The extent of our territory, the vast resources of the several States, our wealth in commerce, manufactures, minerals, agriculture—these have often been rehearsed. Liberty of speech, of the press and of the individual conscience—these things we have inherited from our fathers. Educational and religious advantages, with the deep love of home and the opportunity for every industrious man to have and to hold one of his

In like manner I affirm that when the Constitution reserved to the States or the people all political powers not granted to the Federal Government, it meant to preclude every ground of necessity for the assumption by that government of the powers thus withheld.

In fact, the idea of a written constitution—a fixed and supreme law—is utterly irreconcilable with the theory that the administrators of such a government can resort to their own judgment of public necessity, and act contrary to that supreme law, and that good citizenship requires the people to acquiesce in that judgment. They who set up such a claim for our rulers claim for them an entirely irresponsible power. We are required, for example, to believe that what are called "arbitrary arrests" are necessary, but no one explains to us the grounds of that necessity. No account is rendered. We are to *assume* the existence of causes of justification, but no one tells us what those causes are. They may remain forever locked in the bosoms of those who do the acts of which we complain. Why should American citizens, filling high places of public trust, act upon such a principle as this? Can any thing be more degrading, more injurious to the public conscience of a people, than to form a habit of implicit belief in the existence of necessities which nobody explains, and of which nobody is required to give an account? You may hear a hundred men in a day, speaking of some particular case of this kind, profess its necessity; and not one man in the whole hundred can tell you what the necessity was.

My friends, these false theories of loyalty—for false I must deem them—are infusing into our national character a fatal poison. They are leading those who cherish them to impute factious and interested motives to all pure and manly efforts in defense of the principles of civil liberty. They who indulge in this dangerous work of deriding the defenders of constitutional rights, can have but a very inadequate conception of the convulsions that must precede the final loss of those rights. They take but a very superficial view of the depth of those feelings which lead men in all free countries to resist every form of mere arbitrary power. They make no account of the principles implanted in our breasts, and cherished into dictates of nature by generations of training in the practice of liberty; those principles on which depends the primary office of an opposition in a free government, and by means of which all constitutional rulers are restrained from abuses of power. Impatient of those restraints, such persons rush to methods which can not be employed without undermining the foundations of liberty; and for a supposed temporary advantage barter away the strength and the supports, the vigor and the health of the body politic. This has been in all ages the downward course of nations, who have substituted for free institutions and systems of fundamental law a blind and unquestioning faith in public necessities, and have then welcomed some despotic power. Thus did the Roman Empire succeed the Republic, and thus we may be preparing ourselves for a like destiny. Let us be warned in time.

I have endeavored to state with due precision and fairness one very important part of the conditions of a true loyalty. But I should leave this subject in an imperfect state, if I omitted, on the other hand, to give equal prominence to certain principles of our political system which limit the mode in which States and individuals are to exercise their constitutional rights of opposition to the measures of the Federal Government. I have briefly adverted to this already; but a more extended statement of the principle is necessary.

I will assume then that a measure, having all the forms of law, is believed upon good grounds to be a violation of the constitutional rights of States and individuals. What is the rule of action under such circumstances? There is no difficulty whatever in finding the answer. By the establishment of a judicial system within the Federal Constitution, having ultimate cognizance of all cases arising under that Constitution, *one* mode is provided by which both States and individuals can ascertain whether their reserved rights are invaded by the Federal authorities.

This remedy is at all times open; and there is no valid reason why a State should forcibly assert its constitutional rights, any more than that an individual should do the same thing. While a State remains a member of the Union, it is bound to vindicate its constitutional rights and powers in that mode which is consistent with the preservation of that Union; and it can at any time, under any supposed violation of its rights or the rights of its people, make a case for judicial determination. Forcible resistance is open revolution; and nothing but an intolerable oppression, cutting off all judicial remedy, can make revolution a necessity and a duty.

Again:—there is another equally good reason, which shows that no popular tumults, and no forcible resistance, are either legally or morally justifiable, while the ballot-box remains untouched. If the people of a State have reason to believe that measures of the Federal Government are subversive of the Constitution, it is their right and their duty to correct the evil by a change of their rulers. In cases of supposed extensive violations of the Constitution, to which the attention of the whole country is called, the remedy of elections is ordinarily sufficient to reverse, and is in our system held to reverse, erroneous constructions of that instrument, as well as errors of policy. The popular tribunal may not be quite so precise in its action as the judicial; but there can be no mistaking the judgment of the people, when it is pronounced upon an issue clearly made with an Administration which is charged with infringing the Constitution.

These principles no one, I presume, will be inclined to dispute. But there is thrust in, to intercept their application to the present crisis in our affairs, a doctrine which I for one distinctly repudiate. That doctrine is, in substance, that *all* questioning of the measures of the Administration should be postponed while we are in a civil war; that there should be but one party; and that all should rally in an "*unconditional support* of the constituted authorities." This dogma needs examination. If by an unconditional support of the constituted authorities, it is intended to claim that we must all recognize the fact that we are engaged in a civil war, and that we must conduct it, while it lasts, *through* those authorities, and must hold no irregular intercourse with the public enemy, I readily accede to the proposition. But if it is meant that we are not to question the *methods* which the Administration pursue in the prosecution of the war; that we have no rightful control over their *measures;* or that we are to refrain from demanding a change of their *policy*—I reject the doctrine without the slightest hesitation. The very issue which you make with the Administration of itself refutes that doctrine. That issue is, that their course of action subverts the Constitution; makes the war an attack upon the social system of the South; and renders it impossible to succeed in that war, without destroying, for the South and for the North, the whole principle of State sovereignty on which the Union was necessarily founded as *one* of its corner-stones. It is in vain to say that the acts of the Administration, of which you complain, are *military* measures. In every civil war there are political considerations which must qualify the military action, or that action can result only in disaster. A government that undertakes to suppress a great revolt of powerful and organized communities, at the same time furnishing the strongest of moral motives for resistance, is in the same situation as he who fights his enemy with one hand and supplies him through the other with the munitions of war. In the present case we have made the conquest one of infinite difficulty, by first declaring that we waged the war solely for the supremacy of the Constitution, and then turning round and making the overthrow of the Constitution a too probable result of our success.

This result will not be confined to the condition of the revolted States, if the war continues to be prosecuted as it has been for the last six months. You can not acquiesce in the measures of the Administration, involving, as they do, the exercise of many powers that lie wholly outside of the Constitution, without leaving this country hereafter to be ruled by powers that will rest upon nothing but what the judgment of a party, or a faction, or a clique, shall deem to be public necessities. In this aspect of our affairs I can not avoid a word of earnest appeal to all reflecting men, to consider what fate must attend the securities of property, as well as the rights of person, if we permit the Constitution to be lost.

There are five great securities of property, the continuance of which in this country is dependent on the preservation of the Constitution of the United States. Let me enumerate them. They are:

1. A uniform metallic currency, as the basis and standard of all values.

2. The power to establish a uniform system of bankruptcies, whenever the interests of commerce require it.

3. The inviolability of contracts by State Legislatures.

4. The provision which places property under the protection of the Constitution, as against Federal power, so that no man can be deprived of it without legal process.

5. The prohibition which restrains the Federal power of *eminent domain*, so that private property can not be taken for public use without just compensation.

Now no rational being can suppose that these guaranties can be extorted anew from that centralized despotism which is but too likely to be the only successor that the Constitution of the United States can ever have. I care not what ideas men may form of that "stronger government," which some allow themselves to wish for in the place of our present system. My reason and my instincts both teach me that that government will be an unchecked and uncontrolled despotism; and we need not look far for the signs of its approach. Consciously or unconsciously, there are many agencies at work to promote its advent; one of the most potent of them is the false doctrine of "loyalty," against which I contend, and another is the perilous idea that you can safely trifle with a fixed constitution. We have made such vast strides towards a system entirely unknown to the Federal Constitution, that we can now see the nature of the only power that will ever replace it. When that power has fully come, the present securities of property will have been swept away with the securities of person. Both will disappear with the Federal Constitution; and we shall never extort them as concessions from the new power, or place them beyond reach, if we can extort them. There are no Barons on this our American earth to make a new *Magna Charta;* our race will never see another Runnymede; and *we* shall never see another Washington, another Madison, another Hamilton, another Jay, another Patrick Henry, another Samuel Adams. Even the States, with their separate constitutions, their bills of rights, and their present capacity to protect their people, will fall beneath the new and unchecked power to which the nation will surrender itself, when it cuts aloof from the Federal Constitution; and if they should not, every intelligent man, who has had much to do with accumulation, knows, or should know, that property, deprived of the supports which it derives from the Federal Constitutional system, can maintain but a feeble and precarious existence. We must remember that long, long centuries ago—in a state of society in one sense rude, but when the manly virtues of our ancestors gave them a historic splendor that we can only reflect, it providentially happened that the rights of property and the rights of person were indissolubly blended in one immortal maxim, that was laid, for all time, at the basis of the civilization of our race. Whatever may happen in other civilizations, or in other climes, Liberty and Property for us must flourish or perish TOGETHER.

My friends, it is time that the warfare upon opinion, and thought, and speech, should cease. It is time we had ascertained that our national difficulties can never be cured without the action of the people. It is time we had exploded the fallacy that patriotism and party are incompatible in any conceivable circumstances of our country. You, at any rate, let me hope, reject this dogma as a delusion; for in all the gloom of the present, in all the dark uncertainties of the future, I put my hopes in the great Democracy of the Union. I see nothing else to which we can look. I see you, it is true, occasionally distracted by the tactics of your opponents, occasionally disturbed by the indiscretion of friends. But I also see you animated by a patriotism which I fully believe will guide you aright, and which, in spite of all that men may say of you, commands my respect and confidence. Permit me then, with such freedom as may be taken by one who neither has nor seeks any special place in your organization, to offer you a word of friendly counsel.

What you need, as it seems to me, is to be fully impressed with a belief in your mission and in your capacity to fulfill it. That mission is to save the Constitution of the United States. By saving it, I mean of course that you are to save it for the whole Union, for the South and the North, for the East and the West, with every right which it protects completely reëstablished. I can see no other mode of saving it; for it is to my mind apparent, that a war prosecuted against the South for the acquisition of powers over their domestic institutions which the Constitution expressly withholds from the Federal Government, can result in nothing but the establishment of a system under which there can be no local rights of self-government left for any section or any State. This it is your mission to prevent. You can not prevent it, by uniting with those who proffer support of the war without the slightest protest against the unconstitutional policy with which it is prosecuted. In all the late popular proceedings looking to the establishment of what are styled "Loyal Leagues," I have not seen one word of indignant remonstrance against the unconstitutional measures of the Administration. You can not expect, and need not look for such remonstrance from assemblies largely composed of those who are the peculiar political supporters of the Administration, and who are more or less responsible for its measures. Public opinion, if it is to make itself *heard* and *felt* against all violations of the Constitution, must make its utterances through the action and the voice of those who have never failed to protest against the policy that has created for us so much peril. If that public opinion fails to recognize this necessary channel of expression — if it yields itself to a fatal apathy, or *will* not see how it can at once save a Government and change an Administration — then all will be lost, and there will remain to us only the consolation that we have individually done our duty.

You are then, permit me to add, to seek by every constitutional and upright method, to obtain the control of all the organisms of government. If in the mean time you can not induce the present Executive of the United States to change his policy, then, remembering his position, possess your souls in patience until you can give him a constitutional successor. Let every thing be prepared with one fixed and unselfish purpose: namely, to make every successive election reverse the doctrines and dogmas and usurpations which you know you should condemn. By this course of action, instead of weakening, you will strengthen your Government; for you will make it apparent to the whole world that the present arbitrary rule is to be succeeded by a period when the Constitution is once more, in all its beneficence and all its power, to be "THE SUPREME LAW OF THE LAND." Fail to do this, and the nation, losing heart and hope, will lose sight of the methods by which a constitutional succession can be preserved to a better day; and will yield itself to the despair which welcomes despotism, or to the rage which welcomes anarchy.

I know the difficulties of your position; but you must not falter, and you must not admit that you can fail. High virtues are demanded of you. You must live down slander, you must despise obloquy, you must watch your own motives, you must chasten your own spirits, you must

> ——"stretch every nerve
> And press with vigor on"

to the salvation of your country. You must win public confidence by your purity; you must challenge public respect by your intelligence. Above all, and before all, without one instant's hesitation, without pleading one solitary excuse, you must be true to the principles of civil liberty. You must learn that those principles are no chance production of the "piping times of peace," but that they are the rules which in all times of tranquillity and all times of commotion have been evolved out of the wisdom of ages, to save us from the mad thirst for arbitrary power that has again and again seized upon highly civilized nations, and destroyed the hopes of mankind.

Preparing yourselves in this way for the great task that is before you, you will be able to approach the difficult problem of this war with a firm and fearless step. You will see that this problem presents to you the alternatives of consenting to a dismemberment of the country, or of preventing that dismemberment by a reversal of the popular and governmental action which has made it so nearly an accomplished fact. You will soon hear it said, by those who have urged on the war upon this most disastrous policy, that it is too late now; that the breach can never be closed; that the South must be permitted to go in peace. Just here, then, precisely here, before all is given up to the control of the extremists North and South, YOU must interpose. You have a right to have other measures and other counsels tried. You are numerically a majority in at least four of the largest States in the Union. You may rightfully demand that the Constitution, with all its guarantees, be tendered to the revolted States; and you may rightfully do all that can assure the people of the South of its protection, without calling upon your government to change its *military* attitude. I know well enough the insidious answer that is made to this suggestion; how confidently we are told that the South would reject your offer with scorn. But I tell you that history has never seen a case of war, foreign or civil, in which a nation could absolve itself from the moral responsibility of doing right, by asserting beforehand that it knew its adversary would do wrong. The elements of a moral judgment do not exist in advance of such an offer, either in the controversies of nations or in the controversies of individuals. Whatever others may think, or say, or do, you, I trust, will act upon a principle which I am persuaded rests upon a moral foundation that no sophistry and no casuistry can successfully assail. If, after such an offer, the war must still be carried on, no language can overstate the advantage that would be gained in the vigor of it's prosecution.

And here, gentlemen, I close. One path of duty is clearly open before us. I can see no other now. Sufficient unto the day is the evil, sufficient unto the day is the duty thereof. He who does that one duty in a firm and humble faith in the providence of God, prepares himself for a clear perception of the next that may arise in the future.

6*

State of New York.

COMMUNICATION

FROM

MAJOR GENERAL DIX,

RELATIVE TO THE ARREST

OF

HAWLEY D. CLAPP.

TRANSMITTED TO THE LEGISLATURE APRIL 13, 1864.

ALBANY:
COMSTOCK & CASSIDY, PRINTERS.
1864.

State of New York.

No. 93.

IN SENATE,

April 13, 1864.

COMMUNICATION

FROM MAJOR GENERAL DIX, RELATIVE TO THE ARREST OF HAWLEY D. CLAPP.

HEADQUARTERS, DEPARTMENT OF THE EAST,
NEW YORK CITY, *April* 11, 1864.

Hon. CHARLES J. FOLGER, *Chairman:*

Sir—Your note of the 9th, inst., was received yesterday, and it affords me pleasure to furnish you with the facts and circumstances attending the arrest and imprisonment of Hawley D. Clapp.

When your note came to hand, I was completing a report to the Secretary of War, (a copy of which, with accompanying papers, I inclose) giving a detailed statement of the atrocious frauds committed upon recruits in this city, and particularly at Lafayette Hall, where Mr. Clapp was the principal bounty-broker, one of a class of agents, who were brought into existence by the system adopted by the committee of the board of supervisors, for procuring recruits, whose services were entirely unnecessary, and whose principal vocation, either by their own direct action or through confederates, was to cheat men entering the service, out of their bounties. The committee, when the frauds had become too palpable and too extensive to be borne, obviated the evil, as far as they could, by the adoption of proper precautions, but not until a military order had been issued, requiring the full amount of bounty to be paid to the recruit.

My report to the Secretary of War, enters into a full detail of these transactions, alike disgraceful to those who were concerned in them, and to the community in the bosom of which they occurred. Mr. Clapp received from the committee of the supervisors, the bounties for a large number of recruits, ($300 each) who, as shown by testimony satisfactory to me, were cheated out of the greater part of it, by him, or the parties confederated with him in the business. As the money was paid into his hands, I consider him responsible for it; and I have deemed it my duty, whenever a clear case of fraud was made out, to see the soldier redressed, if possible.

It is only by the summary process of a military arrest, that these fraudulent transactions can be reached. If they are brought into the civil courts, all remedy is hopeless. The recruits are the only witnesses, and the exigencies of the country will not permit them to be kept from the field.

The only alternatives, therefore, were to allow these stupendous frauds to go unredressed, to let the patriotic men, who are offering their lives on the altar of their country, be robbed of the provision which their fellow citizens have made for their families, and to suffer the plunderers to escape with their ill-gotten gains, or to take, as I have done, some of the principal agents in these frauds into custody, to be held till they make restitution.

The amount of which recruits were defrauded at Lafayette Hall, where and while Mr. Clapp was chief broker, cannot fall short of $400,000. I have succeeded in recovering about $20,000, and am not without hope of adding largely to the amount.

I am fully aware of the responsibility I have taken in these cases, and that the exercise of the power of arrest is only warranted by the circumstances in which the country is placed, and the special facts which my report to the Secretary of War discloses. It has been exerted in a few cases only, and with the confident assurance in each, that I should be sustained by the Government, and by the public judgment.

Although it is technically true, as Mr. Clapp states in his petition to the Legislature, that "he has not held at any time office under the Government, or had any contracts with the Government" itself, he stood in his capacity as bounty broker, in relation to the military service, of which he seems to appreciate neither the scope nor the force. Lafayette Hall, in which his agency was transacted, was occupied for military purposes; it was guarded by sentinels, and the acts for which he was arrested, were performed within the lines; it was, for all essential purposes, a camp, and he was within it, furnished with office room and other conveniences for himself and clerks, and engaged in paying recruits their bounties as chief broker, under an appointment, not directly from the Government, but from General Spinola, the commanding officer. He was personally engaged in services of a strictly military character, and standing in a much nearer relation to the Government than many classes of camp followers and retainers, who are by act of Congress, subject to martial law. My own judgment is strongly inclined to the conclusion, that he may be tried by court martial; and if he has not been brought before one ere this, one chief reason is, that I desired to satisfy myself by consulting the course of proceedings in analogous cases, that I should not err in holding him to account before such a tribunal for the acts with which he is charged.

Almost every imaginable form of outrage and deception has been developed in the cases, in which Mr. Clapp was agent for the payment of bounties. Men, both white and colored, were offered employment as teamsters, wagon-masters and officers' servants, receiving from $20 to $50, as "pay in advance," and finding themselves enlisted as private soldiers, while Mr. Clapp received from $300 to $315, in each case. With what confederates the money was divided, he and they only can tell.

I have considered it enough that it was received by him, and not paid to the recruits, who were entitled to it. In some cases, boys have been seduced from their homes to secure their enlistment; in others, men have been drugged, and enlisted while unconscious; in others, they have been promised furloughs, and, where the full bounty was not paid, they have been told, that they would receive the balance, as soon as they arrived at Riker's Island. In short, there is no artifice or fraud which has not been resorted to, in carrying out this system of pillage. In one case reported to these headquarters, by Mr. Supervisor Blunt, Mr. Clapp was compelled to make restitution, and his conduct was such that he was not allowed to transact business with the supervisors in his own name, but continued it in the name of other parties.

I feel convinced that no class of men would be likely to take part in these outrages upon our gallant soldiers, or sympathize with the perpetrators, unless they cherished a secret sympathy with those who are endeavoring, by force of arms, to overthrow and destroy the government of their country.

Mr. Clapp has been treated since his confinement, with a leniency he does not deserve. He has had the same food as the men whom he has defrauded, and is much more comfortably lodged and sheltered. His counsel has been permitted to hold two private interviews with him, a privilege not usually granted to the inmates of Fort Lafayette. I have indulged the hope that he would consent to disclose the names of others, more prominent than himself, who are believed to have participated in his fraudulent gains. He is not held for this purpose alone, but with the further view to compel complete restitution to those he has wronged, when the extent of the frauds in which he is implicated, shall be ascertained, and also for trial and punishment, if it shall be decided that he is amenable to a military court. It has afforded me pleasure to comply with the request of your committee, and I earnestly hope that the disclosures I have made, may lead to some legislative provision to secure to recruits, the bounties intended to be paid to them. I take the liberty of stating, that in some instances, the authorities of towns have, of the $300 raised for bounties, voted $100 to the recruit, and $200 to the broker or runner; a temptation to cupidity, which has led to every species of unfairness, deception and fraud.

I am satisfied that the Legislature could never have anticipated so gross a wrong to recruits, to tax payers and the public service, and that suitable restraints will be imposed upon local authorities.

I have the honor also to transmit herewith, a certified copy of the order under which Mr. Clapp was sent to Fort Lafayette, by Brig. Gen'l Stannard, commanding New York city and harbor.

I am very respectfully, your obedient servant,

JOHN A. DIX, *Major General.*

HEADQUARTERS, DEPARTMENT OF THE EAST,
NEW YORK CITY, *April*, 1864.

Hon. E. M. STANTON,
Secretary of War, Washington, D. C.:

Sir—On the 2d of January, I addressed a communication to you in regard to recruiting frauds, and enclosed a copy of another which I addressed on the same day to Col. Fry, Provost Marshal General.

When I was informed that recruits were defrauded of their bounties at Lafayette Hall, I sent for General Spinola and communicated to him the information I had received. He denied the truth of the statements, and assured me that the recruiting regulations were fully complied with; that no man was enlisted without being fully apprised of the nature of the service in which he was engaging; that no recruit was defrauded of his bounty, and that where a less sum than that allowed by the county was paid, it was always by voluntary and amicable agreement with the broker. I had no authority, as commander of the department, to interfere with the recruiting service; but the repetition of the complaints of fraud became so frequent, that I felt it my duty to interpose, so far as to ascertain what ground there was for them. Besides the wrong to recruits in defrauding them of their bounty, I found that men were induced to enlist by false representations from the broker, through whom they were presented, and that persons physically disqualified for military duty were mustered into the service in great numbers. Old men, boys and persons laboring under incurable diseases were, in numerous instances, thrust into the service under this system of public plunder, alike fraudulent to the recruits and the government.

I sent for General Spinola several times, and always received from him the assurance that all was fairly conducted by the officers at Lafayette Hall. The evidence to the contrary became so conclusive, that I directed Lieut. Cole and the contract surgeon, Dr. Kerrigan, to be arrested. They have since been tried; the former dismissed the service, and the latter, who holds no military commission, disqualified for future employment. In my interviews with General Spinola, I objected to the whole system of brokerage, as calculated to prevent instead of promoting enlistments. It was my opinion that public complaints of fraud in the payment of bounties, would in many cases deter men from presenting themselves as voluteers, and that the ranks of the army would be filled with recruits who, feeling that the Government had permitted them to be cheated by its own officers, would be very apt to consider themselves released from their engagements, and would not hesitate to desert at the first opportunity.

General Spinola defended the system of brokerage, and said that without it the Government would get no recruits. The result has been precisely the reverse. Since measures have been taken to secure the recruits the whole bounty to which they are entitled, the number of enlistments has been greatly augmented, and a better class of men secured. See letters from Gen. Jackson and Capt. Shannon, A. A. G., marked "A" and "B."

The bounty, in the payment of which these frauds have been committed, is that paid by the city and county of New York, amounting to $300 per man with a fee of $15 to the person presenting the recruit, in case the recruit be white. About 2,000 men were recruited by General Spinola before he was relieved from the recruiting service. The average amount of bounty paid to them, as he stated in an explanation volunteered to one of my staff officers, (see letter of Major Halpine, A. A. G., marked, "Exhibit C") and as further examinations showed, was about $100 per man. The other $200 per man, has been plundered by brokers and their coadjutors. Of the $600,000 which should have been paid to these recruits, they only received about $200,000, and the enormous sum of $400,000 has been plundered by brokers and their associates.

It is one of the most stupendous frauds ever committed in this country. The funds from which the bounties were intended to be paid, were raised on securities which are a lien upon the property of the city. The bounty was intended to go to the recruit as an inducement to him to expose his life in upholding the Government against treason, and as a provision for his family. It has gone for the most part into the hands of public plunderers, some of whom are of notoriously infamous character, and one of whom is known to be a liberated convict, who has been an inmate of the States prison. Among the men engaged in these frauds was Theodore Allen, who was brought to my headquarters and refunded $200 taken by him from a recruit. Other cases of fraud committed by him were subsequently brought to my notice, and orders for his arrest were given, but he has eluded the pursuit of the officers of justice. I annex a letter from the superintendent of the police, (marked "Exhibit D") stating that he "has been known to the police of the city for at least ten years," that "his reputation in the force is that of a thief;" and that he kept "a gambling house before engaging in the substitute broker business." This man swears that "he was well known to Mr. Brennan, the comptroller, and to the supervisors," and that, "through the friendship of the comptroller, and at his suggestion, and with the approval of the supervisors, these enlistment blanks, thus countersigned (see next paragraph) were given by the supervisors in person to deponent (Allen.) This man may be regarded, in his leading characteristics portrayed by the superintendent of police, as a type of the group of depredators who were engaged in plundering recruits.

The system inaugurated by the committee of the board of supervisors was, unfortunately, well calculated to give effect to these frauds. Papers were issued in blank and authenticated by the signature of one of the committee, and it was only on the return of these papers, in each case, that the bounty was paid. It was paid by them to the broker, and not to the recruit. The papers were given only to a limited number of persons, so that the business of furnishing recruits and of plundering them of their bounties was, to a great extent, a monopoly. I called the attention of the chairman of the committee of the board, at an early day, to the mischievous consequences of this system, and the committee subsequently remedied it by requiring the broker, or holder of the paper, before paying him the bounty, to produce a certificate of a mustering officer that it had all been paid to the recruit; but the old practice was continued without redress, until the enormous sum I have mentioned was obtained, through deception and fraud, by the holders of these papers, which were, in effect, drafts at sight on the supervisors; and so valuable were they considered, that they were in many cases, sold at a premium of from $25 to $75 by the first holders, the purchasers relying on his ability to cheat the recruit out of a sufficient sum to repay the premium, and make a handsome profit for himself.

General Spinola, while defending the conduct of his officers, and asserting the salutary working of the system of brokerage, requested me to send some of my staff to Lafayette Hall, to see in what manner the business of recruiting was conducted. Several of them were sent by me at different times, and it was on their statements that Lieutant Cole and Doctor Kerrigan were arrested and brought to trial: See statement of Captain Rives, A. D. C., herewith transmitted, marked "Exhibit E." The officials by whom this system of fraud was continued, after they were cognizant of the frauds committed, and who permitted it to go on without interposing their authority to arrest it, must be held, under my view of the subject, as participators in the wrong, even though they may have derived no pecuniary benefit from it. The whole system is a stain upon the community in which it has been tolerated, and the disgrace can only be removed by the most determined and persevering efforts, not only to bring to punishment all concerned in it, but for recover to the gallant men who are exposing their lives in the field, to preserve the existence of the government, the money of which they have been defrauded by heartless villains, who have neither the virtue nor the courage to sustain the country against its enemies, but who make a mercenary and criminal profit by plundering its defenders.

I have not hesitated, when these frauds have been clearly proved, to arrest the perpetrators, and to hold them in custody until they have repaid the amounts they have fraudulently obtained, satisfied that I should be supported in so doing, by the Government and the public judgment. I have recovered and paid over to the parties defrauded, or deposited in bank until their orders for payment can be obtained, about $20,000. I hope to secure a much larger amount; and I desire to acknowledge the very efficient aid I have received from Marshal Murray and his deputies, in arresting the criminal authors of these frauds and compelling restitution.

I found in numerous instances, that the brokers have made written contracts with recruits, to enlist for sums less than the bounty allowed by the city and county. I have treated all such contracts as void, for want of consideration; and in nearly every case, an investigation has shown that they were obtained by false representations.

The outrages practiced on recruits are too intolerable to be borne with equanimity, and in some cases, too loathsome to be detailed.

Boys have been seduced from their families, enticed into oyster houses, drugged, and then enlisted in a state of semi-unconciousness. Two were so badly drugged that they died, one, the very night of their arrival at Riker's Island, and the other on the following day. I have taken, in some of the worst cases, the responsibility of discharging these boys, where subsequent medical examinations showed them to be unfit for active service, requiring them to refund all the bounty left in their hands by the plunderers. It is deeply to be regretted that in nearly every instance the latter succeeded in eluding detection.

The brokers and runners have frequently, in order to facilitate their schemes of depredation, put on the uniform of the army, representing themselves as officers authorized to enlist recruits, promising them furloughs after their enlistment, and inducing them to leave the greater part, sometimes nearly the whole, of the bounty in their hands. In such cases, I have not only compelled them to repay the moneys thus fraudently obtained, but taking them at their own word as members of the army and requiring them to produce their commissions, and their authority to recruit, I have, on their failure to sustain the assumed character, sent them to the forts as *prima facie* deserters.

These stringent measures have nearly broken up this whole system of fraudulent recruiting. But a great wrong has been done to individuals and the service, and it is impossible, wholly, to repair it. I shall, nevertheless, persevere in my efforts to discover all the guilty parties, and to compel restitution wherever the evidence is sufficiently clear to warrant the exercise of the requisite authority.

I have the honor to be, very respectfully,

Your obedient servant,

(Signed,) JOHN A. DIX,

Maj. Gen. Commanding.

Official copy.

CHAS. G. HALPINE, *Major and Asst. Adjt. Gen.*

HEADQUARTERS, DEPARTMENT OF THE EAST,
NEW YORK, *February* , 1864.

Brigadier General JAMES B. FRY,
Provost Marshal General, Washington, D. C.:

Sir—In reply to your communication of February 8th, I have the honor to state the following in relation to the recruiting in this city, at Lafayette Hall, under the superintendence of Brig. Gen. F. B. Spinola, U. S. Vols.

In the latter part of November, a great many complaints were made to Major General Dix, in reference to the manner in which enlistments were made. These complainants were generally the father, mother, sister, brother, or some near relation, and in the case of negroes, their employers. They stated that the recruits had been swindled out of nearly all of their bounties by brokers, who carried on their business openly at Lafayette Hall; that these brokers would tell the recruits that they would give them the remainder of their bounties when they arrived at Riker's Island, but in no instance did the recruits receive it.

In some case negroes were taken there with the understanding that they were to be hired as hostlers to take care of some gentleman's horse. Such was the case of Anthony Riker, William *alias* Joseph White, Evart D. Keaton, (cases before a general court martial for the trial of Lieut. Cole, the mustering officer,) and many others. The affidavits in the cases have been sent to the War Department. In all these cases (Riker, White and Keaton), they testified that they were taken to Lafayette Hall to become hostlers, and not for the purpose of becoming soldiers. That in the case of Riker, he was promised $25 a month; he signed his name to some papers which he thought was the contract; that he was not sworn into the service of the United States; and had no idea he was a soldier until he started to go away, when the guard stopped him. They (brokers) gave him but $14. The cases of White and Keaton are the same. The mustering officer did not explain anything to them. On the 28th of November, Vincent Ruelland, a sailor of the French corvette "Tissiphone," then lying in the harbor of New York, was drugged by them, and taken to Lafayette Hall, and, while drunk, was enlisted. On the 27th November, L'Hote and Angel, sailors, of the same vessel, were made drunk, and taken by brokers to Lafayette Hall, and enlisted. These men could not speak a word of English, and were so drunk that they could hardly stand, and their signatures to their enlistment papers will prove conclusively that they were drunk. They were in almost full uniform. After this happened, complaints were made to us by the French Consul in this city. I was sent by General Dix to go to Lafayette Hall, and see how they done business. I went, I think, on or about the last of November 29th, perhaps 30th. I was in citizen's dress, for I did not wish them to know me. I saw a great crowd of brokers, who seemed to have full sway. A few days after this I went there again, but as soon as I had entered the room I heard some one screaming. I went immediately to the place from whence it proceeded, which was near the desks where the mustering was going on, I found there a negro boy about 18 to 20 years of age, being held by some men dressed in uniform and whom I took to be guards. I had already received complaints of men being enlisted there against their will, and took this to be one of the same. I considered it my duty to throw off all disguise, and prevent it if such was the case. I went to the soldiers who were holding him and asked what they were doing to the boy. They said it was none of my business. I then told them who I was, and ordered them to let the negro loose. I then asked the negro what they were going to do with him; he said that they were trying to make him enlist as a soldier, and that he did not wish to be one. I then told an officer who was present, (I do not know his name,) and I thought on duty, to have the negro sent away, which he did. No one paid any attention to this, for by the way they acted it seemed to be a common occurrence. The screams of the negro could be easily heard on the street. I left immediately and reported the fact to head quarters. I testified to all this on the court martial in the case of Lieut. Cole. He brought General Spinola and Captain Hanley, A. A. general of his staff to testify that they remembered this circumstance, and they testified that it took place in the latter part of December, certainly after the 24th. I testified that it took place before the 11th of December, and I thought about three or four days after my first visit. I did not see General Spinola on this occasion, as he said I did. I remember the case which he refers to, but but it was a different one from which I testified to.

At another time, I do not remember the day of the month, but was in December, (I took note of this with the names and day of the month,) I saw General Spinola, in person, swear a recruit who was so much under the influence of liquor that he could hardly stand. I saw the man's condition before he was sworn in, and kept back so I would see if they would swear him in that condition; and as soon as I saw General Spinola swearing him in (in person), I went up close, (he did not see me), and heard all that was said. The man was not asked if he wanted to be a soldier; his hand was held up while the oath was being read, but he made no reply to it for his condition was such that he could not understand. I said nothing to General Spinola in reference to this. On the same day I saw a person on the bench about 17 to 19 years of age, who was about five feet high. When the papers were brought up, enlistment papers, the boy's height was put down, as General Spinola said, as five feet two inches. He ordered the orderly to have the boy measured again. I went and saw him measured without General Spinola seeing The boy measured four feet ten and a half inches, and he moved his head easily under this measure. He was then taken back to General Spinola, and the man said he measured about five feet two. General Spinola said put him down five feet three, I reckon he is that. The mustering officer would ask the recruit in some case, "are you satisfied with your bounty that you have?" and they would say yes, for the brokers told them that they were entitled to only so much, and the mustering officer did not tell them as a general thing how much they were entitled to, but simply asked the question "have you received your bounty and are you satisfied with it ?" The negroes who were going as hostlers, did not know what this meant. I spoke to General Spinola on several occasions in reference to this. He said he did not care whether a recruit received a cent or not, and he would take a man if he did not get a cent. Hawley D. Clapp had a man in Lafayette Hall to cash the assignment papers of the brokers. This man had a clerk, and I did not know until some time after my first visit, that this man (C. B. Ellsworth), was not employed by the Government to pay bounties. This man testified in the court that he was employed by Hawley D. Clapp to cash these papers.

Patrick Burns testified that Hawley D. Clapp made from $25 to $50 off of each recruit's papers, on an average about $50, and that the brokers made $100; such is not the case, for all the affidavits will show that they made almost $200, and in some cases 320 odd dollars. Anthony Riker only received $14; Joseph White (alias William), $40; Vincent Ruelland $1 (one); Charles S. Rone (Rosey), $40; Evart D. Keaton $25, and John Santo none. Santo belongs to the 10th U. S. infantry, (a musician); he had a furlough, came to New York from his regiment at Fort Lafayette, was made drunk by some runner, taken to Lafayette Hall, and was enlisted. He had his furlough in his pocket. He does not recollect anything from the time that he was made drunk until he found himself on Riker's island, two days afterwards. All the affidavits will prove that the recruits as a general thing receive but about fifty dollars, and that the brokers were always encouraged. The brokers would tell the men (recruits), that they would pay them the remainder as soon as mustered. All the mustering officers and General Spinola knew of this swindling, for the name of Lafayette Hall and its swindling, was a byword in the mouth of every one. General Spinola was present during the day from 12 M. until night. He saw drunken men daily in the hall, and on the eve of being mustered. Yet these men were never sent away, but were mustered. I know of several cases where he saw me, and sent the drunken men away, yet I never saw a case where a man was not mustered because he was drunk, unless some of the officers of Lafayette Hall saw me there. I noticed this fact in particular. I have seen many men mustered who were under the influence of liquor. When I was there in disguise, for the first three or four times and before my face was familiar, to see drunken men awaiting to be mustered was anything but common. But when my face was known the men would be hurried out and kept there until I left, and I suppose they were then brought back and mustered. I never saw the men (recruits), questioned properly; thy were intimidated by the brokers, and the brokers were assisted in this by the various officers at Lafayette Hall. P. B. Marsh (late detective to Brig. Gen. Hays), testified that he went to see General Spinola in the case of Vincent Ruelland. He asked him (General Spinola), if it was not the duty of the mustering officer, when the party (recruit), could not read, to read the enlistment papers to him, that he (recruit), might know what he was signing. General said, "Damn it, if we did that we could not recruit twenty men a day." I (Marsh), then asked him how it was in the case of the French sailor, Ruelland, that could neither read, write or understand a word of English? he (Spinola), said "Oh, damn it, he signs his name." About the first part of January last, while passing along by the Metropolitan hotel, which is nearly opposite to Lafayette Hall, I saw a boy, apparently about eighteen years of age, coming down the street, (Broadway). He was seized by two runners, (one taking him by the feet and the other by the body,) who tried to carry him across to Lafayette Hall. They had got as far with him as the middle of the street, when his cries and screams attracted so many persons that the runners dropped him and ran into Lafayette Hall. Colonel Van Buren, Asst. Adj. General to the head-quarters, Dept. of the East, witnessed a similar occurrence in the passage way of Lafayette Hall, and made the parties release the man. The sentinel who was stationed at the door paid no attention to this, for the reason that it must have been a common thing. I have received complaints of parties (negroes), who were taken by force to Lafayette Hall and confined there under guard, and did not receive anything to eat until they consented to enlist as a soldier.

These complaints have been sent to the War Department in the form of affidavits.

Major Halpine, of General Dix's staff, has also made a statement which is enclosed. I also forward the letter of Mr. Schultz and detective Kelsy, which will give some information. I would suggest that Brig. Gen. Hays, provost marshal of New York, could, I think, give a great deal of information. The enlistments as carried on at Lafayette Hall, is in the mouths of every one, and with the information now before you I think that it will not require much thought as to who are the guilty parties.

I have the honor to be, sir, very respectfully,

Your obd't serv't,

(Signed,) WRIGHT RIVES,

Capt. and A. D. C.

Official copy.

CHAS. G. HALPINE, *Major and Asst. Adj. Gen.*

OFFICE OF SUPERINTENDENT OF THE METROPOLITAN POLICE,
300 MULBERRY STREET, NEW YORK, *Feb'y 17th*, 1864.

Major General JOHN A. DIX, New York:

Sir—In reply to your enquiry of yesterday I have to state, that the person Theodore Allen, has been known to the police of this city, for at least ten years; his reputation in the force is that of a thief, but he has never been convicted, although arrested and held several times. He was lieutenant in the 25th Regiment, N. Y. S. Vols., Col. Kerrigan, and served his time out. On his return he opened a gambling house in Greene street, and subsequently engaged in the substitute brokerage business.

Very respectfully yours,

(Signed,) JOHN A. KENNEDY,

Superintendent.

HEADQUARTERS, DEPARTMENT OF THE EAST,
April 12th, 1864.

A true copy.

D. T. VAN BUREN, *Col. and A. A. G.*

HEADQUARTERS, DEPARTMENT OF THE EAST,
NEW YORK CITY, *February 18th*, 1864.

To Major General JOHN A. DIX:

General—During the progress of the investigation as to the conduct of affairs at Lafayette Hall, made by me, under your instructions, I was waited upon by General Spinola, who volunteered a statement in explanation and vindication of the manner in which recruits had been enlisted at that place. This statement was volunteered on the part of General Spinola, and was by me deemed so important that I took down on paper, notes of its most important points, as he spoke, begging him to talk slowly and pause at the end of each sentence, until I had so recorded his words. Of that statement, in its more important features, the following is a synopsis.

General Spinola's Statement.

Bad as things are in New York, they are much worse in the New England States. My object is to fill my brigade, and without the help of the brokers this cannot be done. In New England, the towns, cities and counties take an assignment of the United States bounty and State bounty from the recruit, cash them, and give the whole to the brokers. They are not particular as to whom, or what class of men they take, their object being to fill up their quota. Thus a Mr. James Lee, a broker at Lafayette Hall, had three men rejected by my examining surgeon, whom he subsequently took east, and, on his return, told me that he had cleared $1,250 on them. In this manner recruits are taken away from New York at the rate of from 100 to 150 per diem. Not long ago a broker brought down from Dunkirk 28 men, and offered them at Lafayette Hall. On being told that (owing to investigations that were being made) he would have to pay the $300 county bounty into each man's hands, this broker replied: "I spent $1,200 and three weeks of my time getting them—how am I to get paid?" He then took them east and will, doubtless, receive for each of them a full county, State and United States bounty, somewhere between $700 and $800, less the sum of $125 per man, which they had agreed to take. These cases are of daily occurence. General Spinola knows of a case in Brooklyn, where a person, called Hand, had his son taken from him, only fifteen years of age. The broker took him to New Hampshire, and came home in a few days with $450, and the boy sent home $200. The General says that, he has cases every day where recruits refuse, peremptorily, to take more than $150, even when offered, and pressed to receive the whole amount. They say, "No, we have $150 and will receive $300 more on Riker's Island, and we do not want any more; we prefer to give away the balance." Had one case a few days ago in which a boy received $100 from the broker, the broker keeping $200 for himself. This boy wanted to pay him $50 more, only leaving himself $50. He was forcibly restrained from doing so by the officers in Lafayette Hall, but he rolled up a fifty dollar bill, and threw it over the railing to the broker, insisting that he wanted to give it to him. This boy while doing this was, in General Spinola's judgment, perfectly sober.

A gang of sharpers have enlisted, and are now on Riker's Island for gambling purposes, and they "skin" fellows of every cent they bring there. There is a great deal of gambling on Riker's Island.

General Spinola says that he tried hard, at first, to get the recruits paid by the supervisors' committee, but they were kept there all day, and sent away without their money; the offices were so far apart (*i. e.* Lafayette Hall from the county court rooms) that it would have taken a detail of 500 soldiers to carry the recruits to and fro.

General Spinola has seen Supervisor Orison Blunt advance, out of his own pocket, the money to start fresh volunteer brokers, taking their due bills for its payment. He has heard Blunt say, repeatedly, in the presence of Hawley D. Clapp, himself and others, that, "he did not care a damn if the recruit did not get $5; what he wanted was to fill the quota, and get rid of the damned draft." Blunt gives the papers, (see Appendix A and B) authorizing these brokerages to everybody, and anybody who will apply. They are printed certificates of muster, to be signed by the mustering officer, and an assignment of bounty to the broker, to be signed by the recruit. There is another assignment from the broker to Orison Blunt, who, on this latter document, draws money from the comptroller.

General Spinola has no doubt that very many payments have been made on forged papers by the county committee. It is easy. There is only one name to be really forged—that of the mustering officer, with whose signature it is impossible for Mr. Blunt, or those acting in his behalf, to be very well acquainted. The other signature upon the paper, that of the recruit, there is no means whatever of verifying.

It has also to General Spinola's knowledge been a common practice to change men between Lafayfette Hall and Riker's Island. The brokers present a man who is rejected, having all his papers, however, duly made out before presentation. They then send in a second, sound and healthy man, under the same name, have him passed by the doctor, and then between Lafayette

Hall and Riker's Island, by the connivance of the guard, or otherwise, substitute the rejected man for the sound man; and this has taken place repeatedly. He has now one case in which he knows this to have been done, and in which he is endeavoring to cause the arrest of the party engaged in the swindle.

The appointment of Hawley D. Clapp to be chief broker at Lafayette Hall took place in this way. When General Spinola found that the supervisors would not or could not pay the $300 county bounty to each recruit, he said to Mr. Clapp, "Here is a good thing," and gave to him and his clerks permission to have an office, with desks, tables, &c., in Lafayette Hall. Clapp only takes as his share, in each case, the $15 recruiting fee, as payment for the loan of the $300 until such time as he can get the assignment cashed by Mr. Blunt. Is of the opinion that the board of supervisors will insist upon its going on in just this way.

General Spinola says that he was not satisfied with the manner in which one of the doctors in Brooklyn did business; that he knows he was in the habit of signing certificates of physical fitness in blank, and allowing them to be filled up by his assistant; did not like this assistant; thought he was "on the make," and passed men for money paid by the brokers; he did not however arrest either the doctor or his assistant; has now at his house one of these certificates, signed in blank by this doctor; thinks that if the broker system be broken up that recruiting will come to a dead halt; claims that of the 2,000 men enlisted at Lafayette Hall, previous to this statement, they have averaged a receipt of $100 per man; thinks $200 for the broker not too much, as they have in some cases to bring the recruits from Canada, New England, Pennsylvania, Ohio, and elsewhere; is satisfied further that it is not for the good of recruits to have much money paid to them, as they will only buy whiskey with it and get intoxicated.

The General desires that I should see Brig. Gen. Nelson Taylor, Lieut. Col. Daniel Mann, and some other officers, who have been cognizant of the mode of doing business at Lafayette Hall, whom he would send to me. He expresses anxiety that this report should be fairly made, as, otherwise, it might injure his standing as an officer. If he has committed any errors they have arisen solely from his desire to fill up his brigade as rapidly as possible, in order that he might return to the field.

I have further to report, that I had interviews with Mr. Hawley D. Clapp, Captain Hanley, assistant adjutant general to General Spinola and mustering officer at Lafayette Hall, Lieut. Col. Daniel Mann, and several other officers detailed on recruiting service at Lafayette Hall, sent by General Spinola to offer their testimony.

In their statements there was, apparently, full corroboration of all of General Spinola's views in reference to the matter, but no new facts of sufficient importance to claim special attention.

I have the honor to be, General,

your obdt. servant,

CHAS. G. HALPINE,

Major and A. A. Gen.

HEADQUARTERS, DEPARTMENT OF THE EAST,
NEW YORK CITY, *February* 22, 1864.

Brig. Gen. G. I. STANNARD,
Commanding U. S. Troops N. Y. City and Harbor:

General—I am commanded by Major General John A. Dix to direct that you will take charge of Mr. Hawley D. Clapp, and confine him within Fort Lafayette, pending further orders from the War Department in his case.

The charges against Mr. Clapp go to show that he has been portion of a system by which thousands of recruits have been grossly and scandalously defrauded of their bounty money, at Lafayette Hall, and under which unfit men, drunken men, and men suffering under insensibility produced by opium, have been illegally sworn into the service of the United States, and then defrauded of their bounty.

I have the honor to be, General,

Your very obd't serv't,

(Signed,) CHAS. G. HALPINE,

Major and A. A. Gen.

P. S. By further command of General Dix, General Stannard will immediately place Mr. Hawley D. Clapp under charge of an officer, who will be responsible for his delivery at Fort Lafayette before sundown this evening. The officer in charge will allow Mr. Clapp to make such purchases as appear necessary, and also to visit his counsel, Mr. James M. Smith, in Chambers street, but to make no other visit.

Very obediently,

(Signed,) CHAS. G. HALPINE,
Maj. and A. A. Gen.

Official copy.
CHAS. G. HALPINE, *Maj. and A. A. Gen.*

HEADQUARTERS, DRAFT RENDEZVOUS,
RIKER'S ISLAND, N. Y. H., *Feb.* 29, 1864.

General—I have the honor to make the following statements concerning the affidavits of recruits, which have been taken at these headquarters during the past three months.

In the month of December there was a continual stream of complaints from the men relative to their bounties; some in the form of written communications, some verbal statements through their company and battalion commanders, and many through the provost marshal. At first these complaints were not much noticed, because it was not clear how the evil could be remedied here. The men appeared on the rolls as having been properly enlisted, and there was nothing beyond their own statements to show that they had not received the full bounty to which they were entitled. However, the complaints soon became so numerous that the practice of taking affidavits was begun, although with little expectation of recovering the bounties of which it was evident so many had been robbed.

The applicants to have their affidavits taken steadily increased in number, and a special clerical force was employed on this work. It is no exaggeration to say that the office was frequently thronged with recruits, anxiously waiting an opportunity to make their statements. Frequently civilians came to the island in search of relations that had been missed, and when found would bring them to the office, and solicit for them the privilege of making their statements. And, in this connection, the fact may be stated, as it indicates the kind of recruits that were being furnished there, that the father sought and found his missing son, and the son his missing father.

The tenor of these affidavits was generally the same, fraudulent enlistment of recruits, and little or no bounties paid them. The amount of treachery and baseness which they disclose seems almost incredible. Persons who supposed they were hiring themselves to a few months service as waiters, coachmen, sailors and mechanics, suddenly found themselves bound to a three years' term of military service. Many, who had been drugged, could tell nothing of their enlistment, and were wholly unable to account for the suit of blue in which they were clothed. Many received a small part of the $300 bounty, and were told that the remainder would be paid at Riker's island.

It is impossible to state the exact number of affidavits which have been taken, for the records contain notice only of those which were forwarded to the headquarters of Maj. General Dix and Brig. General Hays. Many affidavits were taken and forwarded by mail to the friends and relatives of the recruits, and in many cases delivered to them personally at the office. The number however is large, and may be safely stated at hundreds.

In the beginning the direct object of taking the affidavits was to recover the bounty; and, therefore, many cases were passed by as hopeless; for instance, cases where the recruit had no clear knowledge of the circumstances of his enlistment, and could give neither names nor localities; so that, the actual number of affidavits taken, even though reaching hundreds, can but partially show how great a wrong has been done.

I am, General, very respectfully,

Your obdt. servt.,

(Signed,) R. C. SHANNON,

Capt. and A. A. G.

Brig. Gen. N. J. JACKSON, *Commanding Draft Rendezvous, Riker's Island, N. Y. H.*

Official copy.

CHAS. G. HALPINE, *Major and A. A. G.*

HEADQUARTERS, DRAFT RENDEZVOUS,
RIKER'S ISLAND, N. Y. HARBOR, *Feb'y* 29, 1864.

Major—I have the honor to acknowledge the receipt of your communication of the 18th instant, requesting a statement of my views as to the past system of obtaining recruits at Lafayette Hall under General Spinola, the quality of the men furnished under that system, their condition, spirit, and any other facts which may be regarded in this connection as of public interest.

In reply, I have the honor to state, that my only means of

judging the system is by the recruits furnished under it, and judging by the recruits, I should unhesitatingly say, that the system which is attended with such results must be radically wrong, and if allowed to continue would become nothing less than an outrage on the community, and a disgrace to the Government. I derive this opinion from a comparison of the recruits furnished under that system with those that are received now.

Upon carefully examining the records, I find that during the month of December last, there were received at this rendezvous on the average of eighty-one recruits per diem, and that during the present month of February, there have been received on the average one hundred and twenty-one per diem, being an increase of about 50 per cent.

Under the system of recruiting which prevailed during the month of December last, more young boys and old men were received than now, more men came to the island drugged and intoxicated than now, and finally, (which is the best test of any system of recruiting), the number of strong, healthy able-bodied men that came was very much less than now. This shows that if the system in question is not bad, there can be few others worse.

Again, I am forced to this opinion, by the statements of the men themselves, made under oath, all of the same general character, telling of fraudulent enlistments and little or no bounties received. On this point, I would respectfully call your attention to the accompanying report of Capt. Shannon, A. A. G., with the additional remark, that the practice of taking affidavits has now almost entirely ceased, for obvious reasons.

I am, Major, very respectfully,

Your obedient servant,

(Signed,) N. J. JACKSON,

Brig. Gen. Vols.

Official copy.

CHAS. G. HALPINE, *Major and Ass't Adj't Gen.*

To the Hon. the Senate:

The petition of Hawley D. Clapp, of the town of Mamaroneck, in the county of Westchester, in the State of New York, now confined as a prisoner in Fort Lafayette, respectfully represents: That he is not now and has not been engaged in or connected with the military authorities of this State or of the United States. That he has not held at any time office under the General Government, or had any contracts with the Government. That he has not been guilty of any crime or offence against the laws of the State, or of the United States. That he has not been arrested upon any process issued out of any State or Federal court; but that such arrest and imprisonment is by virtue of an order issued by Major General Dix.

And your petitioner further shows, that on the 17th day of February, 1864, he was arrested and imprisoned in Fort Lafayette, where he has since remained in confinement, subjected to the same treatment and indignities inflicted and imposed upon traitors and pirates. And your petitioner further shows, that he has been informed that such imprisonment and indignities are imposed and inflicted upon him to extort from him information which it is alleged he possesses, though your petitioner has repeatedly averred, and still avers, that he does not possess the information that is attempted to be extorted from him by these inquisitorial acts; and that he has offered to answer under oath any interrogatories relating to his alleged knowledge. That he has repeatedly demanded a hearing upon the charges against him, which hearing has been refused. That he has offered good and sufficient bail to appear and answer any charges against him, and that such offer has been refused. And your petitioner, as a loyal citizen that was never accused of crime, claims the protection of the law of this State, and invokes your honorable body to take some measures that will secure him his constitutional rights and shield him from unjust oppression.

HAWLEY D. CLAPP.

NEW YORK, *April* 5, 1864.

The Death of President Lincoln.

A SERMON

PREACHED IN SAINT PAUL'S CHAPEL, NEW YORK, ON WEDNESDAY, APRIL 19, 1865.

BY THE

REVD. MORGAN DIX, S. T. D.,

RECTOR OF TRINITY CHURCH.

PRINTED BY ORDER OF THE VESTRY.

CAMBRIDGE:

PRINTED AT THE RIVERSIDE PRESS.

1865.

RESOLUTIONS

ADOPTED BY THE VESTRY OF TRINITY CHURCH.

UPON receiving the news of the assassination of the President, the Vestry assembled, on the call of the Rector of the Parish, at 3 o'clock, P. M., on Saturday, April 15th, and adopted, unanimously, the following preamble and resolutions:—

WHEREAS, on the evening of the 14th day of April, 1865, being Good Friday, by an assassin as yet unknown, the venerated and beloved President of the United States, Abraham Lincoln, was suddenly assaulted and slain; and whereas the announcement of that appalling crime has just been made to this community, filling all hearts with a grief, astonishment, and indignation which cannot be described; and whereas this Vestry has been called together by the Rector, to take such action as in their judgment may seem fit and becoming; therefore,—

Resolved, That this Vestry, as sharers in the common distress and affliction, unite in the public lamentation over the untimely death of the honored Chief Magistrate of the Union, and shocked beyond measure at the intelligence which has just been received, remain without words adequate to express their sorrow.

Resolved, That we recognize in this calamitous event one of those visitations, permitted by Almighty God, before which a nation can but bow in silence and awe, with the prayer that they may be overruled for the good of our country.

Resolved, That while we regard the act by which our beloved country has thus been, through indescribable malice and fury, plunged into the deepest affliction, as one of those crimes of which no language can adequately paint the atrocity, of which the history of Europe has not for many centuries furnished a parallel, of which our own history has thus far furnished no example, and than which no history furnishes a more detestable and infamous act to the view, we cannot but hold it to have been dictated by the spirit which, from the commencement of our national troubles, has sympathized with the enemies of the public peace, and aided and abetted the rebellion, now, as we trust, subdued; a spirit whose tendencies and essential character had previously been manifested in the July riots in this city, in 1863, in the attempt to destroy this city by incendiarism, in November last, and in the systematic outrages inflicted on our captured soldiers in the prisons of the South.

Resolved, That this Vestry hereby record their tribute of respect to the memory of the late President with profound sorrow for his loss, recognizing in him a singleness of purpose, an honesty of intention, an ardent patriotism, a fidelity to duty, and a growing mastery of the circumstances of his position, which enabled him, under Providence, to fulfil and bring to successful completion a work almost unprecedented for difficulty; and that in his removal, at the moment in which the labors of his last four years had culminated in the triumph of the national authority and the evident approach of the blessings of peace, we see the completion of a career which the nation will ever look back to with thankfulness, and hold in affectionate and tender remembrance.

Resolved, That the Rector be requested to take order that the churches of this parish be draped in mourning, in token of our sympathy with the distress and anguish which have been caused throughout the length and breadth of the land by the murder of our venerated and beloved Chief Magistrate.

Resolved, That the Rector be authorized to give such publication to the above Resolutions as he may deem expedient; also *Resolved*, That an attested copy of the same be sent to the family of the deceased, and to the Department of State at Washington.

On Wednesday, April 19th, 1865, in compliance with the recommendation of the National Government, funeral solemnities were held, at 12 o'clock meridian, throughout the United States, in honor of the late President. The following Sermon was preached in St. Paul's Chapel on that occasion.

SERMON.

"He that ruleth over men must be just, ruling in the fear of God. And he shall be as the light of the morning, when the sun riseth, even a morning without clouds; as the tender grass springing out of the earth by clear shining after rain." — 2 SAMUEL xxiii. 3, 4.

THESE were the last words of David. He spake them as he saw the time drawing near when he must go the way of all the earth; they were the last song of the Psalmist. Each man knows best the law of his own profession; he, as a ruler, knew what a ruler ought to be, and delivered his judgment on that subject before he died. The sentence on his own performances he left his Lord to utter; but the general law by which he ought to have guided his course, he was moved so to state and express in the moment in which the rod of empire was about to be taken from his relaxing hand.

Those words of David, the ancient king, may be most aptly used as proper to a description of the dead President. We assemble to-day on an occasion without a precedent in our past history. There has been, on this side of the world, no sorrow like our sorrow, so far as we can read back the history of the men who have dwelt here. Regarded in its cause and in its manner of manifestation, it stands beyond comparison in its awful grandeur. By that act, to which the sober judgment of mankind has awarded the crown in degrees of atrocious crime; by that deed, of which language fails to paint the infamy; by that sin, against which Christian civilization cries out as involving the reversal of all progress towards good, and as throwing back mankind into the slough of barbarism, the act, the crime, the sin of murderous assassination, a man has been laid low, who held in his hands the destinies of twenty-five millions of his countrymen, and to whom they were at that moment looking with growing confidence in his honesty of purpose, his integrity of character, and his ability to do his duty in that position unto which it had pleased God to call him. And we are gathered together to mourn and weep with all those millions over a bereavement which every lover of his country feels to be personal to himself. There is a great cry throughout the land; it seems as though there was not a house where there is not one dead. Some few words would I reverently speak at this hour, when, perhaps, a solemn silence might better suit the occasion.

And first, of him who has been wrested from us by the murderer's hand. That sanguinary fiend, that nocturnal demon of the darkness of this world, thought to have done him a harm when he lifted up the weapon against his life. How short-sighted are the calculations of the wicked one! That act has been, not the destruction, but the immortalizing of the venerated and beloved victim. When or where, at any time, in any age, has a man gone to his grave as this ruler of the land is going to his, this hour? Who ever saw or dreamed of a manifestation of sorrow, of anguish, of interest, of devotion to one human being like that which this hour is revealing? Unforced, unasked, the result of no national edict, of no proclamation by authority, it is the simple, unaffected, real demonstration of the heart of this great family of freemen. There is a grandeur in this scene with which no occurrence hitherto can compare. Let the blood-stained felon, wherever he be now skulking, mark what he has done. He thought to spread dismay and confusion through the land. He has but lifted a veil which lay upon the great national heart, and shown the world its greatest strength and glory, in its tenderness, its veneration for goodness, its magnificent collectedness and self-control. His infamous deed has made stronger than ever the people whom he hates; stronger, as they are stronger who have been knit together by the bond of a common affliction. The sound of the funeral hymn, now sternly ascending over the whole land, bespeaks a compactness, a concentration, a mutual devotion, which, up to this hour, lacked the lever of development and the cause of expression; this funeral wail has in it the music of a coming era, through which the dead of to-day shall walk in spirit, canonized and glorified in the undying love and veneration of coming ages. Just as the French look back to the good Henry IV., and love him for the fate which brutal passion inflicted, so will the American people, to their remotest generations, speak tenderly and reverently of that good, that honest, that kindly-hearted man, their sixteenth President.

"He that ruleth over man must be just, ruling in the fear of God." How fairly do these words describe him. Who was just, if he was not? or who, if we may read the man's inmost heart from his words, did ever rule more conscientiously in the fear of God? Honesty and his name were synonymous; and now that he is dead, what more could he ask, what nobler record, than that he was proverbially the honest man? And then, how tender-hearted; men thought at last almost too much so; but let us rather think of that grand, Christ-like trait with thankfulness, that it beamed forth so brightly from his person at the last. When they struck him down he was meditating how to do them good; his last official acts were acts of kindness and leniency, so marked as to excite, in some quarters, alarm; in him they murdered their best friend; his heart was full of plans of conciliation at the moment when they aimed at it their execrable blow. That is enough for every lover of peace to make him look, with moistened eyes, at that untimely grave. There lieth one who, so far as we can judge, bore no ill-will to any creature that lives; who, as he said himself when they told him that he was reëlected, felt sorry to triumph over any one; who was seeking, in those his last few days, to find how he might soften to the enemies of his country the circumstances of their late disastrous defeats, — how he could save them mortification and humiliation, — how much he could safely give them back of that which they had forfeited; who would, I think, have pardoned, if it came to the last, even the chief man of the insurgents; who would have had the blood of no one on his hands; and who, if he knew in those last hours what had happened to him, and who had done it, would, I verily believe, have prayed for his murderer, and been ready to do what no one else can do — forgive him. Oh, if there be a crime more foul, more base, more abominable, than that which has been done on that unostentatious, wise, kind-hearted, friendly man, let it be named, that we may see in the scale of wickedness one degree below any yet known! The people know of nothing worse, and, therefore, is he lamented as none was ever lamented for by them unto this day.

Whither can the assassin fly? Whither, that the justice of Heaven shall not fell him? Whither, that the arm of the government cannot lay hold of him? This is a case in which there need be no impatience, no hurry. The retribution may be deferred; but it will come. The whole earth has not a place where he cannot be known and followed and found. The government does not exist which dare refuse to give him up, if he be within its limits. Only one part of the world is there to-day where he can breathe and walk abroad in safety—in those parts of this country still in an insurgent condition, and not yet reached by our armies. But around that lessening region the circle hourly contracts. He shall not long have shelter there; the years at last shall bring him into our hands, if the months and the days do not do it sooner. There is small consolation in the thought; the evil cannot be repaired. But that man owes a debt to the nation, and sooner or later the hour of its payment will come. Meanwhile we have but to be patient and follow.

Among the thoughts which come upon the mind at such a moment as this, is one of which I will briefly and dispassionately speak. One consequence of this ghastly crime will be, and is already, that an entire population is put on trial before the bar of the opinion of mankind. It has been urged by many — by most — that this act of assassination is but the natural result of a social condition to which such acts seem properly to belong. It is said that the moral and social tone, temper and spirit of the Southern people are such that acts of infamy like this might naturally be expected from them. But there are others who cannot consent to such a view of the case; who claim for Southern civilization a higher tone, a better spirit; who maintain that its principles are the principles of Christianity, and that the moral condition of the people is not below that of the rest of civilized mankind. To that opinion your preacher has adhered. He could not feel that a whole people could have been so brutalized, so degraded, as it has been represented that they are. But now the thing is to be determined — the truth is to be made plain — in the red and bloody light of this cruel and diabolical outrage. There can be no escape from this test, nor any evasion of the issue. By the calm, concurrent, and deliberate judgment of civilized and enlightened nations, assassination is held to be a crime — an act which no circumstances can excuse. That was not the Pagan view. The change in opinion on this point has come with the acceptance of the teachings of Jesus Christ, and with the spread of His religion through the world. To defend assassination is no more possible in this age than to defend suicide; no more possible on Christian principles; it is classed among those frightful enormities with which lower civilizations teem, and to which men are more or less prone in proportion to their higher or lower position in the scale of advancement. Hence we have heard, wherever this deed has been made known beyond our borders, a cry of horror, a cry of detestation from all official mouths — from all who could speak for constituencies. We have heard that cry from those who have never been on our side, and who do not yet alter their feelings concerning us; but as men, and as Christians, they think it due to their manhood and their faith to express, in language not to be misunderstood, their horror at the sudden appearance of that barbarian shape, the political assassin, amid the lights of this age. For two hundred and fifty-five years such a dire shape has not emerged from the outer darkness to alarm and astound the world. Since A. D. 1610, no ruling sovereign of a mighty people has actually thus been hurried out of the world. Have we not, therefore, in this event a test which no ingenuity can evade of the real temper, tone, and quality of that community with which we have been forced into contention? We wait to hear what they will say. They must speak, and the whole world will listen to every word they utter. He who invaded the family circle of the President and did him to death; he who, with a dastardly cowardice which must simply be pronounced immense, entered the chamber of that sick and helpless man, the Secretary of State, and stabbed him in his bed,—these wretches knew not all that they did; for among the results of those ferocious actions was this, — that they have arraigned the whole Southern people before the bar of the opinion of mankind, and put them on trial at that august tribunal. The judgment is set, and the books are opened; Christian civilization waits attentively to hear them speak. There is but one thing to do, if they would stand in this audit. To denounce the act, to join in the common cry against the outrage done to God, to man, to Christ, to the age; to disclaim any responsibility for it; to shrink back from the bloody actors in that murder; to say, We, too, are Christians, civilized beings, men; we abhor as much as you can a deed like this; charge it not on us; it is the work of desperadoes for whom we are not accountable: think not of us as though we would excuse or defend a crime fit only for a barbarous zone, and from which, with the enlightened world, and as acceptors of the principles of Christianity, we equally with yourselves revolt in disgust and horror. Such must be their answer, if their claims be true. And would to God it might come back to us from the other side in unmistakable terms,—a full, clear, hearty, manly voice,—assuring us that the weapons of their warfare are and ever will be those of honorable, though, as we deem, mistaken, men, and not the poisoned chalice, the midnight torch, the secret dagger, the muffled pistol. Then might good come even of this awful catastrophe. We, loving the dead as we do, they, horror-stricken at his murder, might yet join hands over his bloody grave, and ask forgiveness of God and of each other in whatsoever, all through these years, we have done amiss. Would to God it might be so; the blood of the martyr might indeed make fertile the ground of that country, all parts of which he loved. But I fear, I tremble lest it should be otherwise, lest we shall hear some quite different voice, perhaps a brutal cry of approval, perhaps a glorifying of the act even more monstrous than the deed itself; for he who could calmly and in cold blood justify it, must be at heart like those who did it; and if that sullen response should come, if those assassins should be received as heroes, their crime applauded, their persons admired, the judgment of mankind defied,—if such should be the answer, then, of a truth, must the heart grow heavier than it is now, and a thoughtful man must ask himself, "What are those people? What is their normal state? What are their thoughts—their principles? What cause has been at work to keep them back behind the rest of the world, to depress them, to hold them at the old heathen positions, at the old standpoints of Paganism, to keep them blind while all the rest of the world sees? What is that civilization which appropriates and glories in deeds like this, which calls the midnight murderer a hero, the stealthy killer of the old, the sick, the defenceless, a demigod? Is it a work of this age? or is it a thing of the past? Is it a system which rests on Gospel principles and Christian ideas? or is it a remnant of hard old Roman Paganism and an ally and friend of the Thugs? And can there be peace while any vestige remains of those peculiarities, whatever they may be, which make that system what it is, and, under it, debase and distort those people from the very form of man?" Brethren, it is with indescribable anxiety that many are now waiting for the response of the Southern people to these atrocious murders which have been committed in their name. We will not think the worst until all hope is gone; we will yet hope against hope. But if it must be so, then, indeed, will it seem as if all hope were at an end — as if all that has been said were just — as if the charges hitherto made had not been rash; and, so far as defence of that community is regarded, impartial lips must be silent henceforth.

A few words in conclusion. I return to my subject, to him whose memory we honor to-day, for whom we make loud and bitter lamentation. But he is beyond the reach of our cry; he is not, however, beyond that of our praise. His name is with us — in our households, on our national annals, on the roll of the world's prominent men, and in the heart of a great nation while that nation shall endure. I do not enumerate his amazing successes in guiding the ship of state through as heavy a storm as ever beat and blew; in leading us to conclusions of the most wonderful character, as official commander-in-chief of the power of the nation; in emancipating from the fetters of slavery an entire race of human beings. Let the historian write of all these things in his account of that remarkable man. Let me rather repeat the words of King David, spoken concerning the just ruler that ruleth in the fear of God:—For "he shall be as the light of the morning when the sun riseth, even a morning without clouds; as the tender grass springing out of the earth by clear shining after rain." To him, with wonderful accuracy, as we trust, may these words be applied. The rebellion is nearly over; the sun of peace will soon, we trust, be bright over all the land, and a new and grand era is commencing for our country. But the good and honest President will ever stand there, in the memory of the people, surrounded with the light of that morning in which, just as it was rising upon us, he was called to his rest; and his name will be, in the hearts of the American people, as green, as fresh, and as pleasant as is to the eyes the tender grass springing out of the earth by clear shining after the rain. Alas! that rain was the rain of his own blood — the blood of his active brain, of his generous heart; but there is already a great and clear shining upon the earth where that red shower fell; and, while the lights of martyrdom and sacrifice shall continue to shine, they will rest on that venerable place, and glow there, like sacred fires, from generation to generation.

From Rev. George Duffield

Our Soldier-Dead.

AN ADDRESS

ON

DECORATION DAY

Northville, May 30th, 1884.

BY

GEORGE DUFFIELD, A. M.

"All time is the millennium of their glory."—EVERETT.

[PUBLISHED BY REQUEST.]

APP. A

EVER welcome Spring! Both young men and maidens, old men and children bid thee, All hail!

This 'renewing of the face of the earth,' is something to which the most stolid of mortals can never become wholly accustomed. It breaks up the monotony of life like nothing else. Instead of naked and unsightly skeletons, all the trees of the field, and the forest, are dressed in the full magnificence of leaf and flower; and in this there is an intimation of something higher than earth!

The rod that budded, was a sign,
To all who saw, of power divine;
But now the 'anointed eye' may see,
An Aaron's rod in every tree!

Between this season and youth, there is the strongest possible sympathy, and youth enjoy it, to the very utmost! No worm as yet on the leaf, no blossom faded and fallen from the bough, not a single winged seed wafted into air from its parent flower, not a solitary note silenced in the chorus of universal song;—the longest day is not too long to gratify the eye, and feast the ear; and night with envious veil comes all too soon.

With those, however, who have had a deeper experience of life, it is quite otherwise. In the glad chorus we can not fail to recognize a minor strain. We feel a shadow creeping over the landscape, that was once as bright to us, as to others. The beautiful season does not come altogether as it formerly did; a glory has passed away, that we would gladly have retained.

"It is not now, as it hath been of yore!"

Many things it returns with the birds, but there are many more it does *not* return. It gives a new and fresh existence to the leaf, as if it had been just created in Paradise; but once there were hopes, precious hopes—and where are they? It gives back the bud and blossom, as fragrant and as fair as ever; but once there were *affections*, warm and dear as life itself;—does the spring ever renew them? The incense-breathing south blows softly and opens the earth, and makes it soft with showers; but it opens not the grave; it does not restore the precious dust that we have there treasured, out of our sight. It is as cold, and dark, and cheerless as winter itself, and still more silent.

It seems strange that the earth *can* be so beautiful, when those are absent who were once so dear; and who can no longer share with us, in its exuberant beauty; and whose companionship made life itself. In very deed it makes us sad to our inmost soul to see the earth so gay; when our loss has been to us nothing less than that of the spring out of the year,—we almost wish that her next flowers may bloom above ourselves.

Thus it is, that to those who have lost friends in war, or by disease at home, the season naturally becomes one of mournful remembrance; and as there is no fellowship so deep as that of suffering, the observance of such a custom as this, and at such a time, is equally natural and appropriate. I see in it nothing of superstition, but much of gratitude; nothing of ostentation, but much of patriotism; and in the tender sympathy it manifests for the widow and the fatherless, not a little of pure and undefiled religion.

Even death is no exception to the universal rule of cost and compensation—for while it separates us from some whom we love, it brings so much the nearer, and makes the dearer, others who are left to mourn a bereavement that belongs to all.

Tho' I have never before been in these streets, or seen these faces, I cannot but think well of a place, and of a people, to whom such sentiments are welcome and familiar. My only regret is that so brief a time for preparation—permits me to do so great a theme—but imperfect justice.

Perhaps the feeling that underlies this beautiful custom first found expression on the 19th of April, 1861, when the memorable despatch was sent from Boston to the Mayor of Baltimore by Governor Andrew—"I pray you cause the bodies of our Massachusetts soldiers, *dead in battle*, to be immediately laid out, preserved in ice and tenderly sent forward by express to me. All expenses will be paid by this Commonwealth."

But when and where this *day* had its original observance is somewhat uncertain. The first notice your speaker had of it was at New Orleans, and as Pere La Chaise is the parent of modern cemeteries, so the custom of decorating the grave, and thus divesting it in some degree of that indefinable terror with which it is so apt to be regarded, may be borrowed from the French.

The next notice was in a dirge, by HENRY TIMROD, sung on the occasion of decorating the graves of the Confederate dead at Magnolia Cemetery, Charleston, South Carolina; where the victims of a fallen cause are apostrophized in strains more worthy of other and better martyrs!

"In seeds of laurel on the earth,
The blossom of your fame is blown,
And somewhere waiting for its birth,
The shaft is in the stone."

Gradually the custom found its way along the Atlantic coast to Richmond, where to this very hour so many of her daughters dress in the deepest mourning, which to the end of their lives they will never consent to lay aside. Well may these Rachels continue to weep for their children, and refuse to be comforted, if they have no better prayer than this;

"Stoop angels hither from the skies,
"There is no holier spot of ground,
"Than where defeated valor lies,
"By mourning beauty crowned.

Even the First Napoleon could understand that "It was the cause, and not the death, that makes the martyr," and that he himself was only a victim of pride and ambition, and not a martyr at all.

"Who falls for love of God shall rise a star!"

But no such resurrection of national fame, can await those who have lifted a parricidal hand against the life of the Nation ;* "who would have robbed their country of its Nationality! The people of the prerogatives of man!" For them the shaft that is in the stone, will never come out of it!

The universal indignation occasioned by firing on the flag at Sumpter, has long since passed away, with the flags that then waved defiance from every loyal house-top; the deeper and more abiding resentment by which it was followed at the outbreak of a rebellion, so unnecessary and indefensible,† has itself been followed by the calm and irreversible judgment of history; and there is no further occasion for crimination or recrimination. That day has gone by; but there is still need of such a day as this, in which for every patriot heart to bear their annual testimony on the point at issue; it is a privilege they will not be denied.

Willingly do I accord to the men and women of the South, the right of a common humanity to mourn their dead, when and wheresoever they choose.‡ I give the men of

* App. B. † App. C. ‡ App. D.

Stonewall Jackson's division and others, full credit for valor, desperate as was ever seen in all the annals of war; I freely award to those in the opposing armies the name of SOLDIER, they so deservedly possess in common. Heroes all! to depreciate their valor would in the same ratio diminish ours also. Within certain limits as defined by themselves, I do not deny them a sectional rather than American patriotism, that is peculiarly their own. I can even see how under the erroneous instruction of their orators, civil and religious, the decisive test that bound their conscience, was loyalty to the individual State, as ours to the country at large; and therefore in the due exercise of christian charity, I would in nowise impeach the sincerity of their religion. "With malice toward none," like the martyred Lincoln, I certainly cherish toward them no unforgiving spirit. In the South the prevailing sentiment was hatred of the North; in the North not hatred of the South, but love of the Union as a whole; then as ever, love more powerful than hate, and light than darkness!

My own personal testimony may have some interest here. As a member of the Christian Commission, even within sight of our loyal dead and dying, and fully aware of the horrors then passing in Libby, Andersonville, and other prison pens; at different times and places, in the Rebel Wards of the Washington Hospitals, on the bloody field of Gettysburg, and at Bermuda Hundred and City Point, after the battles of the Wilderness, these hands have ministered to their necessities; when hungry and thirsty given them their first bread to eat and water to drink; at their own entreaties —washed and cleansed their wounds from something worse than blood—services, for which, if I may take their own word for it, at the time, they were not altogether ungrateful! Even more than this, at the Yorktown Centennial, I was willing to meet and did meet them, and cordially extend the right hand of American citizenship, to which they were entitled, by a national amnesty as generous as unparalleled! God forbid we should ever have occasion to regret it!

Beyond this, charity no longer rejoices in the truth. The record of the past is forever unalterable. Their "cause" was not our cause, our enemies themselves being judges—for it was "lost." In that mortal strife it was not the color of the uniform that made the difference. There was a difference in fundamental principles of civilization and government. We went into the war for the Union; we fought it through against treason and rebellion. Living or dead, their soldiers must remain what they were, and ours what they were, to the end of time. In the charm of brilliant valor we may forget the injustice of the occasion that called it forth, but it will be only for a moment. The sober second thought of the people will never allow it to be permanent. *Their dead are not our dead, nor our dead theirs.* By a beautiful courtesy we may observe the same day for the expression of our grief; we may put the rose or the lily on the graves of the departed, or combine them both; but never can we mark them with the same flag. Nor if I understand Southern character aright, would they thank us, or even allow us so to do.

About the same time that Richmond began to decorate her graves, Washington, at the National Cemetery at Arlington, and elsewhere, began to decorate ours. The first time I saw the day observed was at Harrisburg, on the banks of my native Susquehanna—in 1868—and never while memory lasts will I forget the weeping eyes of mothers, wives, and daughters in that sorrowful procession;—the feelings with which I joined them and followed to the cemetery—nor the scene that then ensued, when they threw themselves on the graves of their dead, and gave utterance to their grief.

Only once before had I witnessed anything just like it, and of all other days, on the morning that brought the news that Richmond was taken. At the request of two of the Boys in Blue, I had gone nine miles into the country to attend a soldier's funeral. The day was cold and raw, but the road on either side was lined with wagons, and the large school house completely filled. The two soldiers who came as a committee, met me at the door, and gave a word of explanation! "This poor woman has lost a father, and a husband, and a son; but none of them have been brought home! She thought if she could only get her friends together, and have a funeral, it would do her good! We beg pardon for bringing you so far on a sort of false pretense, but we thought *you* would understand it!"

Taking my place in the desk, I said, how many of you in this 'cruel' war (as we were then accustomed to call it), like this poor woman, have lost *fathers?* The number of hands that went up were not a few! How many of you like her, have lost *husbands?* More hands went up than before! How many, *brothers?* The show of hands was still greater. How many of you like her, have lost *sons?* And then there were more hands than ever, amid such weeping as stopped all further inquiry, and made the place a complete Bochim!

When at length I found myself able to speak, and the people to hear, I dared to say among other things for their comfort—that the war in which we were then engaged was a just one, unjustly forced upon us; that our cause was not only that of constitutional liberty, but of humanity itself;—that as such it was well worth all that it would cost;—in the Union preserved and the country saved. Now and then it would so happen, that the calamities of the war would be unusually heavy in particular localities, and so it was here. I did not dare to tell all I knew about the regiment, that went from that vicinity, and in whose history we had a fair sample of too many others.

In the summer of 1861 I saw them take up their line of march, 1,100 strong. After the battle of Gettysburg, so many of them had been killed, wounded, and taken prisoners, and detailed for other duty, that when the roll was called, one of the soldiers whom I met on my way to the White Meeting-house informed me, they only numbered that morning "forty-eight muskets!" All the rest killed, wounded, prisoners, or in the hospital. During its term of service, the losses of that regiment were eight officers, one hundred and sixteen men, killed in action; four officers and 56 men died of wounds; one officer and two hundred and thirty-six men died of disease; total, 408. Besides the triple battle of Gettysburg, Fair Oaks, Malvern Hill, the Wilderness and Petersburg, they participated in fifty of the seven hundred other battles in that gigantic war. And thus it was, that in the eleven regiments of cavalry, the thirty regiments of infantry, etc., amounting in all to ninety thousand seven hundred and forty-seven, Michigan's Roll of Honor stands: Commissioned officers 358, enlisted men 14,855; total, 14,885.

These were the heroes and martyrs who, with others of the 270,000 on the National Roll of Honor, stood by the Republic in the dark hours of Treason, of Suspense, of National Defeat, of Invasion, of Foreign Intervention, of Military Crisis, of Political Crisis, and proved that we still were a Nation; that we still had a Government; that it could no longer be considered an experiment; and who gave due notice that all the boastings of Rebellion would end, in ignominious failure and bitter disappointment!

Occupying a position midway between the East and the West, and close upon an almost hostile frontier, the soldiers of Michigan had the double duty of sustaining the centre and being on the advanced guard. Brave men and true were they as ever shouldered a musket or drew a sword!—men of the mighty heart! men who had souls—" public souls,"—men who could take *in* and feel *up* to their share in the noble cause in which they were engaged! Well worthy they to bear the uplifted shield, and on their colors the symbolic motto of the State, " I will defend!"

Perhaps, instead of mere general terms of eulogy, the peculiar nature of this occasion will permit them to speak for themselves.

Going on the steamer "J. W. Brooks" from City Point to the relief of Washington, I found by my side on the crowded upper deck an artilleryman, to whom the day had been a hard one. Pouring his cold coffee from his canteen, soaking his hard-tack in it, and picking a rind of bacon so clean that he could not find a scrap more, he shut up his knife with the cheerful exclamation, "Many a better dinner have I eaten at home, but never one that I enjoyed more than this!" Before such men the "big skirmish line" of the rebels soon disappeared.

Late one evening, visiting the post hospital at Bermuda Hundred, and finding nearly all asleep but one, I inquired for the man a contraband had that day brought through the lines, who had thirteen rebel buckshot in him. "No," said he, "he has only seven," and suiting the action to the word, he said, "Here are the other six; I am good for the Johnnies yet!"

Just after a battle I found a young man of remarkably intelligent countenance. "Well, my boy, what can I do for you?" "O! nothing; I'm all right!" said he; but perceiving from his tone there *was* something wanting, I repeated my inquiry. "You will think me foolish," he replied, "but in the last skirmish I was left wounded on the field, and my testament was so soaked with blood and rain that it fell to pieces." "That want is easily supplied," I said. "No," said he, "not so easy as you think, for it was a *Greek* testament!" What was his delight when, taking out of my pocket this very copy that I now hold in my hand, he had the pleasure of reading a chapter in the original!

After the battle of Gettysburg, I went into a church that had been converted into a hospital, and inquired if there were any men from Michigan. "Here's one," said a feeble voice of a boy of eighteen; "are you from Michigan?" "Yes." "Well, what do they think at home of the Army of the Potomac *now?*" I told him "Just what we always thought; that it would be all right with the men, when they got the right leaders." "That's so," said he; "I tell you Mr. Duffield, there was not a man who went into this last fight, but had *a heart as big as a meetin' house!*" In the eye of that boy I first saw the strange, unearthly light that convinced me of a divine afflatus, and of the truth of the Cromwellian doctrine, that "Great courages are the gift of the Almighty!"

Not long after I found another soldier, braver still! Having conquered in one battle, he was now preparing for another, and as I looked over his shoulder, I found him deep in Ephesians vi., and putting on the whole armor of God, that he might come off more than conqueror in the last great conflict with the King of Terrors—like many another whom I met—"Every inch a soldier, and every inch a Christian!"

Call the roll of all the heroes of Greek or Roman fame, and I will venture to find their parallels in the heroes of our own Republic, and exhaust the list! With all that has been said in honor of our heroes—either in the State or Nation at large—we can never say too much. LINCOLN stands alone. And where will you find *manhood*, if not in such a king of men, as GARFIELD? Where thunderbolts of war, if not in such leaders as GRANT, and SHERMAN, and SHERIDAN, and CUSTER? Where citizen soldiers, whose every "bayonet thinks," if not in the rank and file of as brave an army as ever trod the crimson field! But pardon me that I thus speak to those who know those men so well already. I only venture on such testimony, that they may confirm it, for the sake of the generation that has risen since.

They are not dead, but rather we seem to be dead who still survive! They live in song, which has no sweeter elegies than those which lament their loss! They live in eloquence—in the impassioned eulogy of the orator, who, since the day of Pericles, can find no theme more grateful to himself, nor more acceptable to his hearer. They live in history, that has no brighter page, than that which records their deeds. They live in our *hearts*, and to live in the hearts of others is the best place for any man to live. They live in their descendants, the sons and grandsons of their noble sires. They live in the life of the country they have rescued, from the mightiest rebellion, since Lucifer attempted to ascend the sapphire steps of the eternal throne.

Glory to God, and honor to their sacred names.

"They live—they live—in blest eternity!"

Those who fell on the Eurymedon, at Marathon, Thermopylæ and Salamis, were honored among the Greeks as equally worthy of remembrance by gods and men. It was not a dirge they sang, but a pæan appropriate to their fallen heroes, its tone not mournful, but triumphant. And how wonderfully significant their inscriptions:

"When on a razor's edge all Hellas stood,
We who lie here preserved her with our blood."

And again—

"Go tell the Spartans, thou that passest by,
That here obedient to her laws we lie."

"'Tis but two lines, and all Greece for centuries had them by heart. *She forgot them!* and Greece was living Greece no more."

—It is good for each State to have its Roll of Honor, in which to record the immortal names—

"That were not born to die."

It is good for our universities and colleges to institute Memorial Halls for those of their number, who have graduated with higher than academic honors on "the high places of the field." It is good for counties and townships to build enduring monuments to friends and kindred, at the expense of whose lives we had "victory at last!" It is good to erect memorial pillars on the field of battle, where stood the unconquerable battery, or where the cavalry made their desperate charge! It is good to lay out national cemeteries—of which there are now eighty-one larger, and several hundred smaller, scattered all over the land. But best of all is it, as each successive year the faithful earth provides the flowers, to decorate their graves!

Go forth, then, fair maidens, to your appointed task, and as ye scatter with grateful hands the vernal flowers above these precious mounds of green, remember, that while honoring others you put no little honor on yourselves.

Remember, since the untimely death of Adonis by the tusk of the cruel boar, it has been the tender custom of the virgins in every age, in some form or other, to walk in procession and lament the fate of those who came to an untimely death by the hand of lawless violence. Remember, as you represent the eight and thirty States, that in all countries there has never been just such another Union as our own—the union of single States, and of the representatives of the people at large—woven together into the truest and strongest government on earth!

As the dew gems the grass of the morning, ye need not be ashamed to drop a kindly tear, for these martyrs are your own.

Of the total number of these who enlisted, the average age was *twenty-two*, and their last word, more frequently than any other, was MOTHER!

Patriotism is only another name for the love of home—and they fought as truly for their altars and their fires—on the other side of the Potomac—as though they fought and fell at their own door.

"Above the dear, brave hearts that cease to beat,
Let loving hands strew flowers on every mound,
Within the lines of the still camping ground,
Where there is no assault, and no retreat,
And victory is not followed by defeat.
Unbroken rest and peace at last are found;
No clash of swords, no trumpet's thrilling sound
Nor roar of guns disturb their slumbers sweet.
Their deeds are writ on memory's sacred scroll;
And patriot love shall touch these hearts of ours,
When, at their graves, Fame comes to call the roll,
And hope, and love, and honor scatter flowers.
Brave souls survive the storms of shot and flame;
Their furlough blossoms in eternal fame."

There is a beautiful German legend that "At the return of every Spring, the Emperor Charlemagne comes back from his grave, to bless the land over which he once held sway; that up and down the Rhine he walks, flinging his blessing on gardens, and vineyards, and fields, to multiply the vintage and the harvest." So with our soldier-dead, who fell under the flag in defense of the Union.

"The spirit of their example is still here. It fills the air. It fills our hearts, and long as time shall last, it will hover in the skies," and rest upon the land for which they died!

Northville Roll of Honor.

Soldiers in the Revolutionary War.

RICHARD LEWIS.

Soldiers in the War of 1812.

ASA SHA.
WILLIAM SICKLES.
WILLIAM DUNLAP
OLIVER WHITAKER.
CAPT. CALEB HARRINGTON..
ISRAEL NASH.
PAUL HAZEN.
GEO. B. DENNIS.
THOS. WATTS.
JOS. WOODMAN, A. M., M. D.
HENRY POMEROY.
AVERY DOWNER, M. D.
ASA SLOAN.
JOSEPH ALLEN.
REV. ANSON SHA.
DEA. E. C. WILLIS.
SAMUEL WHITE.
ABRAM VRADENBURGH.
JOHN BALL.

Soldiers in the Mexican War.

AMOS B. GOOCH, killed, Pueblo, 1847.
DANIEL BROWN.
JOHN BLOYE.

Soldiers who were Killed or Died in the War for the Union.

CHAUNCEY D. RATHBURN, Co. D., 5th M. Cav., killed, Littletown, Pa.
NELSON A. ALLEN, " " " " Gettysburg, Pa.
ALFRED C. ANDERSON, " " " " Boonesboro, Md.
JOHN D. GUDITH, " " " " Winchester, Va.
CHAS. W. HIGGINS, " " " " Cedar Cr., Va.
ALLEN HARMON, 2d Lt., " " " " Chantilly, Va.
JULIUS JOHNSON. " " " " Leestown, Va.
NORTON MARSHALL, 1st Sgt., " " " died of wnds., Fortress Monroe
STEPHEN RYDER, " " " " " Washington, D.C.
JAS. M. GREER, " " " " Hospt., Philadelphia.
JOS. LOUNT, " " " " " Fairfax, C. H., Va.
LEWIS K. VAN GEISON, " " " " Andersonville Prison.
DANIEL H. PALMER. " " " " " "
PHILANDER LEWIS, " " " " " "
CHAS. H. W. MILLER, " " " " " "
WALLACE W. SMITH, " " " " " "
NODIAH C. WARD, " " " " Florence Prison.
HENRY VRADENBURGH, Co. I., 22d Inft., " Libby Prison.
OLIVER S. LEDYARD, " " " Millen Prison.
GEO. SMITH, Co. H., 5th M. Cav., " Hspt., Washington, D.C.
ALFRED WILLIS, Co. C., 24th M. Inft., " Florence Prison, S. C.
HENRY SCRIBNER, Co. H., 9th Cav., " Hspt., Cumberland, Ten.
DAVID PALMER, Co. E., 2d Inft., " " Knoxville, Ten.
ALBERT CLARK, Co. B, 2d Inft., " " Washington, D.C
GEO. FRANKISCH, Co. I., 6th Inft., " Ft Gaines, Ala.
JOSEPH DEZELA, Co. H. 2d Inft., killed, 2d Battle Bull Run.
DELOS ANDREWS. Co. H., 2d Inft., " Campbell Hspt., Tenn.
WM. HAWKINS, Co. H., 2d Inft., died, unknown.
TRUMAN BARKER, Co. H., 2d Inft., died of wounds, Hospt., Washington.
FRANKLIN EMORY, 2d Lt. Co. C, 7th Inft., killed, Fredericksburg, Va.
WM. M. WATERMAN, 2d Lt. Co. C., 1st Cav., killed, Louisa C. H., Va.
ALEXANDER HAMILTON, Co. M., 1st U. S. Cav., killed, Littlestown, Pa.
CHAS. PINKERTON, Co. C., 24th Inft., killed, Wilderness, Va.
DAVID VAN HOUTEN, Co. F., 16th Inft., killed, Chicahominy, Va.
CHAS. D. BOVEE, Co. K., 9th Cav., killed, Blue Springs, Tenn.
JOSEPH REEVES, Co. F., 1st Cav., killed, Gettysburgh, Pa.
ROBT. ANDERSON, Co. H., 1st Cav., killed, Brentsville, Va.
GEO. SMITH, Co. I., 6th Cav., Morganzie's Bend, Miss. River.
WM. KELLOGG, Co. D., 6th Inft.
JAS. BURR, Co. C., 1st Cav., died in hospital, Philadelphia, Pa.
CLARK STEWART, Co. G., 14th Inft., died in hospital, Nashville, Tenn.
JOSEPH PUTNAM, Co. F., 16th Inft., killed, Wilderness, Va.
LEANDER YERKES, Co. E., 23d Inft., died in hospital, Bowling Green, Ky.
JOHN S. RYDER, Co. B., 24th Inft., killed, Gettysburgh, Pa.
LUCIUS LIGNIAN, Co. D., Eng. and Mechs., died in hospital. Hilton Head.
CHAS. L. GOOCH, 14th Union. W. V., killed, Winchester, Va.
HORACE GOOCH, Co. B., 6th Cav., killed, Falling Water, Va.
JNO. H. JANES, Co. C., 24th Inft., died in hospital, Washington, D. C.
WM. HERRINGDEEN, Co. C., 24th Inft., died in hospital, Baltimore, Md.
JOSIAH CRONKITE, Co. F., 16th Inft., killed, Richmond, Va.
GEO. CRANDALL, Co. H., 22d Inft., killed Chicamauga, Tenn.
DAVID DAVISON, Co. B., 20th Inft., Hospt., Crab Orchard, Ky.
M. O. WALKER, Co. –, 6th Inft., killed Fort Donelson.
JOHN HUGHESTON, Co. I., 22d Inft., Hospt., Stevenson, Ala.
HENRY PARMENTER, Co. C., 30th Inft., Hospt., Jackson, Mich.

Northville Soldiers who Survived the War for the Union.

GEO. WELCH, Co. C., 24th Inft.
A B. MARKHAM, " "
J. W. BABBITT, " "
W. U. THAYER, " "
JARED TURRIL, " "
A. POMEROY, 2d Lt. " "
F. T. STEWART, " "
CALVIN MAXFIELD, " "
CHAS. DOBBINS, " "
NORMAN COLLINS, " "
WM. H. BRIGHAM, " "
B. F. BRIGHAM, " "
W. F. HUGHES, " "
GEO. HOISINGTON, " "
JAS. C. BRUCE, Co. F., "
A. W. HOSNER, " "
C. T. RODGERS, Capt. Co. C., "
GEO. CALKINS, Co. H., 8 Inft.
W HORRINGTON, Co. G, 14th Inft.
W. E. SPRINGSTEEN, " "
C. E. CLARKSON, " "
L. CHARTER, " "
*PERRIN WIGHT, " "
*I. B. WILKINSON, Co. I., 16th Inft.
W. CRONKITE, Co. F., "
J. S. GOOCH, Co. ——, Eng. & Mich.
J. GUTHRIE, Co. I, Eng. & Mchs
S. F. HUGHES, Co. D., " "
W. E. DOWNER, Co. L, " "
N. B. HUGHS, Co. F., " "
E. S MOULTON, Co. E., " "
O.W. MOULTON, Co. E, " "
J.F. ANDERSON, Co. F., " "
T. ROGERS, Co. I., " "
*W. SLATER, Co F., " "
M. PALMER, Co. H., 22d Inft.
D. PHILLIPS, " "
H. BARNUM, Co. I., "
J.H. WOODMAN, Cpt., " "
*S. WYMAN, " "
E. VRADENBURGH, " "
SETH NOBLE, " "
*H. B. GOODALL, " "
J. C. BOUGHTON, Co. K., 2d Inft.
JAS. ANDERSON, Co. I., "
*ALBERT E. CLARK, Co.B., 4th Cav.
ALFRED N. REED, Co. K., "
*A. PARMENTER, Co. G., 2d Inft.

JOHN CRONKITE, Co. F., 16th Inf.
C. STEWART, Co., I., 5th Inf.
JAS. HAMILTON, " "
GEO. W. DIBBLE, " "
DANIEL DAKE, Co. D., "
B. F. GOOCH, Corp. Co. F., 3d Inft.
*LOTHROP FULLER, Co.L., 1st Cav.
J. C. BLAUVELT, Co. C., "
9 mos. Andersonville Prison.
G. L. HOLMES, 2d Lt. Co. L., "
JAS. LEYDARD, Co. C., "
H. M. BULLARD, Co. L., "
E. H. BRUCE, " "
9 mos, Andersonville Prison.
J. N. ELLIOTT, " "
WALLACE NICHOLS, " "
HENRY L. REEVES, " 4th Cav.
JAS. PUTNAM, Co. D., "
JER. HAWKINS, Co. C., 1st Cav.
*STEPHEN FULLER, 6th Kentucky.
D. SEVERANCE, Co. D., 28th Inft.
B. G. WEBSTER, Co. F., 20th "
*LESTER WITHEE, Co. K., 23d "
W. A. COPELAND, Cpt. Co. B., 10 "
M. G. B. SWIFT, Co. E., 4th Inft.
*A. BRADLEY, Co. —, 4th Cav.
*WM. HASTINGS, 1st U. S. Inft.
A. FULLER, 2d Lt. 9th Cav.
*WM. MARSH, Co. C., 24th Inft.
*OSCAR LOUD, " "
*JAS. M. LOUD, " "
CHAS. H. HOUK, Co. I., "
*W J. CLARK, 2d Lt. Co.C., 30th Inft.
JNO. L. FULLER, " "
GEO. ALLEN, " "
JOSIAH EMORY, Co. C., 30th Inft.
JNO. B. NORTHROP, " "
FRK. PUTNAM, " "
A. L. VAN DYN, " "
C. L BRIGHAM, " "
E. N. HUGHES, " "
WM. H. YERKES, " "
W. J. LITTLE, " "
LESTER LIKE, " "
DUANE COOK, " "
ROBT. F. ALLEN, 2d Lt. " "
C. PHILLIPS, musician, " 24th Inft.
E. K. SIMONDS, Co. D., 5th Cav.

*Died since the war.

HIRAM LOUNT,	Co. D., 5th Cav.
G. S. WHEELER, 1st Lt.	"	"
AZEL C. BLAIR,	"	"

Andersonville, prisoner 17 months.

WM. WOODBURN, Co. D., 5th Cav.

Andersonville, prisoner 17 months.

JNO. GARDNER, Co. D., 5th Cav.

Andersonville, prisoner 17 months.

H. M. WHITE, 2d Lt. Co. D., 5th Cav.
ANDREW HOUK, " "
M. S. ROOT, " "
JAS. K. LOWDON, " "

Andersonville, prisoner 6 months.

GEO. COX, Co. D, 5th Cav.

Andersonville, prisoner 6 months.

NELSON LLOYD, Co. D., 5th Cav.
*L. W. FERGUSON, Cpt. " "
C. B. VAN DUYN, " "
G. L. VAN DUYN, " "
H. FORCE, " "
B. MILLER, " "
A. BUTTERFIELD, " "
C. B. COSTELLO, " "

17 mos. Andersonville.

*WEL. FORCE, Co. I., 22d Inft.
*JER. LIKE, Co. C., 30th "
E. S. HORTON, Co. D., 5th Cav.
*ALF. BEAL, Co. K., 2d Inft.
G. SMITHERMAN, Co. G. 3rd Cav.
R. SMITHERMAN, Co. C., 30th Inft.
J. L. CAMPBELL, 2d Lt. Eng. & Mchs.

*S. J. LOCKWOOD, Co. D., 5th Cav.
*GEO. S. JEFFERDS, " "
*W. L. STEWART, " "

Andersonville prisoner 6 mos.

*ACMED LAWSON, " "
S. C. WHEELER, " "
C. O'DONNEL, 2d Lt. " "
JOHN A. TUBBS, " "
GEO. KINGSLY, " "
JOHN LEDYARD, " "
E. K. STARKWEATHER, "
GEO. W. NEWMAN, " "

Andersonville prisoner 6 mos.

MAJOR M. BAILEY, " "
JAS. ARMSTRONG, " "
ED. S. HASTINGS, " "
JACOB E. BULLOCK, " "
*A. B. DOWNER, Co. C., 8th N. Y. H. Ar.
*B. PARMENTER, Miss. Flotilla.
P. McCOY, Co. K., 102 U. S. Col. Inft.
WM. HARRIS, " " " "
*CASS. ELIOTT, ——, 69th N. Y. Inft.
*SYL. BABCOCK, Co. I, 30th Inft.
L. L. GOOCH, Co. —, 12th U. S. R Inft
*H. YERKES, Co. B., 3rd N. Y. Cav.
J. M. DOIG, Co. C., 24th Inft.
H. C. DENNIS, " "
GEO. DENNIS, Co. L., 1st Cav.
R. E. MANNING, Co. B., 20th Inft.
D. R. WILSON, " "
C. DOBBINS, Co. —, — N. Y. Inft.

*Died since the war.

Appendix.

(A) NORTHVILLE, MICH., June 23, 1884.

Rev. George Duffield, DD.:

DEAR SIR—Believing that the tribute offered by you to the memory of our fallen comrades is worthy of preservation and should be accessible to every soldier, we, the undersigned, soldiers of Northville and vicinity would respectfully request you to publish the same.

J. H. WOODMAN, 22d Mich. V. Infantry.
MORRIS L. NICHOLS, 6d M. V. "
A. E. ROCKWELL, 1st Wisconsin H. A. V.
GEORGE H. CALKINS, 8th Mich. V. Infantry.
WILLIAM H. BRIGHAM, 24th Mich. V. Inf.
MYRON P. WHITE, 146th N. Y. Vol.
J. W. DOLPH, 22d N. Y. Cav.
H. YERKES, 30th Mich. Vol. Infantry.
W. E. DOWNER, 1st Mich. Engineers.
ALVIN L. VAN DYNE, 30th Mich. V. Infantry.
E. K. SIMONDS, 5th M. Vol. Cav.
E. K. STARKWEATHER, 5th M. V. Cav.
GEO. L. VAN DUYNE, Co. D., 5th Mich. Cav.
B. GLUETSTER, 20th Mich. Inf.
JOHN GUTHRIE, 1st Mich. Engineers Mechs.
H. O. WAID, 108th N. Y. Vol. Inf.
E. VRADENBURG, 22d Mich. V. Inf.
A. W. CARPENTER, 13th N. Y. Inf
JAMES ARMSTRONG, 5th Mich. Cav., Co. D.
A. POMEROY, 24th Mich. Inf., Co. C.
E. S. HORTON, 5th Mich. Cav., Co. D.
EDWARD S. HASTINGS, 5th Mich. Cav.
JOHN SMURDOCK, 151st N. Y. Inf.
H. S. NICHOLS, 1st M. Eng. and Mech., Co. M.
FREEMAN RENSHAW, 1st N. Y. Vet. Com.
M. S. ROOT, 5th Mich. Cav.
A. C. BLAIR, 5th Mich. Cav.
ANDREW HOUK, 5th Mich. Cav.
HIRAM LOUNT, 5th Mich. Cav.
LEONARD CHARTER, 14th Mich. Vet. V. Inf.
JAMES HAMILTON, 6th Mich. Inf.
A. N. HARRISON, 9th Iowa Inf., Co. B.
HENRY M. WHITE, 5th Mich. Cav., Co. D.

NORTHVILLE, MICH., May 31st, 1884.

Rev. George Duffield, DD., Detroit, Mich.:

DEAR SIR—The undersigned, citizens of Northville and vicinity, having listened with great interest and profit to the oration delivered by you in this place, yesterday, on the occasion of decorating the graves of our fallen soldiers, hereby respectfully request a copy of the same for publication.

J. M. SWIFT.	G. S. VAN ZILE.
J. A. DUBUAR.	A. M. RANDOLPH.
J. M. BURGESS.	T. G. RICHARDSON.
W. H. AMBLER.	H. W. NEY.
JAMES HUESTON.	W. P. YERKES.
GEORGE E. BRADLEY.	H. W. GELSTON.
B. A. WHEELER.	ANSON L. CADY.
HARRISON YERKES.	WINFIELD SCOTT.
JOHN G. LAPHAM.	J. O. KNAPP.
J. PERKINS.	REV. JAMES DUBUAR.
H. D. CLARK.	GEORGE C. HUESTON.
J. H. JUNKIN.	C. M. JOSLYN.
W. H. CHEEVER.	E. S. WOODMAN.
J. G. SMITH.	M. A. PORTER.
CHARLES R. STEVENS.	E. K. SIMONDS.
F. S. HARRISON.	D. B. NORTHRUP.
A. E. ROCKWELL.	C. B. HUNGERFORD.

DETROIT, MICH., Dec. 6th, 1884.

Messrs. J. M. Swift, M. D., W. E. Downer, Sec. of N. S. U. and others:

GENTLEMEN—Thanks for the joint request of soldier and citizen to publish the address. With such an endorsement, the sentiments therein contained become your own, and increase their value an hundred fold.

"Decoration Day" always reminds me of All Saints Day as observed in many of our churches in commemoration of the "Blessed Dead." There is much that these days have in common. But for the precious lives so generously sacrificed on the altar of Liberty, by our noble volunteers and veterans, the fire of the altar had gone out, and the temple had this day been a heap of ruins.

As we have learned from past ages that the deterioration of every government begins in the decay of the principles on which it is founded, so let posterity learn from our own age, and be wise enough to take warning. All honor to "the Advance Guard!"

"In the dream of the Northern poets
The brave who in battle die
Fight on in shadowy phalanx,
In the field of the Upper Sky!"

With the permission of the Committee I would like to give with the address the Northville Roll of Honor, to add the letters of Soldiers and Citizens, and possibly an occasional note in the Appendix.

Very respectfully,

Your friend and fellow citizen,

GEORGE DUFFIELD.

(B) "I call the war against the Union, a "Rebellion," because it is one, and in grave matters it is best to call things by their right names. I speak of it as a crime, because the Constitution of the United States so regards it and puts "Rebellion" on a par with "invasion."—*Everett's Gettysburg Oration.*

"I thank God for abolishing slavery as the origin and agent of a treason that is without justification and without parallel."—*Seward at Gettysburg.*

(C) "Gen. Thomas drew his sword to put down a rebellion, which even by Gen. Lee's confession was both unnecessary and indefensible."—*Garfield's Oration, p.* 23 *and p.* 43.

"As a military question, it was in no sense 'a civil war.'"
—*Beauregard.*

Let us never forget this—least of all on "Decoration Day!"

(D) The Greek tragedians teach the duty of burial as a universal custom"—the only limitation, that which forbade interment within the borders of their native land, of sacrilegious persons, and *of traitors who had borne arms against their fellow citizens.*" (Visscher as quoted by Professor Dooge, in his Antigone) a most significant exception indeed! (The italics mine).

(E) "It has been estimated that at least one-fifth of all who fell on the field of battle are now lying in unknown graves."—*Soldier's Monument Dedication, Evergreen Cemetery, Brighton, Mass.*, 1866.

HOW DECORATION DAY WAS OBSERVED.

" Northville people probably never had a finer or more satisfactory celebration of the day, set apart for the commemoration of those who gave their lives for the salvation of their country, than that of last Friday. All the forenoon a crowd of busy workers were engaged in building a platform in the school house yard, and a large number of ladies were no less busy preparing floral gifts. On the arrival of the one o'clock train, strains of music were heard, and in a few minutes the Plymouth Cornet Band in new uniforms, were seen marching up Main street, discoursing excellent music. The band was followed by Eddy Post, G. A. R., of Plymouth, escorted by the Soldiers' Union of Northville.

Owing to the probability of rain, it was deemed expedient to have the Decoration exercises first, and the procession accordingly marched to the cemetery, where thirty-eight young ladies, each wearing a badge, incribed with the name of a State, and carrying a basket of flowers, to scatter on the graves of the fallen heroes, each of which was marked by a small flag.

When all the graves had been thus decorated, the procession marched to the main entrance of the cemetery, where a cenotaph inscribed with the names of the soldiers buried elsewhere had been placed. The procession formed a circle round it, and after the flowers had been strewed about it, a brief address was delivered by A. M. Randolph. The procession and citizens then assembled at the stand.

The exercises were begun with a piece of music by the band. The prayer was offered by Rev. H. W. Gelston. A solo was then sung by M. H. Withee in an excellent manner, and the writer takes pleasure in saying that he never heard that stirring National hymn sound any better.

Dr. Swift as the President of the day, then introduced Rev. George Duffield, DD., of Detroit, who proceeded to deliver an address that stirred the hearts of every ex-soldier present. * * *

The exercises closed with the following

DECORATION HYMN,

BY DR. SWIFT.

We give to memory's sway
All that our hearts can pay,
And all our powers:
These sacred aisles we tread
Beneath which sleep our dead—
With rarest flowers we spread—
Unsullied flowers.

There undisturbed they lie
While hurrying feet go by
And the swift years.
In honored graves they rest
And we at loves behest
Enshrine their memory blest
With flowers and tears.

This land our Fathers gave
This land they died to save,
From traitor's hand
Our flag whose fold of blue
Decked with the stars anew,
In Union firm and true,
Waves o'er the land.

Then rest, brave soldier, rest,
Enshrined in every breast
A sacred trust,
With rarest flowers of May,
As spring yields up her sway,
We'll ever and for aye
Hallow thy dust.

LADIES REPRESENTING STATES.

MINNIE SMITH, N. Carolina.
LIDA STARKWEATHER, Oregon.
GRACE LAPHAM, Maryland.
VENA HAUK, Arkansas.
CARRIE GUTHRIE, Iowa.
GEORGIA PALMER, Massachusetts.
GRACE BLACKWOOD, Nevada.
GEORGIA SIMMONS, Nebraska.
MYRTIE KNAPP, California.
JOSIE GILLESPIE, Maine.
NELLIE GILLETT, Tennesee.
NELLIE WAID, Ohio.
MAUD STARKWEATHER, W. Va.
HATTIE THORNTON, Kansas.
EMELINE GAGE, Michigan.
MYRTIE BLAIR, Georgia.
NORA REED, Minnesota.
MAY BOVEE, New Hampshire.
MAY GREER, Vermont.
BIRDIE POWER, Rhode Island.
HATTIE LOUDEN, Connecticut.
LILIAN LAKE, New York.
ANNA BRIGHAM, New Jersey.
——————, Louisiana.
MARY ROBINSON, Pennsylvania.
MARY SIMMONS, Wisconsin.
JENNIE BABBITT, S. Carolina.
HATTIE CLARK, Delaware.
CORA GREER, Florida.
LEAFA GREER, Mississippi.
MAY JOHNSON, Alabama.
FLORA WAID, Texas.
EMMA SIMONDS, Ill.
CORA WELSH, Missouri.
LIZZIE STARKWEATHER, Ind.
IDA GAGE, Colorado.
ALICE CHARTER, Kentucky.
EVA BEAL, Virginia.

At the adjournment of the public exercises the Soldier's Union met at the Council Room and elected as officers for the ensuing year—

President—H. O. WAID.

Secretary—WM. E. DOWNER.

—*Northville Record.*

P. S.—The publication of this Address was unavoidably delayed to get a complete list of names.

ADDRESS OF THOMAS D. ELIOT,

OF THE 1ST CONGRESSIONAL DISTRICT OF MASSACHUSETTS,

TO HIS CONSTITUENTS.

MY FRIENDS:—I feel impelled to address you by considerations which have pressed themselves upon me recently with an earnestness that I am not able to withstand. They control wholly the unwillingness I have always felt to anticipate or to accompany what I deem it right, as a public servant, to say or to do, by statements explanatory or defensive. These days develope rules of action inapplicable heretofore. As your representative, anxious to advance, here at this time, by personal influence and by vote, your real interests, I am desirous also that you shall know why I have not advocated and why I cannot support the "Compromises" of this year. So far as they are unreal or unsubstantial, or may be understood as surrendering or conferring some privilege or power which we do not intend to surrender or confer, I object to them as frauds upon those who are the other parties to the "Compromise." In this category must be included all propositions for concession which, it is claimed, do not surrender principle. The great question upon which the Southern slave-holders join issue with us is one of principle. If we yield anything that is substantial it must be something of principle. When it is said that we must, at this momentous crisis, be willing to concede and to surrender, provided only we remain faithful to principle, nothing is said, for if we yield nothing that costs us anything we give nothing that is of value. If it be deemed of value it is because the party who receives it is deceived and believes that more is conceded than we intend to yield. A compromise thus effected is secured by false pretences.

But some among the proposed measures of adjustment which have been pressed with earnestness upon Northern men do manifestly involve serious surrender of principle—of all, in fact, that is real and vital—of all that we have contended for, for the vindication of which the Republican party was organized, and in whose vindication it has achieved success. And so far as these propositions are concerned, I object to them as frauds upon the people of the North and West, as frauds upon freedom, whose commission presupposes faithlessness to duty and criminal violation of high trust. As there are two classes of compromise, both objectionable upon the general grounds above stated, so there are two classes of States sought to be affected by them. The Southern seceding States may, it is hoped, be reclaimed, and the middle adhering but threatening States may, it is urged, be retained if these concessions, or some of them, be made. But no one of the seceding States proffers return to allegiance upon concession. By no one of them is compromise desired. And for a reason that is well understood. The design to withdraw from the existing Union and to construct a Cotton Confederacy has been indicated from time to time by Southern politicians for many years. It was entertained by Mr. Calhoun, and has been developed by his disciples; and the election of Mr. Lincoln and consequent loss of political power by the South are availed of as the fit pretext for its consummation. And no one of the able and patriotic men who have spoken for the middle States in the Senate or upon the floor of the House of Representatives has felt authorized to commit his State to a continuance in the Union even if the concessions are made which have been most hopefully advocated. "Concede and we will consider," has been substantially the ground assumed by them. But these men, able and earnest and hopeful, are not secessionists, and do not sympathize with them in their respective States. The secessionists in the middle States mean to bring about disunion for subsequent "reconstruction" probably—but disunion now, as the first step toward such reconstruction as will secure to them permanent power. I have seen no reason to believe that any concession that does not involve unconditional surrender of manhood would affect perceptibly the action of these States. No promise or pledge has been given by any State or made by any representative concerning State action upon "concession;" nor have any authorized assurances been held out to the representatives of the free States of the Union that any middle slave State would probably be satisfied to remain united with them upon concession made. If the secessionists within any State can control the action of their State, no offered compromise would prevent separation. If they have not control, no withdrawal from the Union will occur.

I desire now to review briefly the "question" and the "compromises" proposed. The duty of the free States will be thus developed.

The question is one of political power. From the day of the inauguration of Mr. Jefferson to the day of the election of Mr. Lincoln, with brief interval, the power of the Government has been held by one political party. In course of time, gradually, and by the operation of causes growing out of the character of our institutions, this party has become more and more obviously the party of the South, or, more accurately, of the slaveholding interest of the South. At last it has come to pass that its success has been rightfully deemed the success of the slave power, and its defeat has been as rightfully deemed the success of the free power in the land. Now it was well known that the census of this year would demonstrate certain facts which would materially affect the balance of political power in this country. Among the earlier compromises which it was deemed wise by the founders of our Government to sanction, that one which determines the apportionment of representatives among the several States by adding to the whole number of free persons "three-fifths of all other persons" was destined to secure a political power to the slave interest which the natural forces of freedom could alone control. Those natural forces have been operating hitherto, and it was known that the census statistics of 1860 would add more strength to freedem than the arbitrary provisions of the Constitution had guaranteed to slavery. The election of Mr. Lincoln upon the Chicago platform has demonstrated the power of a present majority, and the necessary withdrawal from office by Southern Democratic States, consequent upon it, has forewarned the extreme South that such majority earnestly operating within the rule of the Constitution, in favor of freedom, would probably indefinitely postpone the recovery of lost power. And the time will come when the historian who shall narrate the occurrences of this year will be obliged to record the fact, that ambitious, designing, and reckless men, flushed with power, and insolent from its long possession, resolved to ruin when not permitted to rule, encouraged and aided by public officers willing at any sacrifice to conceal their own official corruption, have by a series of fraudulent misrepresentations to the people of the Southern portions of the Union, where no Republican voice is permitted to be heard, so poisoned the heart of the people against the Government that within ninety days after the election of the President, six States have enacted ordinances of secession. Two of these States, South Carolina and Georgia, were original members of the Union; but before they became so, the first compromise, "parent of all our woes," was made. In the Constitutional Convention, while the question of the continuance of the slave trade was under consideration, and the eloquent statesmen of Maryland and Virginia were opposed by the delegates from South Carolina and Georgia, it was deemed best to let in these two States upon their own terms and not to exclude them from the Union; and the compromise in the first article of the Constitution was made that States might "import" such persons as they thought proper to admit prior to 1808.

To extend slavery was the purpose and the effect of this first compromise, and now it is proposed that we should for the same purpose, by constitutional amendment, which shall be unchangeable hereafter, covenant and agree that lands now free which may be acquired by purchase, or by force or fraud, lying South of an arbitrary line, shall be doomed to hopeless slavery.

The reasons assigned by secession leaders in the different States to justify their treason are various and somewhat inconsistent. In South Carolina it has been confessed that since the time of Mr. Calhoun, if not from an earlier period, it has been the purpose of that Commonwealth, at a convenient time, to assume its position among the powers of the earth as a sovereign nation. In one of the States the election of Mr. Lincoln has been assigned as the controlling cause; and the legislation of some of the Northern States unfriendly to their interests has been vouched in as one of the reasons impelling them to separation. But the recognized Republican doctrine, that the will of the majority expressed according to the provisions of constitutional law, should control and determine the policy of the Government, has been repeatedly avowed as the radical and underlying grievance which cannot be submitted to. The pretence is that the majority will oppress, and assume powers not conferred by the Constitution. No oppressive measures have been initiated, for as yet the Republican party have had no control or responsibility; and it is obvious that none could be consummated without a majority in the House of Representatives and against a majority in the Senate. But the time is near at hand when the Republican party, if faithful to its principles, would control both the Senate and the House; and the Southern politicians have well understood that now, before the inauguration of Mr. Lincoln, was the time to strike the blow. During the Presidential canvass, when it was ascertained that the hostile wings of the Democratic party could not unite, and that a Democratic defeat must be sustained, there were in the Cabinet at Washington able, ambitious, and unscrupulous men, who, it is now known, were then in conspiracy to overthrow the Government. The Army and the Treasury were in their hands. The money of the Treasury was thrown into Southern States, and used to strengthen Southern power. The military forces of the Government were dispersed and sent far away from home. The arms and munitions of war belonging to the Government were withdrawn from the North, and large sums of money expended in the procurement of other arms and munitions of war, which have been distributed among the forts and arsenals of the South. When it is remembered that these acts of treason were designed and consummated for the purpose of enabling the extreme Southern States more successfully to throw off their allegiance to the Union, and more readily to establish an independent slave Confederacy, it will be appreciated at once that no concession or compromise, however humiliating, could prevent or postpone those ordinances of secession advocated and demanded by the very traitors who, at Washington, had prepared the way for their vindication by arms within the rebelling States.

On the 20th of December, 1860, South Carolina assumed to withdraw from the Union. Mississippi followed on the 9th of January, 1861; on the 11th of January Florida and Alabama enacted their ordinances of secession. Georgia followed on the 18th, and on the 26th of January Louisiana determined to unite her fortunes with those of her sister States. Six separate sovereignties were thus created, and while I write, these rebel States are in convention for the purpose of forming what they term a Provisional Government. The same men who, in the Cabinet of Mr. Buchanan, had initiated, plotted, and arranged these acts of treason against the United States, were found in the conventions of these States, hurrying to their final passage with mad haste the ordinances of separation. And one of them is now the President of the convention of seceding States. During all this time the forts and arsenals and public property of the United States within these States were left unguarded. Months before, the President had been warned and urged and entreated to protect and defend them. But the men who held his ear withheld his hand. With a few important exceptions, every fort and arsenal, and depot of arms within the seceding States, has been seized, and is now occupied by the enemies of the Union. Immense supplies of arms, ammunition, and implements of war have been fraudulently and traitorously possessed under color of authority from the States in which they were situate. And they are now held, with large deposits of money also seized, against the will of the Government to which they belong, under a pretence of right! It is proposed to retain and to use them all if necessary to defeat any attempt which shall be made by the Government to recover its own property!

It is obvious that no action of the Republican party could have stayed for one day the progress of events during the month of January. If the President had been faithful to his duty, those various acts of treason could not have been consummated. But the consequences of his criminal inaction cannot be visited upon us. And when it is remembered that among the most persistent and uncompromising leaders of the secession rebellion are found the men who have from its organization most bitterly opposed the principles and denounced the men of the Republican party, it will be appreciated at once that no action of that party short of its dismemberment could have been effective to control the course of events which have brought the Union to its present distracted condition. In the record of the past, no history is found of such gigantic national crime, as that which will blacken the page that shall describe fitly events recently enacted and now occurring among us. The means adopted by the traitors, official and political; the consequences risked and defied, and the end to be secured, must be regarded together, if we would estimate aright the unparalleled atrocity of the great act of treason. To overthrow a popular political party; to establish slavery as a national institution; and to recover and perpetuate political power, are now recognized as the threefold end sought to be brought about by preliminary secession and subsequent reconstruction. It is not impossible that the hurried and illconsidered, and insolent action of the first seceding State may result in permanent separation of the Gulf States; and whether such result was originally contemplated or not, it may in the progress of events be made inevitable. It must be so, unless such humiliating surrender by the free States of the rights of freemen shall be made, as will demonstrate that we are indeed a nation of slaves; or unless, in the mysterious providence of God, events shall occur, at which the heart of the nation, is shaken in advance with dread, that may call for reconstruction without the presence of a slave.

But the "question" is not fully stated when we have considered the causes of this rebellion or its progress hitherto. There are border slave States, where radical secessionists are now working with that zeal which avowed treason stimulates to unwearied anp unscrupulous efforts, and where noble and patriotic men are striving to stem the mad tide that must otherwise overwhelm them, and their families, and their fortunes! And the Republican party is called upon to strengthen the hands of those men against their common enemy. I frankly confess that it is here I feel the pressure of the call for concession. There are men in all those States who recognize as clearly as we can do the weakness, folly, and wickedness of what is called secession. Their hopes centre in the Union, and their personal fortunes are involved in its existence. In Missouri, the most western, and in Maryland, the most northern of the border States, the great interests of the people seem to be so dependent upon their continued union with the the free States, that their patriotic men may truly say, "it is to the Union alone we must look for continued prosperity and peace."

But there is one prominent and controlling objection to the measures of concession and guaranty proposed, not affecting their character—itself objectionable—which is applicable to the position assumed by the middle or border States.

All the "compromises" are concessions merely, without equivalent. It cannot be said properly that the equivalent is that the border States will not attempt to withdraw from the Union. That, if true, would be no equivalent. It would be a demand for concession upon threat and not for value. But it is not true. No party or party man has declared or claimed a right to do so, that any of these States would not withdraw if these compromsises are granted; but only that being made, the hands of Union men would be strengthened in their contest with disunionists. Whether, thus strengthened, they can uphold the flag of the Union is uncertain. But if it shall appear that such strength thus secured will be sufficient for that work, this objection remains: that all or substantially all of those who have from the border slave States asked concession or compromise, that so they could the better at home contend with the enemies of the Union, have stipulated, nevertheless, for one condition, as a political *sine qua non* of permanent union. And that condition is, that no force shall be employed by the Government to recover its own property.

That would be "coercion!" And "if one drop of Southern blood should be spilled, all the Southern States must at once unite." I believe this to be the feeling of the larger number of those who yet ask for concession, to the end that the present Union may not be further, and at once dissolved. But obviously, unless the middle States are willing to belong to the Union, and to support the Government and to "enforce the laws," their continuance with us would be a source of weakness, and not of strength. For one thing is certain, we must ascertain whether we have or not a Government! If we have not, one must be made, and that would be a Free Republic. If we now have a Government, its laws should be obeyed and enforced, and the traitors who have taken forcible possession of the forts, arsenals, military depots, mints, and hospitals of the Federal Government should be brought to punishment, and the property recovered. This question of Government or no Government, must now be settled. It must be determined in the only feasible, and, indeed, possible way, by retaking what has been wrongfully, and in violation of law, wrested from our control. To do that may require time and money, and the shedding of blood. They alone who have committed the treasonable crime, are responsible for this. At whatever cost of time, or money, or human life, it must be done, if this Government is a Fact and not a Fiction.

With this question another is connected, which involves the abstract right of secession. I need not argue to you the absurdity of that right as claimed. It is said "six States *are out*, why discuss the right?" Because the adhering border States are also threatening States! They claim that they will withdraw, if "guarantees are refused." Shall we give them guarantees, even if thereby kept within the Union, and thus impliedly recognize the right to secede? Would such settlement permanently benefit them or us? But if these States have a right to withdraw, other States may also withdraw, if guarantees are refused to institutions or interests claimed to be essential to their prosperity. If the iron of Pennsylvania, or the zinc of New Jersey or Wisconsin, shall be refused protection, or the manufactures of New England shall be prejudiced by unfriendly legislation, any offended State has the same right to secede that the hitherto seceding States have had, or the threatening States now have; therefore it must now be settled whether such right exists. If the middle States insist upon such right, to be exercised by each State when it may choose, and as it may choose, it is worse than useless to attempt concession or compromise. We can have no Government entitled to respect among the nations of the earth, if each State being offended may withdraw. Secession is rebellion. It is revolutionary. If the men who set the laws at defiance fail, they are liable to the punishment of traitors. If they succeed, they vindicate by force the right of revolution. But it is a question of force. I do not forget that six States claim to have seceded, and that one more will probably soon follow them. I am not discussing what ought to be done by the Government with respect to them. Where one man commits a crime he may be punished. Where 50,000 men commit a crime, the course which it may be most proper to pursue, is not so obvious. But I am considering rather this assumed right of secession, in view of the compromises we are called upon to make. For manifestly, concessions are useless, unless such right as claimed is abandoned. I do not believe that it will be deemed right to attempt to keep by force any State within the Union. But its right to secede must not be admitted expressly, or by implication. Let the revenues be collected. Let the property of the Government be recalled, and the evils of separation will work out their own remedy. But when we are called upon, as we now are, to make constitutional surrenders and concessions and guarantees, in order that States now in, shall be induced to remain loyal to the Union, no doubt should be left concerning the future exercise of that right by any State South or North. I have seen no reason to believe that any one State which has discussed the question of concession or secession, would hesitate to claim the right at any time peaceably to secede. I cannot hearken to any proposition, while such right is maintained. The "right of revolution"—we all understand. The right of peaceable secession, as now claimed, is a very different thing. The one confesses a Government, and seeks to overturn it. The other is inconsistent with the existence of a Government. A Government must assume to maintain its laws, and to enforce obedience.

But the concessions, or compromises, or constitutional guarantees demanded by the slaveholding power of the South from the Republicans of the Union, ought not to be made or given for reasons intrinsic to and suggested by the character of the concessions or guarantees themselves. The Committee of Thirty-three have reported for the action of Congress certain general resolutions and a proposition to admit New Mexico as a State, and an amendment to our Constitution and an additional fugitive slave law. Besides these, the compromises known as the "Crittenden" propositions are under consideration. I can give my support to none of them, or to none like them. Eleven resolutions have been reported. Probably no one believes that the passage of all of them would have any effect to change a vote in any State upon the question of secession. One of them announces that "all attempts" by State Legislatures to obstruct or hinder the recovery and surrender of fugitives from service or labor are in derogation of the Constitution of the United States. An "attempt" to obstruct by legislation would presuppose legislation *with intent to obstruct*. The Constitution provides for the delivery, on claim, of the person owing service who has escaped; and legislation with intent to defeat that provision of the Constitution would be "in derogation" of it. But no one believes that after a month of labor thirty-three gentlemen have agreed to offer a resolution for the purpose of announcing that fact! Who doubts that a law made for the purpose of defeating a provision of the Constitution is "in derogation" of it? But the objection to that resolution is this: Every Southern man and every Northern Democrat, as I believe, who has discussed or referred to the "liberty bills" or the "laws preventing kidnapping," now upon the statute books of many of the Northern States, has spoken of them as attempts to violate the constitutional provisions concerning the rendition of fugitives from service. And this resolution by the terms "all attempts to obstruct," means to affirm, and is understood to affirm, that *all such liberty laws and laws against kidnapping* are "attempts to obstruct" the surrender of fugitives "in derogation of the Constitution." Now that proposition is not true. It is not true in fact or in law. My objection to the resolution is that it is either so weak that it ought not to be offered or so deceptive that it ought not to pass.

One of the resolutions calls upon the Northern States to "revise their statutes." It is not deemed worth while to invite the Southern States to revise or reconstruct their laws. Massachusetts has been revising as far as she deemed it her duty to do so. I decline to advise her to do more. But if it were within the fair scope of my duty to advise my Commonwealth concerning her legislation to protect the personal liberties of her citizens, I should say "repeal no law which assumes to protect our own citizens, and which no court of Massachusetts has declared to be in derogation of the Constitution, without providing also that the repealing act shall not go into operation until the fugitive slave act of 1850 shall be so amended that *the citizens of Massachusetts may have the right to a trial by jury within their own State upon all questions involving their right to personal freedom.*"

The sons of Massachusetts have a right to such protection from their native Commonwealth. What citizen of a southern State will hesitate within his own State to claim the same protection and assert the same right of legislation. Another resolution is a *congressional recognition* of slavery as now existing in fifteen States, and a declaration that no *right exists* outside of a slave State to interfere with slaves or slavery *in disregard of the rights of their owners or the peace of society.* Now, no one pretends that any such right to interfere exists. Every one understands that the Republican party disclaim such doctrine. And the real object of that resolution cannot be to announce a fact so baldly incontrovertible. The object of the resolution must be to secure a congressional recognition of the institution of slavery as now existing in our southern States. I will be a party to no such recognition. What Madison objected to have named in the Constitution, I am unwilling needlessly to recognize by formal resolution.

But I cannot criticise each resolution in detail. Two or three of them are unobjectionable and appropriate. One of them is "that it is the duty of the Federal Government to enforce the Federal laws, protect the Federal property and preserve the Union of these States." I shall vote for that resolution. But when these resolutions assert a proposition which no one denies, but contain recognitions or authorize inferences which will be understood by the southern slaveholder as meaning something which the northern Republican would be unwilling to admit in terms that he did truly mean, I decline wholly to give them my support.

Among the proposed measures of adjustment, is a resolution for an amendment of the Constitution. It is as follows:

"Article XII. No amendment of this Constitution having for its object any interference within the States, with the relation between their citizens and those described in section second of the first article of the Constitution, as 'all other persons,' shall originate with any State that does not recognize that relation within its own limits, or shall be valid without the consent of every one of the States comprising the Union."

I cannot consent as a Representative of the people to propose to the State Legislatures any such amendment to the Constitution. By the provisions of the fifth article of the Constitution, the ratification by the Legislatures of three-fourths of the States, or by Conventions in three-fourths of the States, are required to make valid any proposed amendments thereof. It is apparently not possible that any alteration of the Constitution which the proposed amendment would prevent could be made. It is not contended that such amendment is required because of any possible contingency which could effect such alteration. But it is proposed as a measure of reconciliation. No southern State has asked for such amendment. There is no reason to believe that any southern State would be affected by it or satisfied with it. But if such amendment could have any practical effect, it must be because it would give constitutional sanction to slavery which it has not now, or would furnish guarantees to slavery additional to those now furnished.

I am willing that all the States shall have for all their interests the protection which the Constitution now affords. I am aware that the progress of civilization, the varying interests of society, and the course of events, may require change in our organic law. If a National Convention shall hereafter be called, upon application by the States pursuant to the terms of the Constitution, such amendment as now proposed, if it shall be deemed to furnish additional and substantial guarantees to slavery, may be fitly discussed. But I am wholly averse to the uncalled for initiation by Congress of any amendments, at this period of Christian civilization, which shall give more strength or greater perpetuity to usages, customs, or laws which recognize a right in one man to oppress, or defraud, or enslave another. Next in the order of proposed compromises is the Act for the admission of New Mexico. When this Territory was acquired by the United States, it was free by means of Mexican legislation. Being organized into a Territory, the Territorial legislature wrongfully and by unauthorized assumption of power, enacted a slave code of peculiar, original, and unequalled severity. That code now operates within the Territory, and would operate within the State we are called on to make. It is now a slave Territory. It is proposed to make it a slave State. It is said that slavery will not go there because slave owners can do better with their slaves elsewhere. So long as that is true, slavery will not be to any great extent introduced. How long it may be true no one can tell. But slaves are there now by force of Territorial law. The fact that the number is small cannot affect the principle. I do not believe it to be right, nor do I believe it to be for the welfare of the Union that another slave State shall be at this time admitted. If it shall come in as a free State, or if being admitted it shall, as is believed by many, repeal the slave code and abolish slavery, the South will say, and I think with good reason, that they have been deceived, and the precise question now disturbing the condition of the country when the next southern territory shall be acquired will again distract us. New Mexico is not fit to be a State. Her citizens have not asked to be admitted as a State. The slave interest of the South will be deceived if being admitted she establishes free institutions. The Republicans will be deceived if being admitted now, she adheres to the code by which the Territorial Legislature attempted to legalize slavery.

The amendment of the act for the rendition of fugitives from labor, is advocated as being an improvement of the law of 1850. And it is, as a piece of legislation, an improvement upon that law. It would not be easy to change for the worse the law of 1850. And, until it can be repealed or more humanely amended, I prefer to leave it as it is. My own views upon this subject are well known to you. I am of the opinion held by Mr. Webster, and more recently expressed by the South Carolinian disunionists in their Convention, that it was not the intention of the framers of our Constitution to confer upon Congress the power to legislate concerning the rendition of fugitives from labor.

Mr. Crittenden has proposed amendments to our National Constitution in six articles.

The first article provides that in all territory now held or hereafter acquired by the United States south of the line of 36° 30', slavery of the African race is hereby recognized as existing, and shall not be interfered with by Congress, but shall be protected as property by all departments of the Territorial government.

That article would doom to slavery by law, in advance of our ownership of the territory, all the regions of Mexico and Central America now free! When the people of the United States shall consent to such an amendment of their organic law, they will become a "slave nation." That time has not yet come.

The second article takes from Congress the power to abolish slavery in places *under its exclusive jurisdiction* within the slave States.

The third article abolishes their power to act within the District of Columbia, while Virginia or Maryland hold slaves, without their consent, or without consent of the inhabitants of the District or compensation to dissenting owners.

The next article provides that Congress shall have no power to hinder the transportation of slaves, by land or water, from one State to another where slavery is recognized. This amendment would secure a transit through the free States.

There are other amendments proposed, but these are the most important,

When the people of the free States of the Union are prepared to incorporate these provisions into their organic law, another "Preamble" should be made, for these amendments would not be to "secure the blessings of liberty," but to inflict the curse of slavery upon ourselves and our posterity.

No changes in our law could be suggested which would more truly make slavery a National Institution. These propositions can receive no favor, and I have stated them now because I believe that no argument against them will be desired except what the statement itself affords.

Such are the compromises of this year! The people have rendered their judgment in favor of freedom in the Territories. The political power of slavery thereupon sunders the Union, demanding concession and new guarantees; and being defeated at the polls; insolently requires that the principles of its own political platform shall become constitutional law.

The crisis in our National affairs is one of gravest moment. I assume with awe the profound responsibility that rests upon those who now represent the People. I was not chosen by you in view of such events. But I have regarded with jealous watchfulness the causes that have produced them, and I recognize the duties they enjoin.

I am entreated in your behalf to make "concession" to slavery—to make the slave power which has ruled us heretofore more potent by Congressional legislation and by Constitutional amendment—so that it shall rule us hereafter also. It is said the Union may be saved by concession. I believe the Union has been dismembered now, because of power gained by unwise concessions heretofore made. I believe that only firm adherence to the principles of our present Constitution will restore to us a more perfect union and establish justice and insure to us domestic tranquility.

THOMAS D. ELIOT.

WASHINGTON, *February*, 1861.

H. Polkinhorn, Printer, Washington.

From the Author
Jan 15 96

THE NEGRO AS A SOLDIER

WRITTEN BY

Christian A. Fleetwood,

Late Sergeant-Major, 4th U.S. Colored Troops,

FOR

THE NEGRO CONGRESS,

AT THE

Cotton States and International Exposition,
Atlanta, Ga.,

November 11 to November 23, 1895.

PUBLISHED BY PROF. GEO. WM. COOK.

WASHINGTON, D.C.:
HOWARD UNIVERSITY PRINT.
1895.

THE NEGRO AS A SOLDIER

WRITTEN BY

Christian A. Fleetwood,

Late Sergeant-Major 4th U. S. Colored Troops,

FOR

THE NEGRO CONGRESS,

AT THE

Cotton States and International Exposition, Atlanta, Ga.,

November 11 to November 23, 1895.

PUBLISHED BY PROF. GEO. WM. COOK.

WASHINGTON, D. C.
HOWARD UNIVERSITY PRINT.
1895.

COTTON STATES AND INTERNATIONAL EXPOSITION,
Atlanta, Ga., 1895.

COMMISSION FOR THE DISTRICT OF COLUMBIA COLORED EXHIBIT.
Jesse Lawson, Chief Commissioner.

Edward E. Cooper, Vice Chairman,
Thomas L. Jones,
W. S. Montgomery,
James H. Meriwether,
Joseph H. Stewart,
Henry E. Baker, Treasurer,
A. F. Hilyer,
Geo. Wm. Cook,
Col. Nathan Toomer,
J. E. Johnson, Secretary.

Ladies' Auxiliary Committee.

Mrs. B. K. Bruce, President,
Mrs. J. T. Layton, 1st Vice Pres.,
Mrs. A. F. Hilyer, 2d Vice Pres.,
Mrs. Jesse Lawson, Secretary,
Mrs. Charles R. Douglass, Treas.

Men's Auxiliary Committee.

David A. Clark, Chairman,

OFFICE OF THE COMMISSION,
Room 4, 609 F Street, Northwest,
Washington, D. C. August 5, 1895.

Major C. A. FLEETWOOD.

Dear Sir:—At a meeting of the Committee for the District of Columbia on National Negro Congresses at the Atlanta Exposition, held this day, you were appointed a speaker to represent the District on the subject, "Military."

Will you kindly favor us with an early notice of your acceptance?

Very respectfully,
WALTER H. BROOKS, Chairman
W. J. HOWARD,
EDWARD H. LIPSCOMBE, Sec.
Committee.

THE NEGRO AS A SOLDIER.

IN THE WAR OF THE REVOLUTION.

For sixteen hundred years prior to the war between Great Britain and the Colonies, the pages of history bear no record of the Negro as a soldier. Tracing his separate history in the Revolutionary War, is a task of much difficulty, for the reason that while individual instances of valor and patriotism abound there were so few separate bodies of Negro troops, that no separate record appears to have been made. The simple fact is that the fathers as a rule enlisted men both for the Army and Navy, just as now, is only continued by the Navy, that is to say, they were assigned wherever needed, without regard to race or color. Varner's Rhode Island Battalion appears to have been the only large aggregation of Negroes in this war, though Connecticut, New York, and New Hampshire each furnished one separate company in addition to individuals scattered through their other organizations, so that ere the close of the war, there were very few brigades, regiments, or companies in which the Negro was not in evidence.

The free Negro appears to have gone in from the beginning without attracting or calling out special comment. Later, as men grew scarcer and necessity more pressing, slaves were taken in also, and then the trouble began. Those who held slaves did not care to lose them in this way. Others who had not, did not think it just the thing in a war for avowed freedom to place an actual slave in the ranks to fight. Some did not want the Negro, bond or free, to take part as a soldier in the struggle. So that in May, 1775, the Massachusetts Committee of Safety voted that thereafter only free men should be enlisted. In July, Gen. Gates issued an order prohibiting further enlistments of Negroes, but saying nothing of those already in the service.

In October, a council of war, presided over by Gen. Washington, comprising three Major Generals and six Brigadier Generals, voted unanimously against the enlistment of slaves, and by a decided majority against further enlistments of Negroes. Ten days later in a conference held at Cambridge, Mass., participated in by Gen. Washington, Benj. Franklin, Benj. Harrison, Thos. Lynch, and the deputy governors of Connecticut and Rhode Island, the same action was taken.

On the 7th November, 1775, Earl Dundore, commanding the forces of His Majesty the King, issued a proclamation offering freedom and equal pay to all slaves who would join his armies as soldiers. It did not take the the colonists long to find out their mistake, although Gen. Washington, in accordance with the expressed will of his officers and of the Committee of Safety, did on the 17th Nov., 1775, issue a proclamation forbidding the further enlistment of Negroes. Less than two months later, that is to say on the 30th Dec., 1775, he issued a second proclamation again authorizing the enlistment of free Negroes He advised Congress of his action, and stated that he would recall it if so directed. But he was not. The splendid service rendered by the Negro and the great and pressing need of men were such, that although the opposition continued from some sections, it was not thereafter strong enough to get recognition. So the Negroes went and came much as did other men.

In all the events of the war, from Bunker Hill to Yorktown, they bore an honorable part. The history of the doings of the armies is their history, as in everything they took part and did their share. Their total enlistment was about 3,000 men. A very fair percentage for the then population. I might instance the killing of Major Pitcairn, at Bunker Hill, by Peter Salem, and of Major Montgomery at Fort Griswold by Jordan Freeman. The part they took in the capture of Major-General Prescott at Newport; their gallant defense of Colonel Greene, their beloved commander, when he was surprised and murdered at Croton River, May 13, 1781, when it was only after the last of his faithful guards had been shot and cut down that he was reached; or at the battle of Rhode Island, when a battalion of 400 Negroes withstood three separate and distinct charges from 1,500 Hessians under Count Donop, and beat them back with such tremendous loss that Count Donop at once applied for an exchange, fearing that his men would kill him if he went into battle with them again, for having exposed them to such slaughter; and many other instances that are of record. The letter following, written Dec, 5, 1775, explains itself;

To the Honorable General Court of the Massachusetts Bay.

The subscribers beg leave to report to your Honorable House which we do in justice to the character of so brave a man), that under our own observation we declare that a Negro Man named Salem Poor, of Col. Frye's Regiment, Cap. Ames' Company, in the late battle at Charleston, behaved like an experienced officer as well as an excellent soldier. To set forth particulars of his conduct would be tedious. We would only beg to say, in the person of this Negro centers a brave and gallant soldier. The reward due to so great and distinguished a character, we submit to Congress.

JONA. BREWER, Col.
THOMAS NIXON, Lt. Col.
JOSEPH BAKER, Lieut.
JONAS RICHARDSON, Capt.
EBENEZER VARNUM, 2 Lt.
WILLIAM SMITH Capt.
RICHARD WELSH, Lieut.
WM. PRESCOTT, Col.
EPHM. COREY, Lieut.
JOSHUA ROW, Lieut.
ELIPHALETT BODWELL, Sergt.
WM. HUDSON BALLARD, Capt.
JOHN MORTON, Sergt.

This is a splendid and well attested tribute to a gallant and worthy Negro. There were many such, but, beyond receiving and reading no action was taken thereon by Congress. There is no lack of incidents and the temptation to quote many of them is great, but the time allotted me is too brief for extended mention and I must bring this branch of my subject to a close. It is in evidence that while so many Negroes were offering their lives a willing sacrifice for the country, in some sections the officers of the Continental Forces received their bounty and pay in Negroes, "grown" and "small," instead of "dollars" and "cents." Fighting for *Liberty* and taking pay in *Slaves!*

When the war was over the free men returned to meet their same difficulties; the slaves were caught when possible and reenslaved by their former masters. In Boston a few years later we find a party of black patriots of the Revolution mobbed on Boston Common while celebrating the anniversary of the abolition of the slave trade.

The captain of a vessel trading along the coast tells of a Negro who had fought in the war and been distinguished for bravery and soldierly conduct. He was reclaimed and reenslaved by his master after the war, and served him faithfully until old age rendered him useless. The master then brought the poor old slave to this captain and asked him to take him along on his trip and try to sell him. The captain hated to sell a man who had fought for his country, but finally agreed, took the poor old man to Mobile, and sold him for $100 to a man who put him to attending a chicken coop. His former master continued to draw the old slave's pension as a soldier in the Revolution, until he died.

THE WAR OF 1812.

The war of 1812 was mainly fought upon the water, and in the American navy at that time the Negro stood in the ratio of about one to six. We find record of complaint by Commodore Perry at the beginning because of the large number of Negroes sent him, but later the highest tribute to their bravery and efficiency. Capt. Shaler, of the armed brig General Thompson, writing of an engage ment between his vessel and a British frigate, says:

"The name of one of my poor fellows, who was killed, ought to to be registered in the book of fame, and remembered as long as bravery is a virtue. He was a black man, by name John Johnson. A twenty-four pound shot struck him in the hip, and took away all the lower part of his body. In this state the poor brave fellow lay on the deck, and several times exclaimed to his shipmates: 'Fire away, my boys; no haul a color down!' Another black man, by the name of John Davis, who was struck in much the same manner, repeatedly requested to be thrown overboard, saying that he was only in the way of others."

I know of nothing finer in history than these.

As before, the Negro was not universally welcomed to the ranks of the American army; but later continued reverses and a lack of enthusiasm in enlistments made it necessary to seek his aid, and from Mobile, Ala., on September 21, 1814, General Jackson issued a stirring call to the free colored people of Louisiana for aid. It began thus:

"Through a mistaken policy you have heretofore been deprived of a participation in the glorious struggle for national rights in which our country is engaged. This no longer shall exist."

In a remarkably short period, two battalions were raised, under Majors LaCaste and Savary, which did splendid service in the battle of New Orleans. New York enrolled two battalions, and sent them to Sacketts Harbor. Pennsylvania enrolled twenty-four hundred, and sent them to Gray's Ferry at the capture of Washton, to prepare for the invading column. Another battalion also was raised, armed, equipped and ready to start to the front, when peace was declared.

Let us hear the testimony of that original democrat, General Jackson. Under the date of Dec. 18, 1814, he writes as follows:

"To the men of color, soldiers: From the shores of Mobile I called you to arms. I invited you to share in the perils and to divide the glory of your white countrymen. I expected much from you; for I was not uninformed of those qualities which must render you so formidable to an invading foe. I knew you could endure hunger and thirst, and all the hardships of war. I knew that you loved the land of your nativity, and that, like ourselves, you had to defend all that is most dear to man. But you surpass my hopes. I have found in you, united to those qualities, that noble enthusiasm that impels to great deeds.

"Soldiers: The President of the United States shall be informed of your conduct on the present occasion, and the voice of the representatives of the American nation shall applaud your valor, as your general now praises your ardor. The enemy is near. His sails cover the lakes, but the brave are united, and if he finds us contending among ourselves, it will be for the prize of valor, and fame its noblest reward."

In one of the actions of this war, a charging column of the American army was repulsed and thrown into great disorder. A Negro private, seeing the disaster, sprang upon a horse, and by heroic effort rallied the troops, led them back upon a second charge, and completely routed the enemy. He was rewarded by General Jackson with the honorary title of Major. Under the laws he could not commission him.

When the war was over, this gallant man returned to his home in Nashville, Tenn., where he lived for years afterward, highly respected by its citizens of all races.

At the age of seventy years, this black hero was obliged, *in self-defense*, to strike a white ruffian, who had assaulted him. Under the laws of the State he was arrested and given nine and thirty lashes on his bare back. It broke his heart, and Major Jeffreys died.

THE WAR FOR THE UNION.

It seems a little singular that in the tremendous struggle between the States in 1861–1865, the south should have been the first to take steps toward the enlistment of Negroes. Yet such is the fact. Two weeks after the fall of Fort Sumter, the "Charleston Mercury" records the passing through Augusta of several companies of the the 3rd and 4th Georgia Regt., and of sixteen well-drilled companies *and one Negro company* from Nashville, Tenn.

"The Memphis Avalanche" and "The Memphis Appeal" of

May 9, 10, and 11, 1861, give notice of the appointment by the "Committee of Safety" of a committee of three persons "to organize a volunteer company composed of our patriotic freemen of color of the city of Memphis, for the service of our common defense."

A telegram from New Orleans dated November 23, 1861, notes the review by Gov. Moore of over 28,000 troops, and that one regiment comprised "*1,400 colored men.*" "The New Orleans Picayune," referring to a review held February 9, 1862, says: "We must also pay a deserved compliment to the companies of free colored men, all very well drilled and comfortably equipped."

It is a little odd, too, that in the evacuation of New Orleans a little later, in April, 1862, all of the troops succeeded in getting away except the Negroes. They "got left."

It is not in the line of this paper to speculate upon what would have been the result of the war had the South kept up this policy, enlisted the freemen, and emancipated the enlisting slaves and their families. The immense addition to their fighting force, the quick recognition of them by Great Britain, to which slavery was the greatest bar, and the fact that the heart of the Negro was with the South but for slavery, and the case stands clear. But the primary successes of the South closed its eyes to its only chance of salvation, while at the same time the eyes of the North were opened.

In 1865, the South saw, and endeavored to remedy its error. On March 9, 1865, the Confederate Congress passed a bill, recommended by Gen. Lee, authorizing the enlistment of 200,000 Negroes; but it was then too late.

The North came slowly and reluctantly to recognize the Negro as a factor for good in the war. "This is a white man's war," met the Negroes at every step of their first efforts to gain admission to the armies of the Union.

To General David Hunter more than to any other one man, is due the credit for the successful entry upon the stage of the Negro as a soldier in this war.

In the spring of 1862, he raised and equipped a regiment of Negroes in South Carolina, and when the fact became known in Washington and throughout the country, such a storm was raised about the ears of the administration that they gracefully stood aside and left the brave general to fight his enemies in the front and rear as best he might. He was quite capable to do both, as it proved.

On the 9th of June, 1862, Mr. Wickliffe, of Kentucky, introduced a resolution in the House of Representatives, which was passed, calling upon the Secretary of War for information as to the fact of these enlistments and by what authority this matter was done.

The Secretary of War replied under date June 14, 1862, disavowing any official knowledge of such a regiment and denying that any authority had been given therefor. He referred the resolution to Gen. Hunter' His reply is one of the best things of the war I quote it entire.

Headquarters, Department of the South,
Port Royal, S. C., June 23, 1862.

Hon. Edwin M. Stanton, Secretary of War,
Washington.

SIR : I have the honor to acknowledge the receipt of a communication from the Adjutant-General of the Army, dated June 16, 1862, requesting me to furnish you with the information necessary to answer certain resolutions introduced in the House of Representatives June 9, 1862, on motion of the Hon. Mr. Wickliffe, of Kentucky, their substance being to inquire : First, whether I had organized, or was organizing, a regiment of fugitive slaves in this department; Second, whether any authority had been given to me from the War Department for such organization; and Third, whether I had been furnished by order of the War Department with clothing, uniforms, arms, equipments, etc., for such a force.

Only having received the letter conveying the inquiries at a late hour on Saturday night, I urge forward my answer in time for the steamer sailing to-day (Monday), this haste preventing me from entering as minutely as I could wish upon many points of detail, such as the paramount importance of the subject calls for. But in view of the near termination of the present session of Congress, and the widespread interest which must have been awakened by Mr. Wickliffe's resolution, I prefer sending even this imperfect answer to waiting the period necessary for the collection of fuller and more comprehensive data.

To the first question, therefore, I reply that no regiment of "fugitive slaves" has been or is organized in this department. There is, however, a fine regiment of persons whose late masters are "fugitive rebels," men who everywhere fly before the appearance of the national flag, leaving their servants behind them to shift as best they can for themselves. So far, indeed, are the loyal persons composing this regiment from seeking to avoid the presence of their late owners that they are now, one and all, working with remarkable industry to place themselves in a position to go in full and effective pursuit of their fugacious and traitorous proprietors.

To the second question, I have the honor to answer, that the instructions given to Brig.-General W. T. Sherman by the Hon. Simon Cameron, late Secretary of War, and turned over to me by succession for my guidance, do distinctly authorize me to employ all loyal persons offering their services in defense of the Union and for the suppression of this rebellion in any manner I might see fit, or that the circumstances might call for. There is no restriction as to the character or color of the persons who might be employed, or the nature of the employment; whether civil or military, in which their services should be used. I conclude, therefore, that I have been authorized to enlist "fugitive slaves" as soldiers, could any be found in this department.

No such characters have, however, yet appeared within our most advanced pickets, the loyal slaves everywhere remaining on their plantations to welcome us, and supply us with food, labor and information. It is the masters who have, in every instance, been the "fugitives"—running away from loyal slaves as well as loyal soldiers, and whom we have only partially been able to see—chiefly their heads over ramparts, or, rifle in hand, dodging behind trees, in the extreme distance. In the absence of any "fugitive master" law, the deserted slaves would be wholly without remedy, had not the crime of treason given them the right to pursue, capture, and bring back those persons of whose protection they have been thus suddenly bereft.

To the third interrogatory, it is my painful duty to reply, that I never have received any specific authority for issues of clothing, uniforms, arms, equipments, etc., to the troops in question. My general instructions from Mr. Cameron, to employ them in any manner I might find necessary, and the military exigencies of the department and the country being my only, but, in my judgment, sufficient justification. Neither have I had any specific authority for supplying these persons with shovels, spades and pickaxes when employing them as laborers, nor with boats and oars when using them as lightermen; but these are not points included in Mr. Wickliffe's resolution. To me it seemed that liberty to employ men in any particular capacity implied with it liberty also to supply them with the necessary tools; and acting under this faith I have clothed, equipped and armed the only loyal regiment yet raised in South Carolina.

I must say in vindication of my conduct that had it not been for the many other diversified and imperative claims on my time, a much more satisfactory result might have been hoped for; and that, in place of only one, as at present, at least five or six well-drilled, brave, and thoroughly acclimated regiments should by this time have been added to the loyal forces of the Union.

The experiment of arming the blacks, so far as I have made it, has been a complete and even marvellous success. They are sober, docile, attentive, and enthusiastic, displaying great natural capacities for acquiring the duties of a soldier. They are eager beyond all things to take the field and be led into action; and it is the unanimous opinion of the officers who have had charge of them, that in the peculiarities of this climate and country, they will prove invaluable auxiliaries, fully equal to the similar regiments so long and successfully used by the British authorities in the West Indies.

In conclusion I would say it is my hope, there appearing to be no possibility of other reinforcements owing to the exigencies of the campaign in the peninsular, to have organized by the end of next fall and to be able to present to the Government from forty-eight to fifty thousand of these hardy and devoted soldiers.

Trusting that this letter may form part of your answer to Mr. Wickliffe's resolution.

I have the honor to be, most respectfully, your obedient servant,

D. HUNTER,

Major General Commanding.

The reading of this famous document in the House brought out such a storm of laughter, from both friends and foes that further action was impossible. The Hon. Sunset Cox speaking of the matter some years later said: "I tell you that letter from Hunter spoiled the prettiest speech I had ever thought of making. I had been delighted with Wickliffe's motion, and thought the reply to it would furnish us with first-rate democratic thunder for the next election. I made up my mind to sail in on Hunter's answer no matter what it was—the moment it came, and to be even more humorously successful in its delivery and reception than I was in my speech against war-horse Gurley of Ohio. Well you see, man proposes, but Providence orders otherwise. When the clerk announced the receipt of the letter, and that he was about to read it, I caught the Speaker's eye, and was booked for the first speech against your Negro experiment. The first sentence being formal and official was very well; but at the second the House began to grin, and at the third, there was not a man on the floor, except Father Wickliffe, of Kentucky, perhaps, who was not convulsed with laughter. Even my own risibles I found to be affected, and before the document was concluded, I motioned to the Speaker that he might give the floor to whom he pleased, as my desire to distinguish myself in in that particular tilt was over."

The beginning of 1863, saw the opening of the doors to the Negro in every direction. General Lorenzo Thomas went in person to the valley of the Mississippi to supervise it there. Massachusetts was authorized to fill its quota with Negroes. The States of Maryland, Missouri, Delaware and Tennesee were thrown open by order of the War Department, and all slaves enlisting therefrom declared free Ohio, Connecticut, Pennsylvania and New York joined the band and sent the stalwart black boy in blue to the front singing, "Give us a flag, all free, without a slave." For two years the fierce and determined opposition had kept them out, but now the bars were down and they came pouring in. Some one said he cared not who made the laws of a people if he could make their songs. A better exemplification of this would be difficult to find than is the song written by "Miles O'Reilly" (Col. Halpine), of the old 10th Army Corps. I cannot resist the temptation to quote it here. With General Hunter's letter and this song to quote from, the episode was closed:

Some say it is a burning shame to make the Naygurs fight,
An' that the trade o' being kilt belongs but to the white:
But as for me, upon me sowl, so liberal are we here,
I'll let Sambo be murthered, in place of meself, on every day of the year.
On every day of the year, boys, and every hour in the day,
The right to be kilt I'll divide wid him, and divil a word I'll say.

In battles wild commotion I shouldn't at all object,
If Sambo's body should stop a ball that was coming for me direct,
An' the prod of a southern bayonet, so liberal are we here,
I'll resign and let Sambo take it, on every day in the year,
On every day in the year, boys, an' wid none of your nasty pride,
All right in a southern bagnet prod, wid Sambo I'll divide.

The men who object to Sambo, should take his place and fight,
An' it is betther to have a Naygur's hue, than a liver that's weak an' white,
Though Sambo's black as the ace of spades, his finger a thryger can pull,
An' his eye runs straight on the barrel sight from under its thatch of wool,
So hear me all, boys, darlin, don't think I'm tipping you chaff,
The right to be kilt, I'll divide with him, an' give him the largest half.

It took three years of war to place the enlisted Negro upon the same ground as the enlisted white man as to pay and emoluments; *perhaps* six years of war might have given him shoulder-straps, but the war ended without authorization of law for that step. At first they were received, under an act of Congress that allowed each one, without regard to rank, ten dollars per month, three dollars thereof to be retained for clothing and equipments. I think it was in May, '64, when the act was passed equalizing the pay, but not opening the doors to promotion.

Under an act of the Confederate Congress, making it a crime punishable with death for any white person to train any Negro or mulatto to arms, or aid them in any military enterprise, and devoting the Negro caught under arms to the tender mercies of the "present or future laws of the State" in which caught, a large number of *promotions* were made by the way of a rope and a tree along the first year of the Negro's service (I can even recall one instance as late as April 1865, though it had been long before then generally discontinued).

What the Negro did, how he did it, and where, it would take volumes to properly record, I can however give but briefest mention to a few of the many evidences of his fitness for the duties of the war, and his aid to the cause of the Union.

The first fighting done by organized Negro troops appears to have been done by Company A, First South Carolina Negro Regiment, at St. Helena Island, November 3–10, 1862, while participating in an expedition along the coast of Georgia and Florida under Lt.-Col. O. T. Beard, of the Forty-eighth New York Infantry, who says in his report:—

"The colored men fought with astonishing coolness and bravery. I found them all I could desire, more than I had hoped. They behaved gloriously, and deserve all praise."

The testimony thus inaugurated runs like a cord of gold through the web and woof of the history of the Negro as a soldier from that date to their final charge, the last made at Clover Hill, Va., April 9, 1865.

Necessarily the first actions in which the Negro bore a part commanded most attention. Friends and enemies were looking eagerly to see how they would acquit themselves, and so it comes to pass that the names of Fort Wagner, Olustee, Millikens Bend, Port Hudson and Fort Pillow are as familiar as Bull Run, Antietam, Shiloh and Gettysburg, and while those first experiences were mostly severe reverses, they were by that very fact splendid exemplifiers of the truth that the Negroes could be relied upon to fight under the most adverse circumstances, against any odds, and could not be discouraged.

Let us glance for a moment at Port Hudson, La., in May, 1863, assaulted by General Banks with a force of which the First and Second Regiments, Louisiana Native Guards, formed a part. When starting upon their desperate mission, Colonel Stafford of the First Regiment in turning over the regimental, colors to the color guard, made a brief and patriotic address, closing in the words:

"Color Guard: Protect, defend, die for, but do not surrender these colors." The gallant flag-sergeant, Plancianos, taking them replied: "Colonel: I will bring back these colors to you in honor, or report to God the reason why."

Six times with desperate valor they charged over ground where success was hopeless, a deep bayou between them and the works of the enemy at the point of attack rendered it impossible to reach them, yet strange to say, six times they were ordered forward and six times they went to useless death, until swept back by the blazing breath of shot and shell before which nothing living could stand. Here fell the gallant Captain Cailloux, black as the ace of spades; refusing to leave the field though his arm had been shattered by a bullet he returned to the charge until killed by a shell.

A soldier limping painfully to the front was halted and asked where he was going, he replied; "I am shot bad in de leg, and dey want me to go to de hospital, but I guess I can give 'em a little more yet."

The colors came back but crimsoned with the blood of the gallant Plancianos, who reported to God from that bloody field.

Shall we glance from this to Millikens Bend, La., in January, 1863, garrisoned by the Ninth and Eleventh Louisiana and the First Mississippi, all Negroes, and about one hundred and sixty of the twenty-third Iowa (white), about eleven hundred fighting men in all. Attacked by a force of six Confederate regiments, crushed out of their works by sheer weight of numbers, borne down toward the levee, fighting every step of the way, hand to hand, clubbed musket, bayonets and swords, from three a. m. to twelve, noon, when a Union gun-boat came to the rescue and shelled the desperate foe back to the woods, with a total loss to the defenders of 437 men, two-fifths of their strength.

Shall we turn with sadness to Fort Wagner, S. C., in July, 1863, when the Fifty-fourth Mass. won its deathless fame, and its grand young commander, Col. Robert Gould Shaw, passed into the temple of immortality. After a march of all day, under a burning sun, and all night through a tempest of wind and rain, drenched, exhausted, hungry, they wheel into line, without a murmur for that awful charge, that dance of death, the struggle against hopeless odds, and the shattered remnants were hurled back as from the mouth of hell, leaving the dead bodies of their young commander and his noble followers to be buried in a common grave. Its total loss was about one-third of its strength.

Here it was that the gallant Flag-sergeant Carney, though grievously wounded, bore back his flag to safety, and fell fainting and exhausted with loss of blood, saying, "Boys, the old flag never touched the ground!" Or another glance, at ill-starred Olustee, where the gallant 8th U. S. C. T. lost 87 killed of its effective fighting force, the largest loss in any one colored regiment in any one action of the war. And so on, by Fort Pillow, which let us pass in merciful silence, and to Honey Hill, S. C., perhaps the last desperate fight in the far south, in which the 32nd, 35th and 102nd U. S. C. T. and the 54th and 55th Mass. Inf. won fresh and fadeless laurels for splendid fighting against hopeless odds and insurmountable difficulties, and then to Nashville, Tennessee, with its recorded loss of 84 killed in the effectives of the 13th U. S. C. T.

These were all brilliant actions, and they covered the actors with and reflected upon the race a blaze of glory. But it was in the armies of the James and of the Potomac that the true metal of the Negro as a soldier rang out its clearest notes amid the tremendous diapasons that rolled back and forth between the embattled hosts. Here was war indeed, upon its grandest scale, and in all its infinite variety. The tireless march under burning sun, chilling frosts and driven tempests, the lonely vigil of the picket under starless skies, the rush and roar of countless "hosts to battle driven" in the mad charge and the victorious shout that pursued the fleeing foe;

the grim determination that held its line of defenses with set teeth, blood-shot eye and strained muscle beating back charge after charge of the foe; the patient labor in trench and mine, on hill and in valley, swamp and jungle, with disease adding its horrors to the decimation of shot and shell.

Here the Negro stood in the full glare of the greatest search light, part and parcel of the grandest armies ever mustered upon this continent, competing side by side with the best and bravest of the Union army against the flower of the Confederacy, the best and bravest of Lee's army, and losing nothing in the contrast. Never again while time lasts will the doubt arise as in 1861, "Will the Negro fight?" As a problem, it has been solved, as a question it has been answered, and as a fact it is as established as the eternal hills. It was they who rang up the curtain upon the last act of the bloody tragedy at Petersburg, Va., June 15, 1864, and they who rang it down at Clover Hill, Va., April 9, 1865. They were one of the strong fingers upon the mighty hand that grasped the giant's throat at Petersburg and never flexed until the breath went out at Appomattox. In this period it would take page on page to recount their deeds of valor and their glorious victories.

See them on the 15th of June, 1864, carrying the outpost at Baylor's field in early morning, and all that long, hot, summer day advancing, a few yards at a time, then lying down to escape the fire from the works, but still gradually creeping nearer and nearer, until, just as the sun went down, they swept like a tornado over the works and started upon a race for the city, close at the heels of the flying foe, until mistakenly ordered back. Of this day's experience Gen. Badeau writes: "No worse strain on the nerves of troops is possible, for it is harder to remain quiet under cannon fire, even though comparatively harmless, than to advance against a storm of musketry." General W. F. "Baldy" Smith, speaking of their conduct, says: "No nobler effort has been put forth to-day, and no greater success achieved than that of the colored troops."

In his order of the day he says:

"To the colored troops comprising the Division of General Hinks, the general commanding would call the attention of his command. With the veterans of the Eighteenth corps, they have stormed the works of the enemy and carried them, taking guns and prisoners, and in the whole affair they have displayed all the qualities of good soldiers."

Or, again, at the terrible mine explosion of July 30, 1864, on the Petersburg line, and at the fearful slaughter of September 29, 1864, at New Market Heights and Fort Harrison. On this last date in the Fourth U. S. Col. Troops, out of a color-guard of twelve men, but one came off the field on his own feet. The gallant Flag-sergeant Hilton, the last to fall, cried out as he went down, "Boys, save the colors;" and they were saved.

After the magnificent fighting of this last date, under date of Oct. 11, 1864, Maj.-General B. F. Butler issued an order, a portion of which I quote, as follows:

"Of the colored soldiers of the third divisions of the 18th and 10th Corps and the officers who led them, the general commanding desires to make special mention. In the charge on the enemy's works by the colored division of the 18th Corps at New Market, better men were never better led, better officers never led better men. A few more such gallant charges and to command colored troops will be the post of honor in the American armies. The colored soldiers, by coolness, steadiness, determined courage and dash, have silenced every cavil of the doubters of their soldierly capacity, and drawn tokens of admiration from their enemies, have brought their late masters even to the consideration of the question whether they will not employ as soldiers the hitherto despised race."

Some ten or more years later, in Congress, in the midst of a speech advocating the giving of civil rights to the Negro, Gen. Butler said, referring to this incident:

"There, in a space not wider than the clerk's desk, and three hundred yards long, lay the dead bodies of 543 of my colored comrades, slain in the defense of their country, who had laid down their lives to uphold its flag and its honor, as a willing sacrifice. And as I rode along, guiding my horse this way and that, lest he should profane with his hoofs what seemed to me the sacred dead, and as I looked at their bronzed faces upturned in the shining sun, as if in mute appeal against the wrongs of the country for which they had given their lives, and whose flag had been to them a flag of stripes, in which no star of glory had ever shone for them.—feeling I had wronged them in the past, and believing what was the future duty of my country to them— I swore to myself a solemn oath: 'May my right hand forget its cunning, and my tongue cleave to the roof of my mouth, if ever I fail to defend the rights of the men who have given their blood for me and my country this day and for their race forever. And, God helping me, I will keep that oath."

Or another instance: when under Butler first and Terry later, driven by storms and tempestous seas to powerful Fort Fisher, cooperating with our gallant Navy in its capture, and thence starting on the long march that led through Wilmington, and on to Goldsboro, N. C., where Johnson's army, the last large force of the Confederacy in the field, was caught between the forces under Terry and the forces under Howard; and the war as such was ended with his surrender, April 26, 1865.

A little of statistics, and I will close.

The total number of colored soldiers in this last war was 178,975, and the number of deaths 36,847.

Of enlistments the United States made 96,337, and the several States 79,638.

Enlistments were divided as follows:

Alabama	2,969	Mississippi	17,869
Louisiana	24,052	Maine	104
New Hampshire	125	Vermont	120
Massachusetts	3,966	Rhode Island	1,837
Connecticut	1,764	New York	4,125
New Jersey	1,185	Pennsylvania	8,612
Delaware	954	Maryland	8,718
Dist. of Columbia	3,269	Virginia	5,723
North Carolina	5,035	West Virginia	196
South Carolina	5,462	Georgia	3,486
Florida	1,044	Arkansas	5,526
Tennessee	20,133	Kentucky	23,703
Michigan	1,387	Ohio	5,092
Indiana	1,537	Illinois	1,811
Missouri	8,344	Minnesota	104
Iowa	440	Wisconsin	165
Kansas	2,080	Texas	47
Colorado Ter.	95	Miscellaneous	5,896

The completed organizations were as follows:

138 regiments of infantry.
6 " " cavalry.
14 " " heavy artillery.
1 " " light artillery.

On 449 occasions their blood was spilled.

These are a few of the regiments having the largest number of men killed in any one engagement.

The	8th U. S. C. T., at	Olustee,	87 killed.
"	13th "	Nashville,	84 "
"	23rd "	Petersburg,	81 "
"	7th "	Fort Gilmore,	68 "
"	5th "	Chaffin's Farm	63 "
"	6th "	" "	61 "
"	54th Mass. Inf.,	Fort Wagner,	58 "

The regiments having more than fifty men killed during their period of service are as follows:

Seventy-ninth	U. S. C. T.	Total Killed,	183
Eighth	"	"	115
Fourth	"	"	102
Thirteenth	"	"	86
Seventh	"	"	84
Twenty-third	"	"	82
Sixth	"	"	79
Fifth	"	"	77
Twenty-second	"	"	70
First	"	"	67
Forty-ninth	"	"	59

Sometimes a comparison will illustrate better than figures alone. I give a single instance: Every one has heard of the charge of the Light Brigade, at Balaklava. I will put beside it a Black Brigade of about the same number of men.

Here they are:

Duncan's Brigade, comprising the Fourth and Sixth Regiments at

New Market Heights,	Had	683	Lost	365	Percent	53.7
Light Brigade, Balaklava,	"	673	"	247	"	36.7
Excess in Duncan's Brigade,		10		118		17

Sanford B. Hunt, M. D., late surgeon of U. S. Volunteers, made an exhaustive research into the capacity of the Negro as a soldier. As to his—

1. Aptitude for drill.
2. Capacity for marching.
3. Endurance of fatigue and hunger.
4. Powers of digestion and assimilation.
5. Immunity from or liability to disabling diseases.

All of which points are treated with great detail, and summed up as follows:

"For the purposes of the soldier he has all the physical characteristics required, his temperament adapts him to camp life, and his morale conduces to discipline. He is also brave and steady in action. In all subsequent wars the country will rely largely upon its Negro population as a part of its military power."

Under the act of Congress passed July 12, 1862, the President of the United Stases was authorized to have prepared, with suitable emblematic devices, Medals of Honor to be presented in the name of the Congress to such soldiers as should most distinguish themselves by their gallantry in action and other soldierly qualities. So chary has the Government been in their issue that the award has not reached two thousand among the three millions of volunteers and regulars in the Army and Navy. So that these medals are more rare than the "Victoria Cross" of England, the "Iron Cross" of Germany, or the "Cross of the Legion of Honor" of France.

I copy the list of those issued to Negro soldiers as they stand upon the records, that is, in the numerical order of the regiments to which the recipients belonged. It will be therefore understood that this order does not indicate priority of time or degree of excellence.

Christian A. Fleetwood,	Sergeant Major,	Fourth	U. S. C. T.
Alfred B. Hilton,	Color Sergeant,	"	"
Charles Veal,	Corporal,	"	"
Milton M. Holland,	Sergeant Major,	Fifth	"
James Brownson,	First Sergeant,	"	"
Powhatan Beatty,	First Sergeant,	"	"
Robert Pinn,	First Sergeant,	"	"
Thomas R. Hawkins,	Sergeant Major,	Sixth	"
Alexander Kelly,	First Sergeant,	"	"
Samuel Gilchrist,	Sergeant,	Thirty-sixth	"
William Davis,	Sergeant,	"	"
Miles James,	Corporal,	"	"
James Gardner,	Private,	"	"
Edward Ratcliffe,	First Sergeant,	Thirty-eighth	"
James Harris,	Sergeant,	"	"
William Barnes,	Private,	"	"
Decatur Dorsey,	Sergeant,	Thirty-ninth	"

After each war, of 1776, of 1812, and of 1861, history repeats itself in the absolute effacement of remembrance of the gallant deeds done for the country by its brave black defenders and in their relegation to outer darkness.

History further repeats itself in the fact that in every war so far known to this country, the first blood, and, in some cases, the last also, has been shed by the faithful Negro, and this in spite of all the years of bondage and oppression, and of wrongs unspeakable. Under the sun there has nothing been known in the history of any people more marvellous than these facts!

Oh, to the living few,
  Comrades, be just, be true.
Hail them as heroes tried,
  Fight with them side by side;
Never in field or tent,
  Scorn the Black Regiment.

It is but a little thing to ask, they could ask no less: *be just;* but, oh, the shame of it for those who need be asked!

There is no need for panegyric, for sounding phrases or rounded periods. The simple story is eloquent with all that is necessary to make the heart swell with pride. In the hour allotted me to fill, it is possible only to indicate in skeleton the worth of the Negro as a soldier. If this brief sketch should awaken even a few to interest in his achievements, and one be found willing and fitted to write the history that is their due, that writer shall achieve immortality.

LETTER

OF

GEN. A. J. HAMILTON,

OF TEXAS,

TO

THE PRESIDENT OF THE UNITED STATES.

LETTER OF

GEN. A. J. HAMILTON,

OF TEXAS,

TO THE PRESIDENT OF THE UNITED STATES.

New York, July 28th, 1863.

My dear Sir,—The deep interest felt by me, as a Southern Union man, in the result of measures adopted by you for the maintenance of the National authority in all the States, by the complete and permanent suppression of the rebellion against the Union and the Constitution, will, I trust, excuse the freedom of this letter and my request for your patient consideration of what I write.

I am sure that your desire to have the great issues involved in the present struggle properly and forever stettled is not less ardent and constant than my own. Our common wish has common roots in our common aspirations for the honor, prosperity, and unity of the Republic; that which you cherish derives peculiar strength from the great responsibilities of the chief magistracy, and that which animates every pulsation of my heart derives a strength not less peculiar from the fact that the rebellion which imperils our country, desolates my once happy home—deprives of their liberties and puts in jeopardy of their lives my family, my kindred, my friends, and my neighbors.

But it will avail little to procure a temporary adjustment; and I am prompted to address you now because I observe in some quarters indications of a disposition to accept, if not to invite, a peace which would inevitably lead to new convulsions more disastrous than the present.

By some persons of considerable political prominence, and by some leading presses, a systematic effort appears to be put forth to reconcile the public mind to the idea that the future policy of the Government may be formed on the basis of a compromise with the cause of the existing rebellion, which will admit of the re-establishment of slavery in the States where it has been abolished by your proclamation of January last.

To pave the way, apparently, for such a compromise, northern sympathisers with rebellion and some too who cannot justly be so designated, constantly endeavor to impress on the public mind the notion that our National and State Constitutions were made for the white race alone; and that therefore other races can have no rights under them.

No one denies, I believe, that the people of the white race were much more considered in framing our Constitutions than the people of the black race; but the impression sought to be made is that the blacks are *excluded*, by their terms, and by inference, from being regarded as a part of the people for whom they were made.

The proposition so understood I propose briefly to consider; and then to add a few words on the policy to which, it seems to me, it is intended to lead—namely, peace through a full and complete amnesty and the abrogation of your Proclamation of Emancipation.

The Constitutions from which the black population is supposed to be excluded can be only the Federal and State Constitutions.

First, then, is it true of the Constitution of the United States, that it excludes the black race? I have sought in vain for a section or provision in that instrument which, in terms, sustains the proposition, or which can, by any possible construction, give color to it. I find, in fact, in the Constitution, the converse of the proposition. The third clause of the second section of the first article of the Constitution, is as follows: "Representatives "and direct taxes shall be apportioned among the several "States which may be included within this Union according to "their respective numbers, which shall be determined by "adding to the whole number of *free persons*, *including those* "*bound to service for a term of years* and excluding Indians "not taxed, three-fifths of all other persons." The great constituent body which forms the basis of the political department of the Government, is here defined. Of what classes of persons is this body composed? 1st. "*Free persons*," without reference to color or nationality (for no such qualification is expressed, or can be implied), and including in this class of "*free persons*" "those bound to service for a term of years" and "excluding" from the class of "*free persons*" "Indians not taxed;" then added to the body of "*free persons*, including," &c., "three-fifths of *all other persons*," meaning by this description of "all other persons," the slaves of the South. Who then were the "free persons, including those bound to service for a term of years?" They are not *slaves* of whom only three-fifths can be counted—nor are they Indians not taxed. Is it true that they who are white alone belong to this class? Whence comes the idea, and what are the proofs Who were the persons who, for the most part, were held to service for a term of years, at the period of the adoption of the Constitution? I believe it is a part of the history of the country, that in some of the States, at that very time, Africans or their descendants were held to labor for a term of years. If so, they were included in the class of "free persons," in the very *terms* of the provision referred to, and were *intended* to be included. So too the black man who was neither held to labor for a term of years nor for life, but who was a "free person," was included in the language and the spirit of the Constitution. To this obvious construction the Southern States have committed themselves, by counting the free blacks among their "*free persons*" in determining their representation.

If those who maintain the theory of exclusion will point to some clause or provision in the Constitution which sustains it, the country will be better prepared for its consideration.

Even the slaves are not thought unworthy of recognition, and are, to the extent of three-fifths of their number, made a part of the aggregate constituency of the political department of the Government.

But because this and other provisions of the Constitution were made in reference to their condition of slavery, is it to be said that when they shall have ceased to be slaves they are, by some silent and unseen provision of the Constitution, to be excluded from all its provisions? If their condition be changed from slavery to freedom, the effect of such change upon their status under the clause of the Constitution quoted, is to incorporate them with that class from which there is no deduction in fixing the basis of representation. In what manner, then and by what provision of the Constitution of the United States are negroes, when free, excluded from recognition?

If we search the State Constitutions, there will be found in many, if not most of those of the free States, express recognition of the black man.

In that of the State of New York they are, under the description of "men of color," allowed to vote when they shall have been, for three years, citizens of the State, and for one year preceding the election at which they propose to vote, have been seized and possessed of a freehold estate of the value of two hundred and fifty dollars, above all debts and encumbrances thereon, and upon which they have paid a tax. I might refer to the Constitution of Massachusetts, and of many of the other States, for similar provisions, but it is unnecessary. In the face of such clear *affirmative* constitutional recognition, a declaration to the contrary may, perhaps, challenge admiration for its boldness.

If we are now to learn that the black race are ignored and excluded from citizenship by the Constitutions of States, by which they are required to perform all the ordinary duties pertaining to the citizen, and allowed the highest rights of freemen, including the right of suffrage—if the Constitution of New York excludes them, how, under its provisions, can they vote? And why and how is it that to-day, they are being drawn, as conscripts, under the late act of Congress?

Native-born men—free men—wielding a portion of the political power of Government, Federal as well as State, and with arms in their hands to defend the flag of the former—are not, whether white or black, without the pale of constitutional recognition.

The resort for proof of the correctness of the proposition under consideration will be, most probably, to the Constitutions of the Slave States. If so, then I have only to say, they are not the *only*, nor yet a *majority* of the Constitutions of this country, and do not therefore, prove the truth of the proposition—and, that if the extinction of slavery is a result of the rebellion, then it may be that even in the South some meaning and force may be attached to that provision of the Constitution of the United States, which declares that "The citizens of each State shall be "entitled to all the privileges and immunities of citizens in "the several States."

The proposition that the Government can and ought to force the colonization, in distant lands, of the negroes, when free, is as reprehensible in principle, and as unsupported by constitutional authority, as is the one just disposed of. The power to do this is claimed for the Government—(for it would be uncharitable to suppose that its asserters would insist upon the Government taking so important a step without full authority)—to compel the black race to accept expatriation from the United States as a condition of freedom. If this power exists in the Government, I insist that the country shall be informed where it has been so long hidden away, and where it is now lodged. What provision of the Constitution confers it, either expressly, or as an incident of an express power? Every earnest thinker will desire to know, not only the source of the power, but the department of the Government to which it has been confided. Touching these important inquiries those who favor the policy of deportation are entirely silent. Much is said about the physical and mental inferiority of the black race, and we are left no alternative but to infer that the power is claimed for Government: 1st, because they (the blacks) are excluded from recognition by the Constitutions of the country; 2d, because they are physically and mentally inferior to the white race; and, 3d, (for such is a part of the argument), because if the two races are permitted to remain together, after the emancipation of the blacks, amalgamation will soon produce a piebald race, to the great detriment of society and government.

I say again that the favorers of this policy could never have urged it upon the country, unless they believed there was power in the Government to adopt and enforce it. Then, it must be, by application of the facts assumed in argument not to any particular provision, but to the whole body of the Constitution, that they distil the subtle power. The first of these assumed facts I have done with. The second I shall not dispute. I shall content myself with questioning the power of Government *to discriminate against* one class, or description, or nationality, of those within its jurisdiction, because of physical or mental inferiority to some other class, or description, or nationality.

This would cease to be a free government the moment the power should be permitted to it to determine, that because of difference of race—of color—of physical inferiority, or mental development, the right of the citizen could be determined.

If unhappily such power shall ever be exercised, it might, and probably would, upon a principle of impartiality, be applied to all alike. The principle could no doubt find its advocates, while there is just as little reason to doubt that some of them would fall the first victims to its impartial enforcement.

If on account of color—race—or physical or mental inferiority one class of people can be forcibly ejected from the territory of the Government, as a measure of policy, or on the plea of necessity—(the tyrant's plea the wide world over)—where will bounds be fixed to limit its exercise as often and upon whatever class of citizens the majority in power may, from time to time, desire?

Neither the foreign born or native citizens could rest easy under such a precedent.

As to precisely what would result in the way of amalgamation, from the two races living together in freedom, I cannot say. I am not sufficiently versed in physiology to determine what increased physical affinities of the two races would be developed by the blacks becoming free. I feel morally certain that the *facilities* for amalgamation would not thereby be increased.

The final argument in favour of the power claimed for the Government may be yet held in reserve. If so, perhaps it will be found, when pushed forward, to be something like this—"Africans and their descendants are *not and cannot* be citizens under the Constitution of the United States, and have no rights which white men are bound to respect."

I shall not review the Dred Scott decision. The legal and

logical correctness of the opinion of the Court was, at the time it was pronounced, met by two learned Justices, not surpassed, if equalled, in the just estimation of the bar or of the country, by any other members of the Court, in dissenting opinions which have not been, and will never be, successfully answered; and the philosophic historian of our country has already truly traced its inhuman spirit and disastrous reasoning to the attempt of Southern slave owners to overthrow free government for the majority of the white race, the more firmly to rivet the chains upon the black race, which has culminated in this gigantic rebellion. Two and a half years of revolution, while they have been full of sorrows, have not been unfruitful of honest inquiry leading to the discovery and acknowledgment of truth. The great Teacher has from day to day impressed new ideas upon the public mind and suggested means adequate to the necessities of the hour. The despised negro, whose perpetual bondage was the leading object of the effort to overthrow free government, was at last considered by the Government as a possible means of aiding in its preservation. As freemen, they would no longer constitute the chief laboring and producing population of the rebellious States, but become soldiers of the Government, stimulated by its solemn act, which proclaimed their freedom before all the world and in the sight of Heaven. The result of that Proclamation is that they are to-day, many of them, in the ranks of our armies, and have already, on historic battle-fields, vindicated their right to freedom by their heroic defence of the flag of the free. They are native born—they live and have ever lived in the United States. They are free—they are fighting and dying for free government—for *this* Government. Why are they not its citizens? They are citizens in *fact*, in *reason*, and by every right that confers citizenship. And so they will henceforth be considered—the law proceeding from the right—and he who, ten years hence, shall dispute the fact will be pitied rather than blamed.

What shall be said of the final proposition—" full pardon to the rebels, and the abrogation of your Proclamation of Emancipation?" There is nothing of opposition to free government, or of wrong to humanity and civilization, that is not embraced in this proposition. It justifies the rebellion in its acts and purposes—it asks, in effect, that the Government shall become the accuser of those who have labored most zealously to sustain and preserve it. It asks the Government to do more—to descend to a depth of infamy beyond that ever reached by any other—to admit, in the face of Christendom, that the Proclamation of Freedom to the Slaves was a deliberate cheat, meant only to dupe, for the time being, the anti-slavery sentiment of the world; and especially to deceive the negro, to the end that he might be induced to engage in the contest, the sooner to force the rebel master to receive him back and to acknowledge that he holds him under the Constitution of the United States.

In this connection it is well to remember that this *anti-slavery sentiment* is the fixed condition of the public mind of the civilized world. And to this sentiment, more than to all other causes, do we owe the fact that *non-intervention* by foreign governments in the great struggle now pending here, has so far been maintained.

At the period when the governing classes of some of the governments of the Old World, sympathizing with the aristocratic principle of slavery, and deeply interested in the preservation of the privileges of class, were just ready to proclaim intervention in American affairs, the Proclamation of Freedom to the slaves, issued by you as President of the United States and in solemn form, and the concurrent assertion of the rebels in the South, of their determination to maintain slavery as the corner stone of their new government, so awakened that deep sentiment of hostility to slavery in the masses of the people of those governments, and so attracted their active sympathies to this Government, as to effectually forestall intervention.

And to this sentiment thus aroused and stimulated by your grand Proclamation, and now outspoken in England, do we owe it to-day to be thankful that we see the emancipation party holding—*and holding firmly*, under the able guidance of John Bright—the balance of power in that Government.

In France too even Imperial power has not, so far, openly opposed the national sympathy on the side of freedom. If we are destined to encounter foreign enemies in this struggle, it will be most likely when by a vacillating policy in support of the Proclamation, or its abandonment, we have forfeited the confidence, the respect, and moral aid of the friends of freedom throughout the world. With the sympathies of Christendom with us, intervention is but a possibility—against us, it is a certainty.

The effect which a disavowal and retraction of the Proclamation would have upon the public mind of other nations is evident. It would at once paralyze the efforts of those who have hitherto stayed the action of their governments in proposed interference in our affairs.

It would weaken, if not destroy, the liberal party of France and England—it would surely convert them from friends to enemies of this Government, and thus break down the most powerful barrier to intervention and foreign war. Thus self-interest and national safety should alone suffice to prevent such madness.

But there is an argument higher than these which appeals directly to every Christian heart—an argument used by yourself in the terms of the Proclamation.

" *Upon this act—sincerely believed* (so runs the instrument) *to be an act of justice warranted by the Constitution upon military necessity—I invoke the considerate judgment of mankind and the gracious favor of Almighty God.*"

Thus did the chief of a Christian people, before mankind, and in the sight of God, proclaim freedom to the slave, and by his official signature to the great act commit himself to its wisdom, its justice, and its constitutionality, and to the efficiency of its provisions.

That act was in pursuance of an act of Congress authorizing it. The power in the Congress to declare war carries with it, the power to provide the means and prescribe the necessary measures to make the war effective. It was in the exercise of this power that Congress acted. The war-making power, which is also the law-making power of the Government, said to the President, the commander-in-chief of its armies, Do this thing, and it was done. It is unprofitable to attempt to prove to those who are unwilling to believe, that the act was constitutional. The majority of the people of the United States and of the civilized world so believe it and so sanction it.

If your proclamation was not then a mere assumption of power, but a valid act, done in the exercise of constitutional discretion, what power can abrogate or annul it? The act, if constitutionally done, is as irrevocable as is the act of the President in signing an act passed by the Congress. In either case discretion and power cease with the act. When the proclamation was issued it became the *law* of freedom to the slaves therein embraced—a law which I repeat is irrevocable by any power in the Government. Laws which are general in their character and create no vested right in the citizen, may be changed or repealed—but those which create personal rights and vest them in the citizen are protected from infraction by constitutional guarantees. A legislative grant to land cannot be revoked at the pleasure of the power making the grant. The enfranchisement of hundreds of thousands of people by the Government—the solemn act which raises them from slavery to freedom—is surely not less sacred and inviolable. There is no power in this Government to make slaves of freemen, white or black. While the civilized world has hailed the act with joy, it would shudder at an effort to recall it or impair its vital force. The policy of such a course would be as fatal to the peace and welfare of the country as the act would be atrocious in principle.

Those who propose it surely cannot yet comprehend the real design of the rebellion, and the change which it has produced in the relations of the different classes in the South. A restoration of "the Union as it was," to use a cant phrase of the day, is not a possible thing. If it means a restoration with slavery, then it will not be a Union of peace, prosperity, and happiness, but a Union of discord, hatred, and violence in the South which will sink it in barbarism. Can we hope for peace between the sections now at war, with slavery still existing? But if this were possible, how can it be expected that the rebels and loyal men of the South can live in peace in the future, the cause of the trouble—*slavery*—still in existence, the rebel masters more intolerant, jealous, and brutal than ever before, with arrogance increased by the victory which they will have achieved over the people and Government of the United States and the moral and political opinions of the civilized world? I know well that there are those who are impatient when "loyal men South" are mentioned in the consideration of these questions. Nevertheless, I insist most respectfully, but earnestly, that they *are* worthy of consideration because of their devotion to liberty and their Government, because of their sacrifices and sufferings, and because they constitute the only future strength of the Government in the South. They are to-day the *majority* of the South, whatever may be said or thought to the contrary. Their vindication is certain, if slow. Time will prove that the great body of the citizens of the South will gratefully return to the Union of their fathers, while it will more fully develope the undying hatred to free government of less than 300,000 slaveholders.

We need not further shut our eyes to the nature and disposition of the antagonistic forces now in conflict in this war. Men need not wonder at the convulsion resulting from the conspiracy, created solely by the pro-slavery spirit that plotted the rebellion. This conspiracy is now known to have embraced various objects in its scope. The determination to hold in bondage four millions of colored people with their increase, and to make such bondage perpetual, was the main object of the conspiracy. This determination formed the basis of all other measures, whether of intrigue, war, or diplomacy. It entered into every plan and calculation of the rebel leaders. The attempt to destroy the national unity grew out of the conspiracy against the colored man, and became necessary to accomplish the scheme of his perpetual bondage. There was an obstacle in the way. There were seven millions of non-slaveholders in the South. How could it be otherwise than that this population should, at no distant day, stand upon its rights and dictate that policy which should accord with its interests? It was the apprehension of this that led to the conspiracy against the political rights of these masses. It was a truth fully realized by the leading conspirators that slavery could not long exist against a union of the free labor forces North and South, blended by common sympathy; therefore the national unity must be destroyed. They said, "Slavery and democracy are incompatible," and this involved the necessity of a monopoly of political power by the slaveholders in order to maintain in perpetuity their political property in slaves. These are the motives which led them to attempt the destruction of the Government.

What has the nation now to say to this active intrigue to postpone the destruction of slavery, which is the antagonist of free government? Can it be possible that any man of sense, or judgment, desires such postponement? I ask you to contemplate the fruits of that narrow policy which has disfranchised a large portion of the white population South. I ask our countrymen to consider that educational neglect and political debauchment of the South, which have changed it from an element of national strength into an agency for the attempted accomplishment of national ruin. Compare the condition of the Southern white masses in their industrial interests with that of other sections. Let the political economist tell us what it is that gives the annual *per capita* production of $166.00 to every man, woman, and child in Massachusetts, whilst in South Carolina productive labor yields a *per capita* of $56.00 only. He will trace this disparity to the direct influence of slavery. The political philosopher may carry the inquiry farther, and show why it is that so much of the population of the North has become a questionable element of national strength. He will find the reason for it in a long continued sympathy with slavery. The encouragement of the slave system of the South by the North has progressed until it has so far contaminated not only Southern but even Northern society, as to seriously imperil the security of the nation.

It might have been supposed that the teachings of events would have set us right ere this. It seems, however, that the calamities of the country have had no power to instruct the political intriguers. Upon such, the active treason of the South, its attempt to destroy the nationality, the plot to overthrow free government, the claims of the masses of the South for protection, and all consideration of future security, are as nothing compared with the preservation of slavery—their only principle is *slavery conservatism*. The time has come for conservatism in the right direction. I think we have had enough of *slavery* conservatism. If we must still be conservatives, let us be conservatives of freedom; encouragers of humanity; promoters of such policy as makes men patriots, and keeps them so; and radical opposers of whatever tends to destroy republican government.

Every man in the country who still clings to the hope of a great nationality under the old ensign, desires the unity of our people. Upon what basis is this unity to be brought about? Slavery has pronounced democracy to be its opponent. Will unity be brought about by upholding slavery? It has aimed at the destruction of the national life. Will the national life be prolonged and secured by cherishing its antagonist? Slavery has conspired against the political rights of the non-slaveholding masses of the South. Is this in accordance with that just conservatism embraced in that clause of the Constitution which guaranties republican government to the people of all the States? It has unscrupulously aimed at the establishment of an order of nobility in the South, and endeavors to make its escape from under the Constitution which interdicts it. Will the further toleration of an institution which has attempted all this produce unity? Through the intrigues prompted by the pro-slavery spirit, the nation has been precipitated into civil war. The whole number of slaveholders has been more than equalled by the white men who have fallen in the conflict. What kind of a monument does slavery conservatism propose to erect to the memory of those thus sacrificed? Slavery will leave a war debt of gigantic magnitude for free industry to pay. In what way will conservatism reconcile the toil of the nation to the cause of its manifold calamities? Not, I apprehend, by pandering to slavery, and making it the basis of future intrigue and revolution.

The nation has had enough of *slavery* conservatism. It now demands not only a change, but a *radical* change. The future security of the nation depends upon the policy which shall be now adopted. Its strength results from civil liberty and free government—its only weakness has been the institution of slavery, which thwarted the development of those ideas. The great South, embracing more than eleven millions of human beings, all under proper guidance, an effective element of national strength, has one enemy only—that is *slavery conservatism.* The twenty millions of people in the North have had one insidious, mercenary, and atrocious enemy—*Slavery Conservatism!* The nation at large has had one enemy—*Slavery Conservatism!* The example in our country is only a repetition of what has been witnessed in all others. The process in freeing nations of the barbarisms of slavery has generally been slow, owing to the weakness of the anti-slavery forces. We have one advantage. The twenty millions of people devoted to free labor have it now in their power to make short work of American slavery. We shall soon know whether conservatism will make chronic the national disease, or whether a rapid and radical cure shall be effected. In the convalescence of this nation the open traitors may not prove to be its worst enemies.

The nation can no longer afford to indulge party tacticians in that line of intrigue which has heretofore proved its bane. The cause of nationality and free government is not alone in danger from domestic foes. The fall of Mexico, through weakness, created by factions, should warn us. The usurper is already triumphing over the ruins of republican government in that unhappy country. No one can doubt the concurrent desires between that usurper and the anti-democratic spirit which to-day animates and controls the rebellion. At this moment negotiations are pending, if not consummated, between the leading rebels in Texas who despair of success by the so-called Confederacy, and parties in northern Mexico, for a union of Texas with the States of Tamaulipas and Neuvo Leon and Coahuila for the formation of a new government under the imperial sanction and favor of Louis Napoleon. This will give the long coveted opportunity to this despot to interfere in the affairs of this country with sufficient plausibility to relieve the act from the overwhelming censure of the French nation. If we are not now, we will at no distant day be standing upon the law of force and the preparation of the nation for warfare to save us from intervention. This is the only security we have. There are 800,000 colored men in the South, loyal by both nature and circumstance, the enemies of those who would overthrow the nationality, and capable of being made allies in the common cause of freedom, justice, and humanity. This force is not to be despised, for it is a force that can be counted on in any emergency that may call it into requisition. It has one simple platform in the ideal of its future—the desire to be free, and fidelity to the power that makes it free. It is this simple platform that may make the colored man an immense power on the side of nationality. It is worth more to the nation to-day, if properly treated, than all the slaveholders, coupled with all those who are now mouthing that abused word "conservatism." Conservatism for a long time repulsed the colored man and made him the efficient ally of the rebels. Alarm for the cause of nationality changed the policy, and commenced making the colored man the ally of freedom.

I know that there are those who, while they desire the freedom of the slaves, are greatly troubled to determine what should be done with them afterwards. And I have also observed that most frequently those who know least of the slaves of the South are most anxious in mind upon the subject. In three words the proper policy can be stated—

Let them alone.

There is no rightful power in the Government to force them from its territory—besides, it will be found that the late masters in the South and others will clamor more loudly against their speedy deportation than they now do against their freedom.

They will need, and must have, their labor (not forced but paid) until time and a change of population in the South shall furnish an adequate supply of white labor. When this period arrives it is most probable, nay, it is certain, that the black race will begin to desire a home and a government exclusively their own. And then I shall be glad, if living, to see this Government extend a strong and generous hand to assist them. If we will, to-day, take care of the rebellion and its cause, as against domestic and foreign foes, the question of the future of the negro will take care of itself.

By your just Proclamation you gave the highest earthly sanction to the wise and noble policy of the enfranchisement of the black man, and by his enrollment in your armies for the defence of the country, you have confirmed it to the benefit of the nation. You will be urged to revoke that act. God forbid that you should listen to such advisors and so rob yourself of the gratitude and admiration of mankind.

The utterance of these sentiments may by some be deemed out of place and unseasonable. I can better afford to bear the censure of such than to forego my convictions of truth and duty.

With sincere wishes for your health and welfare,

I am very respectfully,

Your obedient servant,

A. J. HAMILTON.

To The President of the United States.

From Pres. Angell May 28, '92

HANCOCK

IN THE

WAR OF THE REBELLION

By FRANCIS A. WALKER

Late A. A. G., 2d Corps

HANCOCK IN THE WAR OF THE REBELLION.

A Paper read by General FRANCIS A. WALKER, *late U. S. V., of Massachusetts, at a Meeting of the New York Commandery, February* 4, 1891.

THE outbreak of the war found Hancock, then in the thirty-eighth year of his age, a captain in the regular army, in charge of the quartermaster's depot at Los Angeles, on the Pacific coast. Christened with the name of America's greatest living soldier, graduated from the military academy in 1844, he had joined Scott's column in time to take part in the later battles of the marvellous campaign which ended in the capture of the Mexican capital. At Molino del Rey he was in the column of attack with Longstreet, Pickett, and Armistead —men whom he was to encounter sixteen years later in another and more memorable assault—and was brevetted for his gallantry at Contreras and Cherubusco.

In the long interval which followed the conclusion of peace, Hancock saw much instructive service as aide-de-camp to General Clark upon the Great Plains, as quartermaster during the troubles with the Seminoles in Florida, in the border war in Kansas, in the Utah expedition of Harney, and upon the Pacific coast. Absolutely destitute of asceticism, full of hearty fellowship, fond of ease, and given to good cheer, his stirring ambition, his intense interest in his profession, and his high standard of duty rendered these fourteen years one long term of military education. I doubt if there was an officer in the United States Army who, during that period while political, social, and industrial forces were preparing the war of secession, learned so much that was to become of use when that great occasion came. Hancock was not a man of lofty intellectuality. He had courage—fiery, enthusiastic courage; positive, active, unfaltering loyalty to country and comrade; he had industry beyond measure; the ambition that stirs to do great deeds, and be worthy of high promotion; the power of patient labor, that has been called genius; above all, an unrest while anything remained to be done; a dissatisfaction with what was incomplete; a repugnance at what was slovenly, coarse, or half made up. I am disposed to believe that this period of Hancock's life was passed to even better advantage than if it had comprised active operations, on the large scale, against a powerful enemy. The time was to come, all too soon, when lives were to be thrown away by thousands and money by millions; when orders of infinite consequence were to be given as the result of one glance over a field as restless as the ocean after a storm; when the conjectures of a single officer on the picket line were to determine the movements of twenty thousand men on the morrow. Meanwhile, the future commander of the Second Army Corps, of the left wing at Gettysburg and in the Wilderness, was being trained for his high duties by conducting the orders and correspondence of a military department, or by fitting out expeditions of a company or a squadron, supplying outlying posts, making long marches with a column that would scarcely have served, a few years later, for his headquarters' escort, or conducting the business of a quartermaster's depot on the plains or on the Pacific coast. To a man who is willing to do things just so well that they will pass without censure from his superiors, caring himself only for pay-day and poker, such a scale of operations is cramping and dwarfing. To a man who is trying to do everything in the best possible way, who is studying his profession, and accumulating experience against the day of larger things, nothing is more instructive, enlarging, and strengthening, if not pursued too long, than such preliminary practice.

It followed that the outbreak of the war found Hancock singularly well endowed and equipped for the responsibilities and duties that were to devolve upon him. What he knew of infantry and could do with infantry, let Williamsburg and

Fredericksburg and Gettysburg and the Salient at Spottsylvania testify. While he was not a master of the science of logistics, like Meade and Humphreys, he could conduct a long march, over bad roads, with artillery and trains, better, in my humble judgment, than any other officer of the war, Federal or Confederate. In a somewhat protracted experience, I never but once knew the Second Corps, while under his command, no matter how extreme the distance or severe the conditions, by day or by night, arrive at its destination in bad form, straggling and broken; and its marches were often very long and trying, as on the 29th of July, 1862, when the corps made thirty-two miles, on a single road, with artillery and trains.

In the supply of troops, Hancock, as the result of thorough training and downright hard work, and with the aid of one of the ablest quartermasters of the volunteer service, Colonel Richard N. Batchelder, now quartermaster-general of the army, achieved almost the highest possible success. Of the uses of cavalry and artillery, Hancock knew enough, first, not to think that he knew everything, or to lead him to interfere in the conduct of those charged with these highly specialized services; and, secondly, to recognize good work whenever and by whomsoever done.

Finally, Hancock's experience before the war had made him a perfect master of the regulations, of the procedure proper to every department of the army and to every occasion of the service, and of the forms of military correspondence and record. A master, I say, not a slave; for, while no man understood better the beneficial uses of red tape, no one knew better how to cut red tape when the occasion required. An essayist—Lord Macaulay, I think—in satirizing the employment in the English language of certain Latin terms, asks us to imagine a Roman consul seated in a back office in Bordeaux, a goose-quill over his ear, making out invoices for the skippers of merchant vessels. But the union of martial and civic functions need not be ludicrous. It would be hard o believe that Scipio at Zama looked one inch more the commander than Hancock at Fredericksburg or Gettysburg, or bore himself more knightly and heroically in danger and hardship, in weariness and wounds; yet Hancock was, perhaps, the greatest hand at "papers" that the army ever knew. Even now my head aches from the long night vigils, when, after some weary march or fight, we pored for hours over reports and returns, and discussed minute points of the regulations *àpropos* of the correspondence appertaining to seventy or ninety regiments and batteries. It is usual to make flings at this sort of work, and express contempt for "papers" and regulations and red-tape. But it is more likely that a mill or factory or railroad will be well managed, whose accounts and correspondence are always in arrears, in confusion, in error, than that a brigade or division or corps will be well administered under the same conditions. The need of order and system is even greater in the latter than in the former case. This Hancock perfectly understood. He deemed it no less important a part of his duty to study the state of his command through the morning reports and the monthly returns than on parade or review; and he knew that he could administer a tonic to a sickly regiment through the order-book and the letter-book not less effectually than at Sunday-morning inspection.

Such, in his qualifications for service, was Hancock, as, at his own request, he was ordered East in the early summer of 1861, that he might take an active part in the war which had broken out, amid such direful portents, on the Atlantic slope. For him there was not a moment of hesitation or of indifference as to the coming struggle. To the very centre of his being he was loyal to the Constitution and the laws; and he never valued his commission in the army so highly as when it gave him a place in the front rank of their defenders. He knew too many of the men who, like his friend Armistead, had reluctantly and painfully broken the main ties of their lives in taking the other side, to indulge in puerile talk about traitors and sour-apple trees; he knew too much of the Southern temper to make light of the task before the nation, or to predict a holiday parade for the Union armies; bu with all his soul he stood by the Government, and never did his faith in the ultimate triumph of that cause waver, even amid disappointment, defeat, disaster, and disgrace.

On his first arrival in the East, he was assigned to duty with General Anderson of Fort Sumter fame; but in every lineament, in every motion, he was so manifestly a commander, that it was soon seen to be absurd to keep such a soldier on staff duty when an army of hundreds of thousands was to be officered; and on the 23d of September he was made a brigadier-general of volunteers and assigned to the Army of the Potomac.

No commander ever more carefully prepared in camp for success in the field than did Hancock here and through all his subsequent career. Doubtless most who have any impression whatever regarding Hancock's personality think of him as a kind of meteor on the battle-field, an object of admiration or of terror, flashing hither and thither, achieving his triumphs by sheer brilliancy of bearing, force of intuition, and mysterious power over men. In fact, it was with infinite labor that he forged the weapon his hand was to wield with such effect. He knew that the greater the force exerted the more likely was the sword to break under the blow unless it were perfectly wrought; and it was with care and pains inexpressible that he shaped and tempered it for the conflict. If at Williamsburg, in his first encounter with the enemy, he met and easily vanquished the Confederate brigade sent against him, led on one wing by D. H. Hill, and on the other by Jubal Early, it was not more by reason of the great tactical skill, calm courage, and majestic bearing which stamped upon him McClellan's epithet, "superb," than by reason of the long and painful training to which his troops had been subjected.

Of Hancock in the winter camps of 1861 two things especially require to be said:

First, while he was a strict and even a stern disciplinarian, he was wholly incapable of any of those brutalities which a few officers of the regular army who were set over volunteer regiments, and many volunteer officers who thought they were imitating regular army methods, practised during the first year of the war.

Second, although a "regular" in every fibre of his being, Hancock was altogether destitute of that snobbishness regarding volunteers which was exhibited by so many small minds in so many great places during the first year of the Rebellion. He recognized the fact that the war was to be waged by volunteers, and that, however much the regular army had to give to the vast masses of earnest soldiers swarming in from east and from west to the defense of the Union, it was, after all, these men who were to bear the heat and burden of that great conflict. He saw that it was of supreme importance to promote the self-respect and self-confidence of volunteer regiments; to lead them to think that they could do anything and were the equals of anybody; and that to be everlastingly talking about the regular army, as so many were, bewailing the lack of its methods and forms, instituting odious comparisons, and sneering at the deficiencies of the new troops, was a very poor way of accomplishing that object.

Hancock not only never sneered at volunteers, he did not even patronize them. He made them feel by his evident respect, his hearty greeting, his warm approval of everything they did well, that he regarded them as being just as fully, just as truly, just as honorably soldiers of the United States Army as if they belonged to the old Fifth Infantry. Such was the spirit in which Hancock met his new command. We know with what assiduity, patience, and good feeling, what almost pathetic eagerness to learn and to imitate, the volunteers of 1861 sought to fit themselves for their part in the great struggle.

Hancock's thorough and cordial acceptance of volunteers was seen again in his choice of staff officers throughout the war. Even after he had become a corps commander, when any captain in the service would have been proud to come at his call, he showed no disposition to prefer an officer of the regular army, as such. Mitchell and Bingham, Batchelder and Wilson, Bronson and Livermore, Miller and Parker, were good enough for him.

At the battle of Fair Oaks, Hancock's brigade, then in the Sixth Corps, was not called to take a part; but while Porter was waging his bitter fight against odds at Gaines's Mill, Hancock's brigade was engaged in holding back the enemy, who sought to break in our lines near the Chickahominy. On the following day, while the Army of the Potomac was beginning the first march of that dreary retreat to the James, the enemy again threw themselves upon Hancock's lines, but were again beaten off by the prompt and resolute action of his well-trained regiments. On both these occasions Hancock displayed that high degree of tactical skill which so strongly characterized his later work in command of a division, of a corps, and of a wing of the army.

The eve of Antietam found Hancock the most conspicuous brigade leader in the Army of the Potomac. There was hardly a question who should succeed to the command of the First Division of the Second Corps, when, at noon of that memorable day, tidings were borne to general headquarters that the gallant Richardson had fallen, never to mount horse or draw sword more. At once Hancock was sent for in haste from his brigade of the Sixth Corps, and despatched to take command of Sumner's old division, as it lay under arms, after its desperate battle around Piper's house.

It is always more or less of an experiment to promote even a capable and efficient brigadier to the command of a division. It may be that the natural range of his powers will be found to be exceeded. Even should he, in time, grow up to the position, it is most likely that the new charge will be exercised at first with too much either of timidity or of rashness, with somewhat less than a full grasp of the situation, with comparative feebleness of authority and influence over the unfamiliar body. No such painful interval of self-distrust or of inadequacy to new and larger commands characterized

Hancock's successive promotions. The very day he was advanced from captain and quartermaster to be brigadier-general he was, in every sense, a general officer, confident of his powers, rejoicing in the exercise of his functions, and master of his place, himself, his staff, and his troops. An hour after Hancock rode down the line at Antietam to take up the sword that had fallen from Richardson's dying hand, one could not have told—he himself hardly knew—that he had not commanded a division for a year. So thoroughly had he prepared himself for promotion during his service with his brigade, so sure was he of his powers, that he stepped forward to the higher command upon the field of battle, amid its wreck and disorder, without a moment of hesitation or doubt, and at once became the leader of the division as fully and perfectly as Sumner had been, as Richardson had been. The staff knew it; the troops felt it. Every officer in his place, and every man in the ranks, was aware before the sun went down that he belonged to Hancock's Division.

In the command of that division, composed of fine material, admirably moulded by the heroic Sumner in the winter camps of 1861–62, and gifted with an extraordinary wealth of brilliant young soldiers destined to great careers, like Barlow, Zook, Brooke, Nugent, Patrick Kelly, Miles, and McKeen, Hancock remained until the 10th of June, 1863.

Time will not serve to tell the story of Fredericksburg and Chancellorsville. Of Fredericksburg, where, on the 13th of December, 1862, Hancock led the brigades of Meagher, Caldwell, and Zook out of the city, through streets commanded by the enemy's guns; crossed bridges by the flank at canister range; and there, deploying his forces, moved forward, over a plain swept from end to end by direct and enfilading fires, up towards Marye's Heights, against two tiers of musketry, to within pistol-shot of the Stone Wall which was held by four ranks of veteran riflemen, only desisting from the hopeless attempt to which he had been assigned when his gallant division had lost 2,013 men, including 156 commissioned officers killed or wounded. Of Chancellorsville, where, on the 3d of May, 1863, when all others had left the neighborhood of the Chancellor House, Hancock held his command in two lines of battle, back to back, one fronting towards Gordonsville, the other towards Fredericksburg, with his artillery firing down the lane between; and so kept the enemy at bay until the roads leading to the rear had been cleared of troops, and the way was open for his own slow and orderly retreat.

Each succeeding battle had but heightened Hancock's reputation for exact obedience to orders, for almost magical influence over men, for great tactical skill, for unflinching resolution, whether in attack or in defence; while his administrative ability and the strict discipline of his command, in camp or on the march, had clearly pointed him out as the rising soldier of the Potomac Army, so that, when that excellent officer, Major-General Couch, relinquished command of the Second Corps, on his assignment to the Department of the Susquehanna, every eye instinctively turned to Hancock as his successor. It was with a stern joy at the fulfilment of his righteous ambition, with a glad confidence in his own powers, yet not the less with an earnest sense of the responsibility thus devolved upon him, that, on the 10th of June, Hancock first drew his sword at the head of the corps which, in losing fifteen thousand men in battle, had never lost a color or a gun; whose fair fame, he was well resolved, should never suffer wrong at his hands.

Already had his reputation so far outrun even this high promotion, that, within three weeks of the day when he ceased to be the commander of a division, General Meade sent him forward to Gettysburg, to stay the disaster of the opening battle; to take command of the three corps at the front, over two officers his superiors in rank; and to report upon the suitability of the position for the concentration of the entire army.

In every great career, whether civil or military, there is some one day which is peculiarly memorable; which, by reason, in part, perhaps, of favorable opportunities or especially conspicuous position ; in part, also, through some rare inspiration quickening the genius of the statesman or the warrior, becomes and to the end remains the crown of that career: the day which the mention of that leader's name instinctively suggests; the day to which, in disappointment or in retirement, his own thoughts go back as for him the day of days.

Such to Hancock was Gettysburg. From the hour when, by his splendid resolution, force of character, and power over men, he checked the rout of the first afternoon, restored order and confidence, and formed the new lines which were to be held unbroken to the end, down to the hour when the divisions of Gibbon and Hays, leaping the stone walls and rail fences which had partially sheltered them during the cannonade and the great charge, gathered in thirty Confederate colors and four thousand prisoners from the shattered divisions of Pettigrew and Pickett, Gettysburg was to Hancock all-glorious, all-fortunate. Even the desperate wound he received in the moment of victory seemed at the time scarcely to cast a shadow upon the great triumph he had achieved during the first month of his career as the commander of an army corps.

That the campaign of 1864 did not bring him a proportional increase of fame was due chiefly to three causes :

First, he had already reached an almost dangerous elevation in popular reputation, from which one was far more likely to fall than to rise.

Second, Hancock's Gettysburg wound continued, almost from the opening of the campaign in May, till his enforced departure from the field in November, to be a source of weakness, suffering, and at times of total disability, requiring him frequently to seek rest in an ambulance or on the ground at times when, according to his pristine habits as a commander, he would have been galloping over the field or leading the march of his foremost division.

Third, the species of warfare that was initiated in May, 1864, against an enemy acting almost wholly on the defensive, behind breast-works protected by slashing and abattis, and largely, also, by swamps ; in a region where clear ground was highly exceptional, and where the uncleared ground was often covered by dense and stubborn growth of trees and underbrush through which a single woodman could with difficulty force his way, was one that offered few opportunities for brilliant actions.

Indeed, the campaign of 1864 was one which, except in the case of a few dashing young brigade commanders, was to destroy reputations and not to make them. Sheridan, it is true, won great fame during the year; but it was by his operations in the fertile and open Valley of Virginia, rather than in the jungles of the Wilderness or of Spottsylvania, or among the swamps of the Totopotomoy or the Chickahominy.

To Hancock the loss of opportunity, through the peculiar character of the campaign, was relatively greater than to any other commander, since those qualities in which he preeminently excelled, namely, tactical skill and personal influence over his soldiers in critical moments, were, on most of the battle-fields of 1864, largely neutralized by the nature of the country. Yet, though that campaign afforded little opportunity for brilliant strokes and great successes, the fame of Hancock suffered no diminution under its trials. He it was who, bringing his troops up to the support of Getty's fine division, on the Orange Plank Road, in the afternoon of the 5th of May, forced back the corps of Hill, which had advanced to seize the Brock Road Junction, and thus intervene between the two wings of the Union army. He it was who, in the early morning of the 6th, encountering, with his own divisions and those of Getty and Wadsworth, the corps of Hill and Longstreet, fought that great battle of the Left, in the Wilderness, which has become a synonym for savage ferocity and unrelenting determination. If the tremendous charge at Cold Harbor failed to secure its object, the high-heaped mounds of patriot dead remain a monument of unsurpassed valor and discipline. And it was Hancock's closely massed divisions, moving under his eye, which broke into that wild, spontaneous cheer, as the red earth of the Salient came into view, on the early morning of the 12th of May, dashed forward against a storm of lead, and all together leaped the Confederate intrenchments. Some of you remember, for you were there, how, from that bloody dawn till 12 o'clock at night, the Second Corps, with the good Sixth fighting on its right, held those captured intrenchments against the utmost efforts of Lee's veteran brigades, roused almost to madness by the losses of the early morning; how trees were cut down by the fire of musketry alone; how the foemen fired their pieces full in each other's faces, or gave bayonet thrusts across the intrenchments on which at times both hostile flags were planted; how, again and again, the trenches had to be cleared of the slain, that the living might have a place to stand. Over that desperate and protracted contest Hancock presided, stern, strong, and masterful; withdrawing the shattered brigades as their ammunition became exhausted, supplying their places with fresh troops; feeding the fires of battle all that long day and far into the night, until the Confederates, at last abandoning their attempts to retake the captured works, retired from the field, full twenty hours after the order "Forward" had been given to the column of assault.

In the brilliant strategic movement upon Petersburg, and in the bloody assaults which followed the miscarriage of the attempt to seize the Cockade City before the arrival of Lee's army, Hancock took a part which was abruptly terminated by an outbreak of his Gettysburg wound.

Recovering from his disability, he conducted in July and August two expeditions to the north bank of the James River, of which time will allow me to speak only so far as to relate an incident strikingly characteristic of Hancock and of the gallant commander of the Union cavalry, who was, at this time, under Hancock's orders.

The July expedition to Deep Bottom, as it is called, had in view two possible results. First, that the enemy's lines on that side of the river might be found so thinly held as to allow our powerful corps of cavalry, after the Confederate infantry should have been pushed back upon Chapin's Farm, to capture Richmond by a rush, or, at least, cut up the railroads on the north of the city.

Second, that failing in this, the movement might serve as a feint to draw a large part of Lee's army away from Petersburg, which the Fifth, Ninth, and Eighteenth Corps were preparing to enter through the ghastly avenue that was to be laid open by the explosion of Burnside's mine.

The first object was defeated by the rapid concentration of the enemy's forces; but, as a demonstration in favor of Burnside, the expedition was an overwhelming success. So alarmed were the Confederates that they drew over to that side the larger part of their entire army. This, while favoring the projected assault upon Petersburg, was, of course, accompanied by no inconsiderable danger to the little column on the north bank of the river. Critical as was the position on the 28th, it was rendered highly perilous when the lieutenant-general, on the evening of that day, ordered Mott, with nearly one-half the Second Corps, back to Petersburg. This was to leave two small divisions, scarcely eight thousand strong, to confront overwhelming odds throughout the succeeding day. It was, however, provided that the cavalry should cross to the south bank, leave the horses there, in charge of every fourth cavalryman, and, returning, help the infantry to hold their extended lines. In such a situation everything depended on the enemy's obtaining not even a suggestion of the weakness of our remaining column. To this end the most precise instructions were issued regarding the crossing; not a man was to enter upon the bridge after the first break of day. Every subordinate commander was required to acknowledge receipt of these instructions; and then the headquarters, worn out by the excessive exertions of the three preceding days, sank to rest. From the sound sleep into which I had fallen, I was awakened by hearing my name called from the general's tent. Running in I found Hancock tossing on his camp-bed. "Colonel," he said, "I am anxious about the cavalry. Go to Sheridan and say to him that he must see to it that not a man goes upon the bridge after it is light." I jumped upon an orderly's horse which was kept saddled for an emergency, and galloped to Sheridan's headquarters. As I approached, the first voice that challenged me was not the sentinel's, not a staff officer's, but the voice of the great cavalryman himself. "Who's that?" I gave my message. "I was thinking of the same thing," was the reply. "Forsythe, go down to the bridge, and if General Kautz has not crossed, tell him to mass his division behind the woods." Forsythe and myself rode together toward the bridge. A division of cavalry was just entering upon it. Fifteen minutes more, and the Confederates, who had all night listened to the low rumbling sounds and the dull jarring of the bridge, and from their lookouts had been straining their eyes to catch the direction of the movement, would have seen our troops passing to the rear, and, in all probability, would have swooped down upon our little force and driven us into the river. As it turned out, when it became light enough for them to see, what they beheld was our dismounted cavalrymen, returning from the south side, with their carbines over their shoulders, looking, for all the world, like honest infantry, seemingly the end of a column which had been crossing all night. The effect was complete. The Confederate leaders did not doubt that every brigade which could be taken from the Petersburg lines had been sent in haste across the James, to force a passage into Richmond. This illusion, aided by the activity and audacity of our skirmish line, under Miles, not only sufficed to save us from an attack which could hardly have failed to result in our destruction, but held the Confederate forces closely in place, twenty miles from Petersburg, where the assault of the 30th of July was impending.

My story carries its own moral. Here were the two men of the Potomac Army regarding whom it was popularly sup posed that they won their successes by daring and brilliant strokes. Yet we see them lying awake at night, after incredible fatigues, to ponder the chances of a possible miscarriage. In how many critical moments of the war, comrades, did the disappointment of well-laid plans, if not disastrous defeat, result because able and skilful officers deemed their duty discharged when they had given the appropriate orders! This was not Hancock's or Sheridan's idea of a commander's work. They gave the right orders, and then saw them executed; and it was to this, fully as much as to their more brilliant qualities of soldiership, that the successes of these two chieftains were due.

Time will not serve to tell the story of that blackest of days in the calendar of the gallant leader of the Second Corps, when, on the 25th of August, after his command had lost twenty-three thousand men in battle since it crossed the Rapidan, two of his oft-decimated divisions, scarce sixty-six hundred strong, caught in the ill-constructed intrenchments at Reams's Station, were driven from a portion of their works by repeated assaults from a superior force, with the loss of seven standards, nine cannon, and seventeen hundred prisoners. The agony of that day never passed away from the proud soldier, who, for the first time, in spite of superhuman exertions and reckless exposure on his part, saw his lines broken and his guns taken. "Were I dead," said Nelson, "'want of frigates' would be found written on my heart." So, one who was gifted to discern the real forces which in us make for life or for death, looking down upon the cold and pallid form of Hancock, as he lay at rest, beneath the drooping flag of his country, there on Governor's Island, would have seen "Reams's Station" written on brow and brain and heart, as palpable as, to the common eye, were the scars of Gettysburg.

Nor can I tell of the honorable expedition to the Boydton Road in October, 1864, which closed the career of Hancock in the field. During November, his wound still distressing him, it was proposed by the President and the Secretary of War that he should relinquish his command, and, returning to the North, during the season when active operations would be impracticable through stress of weather, should raise a corps to be composed wholly of veterans who had served honorably through one term of enlistment. This trust Hancock accepted in the same spirit with which he had received, and so far as lay in him had executed, every commission and order since he left the quartermaster's camp at Los Angeles.

In the opening of the year 1865, he took the field at the head of his new command, officered by well-approved soldiers like Carroll, Brooke, and C. H. Morgan; but before he was called to encounter the enemy, the brilliant combinations of Sheridan, Warren, and Humphreys, the sturdy valor and indomitable energy of Wright and Ord, and the fine soldiership and loyal devotion of Parke and Gibbon, had brought the long contest to a close; Petersburg had fallen, and with it Richmond, the objective point of four years' incessant fighting; Lee's army, attempting to escape, had been beset in flank and rear by troops that seemed for the time to have lost the sense alike of fatigue and of fear; battles had been fought upon the double-quick, divisions and army corps had marched or run, in deployed lines, from daylight until dark; and, at last, at Appomattox Court House, the much-enduring Army of Northern Virginia, after performing prodigies of valor, surrounded and brought to bay before five-fold odds, surrendered without shame; Sherman came sweeping up from the South like a whirlwind, driving Johnston's army before him, and the greatest rebellion of modern times was crushed.

SPEECH

OF

HON. W. D. KELLEY,

OF PENNSYLVANIA.

DELIVERED IN THE HOUSE OF REPRESENTATIVES, DECEMBER 19, 1862.

The House being in Committee of the Whole on the State of the Union, Mr. KELLEY said:

MR. CHAIRMAN, I cannot announce to the House, as the eloquent gentleman from Maryland [Mr. CRISFIELD] who has just concluded, did, when he began his remarks, that what I am about to say is well considered and carefully prepared, for I came to the House this morning with no thought of occupying any portion of its time and attention. But it seems to me that before the week closes some rejoinder should be made to the various suggestions in favor of peace and compromise, and of hostility to the acts and policy of the President of the United States, that we have been hearing from day to day. And, unprepared as I am, I propose to reply to a few of these suggestions. I can promise that my words shall be honest, frank, and earnest, though my argument may lack arrangement.

Permit me to say, sir, that I am in favor of peace. I was for peace when I first raised my voice in this House. I was then, as I am now, for early and enduring peace; for peace on terms honorable to the people of the country, and which shall not dishonor the memory of the wise and patriotic men who established the independence and unity of our country, and ordained its beneficent institutions.

I am, sir, for peace so secured that it shall prevail forever over that broad territory which, at the last presidential election, was covered by thirty-four State constitutions, and that which, as territory, belongs to the United States, but which will come under the jurisdiction of States whose people shall know no sovereignty save that which resides in the Constitution as it came to us from the fathers. How, sir, can such a peace be attained? It can only be done by remembering, first and always, that the supreme law of the land is the Constitution of the United States; and that we, as members of this House, are sworn to support that Constitution; and that the President of the United States is sworn to preserve, protect and defend it. My theory is, sir, that rights and duties are things reciprocal. So long as the people of a State obey the behests of the Constitution, and live in accordance with them, they are entitled to the enjoyment of all constitutional rights. So long as they array themselves against them only in such force that the marshal and his *posse* may suppress their violent demonstrations, they are entitled to all those rights, save as the penal code properly applied may abridge them. But, when, as has been the case in the so-called seceeding States, they assemble in organic conventions and throw off all duty to the Government; when they abjure loyalty and duty, and claim to have established on our soil an independent and foreign government; when they attempt in the name and by the agency of such alleged foreign government, to create a navy, and do assemble armies to contend with the power of the Government, and thereby banish our customs and postal system, and close our courts, they lose their title to constitutional rights, and it becomes the duty of the Government by whatever force it may require, to regain possession and control the territory occupied by them, and to rule the people occuping it with such hostile purposes, irrespective of State lines, or State names, or State institutions or State constitutions. It must maintain the unity of the country; and if the inhabitants will disregard all their duties, it must govern them under the power of the Constitution that makes the President Commander-in-Chief of the Army and Navy of the United States, and that requires him, if so it must be, by military force to maintain the supremacy of the Government over every acre of our territory. When supreme jurisdiction shall be thus established, we may say to whomsoever may occupy the country, or particular portions of it, "adopt your State constitution, whether the one that formerly prevailed or another: open your courts, and let the courts of the United States be opened; let our customs system and our postal system be enforced; avow your allegiance to our Constitution and Government, and as you shall perform the duties, enjoy, also, the rights of American citizens."

Gentlemen on the other side seem to forget that sworn duty, as well as patriotism and the future welfare and peace of the country, demand the maintenance of the unity of our territory, and of the supremacy of the power of the United States over it in its entirety. These are things that must be maintained, if we would avoid standing armies and unceasing war. Where all duties under the Constitution are rejected, no rights can be claimed, and the Government must be maintained by force, That is my position, and it is, I believe, the position of the loyal people of the country. When I say loyal I mean it; as I know no conditions that may accompany its expression. That loyalty which is conditional stretches forth a friendly hand to treason. [Suppressed applause in the gallery.] Indeed, conditional loyalty is partial treason. The President's emancipation proclamation has been the subject of invective and denunciation this morning, and it has been said that no man in the country, save the President of the United States, believes that it will promote peace. Sir, has territory ceased to be territory? Do figures still indicate numbers and power? Has the lesser come, by some new influence, to comprehend the greater? For, if it be not so, the enforcement of that proclamation will promote peace by aiding in the establishment of the supremacy of the Government. Has not the question as to whether four millions of stalwart people shall labor for us or for those with whom we are at war, some importance and a direct bearing on the issue? Will its solution, if it transfer them from one side to the other, have no influence upon the power of the rebellion? I believe, with the President, that it will. There are four millions of brawny right arms, mostly dark-colored, but many of them, through the fell influence of the hell-born institution of slavery, fair as our own; there are four millions of people reluctantly giving their daily toil to the support of this rebellion; and it is proposed by the President to invite them, on the 1st of January next, as wisdom would have done more than a year ago, to withhold their labors from that cause and bestow them, as they desire to, upon the cause of patriotism, freedom, and peace, under the starry flag of our country. Who will tell me that the transfer of the labor of these people will have no influence in suppressing the rebellion?

But, asked the eloquent gentleman from Kentucky, [Mr. YEAMAN]—whose elaborately prepared speech, I regret to say, contained, if I heard him aright, a sneer at those who read written arguments—whoever heard of a belligerent party taking private property on land? Let me ask him a question, to be answered in some of his future speeches, who ever heard of a belligerent prohibiting the people of the opposing power from rallying to his standard? He speaks of property, and I speak of *men*. It is a great thing, sir, to be a man

Mr. YEAMAN. The gentleman will allow me to interrupt him.

Mr. KELLEY. I did not invite an immediate answer. As the gentleman guarded himself yesterday against interruption, so did I to-day propound a question to be answered in the future.

Mr. YEAMAN. Allow me one momant. I answer the gentleman by saying that I have cast no sneer upon anybody for reading written speeches. I answer him, also, by saying that slaves, so far from being persons in the eye of the laws o nations, as he treats them, while they are actually persons, are, by that Constitution which he has sworn to support, the private property of private individuals, and that neither under the Constitution, nor under the laws of nations, can you take private property on land as an act of war.

Mr. KELLEY. I take issue with the gentleman there, and if he will say that they are not designated in the Constitution as "persons," or point me to the clause in which they are designated as property, I will yield the point. The Constitution that I have sworn to support tells me that they—yes, the mothers, the fathers, and the children all—are "PERSONS held to service." They are persons so held by virtue of that Constitution which has been spurned and trampled and spit upon, and yet he asks that those who have heaped these indignities upon that sacred instrument shall enjoy to the last iota the rights of loyal men under it. Did sane man ever utter so preposterous a proposition before? It is the service of these people we need. The proclamation invites them to our standard. He characterizes them as property. I say, with the Constitution, that they are persons, and as such will welcome them to our support. Their advent to freedom will exclude the necessity of the further draft or conscription of our sons and brothers.

Sir, I was remarking that it is a great thing to be a man, in contrast with horses, cows, and other cattle with which these poor people are habitually classified, and to which they have been assimulated by brutalizing laws. Man chains the lightning, makes the sun his servant, whitens the ocean with sails—his messengers to the poles in quest of knowledge—burdens its great waves with the commodities which his genius and toil have produced and which he is exchanging for others, the products of distant lands, more valuable to him. From the conflicting, elements, fire and water, he generates a vapory power that almost annihilates space, and practically removes mountains and levels valleys; and at the close of a life of usefulness, upon the sick-bed, he remembers and reviews the past, cheers, counsels, and blesses those about him, and, looking to heaven, feels that with God he is to live forever. The gentleman looks upon these millions of persons as property; so do bad institutions pervert gentle and generous natures. I say, sir, they are capable of all that ennobles man, and all that endears woman to man, and all that opens to either the great hereafter and its blessed hopes. It is of these women, these children, these men, I speak, and I say that he can point to no case in which a belligerent has refused the aid of such as these when engaged in a war such as that which now engrosses and exhausts the energies of this country. Sir, the only thing about the President's proclamation that struck me as amiss was, that it was not, like the lightning, to take instant effect, and that its beneficent result should be postponed to so distant a day. Are these people, or the relation in which they stand to those who hold them to service, like cotton, leather, railroad depots, bad whisky, and other supposed analogous things suggested by the gentleman from Kentucky, yesterday? No, no. Trace back the laws of war so elaborately described by the gentleman from Maryland [Mr. CRISFIELD] to-day, and you will find that the invading force not only has always welcomed acquisitions from the ranks of the enemy, but that, in the good old days of chivalry, a herald invariably proceeded to the gates of a besieged town and offered immunity and protection to all who would join the invading Power. This chivalric example the President's proclamation pledges him to follow on the coming in of the glad new year. Let us hail the auspicious day!

I come back to the question with which I started. Will the gentleman from Maryland [Mr. CRISFIELD], will the gentleman from Kentucky [Mr. YEAMAN], will the gentleman from Illinois [Mr. RICHARDSON,] who so delights to dance the negro before us in all his various attitudes—will any one of these gentlemen, or of their learned coadjutors, say that it is not the duty of the President to maintain the unity of the country and the supremacy of the Constitution over all our territory? And if they will not say that, is there one of them who will say that he was wrong in thus inviting four millions of the people of the country to abandon rebellion and rally to the standard of loyalty, peace, and the Constitution? No one of them, I apprehend, will say so. Than this, in my judgment, mere sympathy with the rebellion could no further go. Gentlemen deny that slavery was the cause of this war. Let me ask them which one of the non-slaveholding States, from the first, has proposed to participate in it, and which one of the slaveholding States has been free from a desire to participate in it, or from overt acts of rebellion? Why is it that prevailing loyalty and treason find their boundaries just here if slavery be not the controlling influence? I give praise to the border States for all they have done on the side of the country; but I remember that the first of the troops from my State to find service found it in the lower part of little Delaware; I remember that Marylanders were the first to shed the blood of New England in this unholy war; I remember that it is but recently, if indeed the question be at all settled, that Kentucky has been able to say with assurance that she has given more soldiers to the Union than to the rebel army. All honor and glory to the men of East Tennessee——

Mr. WADSWORTH. Will the gentleman permit me to correct him?

Mr. KELLEY. Yes, sir.

Mr. WADSWORTH. The gentleman has fallen into a very common mistake upon this question of the number of troops furnished by the people of Kentucky to the cause of the Union and of the rebellion.

Mr. KELLEY. Well, I will waive that question.

Mr. WADSWORTH. I suppose there have never been seven thousand men from the State of Kentucky in the rebellion. Very early in the fall of 1861 we had thirty-two regiments in the Union army; and I understand from our adjutant general that we now have forty-three thousand men from the State of Kentucky in the Union army. I can say, in addition, that from twenty-five to thirty thousand inhabitants of Kentucky have borne arms this summer and fall, without pay or compensation, in defense of their homes, it is true, but also in defense of the honor of the Union.

Mr. KELLEY. I had supposed that the question had been recently settled in favor of Kentucky's prevailing loyalty. It was, however, very debatable ground when we last assembled in this House, and I do not forget the fact that part of the Kentucky army has been led by a gentleman who—brief as is my legislative experience—was an active member on this floor when I came here in July of last year. Nor do I forget that Gen. Breckinridge and his forces have been sometimes repulsed by our arms.

Mr. WADSWORTH. If the gentleman from Pennsylvania will allow me ——.

Mr. KELLEY. I am simply arguing the point that every slave State has shown large sympathies with the rebellion, while no free State has gone into it, although many persons in the free States have manifested extreme sympathies with it.

Mr. WADSWORTH. I simply want to correct an error of fact.

Mr. KELLEY. I am not in error in remembering that General Breckinridge, the late Democratic Vice-President, came from Kentucky, nor do I forget that Mr. Burnett, of this House, was a member from Kentucky. I am not mistaken in either of these facts. Burnett is in the Senate now, I believe, instead of in the field; but he was in the field as a soldier, and was transferred thence to the senate, to return to the field when the conclave of traitors adjourns.

But, as I was saying, Mr. Chairman, I give all honor to the men of East Tennessee. The heroic devotion to the Constitution they have exhibited, and the barbarous cruelties they have endured, make a chapter which even of the people of the Southern States will, long years hence, dwell on perhaps, with mingled pride and pain, but with more interest than on any other in American history. We know how terribly that State has been ravaged by the prevalence of the rebellion within its limits. And Missouri, which has not only elected unconditional loyalists, but unconditional emancipationists to this House, has also been the bloody battle field in which Missourians have been engaged in either army. If it be not true, sir, that slavery is the root of this rebellion, I ask some inspired man to indicate its moving cause, for human wisdom cannot detect it elsewhere.

Now, can it be possible, Mr. Chairman, that the only right so secured on earth that men cannot abjure it, nor Government divest them of it even to save itself in death struggle, is the right of holding fellow beings in bondage? The pro position that we have not the right to invite these slaves to freedom and our standard involves just this theory—that the rebels cannot by the most flagrant treason divest themselves of the right to hold these people in bondage; that the people cannot aquire freedom for themselves, and that no power in the Constitution, or in the war power, or deducible from history or philosophy, can relieve them from the duty of assisting the enemies of the country to destroy its life. Let the arguments be expressed as they may, with all the eloquence and elegance with which care and time and elaboration have clothed them in the mouths of the gentlemen from Kentucky and Maryland, [Messrs. YEAMAN and CRISFIELD,] they come to this. And until gentlemen can demonstrate this extraordinary proposition, they cannot impair the force of the President's proclamation, in accordance, as it is, with all law and all history, with the best impulses of humanity, and the spirit of our charter of freedom, and with the growing tendency of our age. The gentleman from Maryland asks, "will this bring peace? Will the South ever consent to come in under such an arrangement?" Sir, I do not propose to, nor ought the Government to ask the South on what terms it will come in. What the Government ought to do, and what I trust it will do, is to go straight forward and establish its power by crushing out all armed resistance, and when that is done, let it govern the region as a Territory, if the people will not establish their own government. In this condition, let the contumacious remain; but whenever they will establish governments for themselves, adopt State constitutions, open the courts, elect Legislatures, and by them and the people elect Senators and members of Congres, receive them again as States into the Union, under such designations as they may choose, whether novel or familiar. By this means, the forms and vital principles of our Government will be preserved, and peace and constitutional freedom be secured to the people of distant ages. Whenever this Government puts forth its power to the end that it is bound to assert, there will be no question as to whether we mean to violate the Constitution or whether the people of the South will accept the constitutional terms we offer them.

"But," said the gentleman this morning, "will the border States tolerate it?" To be sure they will. True, many of their citizens may dislike to see the Southern market closed againt their human cattle, but the rebellion has gone so far that, with the 1st of January slavery dies south of the border State line; and when there is no market for men, women, and children, south of Virginia and Kentucky, slavery will have small value in any of the border States. I think I see the hand of God in these movements. The events of the time are deplorable, indeed; but I know that His providences are inscrutable, and that he can make the folly and wrath of man to praise Him. I had long seen that if the Democratic party could continue the misrule which it had enforced on the people for years, and especially its aggressions upon the rights of the laborers of the country, a war would come which would be at the door of every man's home. Let us look at it. "A house divided against itself cannot stand," quoted my friend from Maryland, and with grave deprecation. Did not the leaders of the South divide our house? Let us look at it. Go where you will, Mr. Chairman, in our Northern States, you find, the Constitution of the United States taught in our elementary schools, and its democratic spirit everywhere inculcated. You find our youth growing up at the foot of the hustings; and the great doctrine taught to every child is: "You are as good as any other child. When you come to manhood you are to be the equal, before the State, of every other man. You must watch, guard, and maintain all your rights." Thus is the democratic sentiment stimulated in every school, from every lecture stand, at every political gathering; and the political sentiment of the whole North is that of individualism and equality. And once in seven days comes the Sabbath; and from hillside and valley, from the lanes and alleys, as well as from the broad streets of the city, the children gather in the church and Sunday school: There they learn that Christianty enforces while it refine and exhalts the doctrines inculcated in the secular school; thus the religiou sentiment adds its greater power to the political. "These poor are as good a you," says the teacher. "These blind, and lame, and halt, are the chlidren o your Father; and inasmuch as you do kindness unto them, you perform your duty to Him." Thus the political and religious sentiments blend; and theirs is an ever growing power. Of this we have ample evidence all over the North, in the elaborate comforts of our eleemosynary institutions, and the care that is taken of our prisoners. I had the honor, a few days ago, to receive a number of volumes from our Philadelphia Prison Discipline Society, for the Congressional Library. The deaf, the dumb, the blind, the insane, are cared for. Homes are established for friendless children, where the waifs of society, the offspring of the destitute and fallen, the pauper and the felon, are cared for and reared in these teachings of democracy and Christianity. Thus the sentiment spreads and deepens and grows.

We have one institution in the North, the outgrowth of the perpetual contest between labor and capital, that, could the South have carried its domination a little further, would have made war and bloodshed over the whole country. It consists of hardy working men and is known as the trades union. We at the North live by wages. Our men are familiar with toil; our women do not shrink from it. We recognize the maxim, as true to-day as the day when it was first written in homely English:

> "Man labors from sun to sun.
> But woman's work is never done."

We all labor, and wages is the foundation of the welfare and abundance of our people. The idea that induced this rebellion and the supremacy of which could alone have averted it, was that slavery should be not only extended into the new Territories of the country, but be domesticated in all the States. It was first to be introduced into the States by gentlemen *in transitu* with their colonies. The roll of Mr. Toombs's slaves was to be called at the foot of Bunker Hill. We were told in social intercourse in Philadelphia, by Mr. Yancey, that he would yet visit Independence Hall with his slaves. The re-establishment of the right to hold slaves all over the country was the purpose of the leaders of our "wayward sisters." Nothing less would satisfy them. Sir, had that thing been accomplished, the trade unions of the North would either have throttled the slaveholders, or, under the influence of the prejudices of caste and color, throttled the unhappy slaves, perhaps both. Here let me notice the remark of the gentleman from Maryland, that he does not agree with either of the two factions. Of what factions does he speak? The governments of the Union and the confederacy? Sir, it is the first time I ever heard the Government of the United States denounced as a faction in the Halls of Congress. Nor are they who are devoting all their energies to the support of the President and the Constitution to be denounced as a faction. I look in vain through this House for two factions.

I see that the Government, with a million of men, defending itself and attempting to enforce its laws over its own dominions, has been resisted by a body of armed rebels, and that those who sympathize with them, in a greater or less degree, are attempting to embarrass it; but other faction I have not been able to discover. There were two factions before the war broke out. Anterior to that event, there was a body of men in the North, who, under Christian impulses, believing it to be a duty to labor for the oppressed, and that it is a crime to hold men and women in bondage, were willing to violate all civic restraints in order to give freedom, culture, and hope to the slave. The abolitionists may have been entitled to that epithet. And there were southern men, on the other hand, determined, as I have indicated, to carry their institutions all over the North—to make slavery national by perverting the Constitution. There were, then, two factions—devotion to right and justice, perhaps notrestrained by a proper prudence on the one hand, and love of lucre, power, and lust; that blotted out all spmpathy with humanity, on the other, characterized the leaders of these factions.

Had the Southern faction been permitted to dominate until the roll of Southern slaves had been called in every county in every Northern State, there would have broken out a war—a war coextensive with the country, and bloody, at every hearthstone—a war which might have been of races, or in which those who claimed their human property would have suffered with their unhappy and proscribed chattels. The white men of the North, who, from their own hard-earned and hoarded wages, will support their unemployed craftsmen rather than let him work for under wages, would hardly hav permitted men to work beside them for nothing, and throw their babies as property into the scale with their unrequited toil. [Laughter.]

Sir, I believe this war was inevitable. The insane ambition and mad, craving lust of the South could be checked alone by the results of war. It had closed its ears hermetically against the voice of persuasion and reason. And wherever slavery existed, that ambition and and that lust had root. Slavery did cause this war. It was destined to cause war, and if not put in process of eradication, will involve our posterity in war. Is it not fitting, therefore, that the result of the war shall be the end of slavery? The President's proclamation does not propose to touch the institution in the border States. But, as I have said, with the market for the annual crop gone, it will be found to be of no more value in Kentucky than it is now found to be in Missouri, with her free surroundings. And then we will come to what I am prepared to say very few words upon, the compensated emancipation proposition of the President.

The countless millions, the millions of millions that we have heard from the other side are to be expended in compensated emancipation, will be somewhat reduced when we come to remember that it is only the loyal men of the border States that we will have to deal with.

Missouri is here, asking for $10,000,000 on condition that she emancipates her slaves within a little more than a year. In God's name, let us give it to her; and if Kentucky and Maryland make the same claim, let us give it to them, and pay our full share out of the results of our own hard labor at the North. Let us even, by an addition to our already grievous burden of taxes, imposed by this war—slavery's own offspring—share the losses of those whose slaves shall be exalted into freemen.

But, say the gentlemen, the proclamation is unconstitutional and illegal, and therefore void. I fear self-interest blinds some of them. It is a professional maxim that he has a fool for a client who takes charge of his own case. Certainly, no disinterested lawyer will dispute the validity of the proclamation of the Commander-in-Chief inviting to our flag people of the rebel States, and promising them protection and the enjoyment of constitutional rights. But will the proclamation be enforced? Yes; that is certain as the coming of the new year. And I ask the gentleman from Kentucky [Mr. Yeaman] and the gentleman from Maryland [Mr. Crisfield] to pause in the career they open by their speeches of yesterday and to-day. Both profess, truly, I doubt not, to desire peace; both assure us that they would give utterance to no words that would add to the discord of the country. Let them then look the facts in the face. Gentlemen, do you not see that time and Providence are conspiring with man to put an end to the sole source of discord to the country? Do you not see that it was this institution which created division even in the Convention that formed our Constitution? Do you not see that it has been this institution that, from the early settlement of the country down to the present time, has produced more of discord than all other causes combined.

The eloquent gentleman from Kentucky yesterday asserted that this rebellion had been ripening from 1798. I agree with him that that was one standpoint in its progress. The resolutions of 1798 marked a new epoch. But if he will go further back he will find, in the debates of the Convention which framed the Constitution, abundant evidence that slavery was and had been a source of discord, and that it came well nigh preventing the establishment of a Union. It has been a source of discord, and of discord only; never was it a blessing to any State or people.

I have no special love for the negro. I am proud of the race of which, by the blessing of God, I am a member. It is not for the negro that I plead. The gentleman from Illinois [Mr. Richardson] the other day said that all our sympathy and all our action was for the negro, but not one thing did we propose to do for the white man. Has he never heard of the creature—MAN. I speak for man, the child of God, irrespective of the color of his skin.

Look at the baneful influence of slavery upon both white and black. You point me to statistics from the North to show that poverty and crime prevail with the negro there in undue proportion. I point you back to your laws that made it a felony to teach him to read and write, by which he might have drawn moral precepts and power from the same sources that your white children draw them. I point back to the fact that you have never allowed him the stimulus of hope. I say that your accursed institution, and the cruelty and depression inseparable from it, have not only filled our jails with your victims but has brought poverty to both races wherever it has existed. Why is it that Massachusetts, whose soil is so thin that the rocks peep through nearly every acre, like the knees and elbows through a beggar's garment—Massachusetts, which cannot raise wheat enough per annum to feed her own people for a week, is yet rich and populous; while Maryland, abounding in agricultural and mineral resources, to a degree that few States can compare with, lags constantly dragging in the rear?*

Why is it that old Virginia, possessing, as she did, the finest harbor and leading seaport of the country at the time of the adoption of the Constitution with nobler rivers than flow through any other State; with mineral resources that California herself might envy—untold wealth of iron and coal to encourage and stimulate the influx of intelligent and enterprising people—lying nearer to the West than other States with fine harbors; with every blessing that God could lavish upon a territory; why is it, I say, that the Old Dominion has sunk down and down, until her own children turn from their proud pre-eminence, and sneer at her decrepitude? Why, it was because your lords of the soil converted man into property. It was because you banished hope from your laborers; because you did not permit the toiling mother to love the child she had borne with assurance that it was hers, even through childhood. It is this which has made you poor, notwithstanding your mineral deposits, your rivers, and your vast agricultural resources. You have made the negro a curse to you; for God never permits a great wrong to go unpunished.

When, in another year, Congress assembles in these halls there will be no pictures drawn such as the gentlemen have furnished us with, of homes desolated or destroyed, women ravished, masters murdered by slaves converted into freemen, and grateful for the greatest blessing of life. The voice of thanksgiving and praise will come from every heart to whom freedom has been given. It will come from the white man as well as the freed slaves, in tones of praise and hallelujah.

There is, however, one thing the people of the rebellious States have to guard against. Of that they must beware. Let them not undertake to re-enslave the freed men that the President of the United States delivers by his proclamation, or woe may betide them. Let them not thus invite the horrors of St. Domingo. The voice of history admonishes them fully on this point. If they do it will be their act, and not the President's or ours. He will make them free, and they will rejoice in their freedom, and be humbly grateful. Not in the hour of joy and gratitude, and when singing praises for their deliverance is the tiger let loose in man. As God will have wrought this change He will guide it. But let man attempt to reverse His Providence and who shall answer for his folly?

---

* I extract the following from a letter dated Williamsport, Maryland, November 27, 1862, addressed to me by an officer of a Maryland regiment. The writer is a native of that State:

"While I am writing you I cannot refrain from making a statement or two with regard to the topography of this part of Maryland. Doubtless you have a correct knowledge of it generally, and perhaps, in detail, but no one can know and appreciate it without traveling over it and through it I have gone over it some in reconnoitering; but there are, of course, many peculiarities which I have not seen. Its fertility is unsurpassed, but its chief characteristic seems to be its boundless *water power*. To say nothing of the Patapsco, Monocacy, Middletown Valley Creek, Antietam, Conocheague, and many other large streems, you meet almost at the end of every mile, a stream sufficient to run a gang of mills. As I ride over this country the question comes up in my mind can it be possible that Providence ever designed that these mighty waters should run to waste, or that these wonderful natural facilities should always be unavailable? And the answer comes back—no! The day will come when the busy hum of the factory and the mighty blows of the forge hammer will be heard among these mountains; when the exhaustless treasures which are hidden therein shall be brought forth, and when thousands and thousands of glad hearts and merry voices shall shout a hearty welcome to a new era. This, too, is a correct answer. To accept anything else would be equivalent to an acknowledgment that God never designed intelligence and industry to have any part in mundane affairs."

SEPARATION:

WAR WITHOUT END.

By M. Edouard Laboulaye,

MEMBER OF THE INSTITUTE.

UPON WHOM

RESTS THE GUILT OF THE WAR?

SEPARATION:

WAR WITHOUT END.

By M. Edouard Laboulaye,

MEMBER OF THE INSTITUTE.

New-York:

WM. C. BRYANT & CO., PRINTERS, 41 NASSAU STREET, CORNER OF LIBERTY.

1863.

NATIONAL UNITY:

IT MUST NOT BE SURRENDERED.

[*From the N. Y. "Evening Post," Feb.* 7, 1863.]

NEW YORK, February 7th, 1863.

To PARKE GODWIN, Esq.:

I send you herewith a translation from the French of a remarkable paper, originally published in the *Revue Nationale* of Paris. It has seemed to me that, in this critical hour of our national history, no better service could be rendered the country than to give it, in our own language, the widest circulation amongst the people. To this end may I not ask you to give it a place in the columns of the *Evening Post?*

The author is M. EDOUARD LABOULAYE, member of the Institute and Professor of *Legislation Comparée* in the College of France—a man holding the highest position in the first institution of the world, the University of France—and whose whole life has been devoted to the study of the subject of which he writes.

It may not be generally known that the lectures of the professors in all the colleges and schools of the University of France are open and free to all who may chose to attend them, so that the *seances* of such men as Laboulaye, Michelet, Quinet, and other eminent scholars and scientists are crowded by the most thoughtful of the men and women of all the nations of the world, who make Paris their resort for the winter.

I have before me a letter from a French liberalist, of high character and attainments, now a resident of the United States, who has himself had the advantage of a personal intercourse with M. Laboulaye, in which he says: "For the last two years scarcely has he, in his *chaire de legislation comparee*, given one of his eloquent lectures without introducing the United States—their greatness, their constitution, their trials, and their destinies. It is by thus particularizing his teachings that he has aroused for America a universal interest, for no week passes that the learned professor has not around his desk representatives from all the nations of Europe. Even ladies of all ranks and countries—English, Russians, Germans and Spaniards—seated there, side by side with the students of the *Quartier Latin*, listen to and applaud his eloquent and earnest advocacy of American nationality and free institutions."

M. Laboulaye himself relates the incident by which his thoughts and sympathies were first turned towards the people and the institutions of the United States. Everybody who has been in Paris will remember the long rows of wooden trays, filled with the strangest jumble of old books, that stretch along the river edge of the Quai Voltaire, and the other contiguous quais on that side of the Seine. One may find there books in all the languages of the world, and sometimes stray copies of very rare works. Well, one day, now several years ago, M. Laboulaye amused himself with rummaging amongst the old books exposed for sale on the Quai Voltaire. His eye caught the title of a book in English; he took it up, opened it, read a few moments, demanded its price, paid it, some few sous, and with his eyes still fixed upon its open pages, resumed his walk towards the Champs Elysée. Arrived there, he seated himself upon one of the numerous chairs always ready to be hired, and continued to read on until the last page of his new acquisition was finished; and then, instead of returning home, he went in a state of great excitement to M. Armand Bertin, at that time editor-in-chief of the *Journal des Debats*, and on meeting him exclaimed: "Congratulate me, I have to-day put my hand on a great man." And such was the enthusiasm with which he spoke of his new discovery, that M. Bertin begged him to make his "great man" at once known to France. M. Laboulaye, without delay, set to work, and in a few days there appeared, in successive numbers of the *Journal des Debats*, three masterly articles. The first was "on the works of Dr. WM. ELLERY CHANNING," for it was a stray volume of his sermons that M. Laboulaye had purchased on the Quai Voltaire, and he was the "great man" upon whom he "put his hand" that day. The second article was entitled, "The Progress of Religious Ideas in New England," and the last, "The Present Condition and Probable Future of the Great Republic."

The stray seed of the New England Puritan Reformer took deep root, and from that day to this M. Laboulaye has been an earnest student of American ideas and institutions, and on all occasions, and before all men, the unswerving friend and courageous advocate of the people and government of the Union.

A previous article of M. Laboulaye, originally published in the *Journal des Debats*, entitled "A View of the Causes and Aims of the Rebellion," had a wide circulation in this country through the columns of the *Evening Post* and other public journals, and exerted no little influence upon the formation of a just public opinion, here as well as abroad, as to the true character of the slave-masters' conspiracy to overthrow democratic institutions on this continent.

These latest pregnant words of the distinguished publicist reach us at the very moment of their greatest need. At a moment when the public patience seems well nigh exhausted; when here at the north, even the most loyal seem to lose heart and to doubt, and the disloyal, under the guise of conservatism and in the name of democracy, taking courage, strive so much the more, to bewilder and divide public opinion and confound the judgments of the people upon questions vital to national salvation. At this critical moment there comes from the other side of the Atlantic, from the home of Lafayette and Rochambeau, an answer so direct, so pointed and so conclusive, to the most nefarious of the sophistries of the northern parasites of the slave-power, that it cannot fail to aid in confounding their shameless attempt to shift the guilt of the war from the shoulders of their southern masters and to lay it upon those of the people of New England. This most enlightened and impartial student of American affairs, looking at the whole great conflict, from its inception to the present hour, with a single eye to discover the truth, declares that "the South alone is guilty."

But this is by no means the chief point of M. Laboulaye's argument. To yield the dissolution of the national unity—"the rending asunder of the country," that, in his view, is "the one irreparable degradation." "An abdication," he says, "so shameful, for a people accustomed to liberty, is not even to be thought of, so long as there remains a single man or a single dollar to risk in the struggle to keep the inheritance of the fathers."

And this is the momentous point which, I think, you, and all men like you, who have the ability to speak and a great audience who wait daily upon your words, should press home upon the minds and hearts of the people and their rulers.

For any people to permit themselves to meditate the possibility of a surrender of their nationality, indicates a condition of demoralization, which foretells the approach of utter national decay, the coming on of the final shame. But for a people so planted, so nutured by the Divine Providences, so illustrated by the heroic characters and deeds of their great founders, as the people of the United States—for such a people, in the very bloom of their prime, to yield up their national unity at the arrogant demand of a few thousand slave-masters, would be such an ineffaceable stain upon free institutions, upon democratic citizenship, upon Christian civilization, upon human nature itself, as is not to be paralleled in the history of the world. The ignominious delinquency and partition of Poland would be a national glory compared with it. And yet to-day, even here in the North, not to speak of the abettors of the great treason—the genuine spawn of the Tories of 1776—there are men calling themselves loyal, who begin to quail and to hint at a possible time for surrender—at a possible time to defile the graves and desecrate the memories of Washington, of Adams, of Jefferson, of Hamilton and their great compeers.

I know that the Supreme Ruler of the Ages, has always "the stones" out of which he can "raise up children unto Abraham"—new and faithful nations. Are we to have no other significance in the history of the race, but to illustrate these portentous words of the Divine Master of these Christian centuries?

How many years of almost hopeless toil and bloody sweat did the fathers devote to the acquisition of the great inheritance, to maintain which we have given but less than two, of bewildered and oftentimes aimless preparation? From the meeting of that first Congress of the American people, in this city of New York, in 1765, in which "the brave and noble-hearted" Gadsden, of South Carolina, gave utterance to the first grand formula of American nationality—"Away with your royal charters, and let us stand on the broad, common ground of those natural rights that we all feel and know as men; no more New Englanders, no more New Yorkers on this continent; but all of us Americans"—from that hour onward until 1789, when the people of the United States, in their own common name, established and set in motion a national constitution, the great struggle went on. The men of the first revolution, almost without means, surrounded by all manner of perils, and backed by comparatively but a handful of loyal people, waged a struggle of twenty-four years for the right of independent national existence; a right which, in their judgment, involved all other human rights and interests—social, civil, and political—peace, prosperity, and glory. And in this struggle, let it not be forgotten, was included a bloody war of seven years—Valley Forge and all. Less than three millions of people, without ships, without arms or munitions, without money or credit, but only with an earnest will and stout hearts, against the first naval and military power of the world, fighting for a great idea, for that pearl without price, Liberty, to be set in the golden band of national unity.

National Unity: that is the muniment of title to the inheritance transmitted by the fathers, and which the American people to-day stand pledged before the world, to keep intact in all its integrity, both of exterior estate and of interior idea, at the cost of the last dollar of their wealth and the last drop of their blood. Such, at least, is the judgment of all the enlightened and true friends of freedom and humanity, confirmed by the universal sense of the people, of all the civilized nations of the world.

We must not, we cannot falter, without incurring their contempt, and the curses of our own posterity to the remotest generations.

Your friend,

JAMES McKAYE.

DISUNION:

DEGRADATION WITHOUT REMEDY.

FROM THE "REVUE NATIONALE."

The civil war which for two years past has divided and devastated the United States has produced its evil consequences in Europe also. The scarcity of cotton occasions great suffering. The workmen of Rouen and Mulhouse suffer no less than the spinners and weavers of Lancashire. Whole populations are reduced to beggary, and have no resource, or hope of sustenance during the winter, but private charity or aid from the government. In such a cruel crisis—in the midst of such unmerited sufferings—it is natural that the public opinion of Europe should be unsettled, and that they who prolong the fratricidal war should be charged with culpable ambition. Peace in America, peace at any price, is the urgent need; is the cry f thousands of men among us who are pinched with hunger, the innocent victims of the passions and resentments that embrue in blood the United States.

These complaints are but too well founded. The world today is a compact of mutual interests and obligations. For modern nations, therefore, who live by industry, peace is a necessary condition of existence. But unfortunately, if it is easy to indicate the remedy, to apply it is almost impossible. Until now, it is only by means of war that we could hope to reach the end of the war. To throw ourselves with arms in our hands between the combatants, for the purpose of imposing a truce upon them, would be an enterprise in which Europe would exhaust all her resources, and to what end? As Mr. Cobden has justly said, "It would be far cheaper to feed the laboring classes, who are now starving in consequence of the American crisis, on game and champagne wine."

To offer to-day a peaceful intervention would be to expose ourselves to a refusal, if it did not even exasperate one of the parties and provoke it to measures of violence. It would lessen, too, the chances of our mediation being accepted at a more favorable moment. We are thus forced to remain spectators of a deplorable war, which causes us innumerable evils. We can only pray that exhaustion or suffering may at last appease the maddened combatants, and oblige them to accept reunion or separation. A sad position undoubtedly, but one which neutral powers have at all times been obliged to accept, and from which we cannot escape but at the risk of unknown perils.

But if we have not the right to interfere, we have at least that of complaining, and of seeking to discover who is really guilty of this war, which so disturbs our well-being. The opinion of Europe is something. It may hasten events and bring about peace better than bayonets. Unfortunately, for two years, public opinion in Europe has been led astray and has taken a false direction. In arraying itself on the wrong side, it but prolongs the resistance, instead of arresting it.

The South has found numerous and skilful advocates in France and England. They have presented her cause as that of justice and liberty. They have proclaimed the right of separation, and have not quailed even before the necessity of apologizing for slavery. To-day these arguments begin to loose their force. Thanks to a few writers who do not chaffer with the great interests of humanity—thanks, above all, to M. de Gasparin, light has begun to break forth. We know now what to think of the origin and character of the rebellion. To every impartial observer it is now evident that the wrong lies wholly with the South. It is not necessary to be a Montesquieu to comprehend that a portion of a people, whose rights are in no way endangered, but who are led by pride and ambition to attempt the destruction of national unity and to rend assunder the country, have no claim to the sympathy of the French people. As to canonizing slavery, that is a work we must leave to southern preachers. Not all the ingenuity of the world will ever be able to retrieve that lost cause. Even if the confederates had a thousand reasons for complaining and revolting, there must always remain an ineffaceable stain on their rebellion. No Christian, no liberal thinker, can ever interest himself in men who, in the middle of the nineteenth century, openly and audaciously proclaim their wish to perpetuate and extend slavery. The planters themselves, may indeed listen to theories which have intoxicated and ruined them; but no such sophistries can ever cross the ocean.

The advocates of the South have rendered her a fatal service. They have made her believe that Europe, enlightened or misled, would take sides with her and would finally throw into the scales something more than sterile wishes. This delusion has encouraged and still encourges the resistance of the South. It prolongs the war and our sufferings. If, from the first, as the North had a right to expect, the friends of liberty had boldly declared themselves against the policy of slavery—if the partisans of maritime peace—if the defenders of the rights of neutrals, had spoken in favor of the Union—had discouraged a separation which could only benefit England, it is probable that the South would have entered with less temerity upon a road without an outlet. If, in spite of the courage and devotion of her soldiers, if, after all the skill of her generals, the South fails in an enterprise, which, in my opinion, cannot be too often denounced, let her lay the fault at the door of those who had so poor an esteem for Europe, as to imagine that they could suborn its public opinion to serve a political scheme, against which patriotism protests, and which the gospel and humanity alike condemn.

"Granted," say they, "that the South is wholly in the wrong; but, after all, she is determined to separate. She can no longer live with the North. The war itself, whatever may be its origin, is a new cause of disunion. By what right can twenty millions of men oblige ten millions* of their compatriots to continue a detested alliance, to respect a contract which they are resolved to break at any cost? Is it possible to imagine that two or three years of strife and misery will make the conquered and the conquerors live peaceably together? Can a country, two or three times as large as France, be subju-

* And of these ten millions there are four millions of slaves, whose wishes are not consulted.

gated? Would there not be always ill blood between the parties? Separation is perhaps a misfortune, but to-day the misfortune is irreparable. Let it be admitted that the North has the law, the letter and the spirit of the constitution on her side, there remains always an undebateable point: the South wills to be master at the South. You have not the right to crush a people that fights so bravely. Resign yourselves."

If we were less enervated by the luxuries of modern life and by the idleness of a long peace, if our hearts still retained some remnant of that patriotism which, in 1792, sent our forefathers to the shores of the Rhine, the answer would be an easy one. To-day I fear we can no longer comprehend it. If to-morrow the south of France should revolt and demand separation, if Alsace and Lorraine wished to isolate themselves, what would be, I do not say our right, but our duty? Would we stop to count votes, to know if a third or a half of the French people had a right to destroy the national unity, to annihilate France, to rend in fragments the glorious heritage bought with the blood of our fathers? No, we would take up our muskets and march. Woe to him who does not feel that his country is sacred, and that it is glorious to defend it, even at the cost of all possible sufferings and dangers.

"America is not France; it is a confederation, it is not a nation." Who says that? The South, to justify her crime. The North says the contrary, and for two years, at the price of sacrifices without number, affirms that the people of the United States are one people, and that their country shall not be cut in two. This is noble. This is grand, and what astonishes me is, that France can remain unmoved in view of such patriotism. Love of country—is not that the distinguishing virtue of the French people?

What, then, is the South, and whence does she derive this right of separation, so loudly proclaimed? Is it a conquered people that seeks to recover its independence, like Lombardy? Is it a distinct race that wishes no longer to continue an oppressive alliance? No, they are communities of planters established by American hands, on the territories of the Union, who revolt without any other reason than their own ambition. Let us take a map of the United States. If we except Virginia, the two Carolinas, and Georgia, which were originally English colonies, all the rest of the South is settled upon lands bought and paid for by the Union. That is to say, the North has borne the greatest part of the expense. Louisiana was sold to the United States in 1804, by the first consul, for fifteen millions of dollars. Florida was purchased of Spain in 1820, for about five millions. The Mexican war, with its cost of a billion of money and its cruel losses, was necessary to secure Texas. In short, of all the rich territories that border the Mississippi and the Missouri from their source to their mouth, there is not one inch but has been paid for by the Union, and therefore belongs to it. It is the Union that has driven out or indemnified the Indians. It is the Union that has built all the forts, the docks, the lighthouses, and harbors. It is the Union that made all these desert places of value, and rendered colonization possible. Northern as well as Southern men cleared and planted these lands, and transformed into flourishing States these sterile solitudes. Can old Europe, where unity is everywhere the result of conquest, show us a title to property so sacred as this? A country more entirely the common work of a whole people? And now, shall a minority be permitted to appropriate a territory which belongs to all, and to choose for themselves the best part of it? Can a minority be permitted to destroy the Union and to imperil its first benefactors, without whom, indeed, it could not exist? To say that this revolt is not impious, is to say that caprice constitutes right.

It is not, however, a political reason only, which opposes the separation. Its geography, the situation of the different portions, obliges the United States to form one nation. Strabo, contemplating the vast country we now call France, said, with the foresight of genius, that beholding the nature of the territory and the courses of the streams, it was evident that the forests of Gaul, then thinly inhabited, would become the home of a great people. Nature had prepared our territory to become the theatre of a great civilization. This is no less true of America. She is, in truth, only a double valley with an imperceptible head-level and two great water courses, the Mississippi and the St. Lawrence. No high mountains which separate and isolate peoples; no natural barriers like the Alps and Pyrenees.

The West cannot live without the Mississippi—to possess the mouth of the river is for the farmers of the West a question of life and death.

The United States have felt this from the first. When the Ohio and Mississippi were still only streams lost in the great forests of the Southwest—when the first planters were but a handful of men scattered over the wilderness, the Americans knew already that New Orleans was the key of the whole country. They would not leave it in possession of Spain or France. Napoleon understood this. He held in his hands the future greatness of the United States. It did not displease him to cede to America this vast territory, with the intention, he said, of giving to England a maritime rival which sooner or later would humble the pride of our enemy. He might have dispossessed himself merely of the left bank of the river, and thus have satisfied the United States, who at that time asked no more; but he did more (and here I think he was very wrong), he renounced, with a stroke of the pen, a country as vast as half of Europe, and gave up our last right to the beautiful river, we had ourselves discovered. Very soon sixty years will have elapsed since this cession. The states now called Louisiana, Arkansas, Missouri, Iowa, Minnesota, Kansas, Oregon, the territories of Nebraska, Dacotah, Jefferson, and Washington, which will soon become states, have been established on the immense domain abandoned by Napoleon. Without counting the slaveholding population, which seeks to destroy the Union, there are ten millions of freemen between Pittsburg and Fort Union, who claim the course and mouth of the Mississippi as having been ceded to them by France. It is from us that they hold their title and their possession. They have the right of sixty years' occupancy—a right consecrated by labor and cultivation—a right derived from a solemn contract, and better still, from nature and from God. And for defending this right, we reproach them. They are usurpers and tyrants, because they will not put themselves at the mercy of an ambitious minority. What should we say if to morrow, Normandy, in rebellion, should claim as her own Rouen and Havre? And yet, what is the course of the Seine compared to that of the Mississippi, which extends two thousand two hundred and fifty miles, and receives as tributaries all the waters of the West? To possess New Orleans is to command a valley which comprises two-thirds of the United States. "We will neutralize the river," they say. We all know what such promises are worth. We have seen what Russia did with the mouth of the Danube. The Crimean war was necessary that Germany might regain the free use of her great river. If to-morrow a new war should break out between Austria and Russia, we may be sure that the possession of the Danube would be the stake of the contest.

It cannot be otherwise in America from the day when the Mississippi, for hundreds of leagues, shall flow between two slave-holding shores. Already the effect of the war has been to stop the exportation of wheat and corn, the riches of the West.

In 1861 it became necessary to burn the useless crops, to the great injury of Europe, who is the gainer by these exports. The South understands so thoroughly the strength of her position, that her ambition is to separate the valley of the Mississippi from the Eastern States, to unite herself with the West, and to condemn thus the Yankees of New England to a ruinous isolation. The Confederates use the Mississippi as a bait by which they hope to reconstruct, profitably to themselves—that is to say, in the INTERESTS OF SLAVERY—the Union which they have broken up through FEAR OF LIBERTY.

We see, then, what to think of the pretended tyranny of the North; what truth there is in the assertion that she wishes to oppress and subjugate the South. On the contrary, the North only defends herself. In maintaining the Union, it is her RIGHT, it is her EXISTENCE that she would save.

Thus far I have spoken in the name of the material interests only—legitimate interests, and which, founded on solemn titles, constitutes a sacred right; but if we examine the moral and political interests—interests of a superior order—we shall see still more clearly that the North cannot yield without self-destruction.

The United States are a Republic, the freest and at the same time the mildest and happiest government that the world has ever seen. In what consists this prosperity of the Americans? They are alone upon an immense territory; they have never been obliged to concentrate power and weaken liberty, for the purpose of resisting the ambition and jealousy of their neighbors. In the United States there was no standing army, no great war navy. The immense sums spent by us to avoid or maintain war were used by the Americans to establish schools—in giving to every citizen, rich or poor, that education, that instruction which constitutes the moral grandeur and the true riches of a people. Their foreign policy was contained in a single maxim. Never to intermeddle in the political quarrels of Europe on the sole condition that Europe would never interfere in their affairs, and would respect the liberty of the seas.

Thanks to those wise principles, bequeathed to them by Washington, in his immortal Farewell Address, the United States have enjoyed for eighty years a peace undisturbed but once, in 1812, when they were obliged to withstand England and maintain the rights of neutrals. For the last seventy years, we have spent billions to maintain our liberty or our preponderance in Europe. The United States have employed these billions in ameliorations of all kinds. That is the secret of their prodigious success; their isolation has made their prosperity.

Suppose, now, that this separation should be accomplished, and that the new confederacy should comprise all the slave-states; the North loses at once her POWER and her INSTITUTIONS. The Republic is stabbed to the heart. There would be in America two rival nations, always on the eve of conflict. Peace would by no means extinguish enmities. It would not obliterate the memories of past greatness, nor of the UNION DESTROYED.

The South victorious would be doubtless no less a friend of slavery, no less in love with dominion, than in former times. The enemies of slavery, now masters of their own policy, would not surely be made more moderate by separation. What would the Southern Confederacy be to the North? A foreign power established in America, with a frontier of fifteen hundred miles —a frontier open on all sides, and consequently, always threatening or threatened. This power, hostile by reason of its vicinity, and still more so on account of its institutions, would possess some of the most important portions of the New World. She would own half of the sea-coasts of the Union—she would command the Gulf of Mexico, an inland sea one third the size of the Mediterranean. She would be mistress of the mouth of the Mississippi, and could at her will ruin the people of the West. The remnant of the old Union must, then, always maintain an attitude of defense towards their rivals. Custom-house and frontier difficulties, rivalries, jealousies—all the scourges of old Europe, would at once overwhelm America. It would be necsssary to establish custom-houses over an extent of five hundred leagues—to construct and arm forts along this immense frontier, support a large standing army and navy. In other words—they must renounce the old constitution—weaken municipal independence and concentrate power. Adieu then to the old and glorious liberty! Adieu to those institutions which made America the common country of all those who lacked a breathing place in Europe. The work of Washington would be utterly destroyed, and the new condition of things would be full of difficulty and of peril. I understand how such a future might rejoice the people who can never pardon America her prosperity and her grandeur. History is full of these deplorable jealouses. But I understand, even still better how a people accustomed to liberty should risk their last man and their last dollar to keep the inheritance of their fathers, and I respect it. What I do not comprehend is, that there should be found in Europe, people, calling themselves liberal, who reproach the North for her courageons resistance, and counsel a shameful abdication. The war is a terrible evil; but from the war a durable peace may spring. The South may be worn out by an exhausting struggle. The old Union may be again restored—the future may be saved. But what can be the issue of separation, if not WAR WITHOUT END and miseries without number? The dismemberment of the Union—the rendering asunder of the country, would be a DEGRADATION WITHOUT REMEDY. A fate so shameful is to be accepted, only, when one is utterly crushed out and trodden under foot.

So far I have argued on the hypothesis that the South would remain an independent power. But unless the West should join the Confederates, re-establishing a Union which should exclude New England, this independence is a chimera. It might last a few years, but in ten or twenty years, when the West shall have doubled or tripled its free population, what will the Confederacy-be—weakened, per force, by servile cultivation—compared to a people of thirty millions of men shutting her in on two sides? In self-defence the South would be forced to lean on Europe. Her existence would depend on her being protected by a maritime power. England alone is in a condition to guaranty her sovereignty. This would be a new danger for free America and for Europe. There is no navy in the South, and with slavery there never will be any. England at once would seize the monopoly of cotton, and would furnish the South with capital and ships. In two words, the triumph of the South is the re-establishment of England on the continent, whence she was driven by the policy of Louis Sixteenth and Napoleon. It weakens neutrals, it entangles France again, in all those vexed questions of liberty of the seas, which have cost us already two centuries of struggle and suffering. The American Union, while defending its own rights, had assured the freedom of the seas. The Union destroyed, English supremacy would revive again. It is peace banished from the world; it is a return to a policy which has so far only favored our rivals.

This is what Napoleon felt to be true—this is what we forget to-day. It would seem as if history were merely a collection of pleasant stories to amuse children. No one is willing to understand the lessons of the past. If the experience of our fathers was not lost upon our ignorance, we should see that in defending her own independence, and in maintaining the national unity, the North defends our cause as well as her own. All our prayers would be for the triumph of our old and faithful friends. To weaken the United States will be to weaken ourselves. At the first quarrel with England we shall regret, but too late, that we abandoned a policy which for forty years has been the guaranty of our own safety.

In writing these pages, I do not expect to convert those who have in their hearts an innate sympathy for slavery. I write for those honest souls, who allow themselves to be enticed by the great words of national independence, paraded before their eyes purposely to deceive and delude them. The South has never been threatened. To-day she might come back into the Union, even with her slaves. It is only demanded of her not to destroy the national unity, and not to subvert liberty. We cannot repeat it too often: the North is not the aggressor. It only defends, as every true citizen should, the national compact, the integrity of the country. It is sad that it has found so little support in Europe, and especially in France. They relied on us—in us they placed their trust—and we have abandoned them as if the sacred words of COUNTRY and of LIBERTY no longer awoke a response in our hearts. What has become of the days when the whole of France applauded the young Lafayette, as he buckled on his sword in the cause of America? Who has imitated him, who has recalled that glorious memory? Have we grown so old as to have forgotten all that?

What will be the issue of the war? It is impossible to foresee. The South may succeed. The North may be divided and exhausted by intestine strife. The Union is, perhaps, even now, but a great memory. But whatever may be the future, or whatever fortune may attend it, the duty of every man who does not allow himself to be carried away by the success of the present hour, is to sustain and encourage the North to the last—to condemn those whose ambition threatens to destroy the most perfect and the most patriotic work of humanity—to remain faithful to the end of the war, and, even after defeat, to those, who will have fought to the last moment for RIGHT and LIBERTY.

EDOUARD LABOULAYE.

The Condition and Prospects of the South:

A

DISCOURSE

DELIVERED IN SOMERVILLE, MASS.,

JUNE 4, 1865.

BY REV CHARLES LOWE.

BOSTON:
WALKER, FULLER, AND COMPANY,
245, WASHINGTON STREET.
1865.

DISCOURSE

— ON THE —

CONDITION AND PROSPECTS OF THE SOUTH.

By Rev. Charles Lowe, Somerville, June 4, 1865.

Isaiah 62: 10.—"Go through, go through the gates: prepare ye the way of the people; cast up, cast up the highway; gather out the stones. Lift up a standard for the people."

Since I have been permitted, through your indulgence, to see much that is interesting in connection with great events now being enacted for our people, it is, perhaps, fitting that I should make to you some report of so much as really pertains to important questions of our national life.

The period which has elapsed since I parted from you has been most eventful. It has included the close of this gigantic rebellion as an organized warfare. Most signally did this great fact appear in the region where my visit was made. Last year, when I left you for a season, I saw Charleston from the distance; looking on it from the ramparts of a fort, from which shells were being hurled into its homes, while its stubborn defences made its final capture seem a weary task. Now I could enter its precincts to see our victorious army occupying what were left of its princely dwellings, and dictating to the once haughty citizens. At Fort Sumter, which then reared its battered but still formidable mass, a perfect barrier to our approach, I this time saw Anderson raise the flag which four years ago he had carried away; and the booming of a hundred guns from ships and forts, music of bands and cheers of a loyal multitude, as they greeted the symbol of national authority, told of the victory and progress that had crowned our arms. But even on that day all had not been done, for still some armies were left in the field. Hundreds of workmen were still busy with military and naval preparations at the great depot at Hilton Head, and a week after the Sumter celebration I saw, at Georgetown, the return of a large expedition into the interior of South Carolina, with all the accompaniments of plunder and excitement that show the terrible mercilessness of war.

But before my return the close had really come. At Hilton Head came an order suspending military works; and the day I left I sat on the silent beach, where only a few days before the sounds of axe and hammer had been so incessant, and saw the vessel sail away that bore the late president of the Confederacy, an inglorious captive, taking his last look at his vaunted realm.

The war is over. That part of our duties which pertained to it is accomplished; and it is history now. But this only enables us to realize the better what yet remains—the work of reconstruction—which is only just begun; and which now presents itself to our nation, as mighty a task and as perplexing a problem as that which has thus been ended. There is for us now the work signified by the Prophet. "Go through, go through the gates. Prepare ye the way of the people; cast up, cast up the highway; gather out the stones."

It is because I feel very deeply the magnitude of this work before us, and the need there is that every citizen shall understand whatever may help to illustrate it, that I think it not inappropriate to use this hour to-day for giving such items of information and suggestion in regard to it as my visit has enabled me to offer.

I. And the first point is, as to how far we may count on the reality of peace. To answer this I will state as fairly as I can what my observation has led me to believe in regard to the present attitude and feeling of the Southern people.

Let me speak first of those in civil life. There are in the South a few who have, from the beginning till now, been really loyal to the Union, and by no class of patriots has there been shown more noble devotion or more heroic will. It was harder to remain true to the country there, where not only danger threatened such fidelity, but where malign misrepresentations and continual suppressing of the truth made this fidelity rest on a firm faith in principles alone, than it was to go, under the encouragements which have always attended our cause at the North, to the perils and privations of the battle-field. These persons are now, of course, among the nation's truest friends. But these loyal men were fewer than any of us believed.

There is another class of men, some of whom in the beginning were opposed to the act of secession, but who finally were carried along with the current, who understand that the thing is over, that government is entirely triumphant, and whose only wish now is to have order reëstablished as soon as it may. They take the oath of allegiance with a sincere purpose faithfully to observe it. When you talk with them they will not deny their sympathy with the rebel cause, but you feel that they are thoroughly persuaded of their mistake, and that their present attitude is creditable and safe. I think it is all that we have a right to demand. I regret to say, however, that from my observation this class also is much smaller than is generally believed.

The large majority of persons in civil life are still as unfit to be trusted for any fidelity to the government, except so far as it is enforced, as they were during the prosperous days of the rebellion. Even among those who, for the sake of the protection to their property, have taken the oath of allegiance, there are very many who are as hostile as before. The same idea of honor which justified them to their own consciences when they put into the field their soldiers who had returned on parole, and when, in so many ways, they violated pledged faith, makes them hold this oath no further binding than they are held to it by motives of interest or fear.

Those who have been connected with the army may also be divided into different classes. Some of them have served against their will; others did so only because they felt that honor required that they should be faithful to their State, and they now, tired and sickened by the horrors of war, heartily rejoice that they can honorably return to their relations to the old flag. Others, again, who have been earnest approvers of the rebellion, are willing to own that now, since it has failed, they have no course left but to submit, and are ready to be good citizens again.

But these classes embrace a much smaller proportion of the army than is generally believed. Among the officers, much the larger portion, though they are courteous to their captors and obey the etiquette of war, do not disguise the fact of their undiminished hatred of the Union. There are many things which now tend to make it greater than ever. They go to their homes to find everything changed—and changed in a way to aggravate them, at every point. Their fortunes are destroyed; their neighborhoods broken up. And, what is most galling of all, their proud social position is entirely gone. Enterprising men from the North, out of the industrious class which they so much despised, will come in to take places of increasing influence by their side, and (they see plainly enough) will soon outstrip them in all that material prosperity and intellectual activity which gives a controlling power. And, to crown all, the negro not only is lost as property, but is already claiming, with the likelihood of receiving, equal civil and political rights with themselves. What shall they do? It is not surprising that, with their habits and views, they find it hard to acquiesce, and the number who will patiently return in a frame of mind suited to begin the work of cementing our harmonious relations again is very small. Some declare that, as soon as they recover the wreck of their fortunes, they shall go abroad. Some, believing that the profession of arms affords now their only avenue to success, intend to offer their services to some foreign power, not disguising the hope that they may sometime be again in hostility to the United States. Many are about to go to Mexico, to ally themselves with this intent on the side of Maximilian. Some of them, in that spirit which they call chivalry, out of which duelling and the like practices spring, take comfort in believing that opportunities are yet to be offered for taking vengeance for fancied wrongs in a private way, and say that in travelling abroad, or other ways of exposure, certain obnoxious ones will yet learn the power of the Southern wrath. From all that I could learn of the practices of the Southern army, the war has made this spirit of chivalry more dangerous to civil quiet than it was before.

Among the common soldiers there are probably many who long to become peaceful citizens again, and if circumstances permit, they will begin industrial pursuits, with no desire again to disturb the peace. The only fear as respects these is, (the same as in the case of our own soldiers) that the interrupted habits of industry, and especially the loss of self-reliant enterprise consequent upon the strict habit of obedience required of the soldier, may stand in the way of their thrift, and consequently of their contentment. But there is besides a large mass of ignorant and unprincipled men, whose only political principles are hatred of the Northern "Black Republicans," and support of the sovereignty of States—and their only religious belief, the Divine appointment of slavery. The experience of the last four years has taught them habits of endurance and love of rough excitement. Half a pound of bacon and a quart of meal a day satisfies all their wants; give them that, and a rifle and ammunition, and the chances to maraud, and their highest aspiration is secured. They hope for nothing better than a "border ruffian" kind of life, with power to disturb and annoy at will.

I have thus reviewed the elements, as they now exist, of white Southern society; that is to say, of the only classes who by State laws would have any political voice if the States should have accorded to them now the right to legislate for themselves. By the constitution of South Carolina the qualification for voter is that one be a free, white citizen, two years resident in the State and six months in the district where the vote is cast. I do not pretend to any political knowledge, but I do claim to have had a good opportunity for observing Southern people as they are to-day in South Carolina and Georgia, as I have seen them, in their homes and in their public meetings, and I have no hesitation in saying that, in my judgment, to give them now their wonted political rights would be, if not to imperil again all for which we have fought, at least to retard unnecessarily the establishment of peace and order.

The people of South Carolina and Georgia are beginning now to hold meetings and make loyal professions, in hope that by promptly declaring their desire to be in the Union again they may receive greater leniency and ampler restoration of privileges from the Federal government. I think no one can be really acquainted with the character of these meetings, and of the persons who attend them, and not feel deeply solicitous lest government shall be too much influenced by the representations they make.

I believe the only safe course is to continue to hold military control of the conquered States until the condition of things shall have changed. This will change in two ways. First, by the inpouring of an entirely new element of population. Secondly, by the change in the sentiment of the Southern people themselves. And a year or two hence the people will be prepared to adopt measures that would be impossible now, and will then be hampered by the results of premature action if State organization should be at once allowed.

I spoke of the change likely to occur in the feelings of the South. Some speak as though there was little hope of such a change. I have conversed with prominent Southern men and women who say that it is impossible; that they and their children after them will always hold the feelings of hatred to the Union and its defenders which they now entertain. They say that tenacity of sentiment is one of the characteristics of the Southern race, and that they are not to be moved from convictions once entertained. They urge as proof their constant adherence to certain Southern doctrines. I do not, however, believe in such a representation, but think that on the contrary they are very easily influenced, and the reason why they held so tenaciously to those Southern doctrines was, that the influence was all one way. I have instances in mind of change of feeling through intercourse with Northern men, during the short interval that has now elapsed, which illustrate this, and prove to me that the vehement protestations, on the part of Southern men, in regard to the "impossibility of ever submitting to negro citizenship and social democracy and friendship with the North," no more prove that they may not do so very soon, than their equally positive vauntings about "dying in the last ditch" proved that there must be an entire obliteration of fighting men before their confederacy would yield.

The fact is, they are as easily influenced and versatile as they are intense in the feeling they chance to hold, and I see no reason why, if a proper method of dealing with them is pursued, we may not expect within a reasonable period, a pleasant harmony between the people of the two divided sections of our land.

I say if a proper method is pursued—and this method I believe to be, while affording them protection and kindness, and unrestricted business and industrial opportunities,—*to keep a firm hold upon them that shall restrain them from every act of disobedience and continually compel their respect.*

A little consideration of the principles of human nature, I think, makes the good sense of such counsel to appear. We know that, if a man under excitement is allowed to speak his mind and act his will, the very giving vent to his feelings increases them, while it occasions antagonism on the part of their object such as might lead to violence and harm. I could see at the South many points of irritation where, if the Southern people were allowed to act unrestrained, they might be led to say and do what would lead to equally excited act and word on the other side, and finally to serious difficulty, when I was sure that, if the feeling could be repressed till familiarity with the new state of things enabled the irritation to subside, a gradual acquiescence would be ensured. In fact, it is a simple application of accepted principles of surgery. The treatment of a ragged wound is, while trusting chiefly to nature's recuperative power, yet first to bring the parts together and bind them by a firm bandage in their place till there has been time for the flesh to heal and the ligaments to unite. Precisely the same principle holds for the cementing of these torn ties of sentiment and brotherly feeling. The natural working of social intercourse will be the proper cure; but the parts need bandaging for awhile. *And the simplest compress is a strong military force.*

II. As to the material interests of the South. I reviewed with one of the leading merchants of Savannah the present condition of Georgia, and found, taking as a basis the census of 1860, the following results :

The estimated wealth of the State, according to that census, was :—

	Amount of property saved.	Aggregate of property lost.
443,364 slaves..............		$271,620,405
Merchandise...............		13,531,687
Money and solvent debts....	10,000,000	86,124,701
Capital in manufactures....	1,000,000	3,428,132
Shipping and tonnage......	631,732	
Household furniture.......	2,125,045	
Land, average per acre, $4.43..................	149,547,880	
Bank capital.............		12,479,111
Railroads.................	9,000,000	9,000,000
	$172,304,657	$396,184,036

This state of things necessitates a very radical change in the social and political condition of the State. The property left (supposing that the former owners are permitted to retain it,) is chiefly land, mostly held in large estates. It was the habit of these landholders to invest what remained of their income after paying the expenses of the year, by buying more land and more slaves. Now it will be absolutely necessary for these proprietors, in order to procure means of living and of carrying on the land, to sell portions of their land. It will be purchased chiefly by immigrants from the North, and from Europe, enterprising, industrious men. And this not only secures a new element of population, but changes a system of landed aristocracy into one more nearly approaching that of our New England society. It needs not to be argued what an important feature of hopefulness is here. So important does it seem to me, that I hold it now one of the most useful things towards regenerating the South and aiding in its reconstruction, to encourage the emigration there of the right sort of men, filled with New England habits and ideas. It is no matter what their profession or their taste may be. There is an opening for all. There is need of farmers to carry on that splendid land,—which Southern planters say it is hopeless to try to till except with slaves, but which there is reason to believe will be greatly increased in productiveness under free labor and an application of improved methods of agriculture. There is need of capitalists to build saw-mills and railroads, and give a general start to the activity of business; and the condition of affairs is tempting enough to lure them. There is need of mechanics. It is surprising how entirely they were always dependent for mechanical skill on the North. I saw many pieces of work begun before the war, and in hands of Northern contractors, which were suspended when hostilities compelled the contractors to leave, and have never been touched since. There is need of educated and professional men. The leading men in most professions have either died, or left the country, or suffered forfeiture of political rights, and it seems inevitable that all professional and public service must devolve upon new men who shall move in from abroad. It can easily be seen how vastly important it is that a right class of men shall go into all these branches of service. And I think now that one of the best branches of missionary work will be to induce to locate there, as capitalists, as farmers, as mechanics, as lawyers and statesmen, men of high principle, and enlightened minds, and industrious habits, and correct ideas of the best interests of a State. They will then call for what we commonly term missionaries, viz., teachers and ministers, and will support them themselves. I do not mean by this to discourage sending them other missionaries meantime. For until society becomes sufficiently established to feel the need, there is work for moral and religious teachers in the reconstruction to be achieved, and more can be done these next two years than in ten of ordinary life.

III. I have not yet spoken of one subject, which is vastly important, both in itself and for its bearing upon the prospects of the South. I mean the condition and character of the blacks and the probable effects of emancipation as regards the question of labor and society and the welfare of both races.

It is *the question* of the day, and I made it my especial care to examine into it by careful inquiry in every point of view. In the limits of this discourse I cannot give the facts upon which my conclusions are based, but a few of these conclusions I will attempt to state.

And first a few words in general as to the present condition of the colored people. There are certain localities where the negroes are still living with their masters, substantially the same as before. But wherever our armies have gone the old relations are broken up, and great numbers have left their homes and followed the armies to the cities on the coast. Nothing could exceed the destitution of these people after the weariness and exposure attendant upon such a march. Thousands of them came in to Savannah with Sherman's army, many of them in the most pitiable condition. And in the various expeditions since made from Charleston or Savannah, or other places on the coast, the same has been repeated, and up to the present time some 95,000 in all, under such circumstances as I have described, have been received and provided for by the Superintendent of Freedmen's affairs. I saw over 3,000 arrive one day at Georgetown, with a military expedition from the interior of South Carolina—a medley multitude, with no homes or means of livelihood, no education or habits of independence. Of course there is a necessity that at first they shall be fed and clothed by government. Then they are conveyed to the various islands on the coast which Sherman caused to be appropriated to the purpose, and portions of land are given to them by families, and they are encouraged to go to work. Of course they must still be fed until they have an opportunity to raise something for themselves, and this fact of learning, as their first lesson in freedom, to receive gratuitous support, together with the novel excitement of their position, naturally create no very favorable conditions for stimulus to persistent and energetic industry. In addition to these island colonists very large numbers have congregated in the cities. In Charleston there are now 30,000, who, with comparatively little opportunity to labor, are exposed to all the excitements incident to such a state of things.

To make it worse, many well-disposed but ill-judging friends of the colored people are busy among them, inflaming them by exciting appeals, and giving them exalted ideas of their own position which tend to anything rather than encourage a patient assumption of the duties before them. I mention all these unfavorable circumstances because they add to the value of whatever I may be enabled to testify as to the encouraging symptoms in regard to the behavior and prospects of the race.

You know the apprehensions of massacre and insubordination in connection with the sudden emancipation of the blacks. Certainly, there has been ample opportunity for it, and enough to excite it; but through all this period of confusion there has been nothing of the sort. Many a white family has been living far from any protectors, in the midst of their former slaves. These, perhaps, since they have known of their liberty, may have refused to work, and may have shown the excitement natural to such a condition; but the instances where crime or violence have ensued are very rare, and the few that have occurred can generally be traced to such provocations as make them almost excusable. I did not hear of an instance of intoxication among the blacks during the whole of my stay; and hardly did I hear an angry or excited word. Col. Woodford, who commanded Charleston the first month after the evacuation, told me an incident that illustrates the good behavior of the blacks. The first few weeks of our occupation were attended with much excitement, and the negroes could do little else than manifest their joy. They had frequent meetings, at which many enthusiastic speakers, from the North, made congratulatory harangues. And soon it was proposed to have a grand procession to celebrate the glad event. While arrangements for this were in progress a committee of the former citizens of Charleston waited upon Col. Woodford and made earnest protestations against his allowing this procession. They said they knew, as no one could know who had not lived among them, the nature of these people, and that such a procession would greatly endanger the security of the city. They said their own people, irritated by the sight, might be led to do some indiscreet things which might lead to disturbance, and no one could tell where it would end. They entreated him at any rate to put a formidable guard along the whole route it was proposed to take. Col. Woodford replied somewhat curtly to their representations. He said the procession should take place, and instead of making the additional precautions they proposed, he should remove the usual guards from all the streets through which it was to pass, and he warned them that if the white citizens should attempt any of their "indiscreet things" it would be worse for the city. The procession was held, and numbered thousands of people. They carried garlands and banners, and sang "John Brown," and "Star Spangled Banner," and "Union Forever," and made the streets echo with their cheers; but there was no more disturbance of peace than there was this last week in the funeral procession in Boston. I attended a holiday festival in Charleston, at which 10,000 blacks were assembled with not a single policeman on the ground, and did not hear of a single accident or breach of order.

On the islands their capacity for good demeanor under freedom has been yet more effectually put to the test. According to the policy inaugurated by Gen. Sherman, a certain portion of land, such as they may select, is assigned to the colonists, and they proceed to plant and to prepare a home. It is inevitable that, in the confusion of locating scores in a day, mistakes may be made in boundaries of land, and a thousand occasions of dispute may arise out of such hasty arrangements. Yet during the whole process no serious difficulty has occurred. And out of the whole number thus far provided for, 30,000 are already self-sustaining.

In Georgia the policy has been tried of local governments on the various islands, managed entirely by the blacks, and with gratifying results. The people of the island choose their governor and their other officers from among themselves, and frame their own municipal regulations. I made minute inquiries into their condition, and, so far as I could learn, it is very creditable.

There are two other points in regard to the blacks which bear upon the question of the prospects of the South, and the true policy to be pursued. What I have said has been intended as a testimony to their amenability to discipline, and I think it may be considered as established that there is no danger to be apprehended from any disturbance of peace by the blacks, unless some oppressive course is adopted to provoke it, or unless they are exasperated by irritating treatment on the part of the whites.

It is important to consider, besides, 1. Whether they will work: and 2. Whether they will have any desire or capacity to rise in the moral and intellectual scale.

1. Ask any planter and he will tell you that it is proved by all experience that the negro will not work except on compulsion; and you cannot yet make him believe otherwise. Ask many casual observers who may have been annoyed

by some experience of the negro's shiftlessness and laziness, and they will say it probably is true. But a careful investigation has brought me to the conclusion, in support of which I think I have abundant proof, but no time now to offer it, that the indisposition to labor, and the tendency to shirk, is nothing more than the inevitable result of the long habits of working with no other motive than fear of the lash. It has already been tested and proved (I could mention, if I had time, many very interesting proofs) that with judicious management they can be employed under a voluntary system with as much certainty of service as any other class of people. And there are individual instances of enterprise and thrift (and those not a few) which ought to put this point at rest.

2. As to the aspiration among them for higher things little need be said; though it would be pleasant to say much. For this aspiration is so universal and so apparent that it has been noticed and testified to by all, as has also their intelligence and quickness to learn. Not only do they welcome the teachers sent from the North, and try in all ways to avail themselves of their instruction, but almost their first care, when they are settled for themselves, is to provide for the education of their children. In Savannah the colored people have supported free schools at their own cost, by voluntary subscription, ever since the capture of the city, at an expense of three hundred dollars a month, while there has not been one public school supported by the whites. I met the leading colored people of Savannah in many ways—in their committee meetings, in their churches, in their political gatherings and in their homes—and I found among no class of men a higher tone, a more intelligent appreciation of what was most desirable in life, a purer purpose to do what is right, or a more determined resolution to improve all the opportunities that God has given them.

The question is being agitated in the nation now, Shall the negroes be allowed to vote? To one who has mingled with them, as I have done, the serious discussions upon the propriety of it, were it not so serious a matter, would provoke a smile. I hope that for, at least, one year to come *there will be no voting allowed in the rebellious States;* but when it is permitted, to say that those shall vote who have been laboring to overthrow our government, and who now hate it as much as ever, and are determined to injure it as much as they dare, and that those shall be denied who have been praying for it, and weeping for it, and fighting for it, and now love it with true, loyal hearts, is too unreasonable to be seriously discussed. To be sure, there is a large mass of negroes who are very degraded, and unfit to exercise the privilege of franchise, and I should assuredly hope for a qualification requiring the ability to read and write. But this ignorant mass are no more unfit for voters than that large class of poor white citizens who are not only ignorant and degraded, but vicious, lawless, vagabond and violent, The qualification ought to be, of course, applied to them as well as to the negroes; and there is little doubt as to which will rise above it first. In short, the qualification, whatever it be, must be entirely irrespective of color in order to satisfy whether the demands of justice, or the interests of the State.

I have given thus in a general way, and so as to require, if there were time to go into detail, various qualifications, some of the principal features of the present condition of the South. They are mingled features of prostration and promise. The promise, however, is almost wholly because of the prostration, and the greatest hope for the future is from the completeness with which the old has been overthrown. Little remains (or will remain if a proper degree of rigid justice is exercised in the reädjustment of society) of what has been to the South such a bane in church and in State, in public and in the home, poisoning every member and function of social life, so that it has written everywhere a mark that reads like a curse of God.

But all that is essential to prosperity remains. A fair proportion of most productive soil; a climate generally attractive; ample resources of many kinds; and there remain, also, elements of fascination and worth in the character of Southern people. There is a hope that these advantages may attract those who will carry those principles of morals and religion, those ideas of government and liberty, those institutions of education and of charity, that shall rear out of the ashes of what has been in our nation the constant source of discord and reproach, that which shall henceforth be its best ornament and defence. Whether this shall be so depends largely upon wise legislation and right efforts during this period of regeneration. And in connection with it are many duties, as the care of educating freedmen, and the like, in which every one of us will be called to take a part. And I shall be sorry if this imperfect sketch has failed to leave this suggestion, that if the termination of the war has relieved us from certain civic duties, it opens before us new and brighter ones in which God calls on us to act.

SPEECHES

OF

HON. R. McCLELLAND,

Hon. LEVI BISHOP, Hon. GEORGE V. N. LOTHROP,

AND

RESOLUTIONS

OF THE

MEETING CALLED AT THE CITY HALL, DETROIT, MAY, 1863,

TO EXPRESS SENTIMENTS OF CITIZENS OF DETROIT RELATIVE TO THE

ARREST OF HON. CLEMENT L. VALLANDIGHAM, OF OHIO.

DETROIT:
PUBLISHED BY AUTHORITY OF THE DETROIT DEMOCRATIC ASSOCIATION.
1863.

SHALL WE REMAIN FREE?

All democrats and citizens who are in favor of maintaining the freedom of speech and of the press, and opposed to the violation of that freedom, as exhibited in the late arbitrary arrests by military authority, are requested to meet at the City Hall, in Detroit, on Monday evening, May 25th, at 8 P. M., to give expression to their sentiments on that subject.

Signed by between 500 and 600 citizens.

THE MEETING.

In accordance with the call, so unanimously signed, an immense crowd of people assembled at the City Hall. At an early hour the building was densely packed, every available space being occupied.

At 8 o'clock the meeting was called to order by S. Dow Elwood, who nominated as

President—Hon. Robert McClelland.

The following gentlemen were chosen as further officers of the meeting:

VICE PRESIDENTS.

Dr. Z. Pither, Albert Ives, Esq.,
Hon. A. D. Frazer, Dr. Morse Stewart,
Hon. S. T. Douglass, James Beatty, Esq.,
Hon. B. F. H. Witherell, Geo. W. Rose, Esq.,
Hon. L. M. Mason, Edward Orr, Esq.,
Hon. W. C. Duncan, Wm. Purcell, Esq.,
Hon. A. H. Redfield, Jas. McGonegal, Esq.,
S. P. Bracy, Esq., Dr. Peter Klein,
Theo. H. Eaton, Esq., J. V. Ruehle, Esq.

SECRETARIES.

Allen A. Rabineau. Jacob Barns.

SPEECH OF GOV. McCLELLAND.

After the election of these officers, Hon. R. McClelland arose and said:

In considering and discussing the object of this meeting, I hope, and doubt not, the proceedings will be conducted with calmness and forbearance, and be governed by that wisdom and moderation which should characterize the action of so intelligent an audience. The gravity of the occasion should be remembered, and nothing should be said or done which by the most mischievous, could be distorted into a departure from our grand purpose of restoring the Union and preserving the constitution.

We had reason to believe, until very recently, that arbitrary and military arrests had been abandoned. Every one breathed easier, and seemed ready to admit that no good, but much evil, had resulted from them to the Union, cause. And I doubt not there were few who were not startled at the news that Mr. Vallandigham had been made a victim of military power. I differ widely from him in the course he has pursued, and the principles he has enunciated, but cannot help admiring the bold, fearless and able manner in which he has advocated his views, and vindicated himself. We have now nothing to do with the man or his character, but his arrest and trial before a military tribunal involve great principles which underlie the most sacred rights of American citizens, and are the life blood of the Republic. To those principles should our attention be especially directed.

The constitution guarantees "freedom of speech; the right of the people peaceably to assemble, and to petition the government for a redress of grievances; the right of the people to be secure in their persons, houses, papers and effects, against unreasonable searches and seizures; that no person shall be deprived of life, liberty, or property, without due process of law; and that in all criminal prosecutions the accused shall enjoy the right to a speedy and public trial by an impartial jury of the State and district wherein the crime shall have been committed."

In the case presented have not all these guarantees been violated? Mr. Vallandigham was arrested in his own house, and deprived of his liberty without due process of law. He neither belonged to the army or the navy, nor was he subject to military law; yet he was tried by a court-martial—and not by an impartial jury of his country—for addressing the people peaceably assembled for a legitimate purpose, and was convicted and sentenced to a punishment unknown to our laws. The privilege of the writ of *habeas corpus* had not been suspended in his district; the civil courts of the State were open, free and independent, and the act of Congress of the 3d of March 1863, specially enacted to provide for all such cases, was in full force, and cited by his counsel before the court to which application for the writ of *habeas corpus* had been made, and yet the learned and experienced Judge refused to grant it upon the most frivolous pretenses. Notwithstanding the great rights for which ages have contended—and which our fathers supposed they had secured for our enjoyment forever—have been ruthlessly trampled under foot, an apathy has been exhibited by the people that is truly appalling.—If Mr. Fox—the distinguished leader of the opposition to the ministry of England, during the French revolution, which shook the throne of Great Britain to its very foundation—had been thus arrested and sent to the Tower, or before a military court for trial, contrary to the fundamental law of the land, the people would have been electrified with astonishment, and Mr. Pitt, the most powerful and popular man and minister in the kingdom, would have been instantly hurled from his pre eminently high position with ignominy and disgrace

When the famous Wolfe Tone was arrested in Ireland, and improperly tried by a court martial, Curran, the dauntless advocate, presented an application to the King's Bench, calling upon it to support the law, and moving for a writ of *habeas corpus*—it was instantly granted—and when Mr Curran informed the court that his client might die whilst the writ was preparing, the Chief Justice directed the Sheriff to proceed to the barracks, where Tone was confined, and acquaint the Provost Marshal that the writ was preparing to suspend Tone's execution, and see that he was not executed And on being further informed that the Provost Marshal and the Major commanding would not obey the writ, the Chief Justice ordered both into custody. Thus was the majesty of the law sustained even in Ireland.

When the Bellerophon, the prison ship of Napoleon Bonaparte, approached the shores of England, the Ministry, learning that an effort would probably be made to take the Emperor before the civil courts, was so alarmed at the idea of a conflict between the civil and military authorities upon the inviolable principles of the Great Charter, that Lord Keith, on whom any process issued must have been served, was instructed to keep his barge out of the way so as to prevent service, and as soon as possible the ship was hurried off to her point of destination

Such was the veneration known to be entertained by the people for the supremacy of the law, that the Ministry dare not risk the issue, although Napoleon was denounced as a great disturber of the world, by all the sovereigns of Europe, whose armies were required to crush and despoil him of his power.

Many other cases might be adduced to show the extreme jealousy and sensitiveness of the people of Great Britain at every attempt to violate these great rights secured to them by their constitution. And why should they not be equally dear to us who claim them as our birthright and the very basis of self government?—If the precedent established is not abandoned, but justified, by the authorities of the land, how long will it be before we may see an effort made to establish in our midst a military despotism.

Although Mr. Vallandigham was opposed to many of the recent acts of Congress and measures of the administration, I do not understand that he counselled resistance to them — Laws may, in our opinion, be unjust, oppressive and even unconstitutional, but we are not the judges, and have no right to decide upon their validity, because there are appropriate tribunals constituted for this purpose and to them we can appeal, and by their decision we must be bound and governed. We profess to belong to the party of law and order, and advocated this doctrine in all the severe trials encountered in the execution of the fugitive slave law, and how can we recognise or be governed by any other principle now. We stand upon the constitution, and declare ourselves obedient to the laws of the land, and it is our imperative duty to honestly maintain them. Whilst I am for free speech, and advocate an independent and fair discussion of public men, and public measures, I am for observing the laws and supporting the administration in good faith in all constitutional measures to suppress the rebellion, and secure an honorable peace. At the same time I feel bound to do all in my power to thwart any scheme which has for its object the destruction of the Union, and the infringement of the constitution and the rights of the States.

I have an abiding faith in the intelligence and patriotism of the people. If their conservatism is aroused and exercised, as I doubt not it will be, our glorious Union will be restored, our constitution preserved, and the principle of self-government fully vindicated.

COMMITTEE ON RESOLUTIONS.

Wm. P Wells Esq, moved the appointment of a committee of nine to report suitable resolutions. The following were appointed, William P. Wells, Stanley G Wight, J. Logan Chipman, William A Moore, Theo. Romeyn, M. I. Mills, John Patton, Caleb Ives, Edward Kanter.

GRAND RAPIDS SPEAKS.

The President read the following telegram, which had just been received:

GRAND RAPIDS.

Freedom of Speech—Grand Rapids pledges her sympathy and hearty co-operation to the object of the meeting.

SPEECH OF HON. LEVI BISHOP.

MR. PRESIDENT AND GENTLEMEN:—This large and respectable meeting of citizens assembled on short notice, furnishes evidence if evidence were necessary, that the late acts of official violence perpetrated against the constitutional liberties of the country, and especially the one against the person of Mr. Vallandigham, have made a deep impression upon the public mind. It is most natural that it should be so. Political liberty has been the great desideratum of our race, since its first creation. Men have sought it, worshiped it, and sometimes enjoyed it, in the Old Word. But there, its appearance has been like flashes of light, across a dark ground work of aristocratic and despotic establishments. The flash once passed, the old order of things returned and millions again groaned in political fetters.

This western hemisphere was discovered, and settled in a manner that, to a great extent, freed it from the systems of political tyranny, and usurpation, which had bound and desolated other parts of the globe; and for two hundred years, our people have gone on in the engagement of that liberty which mankind had sought for, but rarely ever found.

Our political rights and liberties were confirmed by the sacrifices and virtues of our revolutionary fathers; and since then, while our political campaigns have been various in their results, and in their spirit, as the question involved in them have been various in their character, never, until the present administration came into power, have deadly blows been aimed at the vital principles of our system of free government.

In this there is something which surpasses our comprehension. The present dominant party came into power with those high-sounding platitudes on their lips, "free speech, free press, free men;" and yet that party in the North has been the first in our country's history to strike down these cherished rights of the citizen.

To assert that there is a "military necessity" for these outrages, in States which are thoroughly loyal, where no rebel standard has ever been raised, and where no rebel foot has ever trod, where the civil courts are always open and grand and petit juries are ready to do their duty, and where the ministerial officers of the law are not only willing, but eager to act, is to add cruel and bitter insult to the greatest injuries. In the name of constitutional liberty —in the name of our common humanity—in the name of the common civilization of the age I denounce these acts as tyranical usurpations, having the sanction of no law, of no necessity, and of no wise public policy.

The question therefore comes home to every man, *am I a freeman or am I a slave!* The question now is not how shall the Southern rebellion be dealt with, or what has been the course of Mr. Vallandigham; but the question now is, shall he, and you, and I, and every citizen, be protected in het freedom of speech by the constitution of the country? And here I would acknowledge the everlasting obligations of the nation to the Empire State for the bold and determined stand she has taken on this subject. She has sent more men into the field than any othe State, and made more sacrifices than any other She has more to lose than any other, but she and her chosen chief-have not proven recreant to themselves and to their country in this great contest for constitutional freedom.

I have sometimes thought that this question was even more important than that other question, "Shall the Southern rebellion be crushed?" for if it has been decreed in the councils of Heaven, by that just Providence, which has thus far watched over, prospered and cherished us as a nation, that this country must be divided, and that we must ultimately bow to the painful necessity of a separation into two, and probably into several, independent nations —which may God in his mercy forbid; yet in that case the next thing for us to look after and secure, is the spirit with the forms and substance of our free system of government in our own Northern States. We might even, with a dismembered Union, still have free institutions, free States, free Confederacies, and national prosperity to a reasonable extent.

But our individual, constitutional and social freedom, swallowed up and destroyed in the mighty vortex of national dissolution, would present a combination of national calamities without a parallel in the history of the world. That true patriot and venerable statesman of Kentucky, Mr. Crittenden, would crush the rebellion first, and then look after the constitution But, with unbounded deference and diffidence, I would inquire of him, what he will do if, after crushing the rebellion, or after failing to crush it, he and we shall find nothing of the constitution left to be looked after?

It is high time that the nation became alarmed, when a pliant judiciary, which was erected expressly as one of the barriers to guard the citizen against these very aggressions of despotic authority, cooly acknowledges that it "*dare not*" assert the process of the law; and when unsuccessful commanders, over sensitive to the just criticisms upon their conduct, turn their valiant swords with equal coolness, and much more effect, from the public enemy in arms in front of them, against the unarmed and peaceful citizen in their rear. What a worthy campaign! What a worthy conquest! The public enemy still bids defiance in front.

"While peace and liberty lie bleeding."

in the rear. Such is the condition to which our country has been reduced, from its high state of prosperity, in the short space of a little over two years.

And what is to be the next step in our great political tragedy? Have the men in power reflected well upon their future steps, rendered necessary by those they have already taken? Or, are the stupendous events now passing before us with fearful rapidity, regarded but as a huge joke, to be laughed over in the Presidential mansion?

Presses have been demolished and freemen have been incarcerated in military prisons, in order to crush out the free expression of our opinions on the subject of our national difficulties. But a more important medium for the expression of public opinion yet remains. Will the powers that be in Washington and elsewhere strike at that also?

It is a far more dangerous instrument against usurped authority than lead type, or the tongues of men. Will they attempt to destroy it? Will they send their Provost Marshals and their armed bands through our twenty thousand towns and cities, with orders to drive their bayonets through the ballot-box, and thus throttle its potent voice? The first step against the freedom of speech and of the press should not have been taken, unless the last one was resolved on. Will they venture upon that last step?

And other most important steps lie still beyond. Dictatorships and royal and imperial crowns, the overthrow of State governments, State Legislatures, and State judiciaries, and the Congress of the nation. Have our rulers resolved upon all these? Are our *loyal* leagues but *royal* leagues in embryo? Are these secret associations to be the drilled and sworn and armed auxiliaries in one great national usurpation? to be sustained also by a system of public corruption which it is but mockery to call public patronage? All these high-handed measures would seem to be necessarily consequent, upon the attempt to destroy the freedom of speech, and of the press. They all belong to the one great national crime, upon which it would seem that our rulers have entered.

I am not in a position to volunteer advice to the administration, and I am the last man to sound an unnecessary alarm, or to counsel violence in any circumstances, unless it shall become absolutely necessary in self defense; but if my voice could reach the Cabinet, I would remind them, and I will take the liberty to remind those among us who are known to be in the confidence of the administration, that the passions of man have not changed since his fall; that they but slumber under the discipline imposed by a long acquiesence in the mute supremacy of the law, and if these arbitrary acts against the liberty of the citizen are continued, the public patience may be provoked by them beyond endurance, and we may yet hear swelling throughout the land like the thunders of Niagara, those words which rang through the terrible march from Versailles to Paris:

"Aux arms! citoyens."—

It took the first stage of the French Revolution six years to run its career from the meeting of the States General in 1789, to the fall of Robespierre in 1795: then it took five years more for the Directorial government to run its race from 1795 to the Consulate in 1800; and then four years till the Imperial Crown was placed on the head of Napoleon in 1804. The changing scenes of that great political drama, rushed onward with greater rapidity than any other like changes the world had ever known; and yet, it took fifteen years to bring that revolution to its final termination That was a slow space compared with ours. How much more rapidly have we progressed! With us two short years have sufficed to accomplish nearly all, except the placing of the "Iron Crown" on the head of the despot.

And yet we may still ask, is our free government at an end? Have we already a royal or an imperial despotism? Have the best hopes of mankind, save those which rest on the redemption of the world through Christ, already suffered shipwreck, and passed away among the things that were? These are questions of fearful import.

The question then recurs, what is the duty of the citizen in this fearful condition of public affairs? Three great motives of action at once present themselves, each one of them of incalculable importance to us, and our common country First to crush the rebellion and maintain the Union. Second, to preserve constitutional freedom and prevent a central despotism. Third, to prevent anarchy by maintaining the supremacy of the law. These propositions are all more or less connected with each other, but to name them, is sufficiently them to discuss at least for the present occasion.

The democratic party is in every sense loyal to the governmment. With them the constitution, the laws, and the personal liberty of the citizen, are watchwords. Two years ago they were asked to sustain an administration with whose political principles they could not sympathize, in its efforts to maintain the constitution and overthrow the rebellion; and upon being assured that these were the objects for which the war was to be waged, they laid party aside, came up to the work, and did their whole duty. *And to day, the silent voice of the slain,* ON A HUNDRED BATTLE FIELDS, PROCLAIMS THE LOYALTY OF THE DEMOCRATIC PARTY. But no sooner was the North thus united in one grand patriotic movement for national existence, than the policy and objects of the war were changed, from an effort to maintain the Union into an abolition crusade; and the struggle itself from its high national purpose into a political partisan war. And still the democratic party stand by the Union and laws, and only see but too plainly in our rulers a fixed determination to overthrow them.

A good democrat and a good citizen will annex good terms or conditions to his allegiance to *government* But every man has a right to name the conditions upon which he will support the peculiar measures or policy of a given administration. What right, then, has the Cabinet at Washington to expect our support, when the primary objects of the war have been ignored; when new issues of a partizan character have been by them presented; and when the dearest rights of freemen have been by them trampled in the dust?

I would say to the President and to his advisers, in all candor and sincerity, we cannot sustain you in your unlawful measures. We must, by all means in our power, if need be, resist your arbitrary acts, against the personal liberty of peaceful citizens, and against the fundamental principles of our national magna charter. But, come back again to your starting point, put yourselves again upon the resolves of Congress, as embodied in the Crittenden resolution, bring back your legions into a "strict subordination to the civil authority," let the judiciary "*dare*" to use the process of the court, turn the arms of the nation against the public enemy, and let unarmed citizens at home express their wisdom or their folly as they please, abandon your wild schemes of emancipation, rise for once into the regions of true statesmanship and proclaim the sole objects of the war to be to maintain the constitution and the laws, and to restore the Union. Do this, and you shall again have our sympathy and support; do this and you shall hear from house to hamlet, from hamlet to city, from river to river, from lake to ocean, and from mountain top to mountain top, that glorious national symphony in which no discordant sound shall be heard, "The Union, it must and it shall be maintained."

Have we any reason to expect this? Have we any reason to hope for it? I fear not, for the man at the head of affairs acknowledges himself unable to resist the "pressure" from without. In other words, he acknowledges himself to be unable to fill his high position. Oh! for the will and arm of a Jackson, to hurl the authors of such "pressure" from his presence. And still we must hope, even against hope, for we must not despair of the Republic.

The country is prepared to sustain all constitutional means, at any sacrifice of life and treasure for the restoration of the Union, and the overthrow of the rebellion. Nor would there be much nicety in pointing out sins of omission and commission if an honest purpose in this direction could be seen in the Cabinet; but how can such support be zealous and effective, when the whole country sees and knows, as well as anything can be known, that the administration will not confine themselves to constitutional means, will not even respect the constitution, when it stands in the way of their schemes, and that they appear determined to set it aside altogether.

And there is something peculiarly mortifying and humiliating in the contemplation of this subject. The Pisistratidæ were able statesmen; the old Roman could feel proud of the Cesars amid the ruins of the Republic; Cromwell was one of the ablest Generals and statesmen of his time; and the Napoleons could raise the prosperity and renown of their country to the highest pitch, upon their own usurpations. But we Americans have not the poor consolation to know that our usurpers are even respectable in the eyes of the world. We are commanded to respect the powers that be, and I should be inclined, as a general thing, to respect them without the command; but I sometimes feel, in view of the low order of statesmanship now occupying the places of Webster and Madison and Jefferson and Hamilton, and in view of the sycophancy and servility which hang everywhere about it, that turkey buzzards are pecking at the American eagle, and that jackalls are gnawing at the vitals of the Republic

But we are not yet fallen so low. The spirit of liberty is not yet extinct. The example of our fathers is not yet forgotten. The spirit of Otis and Hancock and of Henry, revolving around that of Washington, while that of Hampden and even that of Brutus, are seen in the background, are moving through the land and calling upon their countrymen to assert and maintain and defend the liberties of the nation.

Let us obey the call, and be faithful to them, to ourselves and to our posterity, remembering always that it is "better to defend our rights at the door-sill than at the hearthstone," and "that eternal vigilance is the price of liberty."

THE RESOLUTIONS.

The committee on resolutions here announced that they were prepared to report, and through their Chairman, Wm. P. Wells, Esq., they submitted the following:

RESOLUTIONS.

Whereas, The Hon. Clement L. Vallandigham, "citizen of Ohio, has been recently arrested by military authority, tried before a military commission, and sent into exile, upon no other charge and for no other reason than words spoken in a public address before a lawful and public assemblage of his fellow citizens;—therefore,

Resolved, That we, citizens of Detroit, assembled in no partisan or factious spirit, but declaring our loyalty to the cause of the Union, and our determination to sustain the government in all constitutional and lawful measures for the suppression of the rebellion, denounce the trial of Mr. Vallandigham by a military tribunal as an arbitrary and unwarrantable interference with the freedom of speech, and as an illegal assertion of the supremacy of the military over the civil power in a State where the courts of law, both State and Federal, are in the uninterrupted exercise of all their functions, their process unimpeded and their powers effectual for the administration of justice.

Resolved, That this assumption of power by a military tribunal, if successfully asserted, not only abrogates the right of the people to assemble and discuss the affairs of government, the liberty of speech and of the press, the right of trial by jury, the law of evidence and the privilege of *habeas corpus*, but it strikes a fatal blow at the supremacy of law and the authority of the State and Federal constitutions.

Resolved, That the constitution of the United States—the supreme law of the land—has defined the crime of treason against the United States to consist "only in levying war against them or in adhering to their enemies, giving them aid and comfort;" and has provided that no person shall be convicted of treason unless on the testimony of two witnesses to the same overt act, or on confession in open court. And it further provides that "no person shall be held to answer for a capital or otherwise infamous crime unless on a presentment or indictment of a grand jury, except in cases arising in the land or naval forces or in the militia, when in actual service, in time of war or public danger," and further, that "in all criminal prosecutions the accused shall enjoy the right to a speedy and public trial, by an impartial jury, of the State and district wherein the crime shall have been committed."

Resolved, That these safeguards of the rights of the citizens against the encroachments of arbitrary power were intended more especially for his protection in times of civil commotion. They were secured substantially to the English people after years of protracted civil war, and were adopted into our own constitution at the close of the revolution. They have stood the test of seventy-six years of trial under our republican system, under circumstances which show that while they constitute the foundation of all free government they are the elements of the enduring stability of the Republic.

Resolved, That adopting the language of Daniel Webster, we declare, "It is the ancient and undoubted prerogative of this people to canvass public measures and the merits of public men. It is a 'home-bred right'—a fireside privilege. It has been enjoyed in every house, cottage and cabin in the nation. It is as undoubted as the right of breathing the air or walking on the earth. Belonging to private life as a right, it belongs to public life as a duty, learning at all times to be courteous and temperate in its use, except when the right itself is questioned, we shall plant ourselves on the extreme boundary of our own right, and bid defiance to any arm that would move us from our ground. This high constitutional privilege we shall defend and exercise in all places; in time of war, in time of peace, and at all times. Living, we shall assert it; and should we leave no other inheritance to our children, by the blessing of God we will leave them the inheritance of free principles, and the example of a manly, independent and constitutional defense of them."

Resolved, That the revival of the system of arbitrary arrests can have but one result—to divide and distract the North and destroy its confidence in the purposes of the administration; that we deprecate it as an element of confusion at home, of weakness to our armies in the field, and as calculated to lower the estimate of American character and magnify the apparent peril of our cause abroad. And that regarding the blow struck at a citizen of Ohio as aimed at the rights of every citizen of the North, we denounce it as against the spirit of our laws and constitution, and most earnestly call upon the President of the United States to reverse the action of the military tribunal which has passed a "cruel and unusual punishment" upon the citizen arrested, prohibited in terms by the constitution, to restore him the liberty of which he has been deprived, and leave to the civil tribunals, where he may be tried by the judgment of his peers, the cognizance of any offences of which he may be accused.

Resolved, That while we thus earnestly remonstrate against these violations of personal liberty and free speech, we are not now called upon to indorse or condemn the peculiar views of Mr. Vallandigham, but we mean to assert the right of personal security, and the supremacy of the civil over the military authority, irrespective of persons or parties.

Resolved, That in our earnest desire for the suppression of the rebellion, we rejoice at the intelligence received to day, of the conquest of Vicksburg, and the consequent opening of the Mississippi by the army under General Grant, and that the gratitude of the country is due to him and the brave soldiers under his command.

The resolutions were unanimously adopted.

SPEECH OF HON. GEO. V. N. LOTHROP.

I deem it, fellow citizens, of good omen that the dark shadow which has recently rested on men's minds, has been to-day brightened by the glorious news from the Army of the Southwest. [Applause.] The great Mississippi is emancipated. I rejoice in the belief that every ripple of that great stream from its source to its mouth now dances in the light of our great national flag. And I think that the day is not far distant when this great nation, wholly emancipated from baleful rebellion, shall once more stand before the powers of earth crowned with union, with prosperity, and with peace. [Applause.]

I come, fellow-citizens, to speak to you to-night in no terms of partisanship. From the beginning of this war I have avoided this Though I have surrendered none of my political convictions, though, in fact, they are daily confirmed by the startling progress of events, yet I have deemed it my duty hitherto to discountenance party action.

Nor could I, if I would, claim to-night the right to speak as a partisan. No, sir, the great protest which is now rising from all parts of the North, belongs rightfully to no party. It should be the voice of every man, and of every party loving and maintaining the great ideas of constitutional liberty. [Applause.] It was long ago said by Lord Chatham, "that America was settled upon ideas of liberty." And so fundamental are the great ideas of free speech and immunity from arbitrary arrest, that they underlie all parties. No party, no man can disclaim them without becoming a renegade to the distinctive faith and political civilization of America. [Applause.]

I shall aim to speak to night, fellow-citizens, in no language of passion. I come in full consciousness of the cala itous times on which we have fallen. I come with prepared impressions of the great duties, political, social and individual, that rest on us all. So coming, I stand to uphold so far as in me lies, on the one hand the flag of my country, on the other its sacred institutions against every foe and against all assaults. [Applause.] I at the same time remember that in so doing I act not for the triumph of any one section or of any one party; but because this great cause stands as the representative of Union and liberty and as such is, in my judgment the cause of humanity and civilization. [Applause.]

I think I shall speak no words which can be fairly construed by the most zealous defenders of the administration to be hostile to the government. I desire to support the government against the insurrection. I have unreservedly done so. From my whole heart I desire to see this hateful rebellion crushed. And as dear to me as is life—as dear to me as is home and children—before God, I believe, that if, by laying all the these down in the bloody grave, I could restore the Union as our sires gave it to us, I would go to the sacrifice more cheerfully than I ever went to triumph. But while we would sustain the administration, we must above all sustain the constitution. The administration and we alike owe obedience to the constitution. The rules of duty and allegiance for them and we are to be sought for in that great charter. And, rightly considered, we shall find that *we only truly support the government when we support the administration in lawful action under the constitution.* [Applause.]

So far we will go to a man. Beyond that we cannot go. Beyond that if true to our fathers, to ourselves and posterity we dare not go—we dare not permit ourselves to go. [Applause.]

Well now, why are we here to-night? Why are you so moved? Why are men like you are—all the Republic so moved? Nay, why beyond any visible mention, do we all know that there lies down in the hearts of men all over the country a deeper unspoken emotion? It is because of all the remarkable, incredible events of the late months, one is prominent, so pointed, that we can no longer remain silent, if we would remain secure or free.

An eminent citizen of Ohio, but of unpopular opinions, at his own home, in the night time, without any warrant, without any charge known to the law, is siezed by a file of soldiers, hurried from his own neighborhood to a distant city, and arraigned before a tribunal unknown to the law. And when he lifts a cry which should be more potent than that of the old Roman, "I am an American citizen—I appeal to the law," the law is palsied—or worse, falls dead—strangled by the hands of its own minister! [Applause and deep sensation, with cheers for Vallandigham.]

These, I believe, are cheers by constitutional lovers of liberty, not because of sympathy with the opinions of the man, but because the meanest man, when smitten by tyranny or wrong, becomes as sacred as if laid on the altar of God. [Applause.]

An act like that which I have described would be startling at any time. This was more startling as the culmination of a series of like outrages. And still more startling because of the bold avowals of the military arm, and the servile acquiescence of the judiciary which attended it.

This brings directly home to us two great questions. These two questions are,

1. Arbitrary imprisonment.
2. Freedom of speech.

No greater questions can appeal to a free people.

These questions I propose here to discuss with the utmost calmness, but with the utmost plainness, also.

"Arbitrary imprisonment," said Hume, the great historian, "is a grievance which finds a place in some degree in almost every government except that of England." It was a noble boast, and it was not an idle one. When those works were written England held, as she still holds, a conspicuous place for constitutional freedom. She stood, indeed, alone among the nations, for then this sunlit pillows of our own great constitutional structure had not risen.

It was the immortal work of our patriot fathers to adjust and perfect English liberty. It was from England, as I once heard Mr. Webster say, that we borrowed Magna Charta, the *habeas corpus*, and the right of trial by jury, a magnificent heritage of freedom.

We have all grown up under a constitution embodying those fundamental guarantees of personal liberty, and so thoroughly have those ideas been grounded in us that we have hardly conceived that they could be violoted. We have no more conceived of an imprisonment without process than an imprisonment without a jailor. We have imbibed our ideas on this point with our native air; and if there are any men in this land who do not feel shocked by the late arbitrary arrests, I earnestly beseech them to review their peculiar political notions, and see if there is not some vice in them which corrupts the very fountains of sound republican principles. [Applause.]

We shall all, I think, better appreciate this question if we go back a little and observe its progress.

It is far back, in times almost barbarous, where we find, in England, the subjects insisting that arbitrary arrests should not be allowed. The right to arrest was claimed as a prerogative of the crown. This the subject resisted. He claimed that no man should be subject to arrest except by process of law. And from this struggle resulted, at last, MAGNA CHARTA, wrung by the iron barons from King John. This declared, in explicit terms, the great doctrine of immunity from arbitrary arrest. This was in the thirteenth century. And from that time to this, through usurpations and revolutions, through war and peace, though often violated, this right of the subject has stood an immutable doctrine of English liberty. Though often betrayed and obscured in stormy or despotic times, yet at the first lull of the elements its light has never failed to re-appear to guide the State back to safe anchorage More than thirty acts of Parliament, it is said, have been passed reaffirming the guaranties of the Great Charter. This shows how dear they were to the people of England. And it was thus endeared by centuries of vigilance and sacrifice, that they crossed the ocean with its first settlers and found a new home in America. You see thus that they are literally a part of our inheritance. Nay, more, as our civilization enters into our personal being, they enter into our very bones and marrow.

After the settlement of America there was a memorable struggle. One the more memorable and prominent, because it was one in which, at least by her sympathies and prayers, America took part. Under the reign of the Tudors, the prerogative of the crown was stretched to the utmost. The rights of the subject shrunk beneath the vigorous hands that grasped the sceptre. The Stuarts followed with the same exacting demands, but with less ability to maintain their usurpations. At last Parliament extorted from the reluctant hands of the first Charles that other instrument of freedom, known as the PETITION OF RIGHTS.

Have the men who now hold the reins of power ever read this petition? Do they know that in their late acts they are reproducing the wrongs of Charles I.? Do they know that in resisting their acts, we are retreading the steps of the best patriots of England? You know, fellow-citizens, the general purports of the Petition of Right. But I wish to refresh your memories. I propose to read you some parts of it to show how applicable it is to our present situation. It covers in terms their three grievances: 1. Arbitrary arrests. 2. Returns to the *habeas corpus*, that the prisoner was detained solely by executive command. 3. Trials for civil offences by no military commanders.

Each of these grievances are reproduced in the case of Mr Vallandigham. And this is in the Nineteenth Century—in America, and under the American Constitution! Thus, alas! you will see, that it falls to us to fight again the same battles which the third Parliament of Charles fought with that cruel and despotic King! [Applause]

I will give you the very words of the petition of right.

The petition recites that whereas, "by the statute called the Great Charter of the liberties of England it is declared and enacted, that *no freeman may be taken or imprisoned* * * * *but by the judgment of his peers or by the law of the land.*"

"And in the eighth and twentieth years of the reign of Edward III. it was declared and enacted by authority of Parliament that no man, of what estate or condition that he be, should be * * * taken nor imprisoned nor disinherited, nor put to death *without being brought* to answer by *due process of law.*"

"Nevertheless against the tenor of said statutes and others the good statutes of your realm to that end promised divers of your subjects have of late been imprisoned without any cause shown, and when for their deliverance they were brought before justices by your Majesty's writs of *habeas corpus*, then to undergo and receive as the court should order and their keepers commanded, to certify the causes of their detainer *no cause was certified, but that they were detained by your Majesty's special command*, signified by the lords of your privy council, *and yet were returned back to their prisons without being charged with anything to which they might make answer according to law.*"

"And whereas also * * * of late diver commissions under your Majesty's great sea have issued forth, by which certain persons have been assigned and appointed commissioners, with power and authority *to proceed within the land according to the justice of martial law* * * * *and by such summary course and order as is agreeable to martial law*, and as is used in armies in time of war, to proceed to the trial and condemnation of such offenders. * * * By pretext whereof some of your Majesty's subjects have been by some of said commissioners put to death, *when and where, if by the laws and statutes of the land they had deserved death, by the same laws and statutes they might*, AND BY NO OTHER OUGHT, *to have been judged and executed.*"

These are the words in which those grievances were set forth; AND THOSE GRIEVANCES AN ENGLISH DESPOT CONFESSED WERE SO INTOLERABLE TO THE ENGLISH PEOPLE THAT HE SOLEMNLY RENOUNCED THEM FOREVER!—[Applause.]

I repeat, then, that the grievances against which we here protest to-night are precisely those against which the Parliament of Great Britain made its immortal protest in 1628. How much more, then, in the civilization of to-day, under the precepts of our fathers, and under the guarantees of our constitution, shall we resist the growing of these great abuses in our land? [Applause]

Let us follow this further. This citizen, when seized, applied to a Federal Judge for the writ of *habeas corpus*. This writ, you will remember, was said by Webster to be one of the priceless gifts of the English law to us. Boswell tells us, that Dr. Johnson, though a bigoted tory, declared that "the *habeas corpus* is the single advantage which our government has over that of other countries."

And Macauley declares that "the *habeas corpus* act, though passed during the ascendancy of the whigs, was not more due to the whigs than the tories."

The writ of *habeas corpus* is an old writ. It is not a writ of grace; it is a *writ of right*. It issues on the petition of a prisoner who alleges an unlawful imprisonment. But corrupt or timid judges sometimes refused the writ. To correct this, the English parliament, in the reign of Charles II., visited such refusal with fine and imprisonment.

It was this high writ that was invoked by Mr. Vallandigham. Judge Leavitt [groans and hisses]. I hardly think he will need any groans save those accusing justice will wring from his own conscience. Judge Leavitt, I say, declined to act on the petition, but politely asked Gen. Burnside what he had to say. He turned his ear from the complaint of the prisoner, and asked first the pleasure of the imprisoner! I doubt whether this has a parallel in this country. God forbid that it should have! You will have observed that the complaint of the Petition of *Right* was, not that the writ was refused, but being granted, a return that the prisoner was detained by the King's command was held sufficient. The King's Judges dared not refuse the writ. Their crime was allowing as sufficient a return showing no lawful cause of arrest. Sir John Elliott, whose counsels shaped the immortal Petition of Right, was arrested and thrown into the Tower. Even the servile Judges of Charles dared not refuse him the *habeas corpus*. But when it was returned that he was held by the King's command, they betrayed the liberties of England by allowing the sufficiency of the return. General Burnside notified Judge Leavitt that he detained Mr. Vallandigham by his simple will as a military commander; and the Judge in defiance of Magna Charta, of the Petition of Right, of the *habeas corpus* act, of the American constitution and of the acts of Congress held this sufficient to prevent the writ!

Now the precepts of my profession—my habits of many years, which have almost become instincts, lead me to regard the judiciary with reverence. And I am glad to say that the general high character of the Judges in this country, their learning and purity, justifies this sentiment. For Judge Leavitt I have been accustomed to entertain much respect. I regret that I should feel constrained to arraign any act of his.

I have brought here to-night his published opinion refusing the writ of *habeas corpus*, and sanctioning this arbitrary arrest. I confess to you that I have read this opinion with grief and dismay! It seems to me there is not in it a material proposition which a constitutional lawyer can defend. I am sure that there is not a judicial sentiment which every lover of constitutional liberty will not deplore.

Judge Leavitt affirms the power of the President to arrest Mr. Vallandigham at his will, if he considers it necessary for the protection and preservation of the government. This, he holds, is a discretionary power, which of necessity the President, as the conservator of the republic, must possess.

He says that the President, as Commander-in-Chief of the Army and Navy, "is invested with very high powers, which it is well known have been exercised on various occasions during this rebellion. * * * It is, perhaps, not easy to define what acts are within this designation, but they must, undoubtedly, be limited to such as are deemed essential to the protection and preservation of the government and constitution, which the President has been sworn to support and defend. And in deciding what he may rightfully do under this power, when there is no express legislative declaration, the President is guided solely by his own judgment and discretion, and is only answerable for an abuse of his authority by impeachment, prosecuted according to the requirements of the constitution. The occasion which calls for the exercise of this power exists only from the necessity of the case: and when the necessity exists, there is a clear justification of the act."

And again. "The sole question is whether the arrest is legal: and, as before remarked, the legality depends on the necessity which existed for making it: and of that necessity, for the reason stated, this court cannot judicially determine."

These are his words. They mean simply this: The President, as Commander-in-Chief, possesses an indefinable, illimitable power. By this he may do *any act, anywhere, and touching anybody*, which, in his judgment, is necessary to protect the government; and of the necessity, as well as of the utility of the act, he is the sole judge.

Reasoning more vicious or more dangerous, in my judgment, never fell from any bench. It is on this supposed necessity of clothing the Executive with a prerogative to do any act supposed to be required for the safety of the State, that the power of arbitrary imprisonment is justified.

This plea is not new. Judge Leavitt will find authority that he would be reluctant to invoke. His reasoning is at bottom identical with that of the minions of Charles. They used the same arguments to show that this was a necessary prerogative of the crown, and ought not to be restrained. Hear them, as reported by Hume, in the debate on the Petition of Right:

"But above all branches of prerogative that which is most necessary to be preserved *is the power of imprisonment*. Faction and discontent, like disasters, frequently arise in every political body; and during these disorders *it is by the salutary exercise alone of this discretionary power that rebellious and civil wars can be prevented*. To circumscribe this power is to destroy its value; entirely to abrogate it is impracticable, and the attempt itself must prove dangerous, if not pernicious to the public. The supreme magistrate; in critical and turbulent times will never agreeably either to prudence or duty, allow the State to perish, while there remains a remedy, which, how irregular soever, it is still in his power to apply."

But this reasoning was rejected by the jealous guardians of English constitutional liberty. Thank God that they did reject it! And rejected it must be by every people who would maintain the rights of a free constitution. [Applause.]

Nor can I stop here. Mr. Vallandigham was seized in the midst of a peaceful and loyal community, in a State where no insurrection existed or was threatened; on the soil of which no armed rebel ever set his foot; in which all the local courts were in the full exercise of all their functions; in which two great Federal courts were organized; carried to Cincinnati and tried before what is called a military com-commission—a tribunal which, I declare to you, gentlemen, was wholly unknown to any law whatever; a trial which was a cruel mockery.

It is indeed said that he was tried by a court-martial. This I deny to be true in any accurate sense. For the purpose of the trial of Mr. Vallandigham a court of the Star Chamber would have been just as lawful as was any court martial, or court of miltary commission whatever.

There is, I believe, a designed confusion maintained on this subject of martial law and military law. Like the phrase "military necessity," they are used vaguely. So long as they contain no precise meaning they furnish convenient cover for usurpations.

Martial Law and Military Law are altogether different things. What, then, is the difference?

Martial Law is simply the will of a commander when at the head of an army, in a hostile country or insurrectionary district, when the whole civil society is subjected to the law of force; and when martial law is proclaimed, it supercedes and overrides all civil laws whatever. This is Martial Law.

Military Law, on the other hand, in this country, is that system of law enacted by Congress for the government of the army and navy. Not for the government of the citizen, of the people, but of the army or navy and of persons attached to it, in war and in peace. This law is founded in legislation, and has its origin and extent in the acts of Congress. This is Military Law.

"Martial law," says Blackstone, taking his reading from Lord Hale, "is built on no settled principles, but is entirely arbitrary in its decisions, and, in truth, is no law. * * * It ought not to be permitted in time of peace, when the King's courts are open for all persons *to receive justice according to the laws of the land*."

"Military law," says Chancellor Kent, "is a system of regulations for the government of the armies in the service of the United States, authorized by Congress and known as the Articles of War, but *Martial Law* is quite a distinct thing, and is founded on paramount necessity, and proclaimed by a militar chief."

In 1792 Lord Loughborough, in giving judgment in the Court of Common Bench in the case of Grant vs. Gould, declared that "Martial Law, such as is described by Hale, and such, also, as is marked by Mr. Justice Blackstone, does not exist in England at all," and he added that it was contrary to the constitution, and had "been for a century totally exploded."

In truth, martial law cannot, by its own force, supercede or overthrow *the civil constitutions and laws in this country at all*. It can have no place except in two cases: 1st In the country of a foreign enemy, over which our laws do not extend. 2d. In an insurrectionary district where the civil organization has already been overthrown or impaired by the rebellion. And in each case the operation of martial law is limited by the actual dominion of the military chief.*

President Lincoln may lawfully occupy Virginia and declare martial law there, because the civil authority has disappeared in rebellion. If Gen. Grant is in Vicksburg to-day—and I trust in God he is—it is competent for him to declare martial law and enforce it within the district actually subject to his military forces. But no commander can declare it where no war or insurrection exists. Nor can he declare it beyond the limits of his actual military dominion. For in all forms of law obedience and protection are relative terms.

Now, under which of these laws was Mr. Vallandigham seized and tried?

* Perhaps the right to declare martial law may extend to the case of a beleaguered city or to the territory covered by the camp or lines of an army actually engaged in military operations against a hostile force. Some instances in point probably exist. But this falls within the general principle above stated. It can only be allowed when the military operations are in the presence of an enemy, and of such a nature or under such circumstances as to make the ordinary course of law impracticable.

Valuable information on the subject of martial law may be found in the learned opinions of Justice Woodbury, in the case of Luther vs. Borden, 7 Howard's U. S. Reports.

Not under the law martial; for no war, no insurrection existed in Ohio. There was no civil commotion. The courts were all open. The administration of civil justice was as perfect there as here. The constable in the name of the law could arrest whomsoever the law charged: The Sheriff could execute all the sentences of the law. Martial law did not and could not exist. And so says Judge Leavitt explicitly. He says: "It cannot be claimed that this law was in operation in General Burnside's department when Mr Vallandigham was arrested."

Was he arrested and tried under the *military law?* The definitions already given answer that question. Mr. Vallandigham was not a soldier or sailor nor in any way attached to the army or navy and the articles of war did not in any way apply to him.

In the name of law and reason I then ask under what was he seized and tried?

Judge Leavitt answers vaguely that it was under an undefined power of the President as commander-in-chief. This power he says is not defined either by the constitution or legislation. Nor can he tell what it is; it is wide as executive discretion and as boundless as necessity!

I utterly deny any such power. The power of the Commander-in-Chief is such as he has under the law military or the law martial. If an assumed power cannot be referred to one of these it has no rightful existence. It is a sheer usurpation. And for God's sake who ever else shall assert this doctrine, let not the bench tell us that there is in this land, in the midst of civil society, a power until now unheard of, wholly indefinable and irresponsible, and finding its occasion, its necessity and its limits in the breast of one man only. [Applause]

Yet this Judge after telling us that this right of arrest existed in the indefinable powers of the Commander-in-Chief, and that Burnside was the rightful delegate of this power, goes on to say that Burnside had no authority to dispose of the prisoner without a trial by a military court. Why not? What law required or authorized a court? This assumed power is more indefinable than the law martial. And that we have seen is merely the unrestrained will of the commander. The same will that arrests can punish. So under this nameless power which Judge Leavitt has evoked, if the President deem it necessary to arrest, he may deem it necessary to punish. His judgment is his only law, his only tribunal.

In plain words, we have this result. The Burnside Military Court is conceded not to have been authorized by martial law. It plainly was not authorized by military law. And as we now see that the claim for any other indefinite, nameless power in the President is indefensible, it is clear that this Military Court was wholly unknown to any law whatever. It was a sheer usurpation. It had no lawful jurisdiction, and its judgment in the eye of the law are nullities.

The Judge says that he had no power to revise or reverse the proceedings of this commission. This would be true, *if it had any jurisdiction*. But it was his imperative duty to inquire if it had any lawful jurisdiction of the prisoner, and, if not, then to rescue him from its illegal grasp. And he also knew that this pretence of holding him for a trial by a military court was in plain defiance of the late acts of Congress.

I have thus shown, I think, how unlawful

and how dangerous are these arbitrary arrests. And now I will only add that we cannot safely acquiesce in them. We cannot for a moment assent to this claim of irresponsible power To day it prevails in Ohio. To-morrow it may prevail here. We may be arrested for this meeting here to-night. And if the Burnside-Leavitt doctrine prevails, there is no peaceful redress beneath the throne of Almighty God! Our English ancestors built high and strong the barriers against these despotic claims. Our Revolutionary Fathers placed them among the most sacred guarantees of our constitution; and, by the blessing of God, we will stand faithfully by them [Loud applause]

And now, fellow-citizens, I pass to the other questions.

For what was Mr. Vallandigham arrested? What was his alleged offense?

As I understand it, simply for standing up in a popular assembly, in Ohio, in open day, and expressing his opinion of the war and of the policy of the administration. This he might do by the constitution of Ohio. Nay, this he might do by the constitution of the United States. "Congress shall make no law respecting an establishment of religion, or prohibiting the free exercise thereof: or *abridging the freedom of speech or of the press;* or of the right of the people peaceably to assemble and to petition the government for a redress of grievances," says the constitution.*

Can it be, then, that I state the offense of Mr. Vallandigham truly?

I have the charge before me. It reads thus:

"Publicly expressing, in violation of General Orders No. 38, from Headquarters Department of Ohio, sympathy for those in arms against the government of the United States, and declaring disloyal sentiments and opinions with the object and purpose of weakening the power of the government in its efforts to suppress an unlawful rebellion."

Under this charge it is specified that on the 1st of May, at a large meeting of citizens at Mt. Vernon, Ohio, in public, he declared the war "A wicked, cruel and unnecessary war," "a war not being waged for the preservation of the Union," "a war for the purpose of crushing out liberty and erecting despotism," "a war for the freedom of the blacks and the enslavement of the whites;" "if the administration had so wished the war could have been honorably terminated months ago;" "peace might have been honorably obtained by listening to the proposed intermediation of France;" "the government of the United States were about to appoint military marshals in every district to restrain the people of their liberties, to deprive them of their rights and privileges"—characterising order 38 "as a base usurpation of arbitrary authority;" saying "the sooner the people inform the minions of usurped power that they will not submit to such restrictions upon their liberties the better," and that "he was at all times and upon all occasions resolved to do what he could to defeat the attempts now being made to build up a monarchy upon the ruins of a free government"

The above were all the words which Mr. Vallandigham was found to have uttered.

Now I hold this up to your scrutiny and ask you what is Vallandigham's offense? It may be unwise speaking, injudicious speaking, ill-timed speaking, false opinions, unpatriotic opinions and all that. With much of it I do not agree. I have wholly differed with this gentleman since the war begun. But that is not the question. What is the offense? What law is violated? That is the question, and the country demands that this be answered without evasion.

Turn back to the charge. What does that say? Publicly expressing sympathy for rebels, declaring disloyal sentiments and opinions with a view to weaken the power of the government.

Now, without inquiring whether the words used will fairly bear this construction, let us assume that they do. I then ask, is this charge *any legal offence?* Does the law denounce *sympathy*, even for a bad cause? Is the utterance of "disloyal sentiments and opinions," followed by no acts, unlawful? I dwell not on the uncertainty of what is disloyal; but, the point I make is whether a man can be arrested for any quality of opinions on public affairs?

Sympathy with a bad cause and the utterance of disloyal sentiments may be unwise, improper, unpatriotic; may persuade us that the man is of unsound head or bad heart; but does the *law* denounce these things? If so, what law? The law deals with *acts;* not abstract motives nor opinions, nor sympathies. [Applause.]

The charge refers to no law. It says, "*in violation of Order No.* 38." Is Order No. 38 *law* over the people of the Northwest? How became it so? How Became Burnside our lawgiver? Who put Burnside and Order No. 38 above the Constitution of the United States?

Congress can make no law abridging freedom of speech. Can Burnside, by a dash of his pen, make such a law? Unless he can, then Order 38 is an imposition.

Now I lay it down as a postulate on this subject that *without free discussion there can be no free government.*

This is the ground of the constitutional guaranties above cited. Hence we can readily see at what price we must lay down this right. A surrender here is a surrender of all.

What is free speech under the constitution?

Clearly the right to canvass and discuss without reserve public measures and acts. Anything short of this is inadequate.

And I claim that Mr Vallandigham had the full right to approve, criticise or denounce the war and all acts and measures of the administration at his pleasure. As a citizen he might form any opinion on these subjects and freely express them. He was certainly free to approve and applaud. This his accusers would

*It will be remembered that this provision was not in the constitution as originally adopted. The absence of these and other important guarantees gave great dissatisfaction. Mr. Jefferson was abroad when this constitution was framed, but his eye was ever watchful in behalf of freedom. He at once set the ball in motion for an amendment. Writing from Paris to Mr. Madison, Dec. 20, 1787 he used these memorable words: "I will now tell you "what I do not like. First, the omission of a bill of "rights, providing clearly, and without the aid of "sophism, for freedom of religion, *freedom of the* "*press* protection against standing armies restric- "tion of monopolies, *the eternal and unremitting* "*force of the habeas corpus laws, trial by jury in all* "*matters of fact triable by the laws of the land*" And he closed by adding: "Let me add that a bill of "rights is what the people are entitled to *against* "*every government on earth, general or particular;* "and what no just government should refuse or "rest on inference."

consider meritorious. But they object when he condemns and denounces.

"But," said a friend to me one day, "this arrest does not infringe freedom of speech; freedom of speech is not license of speech"

What is license of speech? If he meant that no one was entitled to indulge in indecent or profane language, I assent; for the utmost free dom of discussion does not need the use of such language.

He meant that the expression of opinions regarded as unsound, unpatriotic, or of evil tendency, should be deemed not a true free dom, but a license to be restrained. But this obviously destroys all free discussion. It leaves no freedom except such as exists in Austria or France. It makes, if I apply the rule, all opinions that I reject, contraband to all other persons. But the very fact of a a guaranty of freedom of speech implies that men will honestly differ, and that the privilege of expression is to be equal to all. The right of expression shall not depend upon on the quality of the opinions in the judgment of another. The guaranty means this or it means nothing By any other rule, what I deem legitimate my neighbor would reject as a license. We should come back to the old controversy—to which there is but one true solution—liberty of speech to all.

Let me illustrate. The guaranty for the free exercise of religion and of speech is the same. Now suppose my friend to be a Presbyterian Suppose Burnside to become theologically inclined and to issue a theological order 38 making the exercise of Presbyterianism dis loyal and dangerous to government? Would my friend bow to the official logic demonstrating the difference between freedom and licence, or would the blood of the Old Covenenters be up? [Applause]

I have said I do not agree with Vallandigham's opinions. I strongly discent from some of them But he has the same right to utter them as I have mine. His audience will weigh his and mine and choose between them.

What do our friends mean by license of speech? See where this false position places them. What is their style of daily speech of that large body of the people, now almost certainly a majority—I mean those who think this administration a deplorable, disastrous failure? Yet day by day this large body are denounced as traitors and copperheads. Is this license of speech? [Laughter.] Then let all such beware the coming of a new Burnside and a new order 38. [Laughter and applause] When tyranny reigns transitions are unpleasantly sudden. He who is top to-day, may be below to morrow. He who when his fellow man had his head cut off sat and enjoyed the bloody spectacle, may himself furnish the spectacle to-morrow. It is a long lane, says the adage, that has no turn.

Talk not to me of license of speech! What in God's name was your constitutional guaranty framed for except to protect what you call license? What needs to be protected? Is it not the *unpopular* opinion of to-day that needs these guaranties? The man who runs with the majority needs no guaranty. He is never disloyal. [Applause] Under Charles I, Buckingham needed no protection. Sir John Elliot was then the odious man; his opinions ran to license and it was he who needed guaranties. He went to the Tower and died there because Charles' Judges said he was guilty of license of speech in Parliament.

These guarantees, I repeat, are expressly made for the man who utters unpopular sentiments—they are needless for any other. Mr. Chandler [groans and hisses] is a friend of the administration. He may use any language he pleases: He may vilify the General who, at the head of our armies holds our fate in his hand, till confidence is so impaired that assured victory becomes defeat and ruin. His counsels may culminate in a successon of generals whose record of continuous defeat and dishonor hangs like a pall over the whole Heaven. He runs with those in power, and needs to-day no protection. But to morrow this may change The curses of a ruined people may be hurled against him. The "loyal" utterance of to day may be disloyal to-morrow. What we demand for the odious and unpopular Vallandigham may be needed for those who, I think, must soon become as odious and unpopular as he. [Applause]

We then demand that this constitutional guranty shall be firmly maintained; especially must it be maintained in critical times like the present, when passions are high, and it may seem easier to suppress an argument than to refute it

This freedom of opinion is the crowning glory of our civilization. "Opinion in good men," said John Milton, "is but knowledge in the making" It is by the collision of conflicting opinions that man instead of standing petrified in his track, presents the grand spectacle of marching on with intelligent progress. With all their attainment, the ancient republics did not realise this freedom. There was, indeed, a noble aspiration for it. Milton places at the head of his eloquent plea for unlicensed printing these striking lines, from the Greek poet Euripides:

"This is *true* liberty, when freeborn men
"Having to advise the public *may speak free*,
"What can be juster in a State than this?"

This, which was but an aspiration at Athens, has become a law in our constitution. And it is because free born-men may speak free, and must speak free, that I demand this right for Mr. Vallandigham. What can we fear? Is he so strong in his errors that we cannot be stronger in our truth? Cannot we meet opinion with opinion. "Who ever knew truth put to the worse in a free and open encounter?" Mr. Vallandigham belives this war could have been avoided. He believes that it cannot restore the Union. He believes instant peace better than a continuance of the war. He has a right to say so. He has a right to argue it freely to the people, and win them to the adoption of these views if he can. If he is right he may succeed. If he is wrong he will certainly fail But right or wrong his privilege must be maintained. For, when his right goes down, there goes down with it my right, and yours, and every man's. [Applause]

I have a consciousness that this has always been my ground. When I have stood with the majorities I have vindicated this right for those in the minority. I have no sympathy for the mischievous opinions of Sumner. but when he was struck down by a brutal ruffian for the exercise of free speech, I unreservedly condemned the outrage. Yet here there was no denial of the legal right, but only a wanton invasion of the right by an individual!

I have thus shown that Vallandigham was

guilty of no offense. But suppose this were doubtful. What then¿ He was a civilian. His offense if anything was a civil one Why not take him into the civil courts and try him? The act of Congress of March 3d, 1863, especially required that all persons seized by military arres: should be reported to the civil courts for presentment and trial, and it provided that the failure of a grand jury to indict should be a good ground for instant discharge. Ohio is unimpeachably loyal to the Union. She has sent her sons by the thousands, by the hundreds thousands to fight for it. Where blood has flowed or bones been left to bleach in the inclement air—and alas! where are they not? there are the blood and the bones of Ohio. There can be no fear of her courts Not only your constitutions, not only your acts of Congress, but the most elementary ideas of justice require that a man shall be tried and condemned only by regular judicial proceedings, and by fixed and certain laws. "Every man in civilized society," exclaimed Lord Erskine, "has a right to hold his life, liberty and property and reputation under plain laws that can be well understood, and is entitled to have some specific part of his conduct compared and examined by their standard" The great and good Lord Hale has warned us that "where the law is broken down *injustice knows no bounds*, but runs as far as the wit and invention of accusers, or the detestation of the person accused will carry it."

Not one of us, fellow citizens, have any safety except in the permanent laws of the land and their regular administration. When we fall under the arbitrary code of military orders we shall find ourselves tried by the invention of our accusers, or by our own unpopularity. Let no man say that the danger is trifling in the hands of a mild, constitutional President The precedent is of bad omen. A military chieftain may to-morrow leap into the seat today filled by a constitutional President. [Applause]*

I have thus imperfectly discussed the two topics with which I started. I have not made known to you their value. That you instinctively know. But I have sought to make known the grounds on which we claimed and must claim immunity from arbitrary arrests and perfect freedom of speech.

Against the policy of the administration in this behalf—if it has grown to be a policy—we enter our earnest protest. We say to it firmly, decisively, that arbitrary arrests must not be permitted. [Applause.] Freedom of speech must not be abridged. [Applause.] We say to them, we, with you, are haters of rebellion We, with you, will fight to the last against this wicked attempt to disunite us, to overthrow the republic, and to trail our flag in the dust; but we also say to them, when you turn your arm against the liberties of the ci izen—when you imprison without law and deny freedom of speech, you yourselves overthrow the constitution, and commit the same crime the rebels are guilty of. [Enthusiastic applause.]

There we stand inexorably against you. We therefore stand armed against secession and rebellion on the one hand—and with the same inflexible resolution armed against the assaults of the domestic enemies of the constitution on the other. [Applause]

I say to the administration, here we must oppose you. How? We do not propose to go into rebellion, because this is the very crime for which we justly condemn the South [Applause.] But whenever you strike down a constitutional right, we will for ourselves declare that we are not consenting to this death. We will not by silence seem to consent to your crime, nor be driven ourselves into any violence against the constitution [Applause.]

I declared at the Sumpter meeting two years ago, that the South could not be justified in rebellion, because, if wrongs there were, *the constitution provided a peaceful mode of redress.* Arms are only the last resort. That is our impregnable ground before the world So with us to-day. Against the outrages of our rulers the constitution gives a peaceable remedy. We have them in the ballot-box and free discussion. [Applause] These are sufficient. No false administration can stand against them. We will fearlessly drag its crimes to condemnation at the bar of free speech. At every invasion of the constitution we will protest! *protest!* PROTEST! Let us have patience. Let us have free speech. Let us have free voting, and we shall need nothing more. They are better than all the cannon of the universe. We shall find our feet on a rock, and in good time the country must swing around to us. [Great applause]

We must bring the constitution through this terrible ordeal safe, "from turret to foundation stone." We have proven its grandeur in peace: we must now show its adequacy in war In our hands, not one of its glorious provisions must fail. We must vindicate in war, as we have in peace, the entire sufficiency of the institutions of a free people

Momentous as is the crisis, the constitution is sufficient. Let the President stand by this faith and it shall not fail him. By our free suffrage he has been furnished men and money in such measure as no despotism could comel. Let him only keep to the broad, plain way of the constitution. It stretches before him like one of the great ways of Imperial Rome, ample enough for the legions of war or the triumphal processions of peace. Let the President take his stand there. And standing there defending the flag, upholding the constitution and maintaining its priceless guaranties, he will find himself armed with the invincible power of the united North. He will then wield a power grander than ever depended from a sceptre —a power great alike in i s moral and physical strength. And then, unless an inexorable Providence has decreed against us, we shall soon behold this great rebellion, smitten with death, shrink away to the caves of eternal night. [Long continued applause.]

REMARKS OF THE PRESS.

The meeting was mos harmonious, and was a success in the fullest sense of the word The hall could not contain one half of those who assembled. The crowd outside was addressed by Messrs. Chipman, Brown, Wheaton and others. The speeches were all received with vociferous demonstrations of applause At a late hour the meeting adjourned with three rousing cheers for the Union as it was and the constitution as it is.

* The French have this proverb: "*It is only the first step that costs.*" This is as t ue of public as of private conduct. The plea of public necessity which suppresses freedom o speech to-day will be found available for a new aggression to-morrow. If to oppose the administration by speech is held dangerous to the government, it will be easy to hold it still more dangerous to oppose it by voting. That transition is so easy and so imminent that the popular sagacity has detected the peril, and a wide uneasiness already prevails.

From Corporal Skelly Post
Jan. 2, 1894

Dedication of Adams County Soldiers' Monument,

Gettysburg, Pa., February 22nd, 1892.

Oration of Hon. Edw. McPherson.

Mr. President, Members of Corporal Skelly Post, Ladies and Gentlemen:

We are here to dedicate, so far as we can, a Monument to the Soldiers from Adams county who fell in that ghastliest and bloodiest of public tragedies—the War of the Rebellion. I call it the war of the Rebellion—because that is the official title then given, and still maintained, by the Government of the United States, and because that is the title which best describes it. There are many who use other titles. Some call it the "War between the States." Others, the "Civil War in America." Others, the "War of Secession." Others, the "War for Southern Independence." Others, the "American Conflict." Each of these names ignores the essence and origin of the movement and describes it by an incident. The War was in a sense either of these things, but it was more than either title implies. It was primarily and actually a Rebellion against the lawful authority of the United States. It was an overt refusal to abide by the result of a peaceful election of President lawfully, honestly and constitutionally made; and it was a final taking up of arms to make effective such refusal to abide by such result. And that is the primal, actual and controlling fact which marks and makes its distinctive character as a historical event.

The immediate occasion of it was the election in 1860 by the people of the United States, in the constitutional method, of a candidate for the Presidency whom its participants regarded as objectionable. His name was Abraham Lincoln. He was largely a minority President on the popular vote; and his election was effected solely by reason of the division existing among his opponents—a division which was instigated by the Secessionists of the South with a view to produce the result reached. The open movement began the day after that result was ascertained. This was in South Carolina. It was carried forward with such heat and excitement and terrorism that, by the 4th of February following—only three months after the election—a Congress representing seven States, and claiming to represent the people of those seven States, and hostile to the authority of the United States, was met within the territory of the United States under a Constitution adopted in usurpation of the rights of the people of the United States; and by the 18th of February, a President and Vice-President were chosen and inaugurated within the territory of the United States who had sworn fidelity to the Constitution of the "Confederate States of America." All this occurred *before* the newly-elected and objectionable President and Vice-President were inducted into office, and *while* the old President and the old Vice-President, for whom these seceding States had all voted, were yet exercising the high functions of their offices. The movement of Secession was then and there begun, in order to divide this one country of our fathers and ourselves into two countries; and those who made that movement were, and their apologists are unable to this day, to point, for its justification, to a single established right which had been destroyed by the Union, or to a grievous injury which had been inflicted by the Union, or to a means of redress for any fancied grievance which had been asked of, and refused by, the Union. So unreal and so undefined were the "grievances" which were made the pretext for Secession, that one of the most distinguished members of the Secession Convention of South Carolina, in December, 1860, in expressing his want of approval of the reasons given in the papers reported to the Convention, expressed the opinion that if every one of the one hundred and fifty-two members of the Convention should draw up an indictment against the people of the "unfaithful" States, probably "no two would be very nearly alike." No abandonment of a Government by its people was ever before asked on so flimsy and baseless pretexts, and none was ever pressed by its leaders with such indifference to the vast and far-reaching consequences involved in their reckless action.

MR. LINCOLN'S INAUGURAL STATEMENTS AND PROMISES.

President Lincoln was thus confronted, upon his inauguration on March 4, 1861, with a frowning and hostile and completed organization which demanded of him recognition of its independence, and surrender by him to it of all the forts, arsenals and property of the Union which lay within the seceded territory. In what spirit did President Lincoln meet this extraordinary proposition? He assured the whole country that the property, peace, and security of no section are to be *in anywise endangered* by the now incoming administration. He proclaimed that "all protection which, consistently with the Constitution and the laws, can be given, will be cheerfully given to all the States when lawfully demanded, for whatever cause—*as cheerfully to one section as to another.*" He declared a purpose to execute faithfully in all the States the laws of the Union, but that in doing this there need be no bloodshed or violence; and he added: "THERE SHALL BE NONE, UNLESS IT BE FORCED UPON THE NATIONAL AUTHORITY." He declared that the "Chief Magistrate derives all his authority from the people, and THEY HAVE CONFERRED NONE UPON HIM TO FIX THE TERMS FOR THE SEPARATION OF THE STATES. The people themselves can do this also if they choose; but the Executive, as such, has nothing to do with it—his duty "being to administer the present government, as it came to his hands, and to transmit it, unimpaired by him, to his successor." He asked his countrymen to "think calmly and *well* upon this whole subject," and he pleaded that no step be taken which is not *deliberately* taken. He closed his Inaugural with these touching paragraphs:

"In *your* hands, my dissatisfied fellow-countrymen, and not in *mine* is the momentous issue of Civil War. The Government will not assail *you*. *You* can have no conflict without being yourselves the aggressors. *You* have no oath registered in Heaven to destroy the Government, while I shall have the most solemn one to 'preserve, protect and defend it.'

"I am loth to close. We are not enemies, but friends. We must not be enemies. Though passion may have strained, it must not break our bonds of affection. The mystic chords of memory, stretching from every battlefield and patriot grave to every living heart and hearth-stone, all over this broad land, will yet swell the chorus of the Union, when again touched, as surely they will be, by the better angels of our nature."

I heard every word of that incomparable Inaugural, as it fell from Mr. Lincoln's lips. It moistened every eye, touched every heart, and softened every soul of those who heard it—save the eyes, and hearts and souls of certain embittered Senators and Representatives of the South, yet loitering around the Capitol, whose curling lips and sneering faces gave token, as they listened to these tender words, of their traitorous purpose to make sure that the blow then threatened should descend upon the brow of a patient, much-enduring, and magnanimous Nation. Quickly these conspirators sped southward to "fire the hearts" of their co-workers already at Charleston and Montgomery and to undo, as quickly as possible, the effect upon the Southern people of this touching appeal of the new President of the Union. These words, as far as permitted to be known, had had a powerful effect. They had checked the work of disintegration, and had even imperiled the permanency of the disintegration already wrought.

HOW THEY WERE ANSWERED.

There is cotemporary record among themselves that what the conspirators called a "fatal apathy" was at that time settling upon the Southern country. That was simply the "sober second thought" of the people asserting itself—that "sober second thought" which can always be relied upon, if not disturbed, to recall the hasty and to correct the imprudent in public action. Its presence was a menace to the conspirators. How to break this "apathy" was the problem. How to revive excitement and stir up prejudice so as to force forward the work of destruction and to draw the Border States—and especially Virginia, their pivot—into the yawning gulf of Secession, was the difficult point for solution in the early days of April, 1861, at Montgomery, the Capital of the Confederacy. Pressure was determined to be brought by the conspirators. Mass meetings for tempestuous oratory were resorted to at important points. We have record of some of these demonstrations and proof of their quality, and we can readily recall the objective point at which they aimed. The Convention of Virginia was in session and had been since February. It had not affirmatively acted. It was sluggish about plunging into the abyss. The conspirators determined to dragoon it into passing an Ordinance of Secession, for with that done the other Border States south of the Potomac must needs follow. A Committee of that body had been sent under thin disguises to entrap into imprudence President Abraham Lincoln, not yet known as among the most astute of human beings, in order that thereby the predetermined policy of Disunion might be promoted. But the Committee had returned foiled and disappointed. The leaven of Secession worked slowly. When it became apparent that suasion was ineffectual to loosen Virginia from her moorings, and that force must be used to break the ties which bound it to the Union it had largely helped to administer, a distinct appeal for force was made to the Confederate Government—which being given, the carnival of death and desolation began.

The mass meeting in Charleston, S. C., was the most significant or these demonstrations. Its main speaker was Roger A. Pryor, then lately a Representative from the State of Virginia in the Congress of the United States. He had gone thence on the missionary work of dragging his native State from its high position into participation in the meanest movement of history. His soul was a-fire with this work, into which he threw all the ardor of his impetuous nature. He fervently thanked the people of South Carolina that they had "at last annihilated this accursed Union;" that at last it had been "blasted and riven by the lightning wrath of an outraged and indignant people;" and that "like Lucifer, son of the morning, it had fallen, never to rise again." He besought them to give no countenance to the idea of "reconstruction," then whispered in Virginia. He predicted that Virginia will be a member of the Southern Confederation. And he added these words: "And I will tell you, gentlemen, what will put her in the Southern Confederation in less than an hour by Shrewsbury clock—STRIKE A BLOW! [Tremendous applause.] The very moment that *blood is shed*, old Virginia will make common cause with her sisters of the South. It is impossible she should do otherwise." This was on the 10th of April, 1891. We have also record evidence, that on the 11th of April, there was a Confederate Conference at Montgomery, Alabama. in which the subject of discussion was the "propriety of immediately opening fire on Fort Sumter." There were differences of opinion. The calmer and cooler of the conspirators shrank from the awful responsibility, and the Conference hesitated. Finally one of the participants, an official of the State of Alabama, said: "Unless you sprinkle blood in the face of the people of Alabama they will be back in the old Union in less than ten days." These appeals were conclusive. Davis and his colleagues were nerved to the necessary point of reckless daring. And on the next day, April 12, the "blow" demanded by Pryor "was struck;" fire was opened on Sumter; "the blood" called for by Gilchrist was sprinkled or attempted to be sprinkled in the face of the whole people; the Border States were entrapped; Ordinances of Secession were quickly passed—all of them in secret session and practically without recourse to popular approval by vote; military leagues with the Confederacy were immediately made which bound them in iron chains to the cause of Secession; and War was quickly flagrant along our entire frontier. All this is simple history, but it is history which is little known to many, which has been forgotten by more, and which has been much blurred over, and much misrepresented, by those who desire that it be entirely forgotten. But the World cannot permit it to be forgotten, because it goes to the very root in determining how and why the War of the Rebellion actually came.

All of the active participants in this critical and controlling movement, which actually made the War, are dead—save one, Mr. Pryor. He has recently re-appeared in public life, having been last fall elected—such is the unexampled generosity of the North—a Judge of the Common Pleas Court of the City of New York where, with a salary of $15,000 a year, he can peacefully spend his remaining days passing upon the dearest rights of person, property and life of the citizens of the commercial metropolis of the "accursed Union" of his former fiery denunciation.

WHAT THIS LAST SUCCESSFUL ACT IN THE CONSPIRACY INVOLVED.

The bombardment of Fort Sumter began on the 12th of April, in 1861, In thirty-four hours it was silenced and surrendered and its flag was lowered to the Confederate enemy. On the 15th of April, President Lincoln asked the people, by virtue of the authority of a law, passed in 1795 and approved by Washington, to give him 75,000 of their militia in order to enable him to "suppress unlawful combinations in certain States and duly to execute the laws of the Union."

The War was thus begun, as then announced, by the authority and order of the "Government of the Confederate States." Nothing can blot out that fact. Nothing can unwrite that history. Nothing can change that responsibility. That was the act which decreed death to five hundred thousand young and vigorous lives, and to wounds and life-long suffering five hundred thousand more; which blighted the lives of five millions more as wives, sisters, brothers, parents and children; which wasted four thousand millions of money; which imposed a vast debt of nearly three thousand millions of dollars on the people of the Union, to say nothing of the nearly two thousand millions of Confederate debt never payable or paid; which still demands from the people, for current expenses due to the Rebellion, the large sum of one hundred and eighty-five millions a year, being about a half million of dollars every day, and will still further demand the payment of nearly six hundred millions of funded debt still unpaid; but out of which vast sum of misery and waste have come, as partial compensation for them, the removal of the guilty cause of all this woe, the elevation to, and the inclusion within, the widened borders of our American citizenship of all that multitude of wronged and robbed humanity whose perpetual debasement was the chief object of the Confederacy, and the final placing of our popular institutions, actually as well as theoretically, on the foundation-rock of the EQUAL RIGHTS OF ALL MEN.

WHAT INSPIRED THE SOUTH?

What inspired the South to lift up arms against the Union which had always blessed and never harmed it? What was the interest which absorbed and destroyed love of Union? What was the power which, in a few months' time, violently drew the people of the seceding States into the position of rebels against the authority of that Union whose policy they had for eighty years chiefly controlled, to the steady furtherance of their ambitions? Whose was the call that almost in a night produced such an alliance between States as the Constitution expressly forbids, and which put them in the false position of refusing to be bound by the result of a fair election to which they were voluntary and active parties? Who and what was the despot which demanded the sacrifice at once of patriotism and of political honor? There can be but one answer to these questions. All the world saw and knew the power when those events were transpiring. And the Vice-President of the Confederacy in March, 1861, in expounding the new Constitution, exultingly eulogized it as the first government ever instituted among men which was based upon the principle of "African Slavery" as its corner-stone—a stone rejected by the old builders in 1787, but accepted as the "chief stone of the corner" by the new builders of 1861. The safety of Slavery was thus the motive-power which brought into being the Southern Confederacy; and the permanency of Slavery was the inspiration which nerved that people to meet with patient endurance the disasters which ultimately pressed them to the earth. I would not recall these facts to-day, but for the concerted effort in progress on many hands—in books, in magazines, in lectures, in newspapers—to becloud the issue as then plainly and acutely made, to pervert the positions then deliberately assumed, to blot out the admissions and the boasts then publicly made, to falsely state the history of those great events, and to pretend that instead of fighting for the perpetuation of slavery they were really fighting for "civil liberty." Civil liberty, indeed! It is sufficient to say, in reply to this absurd pretence, that if they fought *for* "civil liberty" with the United States fighting *against* "civil liberty" and they were beaten, why is "civil liberty" not as dead in America as the Rebellion is? But the principles of "civil liberty" have never been so widely operative in America as since the overthrow of the Rebellion, and they have never had so complete possession of the American mind and heart as since the surrender of General Lee.

But the "Border States" Confederates make the special defence that they espoused the cause of the Confederates only after President Lincoln had ruthlessly and unconstitutionally taken away the right of trial by jury and the privilege of the writ of *habeas corpus*, and that they supported the Confederacy, not in the interest of Human Slavery but in order to vindicate those ancient and priceless rights. This plea is rhetoric, not history. Cold dates make its overthrow complete. When did Virginia, the leading Border State, and whose action powerfully influenced the others, with its Convention in session watching and waiting, join the Confederacy? On the 9th of April, by a vote of 128 to 20, it recognized the Independence of the seceding States. This was before the attack on Sumter. On the 17th of April it passed *in secret session* its Ordinance of Secession—88 to 55. On the 25th of April it made a military league with the Confederate States, gave Jefferson Davis command of her military forces, and gave him all her munitions of war. Now, when did President Lincoln "take away," or try to "take away," or threaten to "take away" trial by jury and the *habeas corpus?* Not a step in the direction of either, and then only on a narrow military line for strictly military purposes and under special limitation, was taken till *after* the last of those dates. So that the statement that Virginia, which was the pivotal and decisive State of the Border States, seceded because Lincoln took away *habeas corpus* and trial by jury is impossible to be true.

This specious but false plea has been made, by high authority, with the clear implication that the Confederate Government was entitled to go into history as the one Government which carried on a long War without interfering with the trial by jury and the *habeas corpus*. But he must be very ignorant of history who does not know that the President of the Confederacy as early as March, 1862, declared the suspension of the writ of *habeas cor-*

pus "in cities threatened with invasion;" that he afterward extended martial law over East Tennessee, and suspended all civil jurisdiction and the writ of *habeas corpus;* and that he issued a like proclamation to apply to certain counties named in Virginia —all in 1862.

All these were under authority of law. But what was the policy of that administration on *habeas corpus* and trial by jury, *before* the Confederate Congress authorized the suspension of both? The East Tennessee case in November, 1861, is the crushing answer. Col. Wood, commanding the post at Knoxville, reported the arrest of Judge Patterson, State Senator Pickens, several members of the legislature of Tennessee and others of influence and some distinction in their counties. These persons were not found in arms. They were civilians, some of them public officials, but "their actions and words" were said to have been "hostile to the Confederate cause." Col. Wood said it will be a mere farce to arrest them and then turn them over to courts, for it will be "next to an impossibility to convict them." Some were confined in jail in Knoxville; others were sent to Nashville. Colonel Wood asked instructions from the Confederate Secretary of War, Judah P. Benjamin, then lately a U. S. Senator. What was Secretary Benjamin's reply, no doubt under instructions from the President of the Confederacy? 1st. *All* the prisoners are to be treated as prisoners of War. That removed all of them from the protection of civil law; and put them all under military law. 2d. All such as can be identified as having been engaged in bridge-burning are to be tried summarily *by drum-head court-martial*, and, if found guilty, *executed on the spot by hanging*. The Secretary then interprets the spirit of his order by adding the cold words: "It would be well to leave their bodies hanging in the vicinity of the burnt bridges." This was done, and Confederate regard for trial by jury and *habeas corpus* received an incontestable and imperishable illustration. This was in November, 1861—only six months after the opening of hostilities. So that while "Border States" Confederates were in arms in order to protect "civil liberty" in its two great rights—that of trial by jury and of the writ of *habeas cor-*

pus—the administration for which they were exposing their persons was busy in breaking down both these rights in a spirit of blood-thirstiness, and in the exercise of executive authority alone.

Nor is this all. These inventors of ingenious but untenable theories ought to know the facts that, as late as the Spring of 1865, only three months before the collapse of the Confederacy, their Congress passed a wider act, to suspend the writ of *habeas corpus* in *all* cases of arrest by order of the President, the Secretary of War or the general officer commanding the Trans-Mississippi Military Department. So that, from first to last, the Confederate Government regarded both these great rights as proper to be subordinated to the necessities of the military campaign and not at all as entitled to dominate its policies or to illustrate its record.

WHAT INSPIRED THE NORTH?

What was it that brought the North to the defence of the flag? The North fought for no local interest. Its many thousands took up arms to preserve the Union, not only in the interests of themselves and their children, but as well of the Confederate people and their children, as the one governmental institution whose continued life was of supreme importance to all mankind. The North fought that the great race which inhabit the territory of the Union might continue to have a fitting home, *under one Constitutional Government*, for themselves and their posterity—that this great buttress created by our fathers for the protection of human rights might not be overthrown—that this bright light for the nations then and now resting under the shadow of despotism should not be put out—and that the American Nation might not be lost but might be permitted to fulfill its mission of might and majesty, of beneficence and glory.

SECESSION DESCRIBED.

The act of Secession was an act of political insanity. It had its root in love of the profitableness of Slavery, and its nourishment in hatred and jealousy of the free, growing North.

It was carried on in mad haste, precluding calmness of either thought or action. It was excited by the use of means which terrorized public sentiment and compelled acquiescence in its methods and purposes. In its progress it violated every duty of patriotism, every impulse of prudence, every instinct of conservatism. It was rash, violent, and senselessly destructive. It scorned every suggestion of deliberation. It angrily and causelessly threw away for its "peculiar institution" the security furnished by an established Government in whose recesses it was entrenched, and it put every interest of that people on the perilous edge of battle. It made a desperate but always a losing fight. It took up arms with keen avidity. It laid them down in deep despair. It organized itself for the perpetuation and extension of the principle and practice of Slavery. And as it surrendered it found its Slaves almost in the act of becoming equally entitled with themselves to the privileges, powers and rights of American citizenship. No greater overthrow was ever recorded. None was ever more thoroughly deserved. And the Power which had demanded blood for its preservation was itself dissolved by the dripping blood which it drew from the oozing veins of the soldiers of the Union.

UNIONISM VINDICATED.

No public event has ever been so vindicated by time as the resistance made by the North to the attempted dissolution of 1861. Even those who then, in infatuation, blindly and bravely fought against us have, most of them, come to acknowledge that in their defeat they have gained as much as we have gained in our victory. The Nation has received a new birth, and a new baptism. The fierce fires of War have consumed the dross which had come down to us from the Revolutionary period, and the Republic stands purified of the only taint which weakened its blood and threatened to wreck its life. For all which, let the present generation render thanks to the heroic men who unflinchingly met this issue, who bravely bore all its perils, and who under every trial and discouragement fought it out to final and complete victory.

ADAMS COUNTY'S SHARE IN THE GLORY.

The part taken by the soldiers of Adams County in this achievement was most honorable. President Lincoln's call for troops was issued on the 15th of April, 1861. News of it reached Gettysburg before noon on the 16th. The afternoon train carried to Harrisburg an honored soldier, yet living, who tendered to the Governor a company of soldiers for immediate duty. The tender was accepted that evening. On the 20th the company was mustered into service at York—among the first to leap to the defence of the flag. Others quickly followed, until thirty-one companies, being parts of twenty-three different regiments, making a total of about three thousand men, make the splendid contribution to the cause of the Union from a county whose voting population in 1860 was less than 5,500. Thus, more than one-half the adult male population, and probably three-fourths of the arms-bearing population, of this county were in the Army. The names of those who died in service are inscribed on this Monument. The names of those who live are inscribed on the enduring records of the Republic, to be perpetually preserved, to be forever honored among men—not merely as faithful soldiers but as faithful soldiers in a cause which has stood the test and scrutiny of time and is approved by the matured judgment of mankind. These gallant soldiers were upon nearly every important battlefield of the War. They were part of the legions who faced death at Mechanicsville, at Gaines' Mill, at Charles City Cross-Roads, at Fredericksburg, at South Mountain, at Antietam, at Cold Harbor, at Suffolk, at Shiloh, at Swift Creek, at Harper's Ferry, at Winchester, at Monocacy, at Fair Oaks, in the Wilderness, at Fort Steadman, at Spottsylvania, at North Anna, at Weldon railroad, at Stone River, in the Chickamauga Campaign. They were in the Wheatfield at Gettysburg, and were on duty when the Army of the Potomac reached the field of Appomattox. And our 21st Pennsylvania Cavalry made the last charge which was made in the Army of the Potomac.

They were in quick skirmish, in keen scout, in weary siege, in dreary hospital, in exposed line, in deadly charge. They stood at the mouths of belching cannon, within range of merciless rifle, at the edge of the piercing bayonet, in sweep of sharp saber, in face of breast-works. They marched on solid ground and in morass, over open country, and in thicket, through creeks, bayous and rivers. They waited for death over exploding mines. They were for days foodless, for nights shelterless, resting as and how they could. They languished in prison-pens. They endured everything and dared everything which a brave soldier could endure and dare that the honor of their flag should be vindicated and their country remain undivided, to become, as it already has become, the MASTER-POWER AMONG THE NATIONS. The soldiers were the final power that saved their country from its deep imperilment, and that country, posterity and the World of righteousness owe him more than can ever be repaid him, however great the payment.

The dead whose names are upon this Monument are 178. They were among our bravest and best. A country's love enshrines them. The veneration of a saved Nation will keep their memory green through the endless cycles of time, while there beats a heart for human liberty, while there ascends to Heaven a prayer for the progress of the human race.

In closing, let me remark upon the brilliant military record of this region. While a frontier settlement, and known as the Marsh Creek Settlement, its hardy pioneers were an out-post who freely plunged through forests and rivers and over mountains and valleys to thwart the wily savages and their French allies. As early as 1755 they were at the Great Cove caring for the settlers who had escaped the torch and tomahawk. In 1756 they were at the important capture of the Indian town of Kittanning, and at Wyoming where trouble was already brewing. In 1758, they were the division of honor in the Forbes Expedition against Fort Duquesne, and intermediately they were at Forts Lyttleton and Bedford and elsewhere. In 1775, they marched immediately after Bunker Hill to the help of the colonists of Massachusetts; and thereafter were at Long Island, at Trenton, at Monmouth, at Princeton, at Paoli, at Valley Forge, and whithersoever their country called. In 1814, they were at

Fort Erie, at Chippewa, at Bridgewater or Lundy's Lane on the Canada side of the line, and at Baltimore in defence of their own firesides, And it is an interesting fact that the rendezvous of the Adams county contingent who marched to Canada was but a few feet from the spot on which I now stand. In the Mexican War, they were at Palo Alto, Resaca de la Palma, Monterey and Buena Vista. During the War of the Rebellion they counted no service beyond their desire to supply.

OUR HEROIC DEAD.

Our heroic dead, who died that their country might live, wherever they may be lying—whether in trench or grave, whether shroudless or shrouded, whether their resting-places are known or unknown, marked or unmarked—are there lying on "Fame's Eternal Camping Ground," fairly theirs by service and by suffering. There we tenderly leave them, sweetly sleeping, watched over by angels and venerated by comrades—enshrined in the gratitude of a saved and glorified Nation.

From Prof. H. C. Adams
Oct. 1892

AN ADDRESS

— DELIVERED —

At Orange, N. J., Decoration Day, 1884,

BY A. F. MATTHEWS.

May thirtieth, eighteen hundred and eighty-four! For a day money-getting and money-spending stop. The doors of industry are closed; the gates of a thousand cemeteries open. Processions of sad and thoughtful men, of gay and happy children enter their portals and slowly gather about familiar graves. A tender prayer; a bitter tear; a bright garland; a loving word; an echoing volley, and the day is done. What means it all? A holiday is ended. Strange holiday words are touching prayers and feeling eulogies; strange holiday sounds are muffled drums and mournful dirges; strange holiday sights are falling tears and flower-covered graves. Yet, are they strange? Truly they would be strange in other lands. Not so here, for these words, these sounds, these sights are tributes—yet more than tributes—to dead and living heroes. They are symbols of the triumph of democratic progress. No other land, no other time, ever commemorated day like this, for it is Decoration Day, a day when the hallowed graves of patriot soldiers are strewn with wreaths of love—wreaths woven from the blossoms of democracy, the fairest flower of civilization.

Small need therefore, one might think, to ask the lesson of this day; small need to ask the veterans, the widows, the aged parents. Eighteen hundred and sixty, its call to arms, the quick response, the field, the dying, the defeat, the victory; eighteen hundred and eighty-four, the empty sleeve, the decorated grave—all tell with voice more eloquent than words of orator or poet, what this day means to veteran, to widow and to parent. For whom then is the lesson? For whom? A single glance will tell. A new generation has come upon the stage, and the lesson is for them. No part in the struggle did they bear, and only indirectly have they suffered. Little do they realize the cost of those fearful times. The war was fought when they were children. To them the soldier's cap, the soldier's sword were but playthings for a passing hour. In the mad rush of developing industry they have since grown up. Few of them know the history of the struggle, fewer know its teaching. Fit is it then, that the young should reverently draw near these graves to hear the lesson their dumb voices speak. And this above all is the mission of the day—to instruct the young—the vigorous new element, now entering our national life. These flowers, these songs, honor the living who reverently bring them, far more than the heroes they commemorate. The dead have no need of Decoration Day. It is for the living, especially for the young, and no nobler spectacle in this or other lands was ever seen, than a grateful people, leaving the noisy strife of daily toil, and gathering in the peaceful quiet of ten thousand grave-yards, where standing with uncovered heads in silence they may hear the simple message of these venerated sods.

What then do these graves say? What word would their peaceful inmates voice, could they speak? What word do they speak? To the old they speak of finished work and point with comfort to the glories of the future. For the middle-aged, beset with care, their word is that of soft encouragement; but upon the young they lay a strong injunction. The command is simple: *Continue the work we did not finish.* With enquiring look the young men suddenly start. What! is not the war over? Is not slavery dead? Is there not some mistake? Once more they bow their head, and once more they hear a simple message: Yes, the war is over; yes, slavery is dead. These we destroyed, these we obliterated forever. Yours it is to continue the work; be faithful, be loyal, be true. Here then we are face to face with the meaning of this day. The United States have not yet fulfilled their high destiny. Much remains to be done, and who but the young shall do it. Seen in this light—the ultimate realization of our country's possibilities—we may fully realize that far more than the obliteration of pernicious theories of government, far more than the destruction of slavery, did our heroes accomplish. They worked for the future. They were the successors of the patriots of two hundred years, all laboring toward one end—their country's ultimate good.

If there is one thing above all others which history teaches it is this: that all the hates, all the conspiracies, all the wars of men, free agents though they be, are but instruments in the hands of an unseen force—call it what you will, fate, destiny, or providence,—toward one mighty end, the ultimate emancipation and elevation of the individual, the gradual uplifting of the weak and down-trodden, the awarding to every man a man's dignity, a man's rights, a man's manhood. For as the poet truly says, "thro' the ages one increasing purpose runs." Thus we see our heroes' work was but a step in the progress of civilization, a progress not yet complete, and one in which we who remain, especially the young, must bear a share.

If evidence is needed that this is history's teaching, turn to fifteen hundred and twenty-five. In the South of Germany, in Swabia and Franconia, the peasants, stung to madness by oppression, make one more tremendous effort to throw off the yoke of serfdom. Class presses upon class, the higher upon the lower, until at last, the whole burden of society falls upon the serf. He can endure it no longer. With the sad fate of thousands of his predecessors to warn him, once more he takes his chances. For years in the name of simple justice, he has asked that his burdens be lightened. No impudent demand he makes for high privilege, for political rights, or for liberty. All he asks is bread, and a little release from the fearful toil which is crushing out his very soul. His prayer is spurned. With uplifted eye he turns to Heaven, and as he prays, he hears a sound. For over the land the angel of religious liberty has passed, and beneath the protection of her rustling wings Luther leads a mighty army. Now is his opportunity. The spirit of freedom is abroad. Quck as lightning flash he starts. Wild fanatics are his leaders. No mottoes of religious liberty are inscribed upon his banners. His creed is civil liberty and revenge. What has he to do with church? He wants bread, he wants life. The wrongs of centuries pulse through his veins. A madman he becomes. He burns, he robs, he murders. Women's prayers, women's tears will not stay him. Will he be successful? Ah, no! for see the trained legions of the sleeping nobility are aroused, and amid the dying groans of an hundred thousand heroes, the serf's sun of liberty goes down for centuries.

No longer look upon that awful scene of misery and despair. Turn the pages of history forward three hundred years, and behold what wonder meets our gaze? It is eighteen hundred and twenty-five, and from the bosom of the ocean has sprung America—the marvel of the ages. Peace and prosperity are within her borders. The white sails of her swift-going commerce—every shroud an emblem of democracy—far outstrip her rivals. French decrees and British council orders no longer paralyze her industries, for by a second war with England, and now for the first time, she has really established her independence, and taken her place as a leading power in the great family of nations. In the impulses of her teeming youth there seems nothing to stay her high hopes. For behold her people! All men are free and equal. There is no caste; no standing army saps their life, or threatens their liberties. In the security of his rights the honest toiler eats of the fruits of his own labor. There is no king; the people rule.

What a contrast! The sixteenth century and the nineteenth! Germany, mournful with the groans of despairing serfdom; America, exultant with the smiles of glad freedom! Yes, truly, the exaltation of the individual is the lesson of history, and the ultimate goal of human achievement. And now in eighteen hundred and twenty-five it seems as if this end had come, for here and now all men enjoy the privileges and pleasures of liberty, equality, and fraternity. But hold! Not so, for on this bright picture is a fearful spot—slavery. The cotton gin has been invented, and the South at first as eager as the North—nay, more so—to destroy the evil, now finds slavery essential to her political and material prosperity. In easy going idleness she nestles this viper in her bosom. Thus two opposing systems of labor sprang up in this country—the free labor of the North, and the slave labor of the South. So antagonistic are they that in the same country they cannot live. They begin a struggle of life and death. Which shall go down? Compromise upon compromise mark the history of the fearful conflict. At last, Henry Clay, seeing the inevitable result with a statesman's prophetic eye, rises in the Senate Chamber and proposes to buy the slaves, and thus avert the struggle. He fails, and soon the slowly gathering storm-clouds, "the result of the pride and jealousy of seventy years" burst with awful fury upon the land. "All is shrouded in darkness, resonant with thunder-peal, broken by lurid lightning flash." But why dwell on it further? The completed history of the struggle is written upon the tombstones about which to-day we gather.

Quickly, as of old, the regenerated nation rises, and through her falling tears soon the shining sun of peace arches a rainbow of prosperity. High in the vault of heaven, and against the black clouds of the receding storm it rests, stretching its radiant span over golden harvest fields, whirling spindles, flaming forges, happy homes, from the Atlantic to the Pacific. And now comes the completion of the republic's century. With one accord about the hoary State House in Philadelphia, the nation gathers. "Cheer upon cheer greets the ancient scroll of independence." Surely, now on this glad anniversary day we have reached our goal. Slavery is dead, and the individual is emancipated.

Would indeed that it were so, but once more we are too fast. Scarcely does the vast throng reach its million homes, before the lurid flames of fearful riots, the result of wide-spread discontent, light up the land. From that day to this they have occurred, and here in the real cause of these disturbances, we are face to face with our greatest danger. To peacefully settle this and other momentous questions, as one by one they come, our dead soldiers make imperative demand. Let us, therefore, to-day look fearlessly at a few of these practical problems and mark well their bearings.

Would that we might attribute the unrest and dissatisfaction of the so-called working classes of our country, which finds expression in riots and strikes, to the leadship of unscrupulous demagogues, or to the unfortunate ignorance of these men themselves, for then the danger might be averted by education. Unfortunately, it is not so ; far deeper lies the cause. Through the introduction of steam—that new force—into society, for nearly a century, we have bent our energies mainly toward one thing, money making. And we have made it, but as the years have passed it has become concentrated in the hands of the few. Thus the tendency of the times is for the rich to become richer, and the poor poorer. This is the greatest evil our country can encounter and herein is the real cause of the unrest. This is not the time nor place to take sides in the capital and labor conflict. Whatever views one may privately hold, all agree that there is a conflict, and the point to-day is, to recognize the fact that the conflict is a danger, leaving it to older and wiser heads to suggest the remedies. In the opinion of many thinkers this conflict has arisen in this way : Labor-saving machinery has not saved the labor of the workman. To-day he produces twice as much as of old, and yet to get a competence his hours of labor are not materially shortened. Through the wonderful division of labor he no longer learns a trade ; he must learn a branch. In times of commercial depression, thrown out of employment, he can find no work, for as a rule he can do but one thing. In times of commercial prosperity he sees money which in a fair division should be his in increased wages, go to pay dividends upon watered-stock and fictitious securities. In both cases he is dissatisfied. Heretofore our public lands have been the country's safety-valve. With these in easy reach, the laborer need be no man's slave, for here he has a practical alternative. But in twenty-five years these lands will all be gone, and how then shall we solve this problem of antagonizing classes? That it is a danger who can doubt? Already the workmen have found that if they would live as befits a man, they must fight capital with capital, and to this end in trades-unions and other associations they are capitalizing their labor—an evil, but a necessary one. Thus we may see that our danger lies where at first we would least expect it, in our industrial prosperity. And why? Because to get his living the workman must thwart what we have already seen is the course and goal of history; *he must surrender his individuality* to some society which shall tell him when he may and when he may not work. Unless he does this he must become a slave to capital. They have the ballot, did I hear someone say? Yes, but when a mighty railway or other corporations can in our day—as they do—compel their employees to surrender their franchises for the bread they get in return, what will be the case when the public lands are gone? Ballot indeed—a hollow mockery! It is the boast of many of our constitutional expounders, that our forefathers founded a country which for all time should be free from class distinctions. They forget that since those patriots framed that grand bill of human rights in Philadelphia, a revolution in industries which could not be foreseen, much less predicted, has entirely changed the relations of society. In the development of this revolution a daily increasing gap exists between capital and labor, one which the laborer cannot cross. The child has outgrown the mother and now threatens her. If we would continue the work our soldiers began we must avert this unnatural conflict. For we must remember that if there was any one thing for which the Boys in Blue fought, bled, and died, it was that there should be no more slavery of any kind throughout the land, and that every man should have full enjoyment of his individuality which next to Calvary, is God's greatest gift to man. Therefore, we must remember that workmen are something more than mere hands. They are men, and any system of industry which in any way restricts a man's manhood is fraught with fearful danger to a republic whose highest boast is universal suffrage. By early preparation now while there is time, by wise coöperation, by thorough consideration for mutual rights, we may avert this peril. Already wise measures have begun to prevail, but these must be carried further if we would preserve the sacred trust committed to our charge.

Again, if we would honor our dead we must look to the further purification of our civil service. The nation has not yet forgotten, nor will it soon forget, its tears and sobs three years ago, over a President murdered by a shot which woke the country to the fact that it was far more important that its offices should be conducted on business principles, than that any one man, or any one set of men should parcel them out as a reward for party services, often most corrupt and shocking. Much has been done already in this purification, but it should be carried further, and where it is most needed—to our states and cities. In the opinion of our foremost thinkers, the time is soon coming when the nation can no longer allow an institution so necessary to its welfare as the telegraph, and possibly the railways, to remain in the hands of private parties. As in the case of the postal system, so in these will the government assume control. Until, however, we have a civil service pure and thorough, this can never be accomplished. Offices do not exist that some favored individual may revel in the milk and honey of swindling jobbery, the people paying for it all in exorbitant fees and increased taxation. Rather offices are for a single and simple end, the proper and economical administration of just government. They are for the benefit of the people only.

Were I standing before an audience in any other State than this, I might well point out the danger to this country from the repeated maladministration of justice. New Jersey, thank Heaven, whatever her faults may be, has one virtue of which few of her sister states may boast—a temple of justice, pure and undefiled, and one across whose threshold no money-changer has ever dared to step. Not so in all our other states, for the Cincinnati riots tell a story about whose meaning there can be no mistake.

Great need is there also of municipal reform. The crying evil of our government of cities is that national politics enter into it. Unless a man believes in certain party principles, he is unfit to patrol our streets or gather our garbage. The truth is a city should be entirely free from national politics. A city is nothing more than a colossal corporation, whose charter granted by the state, can at any time be taken away by the state. A city really has nothing to do with the general government, or issues that obtain in general government. It is a large family, and all alike are interested in economical administration. Because one national party believes in free trade and another in protection, that is no reason of itself, why either should be put in charge of the affairs of a municipality. What a city needs is servants who will do its work best, without regard to national politics. We want a policeman who will guard our homes, not one who believes in free trade or protection, as the case may be. Had this truth of complete divorce of municipal affairs from national politics been recognized earlier, the debt of New York city to-day, would not be, as it is, greater than that of all the cities of England combined, and New Jersey would not be compelled to hang her head in shame at the reproach of her defaulting cities. All these and many other reforms must be accomplished if we would interpret aright the meaning of this day. This is the work our soldiers began; this is the work they call upon us to finish. The time will soon come when the survivors of the war will have passed away; all the more reason then for the observance of this day, not only that past heroes may be remembered, but also that the rising generations, as one by one they come, may learn the duty of preserving that for which their forefathers died.

It is recorded in mediaeval history, that the prosperous republic of Florence, proud of her institutions, and rejoicing in the glory of her strength, decreed that a mighty cathedral, greater than the world ever saw—should be built, commemorative of her gratitude to God for her prosperity. And so the towering structure, strongly buttressed, well-arched and pinnacled, daily grew, till it lacked nothing but the dome. Then suddenly its architect and builder died. For more than a century no one could be found to complete the work. Finally, Brunelleschi came forward to place the mighty cap upon the mightier structure. Amid sneers and jibes, patiently he labored, and well he might, for in the end success crowned his labors, and at last, full-topped in rounding beauty and swelling strength, the massive dome stood forth, a source of pride to Florence, to Italy, and to all lovers of art from that day to this.

And so here in America, for more than a century a mighty nation has been building a grand temple of constitutional liberty, grander than the world has ever seen, and one which will outlast the ages, a towering memorial of nineteenth century civilization. Year by year it has grown. When for a time its walls seemed to totter and threatened to fall, the young men—a million strong—rushed to the rescue, and so successfully did they stay the impending ruin, that now for twenty years, firm and immovable as a rock, the structure has stood "four-square to all the winds that blow." For it is founded upon eternal truth, buttressed with the lives of patriot soldiers, "over-arched with justice," pinnacled with high hopes and aspirations. Still not yet is it complete; it lacks the dome. To build this as far as we are able is our work. No need to wait a century for the coming of an architect, for the plan drawn in lines so plain that he who runs may read, has been handed down as our birthright of freedom. As the generations come and go, we shall best honor our patriot dead by adding to the completion of this dome; and so, year by year, decade by decade, century by century, shall the temple grow, till at last perfect in matchless symmetry and stately grandeur it shall stand forth complete, the product of the ages, the glad fruition of human toil, and human sacrifice, and human love.

GENERAL MEADE'S LETTER

ON

GETTYSBURG.

PHILADELPHIA:
COLLINS PRINTING HOUSE, 705 JAYNE STREET.
1886.

GENERAL MEADE'S LETTER ON GETTYSBURG.

THE letter of GENERAL MEADE regarding the Battle of Gettysburg, written seven years after the battle, to Colonel G. G. Benedict, of Vermont, and published for the first time by Colonel Benedict, in the "Weekly Press," of Philadelphia, of August 11, 1886, in refutation of the statements made on the battle-field by General Daniel E. Sickles, on the occasion of the reunion, July 2, 1886, of the remnant of the Third Corps of the Army of the Potomac, on the twenty-third anniversary of the battle.

TO THE EDITOR OF THE WEEKLY PRESS, OF PHILADELPHIA.

SIR: A word of explanation of the circumstances which drew forth the following letter seems to be necessary.

In an oration delivered before the Reunion Society of Vermont Officers in November, 1869, the orator, Colonel W. W. Grout, of that State, who had made the acquaintance of General D. E. Sickles, and had adopted the latter's views upon certain points relating to the battle of Gettysburg, advanced the theory—more familiar now than it was then—that General Sickles's famous movement on the second day of the battle was a fortunate step; that it kept General Meade from retreating to Pipe Creek, and that but for Sickles's movements the battle of Gettysburg might never have been fought, and the victory of Gettysburg never won.

In some editorial comments, published in the Burlington (Vt.) 'Free Press,' on the oration, I took up the points thus made. I had had at that time no correspondence with General Meade, nor had I any personal acquaintance either with him or General Sickles, or any prejudice for or against either general. But having witnessed from the brow of Cemetery Hill on that bloody day the movement of General Sickles's corps and some of its consequences, and having made some subsequent study of the battle, I could not accept the orator's conclusions, though presented by a comrade and friend. I protested against this portion of the oration as a distortion of history and an undue exaltation of a corps commander at the expense of the commander of the army; and, by citation of undisputed facts, of orders on the order-books of the Army of the Potomac, and of General Meade's despatches to General Halleck, I showed that General Meade could not have been contemplating on the 2d of July a withdrawal of his army from Gettysburg, unless compelled to withdraw by a movement of the enemy upon his lines of communication; that, on the contrary, his determination to fight, defensively if he could, but offensively rather than not at all, *at Gettysburg*, was clearly demonstrated, and that the fame of General Sickles for conscious or unconscious achievements must rest on something else than the prevention of the retreat of the Army of the Potomac from Gettysburg.

The newspaper articles* containing this view of the subject were subsequently sent to General Meade, who, in acknowledging them, gave the clear, calm, and convincing presentation of his side of the controversy printed below. This has long been held in confidence, as it was written, but, in view of the recent elaborate attack upon General Meade's military reputation, made by General Sickles in his address at Gettysburg, the interests of truth and justice seem to demand that it be given to the public.

Yours truly,

G. G. BENEDICT.

BURLINGTON, VT., August 7, 1886.

* The substance of these editorials in the Burlington 'Free Press' will be found in the appendix to the second edition of Colonel Benedict's admirable little work, 'Vermont at Gettysburg.'—ED. WEEKLY PRESS.

GEN. MEADE'S LETTER.

HEADQUARTERS MILITARY DIVISION OF THE ATLANTIC.
PHILADELPHIA, March 16, 1870.

[PRIVATE.]

G. G. BENEDICT, BURLINGTON, VT.:

DEAR SIR: I am in receipt of your letter of the 13th inst., as also the copies of the 'Free Press,' with editorials and comments on the address of Colonel Grout before the Officers' Society and Legislature of the State.

I have carefully read your articles, and feel personally under great obligations to you for the clear and conclusive manner in which you have vindicated the truth of history. I find nothing to correct in your statement except a fact you mention, which is a misapprehension.

I did not invite General Humphreys to be my chief-of-staff till after the battle, because I did not see him after assuming command till I met him on the field, and besides I relied on him as a mainstay in handling the Third Corps, and did not wish to withdraw him from that position.* I did ask General Williams to assume the duties in addition to those of adjutant-general, but he declined. I also asked General Warren, then my chief of engineers, to act temporarily as chief-of-staff, but he also declined taking on himself additional duties. Under these circumstances I asked General Butterfield to remain till I had time to make permanent arrangements. On the third day, General Butterfield having been disabled by being struck with a fragment of a spent shell, left the army, and a few days afterwards General Humphreys accepted my invitation.

My defence against the charges and insinuations of Generals Sickles and Butterfield is to be found in my testimony before

* General Meade's recollection on this point seems to be slightly at fault. He did see General Humphreys on the morning he assumed command of the Army of the Potomac, at Frederick City, and he at that time expressed his desire of appointing him his chief-of-staff, but after discussion it was agreed between them that this officer could be of greater service by retaining command of his division in the Third Corps during the impending battle.—[*General Humphreys' testimony before Committee on Conduct of War.*]

the Committee on the Conduct of the War. I have avoided any controversy with either of these officers—though both have allowed no opportunity to pass unimproved which permitted them to circulate their *ex parte* statements, and, as you justly say, to *distort* history for their purposes. Both perfectly understand what I meant by my ante-battle order, referring to Pipe Clay Creek, also my instructions to Butterfield on the morning of the 2d, which he persists in calling an order for retreat, in the face of all my other acts, and of the fact that I did not retreat when I could have done so with perfect ease *at any moment.* Longstreet's advice to Lee* was sound military sense; it was the step I feared Lee would take, and to meet which, and be prepared for which was the object of my instructions to Butterfield, which he has so misrepresented. Now, let me tell you another historical fact. Lieutenant-General Ewell, in a conversation held with me shortly after the war, asked what would have been the effect if at 4 P. M. on the 1st he had occupied Culp's Hill and established batteries on it. I told him that in my judgment, in the then condition of the Eleventh and First Corps, with their morale affected by their withdrawal to Cemetery Ridge, with the loss of over half their numbers in killed, wounded, and missing (of the 6000 prisoners we lost in the field nearly all came from these corps in the first day), his occupation of Culp's Hill, with batteries commanding the whole of Cemetery Ridge, would have produced the evacuation of that ridge and the withdrawal of the troops there by the Baltimore Pike and Taneytown and Emmettsburg roads. He then informed me that at 4 P. M. on the 1st he had his corps, 20,000 strong, in column of attack, and on the point of moving on Culp's Hill, which he saw was unoccupied and commanded Cemetery Ridge, when he received an order from General Lee directing him to assume the defensive, and not to advance; that he sent to General Lee urging to be permitted to advance with his reserves, but the reply was a reiteration of the previous order. To my inquiry why Lee had restrained him, he said our troops coming up (Slocum's) were visible, and Lee was under the impression that the greater part of my army was on the ground and deemed it prudential to await the rest of his—as you quote from his report.

* To move from his right upon General Meade's communications.

But suppose Ewell with 20,000 men had occupied Culp's Hill, and our brave soldiers had been compelled to evacuate Cemetery Ridge and withdraw on the roads above referred to, would the Pipe Clay Creek order have been so very much out of place?

That order was to meet the very contingency here in question, to wit: A part of my army, overwhelmed by superior numbers, compelled to fall back, and a line of battle formed to the rear of my most advanced position thus necessitated.

As to General Sickles having by his advance brought on the attack, and thus compelled the battle which decided the war, you have completely answered—and it is a very favorite theory with the partisans of this officer. But these gentlemen ignore the fact that of the 18,000 men killed and wounded on the field during the whole battle, more than two-thirds were lost on the second day, and but for the timely advance of the Fifth Corps, and the prompt sending a portion on Round Top, where they met the enemy almost on the crest and had a desperate fight to secure the position—I say, but for these circumstances, over which Sickles had neither knowledge nor control, the enemy would have secured Round Top, planted his artillery there, commanding the whole battlefield, and what the result would have been I leave you to judge. Now, when I wrote my report of the battle I honestly believed General Sickles did not know where I wished him to go, and that his error arose from a misapprehension of my orders, but I have recently learned from General Geary, who had the day before been sent by Hancock to hold the left, and who in doing so had seen the great importance of Round Top and *posted a brigade on it*, that on the morning of the 2d, when he received my order that he would be relieved by the Third Corps, and on being relieved, would rejoin his own corps (Twelfth) on the right, after waiting for some time to be relieved he sent to General Sickles a staff officer with instructions to explain the position and its importance, and to ask, if troops could not be sent to relieve him, that General Sickles would send one of his staff to see the ground, and to place troops there on their arrival. He received for reply that General Sickles would attend to it in due time. No officer or troops came, and after waiting till his patience was exhausted, General Geary withdrew and joined his corps. Now my first orders to General Sickles were to relieve the Twelfth Corps division (Geary's) and occupy their position. Here is evidence that he knew the position occupied by Geary's division, or could have known, and yet failed to occupy it. Furthermore, when he came to my headquarters at about noon, and said he did not know where to go, I answered, "Why, you were to relieve the Twelfth Corps." He said they had no position; they were massed, awaiting events. Then it was I told him his *right* was to be *Hancock's left*, his *left* on *Round Top*, *which I pointed out.* Now his right was three-quarters of a mile in front of Hancock's left, and his left one-quarter of a mile in front of the base of Round Top, leaving that *key-point unoccupied*, which ought to have been occupied by Longstreet before we could get there with the Fifth Corps. Sickles's movement practically destroyed his own corps, the Third, caused a loss of 50 per cent. in the Fifth Corps, and very heavily damaged the Second Corps; as I said before, producing 66 per cent. of the loss of the whole battle, and with what result—driving us back to the position he was ordered to hold originally. These losses of the first and second day affected greatly the efficiency and morale of the army, and prevented my having the audacity in the offense that I might otherwise have had.

If this is an advantage,—to be so crippled in battle without attaining an object,—I must confess I cannot see it.

Pardon my writing with so much prolixity, but your generous defence and the clear view you have taken of the battle have led me to wander thus far.

Very truly yours,

GEO. G. MEADE.

No. 1.

Papers from the Society for the Diffusion of Political Knowledge.

THE

CONSTITUTION.

ADDRESSES

OF

Prof. MORSE, Mr. GEO. TICKNOR CURTIS, and Mr. S. J. TILDEN,

AT THE ORGANIZATION.

"WHEN A PARTY IN POWER VIOLATES THE CONSTITUTION AND DISREGARDS STATE-RIGHTS, PLAIN MEN READ PAMPHLETS."

READ—DISCUSS—DIFFUSE.

PRESIDENT, PROF. S. F. B. MORSE,
SECRETARY, WM. McMURRAY,
TREASURER, LORING ANDREWS,

OFFICE OF THE SOCIETY,
No. 13 PARK ROW, NEW-YORK
C. MASON, COR. SEC'Y.,
To whom all communications may be addressed.

Resolved, That it be recommended to all citizens in the various cities, counties, and villages of this and other States, who approve of the objects expressed in this Constitution, that they organize auxiliary societies, and open communication with the New-York Society.

ORGANIZATION OF THE SOCIETY

FOR THE

DIFFUSION OF POLITICAL KNOWLEDGE.

On the 6th of February a number of gentlemen met at Delmonico's, to consult on the best means of diffusing correct political knowledge.

On the 13th of February the same gentlemen, with others, reässembled at the same place, to complete the organization of THE SOCIETY FOR THE DIFFUSION OF POLITICAL KNOWLEDGE—the comprehensive objects of which are set forth in the Constitution adopted.

Prof. S. F. B. Morse, who had been chosen President of the Society at a former meeting, took the chair. Upon calling the meeting to order, he spoke briefly as follows:

Speech of Professor Morse.

GENTLEMEN: I can not take the chair this evening, to which you have been pleased in your kindness to call me, without a few words of definition of my position in relation to the movement which we have inaugurated.

Nothing in these days of our country's trial has so saddened the hearts of patriots, and caused such universal misgiving touching the stability and even the existence of our cherished Government, as the constantly recurring evidences of a deep and wide-spread demoralization, pervading the public mind, to which the rostrum, the press, and, I am sorry to add, the pulpit, in a lamentable degree, lend their powerful influence to strengthen and perpetuate. Fanaticism rules the hour. The *fanatic* is on the throne. I use the term fanatic in no loose sense. Fanaticism is a frenzy, a madness. It is not, as it pretends to be, a zeal springing from enlightened reason, founded on the rock of God's word, but a spirit of the pit, clothing itself in our day in the garb of an angel of light, the better to deceive the minds of the unthinking and the simple. Fanaticism has been well defined, "enthusiasm inflamed by hatred," and the truth of the portrait of the foul fiend is exhibited before us every day.

History, ever repeating itself, as time completes its cycles, has not yet closed its sad volume of disastrous hallucinations. It is preparing its pages and reddening its pen to record the story of the foulest tragedy of earth—the most frightful that is yet to deform the annals of the past.

Can patriotic men, persuaded of such an issue, be silent, be idle? There may be those who fold their arms and shut their eyes, and lull their apprehensions with baseless dreams of a future "visionary, impossible Union," a Union begotten of force and fear, not a Union begotten of peace and love; a Union to be created when the South shall be wiped out of existence, and its soil prepared for Northern colonization; when the Southern earth shall be "without form and void," and has become the desolate habitation for the advent of the new Northern man. But there are others who have awakened to the realities of the times. They can not but read the portentous signs of a coming destruction. If the poisonous seeds sown for long years by a proud, God-defying infidelity in France, have shown their natural fruits in the bloody dramas of the Reign of Terror, how can we believe that the same seeds, exotic though we hope them to be, yet now flowering in an artificial atmosphere and in a hotbed made congenial to their rank growth by American infidelity in church and state—how can we believe, I say, that we shall pluck grapes from these thorns, or figs from these thistles?

But what can we do to root out these noxious weeds? We must put machinery in motion adapted to that end. The heresies of the Church must be grappled with by the untainted theologians of the land, for there are thousands of these who have not bowed the knee to the abolition Baal. The heresies of the state can be and must be reached in a constitutional way by the intellects of the country. If I have read the provisions of the Constitution aright, this meeting in its object and its mode of reaching that object, is wholly and completely constitutional. We have, however, been assailed by those whose record and antecedents should not make either the act or the manner of the act surprising to us. We are instructed, however, that charity "rejoiceth not in *iniquity*," and the injunction in this case is salutary, for the temptation is certainly strong to rejoice, rather than to feel indignation at the gross indecency our opponents have thought proper to perpetrate. It is not, indeed, the iniquity of which these libelers have been guilty, and which has drawn down upon them one universal cry of shame from all decent men, that tempts our rejoicing; it is their having given to the public such an unmistakable manifestation of that reckless, unprincipled spirit which is so rife in the ranks of fanaticism, and which it is our own purpose, if possible, to exorcise. True, it is a matter of surprise that the simple, unostentatious, unannounced assemblage of a few gentlemen in a parlor to concert a plan for diffusing knowledge should have been the potent spear of Ithuriel, at once to reveal in proper shape and character, the presence in the community of the demon of fanaticism.

> "Him thus intent, Ithuriel with his spear
> Touched lightly; for no falsehood can endure
> Touch of celestial temper, but returns
> Of force to its own likeness. Up he starts,
> . . . .
> Abashed, the devil stood."

Now we are told from the best authority that the devil is "the father of lies." If falsehoods, therefore, are evidence of his presence or his agency, surely the spawning of *forty-three*, at one incubation, entitles the prolific reporter to preëminent distinction in the ranks of the prince of evils.

We have been charged with disloyalty. Men use words very loosely in these times of excitement. What is disloyalty? It is unfaithfulness to the sovereign. Where is our sovereign? Will it be said that it resides in the powers that be, and these we are commanded not to resist? If there are any associated with us who propose to resist the powers that be, I have not been acquainted with them. There is one of the powers that be, and that too the very chief of these powers, which seems to be strangely left out of view in our political discussions in these eventful times. There are some, I understand, who believe the sovereign power to exist in the President; others that it rests in the national, executive, legislative, and judicial bodies collectively, and others, in the States; and many, if not most, have very indefinite and confused ideas of these powers that be. Each of these is a power, and there are many others, each of which, in the legitimate exercise in its proper order of its own delegated duties, is not to be resisted without blame. But it seems to be forgotten that there is a power in the State sovereign to each and all these powers, one to which all of them are subject. Can we overlook the great truth that the very foundation of our governmental system is based on the sovereignty of the people? Do I mistake or exaggerate when I say that presidents, and governors, and all the departments, whether of State or federal machinery, are all subordinate to the people? Justice Story, in his work on the Constitution, in his concluding remarks, says:

"It (the Constitution) is the language of the people. The people have established it, and spoken their will; and their will, thus promulgated, is to be obeyed as the supreme law of the land. Every citizen has a right to contest the validity of its construction before the proper tribunals, and bring it to the test of the Constitution. And if the case is not capable of judicial redress, still the people may, through the acknowledged means of new elections, etc., check any usurpation of authority, and thus relieve themselves from any grievances of a political nature."

The order, then, of classification of these powers is, first the people, then the State Government, and then the Federal Government. The people in their sovereign capacity and right have absolute power over and above all other powers. The Declaration of Independence, in its mixture of truths, qualified truths, and fallacious maxims, has (so far as our Government is concerned) announced one truth which they who make that document their political bible will not gainsay. "It is the right of the people to alter or abolish (any form of government) and to institute new government, laying its foundation on such principles, and organizing its powers in such form as to them shall seem most likely to effect their safety and happiness." Can any political power be conceived more absolute than this? It is supreme over all the other powers. To make the case more plain, if it is necessary, reverse the case, and suppose it to read: "It is the right of the President, or the Federal Government, or any of the States to alter or abolish the Government, etc." There is no such power but in the people. And now to whom are we appealing in forming this Society? To the *supreme power*. We have nothing to do with any of the other powers, but to use them, so far as we may in their several subordinate stations, as means of reaching the sovereign; and we intend reaching his throne with our petition only through the well-known constitutional channels of access. We mean to use our rights of free discussion, and look for the answer to our appeal of the ballot-box.

Is this treason? Is this conspiracy? Is this resisting the powers that be? Is it disloyalty to appeal to the *sovereign*, or to exercise that portion of the sovereign power which of right belongs to us as part of the people?

Hon. George T. Curtis, in reporting a draft of a constitution from the committee to which the subject had been referred, spoke as follows:

Speech of Hon. Geo. T. Curtis.

Mr. President and Gentlemen: Since we last met in this place we have been subjected to a gross, wanton, and unprovoked insult. Nevertheless, sir, I presume that we shall go on in the discharge of our rights and duties as free citizens of this free country, and, according to the advice which Hamlet gave to the courtier, that we shall use our assailants not according to their deserts, but according to our own honor and dignity. The committee, sir, who were instructed to prepare and report a constitution for the permanent organization of this Society, have directed me to present the instrument which I hold in my hand. Before reading it, however, I desire to be indulged in a few remarks which it is due to the character of those who were here at the first preliminary meeting, and who are again now here, I should make with all calmness, but at the same time with firmness and frankness. When respectable men, who are to be presumed to be as pure and patriotic as their neighbors, are assailed as traitors and conspirators, it concerns the public good that their objects and purposes should immediately be made known, in order that no excuses may be left for the indulgence of a foolish credulity, stimulated by falsehood and malignity, and therefore, sir, we have requested the attendance here of a person who exercises the honorable employment of a reporter for the public press in an honorable and upright manner, and respects his own calling, and who will doubtless give a faithful and true account of all that may transpire here that it concerns the public to know.

Mr. President, the immediate causes for the formation of this Association are the prevalence of doctrines subversive of the fundamental principles of civil liberty and tending directly to the overthrow of the Constitution of the United States, and a wide-spread popular ignorance of the true nature and character of the institutions under which we live. Under these circumstances, sir, what are good men to do who love their country and value its institutions, and who are not willing that these doctrines should go on to produce their bad work in the entire disorganization of society? For, sir, but one of two things can occur, either these doctrines must be met by discussion and refutation and by the peaceful operations of the ballot-box, or they must go on until they have completed their mischief, and property, government, social order, and all things else sink into confusion, to be followed by such peace and security as an absolute despotism can bring. Sir, I do not propose on this occasion to enter into any argument respecting any of the questions which have come into such alarming significance within the last eighteen or twenty-four months, or into any extended discussion of the theories which prevail respecting the various powers of the different departments of the government. But I do propose very briefly to indicate the nature of some of these questions and the character and tendencies of some of those theories, in order that those who may be induced to reflect on the condition of our country may see whither we are drifting. You all know that there are annexed to the Constitution of the United States certain amendments, which embody, in the form of fundamental laws, superior and paramount to all executive or legislative or judicial power, the fundamental, inalienable, and indestructible rights of the citizen; and you also know that the generation of men who made that Constitution and transmitted it to us were not willing to have it go into operation without annexing to it those limitations on the powers of the government. Now, sir, it is not necessary to repeat, to recite what these limitations are. But you are aware that it is now claimed that in time of war, and because the country is at war, it is legitimately in the power of the President to disregard all those restrictions and limitations, and practically to set aside and annul all these rights of the citizen. That I do not exaggerate or in any degree mistake the nature and extent of this claim, permit me to read a single sentence from a pamphlet, written, published, and largely circulated in the year 1862, by an American lawyer:

"No citizen, whether loyal or rebel, is deprived of any right guaranteed to him in the Constitution by reason of his subjection to *martial law*, because *martial law* when in force is *constitutional law*."

Now, sir, you are aware that the whole of this position, so far as it could affect the American people, is founded on the assumption that there is wrapped up in that phrase which designates the military capacity of the President as that of commander-in-chief of the army and navy, power to declare martial law by proclamation all over the country, when the country is in a state of war and the President has armies in the field. Having seen the form in which this doctrine is promulgated now in our American age and in this country, let me ask you to go back for an instant to the year 1628 in England, and see how the same doctrine was then stated by an English lawyer upholding the side of arbitrary power upon the same description of reasoning, and the coïncidence is astonishing. At a conference between the two houses of Parliament concerning the liberty of the subject, holden April 17, 1628, Mr. Sergeant Ashley, a noted lawyer of that day, held the following language in the presence of the two houses:

"The law martial, likewise, though not to be exercised in time of peace, when recourse can be had to the king's courts, yet in time of invasion, or other times of hostility, when the royal army is in the field, and offenses are committed which require speedy resolution and can not expect the solemnities of legal trials, then such imprisonment, execution, or other justice done by the law martial is warrantable, for it is then the law of the land, and is *jus gentium.*"

I will make no comments, but will simply call to your recollection the fact that the phrase or the thing "martial law" is utterly unknown to the Constitution of the United States; that even Congress — the whole legislative power, the Senate, and the House of Representatives — and the President, acting together, can not make any special mode of arrest or trial applicable to any but persons in the army and the navy, and that as to all other men the Constitution absolutely forbids arrests without due process of law or trials otherwise than by a jury of the vicinage. And yet, sir, we are told that the President of the United States may declare martial law by proclamation, and may subject every citizen to seizure and incarceration by provost-marshal.

Then, sir, there is that other kindred heresy by which the same kind of result is arrived at, but by a somewhat different process. We have all heard a great deal about the doctrine of self-defense on the part of the Government. The right of self-defense — as if Government were a natural person, having all the inherent rights of self-defense which a natural person has; and mixed up with this strangely in men's minds is the idea that the members of the executive government may transcend the law of the land in the exercise of this great inherent right of the government to defend itself, and having transcended the law of the land, and committed an injury upon some citizens, may go to Congress and ask for an indemnity, and so the whole wrong is cured by such indemnity by act of Congress. It is the most singular thing in this world that the American people have not hitherto seen that this idea of resorting to the practice of the British Constitution, and borrowing from it what is called the bill of indemnity, to protect the officers of the government from the reclamations and complaints of the citizen, urged in courts of justice, is utterly inapplicable to our Constitution and our institutions, and that the attempt must repeal it—must pull down the Constitution and destroy those institutions. What is the reason, sir, that in England the executive government can in moments of great emergency and in seasons of great public peril, overstep for the moment the positive law of the land, and then, consistently with the principles of that government, receive what is called an indemnity from Parliament — that is, protection and pardon for the act, and thus the remedy of the citizen be cut off? It is solely and simply because it has always been a received principle of that government, that Parliament — the three branches of the Legislature acting together — make and unmake the constitution at their pleasure, and the fundamental reason is that they have no written constitution, but their constitution is an unwritten one. So that when any officer of the government has overstepped the law of the land from right public motives, and in a season of great emergency and peril, it is according to the practice and according to the legitimate theory of their constitution that an indemnity may be granted, for whatever Parliament solemnly enacts in the form of law is constitution. They may set aside the constitution in any particular by act of Parliament—so much so that they may change the descent of the crown, or make the heir apparent a beggar at any moment. But no such thing as that can be done in this country, for the simple reason that we have a written Constitution, which is paramount to all legislative authority and all legislative power — over which Congress has no more control, and in respect to which, where it guarantees rights to the citizen, Congress can no more act to take away the remedy than it can undertake to legislate respecting the condition of things in the provinces of the British empire. If it were not so, it would be in the power of Congress at any time to set aside first one provision of the Constitution and then another, and so to go on until they had frittered away or overturned the whole of it.

Then there is that great mischievous heresy with respect to the power of the President to annul the writ of *habeas corpus*. It will always remain a serious discredit to the administration of Mr. Lincoln, that having to establish the first precedent on that subject since the establishment of the Constitution, they should have made that precedent in the wrong way, and thus have introduced a train of mischiefs in this country which are incalculable in extent, and of which no man can see the result. Why, sir, look at it for a moment. When these questions first rose in the path of the administration, nothing could have been more simple for them to do, nothing more necessary than to go to Congress, not only to ask for proper authority to suspend the writ, but to define that suspension and regulate it, to determine just how far the writ should run, just when and where the judge should stay his hand in prosecuting an inquiry, and on what certificate, and on what facts he should close the inquiry. And, sir, it is within my personal knowledge that some of the members of the administration at the extra session of Congress in 1861—at least the highest law-officer of the Government was implored to take that course, and had they taken it there is no amount of assistance from the best legal minds in the country which they could not have had at the asking, to have framed the proper law for that subject. I appeal to you, Mr. Tilden—I believe you are the only one of my brethren I see in the room—I appeal to you to confirm my statement when I say that no judge in the land can now receive judicial information on which he can act, that the writ of *habeas corpus* is suspended. What is the present state of things? The writ issues—some body comes into court, some military officer, and instead of making a return and bringing up the petitioner, undertakes to inform the judge that the President says that the writ is suspended. What does suspension mean under those circumstances? What are its limitations? What is its operation? Suppose the petitioner asks to be brought up, saying: "The Constitution guarantees to me, if I am accused of crime, a speedy and impartial trial in the State and district wherein the crime is said to have been committed. I have been incarcerated for eighteen months in a loathsome dungeon, and refused all redress." Is the writ suspended to close that inquiry? And yet that is the necessary consequence of this doctrine of executive suspension of the writ. Those are the reasons, sir, why it is one of the most lamentable, one of the greatest calamities that has ever befallen this country that Mr. Lincoln's administration should have set this precedent in the wrong direction.

Mr. Samuel Tilden said: My friend will excuse me for a moment. I will state that happening to be in Washington just about the period when this question rose, and being spoken with upon the subject by a member of the administration, I advised him that he would have no protection of law in acting upon the assumption that the writ of *habeas corpus* was or could be suspended in this mode, that he had better have just as little to do with it as possible, because when the momentary excitement was over, even if acts of this character were necessary, if arrests and detentions were necessary, he would find it wholly impracticable for him to set up any ground of offense against the several forms of redress that might be sought on the part of the person imprisoned. The suspension if validly made could operate, not to annul the other clauses of the Constitution to which Mr. Curtis has referred, or to suspend them, but simply to enable persons to be arrested and detained—that it did not touch the mode of trial and of punishment. Now, in my own judgment, it was absolutely necessary, as well for the safety of the citizen as for the convenience and fair action of the government, that the whole thing should have been defined by legislative action. It was a mistake of the most extraordinary character, resulting, I presume, from the entire want of acquaintance on the part of the law-officer of the government with the subject of constitutional law, and the fact that the acts had been already committed, and were to be justified when his opinion was asked, and not any future action to be determined.

Mr. Curtis continued: I had no doubt as to what view must be taken by the gentleman, although I never exchanged a word with him on the subject in my life. I have said that this is a very unfortunate occurrence. It has interrupted the chain of that steady, safe, constitutional, and only regular and legitimate line of precedents that had come down to us from our British ancestors for many generations. In five reigns in England, if I remember rightly, the writ of *habeas corpus* has been suspended seven times, always by act of Parliament, always by a statute regulating it, defining it, and determining with the utmost precision what is the duty of the judge under such circumstances.

Then there is that other great heresy which may be called the war measure heresy, as if the Constitution were a thing made of India-rubber, to be stretched in one direction in time of peace and in another direction in time of war, or as if we had one Constitution for a state of peace and another Constitution for a state of war. And so we constantly hear it said, no matter what your complaints are about constitutional provisions—no matter what you may question, or what you may suggest or say, "Oh! that is of no consequence — this is a war measure," and thus it is justified. So one might go on through half of the entire night, respecting these extraordinary ideas which have crept into the minds of educated men, and which they have instilled into the popular mind. There is one especially extraordinary, and, in my judgment, equally dangerous idea—and that is, that the rights of the States will take care of themselves, when the war is over, and things will all fall back to their normal condition. Let us look at that for a moment. Here is the militia — the relations to which of the general government and of the States are defined with the utmost precision by the Constitution—and where there was any room for doubt as to the respective practical duties and rights of either government, all that has been, since the war of 1812, settled by judicial decision of the Supreme Court. Suppose, as is perhaps not unlikely, that the bill shall pass Congress, putting the whole control — constitutional provision or no constitutional provision — of the militia of the several States into the hands of the General Government, or, as I have heard it expressed, putting the sword effectually into the hands of the President. You go on in that state of things throughout this war, you go on to a termination of it, whatever that termination may be. Where is the militia then? What precedent has then been established, and what construction by reason of such a precedent acquiesced in—if it has been acquiesced in by the States and people — has the Constitution received at the hands of all the branches of Government and of the States? Why, a construction which does place and leave the whole "sword" of the whole country in the hands of the President of the United States. "The rights of the States will take care of themselves," we are told, and it is very idle, foolish, and somewhat treasonable talk to think any thing about the rights of the States or say any thing about them. Well, there is actually pending in Congress a bill which proposes to annihilate the jurisdiction of the State courts over personal actions for wrongs and injuries upon the suggestion only by the defendant, when he comes into court, that what he has done and what is complained of was done by order of the President of the United States. Actually, it is proposed that if any man sues another citizen of the same State for a personal wrong or injury in a court of the State—nay, sir, it extends to criminal proceedings also as well as civil — the cause shall instantaneously be transferred into the Federal courts on the suggestion only by the defendant that what he did was done by order of the President. Suppose that takes effect. Suppose that is acquiesced in. What construction have the powers of the General Government *then* received at the hands of all the departments of Government and at the hands of the people in reference to that? That the entire jurisdiction of the State courts over personal wrongs as between citizen and citizen is stricken out of existence, when it is set up in defense, that the President ordered the act to be done. These theories have exerted and are exerting a most mischievous effect on the power of the Administration to cope with the public enemy; and I need not say how they have divided the public sentiment and the feeling of the North. I need not say how necessary they have made it that these things should undergo discussion, should be brought to the issue of the ballot-box. There is a vulgar error prevalent among a certain class of second-rate statesmen, that violence is strength. It is a lamentable mistake, and in constitutional countries and in countries which are under the control of constitutional principles, it is the falsest suggestion upon which men could possibly act. No government in any constitutional country is strong, powerful, able to discharge its duty to the utmost, able to call forth all the resources of the people for the accomplishment of any great public object, that does not faithfully and strictly pursue the fundamental law of the land. Bear with me, sir, one moment longer, while I endeavor to say why it is that I feel every infraction of the Constitution as if it were a wound inflicted upon my own body or a wrong done to my own soul. It is not, sir, I assure you, because I have endeavored in some humble and imperfect way to explore the foundations of our liberties and to explain them to my countrymen. It is because I feel in every fiber of my existence that this is the last written Constitution we shall ever have. It is because I feel an innate and undying conviction that if you suffer that instrument to be overborne — that if you acquiesce in serious and great infractions of its provisions—you will throw every thing into a state of entire confusion, and there will be an end of this experiment of self-government founded on and residing in the text of a written Constitution, explained, illustrated, and enforced by the peaceful operation of a supreme judiciary. I do not forget, sir, that the Southern Confederacy, so called, have framed for themselves a written Constitution founded on that of the United States as a model, and with some amendments which may be of more or less theoretical or practical value; but, sir, it does seem to me that no one can look at their condition and prospects without seeing that, although in point of form they may, if they succeed in obtaining their independence and can maintain their position, go on ostensibly under a written constitution, that their government must necessarily and will inevitably be a military government and be conducted by force. God forbid, sir, that we should follow that example. Let us take care how we acquiesce in any infractions of the Constitution.

Let us take care how we fail to do our utmost to instruct and enlighten the people, and to cause them to reverence and to cling to it as the great salvation rock. (Applause.)

With these remarks, sir, I beg leave to read the Constitution for this Society, which the Committee have instructed me to report.

Mr. Curtis then read the following draft of a Constitution, which was unanimously adopted as the Constitution of the Society:

CONSTITUTION.

ARTICLE I.

This Society shall be styled *The New-York Society for the Diffusion of Political Knowledge.*

ARTICLE II.

The objects of the Society shall be to disseminate a knowledge of the principles of American constitutional liberty; to inculcate correct views of the Constitution of the United States, of the powers and rights of the Federal Government, and of the powers and rights reserved to the States and the people; and generally to promote a sound political education of the public mind; to the end that usurpations may be prevented, that arbitrary and unconstitutional measures may be checked, that the Constitution may be preserved, that the Union may be restored, and that the blessings of free institutions and public order may be kept by ourselves, and be transmitted to our posterity.

ARTICLE III.

The officers of the Society shall consist of a President, a Treasurer, a Secretary, and three Standing Committees, who shall be chosen annually. The Standing Committees shall be a Committee on Publications, to consist of seven members, and a Committee of Finance, to consist of ten members; and these two committees shall constitute the Executive Committee of the Society, of which the President, the Treasurer, and the Secretary shall be members *ex officiis*. Each committee may fill vacancies in its own body.

ARTICLE IV.

The Executive Committee shall have the general direction of the operations and measures of the Society in the promotion of its objects; but no pamphlet, book, or other publication shall be circulated or issued in the name or under the auspices of the Society without being first approved by the Committee on Publications; and no person shall deliver a lecture or other public address in the name or under the auspices of the Society without first receiving a written appointment therefor from the Chairman of the said Committee on Publications.

ARTICLE V.

The Committee on Finance shall collect funds for the use of the Society, and pay them over to the Treasurer, whose duty it shall be to pay therefrom, under the direction of the Executive Committee, all expenses that may be incurred by the Society in the prosecution of its objects.

ARTICLE VI.

Regular meetings of the Society shall be held on the first Saturday in April, October, and January, in each year, and special meetings may be held at any time, under the direction of the President.

ARTICLE VII.

The Secretary shall record all the proceedings of the Society; he shall also act as Secretary of the several committees, and shall notify all meetings of the Society, or its committees.

ARTICLE VIII.

Other citizens of the United States, of full age, and of good moral character, may be admitted as members of this Society, on the nomination of two members, at any regular or special meeting of the Society, by a vote of two thirds of the members present.

ARTICLE IX.

No amendment of this Constitution shall be made without the vote of three fourths of the members present at a regular meeting, and notice thereof shall be given at the preceding regular meeting.

ARTICLE X.

The several committees shall report their doings at each regular meeting, and the Secretary shall record the same in the records of the Society.

SAMUEL F. B. MORSE, President.

MANTON MARBLE, }
WM. McMURRAY, } Secretaries.

There being no further business before the Society, an adjournment was effected. The movement thus inaugurated will be a great power in the community and country.

Resolved, That it be recommended to all citizens in the various cities, counties and villages of this and other States, who approve of the objects expressed in this Constitution, that they organize auxiliary societies, and open communication with the New-York Society.

Letter from Mr. Tilden

IN REPLY TO THE EVENING POST.

To the Editors of the Evening Post:

In the *Evening Post* of this afternoon appears a pretended report of remarks made by me at a private meeting of gentlemen held at Delmonico's, last evening, which, I think, your senior editor would not be likely to credit, even though he saw it in a journal that derives its largest claim to public confidence from the authority his name gives to whatever it contains.

I should not deem this publication, however it might misrepresent me, of sufficient importance to require a public notice, except for one single consideration.

It is a studied attempt to give to the meeting the aspect of a revolutionary intrigue, and imputes to me expressions or implications countenancing in some degree, a resort to revolutionary means to effect a change in the policy of the present Federal Administration.

At an ordinary time, I should treat such an imputation with silent contempt. But the time is not ordinary, very far from it. There is a danger yet unrevealed in our future, transcending the calamities we are now experiencing. The premonitions of it are in the wild ideas, which, discarding the maxims and the habits of constitutional government, for the expediency of the moment, grasp at revolutionary power as an instrument of every successive illusion in our national policy.

It illustrates how contagious this bad example is, when set by these who administer the government during a period of public danger, that we daily hear from their partisans, and sometimes from their antagonists, propositions subversive of all constitutional government and of our private rights and personal safety. There are few journals in this city in whose columns, during the present civil war, can not be found invocations to violence against dissentients from their opinions. Among those failing to use their influence to restrain, but often giving countenance to this dangerous tendency, I lament to recall one whose early renown was earned by its advocacy of free discussion, personal rights, and local self-government. We were fast degenerating into a condition in which violence, exercised under the false pretense of lawful authority, or by mobs, was becoming the ordinary weapon of political discussion and partisan warfare, when the elections last fall reminded the party in power that it is not wholly irresponsible, and did something towards restoring that balance between masses representing different opinions, without which popular government is impracticable.

In a generation which finds itself, as ours now does, in a situation wholly novel; which is inexperienced in the larger politics; all of whose leading minds are the growth of a period of peaceful prosperity, and of liberal self-esteem, I fear to see the public mind gradually becoming familiar with the dangerous instruments and methods of revolutionary action. The temptation to use them in aid of the theory, passion, interest, or partisanship of the hour, is immediate and urgent; the evil consequences are remote, contingent, and dimly seen, without the light of experience. That we have hitherto abstained from them is due mainly to the traditions and habits we inherited from our ancestors, wise through much costly experience. I do not think these traditions and habits can be safely broken up. Never once, on any occasion, at any time, in any place, have I failed to lift my voice against any tendency of this kind, from whatever source it proceeded. I may, perhaps, have carried my solicitude upon this subject too far. That is not my opinion. Often, when honest, patriotic men, writhing under a sense of public danger, intensified by a future into which no eye can penetrate, have appealed to me to say what we could do to save the country, I have had occasion to counsel patience with errors which were drifting us as well as their authors to swift destruction, to revive the sense that the men who at present administer the government are our constitutional and legal agents, and that, though they claim from us our full share of the burdens and sacrifices which their policy imposes, without the slightest deference to our convictions in respect to the public interests and public safety, we must still loyally accept disappointment and national disaster, if they should come before the organism of the government can be reclaimed to a better policy in the due course of the elections.

It was some observations of this precise nature, more forbearing than those I now use, made while I was responding to a similar inquiry, that your reporter, by suppression and inversion, has distorted into exactly the opposite import. I had no information of any thing that was intended to be proposed at that meeting, or who was to be present, beyond what was conveyed by the call shown to me a few hours previously. I attended, not because I deemed the occasion of much practical moment — especially as an informal and preliminary meeting — but out of deference to the solicitude of men whose character and motives I unqualifiedly respect. I heard there no suggestion which was not moderate, patriotic, and constitutional. No allusion to peace was made. Some of the gentlemen I know to be of that class called War Democrats; and one, at least, a Republican. In my opinion, the first proposition for a dishonorable peace will come—not from those who foresaw and endeavored to avert civil war, but from that class of the Republicans who were, in a peculiar degree, its authors.

But the ever-recurring question to the minds of those who think the policy of the Administration has been unwise, and generally inadequate and "too late"—and often totally impracticable, yet remains—what can those who think so do? Is there any remedy, or any relief? Can we influence, in any degree, the Administration that represents us in its calamities, if not in its counsels? Will it listen to any suggestion we can offer—will it heed any warning we can give?

Slowly and sorrowfully, after eighteen months of anxious effort, beginning in November, 1860, I yielded to the conviction that we must experience and exhaust each calamity, before we can make it visible to our brethren and friends, who at present hold unchecked an unbalanced sway over the action of the Federal Government.

The controlling intellects of the Administration accept as the guide of their policy or reflect their own vagaries, through the worst element of their own adherents — blind partisans, visionary theorists, impracticable philanthropists, sensation journalists. The illusion which misled their minds before and at their advent to power is constantly reproduced in new forms and new applications, at every successive stage of their career.

It is the voyage of a ship with a false compass; particular deviations are discovered after they have been committed; but they recur in an indefinite series, because their source remains prolific as at first.

I did not say this at the meeting; but, compelled to restate my opinions, I do not hesitate to avow to the public what I believe to be the truth.

The substance of what I did say was, that the dissemination of documents, teaching the fundamental ideas of civil liberty and constitutional government could do no harm, and might be useful, in a time when men's minds are unsettled; that, in my judgment, party action was at present wholly unnecessary, believing, as I did, that future elections would amply take care of themselves; that great caution should be exercised as to the character of all publications authorized or issued, in respect to their practical bearing on the condition of our affairs; that, after all, if we would preserve free institutions among ourselves, or reconstruct the edifice of our Federal Union, it must be chiefly through the lessons of the great teacher, experience; that in a time of war we could not deal with our government, although disapproving its policy, without more reserve than was necessary in debating an administrative question during a period of peace; that the reason was, that if we should paralyze the arm of our own government we yet could not stay the arm of the public enemy striking at us through it; that it was this peculiarity which had sometimes caused minorities to be suppressed in the presence of public danger; and made such periods perilous to civil liberty; that the generation which embraced Washington, Jefferson, Franklin, Madison and Hamilton, and which framed the glorious fabric of American constitutional federative government, had been educated for their work by a quarter of a century of experience in civil commotions; that their intellects had been employed in studying the fundamental questions of government and society in the lights of history, while they were daily reducing its lessons to practice, until they were able to limit theory by practice, and to enlighten practice by theory; that the next generation, which embraced Jackson, Clay, Webster, Wright and their compeers, had the fresh traditions of their fathers; that within the last ten years that generation had wholly disappeared; that the present generation—not inferior in intelligence, nor, perhaps, in dormant public virtue, had neither experience nor traditions as a practical guide for their conduct; that the statesmen of the present time, had, almost without an exception, been born and educated and attained their political eminence during a period of prosperity and peace, in which the mere mechanical action of the government had surmounted every obstacle it had hitherto met, and in which the political philosophy of our wise ancestors had fallen into desuetude, and a race had grown up formed amid the discussion of the small administrative questions, and amid the competitions of professional politicians, for the petty honors and emoluments of office; that generations like individuals, do not completely understand inherited wisdom until they have reproduced it in their own experience, and, finally, that I supposed we must travel through the whole cycle in order to learn what we ought to have known from the historic past.

The only mention I made of Mr. Lincoln was in illustrating this idea; and what I said was, that a man whose whole knowledge and experience of statesmanship was derived from one term in Congress, a long service in the county conventions at Sangamon, a career at *nisi prius* in the interior of Illinois, and some acquaintance with the lobby at Springfield, had now to deal with the greatest questions and most complicated forces of modern history.

I had met with Mr. Lincoln before he was thought of for the Presidency, and have known much of him from his neighbors and friends. I have never been disposed to treat him so uncharitably as is often done by the factions into which his party is divided under the lead of Mr. Chase and Mr. Seward in his own Cabinet, which have scuffled over his body for power from the very day of his election, to the dissensions of which some of the vacillations of the Administration are to be ascribed; and to the occasional ascendency of the most dangerous of which not only fatal mistakes of civil polity, but most of our military disasters, can be distinctly traced.

I am quite aware how difficult is the conduct of a constitutional opposition, during a period of war; how necessary it is to guard against its degenerating into faction, and to keep its measures directed to attaining the utmost practical good for the country at every varying stage of public affairs. I know, also, that such an opposition is often the only means of preserving civil liberty, or of conducting an existing war to a successful termination. I have hitherto never failed to see the exact line between opposition and faction, or to keep within it, with an impartiality at no moment shaken by interest, passion, prejudice or association. I have not for an instant had out of mind the infinite advantages of using, if possible, those who now sway the government, and must do so, though in a less degree, for two years longer, as the instruments of the national salvation.

It was only when I saw them yielding daily more and more to fatal influences that I looked around for a counterpoise in a constitutional opposition. History affords no example of so liberal and generous—I might say prodigal—a support of an administration by the mass of those who dissent from its policy and disapprove its management. How means more vast than were ever before placed at the disposal of an administration have been employed, and with what results, I pronounce no judgment. I leave it to the testimonies daily coming to the public from those who were largely instrumental in bringing this Administration into existence. My view of duty on this subject has been purely and exclusively a matter of the judgment. As long ago as 1854, having broken all party ties, by firm resistance to the repeal of the Missouri Compromise, Mr. Preston King told me that the politicians of the South would never forgive me; and asked me if I thought my name could pass the Senate of the United States? I answered that it was of very little consequence to me whether it could or not; but that it was of great consequence to me that I should do what I thought best for the country. The termination of an intercourse, during which he had persistently sought to engage me with himself in the work of forming the Republican party, was a letter of warning, in which I said, in substance, that every thing that could be usefully or safely done to protect all the interests and rights of the North, could be even better accomplished without the use of such a dangerous agency; and that such an organization would either be a political blunder, or it would be a political crime, in creating a conflict in which the government would probably perish. This conviction, matured by long meditation in retirement and almost political isolation, governed my action ever after by a motive of patriotic duty so overwhelming that there was no room for any other motive.

When unexpected events swept us near to the fatal brink, this conviction was fully stated through the columns of the *Evening Post*, in October, 1860, with the reasons of it, deduced from the nature of men and of parties, in the light of history and of the principles and practices of the great men who founded free government for this continent. I feel my judgment of what was right and wise, and what is now right and wise for us to do, in this most important crisis of our national existence, assured by the accuracy with which, in that prevision, I estimated every element of the question; and, though ready to accept with candor any new lights, I see, as yet, no reason to question my conclusions. If the *Evening Post*, in the issue, from that time to the present, between its opinions and mine, can stand the same test, it may find some excuse for a dogmatic assault I shall not imitate, upon the opinions and motives of others, not less conscientious and patriotic than itself, and, as private citizens, less exposed than it is to the misleading influences of the turbid current of partisanship and journalism.

S. J. Tilden.

New-York, Saturday evening, Feb. 7, 1863.

Daniel Webster.

Mr. Webster's definition of liberty in his Richmond speech, can not be too often repeated. He said:

"Why, gentlemen, there is a good axiom extant, that the quantity of liberty we possess, is precisely equal to the quantity of restraint we put upon the government. And this is true. If the government is restrained from putting its hand in certain particulars upon you, to that extent you are free, and no more. And if individuals are restrained from putting their hands upon you, you have more freedom. *All liberty, therefore, consists in putting such a restraint upon your governments, and upon individuals, that they can not touch your rights or your liberties.*"

Henry Clay.

Letter of Henry Clay to the Ashland Club, on his birthday:

Ashland, Sept. 2, 1843.

My Dear Sir: Allow me to select a subject for one of your tracts, which, treated in your popular and condensed way, I think would be attended with great and good effect. I mean Abolition.

It is manifest that the ultras of that party are extremely mischievous, and are hurrying on the country to fearful consequences. They are not to be conciliated by the Whigs. Engrossed with a single idea, they care for nothing else.

And yet they would see the administration of the Government precipitate the nation into absolute ruin, before they would lend a helping hand to arrest its career. They treat worse, denounce most, those who treat them best, who so far agree with them as to admit slavery to be an evil. Witness their conduct toward Mr. Briggs and Mr. Adams, in Massachusetts, and toward me.

I will give you an outline of the manner in which I would handle it. Show the origin of slavery; trace its introduction to the British government; show how it is disposed of by the Federal Constitution; that it is left exclusively to the States, except in regard to fugitives, direct taxes and representation. Show that the agitation of the question in the free States will first destroy all harmony, and finally lead to disunion—poverty and perpetual war—the extermination of the African race—ultimate military despotism.

But the great aim and object of your tract should be to arouse the laboring classes of the free States against Abolition! Depict the consequences to them of immediate abolition. The slaves being free, would be dispersed throughout the Union; they would enter into competition with the free laborer—with the American, the Irish, the German — reduce his wages, be confounded with him, and affect his moral and social standing. And as the ultras go both for Abolitionism and amalgamation, show that their object is to unite in marriage the laboring white man and black woman, to reduce the white laboring man to the despised and degraded condition of the black man.

I would show their opposition to colonization. Show its humane, religious, and patriotic aim. That they are those whom God has separated. Why do Abolitionists oppose colonization? To keep and amalgamate together two races in violation of God's will, and keep the blacks here, that they may interfere with, degrade, and debase the laboring whites! Show that the British government is co-operating with the Abolitionists for the purpose of dissolving the Union. I am perfectly satisfied that it will do great good. Let me hear from you on this subject. HENRY CLAY.

Five years earlier than this, (1838,) the U. S. Senate adopted the following resolutions, offered by Mr. Clay:

Resolved, That when the District of Columbia was ceded by the States of Virginia and Maryland to the United States, domestic slavery existed in both of those States, including the ceded territory, and that, as it still continues in both of them, it could not be abolished within the District, without a violation of that good faith which was implied in the cession, and in the acceptance of the territory; nor, unless compensation were made to the proprietors of slaves, without a manifest infringement of an amendment to the Constitution of the United States, nor without exciting a degree of just alarm and apprehension in the States recognizing slavery, far transcending in mischievous tendency any possible benefit which could be accomplished by the abolition.

Resolved, therefore, That it is the deliberate judgment of the Senate, that the institution of domestic slavery ought not to be abolished within the District of Columbia; and it earnestly hopes that all sincere friends of the Union, and of harmony, and general tranquillity, will cease to agitate this disturbing question.

What is the Constitution?

ABOLITION AUTHORITY TWO YEARS AGO.

THE Constitution of the United States is a compact of Union adopted by the thirteen original colonies in 1787–8, and '90, and as equal parties to which twenty more States have since been admitted, all to equal rights.

It was in the beginning optional with each State whether it should adopt the Constitution or not, as is shown by the fact that Rhode Island did not ratify it, and was not one of the United States until the twenty-ninth of May, 1790, which was more than a year after the inauguration of our first President.

This compact derives its authority

from the will of the people of the several States that ratified it, each in its sovereign capacity in Convention assembled.

Its preamble declares that it is ordained "in order to form a more perfect Union, establish justice, insure *domestic tranquillity*, provide for the *common* defense, promote the *general welfare*, and secure the blessings of *liberty* to ourselves and to our posterity;" and by a continued and strict observance of it in all its parts, we might still have enjoyed under it all those blessings.

This article is intended to vindicate the inviolability of this Constitution by which alone was formed our *Union*—which is *in itself*, "our government"—the rampart of our freedom, the rubicon of our rights, and the palladium of our liberties, by the authority of which the very men who seek to exceed its powers hold office *under* it, and "without which neither party nor nation, nor liberty can exist." (See *N. Y. Evening Post*, Aug. 22, 1861.)

WASHINGTON'S WARNING AGAINST DESTROYING THE CONSTITUTION.

It is important, likewise, that the habits of thinking, in a free country, should inspire caution in those intrusted with its administration, to confine themselves within their respective constitutional spheres, avoiding, in the exercise of the powers of one department, to encroach upon another. The spirit of encroachment tends to consolidate the powers of all the departments in one, and thus to create, whatever the form of government, a real despotism. A just estimate of that love of power, and proneness to abuse it which predominates in the human heart, is sufficient to satisfy us of this position. The necessity of reciprocal checks in the exercise of political power, by dividing and distributing it into different depositories, AND CONSTITUTING EACH THE GUARDIAN OF THE PUBLIC WEAL, AGAINST INVASION BY THE OTHERS, has been evinced by experiments, ancient and modern · some of them in our own country, and under our own eyes. To PRESERVE them must be as necessary as to INSTITUTE them. If, in the opinion of the people, the distribution or modification of the constitutional powers be, in any particular, wrong, let it be corrected by an amendment IN THE WAY WHICH THE CONSTITUTION DESIGNATES. But let there be no change by USURPATION; for though this, in one instance, may be the instrument of good, it is the customary weapon by which free governments are destroyed. The PRECEDENT must always greatly overbalance, in permanent evil, any partial or transient benefit which the use can at any time yield.—*George Washington.*

MADISON'S VIEWS OF CONSTITUTIONAL LIMITATIONS.

. . . To hold the union of the States as the basis of their peace and happiness; to support the Constitution, which is the cement of Union, *as well in its limitations as in its authorities; to respect the rights and authorities reserved to the States and to the people, as equally incorporated with, and essential to the success of, the general system; to avoid the slightest interference with the rights of conscience*, or the functions of religion, so *wisely exempted from civil jurisdiction;* to preserve, to their full energy, the other salutary provisions in behalf of *private and personal rights*, and of *the freedom of the press.* As far as sentiments and intentions such as these can aid the fulfillment of my duty, they will be a resource which can not fail me.—*President James Madison.*

THE RIGHTS OF MINORITIES.

All, too, will bear in mind this sacred principle, that, though the will of the majority is in all cases to prevail, that will, to be rightful, must be reasonable; *that the minority possess her equal rights, which equal laws must protect, and to violate would be oppression.—Thomas Jefferson.*

MINORITY REPORT

OF THE

COMMITTEE ON FEDERAL RELATIONS:

BY HON. EV'G. MORTON,

In the House of Representatives, January 30th, 1865.

The undersigned, minority of the committee on federal relations, begs leave respectfully to report:

That it has been the custom for several years, in most, if not all of the State Legislatures, to pass resolutions on the state of the Union. The object of this action has not always been patriotic. The motive, in too many cases, has been to sustain party. For this purpose, they are usually drawn by the party in power, and made to speak partisan sentiment. To some extent, the undersigned believes the resolutions now before the House, by a majority of the committee, have this object in view. Of this he will not complain, for precedents have sanctioned the custom. But if more statesmanlike views are to obtain on this subject, by discarding partisan action and inaugurating a more enlarged and patriotic policy, better calculated to unite all parties in common sentiment for the sacred cause of the Union, the time has come for Michigan, the first State to organize the present dominant party, to set the noble example to her sister States of the Union.

The majority report expresses the opinion that Providence

has determined "that this rebellion shall see no end, except upon the basis of universal, unconditional and perpetual freedom to all people, whatever may be their color." If this be so, and the sudden emancipation by war of three or four millions of human beings from bondage to freedom, is to be mutually beneficial to both races, we shall have abundant reason to thank Providence for a result so unexpected and miraculous. From time immemorial, the unfortunate race enslaved have occupied a position of servitude both in their native land and in all other nations. If American slavery has caused results by which their condition is to be entirely changed, the event, while it may not sanction slavery as Divinely appointed, will be equally astonishing to the world, even in our days of progress. It will prove that slavery in this country, under the direction of Providence, has prepared the way for liberty to a people who have, almost since the days of Canaan, been treated "as persons having no rights a white man is bound to respect." The undersigned, however, cannot so view this important subject. While he believes in an overruling Providence, he must believe that men, as free agents, can settle this war and still retain slavery until the enslaved are prepared for freedom. In their present condition the most of them are not prepared for it, and it is even a question whether Christian philanthropy, or sound political policy, will justify immediate and violent emancipation. We should not throw them upon the charity of the world in such a helpless and hopeless condition as they are. If we do, we should be prepared to sustain them with our charities, for we cannot expect the whites of the South to care for them as we shall dictate, or according to our visionary theories on the subject of slavery. Emancipation will merely change the slavery question to the negro question, and it is difficult at this time to determine which will demand the greater sacrifice and consideration, and challenge most the philanthropy of the country. The undersigned cannot, therefore, with the majority, urge the "freeing of the slaves at once." He believes that the best interests of both races will be promoted by the policy of gradual emancipation by the States burdened with the institution.

The majority report embraces the common fallacy that slavery caused the war. Political ambition made use of the slavery question as a hobby for partizan ascendancy. In the controversy about slavery, by northern and southern parties, that state of excited and bitter feeling was created in the public mind which culminated in war. In all this the abuse of the freedom of speech, and the disregard of law, often under pretence of respect for the higher law, in both sections of the Union, did far more to bring this unjustifiable war upon the nation than the mere existence of slavery, which, without this controversy, might have remained for many years to come, as it has in years past, undisturbed and harmless, until, by the inevitable laws of population pressing upon it, the institution would yield without war or bloodshed, quietly to the demands and progress of freedom.

In this bitter controversy, which the undersigned believes caused the war, it is to be regretted that so many of the embassadors of the Prince of Peace were induced to engage. Without their aid it is extremely doubtful whether the nation could have been so alienated in feeling as to rush madly into such a struggle as the one in which we are now engaged. The history of past ages should have warned the people that, however desirable and necessary the clergy are as spiritual guides, as political leaders they have ever been a scourge to mankind. In the name of the Higher Law in the days of the crusades, they marked their pathway from Europe to Asia with the blood and bones of more than a million martyrs, and it was in the name of God and Humanity that they controlled the mob which nailed the Savior of men to the cross. In their political action they are very apt to mingle blind and plausible theory with religious zeal, which makes them bigoted and intolerant; and the more sincere they are in their visionary and impracticable theories and errors, the more dangerous they become as political guides.

It is, perhaps, useless, at this time, to discuss the cause of the war. It is upon us, and the question now is, how to get rid of it and save the Union. But as the majority report speaks of slavery as the cause of the war, it may not be improper to controvert that position. Henry J. Raymond, of New York, is one of the leading republicans in the Union, and, more than any other editor, the organ of the national administration. In a speech at Albany, in 1860, published in his paper, the New York Times, he alludes to the fact that then there was such alienation of feeling between the people of the Northern and Southern States, that the spirit of unity and fraternity was gone—as much so as if they were two nations. In accounting for this hostile feeling, so soon to lead to war and bloodshed, he asks, "What, then, has produced in the minds and hearts of the American people the remarkable change—the revolution of sentiment we now perceive?" He answers:

"I believe I shall state it with sufficient accuracy and impartiality when I say that it is due, first, *to the direct action of the abolitionists;* second, to the manner in which that action has affected political parties in the North; and third, to the manner in which it has been resisted by the Southern States."

Here the first cause of all our trouble is correctly attributed to abolitionism, not to slavery, but to unnecessary interference with it by those who had no constitutional right or power over it. As Mr. Raymond is the author of the platform of the national convention which nominated Mr. Lincoln for re-election, his testimony is the more valuable to the majority here. In continuing his remarks against abolitionism, Mr. Raymond says:

"It is hardly necessary to say that this change of feeling is of recent growth. Although differences of sentiment prevailed then as now, there was none of this dissension, none of this hostility, none of this intense bitterness now so rife, in the early days of the Republic. The division into North and South—into Free States and Slave States, was gradual. At the outset all the States but one were slaveholding. The Northern States, yielding in the course of time to the pressure alike of their convictions and their interests, relieved themselves of the burden. The policy of emancipation by slow, safe and wise methods, was the policy of the country, and was making its way steadily and against greater and greater objections toward the southern boundary of the Union. As late as 1832, the State of Virginia was earnestly discussing the best practical methods of freeing her slaves. At just about that time, while several of the Slave States were turning their attention to the accomplishment of the same great object, the Abolition movement struck in from the North. Starting from the mild and charitable Christian principle, that any man who suffered himself, under any circumstances, to own a slave, was a pirate and a robber; that every slave had the absolute, indefeasible right to assert his freedom, and to kill any man who should resist his attempt to take it, these societies entered upon their grand crusade against Slavery in the Southern States. The first effect of this movement was to startle and arrest the Southern States in their work of emancipation. They found themselves in danger of being suddenly crushed and buried beneath the walls they were endeavoring gradually and safely to remove. They found their slaves stimulated and urged to grasp by force, what they were trying to give them as a boon, and in such a manner as to make it a boon worth possessing. They found themselves compelled to look out for their own safety in presence of this new and terrible foe. The incendiary appeals of Northern Abolitionism, circulated in speeches, in pamphlets, through the mails and by emissaries and agents everywhere, compelled them to assume an attitude of self-defense."

Mr. Raymond then speaks of the John Brown raid, and after saying that "a portion of the republican press teemed with expressions of sympathy for Brown, and apologies for his acts," he adds:

"It is not strange that under such influences the South should have been—as I believe they were, and still are—profoundly alarmed by what they believed to be the sentiments and intentions of the people of the Northern States. They would be something more, or something less than human, if they failed to be impressed by the demonstrations which have passed before their eyes. They undoubtedly believe to-day—the great mass of the people of the Southern States believe to-day—that the great body of the people of the North sympathize with the act of John Brown, and approve entirely of the attempt in which he failed. And it is to that belief that the hostile movements so rife in that section of the country are mainly due."

The undersigned does not introduce this testimony here to justify the rebellion. There is no justification for it. The object is to show that it was produced, not by slavery, as the majority report infers, but by the angry passions which political leaders had aroused in the public mind for their own promotion by partisan success—by restless and meddlesome interference with slavery by abolitionists north, and the effect their action had in giving power to their restless and meddlesome brothers in mischief—the fire-eaters of the south—and who, without abolition aid, could never have fired the southern heart to madness and bloodshed.

In this stage of the controversy, it may do no good to allude to such unwelcome facts, except to remind the stronger party that many of their leaders are sufficiently identified with the authors of our great national calamity to afford to be magnanimous to their weaker co-laborers in the work of war and disunion, in the final settlement of this unnatural struggle.

The undersigned will hail with delight a return to the spirit and concord, union and mutual respect, which actuated the founders of the government, when the rights and feelings of all the States are once more regarded, and moderation and forbearance, so necessary to harmony in a vast country like ours, with so many interests and pursuits, shall again distinguish our statesmen in the administration of the government. Then we may hope that the people in all sections of the country, left free and unmolested in their right to promote their own interests in their own way, subject only to the constitution and laws, will see no State out of the Union, and provide, as speedily as possible, for a time when there shall not be a rebel or a slave in the Union.

Nor can the minority agree with the majority report in wishing to see half a million of "sable Unionists," as the blacks are called, "in the ranks of the Union army." With such a force, made up of men in their condition, subject to obedience and servitude, under the direction of an ambitious chief, ready to follow his ideas and wishes, as a higher law, he might "pass the Rubicon," and overthrow the liberties of his country. It might prove much easier to enlist such an army than to dispose of it after it had been drilled in the work of obedience and despotism. If wanted "in conquering and holding the rich plains and fertile bottom lands of the rebel States," as the majority report claims, their services will be the more dangerous, as these coveted possessions will not be worth their cost in treasure and blood, if they are to be held only by the sword.

The majority report endorses the Proclamation of Emancipation, which the administration itself regards as unconstitutional. At this very moment we are called upon, by a vote of three-fourths of the States, to so change the Constitution as to make it sanction this very proclamation, lest it shall be pronounced invalid by the courts. Instead of making the proclamation conform to the law, the object is to make the law conform to this executive act, and make even the restoration of the Union depend upon its success. In this policy the minority cannot agree, as he is for the Union, with or without slavery, as the people, and not the executive, by usurpation, shall decide. It is difficult to see how the advocates of this policy can claim to be Union men. The President is asked not to withdraw the proclamation. The advice is unnecessary. For the first time in our history the President places himself above the will of the people and the decision of the courts, and refuses to obey them if they shall determine that executive duty requires him to return to slavery any person freed by the proclamation. even if it shall be determined by the people, or the legal tribunal made by the people to determine the validity of his acts, that the interests of some, if not all of these freed men, and the interests of society itself, will be best promoted by placing such persons under the direction of masters, the President of the United States, the servant of the courts and the people, refuses to discharge a duty required by the laws of the land.

The majority report says: "We find no language fully to express our abhorrence of the rebel barbarities." The report then recommends the President to resort to just such "barbarities," by way of retaliation, which would often subject the innocent to barbarous punishment. No doubt barbarities are common enough. War itself is barbarous, and brings with it in all countries, civilized and uncivilized, crimes and enormities enough to make humanity shudder. It is extremely doubtful whether retaliation, in the manner proposed, would remedy these horrible crimes, or give strength to, or confidence in the Union cause. We have evidence that humane and Christian policy is often best to disarm a foe, especially when the contrary policy punishes the innocent equally with the guilty. Violence provokes violence. This is what made the war, and if resorted to generally in its prosecution, in both sections, it may protract it, making us subject to the control of lawless guerrilla bands, and to the anarchy which destroyed the Republic of Mexico.

The majority report "ardently hopes for the day when we shall be both a government without a king, and a republic without a slave." The undersigned cheerfully coincides in this wish, although he is not yet ready thus to acknowledge the President as a king, even if, at times, he may assume kingly power.

The minority will hail with unbounded pleasure the day when, by the triumphs of our noble armies in the field, and the wisdom of statesmanship in our national councils, peace and union shall be restored to our common country. Let a wise and truly national policy be inaugurated and once more we shall have a united and happy people, we may hope, to learn war no more. We want the Union which God and our fathers gave us, the Constitution which they ordained, and then, moving onward to greatness as a nation, we shall cherish, as our fathers did, love for all the States in our great continental republic, and be animated as they were, with common hopes, sympathies and interests, for generations, after slavery is known in our history as an institution of the past.

The undersigned herewith transmits the following resolutions, as a substitute for those submitted by the majority, and recommends their adoption:

Whereas, By the madness and folly of men, our country has become involved in a fearful rebellion, which threatens the very existence of the Union, and the destruction of the principle of self-government;

And whereas, This gigantic rebellion is without justification before an impartial world, and unnecessary for the accomplishment of any good, or the remedy of any evil; therefore,

1. *Resolved,* (the Senate concurring,) That we hereby reaffirm our declaration of unswerving devotion to the government of the United States, and we hereby declare, that while our hearts are made sad by the terrible ravages of war, our judgments fully approve of the vigorous prosecution thereof, for the life of the nation, until there shall be an unqualified submission to the authority of the government.

2. *Resolved,* That war is a terrible calamity to any nation, and can be justified only to uphold just laws and good government among men, and that for this purpose this war should be vigorously prosecuted by the administration in power, and be abandoned for an honorable peace the moment these ends are accomplished by obedience on the part of the rebels to the constitution and laws of the Union, which God and our fathers gave us.

3. *Resolved,* That we tender our heartfelt thanks to our able officers and brave men who have upheld our standard, both on land and sea, and we assure them of our deepest sympathy, and our moral and material support, while battling for the integrity of the nation and the support of the government.

4. *Resolved,* That we fully approve of the use by the Government, of every means known to civilized warfare for the complete overthrow of the rebellion, and ardently hope for the day when we shall, by the common consent of all parties and sections interested, be a nation without a rebel and a republic without a slave.

5. *Resolved,* That the Governor be, and he hereby is requested to furnish to the President of the United States, and to each of our Senators and Representatives in Congress, a copy of the foregoing resolutions.

All which is respectfully submitted,

EDWARD G. MORTON.

Union Square Panorama Company.

THE GREATEST WORK OF THE CELEBRATED FRENCH ARTIST,

PAUL PHILIPPOTEAUX.

Battle of ✻ ✻ ✻ ✻ Gettysburg,

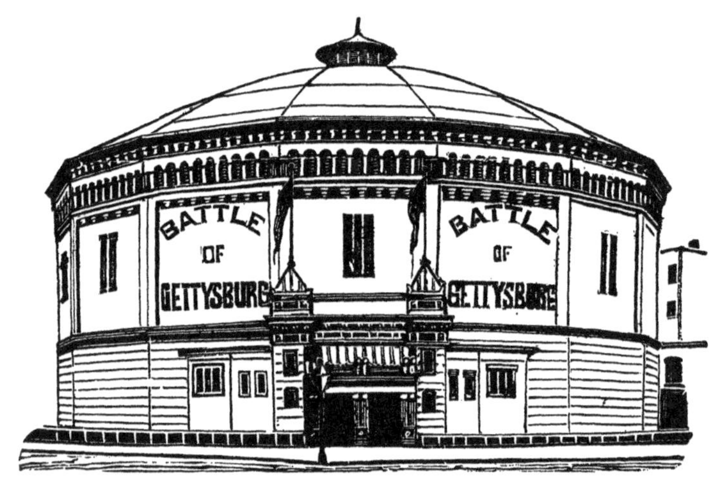

UNION · SQUARE, · NEW · YORK,

(Fourth Avenue, 18th and 19th Streets.)

Open from 9 A. M. to 11 P. M. Sundays Included.

—ADMISSION.—

ADULTS, 50 CTS. CHILDREN, 25 CTS.

PRESS OF BROOKLYN DAILY EAGLE.

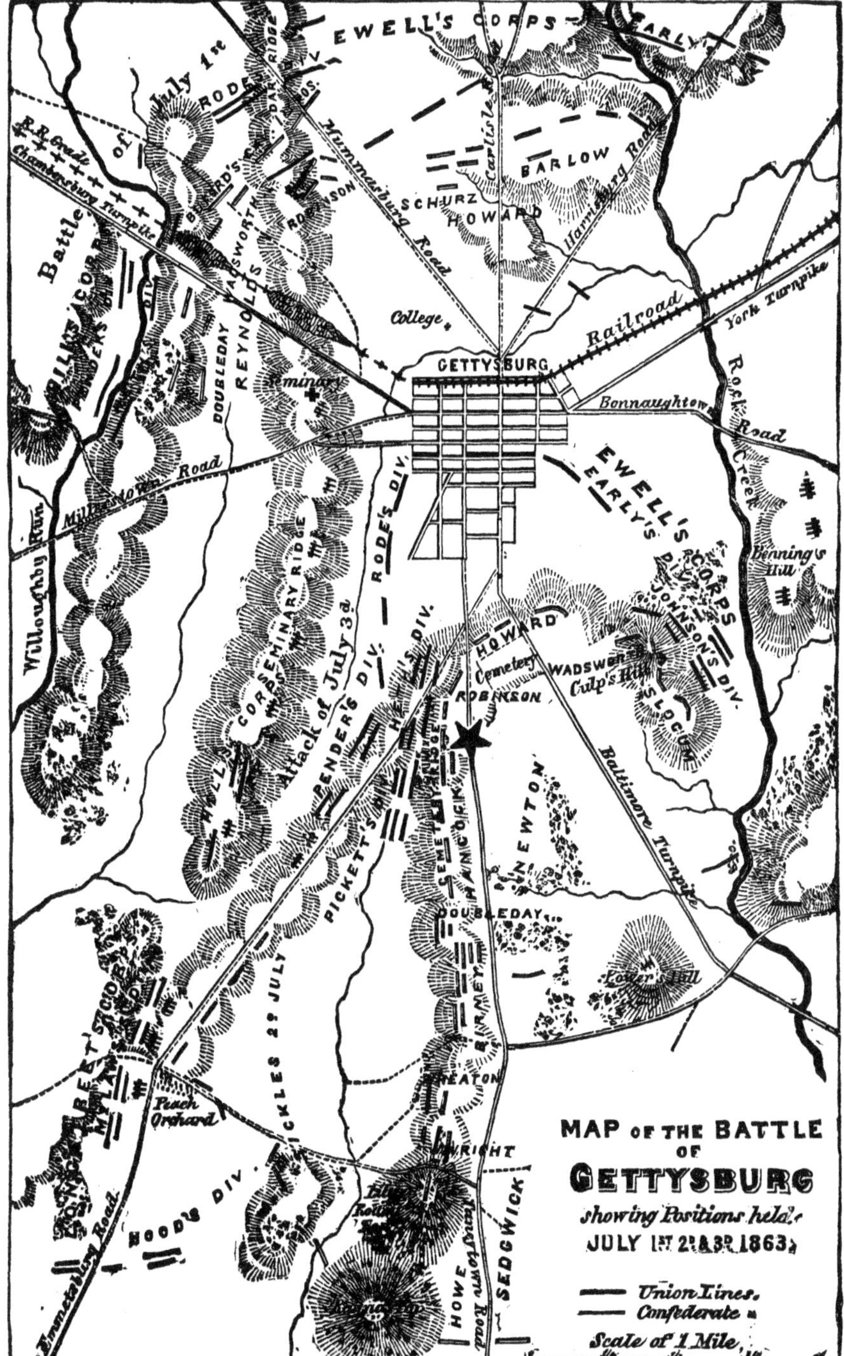

Copyright, 1868, By Harper & Brothers.

The Spectator of the Cyclorama is standing on the spot marked ★

FROM

THE HISTORY OF THE GREAT REBELLION.

HARPER & BROTHERS, Publishers, Franklin Square, N.Y.

This work, containing 1000 illustrations that appeared in Harper's Weekly during the War, is for sale only by McDONNELL BROS., 113 Dearborn Street, Chicago.

BIOGRAPHICAL.

PAUL PHILIPPOTEAUX.

THE celebrated painter of this great work of art was born in Paris in 1846. From his earliest years he showed a remarkable natural aptitude in art matters, and at the age of ten began receiving instructions in the first elements of art painting from his eminent father, the late Felix Philippoteaux, one of the masters of the French School, whose many historical paintings have been bought by the French Government for the Versailles Gallery and other national museums of France.

At the age of sixteen Paul Philippoteaux studied under Cabanel and Leon Cogniet, with both of whom he was a favorite pupil. While at the "Ecole des Beaux Arts" he obtained several first medals, was admitted as No. 1 for the "Prix de Rome" examination, and received other high honors.

He is to-day among the foremost of the artists of Paris, where his paintings in the "Salon" are very highly esteemed, and the general

NOTE.—The portrait of the artist is by himself.

verdict is that Paul Philippoteaux is undoubtedly now the *greatest and most famous historical painter* in the world.

The great success attending the production of his first Cyclorama, The Defence of the Fort d'Issy (1871), (painted in collaboration, and under the supervision of his father, and exhibited fourteen years in the Champs Elysees in Paris, paying 1,450 per cent. to the stockholders), induced him to paint the following Cycloramas :

1. Taking of Plevna (Turco-Russian War).
2. Passage of the Balkans.

Both on exhibition in St. Petersburg.

3. The Belgian Revolution of 1830.
4. The Attack of the Park.

Both exhibited formerly in Brussels.

5. The Battle of Tel-el-Kebir, at the Crystal Palace, London.
6. La Derniere Sortie (with his father).
7. Niagara Falls, now exhibited in London.

And four different Cycloramas of the Battle of Gettysburg, now on exhibition in Chicago, Boston, Cincinnati and New York.

Paul Philippoteaux having conceived the idea of painting the greatest battle of the Rebellion, came to this country in 1880, where Barnet Philipps, the eminent art critic of the New York *Times*, gave him many valuable suggestions on the subject, and introduced him to General Hancock, from whom he gleaned accurate details of the fight ; he went then to the battlefield in person, took sketches, consulted the official maps on file in the War Department in Washington, and then returned to Paris.

The first panorama of this great battle was soon finished and put on exhibition in Chicago. Over half a million people visited it the first year, the receipts being $241,300. It is now in its fifth successful year. Mr. C. L. Willoughby, of Chicago, was so taken with this great success (never attained by any other artist) that he requested Philippoteaux to paint another Gettysburg, which was put up in Boston, and soon sold to a company of that city for $300,000.

It was then determined to place one in New York. In order to execute a canvas still more perfect than the others, Paul Philippoteaux decided to paint it in America, where he could obtain, and copy better, photographs of the prominent heroes of Gettysburg, the coloring of the country and the exact American uniforms and accoutrements of 1863.

Philippoteaux says himself that this *New York Gettysburg is the greatest effort* of his life, and surpasses all his other works in truthfulness, coloring and nicety of detail.

The canvas is four hundred feet in circumference and fifty feet high, consequently measuring twenty thousand square feet.

This Cyclorama of the Battle of Gettysburg, exibited in this costly fire-proof building, is, in every particular, a true and accurate reproduction of the whole mighty struggle, as it actually took place on July 3d, 1863.

Mr. Paul Philippoteaux extends his grateful thanks to General Hunt, of Washington (Chief of Artillery at Gettysburg), to General Alexander Webb, of New York, to Hon. Carleton Coffin, of Boston, and to Mr. Barnet Philipps of the New York *Times*, for their valuable and friendly information on the Battle of Gettysburg.

ADDRESS

DELIVERED AT THE DEDICATION OF THE SOLDIERS' NATIONAL CEMETERY AT GETTSYBURG.

November 19, 1863.

FOURSCORE and seven years ago our fathers brought forth on this continent, a new nation, conceived in Liberty, and dedicated to the proposition that all men are created equal.

Now we are engaged in a great civil war, testing whether that nation, or any nation so conceived and so dedicated, can longer endure. We are met on a great battle-field of that war. We have come to dedicate a portion of that field, as a final resting-place for those who here gave their lives that that nation might live. It is altogether fitting and proper that we should do this.

But, in a larger sense, we cannot dedicate—we cannot consecrate—we cannot hallow—this ground. The brave men, living and dead, who struggled here, have consecrated it, far above our poor power to add or detract. The world will little note, nor long remember what we say here, but it can never forget what they did here. It is for us the living, rather, to be dedicated here to the unfinished work which they who fought here have thus far so nobly advanced. It is rather for us to be here dedicated to the great task remaining before us—that from these HONORED DEAD we take increased devotion to that cause for which they gave the last full measure of devotion—THAT WE HERE HIGHLY RESOLVE THAT THESE DEAD SHALL NOT HAVE DIED IN VAIN—that this nation, under God, shall have a new birth of freedom—and that government of the people, by the people, for the people, shall not perish from the earth.

ABRAHAM LINCOLN.

EXPLANATION

OF THE

BATTLE OF GETTYSBURG CYCLORAMA

1 2 3 4 5

GENERAL HUNT AND STAFF.

1.—Gen. Hunt. 2—Capt. N. T. Craig. 3.—Lieut. Bessell. 4.—Inspector E. R. Warner. 5.—Lieut. Worth.

The Cyclorama represents the decisive action which took place in the afternoon of July 3d, 1863 (the third day of the battle), generally known as

PICKETT'S CHARGE.

The spectator is supposed to be standing on the battle field, near the centre of the Union lines, and from this commanding point views the battle as it actually took place.

It was at 1 o'clock in the afternoon, when a signal gun from the Confederate lines was heard, and from the long stretch of the Seminary ridge, 150 cannon open on the Union lines, their fire being concentrated against the troops commanded by General Hancock.

This portion of the Union line comprised a part of the FIRST CORPS UNDER GENERAL NEWTON ; THE SECOND CORPS UNDER GENERAL GIBBON ; THE THIRD CORPS UNDER GENERAL BIRNEY, and a part of the ELEVENTH CORPS UNDER GENERAL HOWARD.

The object of this tremendous cannonade was to batter the lines of the Federal army, and prepare the way for the final assault with columns of infantry.

GENERAL LEE, who was in command of the Confederate army of Northern Virginia, had planned this last desperate assault, in order to overwhelm the Army of the Potomac, under General Meade, and thus end in victory for the South, the great struggle that for three days had been waged.

NOTE.—The Illustrations are by Paul Philippoteaux.

GENERAL LONGSTREET, second in command to GENERAL LEE, had immediate charge of all the arrangements for the assault, giving directions for the various movements.

When the Confederate guns opened, General Meade at once understood that the critical point of the struggle was at hand, and that the momentous issues, so long wavering in the balance, must soon be decided.

GENERAL W. S. HANCOCK IN 1863.

The ridge occupied by the Union lines was not so long as that held by the Confederates. General Hunt, in command of the Union artillery, had stationed eighty guns (all that the conformation of the ground would admit), along the crest occupied by General Hancock, and at once opened in reply on the Confederate position.

THE THUNDER OF THE GUNS

thus belching forth the hot, hissing storm of solid shots and bursting shells, was tremendous. The ground fairly trembled and shook under the mighty concussions, and as the advantage both in position and the greater number of guns seemed to be with the Confederates, it looked as though the Union lines would be broken and swept from the field.

Several ammunition wagons exploded, and as the smoke of these explosions rolled up the shouts of exultation from the Southern soldiers could be heard for miles along the line.

About 3 o'clock General Hunt ordered a gradual cessation of fire

GENERAL W. S. HANCOCK AND STAFF.

1.—General Hancock. 2.—General Bingham. 3.—Major Mitchell. 4.—Colonel W. P. Wilson. 5.—Captain Miller. 6.—Captain Parker.

from the Union batteries, in order to allow the guns to cool, and also to reserve enough ammunition for

THE FINAL STRUGGLE,

which he knew was soon to come.

This dropping off on the Federal side naturally gave the Confederates the idea that they had silenced the Northern batteries, and at once they made preparations to advance their storming columns that had been awaiting the result of the cannonade in the shelter of the woods back from the line of guns.

GENERAL HUNT, Chief of Artillery.

The commencement of the momentous struggle was now just at hand. GENERAL LONGSTREET, who had assigned the positions of the Confederate troops that were to make the assault, seemed overwhelmed with the responsibility that he had reluctantly assumed, and when Pickett said, "General, shall I advance?" his emotion permitted no reply, and he simply bowed assent. Then Pickett said, proudly, "I shall lead my division forward, sir!" and at once started the movement of his column.

He had been directed to

STRIKE THE UNION LINES

in the centre, and to this end a peculiar shaped clump of trees in Hancock's front had been pointed out to him by General Longstreet, as the objective point where his division was to hurl themselves against the Union stronghold.

THE CONFEDERATE DIVISION,

commanded by General Pickett, consisting of three brigades of Virginia regiments, had taken no part in the fighting of the two previous days, so they were fresh for the contest.

The other forces that were to participate in the Confederate assault were on the right and left of Pickett's troops. When Pickett had succeeded in pushing his way through the Union line, these supporting troops were to help wedge apart the two wings of their enemy so effectually that MEADE's forces would be dispersed in all directions. The number of Confederate troops participating in this movement, it is supposed, numbered 17,000 men.

The distance to be traversed by the Confederates under fire of the Union guns was nearly a mile. Before they came in sight, General Hunt had improved the opportunity to withdraw the disabled batteries, and replace them by others from the reserve artillery. He had also replenished the ammunition chests that were empty, and was prepared for the outcome.

As the head of Pickett's column appeared on the crest of Seminary Ridge, the Union guns at once opened on them a tremendous fire of solid shot, but as steadily as though forming on a parade ground the troops moved forward down the slope. As Pickett's division advanced, the supporting brigades on the right and left also came in view, and then the whole desperate undertaking of the Confederates was revealed to the Union army.

THE SOUTHERNERS CAME ON MAGNIFICENTLY,

and soon the gaps made in their ranks by the plunging cannon shots could be distinctly seen.

From the start, the direction of their march seemed to be towards the divisions of Caldwell and Doubleday, but when about half the distance had been traversed Pickett changed the direction by an oblique movement to his left, thus bringing the advance towards Gibbon's division, which was on the right of Doubleday.

The two Confederate supporting brigades of Wright and Perry, who were on Pickett's right, failed to conform to this oblique movement, but continued straight on to the front; consequently there was soon a wide interval between these brigades and Pickett's line, leaving both flanks unguarded.

By this time the charges of canister shots from the Union guns was working fearful havoc in the ranks of the Confederates, for they had now moved into close range and so were facing death in a thousand terrible forms.

A battery posted on Little Round Top also opened on their flank, increasing their difficulties, but in the face of all this hurricane of death, they continued to move on, steadily closing up the gaps in their ranks, and gathering strength for a final effort.

But there were other movements that bear upon the final result that must be noted :

General Pettigrew, who commanded the supporting Confederate brigades on the left of Pickett's column, had been advancing under the same difficulties that confronted Pickett. The Union guns on the lines of Hays' division of Gibbon's corps, and Schurz's division of Howard's corps, had been playing upon Pettigrew's columns with terrible effect. Hesitating in the face of the increasing difficulties that awaited their nearer approach, the fire of the Union guns was redoubled, and soon Pettigrew's troops were being hurled back in masses.

General Alexander S. Webb.

When the right flanks of Pickett's column had become greatly exposed by the failure of the supporting brigades of Wright and Perry to conform to his oblique movement, General Stannard, of the Union army, who commanded a brigade of Vermont regiments, attached to Doubleday's division, seized upon the opportunity to advance three of his regiments into the gap thus left open in the advancing Confederate lines. One of these regiments was sent to move on the flank of the supporting brigades, and the other two were moved against the exposed flank of Pickett's column. These were also joined by two other regiments from Doubleday's command, and together they delivered a sharp musketry fire on the flanks of

Pickett's column at close range. This resulted in the surrender of some of the Confederates, while others made a desperate attempt to fall back in retreat.

Now came the culmination of the mighty struggle to pierce the Union lines. Squarely in front of the now desperate Confederates was Webb's Philadelphia brigade of Pennsylvania regiments. Veterans of former campaigns in Virginia, now on the soil of their own State, it was their proud distinction to stand in the breach. Although Webb's front had been the centre of the previous artillery fire, and had already lost fifty men and several brilliant officers, their lines held on firm and impenetrable. It thus devolved upon Webb's brigade to meet the final effort of the Confederates, and decide the fate of the day.

For that unforeseen circumstance it would be difficult to find a man better fitted than Webb. He was nerved to great deeds by the memory of his ancestors who had formerly rendered distinguished service to the Republic, and he felt that the results of the whole war might depend upon his holding the position. His men were equally determined.

Cushing's battery, of the 4th United States artillery, and Brown's Rhode Island battery on his left, had been completely destroyed by the cannonade. The horses were killed ; the officers, with one exception, were struck by fragments of shell, and Cushing had but one serviceable gun left. When Pickett's advance had nearly reached the line, young Cushing, mortally wounded in both thighs, ran his last serviceable gun down to the fence and cried :

"WEBB, I WILL GIVE THEM ONE MORE SHOT!"

At the last discharge of his gun, he cried out, "GOOD-BYE,"—and fell dead at his post of duty.

The Confederate brigade of General Armistead, joined with that of Garnett (both of Pickett's division), had forced their way to an advanced position in front of the stone wall just as the fresh batteries had arrived on the ground. General Armistead crossed the stone wall, and the battery was for a few moments in his possession, and the Southern flag floated triumphantly in the Union lines. But Webb, near at hand, led the 72d Pennsylvania regiment against Armistead, encouraging his men as the two lines came in contact.

A portion of the 71st Pennsylvania, behind a stone wall at the right, poured a murderous fire on the enemy's flank, while a portion of the 69th Pennsylvania, with the remainder of the 71st, made an energetic resistance from the left, behind a clump of trees, near the spot where the Southerners had broken the Union line, and where the northern men were fighting with the Southern muskets touching their breasts. At this moment two regiments of Hall's Brigade made a splendid charge and engaged the Confederates in a hand-to-hand conflict.

Armistead was mortally wounded near one of the cannon he had taken.

DEATH OF LIEUTENANT CUSHING.

1.—Lieutenant Cushing. 2.—Sergeant Fuger. 3.—General Alexander S. Webb.

It is said that his last words, which were addressed to one of our officers, were: "Tell Hancock I have wronged him, and have wronged my country."

Gibbon and Webb were both wounded, and the loss of officers and men in all the Union regiments that were engaged at this point was heavy. Two of Pickett's brigade commanders were killed, and another was severely wounded. The number of prisoners taken at this point was double the number of Webb's brigade. Six battle flags were captured, and 1,463 muskets also taken. When Pickett saw that it was *impossible to hold his position*, and that his lines were completely shattered, heart-broken he made his way back, accompanied by the few who had been enabled to get to the rear.

The next day General Lee was found to have moved back, and within a few days his army was once more on Virginia soil. His losses during the campaign were over thirty-one thousand men, and the Union loss was over twenty-three thousand.

Thus was accomplished the repulse of General Pickett's memorable assault at Gettysburg, on July 3d, 1863.

BATTLE OF GETTYSBURG.

CAUSE OF THE CAMPAIGN.

General Grant, by a series of rapid movements, had succeeded in dividing and defeating the Confederate armies by whom he was confronted at Vicksburg and vicinity, and had completely invested that stronghold. General Banks had invested Port Hudson. New Orleans was also in the possession of the Union Army. The complete collapse of the Confederate cause in the West seemed inevitable, and the reopening of the Mississippi throughout its entire length the result.

To offset a disaster so damaging to the Confederate cause, the idea is conceived of an invasion of the North, by which it is hoped that Washington or some of the rich cities of Pennsylvania might be captured and laid under contribution.

Hooker's losses at Chancellorsville, and the withdrawal of some 20,000 troops whose time had expired, made the time opportune. Lee at once proceeded to mobolize his army. Ewell was advanced up the Shenandoah Valley to seize prominent points and to obtain possession of the fords of the upper Potomac, while a large force was concentrated at Culpepper Court House in support. Hill is left south of the Rapidan to hold Hooker in his present position, in the hope that he might throw Longstreet between that commander and Washington by a flank movement.

Hooker began to suspect Lee of some hostile movement and sent General Howe's division across the river to see if the entire army was still in his front. Hill demonstrated in such a manner as to relieve his fears ; but he was soon undeceived by the appearance of Ewell at Winchester and Longstreet east of the Blue Mountains, in possession of both Snicker's and Ashby's gaps. He now made a most precipitate retreat in the direction of the defences at Washington, moving with such celerity as to defeat Lee's purpose of cutting him off.

Finding that Lee does not follow, he concentrates at Bull Run and moves his advance towards Thoroughfare Gap. Lee now withdraws Ewell's forces from beyond the Potomac, where they had in the meantime advanced, by which movement he deceived both Hooker and the people of the North into the belief that the danger of invasion had passed, and that a battle was to be fought in Virginia.

Lee, finding that Longstreet is unable to decoy Hooker from his base, boldly advances into Pennsylvania by the fords of the upper Potomac at Williamsport and Shepardstown. Hooker at once advances by the fords of the lower Potomac, covering Washington. Now, through some misunderstanding with Halleck as to the proper disposition of the troops at Harper's Ferry and Washington, and because it was thought desirable to make a change in commanders, Hooker was asked to resign. General Reynolds was the commander first thought of to succeed him, but for some reason unknown to the writer, General Meade was substituted.

REYNOLDS.

The appointment of this commander was a complete surprise to himself and everyone else. It did not inspire that confidence which ought to possess an army on the eve of battle, but it created a determination in the minds of both soldiers and officers to make up by their own diligence and courage any weakness in the commander.

General Meade at once moved for the enemy's communications, and prepared to give him battle on the best position attainable. Lee, learning of the forward movement of the Army of the Potomac, and seeing the danger of fighting a battle so far from his base, ordered Ewell, who had advanced towards Harrisburg and York, to concentrate at Gettysburg. Hill's and Longstreet's corps were also withdrawn from Chambersburg to the same rendezvous. The backward movement of Lee will bring him on Meade's flank, that commander having started for the same destination. Meade, however, changes the direction of some of his corps, having decided to stand at Pipe Creek, with his right at Manchester. This is about fifteen miles southeast of Gettysburg. But by one of those fortunate accidents which sometimes thrust greatness on a man, the leader of his advance, Reynolds, who was a man of nerve and action, a man not in sympathy with the methods of the past management of the Army of the Potomac, moved forward and precipitated the contest which gave us the victory at

GETTYSBURG.

This little village, which is to be the scene of the first decisive victory of the Army of the Potomac, is situated in an upland valley surrounded by ranges of hills, at the focus of numerous roads which run to every principal point of the compass. Along the roads which lead to this common center, these two hostile armies are approaching ; each unaware of the other's proximity. Lee's army is advancing (Hill's and Longstreet's corps) along the Chambersburg road from the northwest, and Ewell's corps, which had been split up, via the York and Harrisburg roads, while the Union Army, which has been much shattered by the Chancellorsville fiasco, is moving in disjointed and scattered form under the feeble management of its inexperienced commander, along a number of roads. The advance, the 1st and 11th corps, numbering collectively about 24,000 men, are advancing along the Emmetsburg road, which runs from the southeast; the 5th and 12th are moving by the Taneytown road, which runs from the south; the 2d and 3d are moving by the same road, while the 6th is thirty miles away at Manchester, on the Westminster road.

The Union Army, although badly organized, is not a feeble body numerically, neither is there feebleness in spirit or morale. That army, in its long career of hard luck, the sport of cowardly and incompetent commanders, never flinched from its duty, not once, and to-day, as it is marching to its first victory, its spirit is as high and martial as was the army of Cæsar on the plains of Pharasalia. There is a determination on the part of both rank and file to make this invasion disastrous to Lee, and to avenge Fredericksburg and Chancellorsville. The Army had taken the conduct of this campaign into their own hands.

THE BATTLE OF TUESDAY.

Buford, who commanded the cavalry, moved directly upon Gettysburg, where he encountered the advance of Heth's division of Hill's corps, and drove them back on the main body. The main body now coming up, Buford was in turn driven back. The advance of the 1st corps, under Wadsworth, now approaching along the Emmetsburg road, seeing the situation, charged impetuously, driving them through the town. This was about 10 A. M. Doubleday came up in half an hour and took position on the right of the ridge occupied by Wadsworth. Beyond this ridge is an open valley of ploughed fields and meadows. Across the valley Reynolds charged to a ridge beyond. This position was strongly held by the enemy, who met this charge by a countercharge, driving them back. In this movement some of the enemy pressing the right center too hard, were cut off, and Archer and 800 of his men were captured. The enemy's advance was soon checked, when Reynolds once more charged, this time carrying the ridge beyond, and meeting with heavy loss from the enemy's fire. A line of skirmishers was now thrown out, and Reynolds went forward to reconnoitre the enemy's position. While looking through a fence with his field glass he was killed by a sharpshooter.

Doubleday now assumed command. Deeming the enemy too strong in his front, he retired to Seminary Ridge, which lies west of the town, running south. Here he was joined by Robinson's division. Pender's division of Hill's corps now coming on the field, the enemy assumed the offensive, covering his attack by an artillery fire. The assaulting column was received by a fire at short range by the Union batteries, and a sharp infantry fire, before which they retired with severe loss. Being somewhat re-inforced, they again advanced, with no better success. Howard now appeared with the advance of the 11th corps, and assumed command. Schurz was placed in command of the 11th, who were placed on a ridge north of the town, running nearly at right angles with Seminary Ridge. Steinwehr's division was placed on Cemetery Hill, south of the town two miles away. Early, and very soon after Rhodes of Ewell's corps arrived on the field, and joined in the attack. These four powerful divisions under Lee's ablest generals were able to outflank and outfight the Union advance. Howard now sent for Sickles, who was on the Emmetsburg road, to come to his assistance. That commander (without orders) promptly responded. Early on the right and Rhodes on the left attacked the 11th corps, while Pender attacked the left of the 1st corps, and Heath demonstrated on its right. The result of this combined movement was that Rhodes forced his way between the 1st and 11th, while Early broke through Barlow's line of the 11th, attacking both flank and rear, and Pender turned the left of the 1st corps. The 11th broke in disorder and retreated in disorganized form down the Baltimore road and to Cemetery Hill. The first retired with firm front, Buford's cavalry preventing the enemy from following. This critical position of the right wing of the army was due to Meade's determination not to fight at Gettysburg after many of the corps were well advanced in that direction. Meade, on hearing of Reynolds' death, dispatched Hancock to the scene of disaster, to assume command and note the strategetical points of the field. Hancock, like Sheridan at a later day, rode at a frightful gait over the intervening space to meet the shattered remains of the right wing. Like that other commander, he soon restored order and inspired the troops with his own spirit. At his approach the fugitives returned from the Baltimore road, and the stronger ones rallied to his support. Howard, who was his senior, yielded ready obedience to his orders. Noting the strength of the position at Cemetery Hill, he retained that point as the key of the position, and placed troops at Culp's Hill on the right, and Cemetery Ridge on the left, and threw out skirmishers everywhere. Geary, with a division of the 12th, now arrived, and was placed at Round Top on the extreme left. The Union line under Hancock's

HOWARD.

skillful handling presented to the quick eye of General Lee, who had now arrived, evidence that the new commander of the Union army was a man of rare genius, and an enemy worthy of his steel, and he hesitated to attack until all his corps should arrive. This hesitation gave Sickles time to reach the field on the left and Slocomb to arrive with his corps to strengthen the right. Hancock had notified Meade that Gettysburg offered a good position for defence, but was somewhat exposed to be turned at the left. The 2d arrived after dark near the field; Slocomb, at 7 P. M., assumed command. Meade arrived at 11 P. M., in company with Hancock, who had rejoined him at Taneytown. The 5th corps, Gen. Sykes, arrived in the morning.

WEDNESDAY'S BATTLE.

On the morning of Wednesday, Meade commenced to make dispositions for the defence. His troops had all arrived, except the 6th corps, Sedgwick's, who would not reach the field until afternoon. The first move of Meade demonstrated that he had mistaken the natural advantages of his position. He at once commenced to strengthen his right at the expense of his left, accumulating forces in the direction of Culp's Hill and the Baltimore road. Disregarding Hancock's warning that the left was the weak point, he removed Geary, who had been placed on the Round Top by Hancock on Tuesday, and otherwise leaving the line weak on Cemetery Ridge, the force being altogether inadequate to hold the position. Sickles was left unsupported on the extreme left, while Sykes of the 5th was placed on the right. A commander like Hancock, Sherman or McPherson, could have so placed his troops by the aid of his interior lines, and naturally strong position, as to have held Lee at bay, even without the aid of the 6th, and been in condition, in an emergency like that of Thursday, to have taken aggressive action. Fortunately for the Union army, Lee's state of indecision continued until after the arrival of the 6th corps, who were also placed in reserve. Lee now begins to comprehend the situation, that it is Meade instead of Hancock who commands the Union army. He sees the weakness of the left, and of the Union commander, and his indecision is past. His plan is to have Hill threaten the center at Cemetery Hill, and Ewell to assault the right at and beyond Culp's Hill, while the real attack will be delivered at the left, at Round Top and the

GEN. LEE.

south of Cemetery Ridge. He proposes to seize a ridge which lies east of the Emmetsburg road, and from that high vantage ground assault the Union line and throw his troops in the Union rear. Sickles—who was placed on the left, suspects Meade of not desiring to fight on this field, and who now knows the danger of the Union left, he having learned through Berdan's sharpshooters, who had been advanced beyond the Emmetsburg road, that Lee is massing large forces to turn the Union position—advanced his command to the ridge in front, which I have indicated, from which point he can command his present position, and better resist Lee's movements.

'Tis true that in doing this he disconnects with Hancock's too much extended line; but he knows that Meade has two corps in reserve, and can place some division of the 6th in the gap, and Sykes' 5th corps on his exposed left and rear. Meade, instead of doing this, rides forward and remonstrates with Sickles, or his movement. Sickles replies that he considers the movement within his privilege, but expresses a willingness to withdraw to the ridge in the rear, which Meade indicates as a proper line. It now begins to dawn on Meade that Sickles is right, and he promises to support him. Lee now orders Longstreet to strike Sickles with all his might before he can be supported in his new position. But Sickles don't dislodge easily. He holds on, and resists every attack for two hours, thus causing Longstreet to waste his energies and give the Union commander time to concentrate.

SICKLES.

Longstreet's two commanders (Pickett not being present), Hood and McLaws, are ordered to outflank Sickles' right and left, while three brigades of Anderson's division of Hill's corps join the movement at the point of division between Sickles and Hancock. Longstreet's batteries command Sickles both front and flank. It is absolutely necessary to remove Sickles to successfully attack Round Top and the Union rear.

Warren, who is topographical engineer of the Army of the Potomac, has discovered this weakness at the left, and will at the proper time care for it.

Had Meade spent his time in forwarding troops from his reserves to form a second line in Sickles' rear, and to support Hancock's left, and massing his reserve artillery in that direction, he would have checkmated this movement of the enemy, which was necessarily slow, they having a distance to traverse before reaching the Union line. It makes no difference whether the movement was or was not ill advised; such support would have enabled

Sickles to withdraw without disaster if Meade preferred the rear line for defence. It must be apparent to an impartial observer that Meade lacked that prompt aggressive power to think and act on the instant so essential to commanders of large bodies of men in action.

Hood, on his arrival on Sickles' left flank, finds that it extends to the base of Little Round Top. Ward and DeTroiband, who hold the line, stubbornly resist his attemps to break through, and he sends Law's brigade to outflank at Little Round Top. Warren, in the meantime, has detached Vincent's brigade from Barnes' division of the 5th corps, now on its way to Sickles' support, and place them on Little Round Top. He moves Hazlett's battery and some other forces there also. This force is met rather unexpectedly by the enemy, and a severe contest ensues, which results in the complete repulse of the enemy, with severe loss on both sides.

Hood having failed in his attempt to outflank, and seeing the uselessness of trying to break through Barnes' lines, which are now joined to those of DeTroiband and Ward, now redoubles his energies at the western face of Sickles at Peach Orchard. McLaws having joined his left, attacks Humphrey's division in front, while Wilcox and Perry of Hill's corps attack his right flank. Thus assailed front and flank by this strong infantry force and the batteries, which had now got his exact range, he begins to slowly fall back. The centre, which had been weakened to support the right and left, was the real point that the enemy were trying to force. Barksdale's Mississippians are now launched at Graham's line, which gives way, leaving the Peach Orchard in their possession. The victorious Confederates now advanced and force their way through the gap into the wheat field. Humphrey's line now is attacked in the rear. Ward, with two regiments of Gibbon's divisions and Brown's battery, who hold the left of Hancock's line, are at the same time attacked by Wright's brigade of Hill's corps, and completely demolished, and battery captured.

Hancock now assumed the responsibility of sending one of his divisions (Caldwell's) into the break in Sickles' line, who for a brief time held back the victorious enemy though at a fearful cost of men and officers. As well might he try to stay the advancing waves of the sea. Fresh bodies of advancing Confederates are pushed forward in support, and by their momentum carry back this gallant body. Ayers' division are now advanced to the support of Caldwell and are also forced back, with a loss of nearly one-half of the division. Sickles, who had been vainly trying to retrieve the disaster to Birney's division, has been desperately wounded, and has retired from the field.

Meade now orders Hancock to assume command of the left and center, and throws on that commander the responsibility of saving the army. With the rare promptitude which has ever characterized that gallant officer, he brings order out of chaos. He sees that the power of the advancing Confederates is well nigh spent. At the left, Williams' division of the

12th has arrived from the right, and Lockwood's brigade are forcing back the enemy through the Peach Orchard, bringing back on their return Bigelow's captured guns. Wright has been stopped by Gibbon, who has sent a portion of his force on a countercharge, who on their return have brought back the guns of Brown's Rhode Island battery.

MEADE.

Nearly all the troops engaged thus far have been those of Hancock's, Sickles', and portions of the 5th corps, in which work a long distance of Hancock's line has been stripped bare of troops. Into this break Hancock throws the division of Hayes and whatever loose forces are at hand. Thomas' battery is brought into action. The batteries on Cemetery Hill are turned on the enemy, and rake them with an enfilading fire; Doubleday's division, which has advanced from the first corps, is at once brought into action. Robinson's forces from the same corps are placed in front of the enemy, and the line is everywhere established. Hancock's quick eye has detected and his prompt movements have covered every weak point, and the enemy retire to the ridge captured from Sickles, which is the only fruit of this barren victory. A force equal to the number lost in killed and wounded in this battle, properly placed before the action commenced, would have saved the position.

The enemy, baffled in his purpose of turning the left and rear, advance

THE RIGHT AND RIGHT CENTER.

Ewell's first movement is up the craggy sides of Culp's Hill. This position has been weakened by the withdrawal of troops to support the left. Johnson's division press forward, and after a brief resistance capture the outer works, which are nearly bare of troops. They attempt to push their advantage in the direction of the Baltimore road, but are stopped by the determined attitude of Gen. Greene of Geary's division. No further progress can be made in this direction.

The attack is persisted in along toward the center by Early's division of the same corps, two brigades, Hayes' and Avery's, attacking the eastern face of Cemetery Hill, which attack was successful in carrying the outer works, the capture of the 5th Maine battery, and the driving back of Van Gilas' brigade. Hancock, who is expecting some such demonstration, is moving to the support of the center, Carroll's brigade having been advanced to its relief. The enemy are unexpectedly met by this advancing force and driven back, abandoning the captured works and the guns of the 5th Maine. In the meantime Rhodes and Pender have sent some brigades of their divisions to co-operate in the attack on the center on the west face of Cemetery Hill; but the prompt movements of Hancock have so disconcerted them that they retire without completing the attack. Darkness now settles over the combatants; and the second act in the drama ends.

THE BATTLE OF THURSDAY.

On the morning of July 3d, Geary having returned from the left, Slocomb, who was further re-inforced by Generals Shaler and Ruger of the 6th corps, made an advance on Johnson's division, whose advance occupied a position on Culp's Hill, which Ewell had captured from his command late the night before. After a vigorous resistance by the enemy, favored by the rough wooded declivity, he succeeded in dislodging him, and re-establishing his lines. This action lasted until 11 A. M., when quiet prevailed all along the lines.

THE UNION POSITION,

now perfected, extended from the base of Round Top on the left to Culp's Hill on the right. Sykes' 5th corps was on the extreme left, occupying Little Round Top, and extending a short distance up the side of the Big Round Top. Next came the 3d corps, now commanded by Birney, with Birney's division thrown out in front. Next came the 2d corps, Hancock commanding. In his line, sandwiched between Caldwell's and Gibbon's divisions, was Doubleday's division of the 1st corps. Beyond Hayes' division of the 2d corps, which held the right of Cemetery Ridge, is Ziegler's Grove, a little wood which divides Cemetery Hill from the ridge. This position was occupied by Woodward's battery. Cemetery Hill, the apex of the Union position, was held by Howard's 11th corps and Robinson's division of the first. Culp's Hill and the Baltimore road was held by Slocomb's 12th corps and Wadsworth division of the 1st corps. The Union position at a glance presented the form of a bent bow, with the Taneytown road for the shaft, the point of the barb being nearer the right. Along the ridge, which constituted this line, were 100 guns in position to cover the enemy's advance.

LONGSTREET.

THE CONFEDERATE POSITION

was in concave form, extending to a

point about opposite Little Round Top along Seminary Ridge, across the Bonnoughton, York and Harrisburgh roads, thence continuing the circle through the town and over a slight ridge to Rock Creek and beyond to a point opposite the Baltimore road. The Confederate army was in three large corps of three divisions each. Longstreet, right; Hill, center, and Ewell, left. This order was somewhat changed to meet the exigencies of the advance this day. Longstreet, who is to conduct the movement, has been re-inforced by three fresh brigades of Pickett's division, two divisions of Hill's and one of Ewell's corps. He has massed 55 guns on the ridge from which Sickles was driven, and beyond the Emmetsburg road, Hill continuing the circle to a point beyond the roads which I have named above. While Hill has placed some guns (60 in all) along the higher ridge in his rear (Seminary Ridge), which extends to a point nearly opposite the Union left, these will fire over the heads of Longstreet's forces and some of the advance of the Union left, and concentrate on the position at Cemetery Ridge and Hill.

THE ARTILLERY BATTLE.

At a signal from General Lee, at 1 P. M., with the suddenness of a thunderbolt, the stream of shot and shell and shrapnell bursts on the Union position. The enemy have got the exact range and the fire tells. The air is filled with shrieking shot and shell, with fragments of rock torn from the cliffs, branches of trees, clouds of earth, pieces of gravestones from the cemetery, and flying debris. This medley of discordant sounds is taken up and re-echoed along the valley, making a carnage so awful that no one who witnessed it will forget this artillery fire while life lasts. In a few minutes everything which had life was clear from Cemetery Hill. Men and horses were killed while moving through this blinding storm of dust and missiles for shelter. The rocks, ravines, fences and trees were used to protect the non-combatants, while the infantry, who were stationed to resist the assault which is to follow, were instructed to seek such shelter as could be found until the moment of attack. Not so the artillerists, who stand to their guns and give an answering note from the 100 guns along the heights. Not a cannoneer leaves his post, and the guns, though less in number and calibre, are well served. After an hour and a half of this kind of work, the fire slackens down on the Union side ; it may be to allow the guns to cool, or because heavy ammunition is getting low, or for some other cause. This is considered an evidence of defeat by the enemy, and he increases the intensity of his fire. General Hunt, who wishes to confirm him in his belief, ceased firing, except from a few guns. The enemy now prepare for

THE ASSAULT.

The assaulting column, which is two miles long, emerges from the woods into the open plain. Pickett's division, with Kemper and Garnett in front and Armistead in the rear, lead. Heth's division, now commanded by Pettigrew, is on Pickett's left, a little in the rear. Two of Pender's brigades are thrown out on the left as a wing, and two brigades of the same division are in Pettigrew's rear in support. On the right of Pickett, Wilcox's and Perry's brigades are thrown out as a wing, and Wright's brigade is in the rear in support. In front is a cloud of skirmishers. This brilliant array of troops now moved straight onward towards the left face of Cemetery Ridge, amid the deathly silence of expectation, the Union batteries holding their fire until the assaulting columns are within point blank range.

PICKETT.

As the right of the column approached Doubleday's position, seeing that he was very strongly posted five lines deep, the direction was changed so as to strike Gibbon's divisions, which was only two lines deep. The wing (Wilcox and Perry), not understanding the movement, kept straight onward, leaving a gap, thus exposing Pickett's right flank to Hazlett's and McGilvary's batteries at short range. Hancock now ordered Stanard's Vermont brigade of Doubleday's division to attack Pickett's exposed flank. Other portions of Doubleday's force met the wing, who were thrown back in disorder.

This movement also exposed Pettigrew's left flank to Osborn's batteries on Cemetery Hill, also at short range. Pickett's division kept right on, vaulting over fences and other obstructions, until they arrived at the stone wall. Here a most deadly contest ensued in their attempt to beat down Cushing's battery. The enemy now succeeded in penetrating the Union line, but their onset is met by foemen worthy of their steel. Southern dash is met by Northern pluck. This thin line is composed of the very flower of the Northern army, led by such giants as Hancock, Hunt, Chief of Artillery, Gibbon, Hayes and others, who rally to the support of the overborne column, and check the enemy's advance, delivering into their very faces a fire so terrible that they halt and waver. They cannot retreat; they cannot advance; they are pressed on every side. They now surrender. Over 3,000 prisoners are thus captured, leaving their flags in the hands of the victors. Pettigrew's division moves up to the line at the same moment, but its power is spent. It cannot resist the terrible fire of the batteries on Cemetery Hill and the galling musketry fire, and it crumbles and breaks, flying in disorder across the plain, more than two-thirds of its number being lost in this ill-fated assault. Pickett now retires with the remnant of his division, Lee sending Wright's brigade to cover his retreat from the attacking party of flankers sent out from the Union lines.

THE CYCLORAMA

represents the charge when it is well in progress. When the visitor emerges from the staircase to the platform, he faces the rear of the army. His position is at the intersection of the cross fires of Hill and Longstreet cannon. The site of the platform during the artillery fire was occupied by Battery B. This battery was totally demolished and the debris which lie scattered about are some of its remains. The old shattered house where the squad of cavalry are alighting was Meade's headquarters. The old well where the soldiers are drinking, and the ricks of hay in whose shade the wounded soldiers are lying, and the shed where surgeons are at work form a most realistic picture.

ARMISTEAD.

Culp's Hill in the distance forms a most peaceful background to the scene. At your left the green slope of Cemetery Ridge, with its background of trees, hides the cemetery and Howard's position from view. At your right, Wheeler's battery coming down from the Taneytown road through the wheatfield, and the general hurried movement to the front, cause you to turn sharply around, when you face the point where the three Confederate flags are seen, just beside the stone wall where General Armistead's command have penetrated the Union line. General Armistead has been wounded and is falling backward from his horse.

Lieutenant Cushing, who has vainly attempted to hold the position, has been mortally wounded, and as he lies on the trail of his gun is firing his last shot. Coming to the rescue with Hall's Maine brigade is honest John Gibbon, who sits facing you on his big grey horse pointing his men to where the enemy have penetrated the line. General Hall is right behind him on a black horse, and just a little nearer you General Webb is urging his men forward. Looking beyond the batteries coming to and from the field, in the act of crossing a little farm road, is the general who commands the field, Hancock. A staff officer in the act of delivering a message has been shot, and both horse and rider lie dead in the road.

A prominent point, sure to attract the eye, are the figures of two officers, a fine looking young man in artillery uniform (Major Osborn) and a general officer looking through a field glass (General Hunt, Chief of Artillery), their horses standing knee deep in the wheat. At the same time, glancing just beyond, you see beside a stone wall, surmounted by a rail fence, a line of soldiers also knee deep in the wheat. One giant-formed fellow, with his arm in a sling, seems like a modern Goliath. This is known as the death line, no soldier being allowed to pass to the rear alive.

HANCOCK.

The two artillery officers above mentioned are looking in the direction of Pettigrew's advance in the triangle between the stone wall, watching the effect of the fire of Battery A, whose five guns are playing on the advancing enemy, and of Brown's battery who now occupy the place made vacant by the disaster to Battery B, the site of the platform. The shrinking of the forms of Pettigrew's advance in the triangle is caused by the galling fire of those batteries and their infantry support.

Off to the left, beyond Gibbon, is Doubleday's division with his skirmishers out in front in the shape of a triangle. Other lines are obscured by the grove of trees in front. In the meadow beyond them is Stannard's Vermonters with skirmishers thrown out in the apple orchard. The two detached brigades of Confederates coming through the apple orchard are Wilcox and Perry, Pickett's wing. Away beyond in the rear of some houses on the Emmetsburg road is the famous peach orchard of Wednesday's battle. The faint yellow line in the rear is the wheat field so famous at Gettysburg.

The smoke of the batteries on Little Round Top and the little white puffs in the meadow, this side, bear a close relation to the falling forms in your front. One of these missives has killed another of Pickett's brigadiers, General Garnett, who is near the stone wall at the triangle. This officer has not yet fallen from his horse.

General Kemper, the 3d brigadier, has been severely wounded, and is being borne from the field by two soldiers.

The white puffs of smoke along the ridges in your front, mark the positions of Hill's and Longstreet's cannon during the artillery duel.

To your right, as you look over the line of the five guns of Battery A, you see a portion of the village of Gettysburg. Beyond, to the right of the seminary, is a ploughed hillside fringed by a belt of woodland. Beyond the hill is where Buford's cavalry met the advance of Hill's corps and drove them back on the main body. The enemy, who rallied, drove Buford in turn over these fields to the Emmetsburg road.

General Wadsworth, who was advancing up this road, seeing the situation, charged forward impetuously and drove the enemy through the streets of the village. The positions occupied during the first day's battle are hidden from view by Cemetery and Culp's Hills.

General Lee is between the building pierced with numerous tall windows and the cloud of smoke, seen on the brow of the hill beyond the Emmetsburg road. Pickett is seated on a white horse near some houses a little farther down the road.

Lee is watching with anxious eye the progress of Pickett and Pettigrew. The latter already shows evidence of weakness, the terribly destructive fire of the batteries and Hayes' infantry support has decimated his ranks. The end is so plain to both Longstreet and Lee that their only thought is how to save the army from the expected countercharge of Meade with his reserves, when the recoil comes.

General Meade's reserves composed largely of the 6th corps are in two fields near the Taneytown road. General Meade is near the houses at the base of Power's Hill in the field beyond the death line, seated on a bay horse. His chief of staff, Butterfield, is just behind him on a white horse. The Taneytown road which comes in from the south and passes around the base of Power's Hill and disappears over the brow of Cemetery Ridge is the road by which Hancock arrived on the afternoon of the 1st. The road which is seen over the brow of Power's Hill in the dim perspective as it passes through a scattered hamlet, leads to Baltimore.

GARNETT.

The large hill which lies between the Taneytown road and Little Top, which forms south a fine background to the picture, holds no relation, militarily, to the Union position.

There are many points of interest in the foreground and perspective, both in a historic and artistic point of view, which can only be developed by a study of the painting.

In the triangle, between the two stone walls, are three trees, two pines and a tree resembling a poplar; nothing can be truer to nature in coloring, shape and pose than this tree; if you look under its branches to the right, you will see in the distant perspective a little hamlet nestling in a valley in peaceful contrast to the tragic scene being enacted in the foreground.

It was in this line of view that Gen. Pender, of Hill's Corps, who commanded Pettingrew's wing and supports, was mortally wounded while leading his brigades into action.

Seen in the daylight, this picture is so realistic and so true to nature, that you look in vain for the beginning of the canvas.

PENDER.

The hills and the valleys group themselves naturally, and the soft and fleecy clouds of this July afternoon seem to drift lazily over the landscape. Each figure among these thousands is different from any other. Every face wears a different expression. Every footstep casts a shadow.

Seen under the electric light the illusion is perfect. The fields, and the hills and distant vistas are all real, and these are living, moving figures which surround you.

As you stand and gaze o'er the landscape, memory carries you back over the vista of years to the dark and troublous times when this great victory came like a rift of sunlight over an angry sky.

ROSTER OF THE FEDERAL ARMY

Engaged in the Battle of Gettysburg, Wednesday, Thursday, and Friday, July 1st, 2d, and 3d, 1863.

MAJOR-GENERAL GEO. GORDON MEADE COMMANDING.

STAFF.

MAJOR-GENERAL DANIEL BUTTERFIELD, Chief of Staff.
BRIGADIER-GENERAL M. R. PATRICK, Provost-Marshal-General.
" " SETH WILLIAMS, Adjutant-General.
" " EDMUND SCHRIVER, Inspector-General.
" " RUFUS INGALLS, Quartermaster-General.
COLONEL HENRY F. CLARKE, Chief Commissary of Subsistence.
MAJOR JONATHAN LETTERMAN, Surgeon, Chief of Medical Department.
BRIGADIER-GENERAL G. K. WARREN, Chief Engineer.
MAJOR D. W. FLAGLER, Chief Ordnance Officer.
MAJOR-GENERAL ALFRED PLEASONTON, Chief of Cavalry.
BRIGADIER-GENERAL HENRY J. HUNT, Chief of Artillery.
CAPTAIN L. B. NORTON, Chief Signal Officer.

MAJOR-GENERAL JOHN F. REYNOLDS,[1] Commanding the First, Third, and Eleventh Corps on July 1st.

MAJOR-GENERAL HENRY W. SLOCUM, Commanding the Right Wing on July 2d, and July 3d.

MAJOR-GENERAL W. S. HANCOCK, Commanding the Left Center on July 2d and July 3d.

FIRST CORPS.

MAJOR-GENERAL JOHN F. REYNOLDS, PERMANENT COMMANDER.
MAJOR-GENERAL ABNER DOUBLEDAY, Commanding on July 1st.
MAJOR-GENERAL JOHN NEWTON, Commanding on July 2d and 3d.

FIRST DIVISION.

BRIGADIER-GENERAL JAMES S. WADSWORTH COMMANDING.

First-Brigade.—(1) Brigadier-General SOLOMON MEREDITH (wounded); (2) Colonel HENRY A. MORROW (wounded); (3) Colonel W. W. ROBINSON. 2d Wisconsin, Colonel Lucius Fairchild (wounded), Lieut.-Colonel George H. Stevens (wounded), Major John Mansfield (wounded), Captain Geo. H. Otis; 6th Wisconsin, Lieut.-Colonel R. R. Dawes; 7th Wisconsin, Colonel W. W. Robinson; 24th Michigan, Colonel Henry A. Morrow (wounded), Lieut.-Colonel Mark Flanigan (wounded), Major Edwin B. Wright (wounded), Captain Albert M. Edwards; 19th Indiana, Colonel Samuel Williams.

Second Brigade.—Brigadier-General LYSANDER CUTLER Commanding. 7th Indiana, Major Ira G. Grover; 56th Pennsylvania, Colonel J. W. Hoffman; 76th New York, Major Andrew J. Grover (killed), Captain John E. Cook; 95th New York, Colonel George H. Biddle (wounded). Major Edward Pye; 147th New York, Lieut.-Colonel F. C. Miller (wounded), Major George Harney; 14th Brooklyn, Colonel E. B. Fowler.

SECOND DIVISION.

BRIGADIER-GENERAL JOHN C. ROBINSON COMMANDING.

First Brigade.—Brigadier-General GABRIEL R. PAUL Commanding (wounded); Colonel S. H. LEONARD; Colonel RICHARD COULTER. 16th Maine, Colonel Charles W. Tilden (captured), Lieut.-Colonel N. E. Welch, Major Arch. D. Leavitt; 13th Massachusetts, Colonel S. H. Leonard (wounded); 94th New York, Colonel A. R. Root (wounded), Major S. H. Moffat; 104th New York, Colonel Gilbert G. Prey; 107th Pennsylvania, Colonel T. F. McCoy (wounded), Lieut.-Colonel James McThompson (wounded), Captain E. D. Roath; 11th Pennsylvania, Colonel Richard S. Coulter, Captain J. J. Bierer.[2]

Second Brigade.—Brigadier-General HENRY BAXTER Commanding. 12th Massachusetts, Colonel James L. Bates; 83d New York, Lieut.-Colonel Joseph R. Moesch; 97th New York, Colonel Charles Wheelock; 88th Pennsylvania, Major Benezet F. Faust, Captain E. Y. Patterson; 90th Pennsylvania, Colonel Peter Lyle.

---

[1] He was killed and succeeded by Major-General O. O. Howard.
[2] The Eleventh Pennsylvania was transferred from the Second Brigade.

THIRD DIVISION.

MAJOR-GENERAL ABNER DOUBLEDAY PERMANENT, COMMANDER on July 2d and 3d.
BRIGADIER-GENERAL THOMAS A. ROWLEY, July 1st.

First Brigade.—Brigadier-General THOMAS A. Rowley, July 2d and 3d; Colonel CHAPMAN BIDDLE, July 1st. 121st Pennsylvania, Colonel Chapman Biddle, Major Alexander Biddle; 142d Pennsylvania, Colonel Robert P. Cummings (killed), Lieut.-Colonel A. B. McCalmont; 151st Pennsylvania, Lieut.-Colonel George F. McFarland (lost a leg), Captain Walter L. Owens; 20th New York S. M., Colonel Theodore B. Gates.

Second Brigade.—(1) Colonel ROY STONE Commanding (wounded); (2) Colonel LANGHORNE WISTER (wounded), (3) Colonel EDMUND L. DANA. 143d Pennsylvania, Colonel Edmund L. Dana, Major John D. Musser; 149th Pennsylvania, Lieut.-Colonel Walton Dwight (wounded), Captain A. J. Sofield (killed), Captain John Irvin; 150th Pennsylvania, Colonel Langhorne Wister (wounded), Lieut.-Colonel H. S. Huiedekoper (wounded), Major Thomas Chamberlain (wounded), Captain C. C. Widdis (wounded), Captain G. W. Jones.

Third Brigade.—Brigadier-General GEO. J. STANNARD Commanding (wounded). 12th Vermont, Colonel Asa P. Blunt (not engaged); 13th Vermont, Colonel Francis V. Randall; 14th Vermont, Colonel William T. Nichols; 15th Vermont, Colonel Redfield Proctor (not engaged); 16th Vermont, Colonel Wheelock G. Veazy.

Artillery Brigade.—Colonel CHARLES S. WAINWRIGHT Commanding. 2d Maine, Captain James A. Hall; 5th Maine, G. T. Stevens; Battery B, 1st Pennsylvania, Captain J. H. Cooper; Battery B. 4th United States, Lieutenant James Stewart; Battery L, 1st New York, Captain J. A. Reynolds.

[NOTE.—Tidball's Battery of the Second United States Artillery, under Lieutenant John H. Calef, also fought in line with the First Corps. Lieutenant Benj. W. Wilbur, and Lieutenant George Breck, of Captain Reynold's Battery, and Lieutenant James Davison, of Stewart's Battery, commanded sections which were detached at times.]

SECOND CORPS.

MAJOR-GENERAL WINFIELD S. HANCOCK, PERMANENT COMMANDER (wounded).
MAJOR-GENERAL JOHN GIBBON (wounded).
BRIGADIER-GENERAL JOHN C. CALDWELL.

FIRST DIVISION.

BRIGADIER-GENERAL JOHN C. CALDWELL.
COLONEL JOHN R. BROOKE (wounded).

First Brigade.—Colonel EDWARD E. CROSS (killed); Colonel H. B MCKEEN. 5th New Hampshire, Colonel E. E. Cross, Lieut.-Colonel C. E. Hapgood; 61st New York, Lieut.-Colonel Oscar K. Broady; 81st Pennsylvania, Colonel H. Boyd McKeen, Lieut.-Colonel Amos Stroho; 148th Pennsylvania, Lieut.-Colonel Robert McFarland.

Second Brigade.—Colonel PATRICK KELLY Commanding. 28th Massachusetts, Colonel Richard Byrnes; 63d New York, Lieut.-Colonel R. C. Bentley (wounded), Captain Thos. Touhy; 69th New York, Captain Richard Maroney (wounded), Lieutenant James J. Smith; 88th New York, Colonel Patrick Kelly, Captain Dennis F. Burke; 116th Pennsylvania, Major St. Clair A. Mulholland.

Third Brigade.—Brigadier-General S. K. ZOOK Commanding (killed); Lieut.-Colonel JOHN FRAZER. 52d New York, Lieut.-Colonel Charles G. Freudenberg (wounded), Captain Wm. Sherrer; 57th New York, Lieut.-Colonel Alfred B. Chapman; 66th New York, Colonel Orlando W. Morris (wounded), Lieut.-Colonel John S. Hammel (wounded), Major Peter Nelson; 140th Pennsylvania, Colonel Richard P. Roberts (killed), Lieut.-Colonel John Frazer.

Fourth Brigade.—Colonel JOHN R. BROOKE Commanding (wounded). 27th Connecticut, Lieut.-Colonel Henry C. Merwin (killed), Major James H. Coburn; 66th New York, Colonel Daniel G. Bingham; 53d Pennsylvania, Colonel J. R. Brooke, Lieut.-Colonel Richard McMichael; 145th Pennsylvania, Colonel Hiram L. Brown (wounded), Captain John W. Reynolds (wounded), Captain Moses W. Oliver; 2d Delaware, Colonel William P. Bailey.

SECOND DIVISION.

BRIGADIER-GENERAL JOHN GIBBON, PERMANENT COMMANDER (wounded).
BRIGADIER-GENERAL WILLIAM HARROW.

First Brigade.—Brigadier-General WILLIAM HARROW Commanding; Colonel FRANCIS E. HEATH. 19th Maine, Colonel F. E. Heath, Lieut.-Colonel Henry W. Cunningham; 15th Massachusetts, Colonel George H. Ward (killed), Lieut.-Colonel George C. Joslin; 82d New York, Colonel Henry W. Huston (killed), Captain John Darrow; 1st Minnesota, Colonel William Colvill (wounded), Captain N. S. Messick (killed), Captain Wilson B. Farrell, Captain Louis Muller, Captain Joseph Periam, Captain Henry C. Coates.

Second Brigade.—Brigadier-General ALEX. S. WEBB Commanding (wounded). 69th Pennsylvania, Colonel Dennis O. Kane (killed), Lieut.-Colonel M. Tschudy (killed), Major James Duffy (wounded), Captain Wm. Davis; 71st Pennsylvania, Lieut.-Colonel Richard Penn Smith; 72d Pennsylvania, Colonel De Witt C. Baxter; 106th Pennsylvania, Lieut.-Colonel Theo. Hesser.

Third Brigade.—Colonel NORMAN J. HALL Commanding. 19th Massachusetts, Colonel Arthur F. Devereux; 20th Massachusetts, Colonel Paul J. Revere (killed), Captain H. L. Abbott (wounded); 42d New York, Colonel James E. Mallon; 59th New York, Lieut.-Colonel Max A. Thoman (killed); 7th Michigan, Colonel N. J. Hall, Lieut.-Colonel Amos E. Steele (killed), Major S. W. Curtis.

Unattached.—Andrew Sharpshooters.

THIRD DIVISION.

BRIGADIER-GENERAL ALEXANDER HAYS COMMANDING.

First Brigade.—Colonel SAMUEL S. CARROLL Commanding. 4th Ohio, Lieut.-Colonel James H. Godman, Lieut.-Colonel L. W. Carpenter; 8th Ohio, Colonel S. S. Carroll, Lieut.-Colonel Franklin Sawyer; 14th Indiana, Colonel John Coons; 7th West Virginia, Colonel Joseph Snycer.

Second Brigade.—Colonel THOMAS A. SMYTH Commanding (wounded); Lieut.-Colonel F. E. PIERCE. 14th Connecticut, Major John T. Ellis; 10th New York (battalion), Major Geo. F. Hopper; 108th New

York, Colonel Charles J. Powers; 12th New Jersey, Major John T. Hill; 1st Delaware, Colonel Thomas A. Smyth; Lieut.-Colonel Edward P. Harris, Captain M. B. Ellgood (killed), Lieutenant Wm. Smith (killed).

Third Brigade.—Colonel GEORGE L. WILLARD Commanding (killed); Colonel ELIAKIM SHERRILL (killed); Lieut.-Colonel JAMES M. BULL. 39th New York, Lieut.-Colonel James G. Hughes; 111th New York, Colonel Clinton D. McDougall (wounded), Lieut.-Colonel Isaac M. Lusk, Captain A. P. Seeley; 125th New York, Colonel G. L. Willard (killed), Lieut.-Colonel Levi Crandall; 126th New York, Colonel E. Sherrill (killed); Lieut.-Colonel J. M. Bull.

Artillery Brigade.—Captain J. G. HAZARD Commanding. Battery B, 1st New York, Captain James McK. Rorty (killed); Battery A, 1st Rhode Island, Lieutenant William A. Arnold; Battery B, 1st Rhode Island, Lieutenant T. Fred. Brown (wounded); Battery I, 1st United States, Lieutenant G. A. Woodruff (killed); Battery A, 4th United States, Lieutenant A. H. Cushing (killed).

[NOTE.—Battery C, 4th United States, Lieutenant E. Thomas, was in the line of the Second Corps on July 3d. Some of the batteries were so nearly demolished that there was no officer to assume command at the close of the battle.]

Cavalry Squadron.—Captain RILEY JOHNSON Commanding. D and K, 6th New York.

THIRD CORPS.

MAJOR-GENERAL DANIEL E. SICKELS COMMANDING (wounded).
MAJOR-GENERAL DAVID B. BIRNEY.

FIRST DIVISION.

MAJOR-GENERAL DAVID B. BIRNEY, PERMANENT COMMANDER.
BRIGADIER-GENERAL J. H. H. WARD.

First Brigade.—Brigadier-General C. K. GRAHAM Commanding (wounded, captured); Colonel ANDREW H. TIPPIN. 57th Pennsylvania, Colonel Peter Sides, Lieut.-Colonel Wm. P. Neeper (wounded), Captain A. H Nelson; 63d Pennsylvania, Lieut.-Colonel John A. Danks; 68th Pennsylvania, Colonel A. H. Tippin, all the Field Officers wounded; 105th Pennsylvania, Colonel Calvin A. Craig; 114th Pennsylvania, Lieut.-Colonel Frederick K. Cavada (captured); 141st Pennsylvania, Colonel Henry J. Madill, Captain E. R. Brown.[1]

[NOTE.—The Second New Hampshire, Third Maine, and Seventh and Eighth New Jersey also formed part of Graham's line on the 2d.]

Second Brigade.—Brigadier-General J. H. H. WARD Commanding; Colonel H. BERDAN. 1st U. S. Sharpshooters, Colonel H. Berdan, Lieut.-Colonel C. Trapp; 2d U. S. Sharpshooters, Major H. H. Stoughton; 3d Maine, Colonel M. B. Lakeman (captured), Captain William C. Morgan; 4th Maine. Colonel Elijah Walker (killed), Major Ebenezer Whitcombe (wounded), Captain Edward Libby; 20th Indiana, Colonel John Wheeler (killed), Lieut.-Colonel William C. L. Taylor; 99th Pennsylvania, Major John W. Moore; 86th New York, Lieut.-Colonel Benjamin Higgins; 124th New York, Colonel A. Van Horn Ellis (killed), Lieut.-Colonel Francis M. Cummings.

Third Brigade.—Colonel PHILIP R. DE TROBRIAND Commanding. 3d Michigan, Colonel Byron R. Pierce (wounded), Lieut.-Colonel E. S. Pierce; 5th Michigan, Lieut.-Colonel John Pulford (wounded), Major S. S. Matthews; 40th New York, Colonel Thomas W. Egan; 17th Maine, Lieut.-Colonel Charles B. Merrill; 110th Pennsylvania, Lieut.-Colonel David M. Jones (wounded), Major Isaac Rogers.

SECOND DIVISION.

BRIGADIER-GENERAL ANDREW A. HUMPHREYS COMMANDING.

First Brigade.—Brigadier-General JOSEPH B. CARR Commanding. 1st Massachusetts, Colonel N. B. McLaughlin; 11th Massachusetts, Lieut.-Colonel Porter D. Tripp; 16th Massachusetts, Lieut.-Colonel Waldo Merriam; 27th Pennsylvania, Captain Geo. W. Tomlinson (wounded), Captain Henry Goodfellow; 11th New Jersey, Colonel Robert McAllister (wounded), Major Philip J. Kearney (killed), Captain Wm. B. Dunning; 84th Pennsylvania (not engaged), Lieut.-Colonel Milton Opp; 12th New Hampshire, Captain J. F. Langley,

Second Brigade.—Colonel WILLIAM R. BREWSTER Commanding. 70th New York (1st Excelsior), Major Daniel Mahen; 71st New York (2d Excelsior), Colonel Henry L. Potter; 72d New York (3d Excelsior), Colonel Wm. O. Stevens (killed), Lieut.-Colonel John S. Austin; 73d New York (4th Excelsior), Colonel William R. Brewster, Major M. W. Burns; 74th New York (5th Excelsior), Lieut.-Colonel Thomas Holt; 120th New York, Lieut.-Colonel Cornelius D. Westbrook (wounded), Major J. R. Tappen, Captain A. L. Lockwood.

Third Brigade.—Colonel GEORGE C. BURLING Commanding. 5th New Jersey, Colonel William J. Sewall (wounded), Captain Virgel M. Healey (wounded), Captain T. C. Godfrey, Captain H. H. Woolsey; 6th New Jersey, Colonel George C. Burling, Lieut.-Colonel S. R. Gilkyson; 7th New Jersey, Colonel L. R. Francine (killed), Lieut.-Colonel Francis Price; 8th New Jersey, Colonel John Ramsey (wounded), Captain John G. Langston; 115th Pennsylvania, Lieut.-Colonel John P. Dunne; 2d New Hampshire, Colonel Edward L. Bailey (wounded), Major Saml. P. Sayles (wounded).

Artillery Brigade.—Captain GEORGE E. RANDOLPH Commanding. Battery E, 1st Rhode Island, Lieutenant John K. Bucklyn (wounded), Lieutenant Benj. Freeborn; Battery B, 1st New Jersey, Captain A. J Clark; Battery D. 1st New Jersey, Captain Geo. T. Woodbury; Battery K, 4th U. S., Lieutenant F. W. Seeley (wounded), Lieutenant Robt. James; Battery D, 1st New York, Captain George B. Winslow; 4th New York, Captain James E. Smith.

FIFTH CORPS.

MAJOR-GENERAL GEORGE SYKES COMMANDING.

FIRST DIVISION.

BRIGADIER-GENERAL JAMES BARNES COMMANDING.

First Brigade.—Colonel W. S. TILTON Commanding. 18th Massachusetts, Colonel Joseph Hayes;

[1] Colonel Madill commanded the 114th and 141st Pennsylvania.

22d Massachusetts, Colonel William S. Tilton, Lieut.-Colonel Thomas Sherman, Jr.; 118th Pennsylvania, Colonel Charles M. Provost; 1st Michigan, Colonel Ira C. Abbott (wounded), Lieut.-Colonel W. A. Throop.

Second Brigade.—Colonel J. B. SWEITZER Commanding. 9th Massachusetts, Colonel Patrick R. Guiney; 32d Massachusetts, Colonel Geo. L. Prescott (wounded), Lieut.-Colonel Luther Stephenson (wounded), Major J. Cushing Edmunds; 4th Michigan, Colonel Hamson H. Jeffords (killed), Lieut.-Colonel George W. Lombard; 62d Pennsylvania, Colonel J. B. Sweitzer, Lieut.-Colonel James C. Hull.

Third Brigade.—Colonel STRONG VINCENT Commanding (killed); Colonel JAMES C. RICE. 20th Maine, Colonel Joshua L. Chamberlain; 44th New York, Colonel James C. Rice, Lieut-Colonel Freeman Conner; 83d Pennsylvania, Major William H. Lamont, Captain O. E. Woodward; 16th Michigan, Lieut.-Colonel N. E. Welch.

SECOND DIVISION.

BRIGADIER-GENERAL ROMAYN B. AYRES COMMANDING.

First Brigade.—Colonel HANNIBAL DAY, 6th U. S. Infantry, Commanding. 3d U. S. Infantry, Captain H. W, Freedley (wounded), Captain Richard G. Lay; 4th U. S. Infantry, Captain J. W. Adams; 6th U. S. Infantry, Captain Levi C. Bootes; 12th U. S. Infantry, Captain Thomas S. Dunn; 14th U. S. Infantry, Major G. R. Giddings.

Second Brigade.—Colonel SIDNEY BURBANK, 2d U. S. Infantry, Commanding. 2d U. S. Infantry, Major A. T. Lee (wounded), Captain S. A. McKee; 7th U. S. Infantry, Captain D. P. Hancock; 10th U. S. Infantry, Captain William Clinton; 11th U. S. Infantry, Major De L. Floyd Jones; 17th U. S. Infantry, Lieut.-Colonel Durrell Green.

Third Brigade.—Brigadier-General S. H. WEED (killed); Colonel KENNER GARRARD. 140th New York, Colonel Patrick H. O'Rorke (killed), Lieut.-Colonel Louis Ernst; 146th New York, Colonel K. Garrard, Lieut.-Colonel David T. Jenkins; 91st Pennsylvania, Lieut.-Colonel Joseph H. Sinex; 155th Pennsylvania, Lieut.-Colonel John H. Cain.

THIRD DIVISION.

BRIGADIER-GENERAL S. WILEY CRAWFORD COMMANDING.

First Brigade.—Colonel WILLIAM MCCANDLESS Commanding. 1st Pennsylvania Reserves, Colonel William Cooper Talley; 2d Pennsylvania Reserves, Colonel William McCandless, Lieut.-Colonel George A. Woodward; 6th Pennsylvania Reserves, Colonel Wellington H. Ent; 11th Pennsylvania Reserves, Colonel S. M. Jackson; 1st Rifles (Bucktails), Colonel Charles J. Taylor (killed), Lieut.-Colonel A. E. Niles (wounded), Major William R. Hartshorn.

Second Brigade.—Colonel JOSEPH W. FISHER Commanding. 5th Pennsylvania Reserves, Colonel J. W. Fisher, Lieut.-Colonel George Dare; 9th Pennsylvania Reserves, Lieut.-Colonel James McK. Snodgrass; 10th Pennsylvania Reserves, Colonel A. J. Warner; 12th Pennsylvania Reserves, Colonel M. D. Hardin.

Artillery Brigade.—Captain A. P. MARTIN Commanding. Battery D, 5th United States, Lieutenant Charles E. Hazlett (killed), Lieutenant B. F. Rittenhouse; Battery I, 5th United States, Lieutenant Leonard Martin; Battery C, 1st New York, Captain Albert Barnes; Battery L, 1st Ohio, Captain N. C. Gibbs; Battery C, Massachusetts, Captain A. P. Martin.

Provost Guard.—Captain H. W. RYDER. Companies E and D, 12th New York.

SIXTH CORPS.

MAJOR-GENERAL JOHN SEDGWICK COMMANDING.

FIRST DIVISION.

BRIGADIER-GENERAL H. G. WRIGHT COMMANDING.

First Brigade.—Brigadier-General A. T. A. TORBERT Commanding. 1st New Jersey, Lieut.-Colonel William Henry, Jr.; 2d New Jersey, Colonel Samuel L. Buck; 3d New Jersey, Colonel Henry W. Brown; 15th New Jersey, Colonel William H. Penrose.

Second Brigade.—Brigadier-General J. J. BARTLETT Commanding. 5th Maine, Colonel Clark S. Edwards; 121st New York, Colonel Emory Upton; 95th Pennsylvania, Lieut.-Colonel Edward Carroll; 96th Pennsylvania, Lieut.-Colonel William H. Lessig.

Third Brigade.—Brigadier-General D. A. RUSSELL Commanding. 6th Maine, Colonel Hiram Burnham; 49th Pennsylvania, Colonel William H. Irvin; 119th Pennsylvania, Colonel P. C. Ellmaker; 5th Wisconsin, Colonel Thomas S. Allen.

SECOND DIVISION.

BRIGADIER-GENERAL A. P. HOWE COMMANDING.

Second Brigade.—Colonel L. A. GRANT Commanding. 2d Vermont, Colonel J. H. Walbridge; 3d Vermont, Colonel T. G. Seaver; 4th Vermont, Colonel E. H. Stoughton; 5th Vermont, Lieut.-Colonel John R. Lewis; 6th Vermont, Lieut.-Colonel Elisha L. Barney.

Third Brigade.—Brigadier-General T. A. NEILL Commanding. 7th Maine, Lieut.-Colonel Seldon Conner; 49th New York, Colonel D. D. Bidwell; 77th New York, Colonel J. B. McKean; 43d New York, Colonel B. F. Baker; 61st Pennsylvania, Major Geo. W. Dawson.

THIRD DIVISION.

BRIGADIER-GENERAL FRANK WHEATON COMMANDING.

First Brigade.—Brigadier-General ALEXANDER SHALER Commanding. 65th New York, Colonel J. E. Hamblin; 67th New York, Colonel Nelson Cross; 122d New York, Lieut.-Colonel A. W. Dwight; 23d Pennsylvania. Lieut.-Colonel John F. Glenn; 82d Pennsylvania, Colonel Isaac Bassett.

Second Brigade.—Colonel H. L. EUSTIS Commanding. 7th Massachusetts, Lieut.-Colonel Franklin P. Harlow; 10th Massachusetts, Lieut.-Colonel Jefford M. Decker; 37th Massachusetts, Colonel Oliver Edwards; 2d Rhode Island, Colonel Horatio Rogers.

Third Brigade.—Colonel DAVID L. NEVIN Commanding. 62d New York, Colonel D. L. Nevin, Lieut.-Colonel Theo. B. Hamilton; 102d Pennsylvania,[1] Colonel John W. Patterson; 93d Pennsylvania, Colonel

[1] Not engaged.

James M. McCarter; 98th Pennsylvania, Major John B. Kohler; 139th Pennsylvania, Lieut.-Colonel William H. Moody.

Artillery Brigade.—Colonel C. H. TOMPKINS Commanding. Battery A, 1st Massachusetts, Captain W. H. McCartney; Battery D, 2d United States, Lieutenant E. B. Williston; Battery F, 5th United States, Lieutenant Leonard Martin; Battery G, 2d United States, Lieutenant John H. Butler; Battery C, 1st Rhode Island, Captain Richard Waterman; Battery G, 1st Rhode Island, Captain George W. Adams; 1st New York, Captain Andrew Cowan; 3d New York, Captain William A. Harn.

Cavalry Detachment.—Captain WILLIAM L. CRAFT Commanding. H, 1st Pennsylvania; L, 1st New Jersey.

ELEVENTH CORPS.

MAJOR-GENERAL OLIVER O. HOWARD, PERMANENT COMMANDER.
MAJOR-GENERAL CARL SCHURZ, July 1st.

FIRST DIVISION.

BRIGADIER-GENERAL FRANCIS C BARLOW COMMANDING (wounded).
BRIGADIER-GENERAL ADELBERT AMES.

First Brigade.—Colonel LEOPOLD VON GILSA Commanding. 41st New York, Colonel L. Von Gilsa, Lieut.-Colonel D. Von Einsiedel; 54th New York, Colonel Eugene A. Kezley; 68th New York, Colonel Gotthilf Bourney de Ivernois; 153d Pennsylvania, Colonel Charles Clanz.

Second Brigade.—Brigadier-General ADELBERT AMES Commanding; Colonel ANDREW L HARRIS. 17th Connecticut, Lieut.-Colonel Douglass Fowler (killed), Major A. G. Brady (wounded); 25th Ohio, Lieut.-Colonel Jeremiah Williams (captured), Lieutenant William Maloney (wounded), Lieutenant Israel White; 75th Ohio, Colonel Andrew L. Harris (wounded), Lieut.-Colonel Ben Morgan (wounded), Major Charles W. Friend; 107th Ohio, Captain John M. Lutz.

SECOND DIVISION.

BRIGADIER-GENERAL A. VON STEINWEHR COMMANDING.

First Brigade.—Colonel CHARLES R. COSTER Commanding. 27th Pennsylvania, Lieut.-Colonel Lorenz Cantador; 73d Pennsylvania, Captain Daniel F. Kelly; 134th New York, Colonel Charles R. Coster, Lieut.-Colonel Allan H. Jackson; 154th New York, Colonel Patrick H. Jones.

Second Brigade.—Colonel ORLANDO SMITH Commanding. 33d Massachusetts, Lieut.-Colonel Adin B. Underwood; 136th New York, Colonel James Wood, Jr.; 55th Ohio, Colonel Charles B. Gambee; 73d Ohio, Colonel Orlando Smith, Lieut.-Colonel Richard Long.

THIRD DIVISION.

MAJOR-GENERAL CARL SCHURZ, PERMANENT COMMANDER.
BRIGADIER-GENERAL ALEXANDER SCHIMMELPFENNIG COMMANDING on July 1st.

First Brigade.—Brigadier-General A. VON SCHIMMELPFENNIG Commanding (captured); Colonel GEORGE VON ARNSBURG. 45th New York, Colonel G. Von Arnsburg, Lieut.-Colonel Adolphus Dobke; 157th New York, Colonel Philip P. Brown, Jr.; 74th Pennsylvania, Colonel Adolph Von Hartung (wounded), Lieut.-Colonel Von Mitzel (captured), Major Gustav Schleiter; 61st Ohio, Colonel S. J. McGroarty; 82d Illinois, Colonel J. Hecker.

Second Brigade.—Colonel WALDIMIR KRYZANOWSKI Commanding. 58th New York, Colonel W. Kryzanowski, Lieut.-Colonel August Otto, Captain Emil Koenig, Lieut.-Colonel Frederick Gellman; 119th New York, Colonel John S. Lockman, Lieut.-Colonel James C. Rogers; 75th Pennsylvania, Colonel Francis Mahler (wounded), Major August Ledig; 82d Ohio, Colonel James J. Robinson (wounded), Lieut.-Colonel D. Thomson; 26th Wisconsin, Colonel Wm. H. Jacobs.

Artillery Brigade.—Major THOMAS W. OSBORN Commanding. Battery I, 1st New York, Captain Michael Wiedrick; Battery I, 1st Ohio, Captain Hubert Dilger; Battery K, 1st Ohio, Captain Lewis Heckman; Battery G, 4th United States, Lieutenant Bayard Wilkeson (killed), Lieutenant E. A. Bancroft; 13th New York, Lieutenant William Wheeler.

TWELFTH CORPS.

BRIGADIER-GENERAL ALPHEUS S. WILLIAMS COMMANDING.

FIRST DIVISION.

BRIGADIER-GENERAL THOMAS H. RUGER COMMANDING.

First Brigade.—Colonel ARCHIBALD L. MCDOUGALL Commanding. 5th Connecticut, Colonel Warren W. Packer; 20th Connecticut, Lieut.-Colonel William B. Wooster; 123d New York, Colonel A. L. McDougall, Lieut.-Colonel James C. Rogers; 145th New York, Colonel E. L. Price; 46th Pennsylvania, Colonel James E. Selfridge; 3d Maryland, Colonel J. M. Sudsburg.

Second Brigade.[1]—Brigadier-General HENRY H. LOCKWOOD Commanding. 150th New York, Colonel John H. Ketcham; 1st Maryland (P. H. B.), Colonel William P. Maulsby; 1st Maryland (E. S.), Colonel James Wallace.

Third Brigade.—Colonel SILAS COLGROVE Commanding. 2d Massachusetts, Colonel Charles R. Mudge (killed), Lieut.-Colonel Charles F. Morse; 107th New York, Colonel Miron M. Crane; 13th New Jersey, Colonel Ezra A. Carman (wounded), Lieut.-Colonel John R. Fesler; 27th Indiana, Colonel Silas Colgrove, Lieut.-Colonel John R. Fesler; 3d Wisconsin, Lieut.-Colonel Martin Flood.

SECOND DIVISION.

BRIGADIER-GENERAL JOHN W. GEARY COMMANDING.

First Brigade.—Colonel CHARLES CANDY Commanding. 28th Pennsylvania, Captain John Flynn; 147th Pennsylvania, Lieut.-Colonel Ario Pardee, Jr.; 5th Ohio, Colonel John H. Patrick; 7th Ohio, Colonel William R. Creighton; 29th Ohio, Captain W. F. Stevens (wounded), Captain Ed. Hays; 66th Ohio, Colonel C. Candy, Lieut.-Colonel Eugene Powell.

---

[1] Unassigned during progress of battle; afterward attached to First Division as Second Brigade.

Second Brigade.—(1) Colonel GEORGE A. COBHAM, JR.; (2) Brigadier-General THOMAS L. KANE. 29th Pennsylvania, Colonel William Rickards; 109th Pennsylvania, Captain Fred L. Gimber; 111th Pennsylvania, Lieut.-Colonel Thomas M. Walker, Lieut.-Colonel Frank J. Osgood.

Third Brigade.—Brigadier-General GEORGE S. GREENE Commanding. 60th New York, Colonel Abel Godard; 78th New York, Lieut.-Colonel Von Hammerstein; 102d New York, Lieut.-Colonel James C. Lane (wounded); 137th New York, Colonel David Ireland; 149th New York, Colonel Henry A. Barnum, Lieut.-Colonel Charles B. Randall.

Artillery Brigade.—Lieutenant EDWARD D. MUHLENBERG Commanding. Battery F, 4th United States, Lieutenant E. D. Muhlenberg, Lieutenant S. T. Rugg; Battery K, 5th United States, Lieutenant D. H. Kinsie; Battery M, 1st New York, Lieutenant Charles E. Winegar; Knapp's Pennsylvania Battery, Lieutenant Charles Atwell.

Headquarter Guard.—Battalion 10th Maine.

CAVALRY CORPS.

MAJOR-GENERAL ALFRED PLEASONTON COMMANDING.

FIRST DIVISION.

BRIGADIER-GENERAL JOHN BUFORD COMMANDING.

First Brigade.—Colonel WILLIAM GAMBLE Commanding. 8th New York, Colonel Benjamin F. Davis; 8th Illinois, Colonel William Gamble, Lieut.-Colonel D. R. Clendenin; two squadrons 12th Illinois, Colonel Amos Voss; three squadrons 3d Indiana, Colonel George H. Chapman.

Second Brigade.—Colonel THOMAS C. DEVIN Commanding. 6th New York, Colonel Thomas C. Devin, Lieut.-Colonel William H. Crocker; 9th New York, Colonel William Sackett; 17th Pennsylvania, Colonel J. H. Kellogg; 3d Virginia (detachment).

Reserve Brigade.—Brigadier-General WESLEY MERRITT Commanding. 1st United States, Captain R. S. C. Lord; 2d United States, Captain T. F. Rodenbough; 5th United States, Captain J. W. Mason; 6th United States, Major S. H. Starr (wounded), Captain G. C. Cram; 6th Pennsylvania, Major James H. Hazeltine.

SECOND DIVISION.

BRIGADIER-GENERAL D. McM. GREGG COMMANDING.

(HEADQUARTER GUARD — Company A, 1st Ohio.)

First Brigade.—Colonel J. B. McINTOSH Commanding. 1st New Jersey, Major M. H. Beaumont; 1st Pennsylvania, Colonel John P. Taylor; 3d Pennsylvania, Lieut.-Colonel Edward S. Jones; 1st Maryland, Lieut.-Colonel James M. Deems; 1st Massachusetts at Headquarters, Sixth Corps.

Second Brigade.[1]—Colonel PENNOCK HUEY Commanding. 2d New York, 4th New York, 8th Pennsylvania, 6th Ohio.

Third Brigade.—Colonel J. I. GREGG Commanding. 1st Maine, Colonel Charles H. Smith; 10th New York, Major W. A. Avery; 4th Pennsylvania, Lieut.-Colonel W. E. Doster; 16th Pennsylvania, Lieut.-Colonel John K. Robison.

THIRD DIVISION.

BRIGADIER-GENERAL JUDSON KILPATRICK COMMANDING.

(HEADQUARTER GUARD — Company C, 1st Ohio.)

First Brigade.—(1) Brigadier-General E. J. FARNSWORTH; (2) Colonel N. P. RICHMOND. 5th New York, Major John Hammond; 18th Pennsylvania, Lieut.-Colonel William P. Brinton; 1st Vermont, Colonel Edward D. Sawyer; 1st West Virginia, Colonel H. P. Richmond.

Second Brigade.—Brigadier-General GEORGE A. CUSTER Commanding. 1st Michigan, Colonel Charles H. Town; 5th Michigan, Colonel Russell A. Alger; 6th Michigan, Colonel George Gray; 7th Michigan, Colonel William D. Mann.

HORSE ARTILLERY.

First Brigade.—Captain JOHN M. ROBERTSON Commanding. Batteries B and L, 2d United States, Lieutenant Edw. Heaton; Battery M, 2d United States, Lieutenant A. C. M. Pennington; Battery E, 4th United States, Lieutenant S. S. Elder; 6th New York, Lieutenant Jos. W. Martin; 9th Michigan, Captain J. J. Daniels; Battery C, 3d United States, Lieutenant William D. Fuller.

Second Brigade.—Captain JOHN C. TIDBALL Commanding. Batteries G and E, 1st United States, Captain A. M. Randol; Battery K, 1st United States, Captain William M. Graham; Battery A, 2d United States, Lieutenant John H. Calef; Battery C, 3d United States.

ARTILLERY RESERVE.

(1) BRIGADIER-GENERAL R. O. TYLER (disabled).
(2) CAPTAIN JOHN M. ROBERTSON.

First Regular Brigade.—Captain D. R. RANSOM Commanding (wounded). Battery H, 1st United States, Lieutenant C. P. Eakin (wounded); Batteries F and K, 3d United States, Lieutenant J. C. Turnbull; Battery C, 4th United States, Lieutenant Evan Thomas; Battery C, 5th United States, Lieutenant G. V. Weir.

First Volunteer Brigade.—Lieut.-Colonel F. McGILVERY Commanding. 15th New York, Captain Patrick Hart; Independent Battery Pennsylvania, Captain R. B. Ricketts; 5th Massachusetts, Captain C. A. Phillips; 9th Massachusetts, Captain John Bigelow.

Second Volunteer Brigade.—Captain E. D. TAFT Commanding. Battery B, 1st Connecticut;[1] Battery M, 1st Connecticut;[1] 5th New York, Captain Elijah D. Taft; 2d Connecticut, Lieutenant John W. Sterling.

Third Volunteer Brigade.—Captain JAMES F. HUNTINGTON Commanding. Batteries F and G, 1st Pennsylvania, Captain R. B. Ricketts; Battery H, 1st Ohio, Captain Jas. F. Huntington; Battery A, 1st New Hampshire, Captain F. M. Edgell; Battery C, 1st West Virginia, Captain Wallace Hill.

[1] Not engaged. [2] A section of a battery attached to the Purnell Legion was with Gregg on the 3d.

NEW YORK REGIMENTS AT GETTYSBURG.

CAVALRY.

2d, 4th, 5th, 6th, 8th, 9th, 10th Regiments.

ARTILLERY.

Battery B, C, D, E, G, I, K, L, M, 1st Regiment.
1st, 3d, 4th, 5th, 6th, 10th, 11th, 13th, 15th of Independent Battery.

ENGINEERS.

15th, 50th.

INFANTRY.

8th, 10th, 12th, 33d Batteries.

10th, 39th, 40th, 41st, 42d, 43d, 44th, 45th, 49th, 50th, 52d, 54th, 57th, 58th, 59th, 60th, 61st, 62d, 63d, 64th, 65th, 66th, 67th, 68th, 69th, 70th, 71st, 72d, 73d 74th, 76th, 77th 78th, 80th, 82d, 83d, 84th, 86th, 88th, 93d, 94th, 95th, 96th, 97th, 102d, 103d, 104th, 107th, 108th, 111th, 119th, 120th, 121st, 122d, 123d, 124th, 125th, 126th, 134th, 136th, 137th, 140th, 145th, 146th, 147th, 149th, 150th, 154th, 157th Regiments.

LIGHT BATTERY.

3d, 13th, 15th Batteries; SERRELL'S ENGINEERS; 1st Lincoln Cavalry, 2d, 6th Cavalry; 1st Mounted Rifles.

NEW JERSEY REGIMENTS AT GETTYSBURG.

INFANTRY.

1st Regiment,	TORBERT'S BRIGADE,	6th Corps.
2d "	" "	6th "
3d "	" "	6th "
4th "	* " "	6th "
5th "	BURLING'S "	3d "
6th "	" "	3d "
7th "	" "	3d "
8th "	" "	3d "
11th "	CARR'S "	3d "
12th "	SMYTH'S "	2d "
13th "	COLGROVE'S "	12th "
15th "	TORBERT'S "	6th "

CAVALRY.

1st Regiment,	McINTOSH'S BRIGADE,	Gregg's Division.

ARTILLERY.

Battery "A,"	FITZHUGH'S BRIGADE,	Reserve Artillery.
Battery "B,"	ARTILLERY "	3d Corps.
Battery "D,"	" "	3d "

* The 4th Regiment was detached from their brigade, guarding the ammunition train of the RESERVE ARTILLERY.

General W. S. Hancock and Staff.

1.—General Hancock. 2.—General Bingham. 3.—Major Mitchell. 4.—Col. W. P. Wilson. 5.—Captain Miller. 6.—Captain Parker.

RESOLUTIONS

OF THANKS TO

MAJOR GENERAL ROSECRANS,

WITH

GENERAL ROSECRANS' REPLY;

AND THE

ADDRESS OF THE OHIO SOLDIERS TO THE PEOPLE OF OHIO;

TOGETHER WITH

THE CORRESPONDENCE CONNECTED THEREWITH.

COLUMBUS:
RICHARD NEVINS, STATE PRINTER
1863.

RESOLUTIONS

OF THANKS TO

MAJOR GENERAL ROSECRANS,

WITH

GENERAL ROSECRANS' REPLY;

AND THE

ADDRESS OF THE OHIO SOLDIERS TO THE PEOPLE OF OHIO;

TOGETHER WITH

THE CORRESPONDENCE CONNECTED THEREWITH.

COLUMBUS:
RICHARD NEVINS, STATE PRINTER.
1863.

Resolved by the Senate and House of Representatives of the State of Ohio, That twenty-five thousand copies of the resolution of thanks of this General Assembly to Major-General Rosecrans, with the correspondence of the Governor, and the reply of General Rosecrans thereto, and the Address of the Ohio soldiers, with the correspondence connected therewith, be printed for the use of the Members of the General Assembly.

JAMES R. HUBBELL,
Speaker of the House of Representatives.
B. STANTON,
President of the Senate.

April —, 1863.

CORRESPONDENCE.

THE STATE OF OHIO,
EXECUTIVE DEPARTMENT,
COLUMBUS, *January 20th*, 1863.

Major-General ROSECRANS:

Dear General,—In transmitting to you the accompanying Resolutions of our General Assembly—of thanks to the surviving, and of sympathy to the families of the patriot dead, of your command, for your and their victorious bravery in the recent great battle before Murfreesboro, I cannot but express to you the high admiration I entertain for the brilliant generalship and cool courage manifested by you on that most discouraging and desperate battle-field, and also my high appreciation of the great gallantry of your command.

God grant that the success thus far attending you in the brilliant series of battles of Iuka, Corinth and Murfreesboro, may attend you and your noble command, until this unholy rebellion shall be utterly and forever crushed.

Very truly yours,
DAVID TOD

RESOLUTIONS

Relative to a vote of thanks to Major-General Rosecrans.

Resolved by the General Assembly of the State of Ohio, That the thanks of this General Assembly are hereby tendered to Major-General Rosecrans, staff, officers, and the brave men under their commands, for the glorious victory resulting in the capture of Murfreesboro, and defeat of the rebel forces at that place.

Resolved, That the sympathies of the General Assembly are extended to the families of the brave and noble patriots that have fallen in defense of Freedom and Constitutional Liberty, and that their memories will ever be cherished by a grateful people.

Resolved, That the Governor be requested to forward a copy of the foregoing resolutions to General Rosecrans, with the request that they be read to his command.

JAMES R. HUBBELL,
Speaker of the House of Representatives.
P. HITCHCOCK,
President pro tem. of the Senate.

January 14, 1863.

THE STATE OF OHIO,
EXECUTIVE DEPARTMENT,
COLUMBUS, *February* 10*th*, 1863.

To the Speaker of the House of Representatives:

Herewith I communicate a letter from Major-General Rosecrans, acknowledging the receipt of your resolution of thanks,

And have the honor to be,
Respectfully yours,
DAVID TOD, *Governor.*

Letter from General Rosecrans.

HEAD-QUARTERS, DEPARTMENT OF THE CUMBERLAND,
MURFREESBORO, TENN., February 3, 1863.

To the Honorable the General Assembly of the State of Ohio:

The resolution of thanks passed by your honorable body to the Army of the Cumberland, its Commanding General and his staff, has been duly received and published to the troops of this command. On behalf of all, I return you heartfelt thanks.

This is indeed a war for the Constitution and the laws—nay, for National existence—against those who have despised our honest friendship, deceived our just hopes, and driven us to defend our country and our homes. By foul and willful slanders on our motives and intentions, persistently repeated, they have arrayed against us our own fellow-citizens, bound to us by the triple ties of consanguinity, geographical position, and commercial interest.

Let no man amongst us be base enough to forget this, or fool enough to trust an oligarchy of traitors to their friends, to civil liberty, and human freedom. Voluntary exiles from home and friends, for the defense and safety of all, we long for the time when gentle peace shall again spread her wings over our land; but we know no such blessing is possible while the unjust and arbitrary power of the rebel leaders confronts and threatens us.

Crafty as the fox, cruel as the tiger, they cried "No coercion," while preparing to strike us. Bully-like, they proposed to fight us, because they said they could whip five to one; and now when driven back, they whine out, "No invasion," and promise us of the West permission to navigate the Mississippi, if we will be "good boys" and do as they bid us.

Wherever they have the power, they drive before them into their ranks the Southern people, and they would also drive us. Trust them not; were they able, they would invade and destroy us without mercy. Absolutely assured of these things, I am amazed that any one could think of "peace on any terms."

He who entertains the sentiment is fit only to be a slave; he who utters it at this time is, moreover, a traitor to his country, who deserves the scorn and contempt of all honorable men. When the power of the unscrupulous rebel leaders is removed, and the people are free to consider and act for their own interests, which are common with ours under this Government, there will be no great difficulty in fraternization. Between our tastes and social life there are fewer differences than between those of the people of the northern and southern provinces of England or Ireland.

Hoping the time may speedily come when the power of the perfidious and cruel tyrant of this rebellion, having been overthrown, a peace may be laid on the broad foundations of National Unity and Equal Justice to all, under the Constitution and the Laws,

I remain, your fellow-citizen,
W. S. ROSECRANS, *Maj.-Genl.*

THE STATE OF OHIO, EXECUTIVE DEPARTMENT,
Columbus, March 14th, 1863.

To the Senate and House of Representatives :

The soldiers from Ohio in the Western Army, alive to the best interests of our State and people, have seen proper to send back an Address to those they left behind, which they wish me, through you, to communicate to our common constituents.

The address and letter accompanying the same are herewith submitted. Most heartily endorsing the sentiments and action of the brave men who thus speak to us, I respectfully recommend that both the letter and address be spread upon your Journals and published to the world.

Very respectfully,
DAVID TOD, *Governor.*

ADDRESS OF THE OHIO SOLDIERS OF THE WESTERN ARMY TO THE PEOPLE OF OHIO.

THE BATTLE FIELD OF STONE RIVER,
February 1st, 1863.

To the People of Ohio :

The Ohio Soldiers of the Western Army, your Friends, Brothers and Sons, address you from this field of renown, in urgent entreaty, upon matters of such grave import to them and to the country, as to demand your calm and patient audience. Exiles from home for long weary months, away from the petty strife of local politics and the influence of selfish demagogues and party leaders, with the pure and steadfast faith in the holy cause of defending our Government which brought us into the field, and has sustained us in perils, hardships, toils and exposures, which have scarcely a parallel in history, we feel none of the acrimonious bitterness that now enters into the ignoble contentions of home politics, and calmly view the condition of the country from that only true stand-point, the Soldier's and Patriot's devotion to the Great Republic—once blessed of all nations.

We ask, what means this wild, shameless party strife at home ? Why any opposition to this war of self-preservation ? Why any but political demagogues should wish a severance of the Republic ? Wherefore a foolish cry for a cessation of hostilities on our part, to give time to the traitor rebels to strengthen their defences and discipline their armies ? Why should the brave, true men of the great army of the United States, war-broken, toil-worn and battle-stained, be left without sympathy or aid from you, men of Ohio, now enjoying the blessings of peace, careless of dangers of invasion and war's dread terrors, only because we, your brothers and sons, stand "between your loved homes and war's desolation ?"

Are we not in war ? Is not the whole force of the Government employed in defending the nation against a gigantic effort to destroy it ? Has not blood flowed like water, and treasure expended enough to make rich a nation ? Is it not worth preserving ? Can two or more States be carved out peacefully from the present loved Republic ? Can we give away its rivers, lands and loyal people to its destroyers ? Can we afford to divide the Republic into contending petty States and be forever the victims of internecine wars between small principalities ? Can we quietly, calmly, even complacently, sit by and see the grand Republic of the world thus cut off and destroyed by innate weakness ? No honest citizen of Ohio is willing that such should be our fate.

What matters now the cause of the war ? by whose fault, or by the adoption of what mistaken policy ? It exists ! It must be fought out, or ended by giving up all that it is waged for. For the sake of peace; to be rid of the burdens of taxation; for fear of the shedding of blood—would any basely give up his nation and become the citizen of a ruined and dishonored land?

Then wherefore opposition to the war? Because a particular party is in power? because its policy is obnoxious? because it has committed errors? because it has thrown to its surface and given prominence to bad or incompetent men? or adopted political theories and sought to make them practical, which are condemned by many good men? No! the remedies for all these evils, if they exist at all, may be sought in the quiet, but powerful means of the ballot, which has power in our Government to change dynasties, where the armies of the world would fail.

Is it thought that peace and a voluntaray restoration of the Union may be effected by compromise? All that has been tried. Disdainfully, the rebels flung back in our faces every proffered olive branch, before peaceful men became armed soldiers and the booming of Fort Sumter's cannon, with its terrible alarum, called a nation to arms. And now, insolent and defiant, they laugh to scorn all thoughts of peace on any other terms than recognition of their false nationality. They are stronger now than then. The despots and money-changers of Europe have given them substantial aid to destroy a Republic; they have more powerful armies, abler generals, and a firmer determination than when the rebellion began. They know their strength and APPEAL TO IT—not to the poor demagogues of the North, who are their allies. They condemn and despise THEM. Read their proclamations, addresses, army orders and newspapers. At no time have they ever spoken of Northern friends except as ALLIES IN THE WAR! They deride the foolish appeals of their Northern allies for peace and compromise, and preclude all hope of the restoration of the Union on any terms.

What incalculable mischief is being done by these NORTHERN ALLIES,—their speeches and newspapers are quoted, and results of elections reported in Southern newspapers, as evidence, not of any hope of restoring the Union, but to show that the loyal people of the North are becoming willing to submit to any dishonorable and humiliating terms of peace, based even on a full recognition that this fiendish rebellion is right, and that it was well to destroy this Government.

People of Ohio! BUT ONE ALTERNATIVE IS LEFT YOU. YOU MUST PRONOUNCE THIS A JUST REBELLION. YOU MUST SAY THAT IT WAS RIGHT AND JUSTIFIABLE TO DESTROY THIS REPUBLIC; THAT A REPUBLIC IS A WEAK, HELPLESS GOVERNMENT, POWERLESS TO SUSTAIN ITSELF, AND TO BE DESTROYED WHENEVER CONSPIRATORS ENOUGH CAN BE ALLIED FOR THE PURPOSE, OR, YOU MUST SHOW TO THE WORLD the power of self-preservation in the great example of Confederated Republics. That it has a quiet dormant force, which aroused, has gigantic strength and energy. That it not only can protect its citizens in all of their rights and privileges, but can sustain itself as well against foreign attack, as internal treason.

We are fighting for the Republic; to it we have given our hearts, our arms, our lives. We intend to stand between you and the desolating hosts of the rebels, whose most cherished hope and desire has been and is, to take possession of and ravage your own beautiful Ohio. Once already we have stood as a living wall between you and this fate, and we may have to do it again.

Men of Ohio! You know not what this Western Army has suffered. You know not now the hardships and sufferings of your soldiers in their chill tents, their shelterless bivouacs, their long, weary marches, and their battle-thinned ranks. If there be honesty and purity in human motives, it must be found among your long-enduring soldiers. Hear us, and for your Country's sake if not for ours, stop your wild, shameless, political strifes; unite for the common cause, and never think or speak of peace and compromise until the now empty terms mean, The Republic as it was, peacefully if it may be, but forcibly at all events. It is said, war and force cannot restore the Union! What can?

Is there anything else that has been left untried, short of national dishonor and shame? Nothing. Purely physical power has been invoked to destroy the Government, and physical force must meet it. Conquer the rebellious armies, shut in by blockades and victorious armies the deluded people of the rebelling States, and let no peace, no happiness, no prosperity dwell in their land or homes, until they rise against their own tyrants—until popular opinion with them, overthrows their false Government, and dooms their despotic leaders. Whip them and confine them, until "Actæon is devoured by his own dogs."

This is all that can be done, and it must be done with the determined energy of a united people. Thus feel and think the soldiers of the Grand Army of the United States. Are you with us, or will you now desert us, sell your national birthright for a mess of pottage, and for success in local politics, barter away your country—crawl at the feet and lick the hands of the perfidious, cruel and devilish conspirators, who have organized this rebellion, and who boast of their success in destroying your Government, slaying your sons, and wasting your treasure—contemned, derided and despised by them, while you are humbly craving their favor? Not waiting or even hoping for returning loyalty in them, or for terms of peace to be tendered by them? Can you thus dishonor yourselves, your soldiers, and your State?

We ask you now to stay, support and uphold the hands of your soldiers.

Give some of the wasted sympathy so illy but freely bestowed upon the old political hacks and demagogues who SEEK a blessed martyrdom in Lincoln Bastiles, to the suffering but bravely-enduring soldiers who in the camp, the field and the hospital, bear real hardships uncomplainingly. If treason must run riot in the North, keep it there; insult not your soldiers by sending to them the vile emanations of the traitors who are riding into office, place and power, over the ruins of the Government, and making them their stepping-stones. Insult us not by letters, speeches and papers, which tell us that we are engaged as hirelings in an unholy abolition war—which make mob idols of the hour of those whose hypocritical demagoguery takes shape in cowardly, covert treason—whose constant vocation is denunciation of their Government and its armed defenders.

The Army of the West is in terrible earnest—earnest to conquer and destroy armed rebels—earnest to meet force with force—earnest in its hearty detestation of cowardly traitors at home—earnest in will and power to overcome all who desire the nation's ruin.

Ohio's 100,000 soldiers in the field, citizens at home, potent in either capacity, ask their fathers, brethren and friends, by their firesides, and in their peaceful homes, to hear and heed this appeal, and to put an end to covert treason at home, more dangerous now to our national existence than the presence of the armed hosts of misguided rebels in the field.

On the hearing and adoption of this Address by the 1st Brigade, 3d Division, 14th Army Corps, Col. WALKER also reported the following resolution, which was unanimously adopted:

Therefore, Resolved, For ourselves, we are resolved to maintain the honor and integrity of our Government; from the St. Lawrence to the Gulf, and between the Oceans, there shall be but one supreme political power. We are able to defend our birthright; the blood of our sires is not contaminated in our veins; we are neither to be insulted, nor robbed with impunity; the Government we defend was formed for noble purposes; we are the executors of a living, a dying testament, written in the blood of our fathers, which we will re-write in our own; to preserve our Government, is to us a law, unalterable in our hearts as the decrees of Heaven; we stop not now to point the finger of scorn at petty traitors who vainly seek to immortalize themselves by acts of treason—too cowardly to sin with an uplifted hand, too dastardly to stake life for life, as more honorable traitors do—let them bear in mind that there is a time coming when the honest indignation of a loyal people will hurl them headlong into an abyss as bottomless as the pit.

IN CAMP, NEAR MURFREESBORO, TENN.,
Feb. 24th, 1863.

To His Excellency DAVID TOD, *Governor of Ohio:*

It has been deemed proper to send to you, as Governor of Ohio, the inclosed address of the Ohio soldiers, that through you the same may be formally presented to the people and Legislature of Ohio. To that end, at a meeting of officers of several of the regiments, held on the 10th inst., we were appointed a committee to visit the Ohio regiments in this department, and ascertain how many had approved the same, and report to you the address and resolution, and also the regiments that have given their approval to the sentiments of the same.

Our army is scattered over a large extent of territory, and hence we have not yet reached all, but have the pleasure of announcing to you that the following regiments have adopted the address and resolution, and given them their approval:

1st, 3d, 6th, 9th, 10th, 13th, 14th, 17th, 18th, 19th, 21st, 24th, 26th, 31st, 33d, 35th, 38th, 41st, 52d, 64th, 65th, 69th, 74th, 90th, 93d, 94th, 97th, 99th, 101st, 105th Infantry, 1st, 3d, and 4th Ohio Cavalry, and 1st Ohio Battery.

And we have such assurances that we feel positive in saying, that the others (only five, now here) will adopt the same as soon as the same reach the other regiments.

The address and resolution have been cheerfully and enthusiastically and unanimously adopted wherever a vote has been had.

The Ohio regiments in this department are with and for the Government in putting down this rebellion.

We are, Governor,
Respectfully,
Your obedient servants,
Capt. J. W. STINCHCOMB,
Co. B, 17th O. V. I., Chairman.
WM. A. CHOATE,
Lieut. Col., 38th Reg., O. V. I.
WM. H. FREE,
Capt., Co. D, 31st O. V. I.
Committee of Publication.

SPEECH OF

HON. HORATIO SEYMOUR,

Before the Democratic State Convention, at Albany, Sept. 10, 1862.

ON RECEIVING THE NOMINATION FOR GOVERNOR.

Mr. President, having uniformly and decidedly expressed my unwillingness to hold any official position at this time, I did not expect my name would be brought before this Convention. The nomination you have made subjects me to great inconvenience whatever may be the result of this election. I came to this Convention expecting to aid in placing at the head of the ticket the name of one whom I feel to be more fit than myself for that honorable position. But, sir, whatever may be the injury to myself, I cannot refuse a nomination made in a manner that touches my heart and fills me with a still stronger sense of my obligations to this great and patriotic party. In addition to my debt of gratitude to partial friends, I am impelled by the condition of our country, to sacrifice my personal wishes and interests to its good.

Two years have not passed away since a Convention, remarkable for its numbers, patriotism and intelligence, assembled at this place to avert if possible the calamities which afflict our people. In respectful terms, it implored the leaders of the political party which had triumphed at a recent election to submit to the people of this country some measure of conciliation which would save them from civil war. It asked that before we should be involved in the evils and horrors of domestic bloodshed, those upon whom it would bring bankruptcy and ruin, and into whose homes it would carry desolation and death, should be allowed to speak. That prayer for the rights of our people was derided and denounced, and false assurances were given that there was no danger. The storm came upon us with all its fury—and the war so constantly and clearly foretold, desolated our land. It is said no compromises would have satisfied the South. If we had tried them it would not now be a matter of discordant opinion. If these offers had not satisfied the South, they would have gratified loyal men at the North, and would have united us more perfectly.

Animated by devotion to our Constitution and Union our people rallied to the support of Government, and one year since shewed an armed strength that astonished the world. We again appealed to those who wielded this mighty material power, to use it for the restoration of the Union and to uphold the Constitution, and were told that he who clamored for his Constitutional rights was a traitor!

Congress assembled. Inexperienced in the conduct of public affairs, drunk with power, it began its course of agitation, outrage and wrong. The defeat of our arms at Manassas, for a time filled it with terror. Under this influence it adopted the resolution of Mr. Crittenden, declaring,

"That the present deplorable Civil War has been forced upon the country by the Disunionists of the Southern "States, now in arms against the Constitutional Government, and in arms around the Capital; That in this National emergency Congress banishing all feelings of "mere passion or resentment, will recollect only its duty "to the whole Country; That this war is not waged, on "their part, in any spirit of oppression or for any purpose "of conquest or subjugation, or purpose of overthrowing "or interfering with the rights or established institutions "of those States, but to defend and maintain the *supremacy* of the Constitution and to preserve the Union with "all the dignity, equality and rights of the several States "unimpaired, and that as soon as these objects are accomplished the war ought to cease.

Again the people rallied around the flag of the Union. But no sooner were their fears allayed than they began anew the factious intrigues—the violent discussions and the unconstitutional legislation which ever bring defeat and disgrace upon Nations. In vain were they warned of the consequences of their follies. In vain did the President implore forbearance and moderation. No act was omitted which would give energy to the Secessionists, or which would humiliate and mortify the loyal men of the South. Every topic calculated to divide and distract the North was dragged into embittered debates. Proclamations of emancipation were urged upon the President, which could only confiscate the property of loyal citizens at the South; for none others could be reached by the power of the government. The confiscation act had already forfeited the legal rights of all who were engaged in or who aided and upheld the rebellion. These were excited to desperate energy by laws which made their lives, their fortunes, the safety of their families and homes depend upon the success of their schemes.—From the Dragon's teeth, sown broadcast by Congress, have sprung the armies which have driven back our forces, and which now beleaguer the Capital of our Country. The acts of the National Legislature have given pleasure to the Abolitionists, victories to the Secessionists. But while treason rejoices and triumphs, defeat and disgrace have been brought upon the Flag of our Country and the defenders of our Constitution. Every man who visited Washington six months ago could see and feel we were upon the verge of disaster. Discord, jealousy, envy and strife pervaded its atmosphere.

I went to the camp of our soldiers. Amid the hardships of an exhausting campaign—amid sufferings from exposure and want—amid those languishing upon beds of sickness, or those struck down by the casualities of war, I heard and saw only devotion to our Constitution, and love for our Country's Flag. Each eye brightened as it looked upon the National Standard with its glorious emblazonry of Stars and Stripes. From this scene of patriotic devotion I went into our National Capitol. I traversed its Mosaic pavements; I gazed upon its walls of polished marble; I saw upon its ceilings all that wealth, lavishly poured out, could do to make them suggestive of our country's greatness and its wonderful wealth of varied productions. Art had exhausted itself in painting and sculpture to make every aspect suggestive of high and noble thought and purpose. Full of the associations which cluster about this vast Temple which should be dedicaded to patriotism and truth; I entered its Legislative Halls; their gilded walls and gorgeous furniture did not contrast more strongly with the rude scenes of martial life than did the glisten ing putrescence and thin lacquer of Congressional virtue contrast with the sterling loyalty and noble self-sacrifice of our country's defenders. I listened to debates full of bitterness and strife.

I saw in the camp a heartfelt homage to our national flag—a stern defiance of those who dared to touch its sacred fold with hostile hands. I heard in the Capitol threats of mutilation of its emblazonry—by striking down the life of States. He who would rend our National standard by dividing our Union is a Traitor. He who would put out one glittering star from its azure field, is a Traitor too.

THE PRESENT CONDITION OF OUR COUNTRY.

Let us now confront the facts of our condition, and they shall be stated in the language of those who brought this administration into power, and who now are politically opposed to the members of this Convention. After the expenditure of nearly one thousand millions of dollars, and the sacrifice of more than one hundred thousand Northern lives in the language of the *Evening Post*:

What has been the result? Our armies of the West, the noble victors of Fort Donelson and Shiloh, are scattered so that no man knows their whereabout, while the foe they were sent to disperse is a hundred miles in their rear, threatening the cities of Tennessee and Kentucky, and even advancing toward one of the principal commercial cities of the Free States. There is no leadership, no unity of command, apparently no plan or concert of action in the entire region we have undertaken to hold and defend. At the same time, our army of the East, numbering 250,000 thousand troops, fully armed and equipped and admirably disciplined, after investing the Capital of the enemy, has been driven back to its original position on the Potomac, decimated in numbers and unprepared to make a single vigorous movement in advance.

And it adds:—

Now it is useless to shut our eyes to the fact that this is a failure, disgraceful, humiliating and awful.

The *Evening Journal*, the accredited organ of the Secretary of State, now admits the truths uttered in this Hall when we assembled here in February, 1861; truths then derided and denounced as absurd and treasonable. It says:

The War has been a stern schoolmaster to the People of the Loyal States. We have learned the folly of underrating our enemies. We have learned that they are equally brave, equally hardy, equally quick witted, equally endowed with martial qualities with ourselves. We have learned they are terribly in earnest in their efforts to achieve their ends.

The New York *Tribune* declares that

"The Country is in peril. Viewed from the standpoint of the public estimate of 'the situation,' it is in extreme peril. The Rebels seem to be pushing forward their forces all along the border line from the Atlantic to the Missouri. They are threatening the Potomac and the Ohio. They are striking at Washington, Cincinnati and Louisville. This simultaneous movement is both alarming and encouraging. It is alarming because, through the timidity, despondency, or folly of the Federal Government, it may become temporarily successful, giving to the foe a lodgment in some portion of the Free States which may require weeks to break up."

But it is admitted by those who were opposed to us, that debt and defeat are not the heaviest calamities which weigh us down. A virtuous people and a pure government can bear up against any amount of outward pressure or physical calamity, but when rottenness and corruption pervade the legislative hall or executive department the heart of the patriot faints and his arm withers. The organ of the Secretary of State admits:

"There have been mistakes. There have been speculation. Weak men have disgraced, and bad men have betrayed the Government. Contractors have fattened on fat jobs. Adventurers have found the war a source of private gain. Moral desporadoes have flocked about the National Capital and lain in wait for prey. The scum of the land has gathered about the sources of power and defiled them by its reek and offensive odor.—There has been mismanagement in the departments; mismanagement wherever great labor has been performed and great responsibilities devolving. Men—even Presidents and Cabinet officers and Commanding Generals—have erred, because they could not grasp the full significance of the drama, and because they were compelled to strike out on untrodden paths."—*Eve. Journal.*

Hear the voice of a leading Republican orator:

"I declare it upon my responsibility as a Senator of the United States," said John P. Hale, "that the liberties of this country are in greater danger to-day from the corruptions and from the profligacy practiced in the various departments of the Government than they are from the open enemy in the field."

The New York *World* exclaims in an agony of remorse:

It is with dismay and unspeakable shame that we, who have supported the administration from the beginning, observe its abuse of its power of arrest. There is no such thing as either justifying or extenuating its conduct in this particular. Every principle of American liberty, every regard for the loyal cause, every sentiment of justice, every impulse of manhood, cries out against it. The man who thinks at all is absolutely staggered that these things can be. They seem like some hideous dream. One can almost fancy that Mephistophiles himself had got access into the councils of the government, and by some device, fresh from the pit, had diverted its energies from the repression of rebellion to the suppression of liberty.

The New York *Times* demands a change in the Administration, and in the conduct of affairs.

I have thus carefully set forth the declarations and named the witnesses to this awful indictment, against our rulers, for we mean to proceed with all the care and candor, and all the solemnity of a Judicial Tribunal.

It is with a sorrowful heart I point to these dark pictures, not drawn by journals of the Democratic party. God knows that as a member of that patriotic organization, as an American citizen, I would gladly efface them if I could. But, alas, they are grounded upon truths that cannot be gainsaid. Once more, then, our Republican fellow-citizens, in this day of our common humiliation and disgrace, we implore you as respectfully as in the hour of your political triumph listen to our suggestions. We do not come with reproaches, but with entreaties. Follow the pathways marked out by the Constitution and we shall be extricated from our perilous position. On the other hand, if you will still be governed by those who brought us into our present condition, you will learn too late that there are yet deeper depths of degradation before us, and greater miseries to be borne than those which now oppress us. Nay more, the President of the United States appeals to us all, in his communication with the loyal men of the Border States, when he says he is pressed to violate his duty, his oath of office, and the Constitution of the land—pressed by cowardly and heartless men, living far away from the scenes of war, fattening upon the wealth coined from the blood and misery of the land, and living in those localities where official investigations show that this people and Government have been robbed by fraudulent contracts. Such men demand that those who have suffered most in this contest, who have shown the highest and purest patriotism under the terrible trials of divided families, of desolated homes, of ruined fortunes and of blood stained fields, should have a new and further evil inflicted upon them by the hands of a Government they are struggling to uphold. By the help of God and the people we will relieve the President from that pressure.

NECESSITY FOR PARTY ORGANIZATIONS.

An attempt is made to close the ears of our Republican friends to our appeals, because we act as a political organization. Can we do otherwise? Would not the dispersion of this ancient party, identified as it is with the growth, greatness and glory of our land, be looked upon as a calamity, even by our opponents? Did not a shadow fall upon our country when it was torn apart at Charleston; and do not men of all parties point to its disruption as one of the causes of this unnatural war? Is it not just we should have a representation in the State and National government proportioned to our contributions to our armies and the treasury? If we elect all of our ticket at this time, we shall have no more than our proportional share of political power. It may be said we should meet without regard to political organizations, and nominate officers. This destroys the object of such organizations. They would cease to be protections against abuses of power or the inroads of corruption. Let the two great parties be honest and honorable enough to meet in fair and open discussion with well defined principles and policies. Then each will serve our country as well out of power as in power. The vigilance kept alive by party contest guards against corruption or oppression. This watchfulness is most needed when unusual expenditures of money present unusual temptations to the corrupt and selfish.

For another reason we cannot disband our organization. The Union men of the Border and more Southern States, without distinction of party, implore us not to do so. They tell us a triumph of our party now would be worth more than victories upon the battle field. It would re assure their friends, it would weaken their opponents. Every advantage gained over abolitionism puts down the rebellion. While they and we know there are many just and patriotic men in the Republican party, it is still true that its success gives power and influence to the violent and fanatical, and that their party action always goes beyond their party platform.

Every fair man admits there is no way of correcting abuses but by a change of political leaders. The Republican party demanded this when they charged abuses upon Democratic administration. They should concede the principle now.

Experience shows that frauds practiced by political friends are not punished by men in power. It is conceded that gross frauds have been committed in different departments of government; that they have brought distress upon our soldiers, defeat upon our arms and disgrace upon our people. But not one man has been punished, or made to feel the power of that prerogative which is claimed to be an incident of war. Corruption that has done more to destroy the National power than armed rebellion, has gone unscathed. The Sentinel who slept upon his post, has been sentenced to death—the official who closed his eyes to frauds, which destroyed armies, is quietly removed, by and with the advice of the Senate, and represents the Nation's character at the Capital of a friendly power! Citizens in loyal States who became the objects of suspicion or of malignant assaults, have been seized at their homes, dragged to distant prisons without trial and without redress, while each convicted plunderer walks freely and boldly among the people he has robbed and wronged. Maladministration demands change of administration.

At this time issues should be fairly and boldly made. It is no dishonor to be mistaken, but is disgraceful not to be outspoken. Let this war at least settle questions of principle. A few months will decide who is right and who is wrong now, as the past two years have shown who were right and who were wrong heretofore. We are in favor of the rights of the State, as well as of the General Government; we are in favor of local self-government, as well as of the National jurisdiction within its proper sphere.

While we thus meet as a political organization it is not for partisan purposes. We can best serve our country in this relationship. The President of the United States will bear witness that he has not been pressed or embarrassed by us. We have loyally responded to every call made on us by constituted authority. We have obeyed all orders to reinforce our armies. When we were in power we denounced the higher law doctrine—the principle that men might set up their wills against the statutes of the land—as treasonable. We denounced it when uttered by Northern men; we are combatting it now when it is asserted by the rebellious South. We repudiate it by submitting to every demand of our Government made within the limits of rightful jurisdiction. This obedience has not been constrained, but cheerfully rendered, even in support of a party and policy to which we are opposed. We have struggled to sustain not only the letter but the spirit of our laws. We feel that we have set an example of loyalty that will not be lost upon upon those opposed to us. Having done our duty, we now demand our rights, and we shall at this time set in calm and fearless judgment upon the conduct of our rulers. Ours shall not be the language of discord and violence. We deplore the passionate and vindictive assaults of leading Republican journals upon those holding civil or military stations. Above all we protest in behalf of our country's honor and dignity, against their insubordinate and disrespectful language towards the President of these United States. Such language wrecks the authority of Government and tends to anarchy and public disorder.

For another reason, we cannot disband our organization, No other party can save this country. It alone has clearly defined purposes and well settled principles. It has been well said in our Congressional Address, that under its guidance,

From five millions, the population increased to thirty millions. The Revolutionary debt was extinguished.—Two foreign wars were successfully prosecuted, with a moderate outlay and small army and navy, and without the suspension of the habeas corpus; without one infraction of the Constitution; without one usurpation of power; without suppressing a single newspaper; without imprisoning a single editor; without limit to the freedom of the press; or of speech in or out of Congress, but in the midst of the grossest abuse of both; and without the arrest of a single "traitor," though the Hartford Convention sat during one of the wars, and in the other Senators invited the enemy to "Greet our Volunteers with bloody hands and welcome them to Hospitable Graves"!

During all this time wealth increased, business of all kinds multiplied, prosperity smiled on every side, taxes were low, wages were high, the North and the South furnished a market for each other's products at good prices, public liberty was secure, private rights undisturbed; every man's house was his castle; the Courts were open to all; no passports for travel, no secret police, no spies, no informers, no bastiles; the right to assemble peaceably, the right to petition; freedom of religion, freedom of speech, a free ballot, and a free press; and all this time the Constitution maintained and the Union of the States preserved.

WHY THE REPUBLICAN PARTY CANNOT SAVE THE COUNTRY.

On the other hand, the very character of the Republican organizations, makes it incapable of conducting the affairs of the Government. For a series of years, it has practiced a system of coalitions, with men differing in principle, until it can have no distinctive policy. In such chaotic masses, the violent have most control. They have been educating their followers for years, through the press, not to obey laws which did not accord with their views. How can they demand submission from whole communities, while they contend that individuals may oppose laws opposed to their consciences? They are higher law men. They insist that the contest, in which we are engaged, is an irrepressible one and that therefore the South could not avoid it, unless they were willing at the outset to surrender all that abolitionists demanded. To declare that this contest is irrepressible, declares that our Fathers formed a government, which could not stand. Are such men, the proper guardians of this government? Have not their speeches and acts given strength to the rebellion, and have they not also enabled its leaders to prove to their deluded followers, that the contest was an irrepressible one?

But their leaders have not only asserted that this contest was irrepressible, unless the South would give up what extreme Republican demand, (their local institutions,) but those in power have done much to justify this rebellion in the eyes of the world. The guilt of rebellion is determined by the character of the government against which it is arrayed. The right of revolution, in the language of President Lincoln, is a sacred right when exerted against a bad government.

We charge that this rebellion is most wicked because it is against the best Government that ever existed. It is the excellence of our Government that makes resistance a crime. Rebellion is not necessarily wrong. It may be an act of the highest virtue—it may be one of the deepest depravity. The rebellion of our Fathers is our proudest boast—the rebellion of our Brothers is the humiliation of our Nation is our National disgrace. To resist a bad Government is patriotism—to resist a good one is the greatest guilt. The first is patriotism, the last is treason. Legal tribunals can only regard resistance of laws as a crime but in the forum of public sentiment the character of the Government will decide if the act is treason or patriotism.

Our Government and its administration are different things; but in the eyes of the civilized world, abuses, weakness or folly in the conduct of affairs go far to justify resistance.—I have read to you the testimony of Messrs. Greely, Weed, Bryant, Raymond and Marble, charging fraud, corruption, outrage and incompetency upon those in power. Those who stand up to testify to the incompetency of these representatives of a discordant party to conduct the affairs of our Government are politically opposed to us. Bear in mind that the embarrassments of President Lincoln grows out of the conflicting views of his political friends, and their habits and principles of insubordination. His hands would be strengthened by a Democratic victory, and if his private prayers are answered we will relieve him from the pressure of philantrophists who thirst for blood, and who call for the extermination of the men, women and children of the South. The brutal and bloody language of partisan editors and political preachers have lost us the sympathy of the civilized world in a contest where all mankind should be upon one side

Turning to the Legislative Departments of our government, what do we see? In the history of the decline and fall of Nations, there are no more striking displays of madness and folly. The assemblage of Congress throws gloom over the Nation; its continuance in session is more disastrous than defeat upon the battle field. It excites alike alarm and disgust.

The public are disappointed in the results of

the war. This is owing to the differing objects of the people on the one hand, and of the fanatical agitators in and out of Congress on the other. In the army, the Union men of the North and South battle side by side, under one flag, to put down rebellion and uphold the Union and Constitution. In Congress a fanatical majority make war on the Union men of the South and strengthen the hands of Secessionists by words and acts which enable them to keep alive the flames of civil war. What is done on the battle field by the blood and treasure of the people, is undone by Senators. Half of the time is spent in factious measures designed to destroy all confidence in the government at the South, and the rest in annoying our army, in meddling with its operations, embarrassing our generals and in publishing undigested and unfounded scandal. One party is seeking to bring about peace, the other to keep alive hatred and bitterness by interferences. They prove the wisdom of Solomon, when he said: "It is an honor to a man to cease from strife, but every fool will be meddling."

This war cannot be brought to a successful conclusion or our country restored to an honorable peace under the Republican leaders for another reason. Our disasters are mainly due to the fact that they have not dared to tell the truth to the community. A system of misrepresentation had been practiced so long and so successfully that when the war burst upon us they feared to let the people know its full proportions, and they persisted in assuring their friends it was but a passing excitement. They still asserted that the South was unable to maintain and carry on a war. They denounced as a traitor every man who tried to tell the truth and to warn our people of the magnitude of the contest.

Now, my Republican friends, you know that the misapprehensions of the North with regard to the South has drenched the land with blood. Was this ignorance accidental? I appeal to you Republicans, if for years past, through the press and in publications which have been urged upon your attention by the leaders of your party, you have not been taught to despise the power and resources of the South? I appeal to you to say if this teaching has not been a part of the machinery by which power has been gained? I appeal to you to answer if those who tried to teach truths now admittted have not been denounced? I appeal to you if a book, boyond all others, false, bloody and treasonable, was not sent out with the endorsement of all your managers; and is it not true that now, when men blush to own they believed its statements, that its author is honored by an official station? It is now freely confessed by you all that you have been deceived with respect to the South Who deceived you? Who, by false teachings, instilled contempt and hate into the minds of our people? Who stained our land with blood? Who caused ruin and distress? All these things are within your own knowledge.—Are their authors the leaders to rescue us from our calamities? They shrink back appalled from the mischief they have wrought, and tell you it is an irrepressible contest. That reason is as good for Jefferson Davis as for them. They attempt to drown reflections by new excitements and new appeals to our passions. Having already, in legislation, gone far beyond the limits at which, by their resolutions, they were pledged to stop, they now ask to adopt measures which they have heretofore denounced as unjust and unconstitutional. For this reason they cannot save our country.

As our national calamities thicken upon us an attempt is made by their authors to avoid their responsibilities by insisting that our failures are due to the fact that their measures are not carried out, although Government has already gone far beyond its pledges. The demands of these men will never cease, simply because they hope to save themselves from condemnation by having unsatisfied demands At the last Session Congress not only abolished slavery in the District of Columbia, but, to quiet clamorous men, an act of Confiscation and Emancipation was passed, which, in the opinion of leading Republicans, was unconstitutional and unjust. By this act the rebels have no property—not even their own lives—and they own no slaves. But to the astonishment and disgust of those who believe in the policy of statutes and proclamations, these rebels still live and fight and hold their sl ves. These measures seem to have reanimated them. They have a careless and reckless way of appropriating their lives and property, which by act of Congress belong to us, in support of their cause.

But these fanatical men have learned that it is necessary to win a victory before they divide the spoil—and what do they now propose? As they cannot take the property of rebels beyond their reach they will take the property of the loyal men of the Border States. The violent men of this party as you know from experience, my conservative Republican friend, in the end have their way. They now demand that the President shall issue a Proclamation of immediate and universal emancipation? Against whom is this to be directed? Not against those in rebellion for they came within the scope of the act of Congress. It can only be applied to those who have been true to our Union and our Flag. They are to be punished for their loyalty. When we consider their sufferings and their cruel wrongs at the hands of the secessionists, their reliance upon our faith, is not this proposal black with ingratitude?

The scheme for an immediate emancipation and general arming of the slaves throughout the South is a proposal for the butchery of women and children, for scenes of lust and rapine; of arson and murder unparalelled in the history of the world. The horrors of the French Revolution would become tame in comparison. Its effect would not be confined to the walls of cities, but there would be a wide spread scene of horror over the vast expanse of great States, involving alike the loyal and seditious. Such malignity and cowardice would invoke the interference of civilized Europe. History tells of the fires kindled in the name of religion, of atrocities committed under pretexts of order or liberty; but it is now urged that scenes bloodier than the world has yet seen shall be enacted in the name of philanthrophy!

A proclamation of general and armed emancipation at this time, would be a cruel wrong to the African. It is now officially declared in Presidential addresses, which are fortified by Congressional action, that the negro cannot live in the enjoyment of the full privileges of life among the white race. It is now admitted, after our loss of infinite blood and treasure, that the great problem we have to settle is not the slavery, but the negro question. A terrible question, not springing from statutes or usages, but growing out of the unchangable distinction of race. It is discovered at this late day, in Republican Illinois, that it is right to drive him from its soil. It is discovered by a Republican Congress, after convulsing our country with declarations in favor of his equal rights, and asserting that he was merely the victim of unjust laws, that he should be sent away from our land. The issue is now changed. The South holds that the African is fit to live here as a slave. Our Republican Government denies that he is fit to live here at all.

The Republican party cannot save the country, because through its powerful Press it teaches contempt for the Laws, Constitution and constituted authorities. They are not only destroying the Union, but they are shaking and weakening the whole structures of State as well as of the National Government, by denunciations of every law and of all authority that stand in the way of their passions or their purposes. They have not only carried discord into our churches and legislative halls, but into our armies. Every General who agrees with them upon the subject of Slavery is upheld in every act of insubordination and sustained against the clearest proofs of incompetence, if not of corruption. On the other hand. every Commander who differs from their views upon the single point of Slavery, is denounced, not only for incompetency, but constantly depreciated in every act. No man is allowed to be a Christian; no man is regarded as a Statesman; no man is suffered unmolested to do his duty as a Soldier unless he supports measures which no one dared to urge eighteen months since. They insist that martial law is superior to constitutional law, that the wills of Generals in the field are above all restraints; but they demand for themselves the right to direct and control these Generals. They claim an influence higher than they will allow to the laws of the land. Are these displays of insuborbination and violence safe at this time?

The weight of annual taxation will test severely the loyalty of the people of the North. Repudiation of our financial obligations would cause disorder and endless moral evils. Pecuniary rights will never be held more sacred than personal rights Repudiation of the Constitution involves repudiation of National debts. of its guaranties of rights of property, of person, and of conscience. The moment we show the world that we do not hold the Constitution to be a sacred compact, we not only destroy all sense of security, but we turn away from our shores the vast tide of foreign immigration. It comes here now not because there are not other skies as bright and other lands as productive as ours. It seeks here security for freedom—for rights of conscience—for immunity from tyranical interferences, and from meddling impertinence. The home and fireside rights heretofore enjoyed by the American people—enjoyed under protection of written Constitution, have made us great and prosperous. I entreat you again, touch them not with sacrilegeous hands! We are threatened with the breaking up of our social system, with the overthrow of State and National Governments. If we begin a war upon the compromises of the Constitution we must go through with it. It contains many restraints upon our natural rights. It may be asked by what right do the six small New England States, with a population less than that of New York, have six times its power in the Senate, which has become the controling branch of government? By what natural right do these States with their small united populations and limited territories balance the power of New York, Pennsylvania, Ohio, Illinois, Indiana and Michigan? The vast debt growing out of this war will give rise to new and angry discussions. It will be held almost exclusively in a few Atlantic States. Look upon the map of the Union and see how small is the territory in which it will be owned. We are to be divided into creditor and debtor States, and the last will have a vast preponderance of power and strength. Unfortunately there is no taxation upon this national debt and its share is thrown off upon other property. It is held where many of the government contracts have been executed, and where in some instances, gross frauds, have been practiced. It is held largely where the Constitution gives a disproportional share of political power. With all these elements of discord, is it wise to assail constitutional law, or bring authority into contempt. Is it safe to encourage the formation of irresponsible committees, made up of impertinent men, who thrust themselves into the conduct of public affairs and try to dictate to legal rulers? or will you tolerate the enrollment of armies which are not constituted or organized by proper authorities? Are such things just towards those who have placed their fortunes in the hands of the government at this crisis?

We implore you do not be deceived again with this Syren song of no danger. There is danger, great and imminent. of the destruction of all government, of safety for life and property, unless the duty of obedience to law and respect for authorities and the honest support of those in the public service both military and civil, are taught and enforced, by all means within our control.

With us there is no excuse for revolutionary action. Our system of government give peaceful remedies for all evils in legislation.

WHAT THE DEMOCRATIC PARTY PROPOSE TO DO.

Mr. President: It will be asked what do we propose to do We mean, with all our powers of mind and person to support the Constitution and uphold the Union; to maintain the laws, to preserve the public faith. We insist upon obedience to laws and respect for Constitutional authority; we will defend the rights of citizens; we mean that rulers and subjects shall respect the laws; we will put down all revolutionary committees; we will resist all unauthorized organizations of armed men; we will spurn officious meddlers who are impudently pushing themselves into the councils of our Government Politically opposed to those in authority, we demand they shall be treated with the respect due to their positions as the representatives of the dignity and honor of the American people. We do not try to save our country by abandoning its government. In these times of trial and danger we cling more closely to the great principles of civil and religious liberty and of personal right; we will man the defences and barriers which the Constitution throws around them; we will revive the courage and strengthen the arms of loyal men by showing them they have a living government about which to rally; we will proclaim amidst the confusion and uproar of civil war, with louder tones and firmer voices the great maxims and principles of civil liberty, order and obedience What has perpetuated the greatness of that nation from which we derive so many of our maxims? Not its victories upon land nor its triumphs upon the seas, but its firm adherence to its traditional policy. The words of Coke, of Camden and Mansfield, have for long periods of time given strength and vitality and honor to its social system, while battles have lost their significance When England was agitated by the throes of violence—when the person of the King was insulted; when Parliament was besieged by mobs maddened by bigotry; when the life of Lord Mansfield was sought by infuriated fanatics, and his house was burned by incendiary fires then he uttered those words which checked at once unlawful power and lawless violence. He declared that every citizen was entitled to his rights according to the known procedures of the land. He showed to the world the calm and awful majesty of the law, unshaken amidst convulsions. Self reliant in its strength and purity, it was driven to no acts which destroy the spirit of law. Violence was rebuked, the heart of the nation was reassured, a sense of security grew up, and the storm was stilled. Listen to his word:

Miserable is the condition of individuals; dangerous is the condition of the State where there is no certain law, or what is the same thing, no certain administration of law by which individuals may be protected and the State made secure.

Thus, too, will we stand calmly up admidst present disasters. We have warned the public that every act of disobedience weakened their claims to protection. We have admonished our rulers that every violation of right destroyed sentiments of loyalty and duty. That obedience and protection were reciprocal obligations. He who withholds his earnest and cheerful support to any legal demand of his Government, invites oppression and usurpation on the part of those in authority. The public servant who oversteps his jurisdiction or tramples upon the rights, person, property or procedure of the governed, instigates resistance and revolt.

Under abuse and detraction we have faithfully acted upon these precepts. If our purposes were factious, the elements of disorder are everywhere within our reach. If we were as disobedient to this Government and as denunciatory of its officials as those who placed them in power, we could make them tremble in their seats of power. We have been obedient, loyal and patient. We shall continue to be so under all circumstances. But let no man mistake this devotion to our country and its Constitution for unworthy fear. We have no greater stake in good order than other men.—Our arms are as strong, our endurance as great, our fortitude as unwavering as that of our political opponents. But we seek the blessings of peace, of law, of order. We ask the public to mark our policy and our position. Opposed to the election of Mr. Lincoln, we have loyally sustained him. Differing from the Administration as to the course and the conduct of the war, we have cheerfully responded to every demand made upon us. To-day we are putting forth our utmost efforts to reinforce our armies in the field. Without conditions or threats we are exerting our energies to strengthen the hands of government and to replace it in the commanding position it held in the eyes of the world before recent disasters. We are pouring out our blood, our treasures and our men, to rescue it from a position in which it can neither propose peace nor conduct successful war. And this support is freely and generously accorded. We wish to see our Union saved, our laws vindicated, and peace once more restored to our land We do not claim more virtue or intelligance than we award to our opponents, but we now have the sad and bloody proof that we act upon sounder principles of government. Annimated by the motto we have placed upon our banner—"The Union, the Constitution and the Laws"—we go into the political contest confident of the support of a People who cannot be deaf or blind to the teachings of the last two years.

FROM THE

GULF TO VICKSBURG.

A PAPER

READ BEFORE

THE MICHIGAN COMMANDERY

OF THE

MILITARY ORDER

OF THE

LOYAL LEGION OF THE UNITED STATES

DECEMBER 6, 1894.

By Companion
HARRISON SOULE,
Major 6th Michigan Infantry.

FROM THE GULF TO VICKSBURG.

By Harrison Soule,
Major 6th Michigan Infantry.

(Read December 6, 1894.)

April, 1862.—Our troops are encamped on Ship Island. This is one of the numerous small islands which constitutes the southern boundary of Mississippi Sound off the main coast of Mississippi about twelve miles.

Ship Island is about seven miles long and from one to three miles wide. The eastern side is crossed with a heavy growth of timber and plenty of good water may be had anywhere by digging three or four feet in the clean white sand. It is situated about midway between Mobile and New Orleans, and is considered a very important position.

The defence of the island consists of a fort located at the west end, on a point of sand bar extending into deep water, commanding the approach to the harbor, and with a couple of heavy swivel guns on top of the fort almost the entire west and north side of the island is within easy range.

The fort has an armament of six guns mounted in case-mate, which are supposed to be shell proof, and eight heavy brass field guns; also two field Howitzers, twelve-pounders.

The main structure is built of brick, and the top is covered over with heavy pine timber; that covered with plank and with piles of sand from twelve to fifteen feet deep.

Water batteries outside, and at angles with the fort, of heavy nine-inch shell guns sweep all points of the channel. These, with the gunboats which keep vigilant watch over the movements of the enemy along the main land, make the island secure from surprise.

Such is the condition of our surroundings. This position is

the only foothold we have on the so-called Confederate soil at this date.

The daily routine of guard duty has been fairly learned, and all our effort now is centered in trying to master the mysteries of a brigade drill. This is no holiday task, our drill ground being on the southern side of the island, not a tree, shrub or bush; not even a tuft of green grass. Overhead the bright hot sun with its summer scorching heat and the dry, hot sand underfoot. Soldiers ankle deep at every step and the encouragement of a regular army officer to hurry us up in the way we should go.

That courtly gentleman and accomplished officer, Brigadier General Thomas Williams, whom we afterwards learned to respect and revere as one of the brightest of our bright lights that was forever extinguished by the rebellion.

All hailed with joy the orders that came to us that bright April morning to pack up and embark on the good ship, Great Republic, then laying at anchor off the landing.

Only a couple of hours were required, for heavy marching order was the word and our good brigade was snugly stored away. Our own, the Michigan Sixth, Wisconsin Fourth, and Indiana Twenty-first, fully three thousand men on board. However close the quarters, the change is quite agreeable. We can now empty the sand out of our shoes and have solid footing once more.

One of the Navy boats take us in tow and we turn our backs upon Ship Island and gladly bid her farewell forever.

The troops we leave behind us gathered along the shore waving and cheering us good-bye, and doubtless envying the good fortune that took us from that desolate land of sand and fleas.

We are now headed towards the great future, to us the great unknown, and as the shades of evening draw around and envelope us in a long quiet twilight, groups of men, comrades, gather here and there and for long hours talk and surmise as to the future. Past scenes of home life form too tender and loving a theme for common discussion and we are almost unmanned in bringing them vividly to our own mind, so we bury our hopes, our wishes, and our home thoughts deep in our hearts and talk of the dark future, and surmise as to what that has in store for us. We have no intimation as to our future destination. Some think Mobile Bay, some suggest Galveston Harbor, and others are quite certain we are bound for the Mississippi Delta.

Thus the hours wear on far into the night, but gradually the hum of voices cease. Officers and men alike on the floor below, middle and upper deck, and under the clear midnight skies, with the bright moon shining almost straight down upon us, the myriads of stars seeming brighter and more beautiful than ever before with the gentle rippling of the water as our huge vessel is quietly hauled along by the little gunboat far ahead, towing us with her long line and with the steady tramp, tramp, tramp of our faithful sentinel, which is the only sound coming to our ears; thus there in that far off clime, under the bright canopy of heaven, with loving faces of our dear ones at home before us, in mind, we pass into restful sleep which only a tired soldier knows.

Early dawn, the hauling and pulling of ropes and the noise of the sailors working the ship, call us to our feet, and we are made aware that a new state of affairs surround us. We are at sea. No land in sight; our partner, the gunboat, has disappeared, and we are moving along before a good sailing breeze, the sails are being hoisted by the sailors and we are afforded considerable amusement in watching them and listening to the various orders and sailor talk connected therewith, for this is the first time we have ever been on a real sailing ship at sea. The rattle of the drum at guard quarters and the smell of hot coffee soon bring us to a realizing sense that grub is ready. The pint of hot coffee and the plate of boiled rice soon disappear and the weak remembrance is all we have to remind us that we have indulged in such a luxury as a breakfast.

The coffee was very thin and the rice scarce for our first morning meal on the Great Republic. Our dinner is of a more substantial sort, the old army bean is welcome. Hard tack is present and puts us all in good humor.

We have changed our course, and are now sailing directly north, the pilot says, towards the Southwest Pass of the Mississippi. A gunboat or two is seen in the distance, which belongs to the blockading fleet of the gulf squadron. Towards night we sight a number of other vessels and ships, and at sun-set drop anchor amongst them, and in the midst of the fleet of the old commodore, at the Southwest Pass.

The commodore's ships bear a different appearance now from what they did a week ago when they left their anchorage at Ship Island. Then they were clean, bright and shining, everything trim and tidy as only a man-o'-wars-man looks. Flags were gaily flying from every conspicuous place. What a change in appearance! Now not a piece of canvas in sight, not a flag to be seen, the rigging and top gear all down and stowed below; even the long, slender masts are down and short stumpy ones in place. Instead of bright, shining sides, as of old, they are daubed with mud from end to end, as though they had spent the last week wallowing through the mud slough along the shore for which the Delta is noted, thus being disguised so they cannot be so readily seen while lying along the muddy levee in the river where their destiny next takes them.

The fleet are now all ready and during the night, at high tide, all up anchor, pass over the bar and slowly move on up the river. A couple of gunboats give us each a line, we up anchor and take our course in the middle of the channel; all goes smoothly for a time, when our ship's bottom grinds in the sand—slower and slower, and now coming to a full stop; stuck hard aground on the bar.

A beautiful bright morning, April 16, 1862. Hard aground on the bar, Southwest Pass of the Mississippi River.

As we stand on the broad deck of our good ship Great Republic, away to our right across the low marshy plain, almost as far as the eye can reach, we can see the dim outline of a couple of gunboats. They are on blockading duty, and are laying off the Southeast Pass. To the front, and directly north, extends a low marshy plain now covered with a luxuriant growth of pampas grass only known to the great salt marshes along the gulf coast. No tree or shrub in sight to relieve the monotony of this broad waste; deep muddy lagoons winding and twisting all through, with here and there and almost everywhere muddy ponds with not enough solid bottom for grass to get a foothold and not enough water to get a rowboat through.

Here is the home of the alligator, his paradise, where he lives and thrives, only dividing the honors with the musquito. Here they are on their native heath. Winter and summer it is all the same to them, and woe to any living thing who visits their home; they are always there and on the lookout for company. It is said that the terrapin can't stand the pressure and is speedily driven to deeper water.

A half mile to the west and north we can just see the top of several houses, so low down are they nestled in the tall weeds, that only the roof and chimneys are to be seen. Sand has been dredged up from the bar at the mouth of the river and taken up on flatboats to make the foundation on which those houses stand; this is Pilot Town, and the dozen little houses are inhabited by the pilots and their families, whose business in life is to pilot shipping into the Delta and across the bar, coming in, or going out. the fickleness and ever-shifting bottom of the old father of waters making constant watchfulness necessary in order that any use can be made of that great highway. At this time, as may be supposed, Pilot Town is not inhabited, the occupants having taken their lot in the ranks of the confederacy.

Still farther to the north and west, away beyond the little houses, and far across the sea of grass, as it now waves in the gentle morning breeze, may be seen the long line of woods whose tree tops at this distance seem not much above the tall grass, yet we plainly see the dark line which fringes the western bank of the river, and behind which lies Fort Jackson; her heavy armament of large guns and full garrison of troops, the chivalry of the Crescent City, have heralded to the world the invincibility of this stronghold.

Across the river and a mile further up stands Fort St. Philip; she, too, with her heavy guns covering the channel of the river for miles in either direction, flies the rebel flag and bids defiance.

Away to the west as far as the eye can reach, the broad wavy grass only in view, the same wide bayous and deep lagoons for miles and miles along the coast. To the south is the gulf into whose deep blue waters we can plainly see the course of the river tracing it as far as the eye can reach, the clear waters of the gulf repudiating and refusing to mingle with the black muddy river water.

A gunboat away in the distance slowly steaming along off the outer bar or entrance to the Southwest Pass is seen and indicates to us that the blockading fleet are there on duty also. A half dozen small transports with the other troops of Butler's army are in our neighborhood at anchor, waiting for us to get over the bar in order that the entire force may be together when a forward movement is made.

The whole of Farragut's fleet have passed over the bar and gone on up the river, also Porter's fleet of mortar boats have been towed up and are lying in position along the shore on either side of the river ready for business.

This mortar fleet consists of about thirty-five schooners carrying one gun, and each a huge fifteen-inch mortar, the largest size then known, and a gun crew of twenty men each; now, with her many tons of ordnance stores loaded down most to the water's edge, sides hanging with evergreen and bushes even to the top of the masts, they are so trimmed, and can hardly be distinguished even at a short distance as they lay along the grassy and bushy river bank.

April 17th, 1862. This is the day set for the bombardment to begin. Breakfast is over, and all hands set to and arrange as best they can to enjoy the day as soldiers have learned to do, to kill time—can't do anything but wait for high tide, when we hope to get off and up the river.

The story-tellers begin their yarns; the card-players are at it since daylight, and the fishermen get out their tackle and are out in small boats getting clams for bait, clams are thick among the grassy bogs, and notwithstanding the warning of the sailors of alligators and sharks, the swimmers are overboard taking a morning souse in the waters of the Delta.

Ten o'clock. The air reverberates with the shock of the heavy guns. Then another, and still another, which are promptly answered by heavy guns whose sharp report tells us their line of fire is directly towards us and we know the fort has answered. Now the heavy shock of bombs bursting in air, the mortar fleet have opened, and the incessant roar of artillery filling the air, plainly tell us the bombardment has begun.

Stories, games and fishing are laid aside and all eyes are turned up the river. The highest place on the vessel brings a premium. The rigging is filled with officers, men, sailors and cooks, all eagerly striving to get a high place, where they hope to see something of what is going on at the front. No satisfaction is to be had even from the main-top. Nothing can be seen but the clouds of powder smoke, which the gentle winds slowly drift across the distant horizon. And so all day the steady thundering of the distant guns is heard. About three hundred guns in action, the heaviest known in this country are now at work doing destruction and death, and so for long hours, until the daylight waned and night closed in around us; gradually the firing ceases its din, fewer guns are served and finally only the occasional discharge of a bomb as minute guns over the dead, seem, if possible, to deepen the stillness of the night.

We sit up late and the low voices of the men talking of the probabilities of the future and trials of the past, of our prospect in getting across the bar, and as to the probable doings of to-morrow. It is a late hour when the hum of voices cease and balmy sleep covers us with her peaceful wings.

Three o'clock in the morning. All is bustle. Again two of the strongest navy boats are here, each with a stout line hitched to us, ready to take advantage of the high tide and try to take us over the bar.

At a signal they start with a long pull, and a strong pull. We move a little, the bottom of our ship grinds through the sand. We are off with a cheer given all too soon, for again we strike hard and solid, and are now fast, the whole length on the bar. Each boat with a broken line. It is no use. They give it up as a bad job and leave us as before to undergo another day of suspense, just out of the reach of the excitement of visible battle, and not far enough off to be free from its anxieties. Thus a long week is passed, day by day, and night by night, the same thundering of the great guns, the bursting of huge mortar shells continually at work. The same ineffectual efforts to get off the bar, and up into the river. Every expedient has been tried, the shift- of the men and freight to other vessels, but all to no use; our ship is too deep draft and cannot be got over without her entire load is put off, and that is not possible for there is no vessel here on which to transfer our cargo, each being fully loaded with their own stores.

Cheerful news. Word has come that Farragut, with part of the fleet, have run the batteries and are above the forts. Yet we still hear the same incessant roar of the guns and the prompt answering from the fort indicates that we shall have solid work to do before our mission here is ended.

A change of base. Transferred from the deck of our ship to a light draft old river tow-boat with two days' rations and the ever present forty rounds of ammunition. We are taken in tow of a gunboat and are out into the gulf and around the Eastern Passes, up the shore back of Fort St. Philip.

Six miles away across the marshy waste from our upper deck we can see plainly, with the aid of a field glass, the dark outlines of Fort Jackson and more plainly Fort St. Philip and the rebel flag flying from her flag staff. Our ship runs in towards the shore, which is only a sea of long marshy grass growing out of the mud and water, until we stick fast on the bottom. Here we lay during the night, and at early dawn all hands are up, coffee and hard tack for breakfast. Now business begins; the numerous surf boats which we had towed behind and had on board, are hauled to the side of the ship, filled with soldiers stripped for action, one day's rations and forty rounds in the boxes: thus twenty boats are loaded and shoved off. Through deep lagoons and bogs, and marshy places where the water is not deep enough to float boats, muskets and haversacks are deposited inside, and the men take to the water, pulling and shoving the boats over the bogs, through the grass and mud to deeper water, when all hands are in the boats again and shove along with pole and oar, and so the long miles are covered in our slow progress towards the main land.

The middle of the afternoon has long since passed and gone when hard ground is struck, muskets soon in hand, and the foremost, with a cheer, give notice that they are on land.

God's green earth is under our feet once again. Other boats are soon up, and lively the men spring ashore and swing into line, and we are on the levee of the Mississippi, above the forts, which are now cut off from all communication with the outer world.

The navy boats which have run the batteries and are now lying in the river above the fort have already destroyed the telegraph lines along the levee, and on our appearance we are welcomed with cheer after cheer in the old-fashioned way. They are now lying at anchor just off our landing place.

Immediately a couple of boats shove off and bring us a bountiful supply of provision, hot coffee, soft bread, baked potatoes, and fresh meat, which said meat was found straying along the river bank, and fearing it might get lost, they took it in.

Thus after a long day of fasting, we spent a long evening in feasting, and in cleaning and drying our clothes, cleaning guns and making all things ready for a prospective day of activity on the morrow.

Picket lines were put out as usual and it is a late hour when the low hum of voices cease, and the long rows of upturned faces show that tired nature is being reinforced. No firing during the long hours of night, and we rested as peacefully and quietly under the watchful care of our tried pickets and guard line, as though under the skies of far off old Michigan.

At an early hour in the morning we are aroused by a detachment of our pickets from the western shore, who are bringing across the river, with the assistance of the navy boat, a detachment of Rebel troops, who during the night left Fort Jackson and came into our lines, saying there was no use, they had held out as long as they could. Many of their guns had been dismounted by the bombardment, their powder magazine had been blown up, and many of their case-mates fired and burned out. Seeing our troops had surrounded them, and the forts entirely cut off from the upper country, and expecting an assault in the morning, with no hope of a success for them, they had spiked the upriver guns and come over to the Lord's side. Our breakfast, with which the Navy again supplied us, we share with our new converts, then send them aboard the shipping to await developments, which are now close at hand. Having washed up and breakfast over, at sun rise, skirmishers are selected and advanced to positions and our faces turned with determination on Fort St. Philip. The part of our fleet above as agreed open their batteries on the fort, and our storming party are stripped for action and now take the front. As we advance not a shot is fired from the fort in answer to the guns of our fleet, or upon the advancing lines, and we begin to dread the shock of their first opening. We are treated to a surprise. As all eyes are turned towards the fort, a dense volume of smoke and flame bursts into the air, a deafening report, which makes the very earth tremble under our feet, they have blown up their magazine, and as the smoke rises above the parapet of the fort, we see the rebel flag suddenly drop to the ground. They have hauled down the flag. The fort has surrendered. The gunboats stop firing and send off small boats loaded with officers, and men with the old flag. Our troops advance with a cheer over the intervening space of ground, across the parapet and into the fort.

Fort Jackson surrendered at sun rise, Fort St. Philip at ten o'clock, and at half past ten the Stars and Stripes are flying over both forts, and our sentinels posted on the walls. We find Fort Jackson has an armament of seventy-four guns in all, mostly of the old smooth bore pattern, but a few long range rifle guns of heavy power form a very effective water battery.

Fort St. Philip has fifty-two guns mounted and their long range rifle guns cover the river both up and down stream, and is altogether a very substantial and effective fortification. Upon examination we are more and more convinced that in her capitulation we are saved much desperate fighting, for an assault seemed the only thing left for us to do, and we had made all preparations to that end.

With the Union flag flying from the forts, all the shipping from below hauled up and anchored in the river off the landings. Troops are put off in boats and landed to occupy the fortifications and man the batteries. My own company is transferred to the gunboat Wissahickon, and we leave the forts behind and slowly steam along in the wake of the navy boats toward Crescent City.

During the night we are lying at anchor in the middle of the river, finding our beds on the soft side of the deck, resting our tired bones from the fatigue and excitement of the day. At daylight we are slowly moving along up the river, the Rebels having full confidence in the strength of the forts, had expended all their energy in strengthening them and their out-lying batteries, fully believing that no force could capture them; therefore, no preparation has been made to check our advance above the forts or along the river bank, until near the city, where a few field guns are placed to check our approach, and they take wing at the first sight of our advancing fleet of gunboats, without firing a single shot.

As our foremost boats sight the old battlefield at English Bend—Chalmet Battery—where it is understood we may expect trouble, a puff of smoke is seen, then another and another, and a few shots come plunging amongst us. Our advance boats open fire, one by one, as they come around the bend of the river, in range, and the guns of the enemy are soon silenced, and without a halt we pass directly on up the river.

On turning a long bend in the river, we see before us the Crescent City. A dense sheet of black smoke hangs over the city, almost obscuring it from sight, and as we get nearer, we can see the vast sheets of flame and fire all along the river front. The work of destruction and desolation has been going on since the news of our capture of the forts. Thousands of bales of cotton and goods along the levee, piles on piles all along the seven miles of river front has been fired. Ships loaded with cotton lying in the river; steamboats, ferry-boats, almost by the hundred and are mostly burned to the water's edge, the hulks still smudging and smouldering. Scores of steamboat wood, piles of coal, the huge dry-dock, the ship yards, everything which might fall into the hands of the dreaded Yankee has been put to the torch, and millions in value are destroyed, wreathing the city with a thick dark smoke like a funeral pall.

About mid-day we steamed slowly along the seven miles of Crescent levee. Water street, now lined with a living mass of humanity, who view our coming, doubtless, with different emotions, a very few silently welcome the old flag we are bringing to them. The masses look with sorrow and anger illy concealed, and we can hear their low mutterings of disappointment and rage. Now groans for Lincoln and cheers for Jeff Davis; a sudden hustling as a dozen men pounce on one poor darkey, who spoke for the Union flag.

All these scenes come brightly before me after these many years. History can tell, much better than I can hope to do, the situation there in those days. One scene is pictured vividly on my mind after these long years of peaceful life, and will remain with me until the end.

Our good boat moving slowly along the levee, which is packed with the multitude as close to the edge of the charred and smouldering wharf as they could get. Our guns all shotted and run into battery. Gunners at their posts ready for instant action. Amidships our heavy 11-inch Columbiad loaded with shell, in battery, as we slowly moved along, her muzzle passing almost in the faces of the people, sponge and rammer in hand stand the gunners, as if made of blocks of granite. The sergeant of the gun, a short grizzly old tar, with primer inserted and lanyard in hand, points at the old flag flying from the mast's head and pats the big gun even now almost hot from the bombardment of the forts. A pantomime speaking in actions plainer than can be expressed in words: Take whichsoever you choose—but one you must—the flag or destruction; and from these later years I look back on that scene and think those moments were the most eventful of the whole war. One misguided action; a single pistol shot from that infuriated crowd; even an accident at that time, and the horrors of Moscow would have grown pale beside the horrors that would have befallen the Crescent City.

Of our landing; our march along through the packed streets; our occupation of the United States Mint. The detail to bury our dead comrades, among them one of my own company, whom we had brought off the boat with us, and whom we gave a soldier's burial in the street, just outside of the high iron fence which encloses the mint property. Of our first night of occupancy there, with a section of field battery at each of the four corners. Guns covering each street, our pickets stationed a short distance down each street approaching the mint and the entire regiment under arms. Of our weeks there and our first mail from home. Dear old home—bearing dates of two months before and the latest war news from the north with its uncertainties and doubts, I pass over all these, and a week later finds us again on the wing, ourselves and our little belongings.

Now we are on board the large old river steam boat, Lawrell Hill, clumsy old craft as compared with the trim built sea-going ship we have heretofore honored with our patronage. We are bound for up-stream, wherever that means we do not know, and but few of us care, only that to be headed up stream is north, as the boys say, towards God's country. At an early hour we get off convoyed by several gunboats and line of battle ships. How well we remember them all; the Hartford with Farragut, the old commodore, in command of the fleet; the Brooklyn, the Richmond, the Kineo and our old friend Wissahickon, with half a dozen other gunboats and two other river steamers with troops and supplies on board. Thus we bid the Crescent City and our comrades, the balance of the brigade, good-bye. Soon, turning the point of the river above and even the tall chimneys and spires have faded from view; we are as glad to leave them behind, as we were to welcome them to our vision so short a time before.

In passing up the river we find that with the fall of New Orleans, the villages and towns are ablaze with the patriotism of defiance. Guerrilla bands are formed and line the shore on both sides of the river, firing into all passing boats that have the Stars and Stripes flying. After a short experience with the advance of our navy boats, they have enough of it and remain quietly out of sight behind the levee, and hid in the dense growth of weeds and underbrush until the navy boats have passed by, when they again show themselves and are ready to bombard every transport or passenger boat that passes. Thus our journey proceeds slowly along, convoyed by the gunboats from daylight to dark. Towards night we lay up, the gunboats at anchor in mid-channel and our transports run alongside the shore and tie up to a tree, shove out a gang-plank and our pickets are put out from a mile below to a mile above and around the appproach to our steamer. The cooks go ashore and cooking progresses as regularly as clock work; many of the men go ashore and with sheltered tents for a cover, try hard to enjoy the company of the numerous varieties of bugs and musquitoes who seem to be at home along the shore, and on the lookout for company.

Our reserve guard for the picket line usually selects some elevated place or clear ground and enjoy their snooze under the mossy old oaks and magnolia trees of this southern land, unless their slumbers chance to be disturbed by a few shots exchanged along the picket lines.

Halting at the little cities and villages along the route, a patrol is put ashore while the officer of the day calls upon the officials, but few of them express Union sentiments. Yet no resistance is made to our putting up the Union flag. They say if you want it up, you must put it up, we have no force to hinder you. Our force is with Van Dorn and we can't help ourselves. So we put the Stars and Stripes upon the public buildings or on the flag staffs where there were any in the public parks and places. At many places we could not find such a thing as an American flag and we supplied the deficiency from the ample stores of the navy. Thus day by day we passed on up stream; some of the bright moonlight nights the lightest draft of the gunboats would continue onward part or all the night, but such progress was necessarily slow, as sounding had to be continuously made in order to keep the channel of the old muddy river, and our deep draft boats and their navigators are new to such inland navigation. Thus onward we slowly progress until, rounding the bend of the river, the bluffs of Vicksburg with her frowning batteries are in sight.

The advance of our fleet lay at anchor in mid-channel about three miles down stream from the lowest battery. Our transports are soon hauled alongside of the levee and on the west bank about half a mile lower down and just out of range of the batteries. Camp guard and picket are at once put out and our first night before Vicksburg is peacefully and quietly passed. A day or two and others of the gunboats arrive towing some of the mortar fleet; one by one they report and drop anchor along the western shore.

A week passes and we are only waiting for troops which were promised—but never come. Meanwhile, as summer is advancing, the water in the river is fast lowering; already one of the deep draft boats has found the bottom and has to be towed out into deeper water in mid-channel. It is quite certain that whatever is done here, must be done at once. A consultation of the commanding officers is held on the flag ship, and an attack upon the city is agreed upon.

A flag of truce is dispatched to the commanding officer at Vicksburg demanding the surrender within twelve hours, or in the event of a refusal a suggestion is made to remove the women and children as an attack would be made. The reply is come,—if you want Vicksburg, come and take her.

During the night our picket lines on duty on the wetsern bank of the river are attacked by a light force of the enemy. The right wing of our regiment, who are on shore as a reserve, immediately rally to the front on the picket line, and go into action. A sharp but short skirmish routs the enemy, who leave the ground, taking their few wounded. Their dead are gathered in by our forces with our own, and at the same time buried with ours early the next morning under the old mossy oaks which line the river banks, and the three volleys which are fired over their last resting place, that bright May morning, heralded many and many weeks of bloody strife, which was to be enacted so soon in the future around the bluffs of Vicksburg.

May 19, 1862. This is the day decided upon to make an attack; reveille at three o'clock—just at dawn of day a hasty breakfast from yesterday's cooked rations and a tin cup of hot coffee. Details are made and all the small boats in the fleet are ready and alongside of our steamer; hardly enough boat room, but a hundred men are crowded into them and with canteens filled and haversacks packed with two days' rations and the ever-present forty rounds inspected, they are off with muskets in hand for the sacred soil of Vicksburg.

Landing is made about three miles below the city and the boats at once returned for another load of troops. Pickets are put out and at once advance through the little hamlet of Warrenton and are soon out of sight in the dense woods beyond.

A shot or two, and now a full volley, then the rattle of musketry along the entire line, proved the enemy are in full force in the woods in front of our pickets. The fleet can not open fire, as our own men deployed through the woods would be in as much danger as the enemy; therefore, can only await the result of the skirmish. We are not long in suspense, for our entire advance is forced back out of the woods by the enemy, who have a force ten times larger than our own. Our skirmishers now take cover under the levee and the gunboats open fire on the woods with shell, doubtless with very little effect, for the Rebels can disperse through the underbrush and in the ravines which cover the country around Vicksburg, and thus they are comparatively out of danger from the guns of the fleet.

The small boats are sent off with orders to bring us on board again, and by midday we are once more on the transports. Our loss in this engagement is light, owing, in part, to the armament of the enemy—mostly shotguns. It is, however, demonstrated that with our handful of men, scarcely three hundred for duty, and nearly twice that number on the sick list to care for, that we cannot expect to successfully cope with the large force of the enemy, and even if we could meet with success in our attack, assisted as we would be by the fleet, the army must furnish the force of occupation and we cannot occupy, even if we silence their batteries. As the summer advances the weather is getting warmer and our sick rolls are growing frightfully longer; daily we are burying our comrades, and the little head boards are getting thicker and rows of graves growing longer under the old oak trees along the western shore.

Another general consultation among the officers. The commodore insists that the large ships must be gotten down, or they will be stranded in the river, as the water is fast falling, and they must at once start for New Orleans. The order is issued and on the morning of May 26th, our transports steam up, haul away from the shore, and we take our departure for down stream. The gunboats having left their anchorage and preceded up, they leaving at daylight, the Richmond and the flagship Hartford leaving at the same time with us, but being faster, they soon leave us behind. The Brooklyn, being the last one of the fleet left to bring up the rear, and with orders to keep behind us during the passage down, we turn the long bend in the river and the bluffs of Vicksburg are lost to sight. Of course no one knows what may be our destination or fortunes for the future. A dispatch boat was forwarded a week ago, when it became evident that our force was far too light to cope with the fortifications of Vicksburg. Daily we are expecting orders to meet us from General Butler, which will then determine our immediate action.

Slowly we steam along the shore, keeping a sharp lookout for wood; our fuel is getting low, and we have to get our supplies along the shore at the different towns, all of which usually supply the river steamboats.

Grand Gulf; this town we called at on our way up, and the officials put up the Union Flag on their town hall and professed strong Union feeling. The gunboats are far in advance of us and are doubtless supposed to constitute the whole upper fleet; one of our transports being a faster traveler is with them, and ours, the steamboat Lawrell Hill, being short of wood, slow up as we near the little village and head in for the boat landing. We are nearing the shore and almost abreast of the landing and headed in towards it, when a masked battery of six guns opens fire upon us from the levee in the main street, and at this short range the shot and shell comes plunging through the frail old steamer in all directions. Our steam boilers are disabled, and the sound of escaping steam, the shrieking of shell, with the crashing and tearing through the woodwork of our old boat and the rushing of men here and there, all form a picture long to be remembered. Our boat can only drift down with the current, which now we find is altogether too slow, but gradually we are drifted out of range around the bend of the river below the village. Just here we meet a couple of the gunboats returning up the river; they have heard the firing and returned to see the cause.

A towline is put off to us and made fast, and we are again headed up stream rounding the bend of the river and coming in sight of the village again. Here we meet the Brooklyn, our rear guard; having heard the firing she steams along, and is now coming in sight from above.

Having communicated by signal to the gunboats the fact of our being bombarded from the village, and also the fact that we desired to land under cover of the guns of the fleet and if possible capture the battery and troops supporting it.

As we sight the village on our return, we see white flags being hung out from many of the houses, and now one is run up from the flag staff on the town hall. One hour ago and all was different. Then, they were firing into us from their battery and we could hear their loud cheering. Now, peace is suggested by the white flags displayed and silence prevails. Being on duty as officer-of-the-day, I stood by the general when Captain Craven, senior officer of the fleet with us, boarded our transport and with astonishment looked at the condition of things which surrounded us, being literally riddled with shot as we were. Wounded men gathered on the cabin floor and the dead on the deck below. "This is awful, General Williams! What would you advise?" The response came, "I would shell the town until the Stars and Stripes appeared on every white rag now flying over it." "Then open your batteries and I will land the troops." The signal, drop anchor, was made and the order, clear the deck for action, and as the captain regained the deck of his own ship, the signal to commence firing was made, and shots from his 11-inch battery of shell guns went plunging into the doomed town. Women, children, men and animals, all through the streets, were seen hurrying to the hills back of the city, carrying bundles, bales and baggage of all sorts; all rushing for the hills. Shot and shell went plunging and tearing through the town from the thirty guns of our fleet. Our old boat was hauled alongside the levee, and a detail of skirmishers was landed to look for the Rebel battery which fired upon us. It was my fortune to take command of these troops, and as we landed and proceeded from the levee into the town the gunboats ceased firing.

I hope never to see another such scene of desolation, destruction and death as was spread before me. In one place, a house in which a shell had struck and burst was completely shattered. Here a dozen of houses in line, all crushed into kindlings by a single shell; a large brick block crumbled to a heap of debris and ruins, and so all over the little village.

I will not mention the scenes of death before us on that occasion, only say a fearful retribution came upon that little city for their action towards an unarmed and helpless transport that sunny May morning. We found nothing of the battery which had fired upon us from the street. We learned that at the first sight of our returning they had limbered up and taken themselves back into the country. Although our skirmishers patrolled the fields for several miles, we could only learn they were far ahead of us and beyond any possibility of our overtaking them; so we established our picket line over the hills and listened to the noise of our troops all through the dark hours of night, sacking and destroying what remained of the village of Grand Gulf, and when the signal gun was fired to call us in, as we returned through the streets at daylight little could be seen to convey intelligence that a prosperous little village had so recently and defiantly made an assault upon a defenceless transport.

At an early hour we were all on board of our boat, which had been somewhat repaired during the night, and again we head for down stream. Thus we pass on during each day, and at night as usual tie up along the shore until daylight comes. One of the gunboats is now constantly in sight, so we meet with no further trouble. Arriving at Baton Rouge, we overtake the entire fleet, and orders are there for us to disembark and until further orders make ourselves at home. We are soon ashore, our little remnant of baggage snugly stowed away, and we begin housekeeping in the old United States Barracks, which for a brief time is our home, and is the first comfortable quarters we have had since we set foot upon southern soil.

Thus ended in failure one of the best planned and most important campaigns of the war—failure for want of troops.

REMARKS.

The House being in the Committee of the Whole on the state of the Union—

Mr. THOMAS said:

Mr. Chairman, I avail myself of the indulgence of the committee to make some suggestions upon subjects now attracting the attention of Congress and of the country—the relation of the "seceded States" (so called) to the Union, the confiscation of property, and the emancipation of slaves in such States. Sensible how deeply the interests of the country are involved in their right decision, I can only say I have given to them careful and patient consideration, with an earnest hope and desire to learn what my duty is and faithfully and firmly to discharge it.

The questions are novel, as they are momentous. In the discussion of them, little aid can be derived from our own precedents, from the history of other nations, or from writers on constitutional and international law. The solution of the difficult problems of right and duty involved must be found in the careful study of the principles of the Constitution and the just and logical application of them to this new condition of things.

The peculiar feature of our civil polity is, that we live under written constitutions, defining and limiting the powers of Government and securing the rights of the individual subject. Our political theory is, that the people retain the sovereignty and that the Government has such powers only as the people, by the organic law, have conferred upon it. Doubtless these inflexible rules sometimes operate as a restraint upon measures which for the time being seem to be desirable. The compensation is, that our experience has shown that, as a general rule and in the long run, the restraint is necessary and wholesome.

It is, I readily admit, by no narrow and rigid construction of the words of the Constitution that the powers and duties of Congress on these subjects are to be ascertained. Every provision must be fairly construed in view of the great objects the Constitution was ordained to effect, and with the full recognition of the powers resulting from clear implication, as well as express grant. Designed as the bond of perpetual union, and as the framework of permanent Government, we should be very slow to conclude that it lacked any of the necessary powers for self-defense and self-preservation.

But recognizing the profound wisdom and foresight of the Constitution, and its adaptation to all the exigencies of war and peace, when a measure is proposed in apparent conflict with its provisions, we may well pause to inquire whether, after all, the measure *is* necessary, and whether we may not bend to the Constitution rather than that the Constitution should give way to us. When we make necessity our law-giver, we are very ready to believe the necessity exists.

Nor are we to forget that the Constitution is a bill of rights as well as a frame of government; that among the most precious portions of the instrument are the first ten amendments; that it is doubtful whether the people of the United States could have been induced to adopt the Constitution except upon the assurance of the adoption of these amendments; which are our Magna Carta, embodying in the organic law the securities of life, liberty, and estate, which, to the Anglo-Saxon mind, are the seed and the fruit of free government. Some portions of our history have led to the conclusion that the existence of these amendments may, in the confusion of the times, have been overlooked.

In my humble judgment, Mr. Chairman, there has been and is now but one issue before the country, and that is whether the Constitution of the

United States shall be the supreme law of the land. That Constitution was formed by the *people* of the United States. It acts not upon the States, nor through the States upon us as citizens of the several States, but directly upon us as citizens of the United States, claiming on the one hand our allegiance and giving to us on the other its protection. It is not a compact between the States or the peoples of the several States. It is itself a frame of Government ordained and established by the people of the United States.

The sphere of the Government so established is indeed limited, but within that sphere its power is supreme. It is a Government of delegated powers and the powers not delegated are reserved either to the States or to the people. (Amendments, art. 10.)

The powers and functions granted to the national Government by the Constitution are embraced in three general classes: those concerning the relations of the United States to foreign nations, those concerning the relations between the States and their citizens respectively, and certain powers which, though belonging to the home department of Government, to be useful and effective must be general and uniform in their operation throughout the country. A very large proportion of the ordinary and necessary powers and functions of government is left in the States. The powers of the national Government do not extend to or include the domestic institutions or internal police of the States. The separation and distinction between the respective spheres of the State and national governments is an essential characteristic of our system, and is as old as the idea of Union itself. No Union was suggested, no project of one for a moment entertained on any other basis. The colonies in authorizing their delegates to assent to a separation from Great Britain and to form a Union for the general defense, expressly restricted them from consenting to any articles of union which should take from the colonies the power over their internal police and domestic institutions. The resolutions of the colonies of New Jersey, Maryland, and Rhode Island, may be cited in illustration.

The resolution of the provincial congress of New Jersey, passed June 21, 1776, and laid before the Continental Congress on the 28th of June, empowered the delegates of that province to—

"Unite with the delegates of the other colonies in declaring the United Colonies independent of Great Britain, entering into a confederation for union and common defense, making treaties with foreign nations for commerce and assistance, and to take such other measures as may appear to them and you necessary for these great ends; promising to support them with the whole force of this province; *always observing*, whatever plan of confederacy you enter into, *the regulating the internal police of this province is to be reserved to the Colony Legislature.*"

The convention of the colony of Maryland, by a resolution adopted June 28, 1776, and laid before Congress July 1, authorized and empowered the deputies of the colony to—

"Concur with the other United Colonies, or a majority of them, in declaring the United Colonies free and independent; in favoring such further compact and confederation between them; in making foreign alliances, and in adopting such other measures as shall be judged necessary for securing the liberties of America; and that said colony will hold itself bound by the resolutions of the majority of the United Colonies in the premises; *provided the sole and exclusive right of regulating the internal government and police of that colony be reserved to the people thereof.*"—*Journals of Congress*, 1776, pp. 390, 391, 392.

The credentials of the Assembly of Rhode Island, after giving to the delegates power to enter into Union and confederation, add:

"Taking the greatest care to secure to this colony, in the strongest and most perfect manner, its present established form and all the powers of government, so far as relates to its internal police and conduct of our affairs, civil and religious."—*Ibid.*, p. 343.

In the revolutionary government, in the Articles of Confederation, in the Constitution, in its judicial interpretation, in every Administration under the Constitution, and in every department of the Government, the limitation has thus far been carefully recognized and faithfully kept. This familiar, well-settled doctrine as to the independent respective spheres of the national and State government has never, perhaps, been more clearly and strongly stated than in one of the resolutions adopted by the convention which ushered the present Administration into power:

"*Resolved*, That the maintenance inviolate of the rights of the States, and especially the right of each State to order and control its own domestic institutions, according to its own judgment exclusively, is essential to that balance of powers on which the perfection and endurance of our political fabric depends."

It is expressed also, with clearness and strength, in the resolution adopted by the House near the close of the last session of Congress by a nearly unanimous vote:

"*Resolved*, That neither the Federal Government nor the people or governments of the non-slaveholding States have a purpose or a constitutional right to legislate upon or interfere with slavery in any of the States of the Union."

These doctrines as to the supremacy of the national Government within its sphere and of the reserved rights of the States are elementary. Between them there is no necessary conflict. Each is the complement of the other; both vital parts of that political system under whose admirable distribution and adjustment of powers the people of the United States have had for seventy years incomparably the best and most beneficent Government the world has ever known; a Government now imperiled, not by reason of any inherent defect or any want of wisdom or foresight in its founders, not because we have outgrown its provisions, not because it is behind the age, but because it has fallen upon an age not worthy of it, which has failed to appreciate the spirit of wisdom, prudence, and moderation in which it was founded.

Such being the relation of the Government of the United States to its citizens and to the States, the first question that arises is, how far this relation is affected by the fact that several of the States have assumed, by ordinances of secession, (so-called,) to separate themselves from the Union.

The people of the United States in and by the Constitution of the United States, established a national Government, without limitation of time, "for themselves and their posterity." It had been provided under the Articles of Confederation that the Union should be perpetual. The Constitution was established to form "a more perfect union" than that of the Confederation; more efficient in power, and not less durable in time There is not a clause or word in the Constitution which looks to separation. It has careful provisions for its amendment, none for its destruction; capacity for expansion, none for contraction; a door for new States to come in, none for old or new ones to go out. An ordinance of secession has no legal meaning or force, is wholly inoperative and void. The Constitution, and the laws and treaties made under it, the people have declared, "shall be the supreme law of the land, and the judges in every State shall be bound thereby, anything in the constitution or laws of any State to the contrary notwithstanding." The act of secession, therefore, cannot change in the least degree the legal relation of the State to the Union. No provision of the Constitution of the United States, no law or treaty of the United States can be abrogated or impaired thereby. No citizen of the United States residing in the seceded States is, by such ordinance of secession, deprived of the just protection of, or exempted from any of his duties to, the United States. In contemplation of law the reciprocal duties of protection and allegiance remain unaffected. After the act of secession, the province and duty of the Government of the United States are the same, according to the full measure of its ability, as before, to enforce in every part of the Union, and over every inch of its territory, the Constitution and laws of the United States.

It is the necessary result of these principles that no State can abdicate or forfeit the rights of its citizens to the protection of the Constitution of the United States or the privileges and blessings of the Union which that Constitution secures and makes perpetual. The primary, paramount allegiance of every citizen of the United States is to the nation, and the State authorities can no more impair that allegiance than a county court or a village constable. Every proposition, however artfully disguised, which seeks to give any effect or vitality to an ordinance of secession, for evil or for good, is itself a confession of the right. To say that an act of secession is inoperative and void against the Constitution, and that this void act sustained by force is a practical abdication of the rights of the State under the Constitution, is to blow hot and blow cold, to deny and affirm in the same breath, to state a proposition which is *felo de se*.

It is also the plain and necessary conclusion, from the principles before stated, that a *State* cannot commit treason. Under the Constitution of the United States *persons* only can commit treason. How treason may be committed, and how tried and punished, the Constitution points out. (Constitution, art. 3, sec. 3; Amendments, arts. 5 and 6.) The persons who for the time being hold the offices under a State government may individually commit treason, but the acts of the State officers, transcending their authority and in conflict with the Constitution of the United States, involve in their guilt no man who has not himself levied war against the United States or adhered to their enemies, giving them aid and comfort. It is only we, the subjects, that can commit treason or expiate its guilt. No man or set of men can without our consent, involve us in the awful crime, or subject us to the awful penalties of treason.

As a State cannot commit the crime of treason, it cannot incur a forfeiture of its powers and functions as the penalty of treason. The punishment provided for traitors is the result of judicial trial, conviction, and judgment. How to indict a State, the constitution of the court, the mode of trial, the form of judgment, and process of execution yet exist *in gremio legis*. Nor is it material that the acts of the State officers have the sanction and support of the majority of the people of the State. Within the proper sphere of the State government the rule of the majority will prevail, except so far as it is restrained by the organic law. But the majority of the voters of the State cannot deprive the minority of the rights secured to them by the Constitution of the United States. Some of these rights may be kept in abeyance. Their exercise may be overborne by superior physical force

They may sleep, but it is not the sleep of death. They are integral parts of the Constitution, and can only perish when the Constitution perishes.

The State of Tennessee, for example, has passed an ordinance of "secession." She has allied herself with the other seceding States. Her vote of secession is sustained by force. Upon this new and startling theory of the Constitution she has already incurred a forfeiture of all those functions and powers essential to the continued existence of the State as a body-politic. The voice of her eloquent Senator is heard in the Capitol, her venerable judge sits in the highest judicial tribunal, and exercises the highest functions of government, her Representatives mingle in our councils, her loyal citizens greet with tears of joy the banner of our advancing hosts—their hope and our hope, their pride and our pride; yet upon this theory there is no Tennessee, "the Commonwealth itself is past and gone." Its citizens can no longer be represented in this House or the Senate. The courts of the United States are closed against them. (Corporation of New Orleans *vs.* Winter, 1 Wheaton Rep., 91.) The requisition upon the State for troops was a mistake. The direct tax was a mistake. Its citizens, under the shield of the Constitution, are outlaws and in their own homes exiles. If such be the effects of a void act of secession, we should be grateful we are not called upon to witness the results of a valid one. There is nothing in the doctrines of nullification or secession more disloyal to the Constitution, more fatal to the Union, than this doctrine of State suicide. It is the gospel of anarchy, the philosophy of dissolution. Nor by carrying out this doctrine of the destruction or forfeiture of the State organization would anything be gained for the cause of freedom. Slavery exists by the local, municipal law, and would not be abolished unless you go one step further, and hold that, with the loss of the State organization, the institutions, laws, and civil relations of the States perish. Now, in case of conquest, even though the people of the conquered territory change their allegiance, their relations to each other and their rights of property remain undisturbed. The modern usage of nations, which has become law, would be violated if private property should be generally confiscated and private rights annulled. (United States *vs.* Percheman, 7 Peters, 51; 3 Phillemore, p. 743.) When, therefore, States were reduced to Territories, the national Government could not abolish slavery therein, except under the right of eminent domain, and by giving just compensation.

If we are right as to the nullity of the acts of secession, we may proceed to inquire whether the fact that the seceding States have attempted to form a new alliance or confederation will effect the result. Upon the plainest letter of the Constitution, as well as by its entire spirit, these acts of confederation are void. Continuing as States, in spite of their ordinances, they were expressly forbidden to enter into any treaty, alliance, or confederation, or into any agreement or compact with another State or with a foreign Power. (Constitution, art. 1, sec. 10.) Neither by secession nor confederation have they changed their legal relation to the Union and the Constitution of the United States. They are still members of the Union, foregoing for a time its privileges, but subject to its duties, bound to it by a cord which the sword of successful revolution can alone sever.

What, then, it may be asked, is the legal character of this great insurrection? The answer is, it is a rebellion of citizens of the United States against the Government of the United States; an organized effort to subvert and overthrow its authority, and to establish another government in its stead. Nothing can be more explicit than the proclamation of April 15, 1861:

> "The laws of the United States have been for some time past and now are opposed, and the execution thereof obstructed, in the States of South Carolina, Georgia, Alabama, Florida, Mississippi, Louisiana, and Texas, by combinations too powerful to be suppressed by the ordinary course of judicial proceedings, or by the powers vested in the marshals by law:
>
> "Now, therefore, I, Abraham Lincoln, President of the United States, in virtue of the power in me vested by the Constitution and the laws, have thought fit to call forth, and hereby do call forth, the militia of the several States of the Union, to the aggregate number of seventy-five thousand, *in order to suppress said combinations, and to cause the laws to be duly executed.*
>
> "I appeal to all loyal citizens to favor, facilitate, and aid this effort to maintain the honor, the *integrity*, and the *existence of our national Union*, and the perpetuity of popular Government, and to redress wrongs already long enough endured."

The State organizations have been found convenient, and have been used for the purposes of the rebellion. Those of counties and cities have been used for the same ends. In either case it was an entire perversion of their functions, and the action is none the less illegal and revolutionary on that account. A State, as such, having no power to engage in war with any other State, or with the United States, cannot interpose its shield between the Government of the United States and its subjects committing treason by levying war against it; nor is such levying war any the less treason because the traitors held places of trust in the State governments, and perverted the functions of those governments to their base ends.

Morally, it is an aggravation of the offense. It does not change its essential legal character.

In the convention for forming the Constitution of the United States, Luther Martin, of Maryland, was anxious to insert a provision to save the citizens of the States from being punishable as traitors to the United States when acting expressly in obedience to the authority of their own States. The provision offered by him was:

"That no act or acts done by one or more of the States against the United States, or by any citizen of any one of the United States, under the authority of one or more of the said States, shall be deemed *treason*, or *punished as such*; but in case of war being levied by one or more of the States against the United States, the conduct of each party towards the other, and their adherents respectively, shall be regulated by the laws of war and of nations."

This proposition was rejected, Mr. Martin says, with much feeling, because the leading members of the convention meant to leave the States at the mercy of the national Government. The more obvious reason is, that it was inconsistent with the whole theory of the Constitution, which, springing from the people of the United States, acted directly upon them as its subjects, and with a force which no law or ordinance of a State could impair.

This, then, is not a conflict of States, nor is it a war of countries or of geographical lines. It is a conflict between Government and its disobedient subjects. He only is the enemy of the United States who is committing treason by levying war against the United States, or giving aid and comfort to those who do. The loyal, faithful subject of the United States, wherever on the soil of his country he may have his home, is not the enemy of his country. No subtilty of logic, no ingenuity of legal construction, no misapplication of the laws of international war to this contest can change the nature of things, can convert loyalty into treason, or devotion into hostility. If there be to-day in Tennessee, or Georgia, or South Carolina even, a loyal subject of the United States "faithful among the faithless found," the Government is not at war with him. I am aware that as to property taken on the high seas, some of the district courts of the United States have held otherwise. But I venture to predict that the court of last resort will affirm the doctrine, stated by Mr. Justice Nelson of that court, to be good sense and sound law:

"On the breaking out of a war between two nations, the citizens or subjects of the respective belligerents are deemed by the law of nations to be the enemies of each other. The same is true, in a qualified sense, in the case of a civil war arising out of an insurrection or rebellion against the mother government. But in the latter case, the citizens or subjects residing within the insurrectionary district, not implicated in the rebellion, but adhering to their allegiance, are not enemies, nor to be regarded as such. This distinction was constantly observed by the English Government in the disturbances in Scotland under the Pretender and his son, in the years 1715 and 1745. It modifies the law, as it respects the condition of the citizens, or subjects, residing within the limits of the revolted district, who remain loyal to the government."

The difference between a war and a rebellion is clear and vital. War is the hostile relation of one nation to another, involving all the subjects of both. Rebellion is the relation which disloyal subjects hold to the nation, not involving or impairing the rights of loyal subjects. The law may fail to protect obedient subjects, but it never condemns them. As between the government and its subjects in arms against it, the *legal* relation is not that of war, notwithstanding the war power is used to subdue and reduce them to obedience. Though the rebellion has assumed gigantic proportions and the civil power is impotent to repress it, the array of numbers and extent of physical force do not change its essential legal character. It is still treason—the levying of war against the United States by those who owe to it allegiance. For this exigency the Constitution has provided. The war power of the Government may be evoked "to execute the laws of the Union, and to suppress insurrection." In levying war against the United States the rebels do not cease to be traitors, but are doing *the* thing in which the Constitution declares treason to consist. (Art. 3, sec. 3.)

While using the powers and appliances of war for the purpose of subduing the rebellion, we are by no means acting without the pale of the Constitution. We are using precisely the powers with which the Constitution has clothed us for this end. We are seeking domestic tranquillity by the sword the Constitution has placed in our hands. In the path of war, as of peace, the Constitution is our guide and our light—the cloud by day, the pillar of fire by night.

While using the powers of war for executing the laws and subduing rebellion, we are of course bound and restrained by the laws of war. It is our duty and our privilege to respect the maxims of humanity and moderation by which the law of nations and of Christian civilization has tempered the spirit of modern hostilities. During the war we may recognize in the rebels the rights of belligerents, may send them flags of truce, may make with them capitulations, cartels for exchange of prisoners, and extend to them the courtesies which mitigate, to some extent, the iron rigor of war. These things were done in the earliest stages of our Revolution, not only before the separation of the colonies was declared, but before the idea of independence had fairly taken possession of the public mind. But it was never supposed that by adopting the usages of civilized warfare Great Britain was relaxing her hold upon the colonies or elevating them into independent Powers. Nothing is, I think, plainer in principle than that the recognition of these rights and the observance of these usages—*flagrante bello*—cannot affect the legal relation of the parties, does not divest the sovereign of his power, or release the subject from his duties, when the strife of arms ceases. It is only when rebellion has ripened into successful revolution, that the permanent legal relations of the parties are changed. The recognition of the "belligerent rights" of the rebels by foreign Powers can, as between the sovereign and his subjects, have no other or further effect. Such recognition (if known to the law of nations) proceeds upon the ground that the *revolution is not accomplished, and that the connection is not dissolved.* Had this been done, the recognition would have been of their separate national existence.

In my humble judgment, Mr. Chairman, the "seceded States"—so called—and the people of those States are to-day integral parts of the Union, over whom, when the conflict of arms ceases the Constitution of the United States, and the laws made under it, will resume their peaceful sway. Traitors may perish, some institutions may perish, the nation will remain and the States will remain essential parts of the body-politic. "The body is one, and hath many members, and all the members of that body being many, are one body."

With this brief and imperfect development of the principles involved in this great controversy, I proceed to a more direct consideration of the subjects of confiscation and emancipation.

In seeking to know what this Government ought to do in relation to the confiscation of private property, or the emancipation of slaves in the "seceding" States, the obvious question presenting itself to every mind at the threshold is, what is *the end* which the Government and the people are seeking to attain? There can be but one loyal answer to that question. It is to preserve the Union and the Constitution in their integrity, to vindicate in every part of this indivisible Republic its supreme law. No purpose, however humane, beneficent, or attractive, can divert our steps from the plain, straight path of sworn duty. What is writ is writ. In seeking to change it by force of arms, we become the rebels we are striving to subdue.

It is a plain proposition, that in seeking to enforce the law we are, as far as possible, to obey the law. We are not to destroy in seeking to preserve. The people do not desire a bitter and remorseless struggle over the dead body of the Constitution. We may raise armies and navies and pour out as water the treasure and life-blood of the people, but we can neither think nor act wisely, live well or die well for the Republic, unless we keep clearly and always in view the end of all our labors and sacrifices, the Union of our fathers and the Constitution, which is its only bond. No thoughtful man can believe there is a possibility of reconstructing the Union on any other basis, or that it is within the province of Congress in any other but the peaceful way of amendment to make the effort.

The bills and joint resolutions before the House propose, with some differences of policy and method, two measures: the confiscation of the property of the rebels, and the emancipation of their slaves. Some of the resolutions propose the abolition of slavery itself, with compensation for loyal masters. It is my duty to examine, as briefly as I may, the wisdom, the justice, and the constitutionality of the measures proposed; and first of confiscation.

The propositions for confiscation include the entire property of the rebels, real and personal, for life and in fee. Within the class whose estates are to be confiscated are included not only those personally engaged in the rebellion, in arms against the Government, but also those who adhere to them, giving them aid or comfort; so that within the sweep of the bills would be brought substantially the property of eleven States and six millions of people.

The mind instinctively shrinks from a proposition like this. It reluets to include in one "fell swoop" a whole people. It asks anxiously if no consideration is to be had for different degrees of guilt; if the same measure is to be meted to those who organized the rebellion and those who have been forced into it; if no consideration is to be given to the fact that allegiance and protection are reciprocal duties, and that for the last ten months the national Government has found itself incapable of giving protection to its loyal subjects in the "seceding States," neither defending them nor giving them arms to defend themselves, and that deprived of our protection and incapable of resistance they have yielded only to superior force; if a wise Government is to forget the nature of man and the influences of birth, of soil, of home, of society, and of State, by which his opinions are insensibly molded, and that this pestilent heresy of the right of secession, fatal as it is now seen to be, not only to the existence of good Government but of social order itself, has been a cardinal article in the faith of a large portion of the people in the southern States, and that they have been induced by the arts and sophistries and falsehoods of unprincipled leaders to believe that their future safety and well-being required the exercise of the right? Those leaders should atone for their crime by the just penalty of the law. But you cannot, says Burke, "indict a whole people; you cannot apply to them the ordinary rules of criminal jurisprudence." To state the proposition to confiscate the property of eleven States is to confute it; is to shock our common sense and sense of justice; is to forget not only the ties of history and of kindred, but those of a common humanity; is to excite the indignation of the civilized world, and to invoke the interposition of all Christian Governments.

It is said that just retaliation requires the confiscation of the property of the rebels. Doubtless nations may feel compelled to resort to measures of severe retaliation. It may be their only security against future outrage. But a firmly established Government does not resort to cruelty and injustice because its rebellious subjects have done so. It must maintain a higher standard of rectitude and justice. Its object is not vengeance, but to deter men from crime. It knows that harsh and severe punishments but rouse pity for the criminal and indignation against the Government.

Nor will the difference between confiscation by the rebels and by this Government be overlooked. Our acts of confiscation, if within the limits of the Constitution, are effective and permanent; theirs, void in law, are temporary in their effect. The title to one square inch of land will not be changed by any confiscation by the rebel authorities. Every man who has occupied the land of a loyal citizen under their pretended acts of confiscation will be liable for the full rent and damages to the estate. Every man who is in possession of personal property under them will be compelled to disgorge. Every debt paid under them into rebel treasuries will still be due to the loyal creditor. The restoration and indemnity will, I know, be imperfect. Many grievous wrongs will go unredressed. But every rebel, whatsoever functions he may have usurped, judicial or executive, who has invaded the rights of person or of property of a loyal citizen, will be liable to his last farthing for indemnity. So far, therefore, as our Government confiscates the property of rebels to its own use, it takes from the loyal citizen the sources to which he may justly look for redress.

The acts of general confiscation proposed would defeat the great end the Government has in view: the restoration of order, union, and obedience to law. They would take from the rebels every motive for submission; they would create the strongest possible motives to continued resistance. In the maintenance of the confederate government they might possibly find protection; in the restoration of ours, spoliation. "*Spoliatis arma supersunt.*" You leave them the great weapon of despair. Sallust said of the old Romans, "*majores nostri religiosissimi mortales nihil victis eripiebant præter injuriæ licentiam*"—our ancestors, the most religious of men, took from the vanquished nothing but the license of wrong-doing; words, says Grotius, worthy of having been said by a Christian.

It seems to be taken for granted that our efforts to suppress the rebellion will be successful in proportion to the *severity* of the measures we adopt. The assumption is at war with the lessons of history and with the nature of man. The most vigorous prosecution of the war possible is best for the Government and its subjects in arms against it. But the war is means to an end. "Wise men labor in the hope of rest, and make war for the sake of peace." It is only when justice is tempered with mercy that it is justice.

Apart from the injustice and impolicy of these acts of sweeping confiscation, I have not been able to find in the Constitution the requisite authority to pass them. There are two aspects in which the legal question may be viewed—first, the confiscation and forfeiture of property as the punishment for crime; secondly, under what has popularly been called the "war power" of the Government.

Looking at confiscation as the penalty of crime, treason, or any lower grade of offense, some things seem to be plain:

That such forfeiture can be created by statutes applicable only to offenses committed after their passage. Congress cannot pass an *ex post facto* law. (Constitution, art. 1, sec. 9.)

The subject charged with treason may justly claim all the muniments and safeguards of the Constitution.

He cannot be deprived of life, liberty, or property, without due process of law, (Amendments, art. 5;) that is, judicial process as understood from the days of Magna Carta.

He cannot be held to answer for a capital or otherwise infamous crime, except in cases arising in the land or naval forces, or in the militia when in actual service in time of war or public danger, unless on presentment or indictment by a grand jury. (*Ibid.*)

After indictment he must have a trial by an impartial jury of the State and district wherein the crime shall have been committed; which district shall have been previously ascertained by law. (Art. 3, sec. 2; Amendments, art. 6.)

No attainder of treason can work a forfeiture except during the life of the person attainted. (Constitution, art. 3, sec. 2.) By attainder is here clearly meant judicial attainder, as a bill of attainder, that is, an attainder by an act of the Legislature, is by a prior provision of the Constitution expressly forbidden. (Art. 1, sec. 9.)

These sacred provisions of the Constitution, which as common-law muniments of life, liberty, and property, have existed in substance for six centuries, "the least feeling their care, and the greatest not exempted from their power," lie directly in the path and are fatal obstructions to any legislation confiscating property as the penalty of treason, except as the result of the judicial trial and sentence of the offender.

It has been assumed, I think without sufficient reflection, that under our laws against treason the most obnoxious traitors even will escape the righteous punishment of their crimes, because they must be tried by a jury in the State and district wherein the offense shall have been committed. Their only escape will be by exile. Where war is actually levied against the United States, where bodies of men have been actually assembled to effect by force of arms their treasonable purposes, all those who perform any part, however minute or however remote from the scene of action, and who are actually leagued in the general conspiracy, are to be considered as traitors. (*Ex parte* Bolman, &c., 4 Cranch, 75.) We have not indeed adopted the law of constructive presence, which holds that a man who incites or procures a treasonable act, is, by force of the incitement or procurement merely, legally present at the act. But it may be sufficient to constitute presence, if he is in a situation in which he can coöperate with any act of hostility, or furnish counsel and assistance to the parties if attacked. (United States *vs.* Burr, 4 Cranch, 470.) The modern facilities of communication greatly enlarge the field of coöperation. A commander at the end of a telegraph wire, directing the assault upon a fort of the United States, or at a railroad station with troops ready to be moved to the assistance of the rebel army in action, is, in law, present at the overt acts of treason. The leaders of this rebellion will be found, therefore, to have committed treason, and to be liable to indictment and trial in many States and districts in which a jury will be ready, upon adequate proof, to convict.

In the proposed measures, the thing sought to be done is the confiscation of the property of the rebel as the penalty of his offense, and the attainment of this end without the trial and conviction of the offender. Though under the Constitution upon a trial and *conviction* of a traitor you can only take the life estate, these measures assume that without any trial or conviction you may take the fee simple. Our legal instincts shrink from such a proposition. Its intrinsic difficulties have been seen and felt, and a resort has been had to analogies and precedents, judicial and legislative, to find for it some sanction and support: I think without success.

1. It is true, as has been said, that under the Constitution men may be deprived of life and property without trial by jury. Cases arising in the land and naval forces, and in the militia when in actual service in time of war or public danger, are in terms excepted from the general rule, (Amendments, art. 5,) but the exception, instead of impairing, by the law of logic as of common sense, confirms the rule.

2. Property is taken for taxes, and certainly without trial by jury, where the tax and mode of assessment are valid, but this is under an express grant of power to Congress "to lay and collect taxes;" (Art. 1, sec. 8,) the principle and general method of which were perfectly well understood when the Constitution was adopted. Nor does the exercise of this power, as has been suggested, take private property for public use without just compensation; on the contrary, the true and just theory of taxation is that the price paid is the reasonable compensation for the protection and security of life, liberty, and property, which a wise and efficient Government affords.

3. The forfeiture of goods for breach of the revenue laws has slight, if any, analogy to the confiscation of property as a punishment for the crime of its owner. To Congress is given the power to "regulate commerce," and "to levy and collect imports," and, of course, to prescribe the terms and conditions upon which goods may be imported. It may well avail itself of a familiar principle by which property used in violating, defeating, or defrauding the law, is liable to forfeiture. Though the forfeiture of the common law did not, strictly speaking, attach *in rem*, but was a part or consequence of the judgment of conviction of the offender, this doctrine was never applied to seizures and forfeitures created by statute *in rem* and cognizable on the revenue side of the exchequer. The thing was then primarily considered as the offender, and the offense was attached to *it*. The same principle is applied to proceedings *in rem* and seizures in the admiralty. (2 Wheaton, The Palmyra.) It is upon this distinction that the statutes of July 19 and of August 6, 1861, find their

support. The principle is, that the thing used in violating the law may be seized and condemned without a judgment upon the guilt of the owner.

I proceed to inquire how far, if at all, the powers of Congress are enlarged by the existence of this rebellion, and the use of the appliances of war to subdue it.

It would seem to be plain that the resistance of any portion of the people to the Constitution and laws cannot operate to confer upon Congress any new substantive power, or to abrogate any limitations of the powers of Congress which the people have imposed. When the Constitution intends that the existence of war or rebellion shall put an end to any restriction on the power of the Government, it says so. When it does not say so, the fair inference is that it does not mean so. Examples of such removals of restraint are found in article one, section eight, providing that the privilege of the "writ of *habeas corpus* shall not be suspended unless when in cases of rebellion or invasion the public safety may require it;" and in article three of the Amendments, forbidding in time of peace the quartering of soldiers in any house without the consent of the owner, but in time of war permitting it to be done "in a manner to be prescribed by law."

Engaged in suppressing a great and formidable rebellion, the Government may use the instrumentalities of war so far as they are adapted to the end. But it is never freed from the restraints of the Constitution, can never rise above it. The Constitution is never silent in the midst of arms. In war, as in peace, it is the supreme law—itself *salus populi et suprema lex*.

When Government is compelled to use the power of war it observes its limitations. How far in the use of this power it may confiscate or subject to forfeiture private property is the next question before us.

Some things are tolerably well settled. That property used in promoting the rebellion, in levying war against the United States, is lawful prize of war. This would include the arms, munitions, and provisions of war in actual use or procured for the purpose. The rule extends to goods used, not strictly as munitions or implements of war, but so as to defeat the military and naval operations resorted to to subdue the rebellion, as goods on their way to relieve besieged towns or forts, or ships or cargo violating a blockade or proceeding to or from ports with which commercial intercourse has been interdicted. It may extend to ships and cargo upon the high seas, the property of those levying war against the United States; enemies, not because of their domicil or residence upon one part rather than another of the territory of the Union, but because they are in arms against it.

Perhaps we should add to these, requisitions or contributions within military districts, levied upon those at war with the Government, for the support of the invading army. Such requisitions were, however, regarded by Wellington, a great statesman as well as great commander, as iniquitous, as a system for which the British soldier was unfit. I would refer also to the excellent remarks on this subject by President Woolsey, in his admirable Introduction to International Law. (Page 304.)

Beyond the points suggested, it is believed the usages of international war do not extend. By the modern usages of nations private property on the land is exempt from confiscation. This exemption, Mr. Wheaton says—and there is no higher authority—is now held to extend "to cases of the absolute and unqualified conquest of the enemy's country." (Wheaton's Elements of International Law, p. 421.) We refer also, as tending to the same result, to Vattel, book 3, chapter 8, section 147; to 1 Kent's Commentaries, pages 102, 104; 3 Phillimore, page 140; Woolsey, page 304. To this mitigated rule of war there are doubtless exceptions. Of these, Mr. Wheaton says:

"The exceptions to these general mitigations of the extreme rights of war, considered as a contest of force, all grow out of the same original principle of natural law, which authorizes us to use against an enemy such a degree of violence, and such only, as may be necessary to secure the object of hostilities. The same general rule which determines how far it is lawful to destroy the persons of enemies, will serve as a guide in judging how far it is lawful to ravage or lay waste their country. If this be necessary in order to accomplish the just ends of war, it may be lawfully done, but not otherwise. Thus, if the progress of an enemy cannot be stopped, nor our own frontier secured, or if the approaches to a town intended to be attacked cannot be made without laying waste the intermediate territory, the extreme case may justify a resort to measures not warranted by the ordinary purposes of war.—Page 421.

The exceptions growing out of military exigencies, and measured and governed by them, cannot be foreseen and provided for by legislation, but must be left, where the law of nations leaves them, with the military commander.

It has been said that these acts of general confiscation find support under the provision of the Constitution which authorizes Congress "to make rules concerning captures by land and water." The Constitution does not define the meaning of the word "captures." It refers us in such cases to the law of nations, as in others to the common law. Congress has power to declare "war."

What war is, the just causes of war, the rights and duties of nations in conducting it, are to be found in the law of nations. The "captures" referred to are very plainly not seizures of property under legal process, confiscation or forfeiture, but the taking of enemy's property by force or strategy, *jure victoriæ*. The title is acquired by capture, and liable to be lost by recapture. To make rules concerning "captures" is not to make rules in conflict with or beyond the law of nations. The extent to which the power conferred by the law of nations shall be exercised, and the disposition to be had of captures when made, are the proper subjects of municipal law and of the provision of the Constitution.

The case of Brown *vs.* The United States, (8 Cranch, 110,) has been cited as expressly deciding that Congress has power to pass a confiscation bill. I submit, with great respect, that it decides no such thing. The only point *decided* in the case was that British property found in the United States on land at the commencement of international hostilities (war of 1812) could not be condemned as enemy's property without an act of Congress for that purpose. The court dealing with a question arising under war with a foreign nation had no occasion to consider the powers or duties of Congress in the case of rebellion. The *discussions* of the court recognize a distinction between the right of the sovereign to take the persons and confiscate the property of the enemy wherever found, and the mitigations of the rule which the humane usages of modern times have introduced. With all my reverence for the great magistrate who delivered the opinion of the court, I must be permitted to say that usage is itself the principal source of the law of nations, and that these humane usages have become the rules of war in Christian States. The law of nations, says Bynkershoek, is only a presumption founded on usage. (*De foro legatorum*, chap. 18, sec. 6.)

It is suggested that if the confiscation of private property violated the law of nations the courts could not overrule the interpretation of that law by the political department of the Government, and that no other power could intervene. Possibly this may be so; but surely it is not intended that we shall violate the law of nations in dealing with our subjects, because there is no appeal or redress for the subject. It is in the exercise of irresponsible power that the nicest sense of justice and the greatest caution and forbearance are demanded. In suppressing a rebellion so atrocious, marked by such fury and hate against a Government felt only in its blessings, forbearance sometimes seems to us weakness, and vengeance the noblest of virtues. But in our calmer moments we hear the Divine voice, "vengeance is mine; I will repay."

I conclude what I have to say upon this branch of the subject with the remark that, in substance and effect, the bills before the House seek the permanent forfeiture and confiscation of property, real and personal, without the trial of the offender. I am unable to see how under the Constitution that result can be reached.

The temporary use of property in districts under military occupation, and of estates abandoned by their owners, rests upon distinct principles which it is not now necessary to consider. We have only to remark, in passing, that the use of such property and the rule in such districts can be provisional only, waiting the regular action of the State governments, and in no way impairing their permanent powers. Upon this subject I intend at some future day to trouble the House with a few suggestions.

I proceed to the question of the deepest interest involved in this discussion, the emancipation of slaves in the "seceding States." There is no subject on which our feelings are so likely to warp our judgment, in which calmness is so necessary and so difficult, and declamation so easy or so useless. The general principles stated in relation to the power and duty of Congress as to confiscation are applicable to the subject of emancipation.

On the question of policy the plausible and attractive argument is that the only effectual way to suppress rebellion is to remove its cause. The position when thoroughly probed is, not that the national Government has not the power to put down the rebellion without resort to emancipation, but that the continued existence of slavery is incompatible with the future safety of the Republic. This plainly is not a question of present military necessity, but one affecting the permanent structure of the Government, and involving material changes in the Constitution. This can be done in one of two ways. In the method the Constitution points out, or by successful revolution on the part of the free States and the entire subjugation of the slave States. No man can foresee to-day what policy a severe and protracted struggle *may* render necessary. It is sufficient to say that into such a war of conquest and extermination the people of the United States have no *present* disposition to enter. They have too thorough a conviction of the capacity of the Government to subdue the rebellion by the means the Constitution sanctions to be desirous of looking beyond its pale

Upon the legal aspect of the question, it may be stated as a general proposition, that Congress in time of peace has no power over slavery in the States. By that is meant the institution itself; for the national Government may, in my judgment, forfeit the right of the master in the labor of the slave as a penalty for crime of which the master shall be convicted. And when so forfeited, it may dispose of the right as it sees fit. Nor is there any intrinsic difficulty in the use of this species of property under the right of eminent domain. If the Government were constructing a fort or digging an intrenchment, it might hire this species of labor, or, if necessary, take it, as it might other labor or property, giving reasonable compensation therefor.

The provision as to the return of fugitives from service cannot be deemed an exception to the general rule before stated; for the provision applies to escapes from one State into another, and not to escapes within the States. Of which we may remark, in passing, that, as to the former class, the power of the Government is strictly civil, to be executed by judicial process; and that as to the latter, the national Government in time of war or peace has no concern.

Nor would an act of the national Government liberating the slaves within a State, having the consent of the State, and providing compensation for the masters militate with the rule. *Conventio vincit legem.* The consent of the State would relieve the difficulty.

But the question arises, how far the existence of the rebellion confers upon Congress any new power over the relation of master and slave. Strictly speaking, no new power is conferred upon any department of the Government by war or rebellion, but it may have powers to be used in those exigencies which are dormant in time of peace. Such, for examples, are the power to call out the militia, (art. 1, sec. 8;) to try by martial law cases arising in the militia, (Amendments, 5;) to suspend the writ of *habeas corpus*, (art. 1, sec. 9;) to quarter troops in private houses, (Amendments, 3.) But when the national Government is called to the stern duty of repressing insurrection or repelling invasion, may not new power over the relation of master and slave be brought into action? Such, I think, is the result.

A plain case is presented by slaves employed in the military and naval service of the rebels. If captured, they may be set free.

The Government may refuse to return a slave to a master who has been engaged in the rebellion or suffered the slave to be employed in it.

It may require the services of all persons subject to its jurisdiction by residing upon its territory, when the exigency arises, to aid in executing the laws, in repressing insurrection or repelling invasion. This right is, in my judgment, paramount to any claim of the master to his labor under the local law. There might be a question of the duty of the slave to obey, but the will of the master could not intervene. His claim, if any, would be a reasonable compensation for the labor of his slave.

But though the power may exist, there is, with prudent and humane men, no desire to use it. Nothing but the direst extremity would excuse the use of a power fraught with so great perils to both races; and the glorious triumphs of our arms, evincing our capacity to subdue the rebellion without departure from the usages of civilized warfare, have indefinitely postponed the question.

There is one other exigency in which the relation of master and slave must give way to military necessity. If the commander of a military district shall find that the slaves within it, by the strength they give to their rebellious masters—by bearing arms, or doing other military service, or acting as the servants of those who do—obstruct his efforts to subdue the rebellion, he may deprive the enemy of this force, and may remove the obstruction by giving freedom to the slaves. This, it is apparent, is not a civil or legislative, but a strictly military right and power, springing from the exigency, and measured and limited by it, to be used for the subduing of the enemy, and for no ulterior purpose. If the Commander-in-Chief and the generals under him shall observe faithfully this distinction, the use of the power ought to be no just ground of complaint. If, in consequence of the protraction of the war, the effect of the use of this power should be to put an end to slavery in any of the States, or to weaken and impair its force, we may justly thank God for bringing good out of evil.

In my judgment, it would be impracticable for the Legislature, even if it had the power, to anticipate by any general statute the exigencies, or prescribe the rules for the exercise of this power. The Legislature and the people will be content to leave the matter to the sound discretion and sound patriotism of the magistrate selected to execute the laws.

To avoid misconstruction, I desire to say that the power of Congress over slavery in this District is absolute; that no limitation exists in the letter or spirit of the Constitution or the acts of cession. All that is requisite for abolishing slavery here is *just* compensation to the master. Equally absolute, in my judgment, is the power of Congress over slavery in the Territories.

Mr. Chairman, in a letter to a friend, published on the first day of the last year, I ventured to say that secession should be resisted to the last extremity, by force of arms; that it cost us seven years of war to secure this Government, and that seven years, if need be, would be wisely spent in the struggle to maintain it; that for this country there was no reasonable hope of peace but within the pale of the Constitution and in obedience to its mandates. The progress of events has served only to deepen those convictions. They are as firmly rooted as my trust in God and His providence. Who ever else may falter, I must stand by the Constitution I have sworn to support. I am not wise enough to build a better. I am not rash enough to experiment upon a nation's life. There is, to me, no hope of "one country" but in this system of many States and one nation, working in their respective spheres as if the divine hand had molded and set them in motion. To this system the integrity of the States is as essential as that of the central power. Their life is one life. A consolidated government for this vast country would be essentially a despotic government, democratic in name, but kept buoyant by corruption and efficient by the sword.

Desiring the extinction of slavery with my whole mind and heart, I watch the working of events with devout gratitude and with patience. The last year has done the work of a generation. By no rash act of ours, much less any radical change in the Constitution, shall we hasten the desired result. If in the pursuit of objects however humane, if beguiled by the flatteries of hope or of shallow self-conceit, if impelled by our hatred of treason and desire of vengeance or retribution, if seduced by the "insidious wiles of foreign influence," we yield to such change, we shall destroy the best hope of freeman and slave, and the best hope of humanity this side the grave.

1 **No. 2.**

PAPERS FROM THE SOCIETY

FOR THE

Diffusion of Political Knowledge.

SPEECH OF MR. TURPIE,

DELIVERED IN THE

SENATE OF THE UNITED STATES, FEB. 7, 1863.

"WHEN A PARTY IN POWER VIOLATES THE CONSTITUTION AND DISREGARDS STATE-RIGHTS, PLAIN MEN WILL READ PAMPHLETS."

READ—DISCUSS—DIFFUSE.

Resolved, That it be recommended to all citizens in the various cities, counties, and villages of this and other States, who approve of the objects expressed in this Constitution, that they organize auxiliary societies, and open communication with the New-York Society, for the purpose of procuring and circulating our papers.

17

SPEECH OF MR. TURPIE.

Mr. President, it would be well at first thought, it would seem, if the whole world could exist under one form of government. It would be a vast economy in the maintenance of foreign relations. It would dispense forever with the armies and navies of the globe, the eternal witnesses of national jealousy. It would settle forever the great question of the balance of power. In the community, however, it has been ordered that the interest of the whole is best promoted by the pursuit of the interest of the individual in his particular sphere. The self-interest of nations and of communities has demanded separation and different nationalities—separation not to be avoided by identity of language, by identity of religion, by geographical contiguity—not to be avoided in any event where the true and real interests of the community may dictate it.

I do not say this, sir, in justification of the crime of secession, but I say it to show how entirely imbecile and weak is the plea for national unity, founded only upon the circumstance of geographical contiguity, and the identity of race, of religion, and of language. Self-interest divides and it separates. The American Union was formed on the principle of different interests of local communities, being protected and more effectually protected by that Union than by any other means. It was formed upon the sole idea that the reserved rights of the States and the people should not be interfered with by the General Government so created.

It is useless to talk about imaginary lines not being sufficient to divide nationalities. Sir, the line which divides your own State from the Canadas is an imaginary line drawn by the compass of the surveyor. Its virtue, its power, its efficiency, are as well known to every negro-larcenous fanatic in this country as it is to that pleasant speaker of parables who darkens the Presidential mansion with his shadow and yet refuses to recognize the efficiency of a line thus drawn. If we would preserve national integrity, if we would extend and keep expanded the national domain, we shall have, above all things, to show that the interests of communities, the interests of States, the interests of Territories, the interests of the future population who are to inhabit this country, will be best subserved and protected by a national Government. The moment you abandon that doctrine, the moment the Federal Government, under any excuse, under any pretense whatever, interferes in such a way as to show that it no longer consults the reserved rights of the States and the people and the self-interest of separate communities composing it, you destroy the only tie which can bind them to our nationality.

The States made the Union; the Union did not make the States. It is a sufficient answer to the dogma that the States have no *status* out of the Union to say that the States existed before the Union, and must have existed out of it. The Union was formed solely upon the idea that certain rights should be reserved. What rights are they? The right of life, of liberty, of the pursuit of happiness; the right of property, its acquisition, its possession, its disposition after the death of the owner; the right of freedom of the press; the toleration of religious opinion; the right of freedom of speech; all the most sacred rights of political, domestic, and social relations are among those reserved to the States and the people, and can not be interfered with by the General Government in any manner whatever. If there had not been such a reservation the Union never could have existed; and if that reservation be destroyed, the Union will perish with its destruction.

The guardians of these rights—you may call them States, you may call them by whatever name you wish—can be nothing less than sovereign. The idea that any paramount authority may exist as to these rights destroys the reservation of the rights themselves, as it destroys the sovereignty of the community which is bound to protect and assert them. Hence, in the constitution of my State, and yours, of all the States, the crime of treason against the State is defined and punished. Treason can not be committed against less than a sovereignty; and I hold that the States themselves have enacted, and as sovereigns prescribed, the punishment for treason against the rights reserved to them and their people.

I do not wish to wrest this doctrine to my own destruction, or to the justification of any who have taken up arms against the Government. I know that the individuals, the officers of a State, may commit treason against the Federal Government. I believe that the officers of the Federal Government may commit treason against the States. The rights, the duties, and the dangers of the States and the Federal Government are mutual and reciprocal. There should be no trespass either upon the one hand or the other. The crime of treason may be committed against State government as well as against Federal authority.

There are many crimes, however, against the rights of the States and against the rights of the people which are below the grade of treason. There are misdemeanors, offenses less than treason. There are vile frauds, there are most contemptible and cowardly impositions, as fatal to State dignity and State sovereignty as treason itself. The proposition embodied in this bill is one of that character. It is worse than a crime. It is worse than a crime because it lacks the boldness of execution. It is meaner than a crime because you can not fasten it upon the person who seeks to perpetrate it, or upon the power which seeks to commit it. What is this proposition? It is a proposition to interfere with the rights of property in the State of Missouri, and to interfere in the most powerful manner—to interfere by an appeal to the basest passion of humanity, the love of money. The loyalty of Missouri, it seems, has been weighed and measured. It is worth ten millions in cash or twenty millions on credit. I will not pursue the tenor of this thought. It would be doing injustice to the people of a great State to say any thing further about it; nor will I vote the value of a penny to bribe the legislative or popular action of the State of Missouri, upon the subject of their domestic institutions, in any way whatever.

This is a direct bribe offered by the Federal Government, under the authority of the Federal Government, for legislative and popular action against the rights of property in the State of Missouri. If you can buy the property rights of Missouri, you can purchase any others. What reasons are assigned for this most extraordinary conduct? In the first place, it is said that Missouri is willing. Does that change *our* constitutional obligations as Senators and conservators of the Federal compact? Does that give us the right to intervene or interfere? We are told that the fidelity of Missouri to the Union is to depend upon the result of the bill now pending. I heard with regret the Senator from that State [Mr. Henderson] say that unless this bill passed, he would not say what the result would be, but he feared it; that he should leave the State and cast his fortunes with the Union; intimating that the State might leave the Union if this bill was not passed.

Mr. Henderson. Mr. President—

The Vice-President. Does the Senator from Indiana give way?

Mr. Turpie. With all due deference to the Senator, I will not.

Sir, I am sorry that any such appeal should be made to the Senate. I will not under such a threat, as I take it, do so great an injustice to the people of

Missouri, or to those of Indiana, as to vote for a measure of this character. Nor do I believe that the triumph of the Federal cause is to be affected either in Missouri or elsewhere by the defeat or the success of this bill. The American people have undertaken a sublime task, the restoration of our nationality. Does the Senator from Missouri doubt the success of that effort? I do not. I never have. There is a God in heaven for the brave. I believe that no power short of that which arrested Saul on his journey from Jerusalem to Damascus can prevent the accomplishment of that result. I believe that no legislation as suggested by this bill can retard or accelerate the result.

The Administration, to be sure, are laboring under difficulties every day increasing. France, England, Horace Greeley, and the other great powers [laughter] are to be watched and conciliated; McClellan, the patriot without a peer, is to be crushed out and forgotten; Giddings and Garrison, and other domestic enemies of the country's peace, are to be pensioned and provided for; the Porters, by land and sea, are to be punished; the rebels are to be driven out of the State of Missouri; and the draft is yet to be enforced in Massachusetts. These are most arduous labors, and I bespeak for those who have undertaken them not only the coöperation of their friends, but the sympathy of their political opponents, and the neutrality at least of all the world and the balance of mankind. [Laughter.]

But, sir, I do not think that what the Administration has undertaken has any thing to do with the great popular task of the country. Senators are continually saying here, day after day, that unless the country is saved during this Administration, it can not be saved at all. I am of the contrary opinion. I think that, as far as the present Administration is concerned, the Executive has lost the confidence of the people of both sections of this land. He has lost the confidence of the North and the South. He is thoroughly imbued with the fanatical abolition notions of the New-England school. It would be impossible for any man, or any set of men, to operate harmoniously and effectually during the existence of this Administration for the purpose of doing the country any good, or taking any important step towards a final restoration of the political relations formerly existing between these States.

A UNION WORTH HAVING.

I know, sir, that Senators are constantly talking about the Union. I do not wish to be exceeded by any man in my devotion to the American Union. I have spoken for the Union; I have written for the Union; I have fought and acted for the Union when those who now claim to be its ardent friends were willing, under certain contingencies, to let it slide. But I ask you, sir, what do Senators mean by the Union? It is by what they mean, not what they say, that we must judge them. If it is meant by the Union to purchase the negro slaves of Missouri or elsewhere, and pay for them out of the people's money and the public Treasury, I am not for it. If you mean by the Union the support of these fugitive contrabands, these pariahs of the South who escape within our military limits, and the feeding and clothing of these creatures, to the desertion, starvation, and destitution of the soldiers of the Federal Army—if you mean that by the Union, I am not for it. If you mean by the Union the absorption by the Federal Government of the reserved rights of the States and the people I am not for it. But if you mean by the Union the restoration of the national authority upon every foot of the national soil; if you mean by the Union the preservation of the national fame and of the national flag; the flag which waved at Bunker Hill, at Saratoga, at Yorktown, at Palo Alto, at Chepultepec, at Shiloh, and at Donelson—that flag with not a stripe obliterated, and with every star undimmed; the only flag in the world which floats over a limited Government and a free people—if you mean that by the Union, I am for it now and forever.

But, sir, it is said as an additional reason why we should pass this measure, that it will aid the State of Missouri in emancipation. The object is said to be humane and philanthropic. It may be extremely charitable; but I ask you, sir, why has Congress, why has the General Government exclusively confined its charities to Africans in servitude, and to the wants of the negro race? Are there no other sufferers upon whom this money might be expended? Whole regiments now serving under the flag of your country have gone upaid for months. The wives and children of soldiers, a vast constituency at home, are begging daily for bread. I should sooner vote an appropriation of ten or twenty millions for such a purpose than for any purpose presented in this bill.

THIS MOVEMENT UNNATURAL.

What is our action, and what can be its result? Do you call this strengthening the hands of the President? Do you call it strengthening the Administration? Do you call it filling up the ranks of the Army and encouraging the Union cause? I say that this course of conduct can bring nothing but danger and dishonor upon the country. It will be seen that millions of the national treasury are squandered for abolition purposes in Missouri and elsewhere, and that the soldier in the field remains unpaid, and sometimes unfed, and unclothed. I take it, that Senators would show their devotion to the Union in passing by such measures as the one at present urged, and giving their attention solely and wholly to the condition of the country, and the wants of that large constituency of unpurchased and unpurchasable patriotism which has shown its love of country by bearing arms in the field. Talk about the loyalty of Missouri—the purchased love of the prostitute; one that has to be bought with money, and paid for with money! Would you foster and cherish that feeling, if such exists? I would not dishonor the State by saying that I believe in its existence; but would you foster and cherish that mercenary affection to the destruction of the interests of all those portions of our fellow-citizens who are demanding this money, and demanding, in fact, all the resources and support of the Government which we can possibly give them?

Why should there be an intervention and interference in the case of Missouri? Pennsylvania and New-York were formerly slave States. At the close of the Revolution a large amount of capital was invested in those States in slave property. The institution has disappeared from those States, and how? By virtue of the voluntary legislative action of the people and their representatives. I ask Senators, why should the slaveholders of Missouri be paid for their property out of the national treasury any more than the slaveholders of New-York and Pennsylvania? I ask those, particularly, differing with me in political faith; I ask those Senators who have built up political fortunes upon their pretended hatred of this institution, and their pretended opposition to Southern rights, why they now propose to tax the free people of the loyal North and South; why they propose to tax the national treasury for the special benefit of the slaveholder, the slave-breeder, and the slave-driver, of Missouri?

Sir, the State which I in part represent will yield to no State in the Confederacy in its devotion to the Union. Indiana, the gift of Virginia to the nation, loves the Union for the giver's sake. She hopes yet to see the mother of States and statesmen restored and reconciled to all her children. Although the people of Indiana, at any time before the existence of war by the act of the public enemy, at any time before the Federal flag was fired upon by the traitor-band of South-Carolina at Sumter, would have accepted the Crittenden proposition, the Border State proposition, or any of those propositions, as a settlement of the difficulties between the sections, yet when war came, she waged war; not because she desired it, but because she believed we must have war, or worse; we must either have war or a dissevered nationality; we must have either war or abandon the Government to its enemies. Indiana still follows the flag of the Union. The bones of her gallant sons, fallen in this great struggle, mingle in the soil of every battle-field from Missouri to the Rappahanock. Indiana now is not for war—she never has been; she is not for peace; she is not for either of these things, except as a means to an end—that end, the restoration of the Union and the unity of the States. If the war is not waged with that purpose, I am for peace to-day. If it is found that that purpose is impracticable or impossible, I am for a cessation of hostilities this moment.

PEACE AND UNION THE END OF THE WAR.

Sir, the people of Indiana have not gone into this contest blindfolded. They surveyed the whole field. They counted the cost. They knew what it would cost to make the effort. They knew it would cost more not to make it. They are not for separation. They are for national integrity at whatever cost, and by whatever means, whether belligerent or pacific, by which that object may be effected. If mediation is to be proposed as a settlement, the people of Indiana will ask why the mediation of New-York, of New-Jersey, of Kentucky, of Illinois; why the mediation of these sovereignties should not be received and accepted, as well as the mediation of France or England, either in regard to the termination of the war or the policy with which it may be conducted. They will ask why was Crittenden rejected as a mediator and any one else preferred? That they will ask, and they will require an answer. As dear as the Union is to Indiana, and as dear as it is to every loyal citizen, it is not of more value than the rights of the States and the people. The same treasure and the same blood that I should be willing to expend in the preservation of the one, I shall spend just as freely in the security and the protection of the other.

THIS MEASURE OUGHT TO ALARM THE STATES.

It is asked, but it is has not been answered, what power under the Constitution we have to make this appropriation. The Chief Magistrate of the country, when he introduced the resolution inaugurating this policy, and since, has declared that there is no power under the Constitution by which it can be carried out and effected. He has admitted that it is extra-constitutional, and beyond the powers specified in that instrument. Have we had any change in the Constitution? How could a change have been effected? We do not distinguish between power and authority. Will it be for a moment claimed that the present Chief Magistrate of the Union has any more authority than the one who preceded him, or the one before that? It can not be. He may have more power. How has he achieved that power? By calling into his hand the military force of the country, by largely increasing the army and navy; but it has given him no shadow of authority more than that which was possessed by his predecessors.

This appropriation is asked for under the war power. It is claimed by Senators to be necessary to crush out the rebellion, to vindicate the national law and the national authority in the State of Missouri. This war power is a most singular article. India-rubber has had some reputation heretofore for being elastic; gold and silver for being malleable and ductile; but sir, they must yield to this war power in all those qualities. Why, sir, it

> "Lives through all life, extends through all extent,
> Spreads undivided, operates unspent."

WAR POWER A COVER FOR REVOLUTION.

The President is the first great reservoir of this war power. He is Commander-in-Chief of the Army and Navy. Why is he Commander-in-Chief of the Army and Navy? Because he is President, and not for any other reason. I take it to be a settled principle of the Government that the military is always subordinate to the civil power. I take it that the powers of the Commander-in-Chief are subordinate to the powers of the President; and that an act of the Commander-in-Chief against the Constitution and beyond the Constitution can not be justified any more than can an act of the President. The war powers of both Congress and the President are subordinate to civil authority. The President is said to be the grand receptacle of these war powers. The heads of departments have, of course, some of them. Some are claimed for Congress. We are now called upon to exercise our share of these extraordinary powers in the passage of this bill. The Governors of the States have claimed some of these powers. They have been distributed down to a multitude, whom no man can number, of provost-marshals, scattered in every village between the two oceans, except Ceredo and Oberlin, which, being inhabited wholly by white and black Africans, needed no such guardians of loyalty.

It is a most remarkable power—this war power of the Constitution — so much so, that I doubt its existence altogether. It is a myth; it is a fiction; it has no existence. The Chief Executive has laid down what this power is. He says it is the power on his part to do any thing which he may consider necessary to crush the rebellion. That is the only limit to it — his own discretion. Can he lengthen his own term of office? Most certainly he can under the war power, if he should think it necessary to crush the rebellion. Can he increase his pay? Most certainly he can, just as easily as he can issue a proclamation affecting the rights of property in any of the States. There is no limit to the power, and there can be none. I take it, sir, that when you thus place the power in the hands of one man to control the army and navy, and the purse of a great nation, without restriction and without limit, you have erected a military despotism. You call him the President. In France he is called the Emperor; in Austria, the Emperor; in Russia, the Czar. The American Czar will find no serfs west of the Alleghanies. It is not proposed to surrender the most sacred rights which were reserved at the time of the formation of the Constitution to the States and to the people; there *can* be no necessity for their destruction.

Why, sir, under this war power you may exercise any authority whatever. It is useless for us to *say* that an act does not conduce to the crushing of the rebellion; if the Executive *thinks* differently, that is the law. I think that the defeat of this Missouri bill will strengthen the Federal Government, not only in Missouri, but elsewhere. I hope it will be defeated; but if Congress, to whom is deputed a part of this remarkable power, thinks differently, away goes your safeguard on the Treasury, and away go all the restrictions and limits which have been thrown around the rights of property in the several States, and the Constitution, instead of being a living ordinance, becomes only a "quiet dogma of the past."

What will be the effect of this continual interference and intervention by the Federal Government with the rights of the States and the people? What has been its effect already? Do we not read it in the signs of the times? As far as one act, treason, is concerned, the officers and people of certain States have taken up arms against the Federal Government. As far as the other act is concerned, it is proposed not to take up arms, but to interfere and intervene by the power of the purse with the domestic institutions of the States. That power, that inference is no more to be justified than the other. Much has been accomplished by indirection since the commencement of the present policy, which no man could have justified or accomplished directly. We find ourselves now in the prosecution of a war where abolition is coïncident with military success, simply by this same method of indirection. Forces have been called out, arms have been placed in their hands ostensibly and avowedly for the purpose of protecting the national Government against the treason of certain States, and after they have been so called out, by this same indirection, the whole force is converted from its original intention, and a crusade is undertaken and waged against the very rights which the General Government is bound to protect; for, as I said before, I believe that the rights of the States and of the General Government are mutual. The General Government guarantees to the States a republican form of Government. It guarantees the safety and protection of the rights of which I have spoken, and it can not interfere with those rights without abandoning its constitutional limitations, and without a breach of the guarantees which it gave the State at the time of her admission.

Hence there are no circumstances which would induce me to vote for the bill under consideration. I regard it as a violation of the reserved rights of the people of Missouri. I regard it as a violation of constitutional obligations upon our part; and let me say that while we are waging a war for the law, we ought to wage it under the law, and we ought not to violate the law. Without the law there is no transgression. Without law there is no rebellion. And if Congress and the General Government insist upon a breach, a serious infraction of the Constitution in regard to the rights of any of the States, we can not tell how far that breach may go, or can tell what effect it may have upon the whole character of the Government.

I say nothing, sir, now, of that new treason which we have heard whispered in high places, that the army of the Union is to be recalled, that there is to be no further effort to save the *Government*, but that the force is all to be exhausted for the purpose of saving the *Administration*. I say nothing about that except this, as far as the State which I represent is concerned, we are not disposed to abandon the Union; we are not yet disposed to accept separation as a necessity; we are not disposed to accept separation as an alternative rather than recognize the right of the Southern States to a peculiar species of property. No, sir; I charge Senators to avoid this crime against nationality. The people of the North-west, the people of the great central States have recently decided upon these very questions. In those States there was no contest as to whether the integrity of the Government should be maintained. The question in the late canvass related to whether there should be a change of its form by our own agency. Upon that question the verdict of Indiana, of Illinois, of New-Jersey, and of other States, was rendered. Determining that, while the Government should be supported, while it should receive money, while it should receive men from the States guaranteeing the vindication of the national sovereignty, there should be no interference whatever by the Federal Government with the rights of the States themselves. Let not Senators mistake this as the verdict or as the action of a *party*. As far as the result of the election in Indiana was concerned, it was distinctly the action of the people, not of any party, against every possible discouragement that could be thrown upon that action. Less attention was paid to party organization, less attention was paid to party drill and party instrumentalities, than in any contest we have ever had in the North-west. It was a pure, plain decision upon the question as to whether, for any purposes, the rights of the people should be violated; as to whether, for any purposes, freedom of speech, freedom of the press, freedom of debate and discussion could be trampled under foot by the hand of military power. That was the question raised and decided. Let us heed that warning. Let us retrace our steps. Let us say some fault has been committed. Let us heed the protest which the States have entered. The Federal Government will do well to regard it. The Government is worth more than this Administration; it is worth more than any other. It should work for perpetuity. It should work for all time to the health and safety of the nation, which I pray may exist forever as the fathers formed it.

TRICK OF THE RADICAL PARTY TO DRAW CONSERVATIVES INTO WAR.

At an early stage of the political contest of which I have spoken, great efforts were used to blind the people as to the questions really at issue. The Republican party in my State disbanded its organization; it claimed to be no party; it claimed to have no issue but a vigorous prosecution of the war; it called itself "Union;" and at a very early stage of the same canvass, a select coterie of negro maniacs, acting under semblance of law, calling themselves a Grand Jury of the United States District Court, affected to present the Democratic party and its organization as disloyal and traitorous to the country. More than that, prominent members and leaders of the party all over the State were arrested, and without cause imprisoned. I myself made a canvass during the last summer under threats, every day, of personal violence, and with my pockets filled with anonymous letters to the same effect. The presses of the party were closed, in some instances; were torn down and destroyed in others. Every effort was made even in that State, always loyal, to suppress a free, clear, plain expression of the people; but the effort failed. The people did speak, and they spoke what I have here said in the Senate.

I know that Senators have disparaged here the discussion of party questions. They have said: "A million men are now in the field, Democrats and Republicans, fighting side by side; with them there is no quarrel; with them there is no difference; why can there not be unanimity and friendship here?" I ask the same question, why? Talk about parties! How do you make parties? How are they created? You can not make them out of conventions and platforms. They are built upon issues. That is the way the present parties are formed and divided. Who are responsible for these issues? The Senators to my right [the Republicans] and their political associates. When the President of the United States issued his proclamation, calling upon the military force of the country to avenge the insult offered to the national flag at Fort Sumter, all men rallied, without distinction of party, to the support of that banner. There was literally no party. And when Congress met here in special session, in the summer immediately succeeding the proclamation, the same unanimity prevailed. Congress then said that this war should not be prosecuted in the spirit of conquest or subjugation, and it should not interfere with the rights, the dignity, or the institutions of the States. Congress adjourned; it went home and found a united constituency. What has divided us? I will tell you, sir. Do you recollect the victory of Fort Donelson? I know you do. You recollect with what rejoicing every loyal heart received the intelligence of the success of the Union arms. Two days after that victory, a special message was submitted to the American Congress. What was it? Congratulating the people on the return of Tennessee to the Union? Inviting again the States of the South to renew their love and allegiance to the General Government? No, sir. It was confined to the sole object of the "abolishment" of African slavery. Why "abolishment?" Why not say "abolition"? Because then the measure would have been christened at once with the approbium and contempt it deserved. An obsolete term, a word almost unheard hitherto in the language, must be selected and placed in this message to discriminate its doctrines from the disgraceful heresies of that school of fanaticism, which has so often met defeat with proclamation, and made victory itself almost contemptible. That was the first thing that presented these issues of which Senators complain. Other measures of a similar character rapidly followed, which have made party in this country a virtue and a necessity.

ABOLITION THE SOLE ANIMUS OF THE RADICAL PARTY.

There was an appropriation here at the last session of $1,000,000 for abolition purposes in the District of Columbia. Who presented it? Who voted for it? Who carried it against the protest of the people? The Senators to my right; those who are complaining about party discussions and party feeling in this hall. When did they do it? When did they propose to squander this vast sum to gratify the fanaticism of a section with which they are connected, and for which they claim all the loyalty? It was when a rebel army was threatening the possession of the capital itself; when, from the dome of this structure, you might have seen the rebel flag floating—when five hundred thousand men were in arms against this Government. It was at such a time that these men could not forget the flesh-pots of Chicago, but must insist upon party action and party legislation. It is that which has divided a once united people. There is no other cause whatever. If this war had been prosecuted in the spirit in which it was commenced, if it was now prosecuted with an eye single to the purpose of restoring nationality, the people of Indiana, the people of other States would require no draft to certify to a compelled loyalty; they would follow the flag of the Union in myriads more countless than those which followed Peter the Hermit to rescue the sepulcher of Christ from the infidel.

But, sir, it is because you have abandoned the original policy of the war, because you have abandoned the constitutional mode of a reconstruction of the Government, that you have divided the people of the loyal States, and that you have again sowed the seeds of party debate and discussion. I know it is asked at such a time as this will you still continue these wranglings? Let me ask of these Senators, will they postpone these abolltion measures which have already dishonored and ruined the country to so great an extent; will they postpone this thing of buying negroes and paying for them out of the public treasury; will they postpone these other enormities; will they postpone this direct infraction upon the rights of the people of Missouri? If they will postpone these things we will postpone discussion and debate, not otherwise; and I here make the offer, and I know that every person acting politically with me will accede to it, that we bury party; that we forget differences; that we cease discussion and debate, provided they will cease the presentation and urgency of these measures with which they have so often hitherto disgraced the country.

It would, indeed, sir, be a felicitous thing if we of the loyal States could look back upon the history of a once united people and say there was no blot on our escutcheon; that we had never transcended constitutional limits, never stopped to interfere with the constitutional reservation of the rights of any of the States. That brings me to the most important consideration in the passage of the bill—the one I have already alluded to—the effect of this policy of interference and intervention. From the beginning it has been disastrous. If I had the power to blot out the words most hateful to me in the history of my section, I would erase the words "Harper's Ferry." We are never done reading of Federal misfortunes which have clouded Harper's Ferry; and why? At other places we have seen the backs of the rebels; there we have shown them ours. At other places victory has perched upon our eagles; at Harper's Ferry we have had nothing but disaster, defeat, and discomfiture. It is the place where first was raised the hand of Northern fanaticism against the reserved rights and sovereignty of a great State of this Union. It is a spot consecrated to eternal shame and infamy; it is the "damned spot that will never out." Sumter shall equal it in dishonor; but Sumter followed. This may be treason; but it is truth also. If our record of the North was clear, was plain, was unclouded, with what virtue, with what force, with what renewed efficacy we might go before the world and ask its judgment in our favor in regard to the present contest. Do Senators still desire to continue to agitate this most odious doctrine of interference with the sovereignty of the States? Do they still desire to continue to agitate this dangerous and disgraceful element in the political history of the country? If they do, let them vote for the Missouri bill.

But, sir, if Senators desire to return to the constitutional landmarks; if they desire to make this war specially for the Union and for nothing else; if Senators desire to place the merits of this contest wholly and solely upon the question of national integrity, let us defeat this bill;

let us say to Missouri: "If slavery is an incubus and an evil, it is one for which the Federal Government is not responsible; it is one for which the people of Indiana, the people of Virginia, the people of Kentucky, the people of no State in this Union are answerable, except the people of Missouri themselves." For good or for evil they chose this institution. They have recognized, cherished, fostered and supported it; and for one, rejoiced as I would be to hear of its disappearance, I am not willing to lift a finger to tax my people or the national Treasury in aid of any such eleemosynary project. We can find other uses for the public treasure more consonant with the national honor, national unity, and national peace.

Extracts from Webster's Reply to Hayne on the Constitution.

Mr. President, the nature of sovereignty or sovereign power has been extensively discussed by gentlemen on this occasion, as it generally is when the origin of our government is debated. But I confess myself not entirely satisfied with arguments and illustrations drawn from that topic. The sovereignty of government is an idea belonging to the other side of the Atlantic. No such thing is known in North-America. Our governments are all limited. In Europe, sovereignty is of feudal origin, and imports no more than the state of the sovereign. It comprises his rights, duties, exemptions, prerogatives, and powers. But with us, all power is with the people. They alone are sovereign; and they erect what governments they please, and confer on them such powers as they please. None of these governments is sovereign, in the European sense of the word, all being restrained by written constitutions. It seems to me, therefore, that we only perplex ourselves when we attempt to explain the relations existing between the general government and the several State governments, according to those ideas of sovereignty which prevail under systems essentially different from our own.

The Constitution of the United States creates direct relations between this government and individuals. This government may punish individuals for treason, and all other crimes in the code, when committed against the United States. It has power, also, to tax individuals, in any mode, and to any extent; and it possesses the further power of demanding from individuals military service. Nothing, certainly, can more clearly distinguish a government from a confederation of States than the possession of these powers. No closer relations can exist between individuals and any government.

On the other hand, the government owes high and solemn duties to every citizen of the country. It is bound to protect him in his most important rights and interests. It makes war for his protection, and no other government in the country can make war. It makes peace for his protection, and no other government can make peace. It maintains armies and navies for his defence and security, and no other government is allowed to maintain them. He goes abroad beneath its flag, and carries over all the earth a national character imparted to him by this government, and which no other government can impart. In whatever relates to war, to peace, to commerce, he knows no other government. All these, sir, are connections as dear and as sacred as can bind individuals to any government on earth. It is not, therefore, a compact between States, but a government proper, operating directly upon individuals, yielding to them protection on the one hand, and demanding from them obedience on the other.

The truth is, Mr. President and no ingenuity of argument, no subtility of distinction can evade it, that, as to certain purposes, the people of the United States are one people. They are one in making war, and one in making peace; they are one in regulating commerce, and one in laying duties of imposts. The very end and purpose of the Constitution was, to make them one people in these particulars; and it has effectually accomplished its object. All this is apparent on the face of the Constitution itself. I have already said, sir, that to obtain a power of direct legislation over the people, especially in regard to imposts, was always prominent as a reason for getting rid of the Confederation, and forming a new Constitution. Among innumerable proofs of this, before the assembling of the Convention, allow me to refer only to the report of the committee of the old Congress, July, 1785.

The people, sir, in every State, live under two governments. They owe obedience to both. These governments, though distinct, are not adverse. Each has its separate sphere, and its peculiar powers, and duties. It is not a contest between two sovereigns for the same power, like the wars of the rival houses in England; nor is it a dispute between a government *de facto* and a government *de jure*. It is the case of a division of powers between two governments, made by the people, to whom both are responsible. Neither can dispense with the duty which individuals owe to the other: neither can call itself master of the other: the people are masters of both. The division of power, it is true, is in a great measure unknown in Europe. It is the peculiar system of America; and, although new and singular, it is not incomprehensible. The State constitutions are established by the people of the States. This Constitution is established by the people of all the States.

Habeas Corpus.

In order to show what great principles of human freedom have been assassinated by this bill, we have only to refer to the well-settled maxims of law. First, it strikes down the writ of *habeas corpus:*

CHIEF-JUSTICE BLACKSTONE SAYS.

"Next to personal security," says Mr. Justice Blackstone, "the law of England regards, asserts, and preserves the personal liberty of individuals. This personal liberty consists in the power of locomotion, of changing situation, or moving one's person to whatsoever place one's own inclinations may direct, without imprisonment or restraint, unless by due course of law.

"By the Petition of Right, 3 Car. 1st, it is enacted that no person shall be imprisoned or detained without cause shown, to which he make answer according to law. By Car. 1st, ch. 10, if any person be restrained of his liberty by order or decree of any illegal court, or by the command of the King's Majesty in person, or by warrant of the council-board, or of any of the privy council, he shall upon demand of his counsel have a writ of *habeas corpus* to bring his body before the Court of King's Bench or Common Pleas, who shall determine whether the cause of his commitment be just, and hereupon to do as to justice shall appertain.

"To bereave a man of life, or by violence to confiscate his estate without accusation or trial, would be so gross and notorious an act of despotism as must at once convey the alarm of tyranny throughout the whole kingdom; but confinement of the person, by secretly hurrying him to jail, where his sufferings are unknown, or forgotten, is a less public, a less striking, and therefore a more dangerous engine of arbitrary government. And yet sometimes, when the state is in real danger, even this may be a necessary measure. But the happiness of our own Constitution is, that it is not left to the executive power to determine when the danger of the state is so great as to render this measure expedient; for it is the Parliament only, or legislative power, that, whenever it sees proper, can authorize the Crown, by suspending *habeas corpus* act for a short and limited time, to imprison suspected persons, without giving any reason for so doing."—*Commentaries on the Laws of England*, vol. i. pp. 135–136.

37TH CONGRESS, } 2d Session. }

SENATE.

{ REP. COM. { No. 41.

IN THE SENATE OF THE UNITED STATES.

MAY 1, 1862.—*Resolved*, That there be printed, in addition to the usual number, for the use of the Senate, fifty thousand copies of the report of the joint committee on the conduct of the present war, without the documents.

Mr. WADE submitted the following

REPORT.

The joint committee on the conduct of the present war beg leave respectfully to submit a report, in part, as follows:

On the 1st day of April the Senate of the United States adopted the following resolution; which was referred to the committee on the conduct of the war:

Resolved, That the select committee on the conduct of the war be directed to collect the evidence with regard to the barbarous treatment by the rebels, at Manassas, of the remains of officers and soldiers of the United States killed in battle there; and that the said select committee also inquire into the fact whether the Indian savages have been employed by the rebels, in their military service, against the government of the United States, and how such warfare has been conducted by said savages.

In pursuance of the instructions contained in this resolution, your committee have the honor to report that they examined a number of witnesses, whose testimony is herewith submitted.

Mr. Nathaniel F. Parker, who was captured at Falling Waters, Virginia, testifies that he was kept in close confinement, denied exercise, and, with a number of others, huddled up in a room; that their food, generally scant, was always bad, and sometimes nauseous; that the wounded had neither medical attention nor humane treatment, and that many of these latter died from sheer neglect; that five of the prisoners were shot by the sentries outside, and that he saw one man, Tibbitts, of the New York 27th regiment, shot as he was passing his window on the 8th of November, and that he died of the wound on the 12th. The perpetrator of this foul murder was subsequently promoted by the rebel government.

Dr. J. M. Homiston, surgeon of the 14th New York, or Brooklyn regiment, captured at Bull Run, testifies that when he solicited permission to remain on the field and to attend to wounded men, some of whom were in a helpless and painful condition and suffering for water, he was brutally refused. They offered him neither water nor anything in the shape of food. He and his companions stood in the streets of Manassas, surrounded by a threatening and boisterous crowd, and were afterwards thrust into an old building, and left, without sustenance or covering, to sleep on the bare floor. It was only when faint and exhausted, in response to their earnest petitions, they having been without food for 24 hours, that some cold bacon was grudgingly given to them. When, at last, they were permitted to go to the relief of our wounded, the secession surgeon would not allow them to perform operations, but intrusted the wounded to his young assistants, "some of them with no more knowledge of what they attempted to do than an apothecary's clerk;" and further, "that these inexperienced surgeons performed operations upon our men in a most horrible manner; some of them were absolutely frightful." "When," he adds, "I asked Doctor Darby to allow me to amputate the leg of Corporal Prescott, of our regiment, and said that the man must die if it were not done, he told me that I should be allowed to do it." While Doctor Homiston was waiting, he says a secessionist came through the room and said, "They are operating upon one of the Yankee's legs up stairs." "I went up and found that they had cut off Prescott's leg. The assistants were pulling on the flesh at each side, trying to get flap enough to cover the bone. They had sawed off the bone without leaving any of the flesh to form the flaps to cover it; and with all the force they could use they could not get flap enough to cover the bone. They were then obliged to saw off about an inch more of the bone, and even then, when they came to put in the sutures (the stitches) they could not approximate the edges within less than an inch and a half of each other; of course, as soon as there was any swelling, the stitches tore out and the bone stuck through again. Doctor Swalm tried afterwards to remedy it by performing another operation, but Prescott had become so debilitated that he did not survive." Corporal Prescott was a young man of high position, and had received a very liberal education.

The same witness describes the sufferings of the wounded after the battle as inconceivably horrible—with bad food, no covering, no water. They were lying upon the floor as thickly as they could be laid. "There was not a particle of light in the house to enable us to move among them." Deaf to all his appeals, they continued to refuse water to these suffering men, and he was only enabled to procure it by setting cups under the eaves to catch the rain that was falling, and in this way he spent the night catching the water and conveying it to the wounded to drink. As there was no light, he was obliged to crawl on his hands and knees to avoid stepping on their wounded limbs; and he adds, "It is not a wonder that next morning we found that several had died during the night." The young surgeons, who seemed to delight in hacking and butchering these brave defenders of our country's flag, were not, it would seem, permitted to perform any operations upon the rebel wounded. "Some of our wounded," says this witness, "were left lying upon the battle field until Tuesday night and Wednesday morning. When brought in, their wounds were completely alive with larvæ deposited there by the flies, having laid out through all the rain storm of Monday, and the hot, sultry sunshine of Tuesday." The dead laid upon the field unburied for five days; and this included men not only of his own, the 14th regiment, but of other regiments. This witness testifies that the rebel dead were carried off and interred decently. In answer to a question whether the confederates themselves were not also destitute of medicines, he replied, "They could not have been, for they took all ours, even to our surgical instruments." He received none of the attention from the surgeons on the other side, "which," to use his own language, "I should have shown to them had our position been reversed."

The testimony of William F. Swalm, assistant surgeon of the 14th New York regiment, who was taken prisoner at Sudley's church, confirms the statement of Dr. Homiston in regard to the brutal operations on Corporal Prescott. He also states that after he himself had been removed to Richmond, when seated one day with his feet on the window-sill, the sentry outside called to him to take them in, and on looking out he saw the sentry with his musket cocked and pointed at him, and withdrew in time to save his life. He gives evidence of the careless, heartless, and cruel manner in which the surgeons operated upon our men. Previous to leaving for Richmond, and ten or twelve days after the battle, he saw some of the Union soldiers unburied on the field, and entirely naked. Walking around were a great many women, gloating over the horrid sight.

The case of Dr. Ferguson, of one of the New York regiments, is mentioned by Dr. Swalm. "When getting into his ambulance to look after his own wounded he was fired upon by the rebels. When he told them who he was, they said they would take a parting shot at him, which they did, wounding him in the leg. He had his boots on, and his spurs on his boots, and as they drove along his spurs would catch in the tail-board of the ambulance, causing him to shriek with agony." An officer rode up, and, placing his pistol to his head, threatened to shoot him if he continued to scream. This was on Sunday, the day of the battle.

One of the most important witnesses was General James B. Ricketts, well known in Washington and throughout the country, lately promoted for his daring and self-sacrificing courage. After having been wounded in the battle of Bull Run, he was captured, and as he lay helpless on his back, a party of rebels passing him cried out, "Knock out his brains, the d——d Yankee." He met General Beauregard, an old acquaintance, only a year his senior at the United States Military Academy, where both were educated. He had met the rebel general in the south a number of times. By this head of the rebel army, on the day after the battle, he was told that his (General Ricketts's) treatment would depend upon the treatment extended to the rebel privateers. His first lieutenant, Ramsey, who was killed, was stripped of every article of his clothing but his socks, and left naked on the field. He testified that those of our wounded who died in Richmond were buried in the negro burying-ground among the negroes, and were put into the earth in the most unfeeling manner. The statement of other witnesses as to how the prisoners were treated is fully confirmed by General Ricketts. He himself, while in prison, subsisted mainly upon what he purchased with his own money, the money brought to him by his wife. "We had," he says, "what they called bacon soup—soup made of boiled bacon, the bacon being a little rancid—which you could not possibly eat; and that for a man whose system was being drained by a wound is no diet at all." In reply to a question whether he had heard anything about our prisoners being shot by the rebel sentries, he answered: "Yes, a number of our men were shot. In one instance two were shot; one was killed, and the other wounded, by a man who rested his gun on the window-sill while he capped it."

General Ricketts, in reference to his having been held as one of the hostages for the privateers, states: "I considered it bad treatment to be selected as a hostage for a privateer, when I was so lame that I could not walk, and while my wounds were still open and unhealed. At this time General Winder came to see me. He had been a officer in my regiment; I had known him for twenty odd years. It was on the 9th of November that he came to see me. He saw that my wounds were still unhealed; he saw my condition; but that very day he received an order to select hostages for the privateers, and, notwithstanding he knew my condition, the next day, Sunday, the 10th of November, I was selected as one of the hostages." "I heard," he continues, "of a great many of our prisoners who had been bayonetted and shot. I saw three of them—two that had been bayonetted and one of them shot. One was named Louis Francis, of the New York 14th. He had received fourteen bayonet wounds—one through his privates—and he had one wound very much like mine, on the knee, in consequence of which his leg was amputated after twelve weeks had passed; and I would state here that in regard to his case, when it was determined to amputate his leg, I heard Dr. Peachy, the rebel surgeon, remark to one of his young assistants, 'I won't be greedy; you may do it;' and the young man did it. I saw a number in my room, many of whom had been badly amputated. The flaps over the stump were drawn too tight, and in some the bones protruded. A man by the name of Prescott (the same referred to in the testimony of Surgeon Homiston) was amputated twice, and was then, I think, moved to Richmond before the taps were healed—Prescott died under this treatment. I heard a rebel doctor on the steps below my room say, 'that he wished he could take out the hearts of the d——d Yankees as easily as he could take off their legs.' Some of the southern gentlemen treated me very handsomely. Wade Hampton, who was opposed to my battery, came to see me and behaved like a generous enemy."

It appears, as a part of the history of this rebellion, that General Ricketts was visited by his wife, who, having first heard that he was killed in battle, afterwards that he was alive but wounded, travelled under great difficulties to Manassas to see her husband. He says: "She had almost to fight her way through, but succeeded finally in reaching me on the fourth day after the battle. There were eight persons in the Lewis House, at Manassas, in the room where I lay, and my wife, for two weeks, slept in that room on the floor by my side, without a bed. When we got to Richmond there were six of us in a room, among them Colonel Wilcox, who remained with us until he was taken to Charleston. There we were all in one room. There was no door to it. It was much as it would be here if you should take off the doors of this committee room, and then fill the passage with wounded soldiers. In the hot summer months the stench from their wounds, and from the utensils they used, was fearful. There was no privacy at all, because there being no door the room could not be closed. We were there as a common show. Colonel Wilcox and myself were objects of interest, and were gazed upon as if we were a couple of savages. The people would come in there and say all sorts of things to us and about us, until I was obliged to tell them that I was a prisoner and had nothing to say. On our way to Richmond, when we reached Gordonsville, many women crowded around the cars, and asked my wife if she cooked? if she washed? how she got there? Finally, Mrs. Ricketts appealed to the officer in charge, and told him that it was not the intention that we should be subjected to this treatment, and if it was continued she would make it known to the authorities. General Johnson took my wife's carriage and horses at Manassas, kept them, and has them yet for aught I know. When I got to Richmond I spoke to several gentlemen about this, and so did Mrs. Ricketts. They said, of course, the carriage and horses should be returned, but they never were. "There is one debt," says this gallant soldier, "that I desire very much to pay, and nothing troubles me so much now as the fact that my wounds prevent me from entering upon active service at once."

The case of Louis Francis, who was terribly wounded and maltreated, and lost a leg, is referred to by General Ricketts; but the testimony of Francis himself is startling. He was a private in the New York 14th regiment. He says: "I was attacked by two rebel soldiers, and wounded in the right knee with the bayonet. As I lay on the sod they kept bayonetting me until I received fourteen wounds. One then left me, the other remaining over me, when a Union soldier coming up, shot him in the breast, and he fell dead. I lay on the ground until 10 o'clock next day. I was then removed in a wagon to a building; my wounds examined and partially dressed. On the Saturday following we were carried to Manassas, and from there to the general hospital at Richmond. My leg having partially mortified, I consented that it should be amputated, which operation was performed by a young man. I insisted that they should allow Dr. Swalm to be present, for I wanted one Union man there if I died under the operation. The stitches and the band slipped from neglect, and the bone protruded; and about two weeks after another operation was performed, at which time another piece of the thigh bone was sawed off. Six weeks after the amputation, and before it healed, I was removed to the tobacco factory."

Two operations were subsequently performed on Francis—one at Fortress Monroe, and one at Brooklyn, New York—after his release from captivity.

Revolting as these disclosures are, it was when the committee came to examine witnesses in reference to the treatment of our heroic dead that the fiendish spirit of the rebel leaders was most prominently exhibited. Daniel Bixby, jr., of

Washington, testifies that he went out in company with Mr. G. A. Smart, of Cambridge, Massachusetts, who went to search for the body of his brother, who fell at Blackburn's Ford in the action of the 18th of July. They found the grave. The clothes were identified as those of his brother on account of some peculiarity in the make, for they had been made by his mother; and, in order to identify them, other clothes made by her were taken, that they might compare them. "We found no head in the grave, and no bones of any kind—nothing but the clothes and portions of the flesh. We found the remains of three other bodies all together. The clothes were there; some flesh was left, but no bones." The witness also states that Mrs. Pierce Butler, who lives near the place, said that she had seen the rebels boiling portions of the bodies of our dead in order to obtain their bones as relics. They could not wait for them to decay. She said that she had seen drumsticks made of "Yankee shinbones," as they called them. Mrs. Butler also stated that she had seen a skull that one of the New Orleans artillery had, which, he said, he was going to send home and have mounted, and that he intended to drink a brandy punch out of it the day he was married.

Frederick Scholes, of the city of Brooklyn, New York, testified that he proceeded to the battle field of Bull Run on the fourth of this month (April) to find the place where he supposed his brother's body was buried. Mr. Scholes, who is a man of unquestioned character, by his testimony fully confirms the statements of other witnesses. He met a free negro, named Simon or Simons, who stated that it was a common thing for the rebel soldiers to exhibit the bones of the Yankees. "I found," he says, "in the bushes in the neighborhood, a part of a Zouave uniform, with the sleeve sticking out of the grave, and a portion of the pantaloons. Attempting to pull it up, I saw the two ends of the grave were still unopened, but the middle had been prised up, pulling up the extremities of the uniform at some places, the sleeves of the shirt in another, and a portion of the pantaloons. Dr. Swalm (one of the surgeons, whose testimony has already been referred to) pointed out the trenches where the secessionists had buried their own dead, and, on examination, it appeared that their remains had not been disturbed at all. Mr. Scholes met a free negro, named Hampton, who resided near the place, and when he told him the manner in which these bodies had been dug up, he said he knew it had been done, and added that the rebels had commenced digging bodies two or three days after they were buried, for the purpose, at first, of obtaining the buttons off their uniforms, and that afterwards they disinterred them to get their bones. He said they had taken rails and pushed the ends down in the centre under the middle of the bodies, and pried them up. The information of the negroes of Benjamin Franklin Lewis corroborated fully the statement of this man Hampton. They said that a good many of the bodies had been stripped naked on the field before they were buried, and that some were buried naked. I went to Mr. Lewis's house and spoke to him of the manner in which these bodies had been disinterred. He admitted that it was infamous, and condemned principally the Louisiana Tigers, of General Wheat's division. He admitted that our wounded had been very badly treated." In confirmation of the testimony of Dr. Swalm and Dr. Homiston, this witness avers that Mr. Lewis mentioned a number of instances of men who had been murdered by bad surgical treatment. Mr. Lewis was afraid that a pestilence would break out in consequence of the dead being left unburied, and stated that he had gone and warned the neighborhood and had the dead buried, sending his own men to assist in doing so. "On Sunday morning (yesterday) I went out in search of my brother's grave. We found the trench, and dug for the bodies below. They were eighteen inches to two feet below the surface, and had been hustled in in any way. In one end of the trench we found, not more than two or three inches below the surface, the thigh bone of a man which had evidently been dug up after the burial. At the other end of the trench we found the shinbone of a man, which had been struck by a musket ball and split. The bodies at the ends had been pried up. While digging there, a party of soldiers came along and showed us a part of a shinbone, five or six inches long, which had the end sawed off. They said that they had found it among other pieces in one of the cabins the rebels had deserted. From the appearance of it, pieces had been sawed off to make finger rings. As soon as the negroes noticed this, they said that the rebels had had rings made of the bones of our dead, and that they had them for sale in their camps. When Dr. Swalm saw the bone he said it was a part of the shinbone of a man. The soldiers represented that there were lots of these bones scattered through the rebel huts sawed into rings," &c. Mr. Lewis and his negroes all spoke of Colonel James Cameron's body, and knew that "it had been stripped, and also where it had been buried." Mr. Scholes, in answer to a question of one of the committee, described the different treatment extended to the Union soldiers and the rebel dead. The latter had little head-boards placed at the head of their respective graves and marked; none of them had the appearance of having been disturbed.

The evidence of that distinguished and patriotic citizen, Hon. William Sprague, governor of the State of Rhode Island, confirms and fortifies some of the most revolting statements of former witnesses. His object in visiting the battle field was to recover the bodies of Colonel Slocum and Major Ballou, of the Rhode Island regiment. He took out with him several of his own men to identify the graves. On reaching the place he states that "we commenced digging for the bodies of Colonel Slocum and Major Ballou at the spot pointed out to us by these men who had been in the action. While digging, some negro women came up and asked whom we were looking for, and at the same time said that 'Colonel Slogun' had been dug up by the rebels, by some men of a Georgia regiment, his head cut off, and his body taken to a ravine thirty or forty yards below, and there burned. We stopped digging and went to the spot designated, where we found coals and ashes and bones mingled together. A little distance from there we found a shirt (still buttoned at the neck) and blanket with large quantities of hair upon it, everything indicating the burning of a body there. We returned and dug down at the spot indicated as the grave of Major Ballou, but found no body there; but at the place pointed out as the grave where Colonel Slocum was buried we found a box, which, upon being raised and opened, was found to contain the body of Colonel Slocum. The soldiers who had buried the two bodies were satisfied that the grave had been opened; the body taken out, beheaded, and burned, was that of Major Ballou, because it was not in the spot where Colonel Slocum was buried, but rather to the right of it. They at once said that the rebels had made a mistake, and had taken the body of Major Ballou for that of Colonel Slocum. The shirt found near the place where the body was burned I recognized as one belonging to Major Ballou, as I had been very intimate with him. We gathered up the ashes containing the portion of his remains that were left, and put them in a coffin together with his shirt and the blanket with the hair left upon it. After we had done this we went to that portion of the field where the battle had first commenced, and began to dig for the remains of Captain Tower. We brought a soldier with us to designate the place where he was buried. He had been wounded in the battle, and had seen from the window of the house where the captain was interred. On opening the ditch or trench we found it filled with soldiers, all buried with their faces downward. On taking up some four or five we discovered the remains of Captain Tower, mingled with those of the men. We took them, placed them in a coffin, and brought them home."

In reply to a question of a member of the committee as to whether he was satisfied that they were buried intentionally with their faces downward, Governor Sprague's answer was, "Undoubtedly! Beyond all controversy!" and that "it was done as a mark of indignity." In answer to another question as to what their object could have been, especially in regard to the body of Colonel Slocum, he replied: "Sheer brutality, and nothing else. They did it on account of his courage and chivalry in forcing his regiment fearlessly and bravely upon them. He destroyed about one-half of that Georgia regiment, which was made up of their best citizens." When the inquiry was put whether he thought these barbarities were committed by that regiment, he responded, "by that same regiment, as I was told." While their own dead were buried with marble head and foot stones, and names upon them, ours were buried, as I have stated, in trenches. This eminent witness concludes his testimony as follows: "I have published an order to my second regiment, to which these officers were attached, that I shall not be satisfied with what they shall do unless they give an account of one rebel killed for each one of their own number."

The members of your committee might content themselves by leaving this testimony to the Senate and the people without a word of comment; but when the enemies of a just and generous government are attempting to excite the sympathy of disloyal men in our own country, and to solicit the aid of foreign governments by the grossest misrepresentations of the objects of the war, and of the conduct of the officers and soldiers of the republic, this, the most startling evidence of their insincerity and inhumanity, deserves some notice at our hands. History will be examined in vain for a parallel to this rebellion against a good government. Long prepared for by ambitious men, who were made doubly confident of success by the aid and counsel of former administrations, and by the belief that their plans were unobserved by a magnanimous people, they precipitated the war (at a moment when the general administration had just been changed) under circumstances of astounding perfidy. Without a single reasonable ground of complaint, and in the face of repeated manifestations of moderation and peace on the part of the President and his friends, they took up arms and declared that they would never surrender until their rebellion had been recognized, or the institutions established by our fathers had been destroyed. The people of the loyal States, at last convinced that they could preserve their liberties only by an appeal to the God of battles, rushed to the standard of the republic, in response to the call of the Chief Magistrate.

Every step of this monstrous treason has been marked by violence and crime. No transgression has been too great, no wrong too startling, for its leaders. They disregarded the sanctity of the oaths they had taken to support the Constitution; they repudiated all their obligations to the people of the free States; they deceived and betrayed their own fellow-citizens, and crowded their armies with forced levies; they drove from their midst all who would not yield to their despotism, or filled their prisons with men who would not enlist under their flag. They have now crowned the rebellion by the perpetration of deeds scarcely known even to savage warfare. The investigations of your committee have established this fact beyond controversy. The witnesses called before us were men of undoubted veracity and character. Some of them occupy high positions in the army, and others high positions in civil life. Differing in political sentiments, their evidence presents a remarkable concurrence of opinion and of judgment. Our fellow countrymen, heretofore sufficiently impressed by the generosity and forbearance of the government of the United States, and by the barbarous character of the crusade against it, will be shocked by the statements of these unimpeached and unimpeachable witnesses; and foreign nations must, with one accord, however they have hesitated heretofore, consign to lasting odium the authors of crimes which, in all their details, exceed the worst excesses of the sepoys of India.

Inhumanity to the living has been the leading trait of the rebel leaders; but it was reserved for your committee to disclose as a concerted system their insults to the wounded, and their mutilation and desecration of the gallant dead. Our soldiers taken prisoners in honorable battle have been subjected to the most shameful treatment. All the considerations that inspire chivalric emotion and generous consideration for brave men have been disregarded. It is almost beyond belief that the men fighting in such a cause as ours, and sustained by a government which in the midst of violence and treachery has given repeated evidences of its indulgence, should have been subjected to treatment never before resorted to by one foreign nation in a conflict with another.

All the courtesies of professional and civil life seem to have been discarded. General Beauregard himself, who on a very recent occasion boasted that he had been controlled by humane feelings after the battle of Bull Run, coolly proposed to hold General Ricketts as a hostage for one of the murderous privateers, and the rebel surgeons disdained intercourse and communication with our own surgeons taken in honorable battle.

The outrages upon the dead will revive the recollections of the cruelties to which savage tribes subject their prisoners. They were buried in many cases naked, with their faces downward; they were left to decay in the open air; their bones were carried off as trophies, sometimes, as the testimony proves, to be used as personal adornments, and one witness deliberately avers that the head of one of our most gallant officers was cut off by a secessionist to be turned into a drinking cup on the occasion of his marriage. Monstrous as this revelation may appear to be, your committee have been informed that during the last two weeks the skull of a Union soldier has been exhibited in the office of the Sergeant-at-arms of the House of Representatives, which had been converted to such a purpose, and which had been found on the person of one of the rebel prisoners taken in a recent conflict. The testimony of Governor Sprague, of Rhode Island, is most interesting. It confirms the worst reports against the rebel soldiers, and conclusively proves that the body of one of the bravest officers in the volunteer service was burned. He does not hesitate to add that this hyena desecration of the honored corpse was because the rebels believed it to be the body of Colonel Slocum, against whom they were infuriated for having displayed so much courage and chivalry in forcing his regiment fearlessly and bravely upon them.

These disclosures establishing, as they incontestably do, the consistent inhumanity of the rebel leaders, will be read with sorrow and indignation by the people of the loyal States. They should inspire these people to renewed exertions to protect our country from the restoration to power of such men. They should, and we believe they will, arouse the disgust and horror of foreign nations against this unholy rebellion. Let it be ours to furnish, nevertheless, a contrast to such barbarities and crimes. Let us persevere in the good work of maintaining the authority of the Constitution, and of refusing to imitate the monstrous practices we have been called upon to investigate.

Your committee beg to say, in conclusion, that they have not yet been enabled to gather testimony in regard to the additional inquiry suggested by the resolution of the Senate, whether Indian savages have been employed by the rebels in military service against the government of the United States, and how such warfare has been conducted by said savages, but that they have taken proper steps to attend to this important duty.

B. F. WADE, *Chairman.*

THE STATE OF THE UNION.

SPEECH

OF

BENJAMIN WOOD, OF NEW YORK,

IN THE

HOUSE OF REPRESENTATIVES,

MAY 16th, 1862.

SPEECH

OF

BENJAMIN WOOD, OF NEW YORK,

ON

THE STATE OF THE UNION,

IN THE

HOUSE OF REPRESENTATIVES, MAY 16TH, 1862.

WASHINGTON, D. C.:
McGILL, WITHEROW & CO., PRINTERS.
1862.

SPEECH.

Mr. WOOD. Mr. Chairman, I have hitherto avoided troubling this House. Content to be a listener, without any other participation in its proceedings than to oppose my solemn individual negative against measures which my conscience and my principles would not approve, I have said nothing. Indeed, sir, I have not had the heart to rise here and speak. A glance at this Hall, of itself, has been enough to prevent. When I look around and see one third of the Union unrepresented here, and find myself in a body, purporting to be one branch of the Congress of the United States, really in fact but a fragmentary part of it, my heart sinks within me. It appears to be a sectional body—a gathering of the representatives of a sectional party. With these feelings, and with this spirit, I have until now avoided participating in debate.

Besides, sir, during the earlier period of this session, disaster had accompanied the efforts of the Federal arms. I felt that the hour of defeat was not a fit one in which to strive to awaken the great soul of the North to thoughts of peace; I felt that something was due to the sense of mortification, something to the natural desire to retrieve the shame of discomfiture. I hoped, too, that when victory should perch upon our banners, others than myself would seize the occasion to urge a plea in behalf of peaceable measures; and that this Government itself, feeling secure and strong enough to be magnanimous, would take the lead and be the pioneer in opening a path for the settlement of our difficulties without further recourse to bloodshed. I even hoped that the leaders of the now dominant party, moved by the sore distress which has visited our country, would relent from the stern rigor of their doctrine of subjugation, and, in the flush of triumph, would lean a little towards a gentler policy than that which they have heretofore championed with so much zeal and with so little forbearance.

I hoped in vain. The triumph came; a long train of successes has relieved the North from its humiliation. The Government claims now to stand as a rock against which the tempest of opposition must waste itself in futile efforts. The partisans of the ultra war party laugh to scorn the idea that any effectual resistance can be offered to the onward march of our triumphant armies, and yet no single effort has been made in these congressional Halls to stay the effusion of blood. It has been left for me, powerless as I am, to speak the first conciliatory word in behalf of my countrymen. And I do it, sir, in the hope that others, more capable, will not be too much engrossed with the lust of conquest and the pride of victory, to follow my example.

Sir, it is an ineffaceable reproach to those either deluded or wicked men who, in the North, by their unwearied agitation of abolition schemes, have stirred the embers of this strife; it is an eternal reproach to them that, through defeat and victory, throughout every phase of this unhappy struggle, with the groans of their distressed and tortured country smiting upon their ears, they have clung, and still cling, with unpitying pertinacity, and even with ferocity, to the doctrine which has been the germ of all the mischief. With the first exulting shouts of Federal victories they set up the echoing cry of emancipation. With all the energy of fanaticism, with all the subtile arts and intrigues of scheming demagogues, with all the appliances of cunning, intellect, and patronage at their command, even at this eventful crisis, when every American brain should be at work to bring about a fair and honorable peace, they have no thought, no hope, no duty but to propagate their creed, extending its influence into every nook and corner of the land, and poisoning the atmosphere of these sacred Halls with its interminable discussion. Openly and in secret, by the agency of the press, the pulpit, and the political rostrum, in the camp, in the city, and in the open field, they are spreading the contagion; they are innoculating the country with this moral pestilence which has already brought us where we are, to the very brink of the grave of our nationality.

Sir, to these apostles of abolitionism will be traced hereafter whatever of evil has befallen or may befall our country. They are building its sepulchre with the bones of their slaughtered countrymen. I do believe there are gentlemen within my vision now, whose sworn purpose, whose first desire, paramount even to the preservation of Republicanism, is emancipation. They and their disciples first threw the apple of discord. They first applied the torch, and are now more busy than ever with throwing fresh fuel to the flame. Should history ever trace—which God forbid—the record of this country's ruin, that page will seem the strangest to those that read which shall tell of the madness and wickedness of the arch-fanatics of abolitionism. In the dark recesses of the temple of infamy, the gloomiest niches will bear the inscription of their names.

Sir, I counsel none but a moral interference with the work of these mischief-makers. I would not have even fanaticism deprived of the right of free speech! nor would I, in any emergency, advocate the slightest infringement by the Government upon the liberty of the press. Let them sow the seeds of their infamous doctrine broadcast over the land. Whatever may be the danger, I will not countenance the greater danger of establishing a dictatorship over the thoughts of my fellow-countrymen.

But if the abominable theme must be brought into the Council Chambers of the nation, for the sake of decency, if not of justice, let it be at a more suitable time. If there remains one Union man at the South, let us remember that he is unrepresented here; that the subject of slavery particularly concerns him, and that it is ungenerous and unjust, if not cowardly, to take advantage of his absence to push forward measures in regard to the local institutions of his section; measures against which, were he present, he would give his earnest opposition. It will quench whatever remains of Union feeling at the South, if it has not already done so. It will destroy the last hope of a reconstruction of the Union on a friendly basis. It will prove that the first idea of the dominant party in the North is active and unwavering antagonism to slavery, and a fixed purpose to legislate it out of the land at all hazards. Is it thus that we are to conquer a peace? Sir, we are flinging away the last chances of reconciliation as recklessly as madmen cast their treasures into the sea. The agitation of the subject has been the country's bane at every period of its history; its discussion at this crisis is desperate self-destruction. Is it while the magazine is beneath us and about us, bursting with the agencies of ruin, that we must choose to sport with the flaming torch of the incendiary? Sir, until our beloved country shall be saved, the word "emancipation" should, by common consent, be banished from the language of debate in this assemblage. It is a spell which has wrought enough already of desolation. It is a hellish formula of incantation which has conjured up the fiends of discord and civil war; and it never was so potent in its evil tendency as now, when it is being passed, like the breath of the plague, from mouth to mouth, in the Council

Chambers of the country which it has ruined. It should be spoken in a whisper and with a prayer linked to it, as a thing that brings a curse and spreads a pestilence. I despair of my country, I despair of ever living once more in a blessed Union of fraternal States, when I hear all around me the utterance of that ruin-breeding word "emancipation," mingling with the shouts of battle, the fierce huzzahs of triumph over fallen brothers, and the groans of our dying countrymen.

Sir, if in place of making the negro question a subject-matter of debate, this Congress would take into earnest, solemn consideration some expedient for securing peace, I do believe that success would crown our efforts. If they would enter upon that task, not with hearts embittered and intellects swayed by sectional antipathies and mock philanthropy, but with all their souls devoted to that one sacred purpose—the reconstruction of the Union and our redemption from civil war; if they would do this, in the spirit of conciliation, of forgiveness, of tolerance, of brotherhood, and kindly feeling, it is my conviction that before the close of this eventful session, the preliminaries of a peace would be arranged. But while, with the obstinacy of a blind fanatic, and the instinct of a brutal gladiator, the first object is to promulgate a party creed, and the second to crush an opponent and wear the badge of victory, I see no fairer prospect than, at some distant period, reached through seas of blood and heaps of carnage, the forced submission of a crushed and devastated section, and the equally unhappy spectacle of a Government triumphant, but exhausted by its triumph, detested by a moity of those sovereignties that gave it birth, and gazing with horror and remorse upon the desolation it has wrought.

Sir, it is not my intention to vent reproaches, even where I believe them best deserved. I have risen to enter my protest against the discussion, in this Chamber, of any anti-slavery scheme whatever at this crisis, and to offer an earnest appeal to this Congress that its legislation shall embrace every means of securing an immediate peace. If, as the Government claims, the confederate cause is hopeless, the leaders of the secession movement cannot be ignorant of the fact; and knowing it, they will be naturally inclined to lend a willing ear to whatever proper overtures this Government may present. At some period of this struggle there must be negotiation; it must be resorted to, sooner or later; why not now?

Is it because pride forbids that we should be the first to stretch out the hand of conciliation? Heaven forefend that thousands of human lives and a country's welfare should depend upon so false a principle. Is it because the South has not been sufficiently punished, humbled, and subdued? Then let us confess that chastisement and vengeance are the objects of this war. Is it because the anti-slavery movement has not yet received a sufficient impetus? If so, go tell it to the armies that have won your victories! Make abolition the war-cry! Place a banner with that device in the vanward, and lure those armies on to conquest with it—if you can. Your soldiers would rend the treacherous ensign into shreds, and would march to their homes with the same alacrity with which they pushed on to the battle-field.

What, then, is the cause that withholds negotiation? You will not parley with armed treason! But you have parleyed with armed treason, if that be the word; parleyed for the mere convenience of an exchange of prisoners, and other purposes to mitigate the grievances of war. It was your duty so to do. And shall you not do so to accomplish all that your troops are fighting for—the reconstruction of the Union?

Let us suppose that the South is anxious to embrace an opportunity of return, and is withheld from making advances by doubts as to the intentions of the North: is it not right that we should confer with them, that those doubts may be removed? What do the people care for such miserable punctilios in the hour of a nation's agony? Sir, an honorable peace is within the grasp of this Congress without further bloodshed. This Congress knows that it is so, and when the people shall realize that it is only the infamous design to strengthen the anti-slavery movement that prevents an effort to obtain that peace, woe to the chiefs of the abolition party in the land.

But, enough of them. Words are thrown away upon their stubborn fanaticism. I appeal with better hope to the loftier feelings that should pervade humanity, and especially pervade this august assemblage; that should, by the nature of its sacred functions, be far removed from the miserable ambition of reducing a section of our common country to the extreme and therefore dangerous condition of despair.

Sir, there may be a fascination in the gory magnificence of war. There may be a craving for martial glories in the hearts of men, and an instinct of contention which we share in common with the brute creation. But if ever there can be a time when a more Christian impulse should possess our souls, it is now; now, when triumph and the consciousness of strength give us the noble privilege of extending the hand of conciliation without fear of degradation, or of self-reproach for cowardice. If adversity has been our excuse for sternness, let success be our plea for magnanimity. Providence has placed within the reach of the North a greater triumph than countless armed legions could conquer; the triumph of subduing a brave enemy with a generous and merciful policy, will disarm resentment and rekindle the old brotherly flame that perhaps is not yet totally extinct. For, after all, they are our brothers, sir; and some softening of the stern Roman rigor which our rulers have assumed is due to that brotherhood, which, by untimely severity, may be canceled now forever. There are gentlemen who will say that the South must be subdued; that every armed southerner must throw down his weapon and sue for mercy. Should a freeman ask so much of his brother freeman? Would they be worthy of companionship in our fraternity, being reclaimed at such a sacrifice of manly feeling? What would you have them do? Would you have them crouch and cringe and strew their heads with ashes and kneel at your gates for readmission? They are *Americans*, sir, and will not do it. No! though Roanoke and Henry and Donelson should be re-enacted from day to day through the lapse of bloody years, they will not do it. Give them some chance for an honorable return, or you will wipe out every hope, and the two sections will be twain forever. Yes, sir! you may link them to each other with chains, and pin their destinies together with bayonets, but at heart they will be twain forever. They are the children of the same heroic stock, the joint inheritors with ourselves of the precious legacy of freedom; and it is a sacrilege and an insult to the memories of the past, that so many, sir, should sit in your presence here to-day to goad them on to desperate resistance, and so few—alas! so very few—to mediate and restrain.

Of those few, I thank my God that I am one. I am proud to proclaim it here beneath the dome of the Capitol. I shall proclaim it, here and everywhere, until the wings of peace shall be once more folded over the bleeding bosom of my country. I shall proclaim it aloud and honestly, although to do so would make me the next victim of this cruel strife.

Sir, it may be said that I speak of peace, while its attainment, without further recourse to arms, remains impossible. I do not believe it impossible. What effort has been made? What door has been opened through which the passions and ill-feelings of the contestants might pass out and reason enter? None. The single idea has been forced upon the people that the sword, and the sword alone, must decide the issue. It has been pronounced treason to hold an opposite opinion. Sir, if to have but little faith in the efficacy of the sword for joining severed friendships, if to earnestly desire peace and deprecate the horrors of war, be treason, then am I a traitor; and I am prouder of such treason than others can be of their vindictive, flaming, and pretentious patriotism.

I conjure this Congress, in the name of our suffering country, in the names of wives that may be widows, of children that may be orphans, in the name of gallant men, now strong in health, and who, to-morrow, may be stretched in death upon the gory ground, or writhing, maimed, and disfigured, with tormenting wounds—in the name of humanity, that sickens at the daily record of this terrible strife, I conjure this Congress to seize at the merest chance that may exist of a present termination of this tragedy. Let something be attempted in the spirit of mediation. Sir, the people will respond to it. They will thank this Congress for it. They will bless this Congress for any measure that breathes of the spirit of reconciliation. They are weary of this war, weary in despite of the excitement of present victory. They will awake soon to the consciousness that such victories are purchased at a sacrifice terrible to contemplate; that a national debt is created, which, in its rapid accumulation, is appalling—a debt which, if ever paid, will press like an incubus upon future generations, stunting the growth and paralyzing the vigor of our young Republic; or, if repudiated, resting a blot upon our annals.

If we look abroad the spectacle tends only to our shame. We see the sceptered hands of Europe planting their royal banners upon the soil of this western hemisphere, which it is our natural duty to consecrate to republicanism, and which we might at least have guarded from the greed of foreign despots. The flag of Arragon and Castile flaunts in the air of San Domingo, and, united with the blazonries of France and England, is unfurled upon the walls of San Juan d'Ulloa. Where may they not float a twelve months hence, if we, the natural guardians of this continent, should still be busy dabbling in each other's gore? Sir, if there must be war, let it be against the natural enemies of republicanism; if we must humble our national pride to conciliate the British lion, let us make some sacrifice to win back in amity the South, that we may stand once again as comrades in arms, to scourge these foreign interlopers within their proper limits.

I am no advocate of bloodshed, but if a foreign war should be the alternative of submission to foreign insolence, I trust that I should be among the last to fall prostrate that the hurricane might sweep harmless by. To subserve the schemes of a party, we have already humiliated the American people in the eyes of scoffing Europe! It will be a task hereafter to regain the caste we have lost in the family of nations. No greater evil could befall us than to be forced from the position we have hitherto assumed towards foreign Powers! I would not have my country swerve one inch from any vital principle of her foreign policy in any emergency whatever. Above all things I hold dear that national honor which we have ever, till of late, preserved untarnished. However gloomy may be the aspect of things at home, I would have our flag float as proudly as ever abroad, not deigning to make domestic affliction a plea for humility, an excuse for cowardice, or a palliation of national dishonor. Whenever the occasion demands that a stand should be made against foreign aggression, or a rebuke administered to foreign pride, or a chastisement inflicted upon foreign insolence, I would have the gauntlet thrown down upon the impulse of the national sentiment, without reference to domestic exigencies, or pausing to measure the strong proportions of the foe.

In the heat of our private discord, we seem to have forgotten that our great mission as a people, is to republicanize the world, to advance the principle that men are capable of self-government, and to check the progress of monarchy. Sir, we are losing ground in the fulfillment of that sacred mission, and monarchy has gained a new foothold, while we have been weakening our sinews with intestine strife. To what purpose? Is it possible that gentlemen can hope to reconstruct the Union by pursuing a policy of unrelenting severity? Can they expect to re-establish concord and brotherly love by pushing hostilities to the extreme verge? What is the Union worth without mutual respect and reciprocal amity to bind the sections? What! a Union of unwilling States, driven into companionship at the point of the bayonet, and held there by military power! Such a Union would not be worth the shedding of one brave man's blood. We want their hearts, or we want them not at all. And we cannot conquer hearts with bayonets, although they should outnumber the spears of Xerxes. If not brought back by negotiation, they are gone from us forever. To conquer them may be possible. To slay their soldiers, lay waste their lands, and burn their cities may be within our power. But to hold them in subjection, would, in itself, be a final repudiation of the first principle of republicanism. Prosecute this war until you have accomplished the necessity of holding a subdued section in subjection, and the world will look in vain for a republic on the western hemisphere.

Sir, I love to entertain the hope that our Union will be restored upon the foundation laid down by our fathers; and I desire no changes in the plan of that glorious superstructure. But I am not so unnatural a worshiper of the Union as to seek its salvation with the destruction of those for whose welfare it was conceived; to build it up upon the dead bodies of my countrymen. I would purchase its redemption otherwise than by anarchy and ruin. I would not fling away the substance to perpetuate the name. Every drop of blood that is shed in this struggle will weaken the bond of union between us. One word of conciliation at this crisis will do more to save the country than all the achievements, past and to come, of your victorious soldiery.

Why should not that word go forth, even now, in the hour of the triumph of the Federal arms. If there has ever been a period in the history of republics when prolonged civil strife has failed to curtail the liberty of the masses, I have not read that history aright. Already, with one year's bitter experience, we have beheld some of the dearest privileges of American citizenship wrested from our grasp. And how long, at the same rate, before, upon the convenient plea of necessity, shall we be stripped of other rights which heretofore have made us deem ourselves freemen? How long, while personal liberty even now depends on the nod of an official? How long, while free-born American citizens can be left to languish in bastiles, beyond the reach of the constituted tribunals of the land and at the mercy of the Executive? How long, while the press, the guardian of liberty, the friend of the masses, is shackled, gagged, cowed down to sullen silence, or, worse yet, become the minion of a party? How long, while voters are arrested at the polls by military process, and legislators are hurried off to prison before they can assume their sacred functions? How long, while the partisans of the abolition party are coining money out of the blood of their countrymen, parading their showy patriotism and shouting "Union," with their arms up to the elbows in the public Treasury? How long, sir, will the people of the North, taxed beyond endurance, robbed and cheated by an ever-craving horde of political hyenas—how long will they have a choice between freedom and anarchy, between a republic and a despotism? Alas! we still cling to the name of a republic, but have we the reality? It is entirely at the option of one man, or of a council of men, whether the citizen shall breathe in freedom the free air of Heaven. At the "*open sesame*," of the Executive, the gloomy portals of the Bastiles La Fayette or Warren will gape to receive him. And this is the Republic I was taught to love.

Sir, this is only a symbol of what must inevitably be, should the South be *crushed* into the Union. You may bring the South to terms with your bayonets, but when you have done so, you will have made a bond of air; a covenant whose seal will be a military despotism; and to break it at the first opportunity will be an aim and a purpose on the part of the subdued section. What they have attempted once they will not fail to attempt again, when smarting under the remembrance of defeat, when cherishing the deadly hate that a war to the utterance will engender.

For the sake of union now and of union hereafter—not an enforced union, but the strong union of willing hearts—let the word of peace go forth, let the hand of reconciliation be extended. Why, sir, I have heard such words of bitter hatred expressed towards these southerners by northern lips, that I fear it may be already too late ever to renew the bonds of fraternity. Such sentiments, I have heard of implacable resentment, of thirsting vengeance, of sectional antipathy, as Hannibal was taught to nurture against Rome, as Rome, in her quenchless jealousy, conceived towards Carthage to the end. And the doom of Carthage may be accepted by the South rather than reunion at the bayonet's point.

I appeal to this Congress to avert that fate as inglorious to the victor as to the vanquished. Let the door of negotiation be flung wide open, flung open now, while we can make advances with good grace, and with laurels upon our brow. To the winds with the doctrine that you will not treat with armed traitors. It is a sentiment fitter for the epoch of a purpled Roman, than for the Christian age in which we live. It is the sentiment of one who rules with a rod of iron, not of a great and generous people who assume to rule themselves. Enough has been done in proof of the valor of the North, and the resources of the Government. Let something be now done for the sake of the past; for the sake of the memories of the Revolution, of the struggle of 1812, of the battle-fields of Mexico; for the sake of a Union whose cement shall be forgiveness for the past, and friendship and forbearance for the future.

In place of exulting over victories, and longing for new triumphs, how much more pleasant and more holy to draw a picture of the joy that will pervade many a now gloomy household when the glad tidings of peace shall be borne from city to village, from village to homestead, from lip to lip, and heart to heart. A nation's jubilee would well repay you for some little yielding of your stern policy. How many arms would be outstretched, how many hearts would bound to give a "welcome home again!" to the war-stained volunteer. Oh! sir, those meetings at the cottage threshold, those claspings at the farm-house porch, those cleavings of the throbbing bosoms of women to scarred and manly breasts, were worth all the laurels that were ever snatched from blood-stained fields. The news of our victories have been hailed with peans and illuminations; but, with the first tidings of peace, there is not a hovel in the land that would not have a candle at its window; not a palace that would not blaze with splendors in token of the advent of a blessing, priceless beyond all earthly triumphs.

Then, sir, let us lower the points of our victorious swords, and parley with the foe while the bugle blasts of victory are yet ringing in our ears. If we are free in anticipation from the peril of future reverses; if we are sanguine that the Federal arms are henceforward gifted with invincibility, that is the noblest reason why we should say to our opponents, "pause, if you will; reflect." Let us yield them one chance for reconcilement, before we drive them to the resistance of despair. There can be no victory where kith and kin, where brothers and fellow-countrymen, where men who are bound to each other by the holiest of past associations, are struggling for supremacy. All is defeat; all is disaster; all is misfortune, tears, and mourning. Do not let us efface with blood every sacred memory that may yet bind these men to us as brothers. Give one sign of invitation before the death struggle is renewed. Let the spirit of forgiveness pass between the lines of those opposing hosts, and with the blessings of Providence, those armed legions will take a lesson from Sabina and early Rome, whose soldiers, united by domestic ties, threw down their weapons upon the battle's verge, and sprang to each other's embrace.

Sir, I have spoken freely, studying only to make my words an index to my thought. My opinions have brought upon me the censure, often most discourteously expressed, of many who differ with me; but for that I care but little. I am content to bide the hour that shall set me right before my countrymen. As I have believed the prosecution of this war to be a widening of the gulf that separates the sections, I have earnestly opposed it. I have always looked upon the subjugation of the South as a project, whose fulfillment would strike a heavy, perhaps a fatal blow, to true republicanism; and although I will yield to no man in devotion to the Union, although I would make any and every personal sacrifice to restore its glory and integrity, I will never consent, even for the sake of that Union, to yield up my birthright as a free man; to sacrifice those principles of self-government, those rights of free speech, free thought, and personal liberty, without which Union is but a mockery and a name.

It is not grandeur and extent of territory that I covet as the chief attributes of the Government under which I am to live. Were I one of but a single community, insignificant in numbers, but secure in a guarantee of pure republican ministration of affairs, I would be proud of my citizenship. But the union of a thousand States, each one as great and populous as the noble one among whose Representatives I have the honor to be, I would detest, yes, sir, in my most inmost heart I would detest it, if the holding together of its component parts should create a necessity for the assumption of despotic power.

Self-government is the god of my political idolatry, and the Union is but a temple in which I have worshipped it. Should that temple be destroyed, I would not forsake the creed, nor would the mighty principle be buried in the ruins. I love and would preserve the temple, for beneath its roof are gathered the treasures of holy past associations; upon its hallowed walls are inscribed the names of patriots, from the North and from the South, whose blood has been its cement. But rather would I have the glorious fabric crumble to the dust, than see the spirit of despotism enshrined within its sacred precincts.

I have seen already the silent but lengthening shadow of absolutism creeping into this sacred asylum. And when the Executive hand, for the first time in our history, was interposed between the citizen and his rights, the germ was planted of a danger mightier than rebellion in its most gigantic phase; for I believe encroachments by an Executive to be in itself rebellion against the only sovereignty I acknowledge—the majesty of the people. I believe each step towards absolutism to be more fatal to the welfare of the Republic than any possible act within the power of the citizen to conceive and execute. I will resist every grasp that may be made upon an attribute of sovereignty not heretofore acknowledged to the Chief Magistracy; for reason and instinct, no less than the fearful examples that history has furnished from the ashes of republics, teach me that the first step, unchecked, will not be the last, but only the precursor of those giant strides by which, over the necks of betrayed freemen, ambitious men have mounted to a throne.

We want a Union, sir, of sovereigns, not of subjects. And that our Government shall extend over a vast area, to me is of less moment than that it should be purely, strictly, and unequivocally republican at all times and under all conditions.

Sir, I have done. I have only to reiterate my hope and my entreaty that this Congress, which has in sacred charge the welfare of our country, will adopt some measure which may bring about a cessation of hostilities, with a view to negotiation. That done, I am firm in my belief that hostilities will not be resumed.

THE NATIONAL ENTAIL.

A

SERMON

PREACHED TO THE

FIRST CONGREGATIONAL CHURCH

IN BROOKLINE,

ON THE

3D JULY, 1864.

PUBLISHED BY REQUEST.

BOSTON:
WRIGHT & POTTER, PRINTERS, No. 4 SPRING LANE.
1864.

THE NATIONAL ENTAIL.

A

SERMON

PREACHED TO THE

FIRST CONGREGATIONAL CHURCH

IN BROOKLINE,

ON THE

3D JULY, 1864.

PUBLISHED BY REQUEST.

BOSTON:
WRIGHT & POTTER, PRINTERS, No. 4 SPRING LANE.
1864.

SERMON.

EXODUS xx. 5.

I THE LORD THY GOD AM A JEALOUS GOD, VISITING THE INIQUITIES OF THE FATHERS UPON THE CHILDREN.

THESE threatening words are a popular statement of a natural law and a well-known historical fact—the propagation of natural and moral qualities by genealogical descent. The consequences of our actions extend to our posterity; what is sown by one generation is reaped by another; as the fathers, so the children; every age in its turn is blessed by the virtues, or must expiate the vices and the crimes of the age preceding. This law and fact the Hebrew, like other ancient religions, represented as the vengeance of God, who visits the guilt of the fathers with retributory evil on the children.

The fact is indisputable, the law inevitable—the law of natural and moral entail. An established principle of physiology is the propagation of physical traits in vegetable and animal kinds. What we call species in natural history, whether we view it as original creation, or whether with some recent English naturalists we view it as accidental modification of a single primitive type, is a constant, everywhere present illustration of this law. Two seed kernels, scarcely, if at all, distinguishable in form and color, sown in the same soil, will produce very different fruits, and the seed of those fruits will produce the same kinds respectively from age to age. Who can analyze the subtle individuality inherent in those tiny forms which constitutes and perpetuates their proper type? The brute creation and the human animal exhibit the same persistency,—the identity of the species surviving the constant destruction of all the individuals composing it and all the revolutions of time.

And not only the species in general, but every variety within that species—every variety of human kind, so long as it continues to exist, preserves its physical characteristics unchanged. The negro of to-day is the same with the negro depicted on Egyptian monuments three thousand years ago, the same that he was at the start, the same that he will be, in all likelihood, until the race is extinct. The modern Jew, whether found on change, or pilgriming with the peddler's pack, or seated among the fish-stalls of the Ghetto at Rome, is the Israelite still, the veritable son of Jacob, in all the distinctive characteristics of the race. The vagabond Gipsies have been circulating in Europe for centuries—long enough to change the features of a race, if the features of a race were merely extrinsic and accidental. But these people retain not only their customs, their laws and language, but their very looks, the physical peculiarities which they brought with them from the banks of the Indus when flying before the arms of Tamerlane.

Finer and more distinctive traits are propagated in families. There is a family type, a stamp of countenance, a peculiar conformation of the features, which is handed down from generation to generation. The features of the ancestral portrait shall reappear in some remote descendant with an impress so exact that with altered costume the hereditary painting, the work of another century, might pass for the likeness of its modern possessor.

The law of hereditary transmission involves the descent of diseases and defects as well as of the national or family type. The operation of this law in the vegetable world has passed into a proverb: "A good tree cannot bring forth evil fruit, neither can a corrupt tree bring forth good fruit." A good scion cannot come of a base stock nor a sickly scion furnish a healthy graft.

In the human family hereditary disease is one of the most common forms of disease. Constitutional defects, imperfections of the senses, organic disorders, humors, consumption, insanity, descend from parent to child through many generations.

Finally, the law of hereditary transmission is applicable to moral as well as to physical traits and fortunes. Good and evil qualities are hereditary in families. There is a lineage of virtue and vice. It is not of such binding force as to neutralize moral accountableness, but sufficient to constitute a moral relation between one generation and another. Traits of character are transmitted by a law of entail. No man lives to himself alone, and no man dies to himself. This is as true in the order of time as it is in space. Each individual is a link in a chain of lineal transmission; he inherits from all the past, he bequeathes to all the future. Each possesses in addition to his own individuality which distinguishes him by characteristic differences from all his kind, a transmitted type which connects him by characteristic resemblances with all his tribe. That type has come to him from an unknown ancestry; it descends through him to an unknown posterity; it is a part of his Providential heritage; he may modify it indefinately, he may turn its very evil into good, may

———"change the thistles of a curse
To types beneficent;"

he may make hereditary vices and defects the occasion of excelling virtue; or he may by his misdeeds propagate an evil which he did not inherit and inflict on his progeny a curse which shall blight the fortunes of successive generations. This is what is meant by visiting the sins of the fathers on the children. History presents some remarkable instances of this hereditary curse, connected with moral traits, attaching to certain families of which the Herods of Judea, the Claudian family in Rome, and the Stuarts in England and Scotland are conspicuous and familiar examples.

This propagation of national and family traits was deemed by ancient nations a fact of prime significance. Ancient literature abounds in allusions to it. The idea of an hereditary doom, a moral entail, a transmitted curse—the penalty of ancestral crime—is the staple theme of Greek tragedy.

Not less prominent is this idea in the Hebrew Scriptures, where it figures as an organic principle in history and theology. The twelve tribes of Israel are characterized by moral traits, and fortunes corresponding thereto, derived from their respective ancestors, the twelve sons of Jacob. The patriarch is represented as predicting on his death-bed the future destinies of his children. Judah is to rule and Issachar to serve, Joseph shall be a fruitful bough and Benjamin a ravening wolf. The Hebrew Scriptures moreover present the idea of a doomed race. The descendants of Canaan, son of Ham, are condemned to a state of subjection and bondage. This doom is represented in the story as the penalty of filial impiety. The patriarch Noah pronounces a curse on the progeny of his offending son: "Cursed be Canaan; a servant of servants shall he be to his brethren. Jehovah blessed shall be the God of Shem, and Canaan shall be his servant. God shall enlarge Japheth and he shall dwell in the tents of Shem and Canaan shall be his servant." This may be taken as a popular and poetic statement of an historical fact. The fact is that certain vicious traits in the character of Canaan were transmitted to his descendants and exhibited themselves in the moral depravity and consequent civil depression of that race.

The defenders of African Slavery on this continent have rejoiced in this passage as affording Scriptural authority for that institution. They have sought to identify the descendants of Canaan with the natives of South Africa, and would have us believe that Noah's curse changed the color of the skin and the physical structure of his posterity. There needs no other refutation of this absurdity than the Bible itself which flatly contradicts it, showing that the posterity of Canaan occupied the region which bears that name before they were conquered and brought into subjection, according to the patriarchal prophecy, by the Hebrews, the descendants of Shem. Portions of them, after the invasion of the Israelites, are said to have settled in North Africa, in the Baleraric Islands and in Spain, as we learn from an ancient historian* who speaks of columns in Africa bearing the inscription, "We, the princes of Canaan, fled hither from the arms of the robber Joshua." That any portion of them colonized South or Central Africa there is not the shadow of a proof; that they were turned into negroes is regarded by competent authorities as a physiological impossibility.

The main point is, that moral qualities, and the good or evil consequences of those qualities, are hereditary; that whilst a virtuous ancestry insures a prosperous progeny, the sins of the fathers are visited on the children to the third and fourth generation. And this transmission, be it observed, is not only a lineal and genealogical descent—an inheritance by kindred blood—but propagation by example, by tradition, by the influence of precedent and custom on

* Procopius.

succeeding ages. An important feature in the popular theology is founded on this fact. The fundamental doctrine of the popular theology is hereditary sin. The common statement of this doctrine as the imputation of Adam's guilt to his offspring is a moral absurdity. But the doctrine contains a germ of truth, and that truth is the fact we are considering—the propagation of moral qualities and the consequences of moral qualities from age to age. Doubtless, if all the progenitors of the human race, if all who have preceded us in the order of time, had perfectly obeyed the moral law, the human condition at this present would be far safer and happier than it is. A large portion of the evils and miseries to which flesh is heir —the ancient burden of humanity—is the penalty and fruit of ancestral transgression. The sins of our progenitors are not visited upon us as guilt—"the son doth not bear the iniquity of the father" in that sense —but they are visited upon us as individual and social wrongs and sufferings, as evil propensities, bad customs, bad laws, political corruption, civil discord, sedition, war. We are not responsible for ancestral crime; we are responsible for no sins but our own. And for these we are responsible not only to ourselves and our contemporaries, but equally so to our posterity, whether by lineal descent or succession in time.

To a conscientious mind this moral relation between the present and the future—the position we sustain toward those who shall come after us in the order of time—will be a cogent motive power suggesting important and sacred duties. It is natural to man to wish to outlive himself, to survive in his character and works, in the influence of these on his posterity, when as person he has ceased to act in earthly places. The wish so to live is the noblest instinct, the power so to live is the grandest faculty, of the human mind. It is this which distinguishes man from other creatures that know no future and live only in the dim sensations of the hour. To him it is given to cast his thought and activity forward into distant time and to live and act as an influence in human affairs when the instruments of his activity, the cunning hand and the guiding brain, are dust. And never does man appear so great and godlike as when acting in the sense and spirit of this earthly immortality, planting into ages yet unborn the tree whose fruit he shall never behold, but whose hereafter shall be the healing of nations. So to live that they who come after us may find the sphere into which they are born more privileged and blest for that we have lived in it and wrought in it, is a principle which commends itself to every thoughtful and generous mind, and a principle practicable to all however placed or endowed.

The principle is important, and preëminently so in a national view. As a nation we are responsible to our posterity. We are responsible for the use we make of our position and the way in which we answer the call and satisfy the exigency of our time. We are responsible for our action or neglect to act in all that concerns the national well-being. In a country where the people are theoretically the government, where national institutions are committed to popular action to mould and apply, to perpetuate or abolish, this responsibleness falls upon all in the measure of their means and opportunity, and none, from the highest functionary to the humblest citizen, can escape the common burden. In nothing is the action of one generation on another more inevitable than in matters relating to the character and destiny of nations. What we call nationality is an heirloom handed down from age to age—an aggregation of civil and moral characteristics in which one generation reaps what another had sown, where the virtues, the labors and sacrifices of a brave and God-fearing ancestry are recompensed in the character and condition of their posterity, and where the sins of the fathers are visited upon the children from generation to generation.

Look at any nation that is old enough and civilized enough to have a history, and see the law of hereditary transmission exemplified in that history. England is what she is at this day by the action of her barons who wrung from a base and recreant king the great charter of her liberties; by the action of the Puritans who resisted unto blood the attempt to reimpose on a Protestant people the rule of hierarchical Rome. Spain is what she is at this day by the tame submission of her fathers to the priestly yoke and the cruel persecutions of the Inquisition. Holland is what she is by the labors and sacrifices of heroic ancestors who trampled on that yoke. Nowhere are the retributions of God more signally manifest than in the destiny of nations. Centuries may be required to develop and exhibit those retributions, but they are developed and perfectly exhibited in time. The sinning nation must pay to the uttermost farthing the debt of suffering due to violated justice, and drain to the last dregs the cup which it mixed and poured out in the day of its prosperity. A people can no more escape retribution in their national destiny than an individual can escape it in his individual destiny. The same law which ordains that the soul which sinneth shall die, has also ordained that the nation which sinneth shall die. The penalties of national transgression may not be realized or very imperfectly realized by those "by whom the offence cometh," but those penalties are inevitable. As God liveth they are inevitable. One generation of offenders after another may pass away, but the sinful nation survives; its identity is perpetuated from age to age. What the present generation does not expiate posterity will. For the sins of the fathers are visited upon the children.

We, as a people, young as we are, exhibit in our short day, as perfectly as any nation that ever existed in the world, the moral relation which connects together the present and past of national history—the good and evil of national entail. We, as a people, rejoice in a worthy ancestry, than whom a wiser and a braver never laid the foundations of a state. We inherited from them blessings so peculiar and so precious, that scarcely is it possible to prize them as we ought. No extravagance of national boasting, no rhetoric of patriotism, can overstate their worth. The fathers were wise in their generation, but all wisdom was not theirs. They were equal to most but not to all of the exigencies which tried their prudence and their virtue. They sowed good seed in these apt and virgin furrows, which it cost so much toil, and treasure, and blood to clear and prepare. They sowed industry, humility, education, good government, freedom. But while men slept, while vigilance paused, an enemy came and sowed tares among the wheat. We enjoyed the good; for successive generations we lived and flourished on the character and recent example of our founders. "But when the blade was sprung up, and brought forth fruit, then appeared the tares also." We would not, or could not pluck them up, for fear of destroying the wheat with them. We let both grow together until the harvest. And it came at last, and still pends—the bloody harvest that is to separate the evil from the good. To-morrow we celebrate the Eighty-eighth Anniversary of our National Independence. We celebrate it in the midst of fears and fightings; of agonies and alarms; of wounds and deaths, and wide-spread grief. How many families throughout this broad land made desolate and sad by the loss of some brave son, or brother, or husband whose precious life has gone to swell the enormous ransom with which a nation is struggling to free itself from the grasp of treason, and redeem its lost estate! A breach has opened between North and South which one party is endeavoring to repair, the other to make irreparable; both casting into it the children of their bosom—the one for a binding bridge, the other for an impassable barricade.

Here it is, here especially, that the principle I am seeking to illustrate—our obligation to the future, the responsibility we bear as a nation to our posterity—operates as incentive and support. Were it only for ourselves and our own time that this war is waged; were it only for present convenience, profit or pride, could we justify to ourselves the fearful carnage? Who would not rather bear shame and wrong? For one, I would say, let treason do its worst; let the schism spread; let the Union slide; let the flag of our pride be trampled in the dust! Better humiliation, insult, outrage, bonds! Better all this than uncover the hells of war, and let loose the demons of the pit to set the course of nature on fire. But, when we think of the coming generations in the long to-morrow of this land, for whom our doing or faltering, our resistance or surrender to-day may be national life or death for incalculable time; when we think of the brave forefathers, who paved this soil with their bones to erect thereon a commonwealth where humanity new-born might rejoice to run its new career; when we think of the heroes who built this Union with their counsels and their deeds, and cemented it with their blood, we cannot choose but strike the blow which shall either kill the serpent Secession, or disfang and disable it for future harms; which, if it does not restore all that was lost, shall avail to preserve what remains. For we deeply feel that this land is not our land, nor this Union our Union, in absolute allodial right, to keep or surrender as we list. It is a feudal tenure by which we hold it; we are but lieges and vassals in this estate. It comes to us a feoff from the past, to be delivered up unimpaired to the future. No remissness of ours, no flinching in the day of trial, must defraud posterity of their dues. They must not rise up in their generation and charge us with defection in ours. Neither with active plotting against their inheritance must they charge us, nor yet with the passive treachery of sloth or fear. We must have it for our record, and the epitaph of our time: "We did what in us lay to preserve for you, O Posterity, untarnished and entire, the heritage bequeathed to us by our fathers. If we failed, it was Heaven's doom, and no sluggishness of ours, that curtailed your estate."

Thanks to our decision, by the blessing of God, we are not utterly dismembered and dissolved, nor minced into fragments too minute to be re-collected in any future resurrection, or to make successful stand against foreign arms. If the war should end to-day, we should be, with altered boundary, still a nation, more than ever a nation I should dare to hope, since welded and fused by the fiery experience of the last three years.

The regiments that have fought in one brigade,—the men who have stood shoulder to shoulder in the groaning field,—who have suffered one thirst in the long and dusty march,—who have sat by one camp-fire on the banks of the James, and in the mountains of Tennessee, will not part company when their muskets are returned to the armory, and their tattered and drooping banners, that once floated in the same breeze, are hung up for an everlasting memorial in their several capitols. The memory of shared triumphs, and a common heat, will bind them together, and bind their children for future peaceful service, and, if need be, for future mutual defence.

As a nation we are still young; the first century of our national existence has not yet expired. A single life, of the length to which human life is sometimes prolonged, comprehends within its limits our history as a nation, dating from the end of colonial dependence and the birth of Federal existence in 1776. Such a life, in a neighboring town, has just been brought to a close. On the eve of our eighty-eighth birthday, one who had seen his ninety-second,—a cherished fellow-citizen, largely and honorably associated with the civil and academic history of the country—has passed away full of years and honors, in the midst of all that should accompany old age.

It was hoped that he might have been spared to behold the end of our national troubles ; that the bells which shall one day ring in the return of peace to this land, should have been his summons to a world of peace, where nations war no more. How willingly then should our hearts have responded to his own *Nunc dimmittis*—"Now lettest thou thy servant depart in peace, for mine eyes have seen thy salvation."

As it is, we would fain accept the death of the patriarch, whose life embraces two revolutions, as an omen that the wished for end is near. We *will* accept it as a solemn admonition, and a lesson of faithfulness and trust. The patriotic zeal of that strenuous soul, which age could not quench; his never-faltering faith in the destinies of the nation of which he had seen the cradling; his ready tongue and pen, to the very last, wherever a word was needed from him of counsel or cheer, shall be to us a fresh incentive to brave and faithful service in war and in peace, and his example an aid and support under all the Providential burden of our time.

www.ingramcontent.com/pod-product-compliance
Lightning Source LLC
LaVergne TN
LVHW021308110826
845150LV00003B/518

* 9 7 8 1 4 2 5 5 5 8 9 8 7 *